TRAINING & REFERENCE

murach's PHP and MySQL

Joel Murach

Ray Harris

MIKE MURACH & ASSOCIATES, INC.

1-800-221-5528 • (559) 440-9071 • Fax: (559) 440-0963
murachbooks@murach.com • www.murach.com

Authors:	Joel Murach
	Ray Harris
Editor:	Mike Murach
	Ben Murach
Cover Design:	Zylka Design
Production:	Cynthia Vasquez

More books for web developers

Murach's HTML, XHTML, and CSS

Murach's JavaScript and DOM Scripting

Murach's ASP.NET 4 Web Programming with C# 2010

Murach's ASP.NET 4 Web Programming with VB 2010

Murach's Java Servlets and JSP (Second Edition)

Books for database programmers

Murach's Oracle SQL and PL/SQL

Murach's SQL Server 2008 for Developers

Murach's ADO.NET 4 Database Programming with C# 2010

Murach's ADO.NET 4 Database Programming with VB 2010

Books on Visual Basic, C#, and Java

Murach's C# 2010

Murach's Visual Basic 2010

Murach's Java SE 6

Books for IBM mainframe programmers

Murach's OS/390 and z/OS JCL

Murach's Mainframe COBOL

Murach's CICS for the COBOL Programmer

DB2 for the COBOL Programmer, Part 1

For more on Murach books, please visit us at www.murach.com

ISBN-13: 978-1-890774-56-1

Contents

Introduction

Section 1 Get started fast with PHP and MySQL

Chapter 1	Introduction to web development with PHP	3
Chapter 2	How to code a PHP application	45
Chapter 3	Introduction to relational databases and MySQL	93
Chapter 4	How to use PHP with a MySQL database	123
Chapter 5	How to use the MVC pattern to organize your code	159
Chapter 6	How to test and debug a PHP application	189

Section 2 Master PHP programming

Chapter 7	How to work with form data	207
Chapter 8	How to code control statements	231
Chapter 9	How to work with strings and numbers	259
Chapter 10	How to work with dates	291
Chapter 11	How to create and use arrays	311
Chapter 12	How to work with cookies and sessions	347
Chapter 13	How to create and use functions	379
Chapter 14	How to create and use objects	413
Chapter 15	How to use regular expressions, handle exceptions, and validate data	461

Section 3 Master MySQL programming

Chapter 16	How to design a database	503
Chapter 17	How to use SQL to create a MySQL database	537
Chapter 18	How to use SQL to work with a MySQL database	573
Chapter 19	Professional PHP for working with MySQL	611
Chapter 20	A database-driven web site	645

Section 4 Master the advanced skills for building web sites

Chapter 21	How to create secure web sites	675
Chapter 22	How to send email and access other web sites	707
Chapter 23	How to work with files, uploads, and images	743
Chapter 24	An eCommerce web site	779

Reference Aids

Appendix A	How to set up your PC for this book	801
Appendix B	How to set up your Mac for this book	817
Index		832

Expanded contents

Section 1 Get started fast with PHP and MySQL

Chapter 1 Introduction to web development with PHP

The architecture of a web application 4
How a client-server architecture works 4
How static web pages are processed 6
How dynamic web pages are processed 8
A survey of web application software 10
Highlights in the history of PHP 12
Highlights in the history of MySQL 12

The Product Discount application 14
The user interface 14
The HTML file 16
The CSS file 18
The PHP file 20

How to edit and test a PHP application 22
How to edit a PHP page with a text editor 22
How to start and stop Apache and MySQL on your own computer 24
How to deploy a PHP application 26
How to run a PHP application 28
How to test and debug a PHP page 30
How to view the source code for a web page 32

How to use NetBeans to develop a PHP application 34
How to work with PHP projects and files 34
How to edit and test a PHP application 36
How to import and configure a PHP project 38

Chapter 2 How to code a PHP application

Basic PHP skills 46
How to embed PHP in HTML 46
How to code comments and statements 48
The six PHP data types 50
How to declare variables and constants 52

How to get data from a request 54
How to use the built-in $_GET array 54
How to use the built-in $_POST array 56
When to use the HTTP GET and POST methods 56

How to work with data 58
How to code string expressions 58
How to code echo statements 58
How to code numeric expressions 60
How to use the compound assignment operators 62
How to use some built-in functions 64

The Product Discount application 66
The user interface 66
The form in the HTML file 66
The PHP file 68

How to code control statements **70**
How to code conditional expressions 70
How to code if statements 72
How to code while and for statements 74
How to pass control to another page 76

The Future Value application **78**
The user interface 78
The code for the index.php file 80
The code for the display_results.php file 82

How to use the PHP documentation **86**
How to access the PHP manual 86
How to find the documentation you need 86

Chapter 3　Introduction to relational databases with MySQL

An introduction to relational databases **94**
How a database table is organized 94
How the tables in a relational database are related 96
How the columns in a table are defined 98

The SQL statements for data manipulation **100**
How to select data from a single table 100
How to select data from multiple tables 102
How to insert, update, and delete data 104

An introduction to MySQL **106**
What MySQL provides 106
Two ways to work with MySQL 108

How to use phpMyAdmin **110**
How to start phpMyAdmin 110
How to log in, log out, and change your password 110
How to import and run a SQL script that creates a database 112
How to review the data and structure of a table 114
How to run SQL statements 116
How to create users with limited privileges 118

Chapter 4　How to use PHP with a MySQL database

PHP for working with MySQL **124**
How to connect to a MySQL database 124
How to execute SELECT statements 126
How to execute INSERT, UPDATE, and DELETE statements 128
How to use a try/catch statement to handle exceptions 130

How to get data from a result set **132**
How to work with arrays 132
How to get the data from the first row of a result set 134
How to get the data from all the rows of a result set 136

The Product Viewer application **138**
The user interface 138
The code 140

The Product Manager application **146**
The user interface 146
The code 148

Chapter 5 **How to use the MVC pattern to organize your code**

How to use the MVC pattern **160**
An introduction to the MVC pattern 160
How to code functions 162
How to redirect requests 164

The Product Manager application **166**
The user interface 166
The model 168
The controller 170
The view 172

The Product Catalog application **178**
The user interface 178
The model 180
The controller 180
The view 182

Chapter 6 **How to test and debug a PHP application**

An introduction to testing and debugging **190**
Typical test phases for a PHP application 190
The three types of errors that can occur 190
Common PHP errors 192
An easy way to trace the execution of your PHP code 194

How to debug with xDebug and NetBeans **196**
How to set and remove breakpoints 196
How to step through code 198
How to inspect variables 198
How to inspect the stack trace 200

Section 2 **Master PHP programming**

Chapter 7 **How to work with form data**

How to get data from a form **208**
How to get data from text boxes, password boxes, and hidden fields 208
How to get data from a radio button 210
How to get data from a check box 212
How to get data from an array of check boxes 214
How to get data from a drop-down list 216
How to get data from a list box 218
How to get data from a text area 220

How to display data on a web page **222**
How to format special characters 222
How to format line breaks 224
How to display data with echo and print statements 226

Chapter 8 **How to code control statements**

How to code conditional expressions **232**
How to use the equality and identity operators 232
How to use the relational operators 234
How to use the logical operators 236

How to code the selection structures **238**
How to code if statements with else clauses 238
How to code if statements with else if clauses 240
How to use the conditional operator 242
How to code switch statements 244
How to use a switch statement in the controller 246

How to code the iteration structures **248**
How to code while loops 248
How to code do-while loops 250
How to code for loops 252
How to use the break and continue statements 254

Chapter 9   How to work with strings and numbers

How to work with strings **260**
How to create strings 260
How to use escape sequences 262
How to work with string length and substrings 264
How to search a string 266
How to replace part of a string 266
How to modify strings 268
How to convert strings to and from arrays 270
How to convert strings to and from ASCII values 270
How to compare strings 272

How to work with numbers **274**
How to assign integers 274
How to assign floating-point values 276
How to use the math functions 278
How to generate random numbers 280

Other skills for working with strings and numbers **282**
How to use the sprintf function to format strings and numbers 282
How to convert strings to numbers 286

Chapter 10   How to work with dates

How to use timestamps to work with dates **292**
How to create and format timestamps 292
How to work with timestamps 294
How to use the strtotime function 296
Examples of working with timestamps 298

How to use objects to work with dates **300**
How to use the DateTime class 300
How to use the DateInterval class 302
How to use the DateInterval and DateTime classes together 304
Examples of working with DateTime objects 306

Chapter 11   How to create and use arrays

How to create and use an array **312**
How to create an array 312
How to add and delete elements 314
How to work with variable substitution 314
How to use for loops to work with arrays 316

How to create and use an associative array 318
How to create an associative array 318
How to add and delete elements 320
How to work with variable substitution 320
How to use foreach loops to work with arrays 322

How to use functions to work with arrays 324
How to fill, merge, slice, and splice arrays 324
How to work with queues and stacks 326
How to get the sum and product of elements 328
How to search arrays 328
How to sort arrays 330
How to modify arrays 332

How to work with arrays of arrays 334
Understanding an array of arrays 334
How to create and use an array of arrays 336

The Task List Manager application 338
The user interface 338
The code for the controller 338
The code for the view 340

Chapter 12   How to work with cookies and sessions

How to work with cookies 348
An introduction to cookies 348
How to set and get a cookie 350
How to enable or disable cookies 352

How to work with sessions 354
Why session tracking is difficult with HTTP 354
How session tracking works in PHP 354
How to start a session 356
How to set and get session variables 358
How to end a session 360
How to manage a session 362

The Shopping Cart application 364
The user interface 364
The controller 366
The model 368
The Add Item view 370
The Cart view 372

Chapter 13   How to create and use functions

Basic skills for working with functions 380
How to create and call a function 380
How to pass arguments by value and by reference 382
How variable scope works 384
How to provide default values for parameters 386
How to use variable-length parameter lists 388

How to create and use a library of functions 390
A library of functions 390
How to set the include path 392
How function scope works 392
How to create and use namespaces 394

Advanced skills for working with functions **396**
How to work with variable functions and callbacks 396
How to work with anonymous functions 398
How to work with closures 400

The Shopping Cart application **402**
The user interface 402
The model 404
The controller 406
The view 406

Chapter 14   How to create and use objects

How to create and use classes **414**
The code for the Category class 414
The code for the Product class 416
How to code properties 420
How to code constructors and destructors 422
How to code methods 424
How to create and use objects 426

How to code class constants, properties, and methods **428**
How to code class constants 428
How to code static properties and methods 430

The object-oriented Product Manager application **432**
The user interface 432
The model 434
The controller 438
The view 440

Additional skills for working with objects **442**
How to loop through an object's properties 442
How to clone and compare objects 444
How to inspect an object 446

How to work with inheritance **448**
How to inherit a class 448
How to use the protected access modifier 450
How to create abstract classes and methods 452
How to create final classes and methods 454
How to work with interfaces 456

Chapter 15   How to use regular expressions, handle exceptions, and validate data

How to use regular expressions **462**
How to create and use regular expressions 462
How to match characters 464
How to use the character class 466
How to create complex patterns 468
How to use look-ahead assertions 470
How to use a multiline regular expression 472
How to use a global regular expression 472
How to replace a regular expression with a string 474
How to split a string on a regular expression 474
Regular expressions for data validation 476

How to handle exceptions **478**
How to create and throw exceptions 478
How to use the try-catch statement 480

The Registration application 482
The user interface 482
The file structure 482
The model 484
The controller 492
The view 494
A long version of the Registration application 496

Section 3 Master MySQL programming

Chapter 16 How to design a database

How to design a data structure 504
The basic steps for designing a data structure 504
How to identify the data elements 506
How to subdivide the data elements 508
How to identify the tables and assign columns 510
How to identify the primary and foreign keys 512
How to enforce the relationships between tables 514
How normalization works 516
How to identify the columns to be indexed 518
How to normalize a data structure 520
The seven normal forms 520
How to apply the first normal form 522
How to apply the second normal form 524
How to apply the third normal form 526
When and how to denormalize a data structure 528
A database design tool 530
An introduction to MySQL Workbench 530
How to use MySQL Workbench to create database diagrams 532

Chapter 17 How to use SQL to create a MySQL database

How to work with databases 538
How to create a database 538
How to select a database 538
How to drop a database 538
How to work with tables 540
An introduction to MySQL data types 540
How to create a table 542
How to code a primary key 544
How to alter a table 546
How to drop a table 548
How to work with indexes 550
How to create an index 550
How to drop an index 550
How to work with users and privileges 552
A summary of privileges 552
How to create, rename, and drop users 554
How to grant privileges 556
How to revoke privileges 558
How to view privileges 560

Other skills for creating a database **562**
How to load data from text files 562
How to dump a database to a SQL script 564

The script for the Guitar Shop database **566**

Chapter 18 How to use SQL to work with a MySQL database

How to select data from a single table **574**
How to select columns from a table 574
How to use an alias for a column 576
How to select rows with a LIMIT clause 578
How to select rows with a WHERE clause 580
How to use the logical operators 582
How to use the IS NULL operator 584
How to use the LIKE operator 586
How to sort rows with an ORDER BY clause 588

How to select data from multiple tables **590**
How to code an inner join 590
When and how to use table aliases 592

How to code summary queries **594**
How to code aggregate functions 594
How to group queries by column 596

How to code subqueries **598**
Where to use subqueries 598
How to code correlated subqueries 600

How to insert, update, and delete rows **602**
How to insert rows 602
How to update rows 604
How to delete rows 606

Chapter 19 Professional PHP for working with MySQL

Three ways to use PHP to work with MySQL **612**
PDO (PHP Data Objects) 612
PHP's mysqli extension 612
PHP's MySQL extension 612

How to work with PDO **614**
How to work with prepared statements 614
How to set the error mode for PDO 618
A model in PDO 620

How to work with mysqli **626**
How to connect to a database 626
How to select data 628
How to insert, update, and delete data 630
How to work with prepared statements 632
The object-oriented style compared to the procedural style 636
A model in mysqli 638

Chapter 20 A database-driven web site

How to work with large text columns **646**
A simple content management system 646
How to add HTML tags to text 648

The include files for the Guitar Shop web site 650
The home page 650
The directory structure 650
The utility files 652
The view files 652

The Product Catalog application 658
The user interface 658
The controller 658
The view 658

The Product Manager application 662
The user interface 662
The controller 664
The view 666

Section 4 Master the advanced skills for building web sites

Chapter 21 How to create secure web sites

How to use a secure connection 676
An introduction to secure connections 676
How SSL authentication works 678
How to get a digital secure certificate 680
How to request a secure connection 682
How to redirect to a secure connection 684

How to use authentication 686
Three types of authentication 686
How to store and validate a password 688
How to use form-based authentication 690
How to use basic authentication 696

How to work with encrypted data 700
How to encrypt and decrypt data 700
A class for storing encrypted data 702

Chapter 22 How to send email and access other web sites

How to send email 708
How email works 708
How to install the PEAR Mail package 710
How to set up a test email account 712
How to use PEAR Mail to send an email 714
A helper function for sending an email 718
How to use the helper function to send an email 722

How to get data from other servers 724
How to enable the cURL library 724
How to use cURL to connect to another web server 726
How to use an API provided by another server 728

The YouTube Search application 730
The user interface 730
The controller 732
Search view 736
Email view 738

Chapter 23 How to work with files, uploads, and images

How to work with files 744
How to get a directory listing 744
How to read and write an entire file 746
How to read and write part of a file 748
How to read and write CSV data 750
How to copy, rename, and delete a file 752

How to upload a file 754
HTML for uploading a file 754
PHP for working with an uploaded file 754

How to work with images 756
How to get information about an image 756
How to read and write images 758
How to resize an image 760
How to work with transparency 762

The Image Upload application 764
The user interface 764
The utility files 766
The controller 772
The view 774

Chapter 24 An eCommerce web site

An introduction to the web site 780
Prototyping and stepwise refinement 780
The directory structure of the web site 782

The user interface for end users 784
The Catalog application 784
The Cart application 786
The Checkout and Account applications 786
The My Account page 788

The user interface for administrators 792
The Admin Login and Admin Menu pages 792
The Product Manager application 794
The Category Manager application 794
The Order Manager application 794
The Account Manager application 794

Reference aids

Appendix A How to set up your PC for this book

How to install Firefox and Notepad++ 802
How to install the Firefox browser 802
How to install Notepad++ 802

How to install and configure XAMPP 804
How to install XAMPP 804
How to configure phpMyAdmin 806

How to install and configure NetBeans 808
How to install NetBeans 808
How to configure xDebug 808

How to install the book applications and databases 810

How to install the source code for this book 810

How to create and restore the databases 812

How to fix a possible problem with the time zone 814

Appendix B How to set up your Mac for this book

How to install Firefox and TextWrangler 818

How to install the Firefox browser 818

How to install TextWrangler 818

How to install and configure XAMPP 820

How to install XAMPP 820

How to configure phpMyAdmin 822

How to install NetBeans and xDebug 824

How to install NetBeans 824

How to install xDebug 824

How to install the book applications and databases 826

How to install the source code for this book 826

How to create and restore the databases 828

How to fix a possible problem with the time zone 830

Introduction

Ever since it was created in 1995, PHP has been a favorite of developers for server-side web programming. In fact, in some surveys, it now stands as today's most popular web programming language. By most counts, over a million web sites have been written in PHP, including portions of today's largest, most recognizable sites, and often in tandem with MySQL as the database. As a result, there's a continuing demand for web developers who know how to use PHP and MySQL at the professional level. And with this book, you can become one of them.

Who this book is for

This book is for anyone who wants to learn how to build and maintain web sites that use PHP and MySQL. The only prerequisite for this book is that you have basic HTML and CSS skills. If you don't have these skills, you can get them by reading the first 10 chapters of *Murach's HTML, XHTML, and CSS*.

What this book does

This book gets you started with PHP and MySQL as quickly as possible and then builds out your skills in a professional way. To present the whole array of PHP and MySQL skills in a manageable progression, it's divided into four sections.

- Section 1 is designed to get you off to a fast start whether or not you have any programming experience. So chapter 2 presents a complete subset of PHP; chapter 3 shows you how to use a MySQL database; chapter 4 shows you how to develop database applications with PHP; chapter 5 shows how to structure the code in your applications by using the MVC pattern; and chapter 6 shows you how to test and debug your web applications.

  When you finish this section, you'll understand how all the pieces of web applications fit together, and you'll be ready for rapid progress in the sections that follow. Most important, you'll actually be able to build database-driven web applications of your own!

- In section 2, you'll expand your basic PHP skills to include the professional skills you'll need on the job every day. That means you'll soon be coding applications that use arrays, functions, regular expressions, exception handling, libraries, your own objects…and more! The last application in this section illustrates an object-oriented approach to data validation that you can use as a model for data validation in your own applications.

- In section 3, you'll expand your basic MySQL and PHP skills to include the skills you need for building full-fledged database-driven web applications. In chapter 16, you'll learn how to design a database. In chapter 17, you'll learn how to use SQL DDL statements to create a database and control user access to it. In chapter 18, you'll learn how to use SQL DML statements to extract and update the data in a MySQL database. And in chapters 19 and 20, you'll learn the advanced PHP skills that you need for developing database applications.

- The last section in this book rounds out your web development skills by showing you how to secure a web site, how to send email and access other web sites, and how to work with files, uploads, and images. These are the skills you need to ensure that your web applications come across as trustworthy, reliable, and fully professional to your visitors. Then, the last chapter in this section shows how to put all your skills together in an eCommerce web site.

Why you'll learn faster and better with this book

Like all our books, this one has features that you won't find in competing books. That's why we believe you'll learn faster and better with our book than with any other. Here are just a few of those features.

- Because section 1 presents a complete subset of PHP and MySQL in just 6 chapters and 204 pages, you're ready for productive work much faster than you are when you use competing books. This section also uses a self-paced approach that lets experienced programmers move more quickly and beginners work at a pace that's comfortable for absorbing all of the new information.

- Because the next three sections present all of the other skills that you need for developing web applications at a professional level, you can go from beginner to professional in a single book.

- The exercises at the end of each chapter let you practice what you've just learned. However, to make sure you get the most practice in the least time, these exercises start from applications that you download from our web site. This download also includes the solutions to the exercises so you can get help whenever you need it.

- If you page through this book, you'll see that all of the information is presented in "paired pages," with the essential syntax, guidelines, and examples on the right page and the perspective and extra explanation on the left page. This helps you learn faster by reading less...and this is the ideal reference format when you need to refresh your memory about how to do something.

- To show you how all of the pieces of a PHP and MySQL application work together, this book presents the HTML, PHP, and MySQL code for 16 applications, ranging from the simple to the complex. As we see it, the only way to master PHP programming is to study the code in applications like these. And yet, you won't find anything like this in other books.

- Of course, this book also presents dozens of short examples. So it's easy to find an example that shows how to do whatever you need to do as you develop web applications. And our "paired pages" presentation method makes it easy to find the example you're looking for because you don't have to dig out examples that are embedded in the text.

What software you need

To run web applications that use PHP and MySQL, you need the Apache web server, the MySQL database server, and PHP. All three of these can be downloaded and installed for free in a single download called XAMPP.

Then, to edit your PHP code, you can use any text editor that you like. However, a text editor that includes syntax coloring and auto-formatting will help you develop applications more quickly and with fewer errors. That's why we recommend Notepad++ for Windows users and TextWrangler for Mac OS users. Both are available for free, and both can be used for entering and editing HTML, CSS, and PHP code.

To test any web application, including PHP and MySQL applications, you just need a web browser. For that, we recommend Mozilla Firefox. It too is available for free.

Last, if you would like to use an Integrated Development Environment, we recommend the NetBeans IDE for PHP. It includes a text editor that lets you enter and edit code. It provides an easy way for you to run your applications. And it provides special tools that help you debug your applications.

To help you install these products, the appendixes provide the web site addresses and procedures that you'll need for both Windows and Mac OS systems. In addition, chapter 1 provides a quick guide to using Notepad++ and NetBeans.

How our downloadable files can help you learn

If you go to our web site at www.murach.com, you can download all the files that you need for getting the most from this book. These files include:

- the source code for the applications presented in this book
- the source code for the starting points for the exercises
- the source code for the solutions to the exercises

The source code for the book applications is valuable because it lets you run the applications on your own PC, experiment with the source code, and copy and paste any of the source code into your own applications. The exercise starts and solutions are valuable because they let you practice what you've learned on your own to solidify your skills. Here again, the appendixes show you how to download and install these files.

Support materials for trainers and instructors

If you're a corporate trainer or a college instructor who would like to use this book for a course, we offer an Instructor's CD that includes: (1) a complete set of PowerPoint slides that you can use to review and reinforce the content of the book; (2) instructional objectives that describe the skills a student should have upon completion of each chapter; (3) test banks that measure mastery of those skills; and (4) additional student materials.

To learn more about what this Instructor's CD offers and to find out how to get it, please go to our web site at www.murach.com and click on the Trainers link or the Instructors link. Or, if you prefer, you can call Kelly at 1-800-221-5528 or send an email to kelly@murach.com.

Two companion books for every web developer

Today, to build professional web applications, you need three sets of skills. First, you need to know how to use HTML and CSS to markup and format the content that's displayed in the browser. Second, you need to know how to use JavaScript to do client-side processing. Third, you need to know how to use a language like PHP and a database like MySQL to do server-side processing.

When you finish this PHP and MySQL book, you can add to your skill set by getting our two companion books:

Murach's HTML, XHTML, and CSS
Murach's JavaScript and DOM Scripting

If you're new to these subjects, these books get you started fast and present the skills that you need for developing professional web applications. If you have experience with these subjects, these books make it easy for you to learn new skills whenever you need them. And after you've used these books for training, they become the best on-the-job references you've ever used.

Please let us know how this book works for you

From the start of this project, Ray and I had two goals for this book. First, we wanted to make it easier than ever for you to get started with PHP and MySQL. Second, we wanted you to be able to quickly build on that foundation as you raise your skills to the expert level. Now, we hope that we've succeeded.

So, if you have any comments about this book, we would appreciate hearing from you. We thank you for buying this book. And we wish you all the best with your PHP and MySQL programming.

Joel Murach

Joel Murach, Author
joel@murach.com

Section 1

Get started fast with PHP and MySQL

The six chapters in this section are designed to get you off to a fast start with PHP and MySQL. First, in chapter 1, you'll learn how web programming with PHP works and what tools you can use to develop PHP applications. Then, in chapter 2, you'll learn how to use PHP to develop applications that don't require a database.

The next two chapters get you going with MySQL databases. In chapter 3, you'll learn how a relational database works and how to use phpMyAdmin to work with a MySQL database. In chapter 4, you'll learn how to develop PHP applications that get data from and store data in a MySQL database.

The last two chapters in this section round out your skillset. First, chapter 5 shows you how to structure and organize your code by using the MVC pattern. Then, chapter 6 presents the techniques that you will need for testing and debugging applications.

When you complete this section, you'll have all the skills that you need for coding, testing, and debugging significant database applications. Then, you can enhance those skills by reading the chapters in any of the other sections.

1

Introduction to web development with PHP

This chapter introduces you to the concepts and terms that you need for developing web applications with PHP. This chapter also shows you how to deploy, edit, and test a PHP application. When you finish this chapter, you'll have all the background you need for learning how to write the code for PHP applications.

The architecture of a web application **4**
How a client-server architecture works 4
How static web pages are processed 6
How dynamic web pages are processed 8
A survey of web application software 10
Highlights in the history of PHP 12
Highlights in the history of MySQL 12

The Product Discount application **14**
The user interface 14
The HTML file 16
The CSS file 18
The PHP file 20

How to edit and test a PHP application **22**
How to edit a PHP page with a text editor 22
How to start and stop Apache and MySQL on your own computer 24
How to deploy a PHP application 26
How to run a PHP application 28
How to test and debug a PHP page 30
How to view the source code for a web page 32

How to use NetBeans to develop a PHP application **34**
How to work with PHP projects and files 34
How to edit and test a PHP application 36
How to import and configure a PHP project 38

Perspective **40**

The architecture of a web application

The *World Wide Web*, or web, consists of many components that work together to bring a web page to your desktop over the *Internet*. Before you start PHP programming, you need to have a basic understanding of how these components interact and where PHP fits into this architecture.

How a client-server architecture works

Web applications use a *client-server architecture*. This architecture consists of *servers* that share resources with *clients* over a *network*. Figure 1-1 shows the components of a simple client-server architecture.

A *server* can share resources such as files, printers, web sites, databases, and e-mail. A *web server* is a server that shares web sites, and a *web browser* is the client software used to access the web server.

A *network* is a communication system that allows clients and servers to communicate. A *Network Interface Card* (*NIC*) connects the computer to the network. This connection can either be wired or wireless. Ethernet is a common type of wired network. Wi-Fi is a common type of wireless network.

The network is responsible for getting information from one computer to another. This process is called routing. A *router* is a device that is connected to two or more networks. When information comes in from one network, the router determines which network is closest to the destination and sends the information out on that network.

Networks can be categorized by size. A *Local Area Network* (*LAN*) is a small network of computers that are near each other and can communicate with each other over short distances. Computers on a LAN are typically in the same building or in adjacent buildings. This type of network is often called an *intranet*, and it can be used to run web applications for use by employees only.

A *Wide Area Network* (*WAN*) consists of multiple LANs that have been connected together over long distances using routers. A WAN can be owned privately by one company or it can be shared by multiple companies.

An *Internet Service Provider* (*ISP*) is a company that owns a WAN that is connected to the Internet. An ISP leases access to its network to other companies that need to be connected to the Internet.

The Internet is a global network consisting of multiple WANs that have been connected together. ISPs connect their WANs together at large routers called *Internet Exchange Points* (*IXP*). This allows anyone connected to the Internet to exchange information with anyone else.

This figure shows an example of data crossing the Internet. In the diagram, data is being sent from the client in the top left to the server in the bottom right. Here, the data leaves the client's LAN and enters the WAN owned by the client's ISP. Next, the data is routed through an IXP to the WAN owned by the server's ISP. Then, it enters the server's LAN and finally reaches the server. All of this can happen in less than 1/10th of a second.

The architecture of a web application

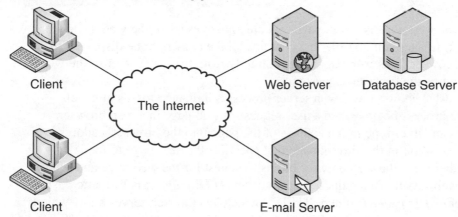

The architecture of the Internet

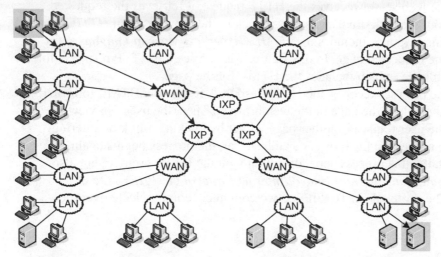

Description

- A *server* makes resources available to other computers called *clients* over a network. A server can share files, printers, web sites, databases, or e-mail.

- A *network* uses *routers* to get information from the sender to its destination.

- A *Local Area Network* (LAN) directly connects computers that are near each other.

- A *Wide Area Network* (WAN) uses routers to connect computers that are far from each other.

- The *Internet* consists of many WANs that have been connected together at *Internet Exchange Points* (IXP). A list of IXPs can be found at http://en.wikipedia.org/wiki/IXP.

- An *Internet Service Provider* (ISP) owns a WAN and leases access to this network. It connects its WAN to the rest of the Internet at one or more IXPs.

Figure 1-1   How a client-server architecture works

How static web pages are processed

A *static web page* is a web page that only changes when the web developer changes it. It is a plain text file that contains all the content to be displayed in the web browser. This web page is sent directly from the web server to the web browser when the browser requests it.

Figure 1-2 shows how a web server processes a request for a static web page. The process begins when a user requests a web page in a web browser. The user can either type in the address of the page into the browser's address bar or click a link in the current page that specifies the next page to load.

In either case, the web browser builds a request for the web page and sends it to the web server. This request, known as an *HTTP request*, is formatted using the *HyperText Transfer Protocol* (HTTP), which lets the web server know which file is being requested. In this figure, you can see the content of a simple HTTP request.

When the web server receives the HTTP request, it retrieves the requested web page from the disk drive and sends it back to the browser as an *HTTP response*. This response includes the *HTML* (*HyperText Markup Language*) for displaying the requested page. In this figure, you can see the HTTP response for a simple web page, which includes the HTML for the page.

When the browser receives the HTTP response, it uses the HTML to format the page and displays the page in the web browser. Then, the user can view the content. If the user requests another page, either by clicking a link or entering another web address in the browser's address bar, the process begins again.

Incidentally, this process depends not only on the HTTP protocol but also on the *Transmission Control Protocol/Internet Protocol* (*TCP/IP*) suite of protocols. The protocols in TCP/IP let two computers communicate over the network.

How a web server processes a static web page

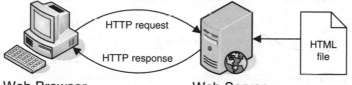

Web Browser   Web Server

A simple HTTP request

```
GET / HTTP/1.1
Host: www.example.com
```

A simple HTTP response

```
HTTP/1.1 200 OK
Content-Type: text/html
Content-Length: 136
Server: Apache/2.2.3

<html>
<head>
    <title>Example Web Page</title>
</head>
<body>
    <p>This is a sample web page</p>
</body>
</html>
```

Two protocols that web applications depend upon

- *HyperText Transfer Protocol* (*HTTP*) is the protocol that web browsers and web servers use to communicate. It sets the specifications for HTTP requests and responses.

- *Transmission Control Protocol/Internet Protocol* (*TCP/IP*) is a suite of protocols that let two computers communicate over a network.

Description

- *HyperText Markup Language* (*HTML*) is the language used to design the web pages of an application.

- A *static web page* is an HTML document that's stored on the web server and doesn't change in response to user input. Static web pages have a filename with an extension of .htm or .html.

- When the user requests a static web page, the browser sends an *HTTP request* to the web server that includes the name of the file that's being requested.

- When the web server receives the request, it retrieves the web page and sends it back to the browser in an *HTTP response*. This response includes the HTML document that's stored in the file that was requested.

Figure 1-2   How static web pages are processed

How dynamic web pages are processed

A *dynamic web page* is a page that's created by a program or script that's running on a server. This means that the page can be changed each time it is viewed.

The changes in the page can come from processing the form data that the user submits or by displaying data that's retrieved from a *database server*. A database server stores information that's organized in tables, and this information can be quickly retrieved by a database query.

Dynamic web pages enable web developers to create interactive web applications. As a result, users can purchase goods and services, search the web for information, and communicate with other users through forums, blogs, and social networking sites. Sites like these would be difficult or impossible to create without database-driven, dynamic web pages.

Figure 1-3 shows how a web server processes a dynamic web page with PHP. The process begins when the user requests a page in a web browser. The user can either enter the URL of the page in the browser's address bar, click a link that specifies the dynamic page to load, or click a button that submits a form that contains the data that the dynamic page should process.

In each case, the web browser builds an HTTP request and sends it to the web server. If the user submits form data, that data will be included in the HTTP request.

When the web server receives the HTTP request, it looks up the file extension of the requested web page to determine which server or program should process the request. For a PHP page, the web server forwards the request to the *PHP interpreter*, which is running on the web server.

The PHP interpreter gets the appropriate PHP script from the hard drive. It also loads any form data that the user submitted. Then, it executes the script. As the script executes, it generates a web page as its output. The script may also request data from a database server and use that data as part of the web page it is generating.

When the script is finished, the PHP interpreter passes the dynamically generated web page back to the web server. Then, the web server sends the page back to the browser in an HTTP response that includes the HTML for the page.

When the web browser receives the HTTP response, it formats and displays the web page. This is called *rendering* a page. Note, however, that the web browser has no way to tell whether the HTML in the HTTP response was for a static page or a dynamic page because all it receives is HTML.

When the page is displayed in the browser, the user can view the content. Then, when the user requests another page, the process begins again. The process that begins with the user requesting a web page and ends with the server sending a response back to the client is called a *round trip*.

How a web server processes a dynamic web page with PHP

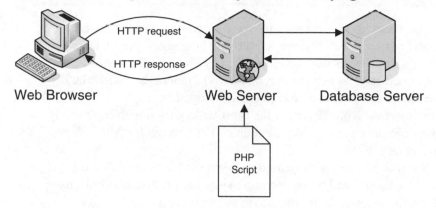

Description

- A *dynamic web page* is a web page that's generated by a server-side program or script. Often, the web page changes according to the information that is submitted by the web browser to the server.

- When a web server receives a request for a dynamic web page, it uses the extension of the requested file to determine which server or program should process the request. If the extension is php, the web server calls the *PHP interpreter* to process the request and the data that's submitted with the request.

- The PHP page can use the data that it gets from the web browser to access the appropriate data from a *database server*. The application can also store the data that it gets from the web browser in the database server.

- When the PHP interpreter finishes processing the PHP page, it generates an HTML page and returns it to the web server. The web server then returns the page to the web browser.

- The browser can't tell whether the HTML that is returned to it was retrieved from a static web page or generated dynamically by the PHP interpreter. Either way, the browser simply displays (*renders*) the HTML that it receives.

- The process that begins with the user requesting a web page and ends with the server sending a response back to the client is called a *round trip*.

Figure 1-3   How dynamic web pages are processed

A survey of web application software

Figure 1-4 summarizes the software for the four components of a web application: web browsers, web servers, server-side languages, and database servers. The first web browser was developed in 1991 by Tim Berners-Lee at the European Council for Nuclear Research (CERN) in Geneva, Switzerland. Since then, dozens of web browsers have been developed.

Microsoft's Internet Explorer (IE) is the most widely used web browser. It is currently available only for Windows, but an earlier version for Mac OS was available until January 2006.

Firefox is the second most widely used web browser. It is available for Windows, Mac OS, Linux, and other operating systems. Firefox was built using source code from the original Netscape Navigator web browser.

Safari and Opera are used by only a small percentage of users. Safari is the default web browser for Mac OS, but it is also available for Windows. Opera is available for Windows, Mac OS, Linux, and other operating systems.

Google's Chrome was released in 2008 and its popularity is growing fast. Chrome is based on the same rendering engine as Safari. As a result, it renders pages similarly to Safari.

The Apache web server, which was developed by the Apache Software Foundation, is the most widely used web server. It is an open-source software project that's available for free. Although there are Apache versions for most modern operating systems, it is typically used on a Linux server.

The other widely used web server is Microsoft's Internet Information Services (IIS). It is included as part of the Windows Server operating system.

Of the *server-side languages*, PHP, Perl, and Python can all be directly installed on an Apache or IIS web server. These languages are referred to as *scripting languages*.

In contrast, JSP and ASP.NET require an *application server* in addition to the web server. For example, JSP applications typically run on an application server such as Tomcat or Glassfish. And ASP.NET applications typically run on an application server for IIS. For more information about JSP and ASP.NET, please see our books on these subjects.

PHP is commonly used with the MySQL database server. This database server is an open-source database server that runs on all major operating systems. However, PHP can also be used with other database servers. Three of the most widely used database servers are Oracle, IBM's DB2, and Microsoft's SQL Server.

Web browsers

Browser	Description
Internet Explorer	Published by Microsoft. It is only available for the Windows operating system.
Firefox	Published by the Mozilla Corporation. It is available for all major operating systems.
Safari	Published by Apple. It is available for the OS X and Windows operating systems.
Opera	Published by Opera Software. It is available for all major operating systems, and it is most commonly used on Cell Phones and PDA's.
Chrome	Published by Google. It is available for Windows operating systems.

Web servers

Server	Description
Apache	An open-source web server that can run on any major operating system. It supports many server-side scripting languages and can interact with many different database servers. The most common configuration is known as LAMP, which consists of Linux, Apache, MySQL, and PHP.
IIS	Microsoft's web server that only runs on Windows operating systems. It primarily supports ASP.NET web development and MS SQL Server.

Server-side languages

Language	Description
PHP	(PHP: Hypertext Processor) Typically used with the Apache web server but also available for IIS. It uses the .php file extension.
JSP	(JavaServer Pages) Requires an application server such as the Tomcat server that's available from the Apache Software Foundation. JSP pages use the .jsp file extension and typically work with servlets that are written in Java.
ASP.NET	(Active Server Pages) Used with the Microsoft IIS web server. ASP.NET pages use the .aspx file extension and typically work with server-side code that's written in C# or Visual Basic.
Perl	Originally developed for use at the UNIX command line to manipulate text, it was later used to build web applications. It uses the .pl file extension.
Python	Used to develop many types of applications in addition to web applications. It is typically used with the Apache web server. It uses the .py file extension.

Database servers

Server	Description
MySQL	An open-source database that is available for all major operating systems.
Oracle	Oracle's database server that is available for all major operating systems.
DB2	IBM's database server that is available for all major operating systems.
MS SQL Server	Microsoft's database server that is only available for the Windows operating system.

Figure 1-4   A survey of web application software

Highlights in the history of PHP

Figure 1-5 summarizes some of the highlights in the history of PHP. To start, PHP 2 was released in 1995 with a name of Personal Home Page. Then, in 1998, PHP 3 was released. With this release, the name of PHP was changed to *PHP: Hypertext Processor*.

In 2000, PHP 4 introduced the Zend Engine. This improved PHP's performance and its popularity too. Finally, in 2004, PHP 5 introduced the Zend Engine II. In addition, PHP 5 introduced improved support for object-oriented programming, the PHP Data Objects extension, and other new features.

As this book goes to press, PHP 5.3 is the current version of PHP. As a result, that's the version of PHP that's used throughout this book. Most of the code in this book also works with other versions of PHP. However, if you're using a different version of PHP, you may notice some differences.

Highlights in the history of MySQL

Figure 1-5 also summarizes some of the highlights in the history of MySQL. To start, MySQL 3.23 was released in 1995. This version of MySQL became widely used by many web sites. Then, in 2003, MySQL 4.0 introduced support for unions. In 2004, MySQL 4.1 introduced support for subqueries and prepared statements. In 2005, MySQL 5.0 introduced support for stored procedures, triggers, views, and transactions. Finally, in 2008, MySQL 5.1 introduced support for row-based replication and server log tables.

MySQL is owned and sponsored by a for-profit firm named MySQL AB. However, in 2008, Sun Microsystems acquired MySQL AB. Then, in 2009, Oracle Corporation acquired Sun Microsystems. As a result, Oracle now has a big say in the future of the MySQL database, which competes with the Oracle database.

Fearing that Oracle will stop developing MySQL, many of the original developers of MySQL left MySQL AB shortly after its acquisition by Oracle and began working on different forks of the open-source code. One of the most popular of these forks is MariaDB. As a result, even if Oracle stops or slows development of MySQL, developers can still consider using MariaDB or other forks of MySQL.

Highlights in the history of PHP

Version	Year	Description
2	1995	This version was named Personal Home Page.
3	1998	This version was renamed *PHP: Hypertext Processor.*
4	2000	This version introduced the Zend Engine.
5	2004	This version introduced the Zend Engine II. It includes improved support for object-oriented programming, the PHP Data Objects extension, and other new features.

Highlights in the history of MySQL

Version	Year	Description
3.23	1995	The original version of MySQL is released.
4.0	2003	This version introduced support for unions.
4.1	2004	This version introduced support for subqueries and prepared statements.
5.0	2005	This version introduced support for stored procedures, triggers, views, and transactions.
5.1	2008	This version introduced support for row-based replication and server log tables.

Description

- MySQL is owned and sponsored by MySQL AB, a for-profit firm.
- In 2008, Sun Microsystems acquired MySQL AB.
- In 2009, Oracle Corporation acquired Sun Microsystems.
- In 2009, many of the original developers of MySQL left MySQL AB and begin working on different forks of the open-source code. One of the most popular of these forks is MariaDB.

Figure 1-5   Highlights in the history of PHP and MySQL

The Product Discount application

To give a better idea of how a PHP application works, this topic presents a simple application. This application consists of three files: an HTML file, a CSS file, and a PHP file.

The user interface

Figure 1-6 shows the user interface for this application. On the first page of the application, the user enters a product description, price, and discount percent, and then clicks the Calculate Discount button. This submits the data to the web server as part of an HTTP request.

When the web server receives the request, it passes the request to the PHP interpreter, which processes the request. It then generates the HTML for the second page of this application and sends it to the web server, which passes the page back to the browser.

The first page (index.html)

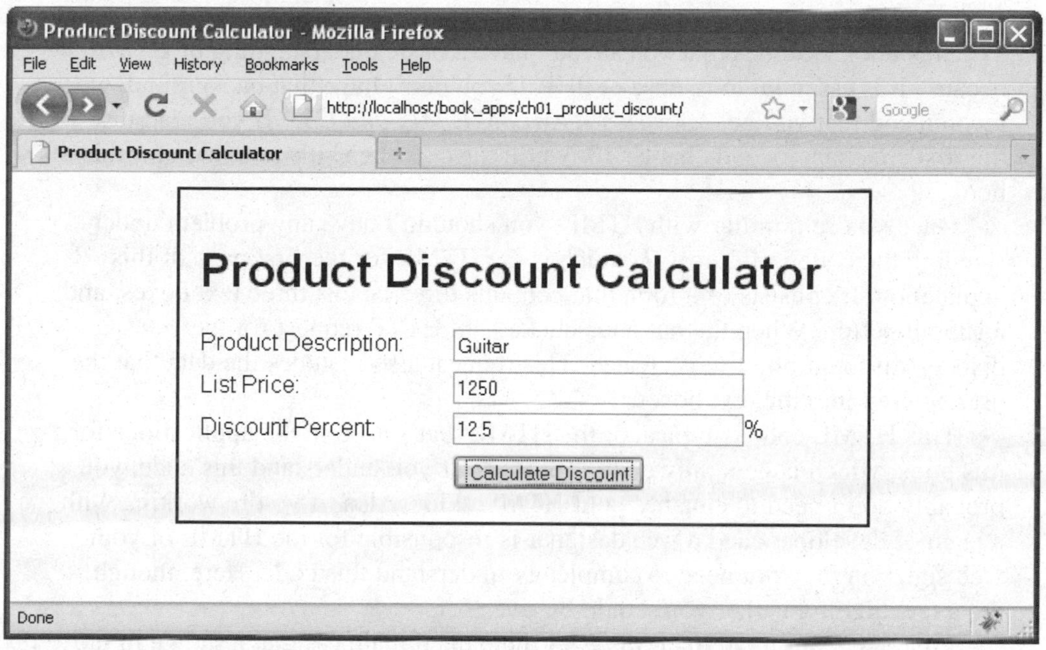

The second page (the response)

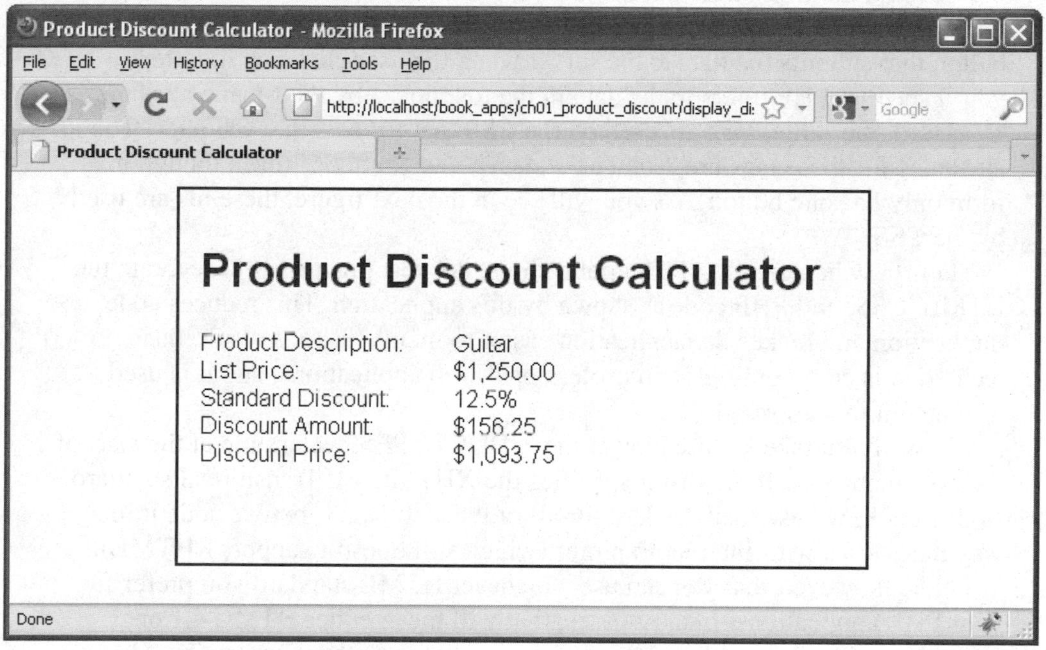

Figure 1-6   The user interface for the Product Discount application

The HTML file

This book assumes that you already have a basic understanding of HTML because it is essential to the use of PHP. If you don't have that background, we recommend that you get *Murach's HTML, XHTML, and CSS*. If you read just the first six chapters and chapter 10, you'll have all the skills you need for this book.

Once you're familiar with HTML, you shouldn't have any problem understanding the code in figure 1-7, which is the HTML for the first page of this application. It consists of a form that contains three labels, three text boxes, and a submit button. When the button is clicked, an HTTP request for the display_discount.php file is created. This request also includes the data that the user entered into the text boxes.

This HTML code is typical of the HTML that's used in the applications for this book, which is generally quite simple. So if you understand this code, you probably don't need to enhance your HTML skills. Also, if you're working with a team of developers and a web designer is responsible for the HTML of your web site, you may not need to completely understand this code. Here, though, are a few highlights that you should be aware of.

First, the <link> tag loads the CSS file named main.css that's shown in the next figure. That file is used to format both of the pages in this application.

Second, the first three <label> and <input> tags create the three labels and text boxes that let the user enter data. Then, the last <input> tag creates the button that submits the data to the server when the user clicks on it. Later, you'll see that PHP refers to the data in the text boxes by their name attributes.

Third, the <div> tags are used by the CSS that formats the web page. The id attributes for these tags are "content", "data", and "buttons" (even though this form only has one button). As you will see in the next figure, these ids are used by the CSS.

Fourth, when creating PHP applications, the best practice is to separate the HTML, CSS, and PHP code as shown by this application. This reduces code duplication and makes the application easier to maintain. As a result, this technique is commonly used in professional web applications, and it is used throughout this book.

Last, if you take a close look at the <!DOCTYPE> declaration at the start of the document, you'll see that it specifies the XHTML 1.0 Transitional standard. In this book, we use that standard for all of the web pages, but we code it in a way that works with Internet Explorer (which still doesn't support XHTML).

Note, however, that you can use whichever HTML standard you prefer for your PHP applications. In most cases, that will mean either HTML 4.1 or XHTML 1.0 Transitional, and the differences between them are trivial. Also, please note that we use the term *HTML* to refer to both HTML and XHTML throughout this book.

The HTML file (index.html)

```
<!DOCTYPE html PUBLIC "-//W3C//DTD XHTML 1.0 Transitional//EN"
    "http://www.w3.org/TR/xhtml1/DTD/xhtml1-transitional.dtd">
<html xmlns="http://www.w3.org/1999/xhtml">

<head>
    <title>Product Discount Calculator</title>
    <link rel="stylesheet" type="text/css" href="main.css" />
</head>

<body>
    <div id="content">
        <h1>Product Discount Calculator</h1>
        <form action="display_discount.php" method="post">

            <div id="data">
                <label>Product Description:</label>
                <input type="text" name="product_description"/><br />

                <label>List Price:</label>
                <input type="text" name="list_price"/><br />

                <label>Discount Percent:</label>
                <input type="text" name="discount_percent"/>%<br />
            </div>

            <div id="buttons">
                <label> </label>
                <input type="submit" value="Calculate Discount" /><br />
            </div>

        </form>
    </div>
</body>
</html>
```

Figure 1-7   The HTML file for the Product Discount application

The CSS file

Figure 1-8 shows the *CSS* (*Cascading Style Sheets*) file for the Product Discount application. Here again, this book assumes that you have a basic understanding of CSS. If you don't, please get a copy of *Murach's HTML, XHTML, and CSS*, and read chapters 4 through 6.

Once you're familiar with CSS, you won't have any trouble understanding the code in this figure. Here, seven *rule sets* are applied to the HTML elements for both pages of the application. The first rule set applies to the <body> element. The second applies to the <div> element that has an id with a value of "content". The third and fourth apply to the <h1> and <label> elements. The fifth and six apply to the <input> elements that are coded in the "data" and "buttons" <div> tags. And the seventh applies to the <br> tag.

Because CSS is incidental to PHP applications, this is the only time that we present the CSS for an application in this book. Note, however, that the CSS for every application is available with the download for this book.

Like the HTML for this application, this CSS is typical of the CSS used for the other applications in this book, which is quite simple. Also, if you are working with a team of developers and a web designer is responsible for the CSS for your web site, you may not need to use CSS at all. In that case, just realize that the CSS does the formatting for the pages.

The CSS file (main.css)

```css
body {
    font-family: Arial, Helvetica, sans-serif;
}

#content {
    width: 450px;
    margin: 0 auto;
    padding: 0px 20px 20px;
    background: white;
    border: 2px solid navy;
}

h1 {
    color: navy;
}

label {
    width: 10em;
    padding-right: 1em;
    float: left;
}

#data input {
    float: left;
    width: 15em;
    margin-bottom: .5em;
}

#buttons input {
    float: left;
    margin-bottom: .5em;
}

br {
    clear: left;
}
```

Figure 1-8   The CSS file for the Product Discount application

The PHP file

Figure 1-9 shows the PHP file for the Product Discount application. In the next chapter, you're going to learn the details for writing PHP code like this. But if you have some programming experience, the explanation that follows should help you understand what's happening right now.

To start, the PHP file gets the data that's stored in the text boxes of the HTML file. To do that, it uses the $_POST array to retrieve the data from the text boxes. This works because the HTML file specifies the POST method for the form that is submitted. To retrieve a value from the $_POST array, this code specifies the name attributes that were used in the <input> tags for the text boxes. For example, a value of "product_description" gets the data that the user entered into the Product Description text box.

After the PHP gets the data for each text box, it stores it in a variable with a name that starts with a dollar ($) sign. For instance, the product description is stored in a variable named $product_description.

After it stores the data in variables, the PHP code calculates the discount amount and discount price by operating on the data in the variables. To do that, the first statement uses the multiplication operator (*) to calculate the discount amount and store it in the $discount variable. Then, the second statement uses the subtraction operator (-) to calculate the discount price and store it in a variable named $discount_price.

These calculations are possible because PHP automatically converts string values to numeric data types if the string value contains numeric characters only. For example, if the user enters 399.95 for the list price, PHP stores this variable as a number, not as a string. As a result, you can perform arithmetic calculations on this variable.

After performing the calculations, the PHP code formats four of the values that the page needs to display. To do that, it uses the number_format function to format three of the numeric variables so they display two decimal places. It also uses the concatenation operator (.) to add a dollar sign ($) to three of the variables and a percent sign (%) to one of the variables. This automatically converts the numeric values to string values.

The rest of the PHP file looks much like a normal HTML page. However, it uses five PHP echo statements to display the data that's stored in the PHP variables within the five <span> tags on the page.

This simple application shows how PHP can get data that's submitted by a user, process that data, and return the processed data to the user. It also shows how HTML, CSS, and PHP work together in a web application. In chapter 2, you'll learn how to write the PHP code for an application like this.

The PHP file (display_discount.php)

```php
<?php
    // get the data from the form
    $product_description = $_POST['product_description'];
    $list_price = $_POST['list_price'];
    $discount_percent = $_POST['discount_percent'];

    // calculate the discount
    $discount = $list_price * $discount_percent * .01;
    $discount_price = $list_price - $discount;

    // apply currency formatting to the dollar and percent amounts
    $list_price_formatted = "$".number_format($list_price, 2);
    $discount_percent_formatted = $discount_percent."%";
    $discount_formatted = "$".number_format($discount, 2);
    $discount_price_formatted = "$".number_format($discount_price, 2);
?>
<!DOCTYPE html PUBLIC "-//W3C//DTD XHTML 1.0 Transitional//EN"
    "http://www.w3.org/TR/xhtml1/DTD/xhtml1-transitional.dtd">
<html xmlns="http://www.w3.org/1999/xhtml">

<head>
    <title>Product Discount Calculator</title>
    <link rel="stylesheet" type="text/css" href="main.css">
</head>

<body>
    <div id="content">
        <h1>Product Discount Calculator</h1>

        <label>Product Description:</label>
        <span><?php echo $product_description; ?></span><br>

        <label>List Price:</label>
        <span><?php echo $list_price_formatted; ?></span><br>

        <label>Standard Discount:</label>
        <span><?php echo $discount_percent_formatted; ?></span><br>

        <label>Discount Amount:</label>
        <span><?php echo $discount_formatted; ?></span><br>

        <label>Discount Price:</label>
        <span><?php echo $discount_price_formatted; ?></span><br>
    </div>
</body>
</html>
```

Figure 1-9   The PHP file for the Product Discount application

How to edit and test a PHP application

Now that you know the components that make up a PHP application, you're ready to learn how to edit and test a PHP application.

How to edit a PHP page with a text editor

Although you can use any text editor to enter and edit HTML, CSS, and PHP files, using a text editor that's designed for working with HTML, CSS, and PHP can speed development time and help reduce coding errors. Some features to look for in a text editor are syntax highlighting and auto-completion.

If you're using Windows, we recommend that you use Notepad++ as your editor because it provides these features. Although there are many other free and commercial text editors, Notepad++ provides all of the features that you'll need for the purposes of this book.

If you're a Mac OS user, we recommend that you use TextWrangler as your editor. This is a free editor that provides syntax highlighting and FTP access, although it doesn't provide auto-completion. Here again, though, you have other choices like commercial editors that do provide auto-completion such as BBEdit (the commercial version of TextWrangler).

To illustrate the use of a text editor for HTML, CSS, and PHP files, figure 1-10 shows Notepad++ as it's being used to edit a PHP file. This editor provides tabs so you can edit more than one file at the same time. In addition, it color codes the syntax of the statements to reflect different coding elements. If you experiment with Notepad++, you'll find that it has many other capabilities that this brief summary doesn't present.

Before you start using Notepad++, you may want to take the time to change the style for comments because the default style is too small on some systems. This skill is summarized in this figure.

Then, when you start a new file, you should let Notepad++ know what language you're working with. To do that, you can either save the file with the .html, .css, or .php extension, or you can use the Language menu to select the language. Once you do that, this editor uses the appropriate color coding.

Notepad++ with three tabs open

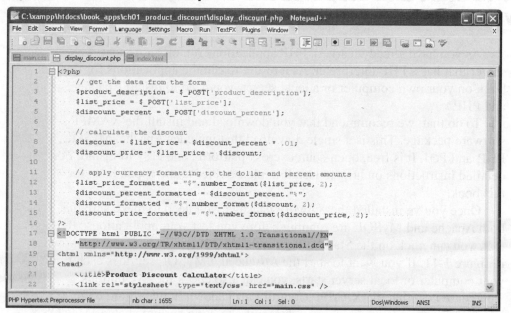

How to open, save, close, and start files

- To open a file, use the Open button in the toolbar. Or, right-click on the file in the Windows Explorer and select the Edit with Notepad++ command.
- To save the current file, use the Save button in the toolbar or press Ctrl+S. Or, to save all open files, use the Save All button.
- To close the current file, use the Close button in the toolbar. Or, to close all open files, use the Close All button.
- To start a new file in a new tab, use the New button in the toolbar.

How to change the style for comments

- Start the Settings→Styler Configurator command, and select PHP in the language list and COMMENT in the style list. Then, change the font name and font size in the drop-down lists to the blank entries at the top of the lists.
- Repeat this for COMMENTLINE for the PHP language, for COMMENT for the HTML language, and for COMMENT for the CSS language.

Description

- You can use many different text editors for editing HTML, CSS, and PHP code. For Windows, we recommend Notepad++. For the Mac, we recommend TextWrangler.

Figure 1-10   How to edit a PHP file with a text editor

How to start and stop Apache and MySQL on your own computer

As you have already learned, PHP applications run on an Apache web server that has a PHP interpreter. As a result, to run the applications for this book on your own computer or a local server, you need to install Apache and PHP.

To do that, we recommend that you download and install the XAMPP software package. This is a single download that includes Apache, MySQL, PHP, and Perl. It is free, open-source, cross-platform, and easy to install. For detailed instructions on how to install it, please refer to the appendixes for this book.

Once you've installed the XAMPP package, you need to make sure that both Apache and MySQL are running before you test your applications. To do that, you can click on the Start buttons in the XAMPP Control Panel as shown in figure 1-11. If you want to start the Apache and MySQL services each time your computer or local server starts, you can also check the Svc buttons.

Please note that the XAMPP Control Panel shown in this figure is for a Windows system. If you're using a different operating system such as Mac OS X, the XAMPP Control Panel will look different than the one shown in this figure, and it will work a little differently too. However, it will still include buttons that allow you to start and stop the Apache and MySQL servers.

The XAMPP Control Panel

```
XAMPP Control Panel Application              _ □ X

        XAMPP Control Panel            [  Shell   ]
        (Apache Friends Edition)       [  Setup   ]

Modules                                [ Port-Check ]
☑ Svc   Apache   Running   [ Stop ]  [ Admin ]   [ Explore ]
☑ Svc   MySql    Running   [ Stop ]  [ Admin ]   [  SCM   ]
☐ Svc   FileZilla          [ Start ] [ Admin ]   [ Refresh ]
☐ Svc   Mercury            [ Start ] [ Admin ]   [  Help   ]
☐ Svc   Tomcat             [ Start ] [ Admin ]   [  Exit   ]

Busy...
Apache service stopped
Busy...
Apache service started
Busy...
Apache service started
Busy...
Apache service started
```

How to start the XAMPP control panel

- On a Windows system, select the XAMPP Control Panel item from the Windows Start menu or double-click on the XAMPP icon on your desktop.
- On a Mac OS system, start XAMPP Control at Applications➔XAMPP or click on the XAMPP Control on the dock. This displays a control panel that is similar to the one above.

How to start and stop Apache or MySQL

- Click on its Start or Stop button.
- To start Apache or MySQL automatically when your computer starts, check its Svc checkbox.

Description

- *XAMPP* is a free, open-source web server package that consists of Apache, MySQL, and interpreters for PHP and Perl.
- XAMPP can be easily installed by downloading and installing one exe file.
- XAMPP is available for Windows, Linux, Solaris, and Mac OS X systems (the X in XAMPP stands for cross-platform).
- To install XAMPP, please refer to appendix A or B.

Figure 1-11   How to start and stop Apache and MySQL on your own computer

How to deploy a PHP application

When you *deploy* an application, you make it accessible from a browser. To do that on your own computer or on a local server when running Windows, you copy all of the directories and files for the application to the \xampp\htdocs directory for the Apache server because that's where Apache looks for applications.

This is illustrated by the first directory structure of figure 1-12. Here, the top-level directory for a guitar store application has been copied to the htdocs directory. In this example, only four subdirectories are shown, including a directory for CSS files and a directory for storing the images that are required by the application. In practice, though, a large application is likely to contain many subdirectories at several different levels.

Note here, that the htdocs directory is called the *document root directory*, while the guitar_store directory is called the *application root directory*. This just means that htdocs is the root directory for all applications, while guitar_store is the root directory for one application.

For this book, you'll be working with many small applications that are designed to help you learn. If you install these applications as described in the appendix, they will be in two directories that are subordinate to the htdocs directory: book_apps and ex_starts. This is illustrated by the second directory structure in this figure. For instance, ch01_product_discount in the book_apps directory is the directory for the application in this chapter. And ch02_ex1 in the ex_starts directory is the directory for the application for the first exercise in chapter 2.

To deploy an application on an Internet server, you copy the application directories and files from the local server to your root directory on the Internet server. To do that, you can use an *FTP program*, which uses *File Transfer Protocol* to upload the files from the local server to the Internet server. To make this work, of course, the Internet server must be running Apache and a PHP interpreter.

In practice, PHP applications are usually developed and tested on a local server before they are uploaded to an Internet server. To make that manageable, the directory structure on the local server is exactly the same as (it "mirrors") the directory structure on the Internet server. That also makes it easier to maintain and enhance a web application later on.

The file structure for a PHP application on a local server

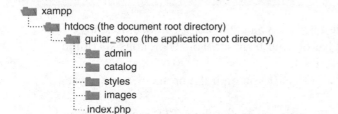

The file structure for the book applications and exercise starts

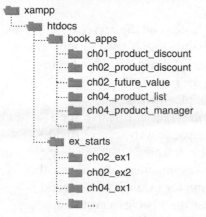

How to deploy a PHP application on a local server

- Copy all of the directories and files for an application to the \xampp\htdocs directory on the server. This is where Apache looks for PHP applications.

How to deploy the downloadable applications on a local server

- Copy the book_apps and ex_starts directories and all their contents to the \xampp\htdocs directory on the server.

How to deploy an application on an Internet server

- Use an *FTP (File Transfer Protocol) program* to upload the tested directories and files to the htdocs directory of the Apache web server.

Description

- To *deploy* a PHP application so you can run it, you need to store the directories and files for the application in the htdocs directory of an Apache server that's on your own PC, a local server, or an Internet server.

- The files for a PHP application usually include HTML, CSS, PHP, and image files. These files are stored in appropriate directories.

- Usually, the directories and files on the local server will mirror the directories and files that get uploaded to the Internet server.

Figure 1-12   How to deploy a PHP application

How to run a PHP application

To access a web page on the Internet, you can enter a *Uniform Resource Locator* (*URL*) into the address bar of your browser. This URL consists of the four components shown in figure 1-13.

In most cases, the *protocol* is HTTP. If you omit the protocol, the browser uses HTTP as the default.

The *domain name* identifies the web server that the HTTP request will be sent to. The web browser uses this name to look up the address of the web server for the domain. Although you can't omit the domain name, most browsers let you omit "www." from the domain name.

The third component is the *path* where the file resides on the server. The path lists the directories that contain the file. A forward slash is used to separate names in the path and to represent the server's top-level directory at the beginning of the path. In the first example in this figure, the path is "/books/".

The last component is the *filename*. In this example, the file is named xhcss.htm. If you omit the filename, though, the web server will search for a default file in the path you specify. By default, the Apache web server provides for default filenames of index.htm, index.html, and index.php.

If you want to view a page that's running on your computer, you can use the localhost keyword as the domain name. In this figure, for example, the second set of examples uses the localhost keyword to access the Apache server that's running on the same computer as the web browser.

If you omit the filename in a URL and there is no default file in the directory that you specify, Apache displays a list of the directories and files within that directory. This is illustrated by the last example in this figure. Here, the book_apps directory doesn't contain a default file. Instead, it contains one directory for each of the applications presented in this book. As a result, Apache displays an index page that lists these directories in the browser.

This is a good way to access the book applications for this book. Then, you can start any application in the book_apps directory by clicking on its link. If you also get an index of the applications in the ex_starts directory and if you bookmark both of these indexes, you'll always have an easy way to run a book application or an exercise.

Incidentally, when you create the directories and filenames for your applications, they should only contain lowercase letters, numbers, the period, and the underscore character because the names in the path may be case sensitive on some servers. Then, if a URL contains a directory named "Images", but the directory on the server is actually named "images", the web server will report that it cannot find the file.

The components of an HTTP URL

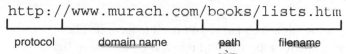

```
http://www.murach.com/books/lists.htm
```

protocol   domain name   path   filename

What happens if you omit parts of a URL

- If you omit the protocol, the default of http:// will be used.
- If you omit the filename, one of the default filenames for the Apache web server will be used: index.htm, index.html, or index.php.
- If you omit the filename and there is no default file, Apache will display an index of the files and directories in the path.

URLs for requesting pages from an Internet web server

A request for a specific page
```
http://www.murach.com/books/xhcss.htm
```

A request for the default (home) page of a web site
```
http://www.murach.com/
```

URLs for requesting applications from a local web server

A request for the default page in an application directory
```
http://localhost/book_apps/ch01_product_discount/
```

A request for a directory that doesn't contain a default page
```
http://localhost/book_apps/
```

An index of the applications in the book_apps directory

Index of /book_apps - Mozilla Firefox

File   Edit   View   History   Bookmarks   Tools   Help

http://localhost/book_apps/

Index of /book_apps

Index of /book_apps

Name	Last modified	Size	Description
Parent Directory		-	
ch01_product_discount/	29-Jul-2010 15:05	-	
ch02_future_value/	04-Dec-2009 12:05	-	
ch04_product_manager/	23-Dec-2009 14:05	-	

Done

Description

- To request a web page or web site on the Internet, enter the URL for the page or site in the address bar of your web browser.
- To request a web page or application on a local server, use *localhost* as the domain name.
- To make it easy to run the book applications and exercise starts for this book, get an index of the book_apps and ex_starts directories, and bookmark those pages.

Figure 1-13   How to run a PHP application

How to test and debug a PHP page

When you finish editing a file for a web page, you need to save it. Then, you can test the web page or application by running it in a browser using the techniques of the last figure.

When the page is displayed in your web browser, you can test it by entering any required data and performing the actions indicated by the controls on the page. In figure 1-14, for example, the Firefox browser shows the first page of the web application that's stored in the ch01_product_discount directory after you enter some data. This of course is the default page (index.html) of the Product Discount application that you saw earlier. After you enter the data, you click the Calculate Discount button to get the results.

Then, if the application doesn't produce the right results or if it doesn't produce any results, your code has one or more errors (or *bugs*). At that point, you need to find and fix those errors, which is commonly referred to as *debugging*. Sometimes, these bugs are syntax errors like omitting a semicolon at the end of a statement; sometimes they are logical errors like omitting a line of required code; and sometimes these errors are caused by statements that the PHP interpreter can't execute. No matter what, though, you need to find and fix the errors.

Usually, when PHP encounters a statement that it can't execute, the browser displays an error message as shown in this figure. In this case, the message shows that the error occurred as the PHP interpreter was trying to execute the statement on line 12 of the file named display_discount.php. As a result, you can begin by taking a closer look at the code near line 12 of that file.

In this case, though, the error occurred because the user entered invalid data for the list price and the discount percent. Here, the first entry starts with a dollar sign, which is illegal in a numeric field, and the second entry ends with a percent sign, which is illegal in a numeric field. In chapter 2, you'll learn how to fix that type of problem by checking the data for validity before processing it.

When you find the causes of the error, you need to edit the file to fix the errors and save the file. Then, to test the application again, you can return to the web browser and click the Reload or Refresh button. This reloads the edited file. At that point, you can check whether the problems have been fixed.

The Product Discount application in the Firefox browser

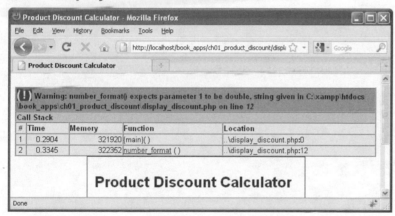

An error displayed in the Firefox browser

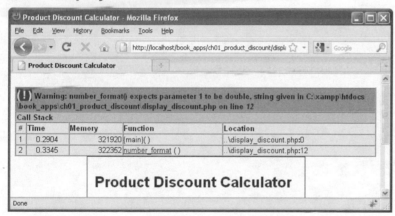

How to test a PHP page for the first time

1. Make sure the Apache and MySQL servers are running.
2. Start a web browser and enter the URL for the application as shown in the last figure.
3. Test the page by entering both valid and invalid data, clicking on all links, and so on.

How to retest a PHP page after you change the source code

*   Click the Reload or Refresh button in the browser. Then, test the page again.

Description

*   If you get an error message, read the message to help determine the cause of the error. Then, modify the PHP code and retest the page.
*   If you discover other types of errors that don't lead to error messages, you also modify the code and retest the page.
*   In chapter 6, you'll learn about finding errors (*bugs*) and fixing them (*debugging*).

Figure 1-14   How to test and debug a PHP page

How to view the source code for a web page

When a web page is displayed by a browser, you can use the techniques in figure 1-15 to view the HTML code for the page in a separate window. If, for example, you use the Firefox browser to view a web page, you can use the View→Page Source command to see the HTML code for that page.

In this figure, for example, you can see the HTML code that's returned to the browser by the PHP file of the Product Discount application. Note that this HTML doesn't include any PHP code. It only contains the HTML code that has been generated by the PHP code.

Why would you want to view the source code? When the page for an application isn't displayed correctly and you want to find out whether the problem is the generated HTML code or something else. If, for example, the PHP code generates the code for an HTML table, you can check to see whether that HTML has been generated correctly.

The source code for a PHP page

```
Source of: http://localhost/book_apps/ch01_product_discount/display_discount.php - Mozilla Firefox

File   Edit   View   Help

<!DOCTYPE html PUBLIC "-//W3C//DTD XHTML 1.0 Transitional//EN"
    "http://www.w3.org/TR/xhtml1/DTD/xhtml1-transitional.dtd">
<html xmlns="http://www.w3.org/1999/xhtml">
<head>
    <title>Product Discount Calculator</title>
    <link rel="stylesheet" type="text/css" href="main.css" />
</head>
<body>
    <div id="content">
        <h1>Product Discount Calculator</h1>

        <label>Product Description:</label>
        <span>Guitar</span><br />

        <label>List Price:</label>
        <span>$1,250.00</span><br />

        <label>Standard Discount:</label>
        <span>25%</span><br />

        <label>Discount Amount:</label>
        <span>$312.50</span><br />

        <label>Discount Price:</label>
        <span>$937.50</span><br />

        <p> </p>
    </div>
</body>
</html>
```

How to view the source code for a page in Firefox

- Use the View→Page Source command.

How to view the source code for a page in Internet Explorer

- Use the View→Source command.

Description

- When you view the source code for a web page in a web browser, the HTML code is opened in a separate window.
- In the source code, you see the HTML that has been generated by the PHP for the page. You can also see that all of the PHP has been removed from the page so it consists only of HTML.
- When testing an application that isn't displaying the information correctly in the browser, you can view the source code to see whether the PHP has correctly generated the HTML code.

Figure 1-15   How to view the source code for a web page

How to use NetBeans to develop a PHP application

Although a text editor is adequate for developing simple PHP applications like the ones for this book, most professional PHP developers use an *Integrated Development Environment (IDE)* that's designed for developing PHP applications. However, an IDE can also be useful as you're learning how to develop PHP applications.

If you're interested, we recommend the NetBeans IDE for PHP. This free IDE runs on all major operating systems, and it provides many features that make it easier to edit and test PHP applications. To learn how to install this IDE, please refer to the appendix. To learn how to get started with this IDE, please read the three topics that follow.

How to work with PHP projects and files

When you use NetBeans, all of the directories and files for an application are grouped within a *project*. You can also have more than one project open at the same time. In figure 1-16, the Projects tab of NetBeans shows that two projects are open: ch01_product_discount and ch02_future_value.

When you work with NetBeans, you can start commands by using the menus, clicking on the toolbar buttons, or right-clicking on an object and using the resulting shortcut menu, just as you would with any application. In this figure, for example, you can see how to open a project, start a new project, or close a project by using the toolbar buttons, but you can get the same results by using the commands in the File menu.

This figure also shows how to identify one of the projects as the *main project* by using the project's shortcut menu. Then, the name of the main project is boldfaced. This is useful when you want to run the main project as shown in the next figure.

To work with the files in a project, you can use the Projects tab to view the files for the project. Then, you can open any file by double-clicking on the filename in the Projects tab. In this figure, for example, three of the files for the ch01_product_discount project are open in the text editor, and the file named display_discount.php is displayed. To start a new file, you can select the project in the Projects tab and click the New File button in the toolbar.

Incidentally, when you create a NetBeans project, NetBeans adds a subdirectory named nbproject to the application root directory. It uses this subdirectory and its files to manage the project. However, this has no effect on the operation of the project, and you can still edit the files using a standard text editor.

NetBeans with three files in the main project open

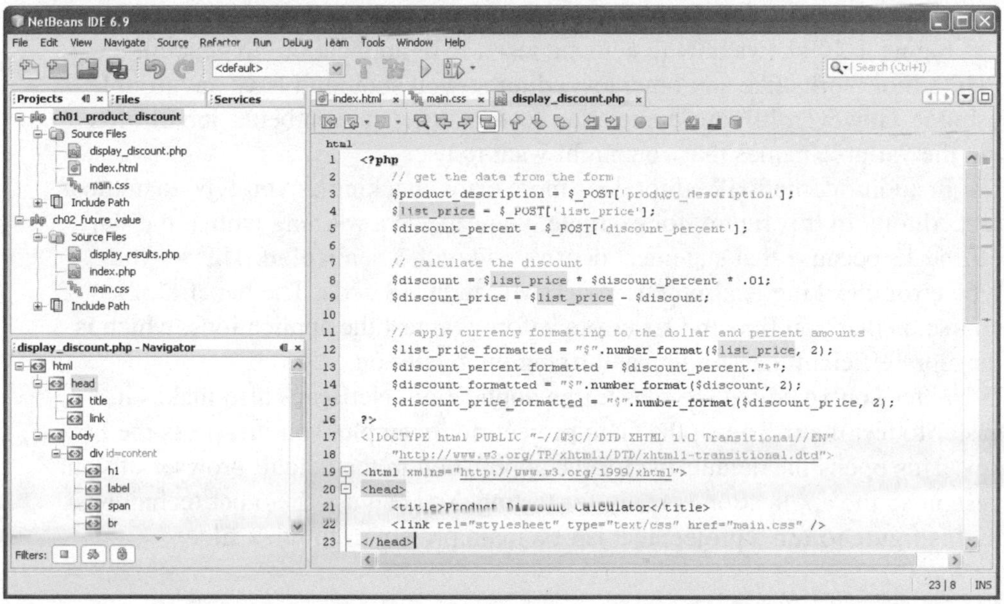

How to work with projects

- To open a *project*, use the Open Project button in the toolbar.
- To start a new project, use the New Project button in the toolbar.
- To close a project, right-click on the project in the Projects tab and select the Close command from the resulting menu.
- To set the *main project*, right-click on the project in the Projects tab and select the Set As Main Project command from the resulting menu.

How to work with files

- To open a file, use the Projects tab to navigate to the file and double-click the file.
- To start a new file, select the project and click the New File button in the toolbar.

Description

- NetBeans is an *Integrated Development Environment* (*IDE*) for developing PHP applications that makes it easier to create, edit, and test all of the HTML, CSS, and PHP files that you need for a web application.
- A NetBeans *project* consists of a top-level directory that contains the subdirectories and files for an application.
- When you create a NetBeans project, NetBeans adds an nbproject subdirectory that contains the extra files that NetBeans needs for managing the project.

Mac OS X note

- To enable right-clicking with Mac OS X, you can edit the system preferences for the mouse.

Figure 1-16   How to use NetBeans to work with projects and files

How to edit and test a PHP application

Figure 1-17 shows how to edit and test a PHP application. In general, the PHP editor works like any other text editor so you shouldn't have any trouble using it. However, its auto-completion feature does an even better job of offering the variable names that you might want to use.

In addition, the PHP editor does more error checking as you type than most text editors. In this figure, for example, you can see a warning icon at the start of line 13 because that statement doesn't end with a semicolon. This as-you-type error checking is also done for HTML and CSS code. The benefit, of course, is that you find and fix errors before you test the applications, which is far more efficient than finding and fixing them later on.

After you've edited the files for an application, NetBeans also makes it easier to test them. To test the main project, for example, you just press the F6 key. This opens the default file for the application in the default browser of your system so the application is ready for testing. You can use the other techniques in this figure to run a project that isn't a main project or to run a file.

NetBeans with an auto-completion list and an error marker displayed

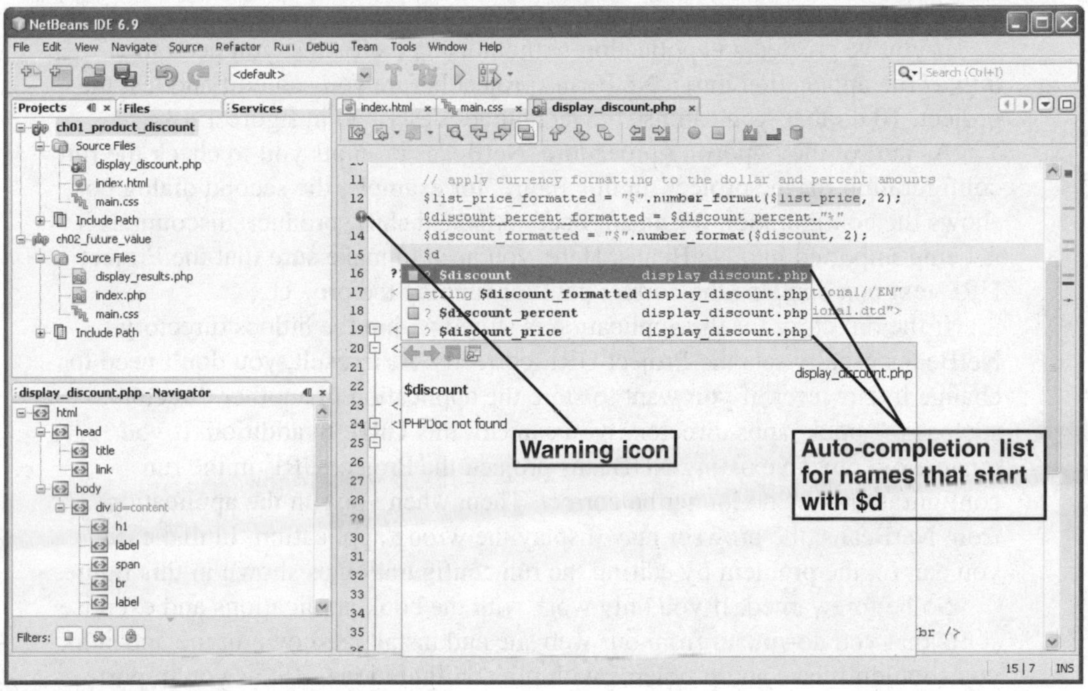

How to edit a PHP file

- Use normal editing techniques as you enter PHP code.
- When you see an auto-completion list, you can highlight an entry and press the Enter key to enter it into your code or you can double-click on it.
- If you see a red error icon at the start of a line that you have entered, you should fix whatever errors the line contains before you test the application.

How to test a PHP application

- To run the main project, click on the Run Project button in the toolbar or press F6.
- To run other projects, right-click on the project and select the Run command.
- To run a file, right-click on the file and select the Run command.

Description

- The auto-completion feature of NetBeans provides lists of possible entries after you enter the starting characters for an entry.
- NetBeans does some error checking as you enter code. Then, if you enter a statement that contains an error, NetBeans puts a red error icon at the start of the line.

Figure 1-17   How to use NetBeans to edit and test a PHP application

How to import and configure a PHP project

If you've created an application without using NetBeans, you need to *import* the application into a NetBeans project before you can edit and test the project. To do that, you can use the techniques described in figure 1-18.

As part of the importing procedure, NetBeans prompts you to check the run configuration for the project. In this figure, for example, the second dialog box shows the configuration for an application named ch01_product_discount as it is being imported into NetBeans. Here, you need to make sure that the Project URL text box contains the correct path for running the project.

If the directory for the application is stored within the htdocs directory, NetBeans usually sets the Project URL correctly. As a result, you don't need to change it. However, if you want to store the application in another directory, such as the book_apps directory, you can edit this URL. In addition, if you rename or copy an existing NetBeans project, the Project URL in the run configuration may no longer be correct. Then, when you run the application from NetBeans, the browser may display the wrong application. In that case, you can fix the problem by editing the run configuration as shown in this figure.

So be forewarned. If you only work with the book applications and exercise starts that you download from our web site and install as shown in the appendix, you shouldn't have any problems with run configurations. But as you import and copy applications of your own, keep the run configuration in mind.

The dialog box for starting a new project

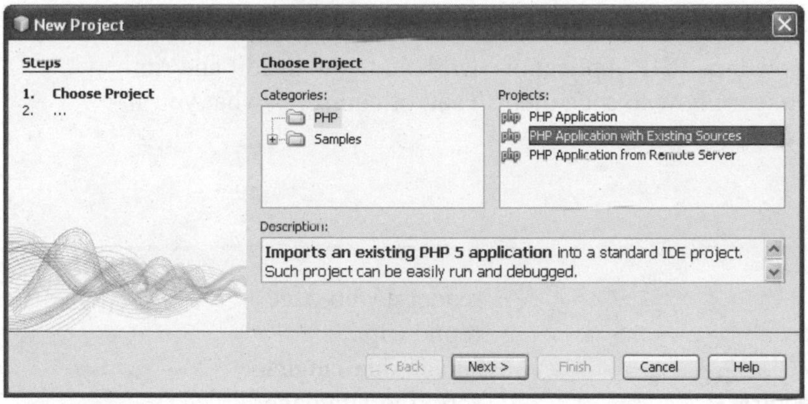

The dialog box for configuring a project

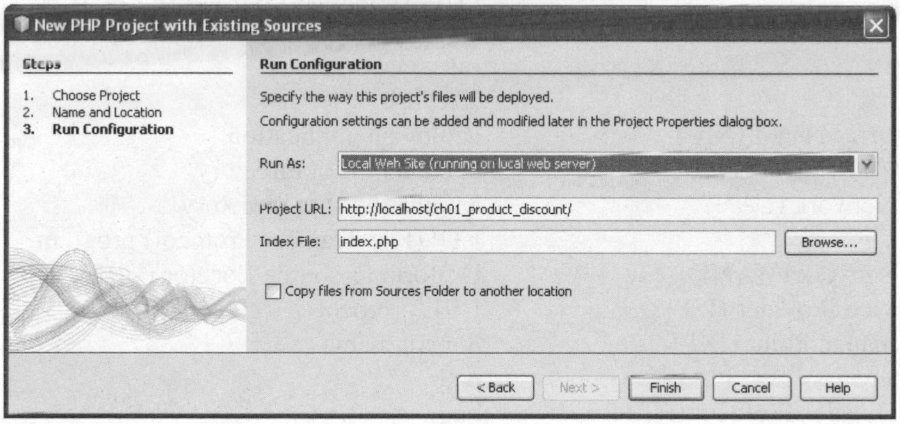

How to check the run configuration for an existing project

- Right-click on a project in the Projects tab and select the Properties command. Then, click on Run Configuration in the Categories list and check the Project URL.

How to import a project

- To import a project, use the New Project command, but select PHP Application with Existing Sources in the Projects list. This will step you through import procedure.

- In the third step, you are asked to check the run configuration. Here, you need to make sure the URL for running the project is correct.

Description

- Before you can run an existing application with NetBeans, you need to import it. Then, NetBeans creates the files it needs for managing the project in its nbproject directory.

- When you import a new Project, you need to check its configuration to make sure the URL for running the project is correct. You also need to check this URL if you copy a NetBeans project from one directory to another and then open it in NetBeans.

Figure 1-18   How to use NetBeans to import and configure a PHP project

Perspective

Now that you know how PHP applications work and how to edit and run them, you're ready to learn how to code them. That, of course, is what you'll learn to do in the next chapter.

Terms

World Wide Web	render a web page
Internet	round trip
web application	server-side language
client-server architecture	scripting language
client	application server
server	PHP: Hypertext Preprocessor (PHP)
web server	Cascading Style Sheets (CSS)
web browser	rule set
network	XAMPP
Network Interface Card (NIC)	deploy an application
router	document root directory
Local Area Network (LAN)	application root directory
intranet	FTP (File Transfer Protocol) program
Wide Area Network (WAN)	Uniform Resource Locator (URL)
Internet Service Provider (ISP)	URL protocol
Internet Exchange Point (IXP)	domain name
static web page	path
HyperText Transfer Protocol (HTTP)	bug
HTTP request	debug
HTTP response	Integrated Development Environment
HyperText Markup Language (HTML)	(IDE)
dynamic web page	project
database server	import an application
PHP interpreter	

Summary

- A *web application* uses an architecture that consists of clients, a web server, and a network. *Clients* use *web browsers* to request web pages from the web server. The *web server* returns the requested pages.

- A *Local Area Network* (*LAN*) connects computers that are near to each other. This is often called an *intranet*. In contrast, a *Wide Area Network* (*WAN*) uses *routers* to connect two or more LANs. The *Internet* consists of many WANs that are connected at *Internet Exchange Points*.

- To request a web page, the web browser sends an *HTTP request* to the web server that includes the name of the requested file. Then, the web server retrieves the HTML for the requested web page and sends it back to the browser in an *HTTP response*. Last, the browser *renders* the HTML into a web page.

* A *static web page* is a page that is the same each time it's retrieved. The file for a static web page has .html or .htm as its extension, and its HTML doesn't change.

* The HTML for a *dynamic web page* is generated by a *server-side program* or *script*, so its HTML can change from one request to another. When a web server receives a request for a web page , it uses the extension of the requested file to find out which server or script should process the request.

* HTTP requests for web pages with .php as the extension are processed by the *PHP interpreter* that runs on the web server. This interpreter processes the request along with any data that is passed with the request. Then, it generates the HTML for the HTTP response.

* *HTML* (*HyperText Markup Language*) is the language that defines the structure and contents of a web page. *CSS* (*Cascading Style Sheets*) is used to control how the web pages are formatted. For this book, you need to be familiar with both HTML and CSS, but the emphasis is on PHP.

* *XAMPP* is a free, open-source, cross-platform web server package that consists of Apache, MySQL, and PHP and Perl interpreters. It is commonly used for PHP applications, and it's easy to install.

* To *deploy* a PHP application on your own computer or a local server, you need to copy all of its directories and files to the document root directory of Apache (\xampp\htdocs).

* To deploy a PHP application on the Internet, you need to transfer the directories and files from your computer or local server to a web server with Internet access. To do that, you can use an *FTP program* that uses *File Transfer Protocol*.

* To run a web application, you can enter the *URL* (*Uniform Resource Locator*) of the application's directory into a browser's address bar. Then, Apache looks for the default file in that directory and runs it. If it can't find a default file, Apache displays an index of the subdirectories.

* If PHP can't execute a statement while you're testing an application, an error message is displayed in the browser. Then, you need to *debug* the application.

* To view the HTML for a web page, you can use your browser's View→Page Source or View→Source command. This can be useful when you want to see whether the PHP application generated the correct HTML.

* To develop web pages, you can use a text editor like Notepad++ or TextWrangler. You can also use an *Integrated Development Environment* (*IDE*) that combines text editing with other development functions.

* NetBeans is an IDE that makes it easier to edit and test PHP applications. NetBeans treats each application as a *project*. You can *import* an existing application into a NetBeans project and then configure it so it will run right.

Before you do the exercises for this book...

Before you do the exercises for this book, you should download and install the software and applications for this book as described in the appendix.

Exercise 1-1   Test the Product Discount application

In this exercise, you'll run the Product Discount application that's described in this chapter. You'll also use your browser to view its source code.

Start the application

1. If necessary, start the Apache web server as shown in figure 1-11.

2. Start your web browser.

3. Run the Product Discount application by entering this URL into the browser's address bar and pressing the Enter key

   `http://localhost/book apps/ch01 product discount/`

   If this application runs, it means that you have installed the software and downloadable applications correctly.

Test the application

4. Enter valid values in the three text boxes. Then, click the Calculate Discount button. This should display the results of the calculation on the second page of the application.

5. Look in the browser's address bar and note that the URL points to a PHP file.

6. View the source code for this application as shown in figure 1-15. Note that this source code only contains HTML, not PHP code.

7. Click on the browser's Back button to return to the first page of the application, enter invalid numeric values like "xx" and "yy" in the second and third text boxes, and click the Calculate Discount button. Then, read the error message that's displayed. You'll learn how to handle errors like this later in this book.

8. Click the browser's Back button to return to the first page of the application. Then, run the application again with valid data.

Exercise 1-2   Run the book and exercise applications

In this exercise, you'll create and bookmark index pages for the book applications and for the applications that are the starting points for the exercises. Then, you'll run some of these applications.

Run some of the book applications

1. Enter this URL into your the browser's address bar and press the Enter key

    ```
    http://localhost/book apps/
    ```

    This should display an index of the book applications.

2. Bookmark this page so you can quickly access it whenever you need it.

3. Run the Future Value application for chapter 2 by clicking on the ch02_future_value link in the index. This should start that application. Then, click on the Back button to return to the index.

4. If necessary, start MySQL as shown in figure 1-11. Then, go back to your browser and start the Product Manager application by clicking on ch04_product_manager. If it starts, this shows that you've installed MySQL and the downloadable MySQL databases correctly as shown in the appendix.

5. Click the Back button and start the Guitar Shop application in chapter 5. This should give you some idea of the types of applications that you'll be able to develop by the time you complete section 1 of this book.

Run some of the exercise applications

6. Enter this URL into your browser's address bar and press the Enter key

    ```
    http://localhost/ex starts/
    ```

    This should display an index of the applications that are used as the starting points for the exercises.

7. Bookmark this page so you can quickly access it whenever you need it.

8. Click on the link for ch02_ex1. This is the link for the application that you'll start with in exercise 1 of chapter 2. It is the Product Discount application of chapter 1, which you'll enhance in this exercise.

9. You are now ready to run any of the book applications or exercise starts with relative ease.

Exercise 1-3   Check out your text editor

If you're going to use a text editor for doing the exercises in this book, this exercise will help you check it out. If you're going to use NetBeans, skip to exercise 1-4.

1. If you're using Windows, use Windows Explorer to review the directories and files for the applications in the /xampps/htdocs directory. If you're using Mac OS, use Finder. Note that each application includes an nbproject directory

that's used by NetBeans, but you can ignore that directory if you aren't using NetBeans.

2. Use your text editor to open the html, css, and php files in this directory:

    `/xampp/htdocs/ex_starts/ch02_ex1`

    To do that, you can use the File Open command of your text editor. But if you're using Notepad++ on a Windows system, you can also select the three files in the Windows Explorer, right-click on them, and select Edit with Notepad++.

3. Review the three files and see how the color coding highlights the syntax in the HTML, CSS, and PHP files.

4. Delete the semicolon at the end of one of the PHP statements and see whether the error is highlighted. Then, re-enter the semicolon.

5. Start a new line in the PHP portion of the PHP file by typing $d and see whether an auto-completion list is displayed. If it isn't, check the settings for your text editor to see whether you need to turn this feature on. Then, delete the code for the line that you started.

6. If you're using Notepad++, you may want to change the style for comments as shown in figure 1-10.

7. If your text editor can't open more than one file at a time or if it doesn't provide syntax highlighting and auto-completion, you should probably switch to a different text editor or to NetBeans.

Exercise 1-4   Check out NetBeans

If you're going to use NetBeans to do the exercises for this book, this exercise will get you started with it.

1. Open NetBeans and then open this project as summarized in figure 1-16:

    `/xampp/htdocs/ex_starts/ch02_ex1`

2. Open the three files for this application as summarized in figure 1-16.

3. Review the three files and see how the color coding highlights the syntax in the HTML, CSS, and PHP files.

4. Delete the semicolon at the end of one of the PHP statements and note the red error icon that appears at the start of the line. Then, re-enter the semicolon.

5. Start a new line in the PHP portion of the PHP file, type $, and note the auto-completion list that's displayed. Then, delete the code for the line that you started.

6. Run the application as shown in figure 1-17. This will start the application in your default browser.

7. Check the configuration for the application as shown in 1-18, and note that the Project URL is correct for this application.

2

How to code a PHP application

In this chapter, you'll learn how to code simple PHP applications like the Product Discount application of chapter 1. That will get you off to a fast start and give you the perspective you need for learning rapidly. If you haven't done much programming, this chapter will move quickly for you. But if you take it slow and do the exercises, you should master all of its skills.

Basic PHP skills 46
How to embed PHP in HTML 46
How to code comments and statements 48
The six PHP data types 50
How to declare variables and constants 52

How to get data from a request 54
How to use the built-in $_GET array 54
How to use the built-in $_POST array 56
When to use the HTTP GET and POST methods 56

How to work with data 58
How to code string expressions 58
How to code echo statements 58
How to code numeric expressions 60
How to use the compound assignment operators 62
How to use some built-in functions 64

The Product Discount application 66
The user interface 66
The form in the HTML file 66
The PHP file 68

How to code control statements 70
How to code conditional expressions 70
How to code if statements 72
How to code while and for statements 74
How to pass control to another page 76

The Future Value application 78
The user interface 78
The code for the index.php file 80
The code for the display_results.php file 82

How to use the PHP documentation 86
How to access the PHP manual 86
How to find the documentation you need 86

Perspective 88

Basic PHP skills

This chapter starts with some basic PHP skills that you need to learn before you can use PHP to store data.

How to embed PHP in HTML

Figure 2-1 begins by showing a PHP file named display.php. This file contains HTML tags for displaying a web page, and it contains some PHP that's embedded within the HTML. The PHP displays data that's passed to the page by the HTTP request. In this figure, for example, a first name of "Ray" and a last name of "Harris" have been passed to the web page by the HTTP request.

To add PHP to a file, you code a PHP tag that begins with <?php and ends with ?>. Then, you enter PHP code between these tags. In this figure, for example, the first PHP tag contains a comment and two PHP statements. These statements get the values from the first_name and last_name parameters of the HTTP GET request and store these values in variables named $first_name and $last_name. Then, the second and third PHP tags contain single PHP statements that display these variables.

When coding PHP files, you usually include a PHP tag before the first HTML tag. This PHP tag contains statements that do some processing and set up the variables to be used in the rest of the page. Then, you usually use shorter PHP tags to display data at various places within the HTML document.

As you work with PHP, you may see other ways to code the PHP tag. However, the technique in this figure is the one that's used the most and the one that we recommend.

A PHP file that includes HTML and embedded PHP

```php
<?php
    // get the data from the request
    $first_name = $_GET['first_name'];
    $last_name = $_GET['last_name'];
?>
<!DOCTYPE html PUBLIC "-//W3C//DTD XHTML 1.0 Transitional//EN"
    "http://www.w3.org/TR/xhtml1/DTD/xhtml1-transitional.dtd">
<html xmlns="http://www.w3.org/1999/xhtml">
    <head>
        <title>Name Test</title>
        <link rel="stylesheet" type="text/css" href="main.css"/>
    </head>
    <body>
        <h2>Welcome</h2>
        <p>First name: <?php echo $first_name; ?></p>
        <p>Last name: <?php echo $last_name; ?></p>
    </body>
</html>
```

The PHP file displayed in a browser

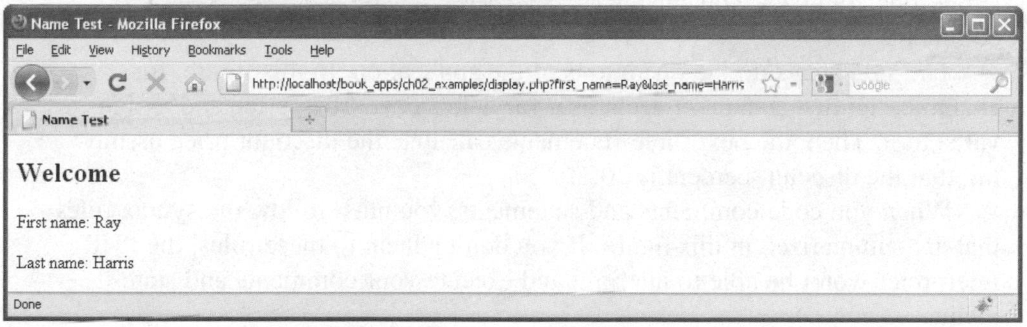

Description

- To embed PHP within HTML, code a PHP tag by beginning with <?php and ending with ?>. Then, you can enter PHP code between these tags.

- Although there are several ways to embed PHP in HTML, the technique above is the one that's commonly used and recommended.

- If you want to do some processing before displaying the HTML, you embed PHP before the start of the HTML document.

- If you want to use PHP to display dynamic data within an HTML document, you embed PHP within the HTML.

Figure 2-1   How to embed PHP in HTML

How to code comments and statements

The *syntax* of PHP refers to the rules that you must follow as you write PHP code. If you're familiar with Java or JavaScript, you'll find that those languages have a syntax that's similar to PHP.

Figure 2-2 begins by showing a code example that contains some PHP code that has both comments and statements. A *comment* helps document what the code does. However, comments are ignored by the PHP engine.

In this figure, the code begins with a *multi-line comment* (also known as a *block comment*) that describes the author and purpose of the program. This comment begins with /* and ends with */. This comment also includes extra asterisk (*) characters to visually set it apart from the rest of the code, but those asterisks have no affect on the comment.

After the multi-line comment, this code uses three *single-line comments* to describe the rest of the code. The first two of these comments are coded on their own lines. However, the third comment is coded at the end of the line after other code. Although it's common to use two forward slashes (//) to begin a single-line comment, you can also use a pound sign (#) to begin this type of comment.

The *statements* do the operations of the application. In this figure, for example, the first statement declares a variable named $list_price and assigns a value to it. Then, the next three statements calculate the discount price assuming that the discount percent is 20%.

When you code comments and statements, you must follow the syntax rules that are summarized in this figure. If you don't adhere to these rules, the PHP interpreter won't be able to interpret and execute your comments and statements.

The first syntax rule is that each PHP statement must end with a semicolon. If you don't end each statement with a semicolon, PHP won't be able to tell where one statement ends and the next begins.

The second syntax rule is that PHP ignores extra whitespace in statements. Whitespace includes spaces, tabs, and new line characters. This lets you break long statements into multiple lines so they're easier to read. As far as PHP is concerned, however, your entire program could be written on one line and it would still work.

PHP code that includes comments and statements

```php
<?php
    /***********************************************************
    * Author:   Joel Murach
    * Purpose: This program calculates the discount for a
    *           price that's entered by the user
    ***********************************************************/

    // get the data from the form
    $list_price = $_GET['list_price'];

    // calculate the discount
    $discount_percent = .20;                    // 20% discount
    $discount_amount = $subtotal * $discount_percent;
    $discount_price = $subtotal - $discount_amount;
?>
```

Another way to code single-line comments

```php
    # calculate the discount
    $discount_percent = .20;                    # 20% discount
```

Syntax rules

- PHP statements end with a semicolon.
- PHP ignores extra whitespace in statements.

Description

- PHP has a syntax that's similar to the syntax of Java or JavaScript.
- A *statement* controls the operations of a program.
- A *comment* helps document what the code does.
- To code a *single-line comment*, code two forward slashes (//) or a pound sign (#) and continue until the end of the line.
- To code a *multiple-line comment* (also known as a *block comment*) code /*, followed by the comment, followed by */. If you code additional asterisks around a block comment to make it easier to read, that's okay, but it isn't necessary.
- To make your code easier to read, you should use indentation and extra spaces to align statements and parts of statements as illustrated throughout this book.

Figure 2-2   How to code comments and statements

The six PHP data types

Before you learn more about coding statements, you need to know that PHP provides for the six *data types* summarized in figure 2-3. Each of these data types is used to store a different type of data. For now, you can focus on the first four data types since they're the most commonly used and are similar across most languages.

The *integer data type* stores integers. An *integer* is a whole number, which is a number that doesn't have any decimal places. You can code a plus or minus sign before an integer to indicate whether it's positive or negative. But if the sign is omitted, the value is treated as a positive value so you usually omit the plus sign.

The *double data type* stores numbers that have decimal places. This data type is also known as the *decimal data type*, and numbers that have decimal places are often called *floating-point numbers*. As with integers, you can precede a floating-point number with a plus or minus sign.

The *Boolean data type* stores a value that is in one of two states such as true/false, yes/no, or on/off. To represent Boolean data, you code either TRUE or FALSE. Note, however, that these words aren't case sensitive so you can code them with or without capital letters. In this book, we usually capitalize them to make them obvious.

Incidentally, PHP words like TRUE and FALSE are *keywords*. This means that they have a special meaning to the PHP interpreter so you shouldn't use them for other purposes.

The *string data type* stores text that can include any characters. To code a string value, you code the *string* within single or double quotation marks. Note, however, that you must close the string with the same type of quotation mark that you used to start it.

The last two data types are for arrays and objects. In chapter 4, you'll be introduced to arrays. And in chapters 11 and 14, you can learn everything you need to know about arrays and objects.

Incidentally, a double value can also include an exponent that indicates how many zeros should be included to the right or left of the decimal point. This lets you express extremely large and small numbers. For instance, the exponent of a number can indicate that the number should have 308 zeros to the left of the decimal point or 324 zeros to the right of the decimal point. Unless you're developing scientific or mathematical applications, though, you probably won't need to use this notation.

The six PHP data types

Type	Description
integer	Whole numbers that range from -2,147,483,648 to 2,147,483,647.
double	Numbers with decimal places that range from −1.7E308 to 1.7E308 with up to 16 significant digits. This data type is also known as the floating-point or decimal data type.
boolean	A TRUE or FALSE value.
string	Text that consists of any characters.
array	A container that holds multiple values of one or more data types. See chapters 4 and 11.
object	A container that contains data (properties) and functions (methods). See chapter 14.

Integer values (whole numbers)

```
15          // an integer
-21         // a negative integer
```

Double values (numbers with decimal positions)

```
21.5        // a floating-point value
-124.82     // a negative floating-point value
```

The two Boolean values

```
true        // equivalent to true, yes, or on
false       // equivalent to false, no, or off
```

String values

```
'Ray Harris'    // a string with single quotes
"Ray Harris"    // a string with double quotes
''              // an empty string
null            // a NULL value
```

Double values that use scientific notation

```
3.7e9       // equivalent to 3700000000
4.5e-9      // equivalent to 0.0000000037
-3.7e9      // equivalent to -3700000000
```

Description

- PHP provides for the six *data types* shown in this figure. Each data type is used to store a different type of data.

- An *integer* is a whole number that can start with a positive or negative sign.

- A *double value* consists of a positive or negative sign, digits, an optional decimal point, and optional decimal digits.

- The *Boolean data type* is used to represent a *Boolean value* that is either TRUE or FALSE.

- The *string data type* contains *strings* that are made up of any characters. A string is coded within single or double quotation marks.

- Exponents can be used for double values that represent extremely large or small values. Unless you develop scientific or mathematical applications, though, you shouldn't need to use this notation.

Figure 2-3   The six PHP data types

How to declare variables and constants

A *variable* stores a value that can change as the program executes. In PHP, variables are easy to spot because they all begin with the dollar sign ($). When you write the code for PHP applications, you frequently declare variables and assign values to them as shown in figure 2-4.

To *declare* a variable, code the dollar sign ($) followed by the *variable name*. Then, to *assign* a value to the variable, code the *assignment operator* (=) followed by an expression that returns the value for the variable.

In the first set of examples, the first five statements assign *literal values* (or *literals*) to variables. A literal is a value that doesn't change. Here, the first statement assigns a *numeric literal* of 10 to $count. This is stored as an integer.

The second statement assigns a numeric literal of 9.50 to a variable named $price. Since this number contains a decimal point followed by one or more digits, PHP stores this number as the double type.

The third statement assigns a *string literal* of 'Bob' to a variable named $first_name. Similarly, the fourth statement assigns a string literal of "Bob" to a variable named $first_name. This shows that you can use either single or double quotation marks to identify a string literal.

The fifth statement assigns a *Boolean literal* of false to a variable named $is_valid. Since Boolean literals aren't case sensitive, this statement works the same with a Boolean literal of False or FALSE.

The next four statements show that you can assign the value that's stored in one variable to another variable. In the sixth statement, for instance, the value that's stored in the $count variable is copied into the $product_count variable.

When you work with variables, you need to remember that they're case-sensitive. As a result, $Count isn't the same as $count. Also, when you create variable names, you must follow the rules shown in this figure, but you can do that just by copying the naming conventions that are used in this book.

Besides the rules, your variables should have meaningful names so it's easy to tell what a variable refers to and easy to remember how to spell the name. To create names like that, you should avoid abbreviations unless they are widely understood. If, for example, you abbreviate the name for monthly investment as $mon_inv, instead of $monthly_investment, it's hard to tell what the variable name refers to and hard to remember how to spell it.

To create a variable name that has more than one word in it, most PHP programmers use underscore characters to separate the words in the name. For example, $is_valid and $list_price use this convention. The alternative is to use a convention called *camel casing*. With this convention, the first letter of each word is uppercase except for the first word. For example, $isValid and $listPrice use camel casing. Although you can use either convention, you should pick a convention and use it consistently.

To define a *constant*, you can use the notation in the last set of examples. Although you can often get the same result by using a variable instead of a constant, using a constant makes sure that the value won't be changed accidentally, and it clearly indicates that the value is not supposed to change.

The assignment operator

Operator	Description
=	Assigns a value to the variable.

How to declare a variable

```
$count = 10;                          // an integer literal
$list_price = 9.50;                   // a double literal
$first_name = 'Bob';                  // a string literal - single quotes
$first_name = "Bob";                  // a string literal - double quotes
$is_valid = false;                    // a Boolean literal - lowercase

$product_count = $count;              // $product_count is 10
$price = $list_price;                 // $price is 9.50
$name = $first_name;                  // $name is "Bob"
$is_new = $is_valid;                  // $is_new is FALSE
```

Rules for creating variable names

- Variable names are case-sensitive.
- Variable names can contain letters, numbers, and underscores.
- Variable names can't contain special characters.
- Variable names can't begin with a digit or two underscores.
- Variable names can't use names that are reserved by PHP such as the variable named $this that's reserved for use with objects.

How to declare a constant

```
define('MAX_QTY', 100);               // an integer constant
define('PI', 3.14159265);             // a double constant
define('MALE', 'm');                  // a string constant
```

Description

- A *variable* stores a value that can change as the application executes.
- To *declare* a variable, code the dollar sign ($) followed by the variable name. Then, to *assign* a value to the variable, code the *assignment operator* (=) followed by the value for the variable.
- PHP assigns a data type to the variable depending on the value that's assigned to the variable.
- A *literal* is a value that doesn't change. To code a *numeric literal*, code the number without quotation marks. To code a *string literal*, code the value within quotation marks. To code a *Boolean literal*, code TRUE of FALSE. These *keywords* aren't case-sensitive.
- To declare a *constant*, you can use the define function to specify the name and value of the constant as shown above. Since the value of a constant can't be changed, you don't code a dollar sign before its name when you declare it or when you use it. By convention, most programmers use capital letters for the names of constants.

Figure 2-4   How to declare variables and constants

How to get data from a request

Most PHP applications operate on data that they get from an HTTP request. That was illustrated in the Product Discount application of chapter 1. Now, you'll learn how to get that data from the HTTP request and store it in your PHP variables.

How to use the built-in $_GET array

When an HTML <form> tag uses the GET method to pass data to a PHP file, the values are stored in a $_GET array. Because this array is part of PHP, it is called a *built-in array*. In figure 2-5, for example, the HTTP request passes two values that have been entered into text boxes to the page named display.php.

Because this request uses the GET method, these values are passed as part of the URL that requests the page. For instance, this portion of the URL in this figure requests the page named display.php and passes two values to it:

```
display.php?first_name=Ray&last_name=Harris
```

Here, the question mark indicates that the data will follow. Then, each data item consists of the name attribute of a text box, the equals sign, and the value that was entered into the text box. The ampersand is used to separate the items.

When the request is received by the web server, the values that are passed to it are stored in the $_GET array. This array contains key/value pairs that consist of the name attribute for each text box and the value that was entered into that text box. In this example, the user entered "Ray" into the text box named first_name and "Harris" into the text box named last_name.

To retrieve the values from the $_GET array, you code $_GET, a set of brackets [ ], and the name of the value that you want. For instance, this code gets the value for the text box named first_name and stores it in a PHP variable named $first_name:

```
$first_name = $_GET['first_name'];
```

Note, however, that if you attempt to retrieve the value for a parameter that doesn't exist in the $_GET array, this code returns a NULL value.

In the last example in this figure, you can see that you can also use an <a> tag to request a PHP file and pass data to it. To do that, you append data to the HTTP request just as the submit method of a form does. This type of request always uses the GET method, and this is sometimes useful in the code for an application.

The built-in $_GET array

Name	Description
$_GET	A built-in array that contains the values passed by the GET method (the default).

An HTML form that performs an HTTP GET request

```
<form action="display.php" method="get">
    <label>First name: </label>
    <input type="text" name="first_name"><br>
    <label>Last name: </label>
    <input type="text" name="last_name"><br>
    <label> </label>
    <input type="submit" value="Submit">
</form>
```

The URL for the HTTP GET request with appended key/value pairs

```
http://localhost/.../display.php?first_name=Ray&last_name=Harris
```

The $_GET array that's created when the GET request is received

Key	Value
first_name	Ray
last_name	Harris

PHP code that gets the data from the array and stores it in variables

```
$first_name = $_GET['first_name'];
$last_name = $_GET['last_name'];
```

An <a> tag that performs an HTTP GET request

```
<a href="display.php?first_name=Joel&last_name=Murach">Display Name</a>
```

Description

- When you use the HTTP GET method with a form, the parameters are appended to the URL when the form is submitted. Then, these parameters are stored in the $_GET array.

- The $_GET variable is an array that contains the keys and values for the data that is passed with the HTTP request.

- When you code or enter a URL that requests a PHP page, you can add a parameter list to it starting with a question mark and with no intervening spaces. Then, each parameter consists of its name, an equals sign (=), and its value. To code multiple parameters, use ampersands (&) to separate the parameters.

- The <a> tag always uses the HTTP GET method when it passes parameters to a page.

- The $_GET variable is a *superglobal variable*, which means it's always available to the PHP code for a page.

Figure 2-5   How to use the built-in $_GET array

How to use the built-in $_POST array

When you use a <form> tag to request a PHP file, there are times when you will want to use the HTTP POST method for the request. To do that, you use POST as the method attribute for the form as shown in figure 2-6. Then, the parameters that are passed to the PHP file aren't shown in the URL.

In this case, you use the $_POST array instead of the $_GET array to retrieve the values for the parameters that are passed with the HTTP request. This works just like the $_GET array in the previous figure.

When to use the HTTP GET and POST methods

So, when should you use the HTTP GET method and when should you use the POST method? In general, you should use the GET method when the page is going to *get* (read) data from the database server. Similarly, you should use the POST method when the page is going to *post* (write) data to the server.

When you use the GET method, you need to make sure that the page can be executed multiple times without causing any problems. In this figure, the PHP file just displays the data to the user, so there's no harm in executing this page multiple times. If, for example, the user clicks the Refresh button, the browser requests the page again, and this doesn't cause any problems.

However, if the PHP file in this figure wrote the data to a database, you wouldn't want the user to write the same data to the database twice. As a result, it would make more sense to use the POST method. Then, if the user clicks the Refresh button, the browser displays a dialog box like the one near the bottom of this figure that warns the user that the data will be submitted again. At that point, the user can click on the Cancel button to cancel the request.

There are also a few other reasons to use the POST method. First, since the POST method doesn't append parameters to the end of the URL, it is more appropriate for working with sensitive data. Second, since the POST method prevents the web browser from including parameters in a bookmark for a page, you'll want to use it if you don't want the parameters to be included in a bookmark. Third, if your parameters contain more than 4 KB of data, the GET method won't work so you'll need to use the POST method.

For all other uses, the GET method is preferred. It runs slightly faster than the POST method, and it lets the user bookmark the page along with the parameters that were sent to the page.

The built-in $_POST array

Name	Description
$_POST	A built-in array that contains the values passed by the POST method.

A PHP page for an HTTP POST request

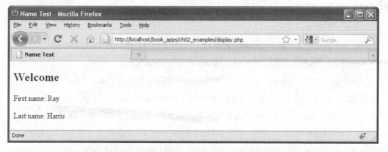

An HTML form that specifies the POST method

```
<form action="display.php" method="post">
```

PHP code that gets the data from the $_POST array

```
$first_name = $_POST['first name'];
$last_name = $_POST['last_name'];
```

When to use the HTTP GET method

- When the request is for a page that gets data from a database server.
- When the request can be executed multiple times without causing any problems.

When to use the HTTP POST method

- When the request is for a page that writes data to a database server.
- When executing the request multiple times may cause problems.
- When you don't want to include the parameters in the URL for security reasons.
- When you don't want users to be able to include parameters when they bookmark a page.
- When you need to transfer more than 4 KB of data.

The Firefox dialog box that's displayed if the user tries to refresh a post

Description

- The HTTP POST method works like the GET method but the parameters aren't appended to the URL.

Figure 2-6   When and how to use the built-in $_POST array

How to work with data

Now that you know the basic skills for retrieving data from an HTTP request and storing it in a variable, you're ready to learn how to work with that data.

How to code string expressions

Figure 2-7 shows how to code *string expressions*. An *expression* can be a single value or a series of operations that result in a single value.

The first set of examples shows how to use single quotes for string expressions. This is the most efficient way to code string expressions with PHP.

The second set of examples shows how to assign empty strings and NULL values to variables. Here, the first statement uses two single quote marks with no characters between them to assign an *empty string* to a variable. The second statement uses the NULL keyword to assign a *null value* to a variable. Since this keyword isn't case-sensitive, it can be coded null or NULL.

The third set of examples uses double quotes to insert variable values into a string. This is known as *interpolation*. When you use double quotes, the PHP interpreter must check the entire string to see if it contains any variables that need to be inserted into the string. That's why PHP works more efficiently when you use single quotes to identify strings. And that's why it's a best practice to use single quotes unless you are taking advantage of interpolation.

The fourth set of examples shows how you can mix single and double quotes to insert a single or double quote within a string. This is something that you'll rarely need to do.

If you need to join (or *concatenate*) two or more strings, you can use the *concatenation operator* (the period). This is illustrated by the first set of examples for the concatenation operator. Here, the third statement joins a string literal of "Name: " with the variable named $first_name. Then, the fourth statement joins the $first_name variable with a single space character and the $last_name variable. As a result, the two variables are separated by a space.

The next set of concatenation examples shows how to join a number to a string. To do that, you just use the concatenation operator. Then, PHP converts the number to a string and joins the two values. In all of these examples, the concatenation operator is preceded and followed by a space, but that isn't necessary.

How to code echo statements

The last two examples show how to use echo statements to send data to the browser. Here, the first example sends the data by embedding the PHP tag within the HTML. This makes the HTML easier to maintain for web developers who aren't familiar with PHP. The second example shows that you can also use an echo statement to send HTML tags to the browser along with the data.

How assign string expressions

Use single quotes for simple strings to improve PHP efficiency

```
$first_name = 'Bob';
$last_name = 'Roberts';
```

How to assign NULL values and empty strings

```
$address2 = '';              // an empty string
$address2 = null;            // a NULL value
```

How to use double quotes to insert a variable into a string

```
$name = "Name: $first_name";            // Name: Bob
$name = "$first_name $last_name";        // Bob Roberts
```

How to use single and double quotes for special purposes

```
$last_name = "O'Brien";                 // O'Brien
$line = 'She said, "Hi."';              // She said, "Hi."
```

How to use the concatenation operator (.) to join strings

How to use the concatenation operator for simple joins

```
$first_name = 'Bob';
$last_name = 'Roberts';
$name = 'Name: ' . $first_name;         // Name: Bob
$name = $first_name . ' ' . $last_name; // Bob Roberts
```

How to join a number to a string

```
$price = 19.99;
$price_string = 'Price: ' . $price;     // Price: 19.99
```

The syntax for the echo statement

```
echo string_expression;
```

How to use an echo statement within HTML

```
<p>Name: <?php echo $name; ?></p>
```

How to use an echo statement to output HTML tags and data

```
<?php
    echo '<p>Name: ' . $name . '</p>';   // <p>Name: Bob Roberts<p>
?>
```

Description

- Although you can use single or double quotation marks to code a string, PHP processes single quotation marks more efficiently.

- An *empty string* is a string that doesn't contain any characters. To assign an empty string to a variable, code a set of quotation marks with no characters between.

- A *null value* indicates that the value is unknown. To assign a null value to a string, you can use the NULL keyword. This keyword isn't case sensitive.

- If you code a variable name within double quotes, it will be converted to a string.

- To join, or *concatenate*, two or more strings, you can use the *concatenation operator*.

- To send data to the browser, you can use the echo statement. This statement can include HTML tags.

Figure 2-7   How to code string expressions and echo statements

How to code numeric expressions

Figure 2-8 begins by showing the operators for coding *numeric expressions*. If you've programmed in another language, you are probably familiar with these operators. In particular, the first four *arithmetic operators* are common to most programming languages.

Most modern languages also have a *modulus operator* that calculates the remainder when the left value is divided by the right value. In this figure, for example, the modulus operator (%) is used to return a remainder of 6 when 14 is divided by 8. It's a common practice to use the modulus operator to determine if a number is even or odd. For example, any number % 2 returns 0 if the number is even and 1 if the number is odd. Another use is determining if a year is a leap year. If, for example, $year % 4 returns 0, then $year is divisible by 4.

In contrast to the first five operators in this figure, the increment and decrement operators add or subtract one from a variable. These operators are commonly used with loops as shown in figure 2-15.

The second set of statements in this figure shows how to calculate the discount for a product. Here, the first statement sets the list price to 19.95, and the second statement sets the discount percent to 20 percent. Then, the third statement calculates the discount amount by multiplying the list price, the discount percent, and a literal value of .01. The literal value shifts the decimal place to the appropriate location. Finally, the fourth statement calculates the discount price by subtracting the discount amount from the list price.

When an expression includes two or more operators, the *order of precedence* determines which operators are applied first. This order is summarized in this figure. For instance, all multiplication and division operations are done from left to right before any addition and subtraction operations are done.

To override this order, though, you can use parentheses. Then, the expressions in the innermost sets of parentheses are done first, followed by the expressions in the next sets of parentheses, and so on. This is typical of all programming languages, and the examples in this figure show how this works.

Common arithmetic operators

Operator	Description	Example	Result
+	Addition	5 + 7	12
-	Subtraction	5 - 12	-7
*	Multiplication	6 * 7	42
/	Division	13 / 4	3.25
%	Modulus	13 % 4	1
++	Increment	$counter++	adds 1 to counter
--	Decrement	$counter--	subtracts 1 from counter

Some simple numeric expressions

```
$x = 14;
$y = 8;
$result = $x + $y;          // 22
$result = $x - $y;          // 6
$result = $x * $y;          // 112
$result = $x / $y;          // 1.75
$result = $x % $y;          // 6
$x++;                       // 15
$y--;                       // 7
```

Statements that calculate a discount

```
$list_price = 19.95;
$discount_percent = 20;
$discount_amount = $list_price * $discount_percent * .01;
$discount_price = $list_price - $discount_amount;   // 15.96
```

The order of precedence for arithmetic expressions

Order	Operators	Direction	Description
1	++	Left to right	Increment operator
2	--	Left to right	Decrement operator
3	* / %	Left to right	Multiplication, division, modulus
4	+ -	Left to right	Addition, subtraction

Examples of precedence and the use of parentheses

```
3 + 4 * 5      // 23 since the multiplication is done first
(3 + 4) * 5    // 35 since the addition is done first
```

Description

• To override the *order of precedence*, you can use parentheses.

Figure 2-8   How to code numeric expressions

How to use the compound assignment operators

When coding assignment statements, you often code the same variable name on both sides of the assignment operator (=). That way, you can use the current value of the variable in an expression and update that variable in a single statement.

Since you often write statements like this, PHP provides the five *compound assignment operators* shown in figure 2-9. Although these operators don't provide any new functionality, you can use them to write shorter code as shown by the examples.

The first set of examples shows how to use the .= operator to append string data to a variable. This is the only operator that can be used with string variables.

The second set of examples starts by showing how to use the standard assignment operator to increment a counter variable named $count. Here, the second statement includes the $count variable on both sides of the assignment operator (=) and adds a value of 1 to it.

Next, this set of examples shows how to use a compound assignment operator to get the same result with less code. Finally, it shows how to use the increment operator to get the same result with even less code. However, the increment operator only works when you want to increment by a value of 1. As a result, if you want to increment by another value, you need to use the compound assignment operator.

The third set of examples starts by showing how to use a compound assignment operator to append numeric data to a string variable. This statement automatically converts the numeric value to a string.

Then, the examples illustrate the use of compound assignment statements with numeric values. Here, the first statement assigns a value of 24.50 to a variable named subtotal, and the second statement uses the += operator to add a value of 75.50 to the value already in subtotal. After this statement executes, the subtotal contains 100.00. Then, the third statement uses the *= operator to multiply the value in subtotal by .9. After this statement executes, the subtotal has a value of 90.

The compound assignment operators

Operator	Description
.=	Appends a string expression to the variable.
+=	Adds the result of the numeric expression to the variable.
-=	Subtracts the result of the numeric expression from the variable.
*=	Multiplies the variable by the result of the numeric expression.
/=	Divides the variable by the result of the numeric expression.
%=	Stores the modulus of the variable and the result of the numeric expression in the variable.

Two ways to append string data to a variable

The standard assignment operator

```
$name = 'Ray ';
$name = $name . 'Harris';        // 'Ray Harris'
```

A compound assignment operator

```
$name = 'Ray ';
$name .= 'Harris';               // 'Ray Harris'
```

Three ways increment a counter variable

The standard assignment operator

```
$count = 1;
$count = $count + 1;             // 2
```

The compound assignment operator

```
$count = 1;
$count += 1;                     // 2
```

The increment operator

```
$count = 1;
$count++;                        // 2
```

More examples

How to append numeric data to a string variable

```
$message = 'Months: ';
$months = 120;
$message .= $months;            // 'Months: 120'
```

How to work with numeric data

```
$subtotal = 24.50;
$subtotal += 75.50;            // 100
$subtotal *= .9;              // 90 (100 * .9)
```

Description

- To perform an operation on a variable and assign the result to the same variable, you can use a *compound assignment operators* (.=, +=, -=, *=, /=, or %=).

Figure 2-9   How to use the compound assignment operators

How to use some built-in functions

PHP provides many *functions* that you can use to work with data. These functions are often referred to as *built-in functions* or *internal functions* because they are part of PHP.

Figure 2-10 shows how to work with five of these PHP functions. To use a function, you code the name of the function followed by a set of parentheses. Within the parentheses, you code any *arguments* that are required by the function, and you separate multiple arguments with commas.

This figure starts by showing how to use the number_format function to format a number. In the syntax for this function, the italicized words represent the arguments that you need to code, and the brackets [ ] indicate that the second argument is optional.

The examples after the table show how this works. Here, the first statement has just one argument, and the number is formatted with a comma to identify the thousands, but no decimal positions. In contrast, the second statement includes the optional second parameter to include a decimal point and two decimal digits. The third and fourth statements show that the number_format function automatically rounds numbers to the specified number of decimal places. Here, for example, .674 is rounded down to .67 and .675 is rounded up to .68.

You can use the date function to get the current date. This function accepts a string argument that specifies the format for the date. This string consists of characters that specify the format that you want. This table for this function summarizes four of these characters. For instance, the first example includes an argument of 'Y-m-d'. As a result, this statement returns the current date in this format: 2010-06-12. In chapter 9, you'll get a complete list of these characters.

This figure ends with a table that presents three functions that are commonly used to check if the data entered by a user is valid. Later in this chapter, you'll see how these functions are used in the context of conditional statements.

When you pass an argument to a function, you must make sure the argument is the correct data type. For instance, the first argument for the number_format function must be the double type, and the second argument must be an integer. If you pass an argument that can't be converted to the correct type, that will cause an error to occur.

A function for formatting numbers

Name	Description
number_format($number [, $decimals])	Returns a number that's formatted with a comma (,). If the second parameter is specified, this function also rounds the number to the specified number of decimal places.

Statements that format numbers

```
$nf = number_format(12345);          // 12,345
$nf = number_format(12345, 2);       // 12,345.00
$nf = number_format(12345.674, 2);   // 12,345.67
$nf = number_format(12345.675, 2);   // 12,345.68
```

A function for getting the current date

Name	Description
date($format)	Returns the current date with the specified format string.

Commonly used characters for formatting a date

Character	Description
Y	A four-digit year such as 2010.
y	A two-digit year such as 10.
m	Numeric representation of the month with leading zeroes (01-12).
d	Numeric representation of the day of the month with leading zeroes (01-31).

Statements that format a date

```
$date = date('Y-m-d');   // 2010-06-12
$date = date('m/d/y');   // 06/12/10
$date = date('m.d.Y');   // 06.12.2010
$date = date('Y');       // 2010
```

Three functions for checking variable values

Name	Description
isset($var)	Returns a TRUE value if the variable has been set and is not a NULL value.
empty($var)	Returns a TRUE value if the variable hasn't been set, contains a NULL value, or contains an empty string.
is_numeric($var)	Returns a TRUE value if the variable is a number or a string that can be converted to a number.

Function calls that check variable values

```
isset($name)         // TRUE if $name has been set and is not NULL
empty($name)         // TRUE if $name is empty
is_numeric($price)   // TRUE if $price is a number
```

Description

- PHP provides many *built-in functions* that can be used to do a wide variety of tasks.

Figure 2-10   How to use some built-in functions

The Product Discount application

Now that you know the basic skills for coding PHP applications, it's worth taking the time to give the Product Discount application of chapter 1 another look. As you will see, it only requires the skills you've learned so far.

The user interface

Figure 2-11 presents the user interface for the Product Discount application. The first page is a static web page that's stored in the index.html file. The second page is a dynamic web page that's stored in the display_discount.php file.

The form in the HTML file

Figure 2-11 presents the code for the HTML file that relates to the PHP for this application. Here, you can see the HTML for a form and three text boxes. When the user clicks on the Calculate Discount button, the form is submitted to the server via the POST method and the file named display_discount.php is requested. The data in the three text boxes is also sent along with the HTTP request.

The first page (index.html)

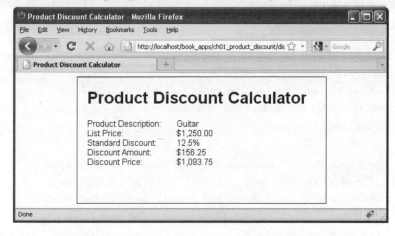

The second page (product_discount.php)

The code for the form on the first page

```
<form action="display_discount.php" method="post">
    <div id="data">
        <label>Product Description:</label>
        <input type="text" name="product_description"/><br />
        <label>List Price:</label>
        <input type="text" name="list_price"/><br />
        <label>Discount Percent:</label>
        <input type="text" name="discount_percent"/>%<br />
    </div>
    <div id="buttons">
        <label> </label>
        <input type="submit" value="Calculate Discount" /><br />
    </div>
</form>
```

Figure 2-11   The user interface and HTML page for the Product Discount application

The PHP file

Figure 2-12 presents the PHP file for this application. It starts with the code in a PHP tag. This code is divided into three parts as shown by the comments.

The first part gets the data from the form by using the $_POST array. This code stores that data in three variables named $product_description, $list_price, and $discount_percent.

The second part calculates the discount and the discounted price. First, it multiplies the list price by the discount percent and then by .01 (to convert the percent to two decimal places). Then, it subtracts the discount from the list price to get the discount price.

The third part applies formatting to the $list_price, $discount_percent, $discount, and $discount_price variables, and it stores the formatted results in variables that have the same names appended by _formatted. For instance, the first statement in this group uses the built-in number_format function to format the list price with two decimal places. But note too that the formatted result is concatenated with a $ sign. As a result, an entry of 1250 will be formatted as:

```
$1,250.00
```

Here, the $ sign is added by the concatenation, while the comma, decimal point, and two zeros are added by the number_format function.

In contrast, the discount percent that the user enters isn't formatted. However, a % sign is appended to it by using the concatenation operator. As a result, an entry of 12.5 is formatted as:

```
12.5%
```

When all four of the variables are formatted, they are ready to be displayed in the web page. Then, the block of PHP code ends and the HTML for the page begins. This HTML consists of a series of labels and <span> tags that use echo statements to display the data. These statements display the three user entries followed by the results of the calculations.

* * *

If you're new to programming, this is a good time to take a break and do exercise 2-1. That will give you a better understanding of how this application works and how the code in the application works.

The PHP file (display_discount.php)

```php
<?php
    // get the data from the form
    $product_description = $_POST['product_description'];
    $list_price = $_POST['list_price'];
    $discount_percent = $_POST['discount_percent'];

    // calculate the discount and discounted price
    $discount = $list_price * $discount_percent * .01;
    $discount_price = $list_price - $discount;

    // apply currency formatting to the dollar and percent amounts
    $list_price_formatted = "$".number_format($list_price, 2);
    $discount_percent_formatted = $discount_percent."%";
    $discount_formatted = "$".number_format($discount, 2);
    $discount_price_formatted = "$".number_format($discount_price, 2);
?>
<!DOCTYPE html PUBLIC "-//W3C//DTD XHTML 1.0 Transitional//EN"
    "http://www.w3.org/TR/xhtml1/DTD/xhtml1-transitional.dtd">
<html xmlns="http://www.w3.org/1999/xhtml">

<head>
    <title>Product Discount Calculator</title>
    <link rel="stylesheet" type="text/css" href="main.css"/>
</head>

<body>
    <div id="content">
        <h1>Product Discount Calculator</h1>

        <label>Product Description:</label>
        <span><?php echo $product_description; ?></span><br>

        <label>List Price:</label>
        <span><?php echo $list_price_formatted; ?></span><br>

        <label>Standard Discount:</label>
        <span><?php echo $discount_percent_formatted; ?></span><br>

        <label>Discount Amount:</label>
        <span><?php echo $discount_formatted; ?></span><br>

        <label>Discount Price:</label>
        <span><?php echo $discount_price_formatted; ?></span><br>
    </div>
</body>
</html>
```

Figure 2-12   The PHP file for the Product Discount application

How to code control statements

Like all programming languages, PHP provides *control statements* that let you control how the statements in an application are executed. To start, this topic shows how to code the conditional expressions that are used in control statements.

How to code conditional expressions

Figure 2-13 shows you how to code *conditional expressions* that use the six *relational operators*. A conditional expression compares two expressions and returns a value of TRUE or FALSE. If, for example, the value of $last_name in the first expression in the first table is "Harrison", the expression returns FALSE. Or, if the value of $rate in the last expression is 10, the expression returns TRUE because 10 / 100 is .1, and .1 is greater than or equal to 0.1.

If you use a relational operator to compare two different data types, PHP automatically converts the data types to the same type and attempts to perform the comparison. For example,

```
10 == '10'
```

returns TRUE because PHP converts both values to the same data type before comparing the values.

To code a *compound conditional expression*, you use the *logical operators* in the second table to combine two conditional expressions. If you use the AND operator, the compound expression returns TRUE if both expressions are TRUE. If you use the OR operator, the compound expression returns TRUE if either expression is TRUE. If you use the NOT operator, the value returned by the expression is reversed.

For example, if the $age variable contains a valid number,

```
is_numeric($age)
```

returns TRUE. Here, is_numeric is one of the three functions for checking variables that are summarized in figure 2-10. Conversely,

```
!is_numeric($age)
```

returns FALSE.

The logical operators in this figure are shown in their order of precedence. That is the order in which the operators are evaluated if more than one logical operator is used in a compound expression. This means that NOT operators are evaluated before AND operators, which are evaluated before OR operators. Although this is normally what you want, you can override this order by using parentheses.

In most cases, the conditional expressions that you use are relatively simple so coding them isn't much of a problem. In the rest of this chapter, you'll see some of the types of conditional expressions that are commonly used.

The relational operators

Operator	Name	Example
==	Equal	`$last_name == "Harris"` `$test_score == 10`
!=	Not equal	`$first_name != "Ray"` `$months != 0`
<	Less than	`$age < 18`
<=	Less than or equal	`$investment <= 0`
>	Greater than	`$test_score > 100`
>=	Greater than or equal	`$rate / 100 >= 0.1`

The logical operators in order of precedence

Operator	Name	Example
!	NOT	`!is_numeric($age)`
&&	AND	`$age > 17 && $score < 70`
||	OR	`!is_numeric($rate) || $rate < 0`

How the logical operators work

- Both tests with the AND operator must be TRUE for the overall test to be TRUE.
- At least one test with the OR operator must be TRUE for the overall test to be TRUE.
- The NOT operator switches the result of the expression to the other Boolean value. For example, if an expression is TRUE, the NOT operator converts it to FALSE.
- To override the order of precedence when two or more logical operators are used in a conditional expression, you can use parentheses.

Description

- A *conditional expression* uses the *relational operators* to compare the results of two expressions.
- A *compound conditional expression* joins two or more conditional expressions using the *logical operators*.
- If you use a relational operator to compare two different data types, PHP automatically converts the data types to the same data type and attempts to perform the comparison.
- Confusing the assignment operator (=) with the equality operator (==) is a common programming error so remember to use == for comparisons.

Figure 2-13   How to code conditional expressions

How to code if statements

An *if statement* lets you control the execution of statements based on the results of one or more conditional expressions. Figure 2-14 shows that an if statement can include three types of clauses. This statement must begin with an *if clause*. Then, it can have one or more *else if clauses*, but it doesn't have to have any. Last, it can have an *else clause*, but that clause is also optional.

To code the if clause, you code the *if* keyword followed by a conditional expression in parentheses and a block of one or more statements inside braces. If the conditional expression is TRUE, this block of code is executed and any remaining clauses in the if statement are skipped over. If the conditional expression is FALSE, the if statement continues with the next clause.

To code an else if clause, you code the *else if* keywords followed by a conditional expression in parentheses and a block of one or more statements inside braces. If the conditional expression is TRUE, its block of code is executed and any remaining clauses in the if statement are skipped over. This continues until one of the else if expressions is TRUE or they all are FALSE.

To code an else clause, you code the *else* keyword followed by a block of one or more statements inside braces. This code is only executed if all the conditional expressions in the if and else if clauses are FALSE.

The first example in this figure shows an if statement with no other clauses. If the price is less than or equal to zero, an appropriate message is stored in the $message variable.

The second example shows an if statement with an else clause. If the $first_name variable is empty, the statement in the if clause executes. Otherwise, the statement in the else clause executes.

The third example shows an if statement with two else if clauses and an else clause. If the $investment variable is empty, the if clause executes. If the $investment variable is *not* a valid number, the first else if clause executes. If the $investment variable is less than or equal to zero, the second else if clause executes. Otherwise, the else clause executes.

The fourth example shows an if statement with a compound conditional expression that tests whether the $investment variable is empty, is not a number, or is less than or equal to zero. If any of these conditions are TRUE, this code executes the statement within the if clause. If all three expressions are FALSE, this code doesn't execute any statements.

The last example shows how to *nest* one if statement within another. Here, the second if statement is nested within the else clause of the first if statement. When these *nested if statements* are executed, an error message is displayed if the $months variable is empty, is not a number, or is less than or equal to zero. This ends the if statement and nothing else happens. But if the $months variable is a number that's greater than zero, the else clause calculates the number of years represented by the $months variable. Then, the if statement that's nested in the else clause checks if the years are greater than 1 and sets the $message variable to an appropriate message.

An if statement with no other clauses

```
if ( $price <= 0 ) {
    $message = 'Price must be greater than zero.';
}
```

An if statement with an else clause

```
if ( empty($first_name) ) {
    $message = 'You must enter your first name.';
} else {
    $message = 'Hello ' . $first_name.'!';
}
```

An if statement with else if and else clauses

```
if ( empty($investment) ) {
    $message = 'Investment is a required field.';
} else if ( !is_numeric($investment) )  {
    $message = 'Investment must be a valid number.';
} else if ( $investment <= 0 )  {
    $message = 'Investment must be greater than zero.';
} else {
    $message = 'Investment is valid!';
}
```

An if statement with a compound conditional expression

```
if ( empty($investment) || !is_numeric($investment) || $investment <= 0 ) {
    $message = 'Investment must be a valid number greater than zero.';
}
```

A nested if statement

```
if ( empty($months) || !is_numeric($months) || $months <= 0 ) {
    $message = 'Please enter a number of months greater than zero.';
} else {
    $years = $months / 12;
    if ( $years > 1 ) {
        $message = 'A long-term investment.';
    } else {
        $message = 'A short-term investment.';
    }
}
```

Description

- An *if statement* starts with an *if clause* and can include multiple *else if clauses* and one *else clause* at the end.

- The if clause of the statement executes one or more statements if its condition is TRUE.

- The else if clause is executed when the previous condition or conditions are FALSE. The statement or statements within an else if clause are executed if its condition is TRUE.

- The else clause is executed when all previous conditions are FALSE.

- You can code one if statement within the if, else if, or else clause of another if statement. Those statements are referred to as *nested if statements*.

Figure 2-14   How to code if statements

How to code while and for statements

The while and for statements let you code loops that repeat a block of statements one or more times. This is illustrated by the statements in figure 2-15.

To code a *while statement*, you code the *while* keyword followed by a conditional expression in parentheses and a block of code in braces. When the while statement is executed, the conditional expression is evaluated. If the expression is TRUE, the block of code is executed and the *while loop* is tried again. As soon as the expression evaluates to FALSE, the block of code is skipped and the while statement is done. If the expression evaluates to FALSE the first time it is checked, the block of code won't be executed at all.

The first example shows a loop that appends the numbers 1 through 5 to a variable named $message. Before the loop, a statement assigns a value of 1 to the $counter variable. Then, the while loop checks if the $counter variable is less than or equal to 5. If so, it executes the two statements in the loop.

Within the while loop, the first statement appends the counter and a pipe character (|) to the $message variable. Then, the second statement uses the increment operator (++) to increment the value in the $counter variable by 1. The loop ends when the value of $counter is greater than 5. As a result, when the while loop finishes, the $message variable contains a string value of "1|2|3|4|5|".

To code a *for statement*, you code the *for* keyword followed by three statements in parentheses and a block of code in braces. The three statements are separated by semicolons. The first of these statements initializes the counter variable. It is executed just once. The second statement is a conditional expression that causes the code in the loop to be executed as long as it's TRUE. The third statement increments the counter. It's executed each time through the *for loop*, but after code in the loop is executed.

The second example shows how to get the same result as the first example with a for loop. Here, the $counter variable is initialized to 1; the loop is executed as long as $counter is less than or equal to 5; and $counter is incremented by 1 after each time through the loop. For a loop like this, a for statement is easier to use than a while statement.

The third example uses another while statement to calculate the future value of a one-time investment at a fixed interest rate. The first three variables store the investment amount, the yearly interest rate, and the number of years. The $future_value variable stores the value of the investment at the end of each year, and it's initialized to the value of the investment amount.

Within the while statement, the variable named $i is used as the counter, so it is incremented by 1 each time through the loop. Within the loop, the year's interest ($future_value * interest_rate) is added to the $future_value variable, and the result is stored back into the $future_value variable. When the loop finishes, the $future_value variable holds the future value of the investment.

The fourth example does the same calculation with a for loop. Here again, $i is used as the counter variable, which is a common programming practice. This name indicates that the variable stores an integer value. Since this variable is only used within the loop, there's no need for a more descriptive name.

A while loop that stores the numbers from 1 through 5 in a string

```php
$counter = 1;
while ($counter <= 5) {
    $message = $message . $counter . '|';  // appends the counter value
    $counter++;                            // adds 1 to the counter
}
// $message = 1|2|3|4|5|
```

A for loop that stores the numbers from 1 through 5 in a string

```php
for ($counter = 1; $counter <= 5; $counter++) {
    $message = $message . $counter . '|';  // appends the counter value
}
// $message = 1|2|3|4|5|
```

A while loop that calculates the future value of a one-time investment

```php
$investment = 1000;          // $investment is $1000
$interest_rate = .01;        // yearly interest rate is 10%
$years = 25;                 // years is 25
$future_value = $investment; // future value starts at $1000

$i = 1;
while ($i <= $years) {
    $future_value = ($future_value + ($future_value * $interest_rate);
    $i++;
}
```

A for loop that calculates the future value of a one-time investment

```php
$investment = 1000;          // $investment is $1000
$interest_rate = .01;        // yearly interest rate is 10%
$years = 25;                 // years is 25
$future_value = $investment; // future value starts at $1000

for ($i = 1; $i <= $years; $i++) {
    $future_value =
        ($future_value + ($future_value * $interest_rate));
}
```

Description

- The *while statement* is used to create a *while loop* that contains a block of code that is executed as long as a condition is TRUE. This condition is tested at the beginning of the loop. When the condition becomes FALSE, PHP skips to the code after the while loop.

- The *for statement* is used to create a *for loop* that contains a block of code that is executed a specific number of times.

- PHP also offers other looping structures that are presented in chapter 10.

Figure 2-15   How to code while and for statements

How to pass control to another page

As a PHP application executes, it moves from one web page to another. To do that, you can use the include and require functions that are summarized in figure 2-16. You can also use the exit function to exit from the current script.

If the include function isn't able to find the specified file, it issues a warning and allows the script to continue. The require function works similarly. However, if the require function fails, it causes a fatal error that stops the script.

The exit function exits from the current PHP script. Most of the time, you don't need to pass an argument to this function. However, if you want this function to display a status message before it exits, you can pass a string argument to it. Since the die function works the same way, you can use either of these functions for exiting.

The first three sets of examples show how to code these statements. Then, the fourth set shows how you can use these functions in an application. Here, an if statement checks the value of a Boolean variable named $is_valid. If this variable is TRUE, the if statement uses the include function to include a PHP file that processes the data. After that, it uses the exit function to skip the rest of the script. In effect, this passes control to the included page.

In other languages, this is commonly called *forwarding a request*, but in PHP, this is better described as a *conditional include*. You'll learn more about that in chapter 5.

The last set of examples shows how to refer to a web page that isn't in the current directory. To navigate down one or more directories, you can include a path. For instance, the first statement in this set of examples includes the header.php file that's in the view directory that's subordinate to the current directory. Or, to refer to the current directory, you can use the dot (.) operator, as in the second statement.

Last, to navigate up one or more directories, you can use two dot operators. For instance, the third statement in this set of examples refers to a file in the directory that's one up from the current directory, and the fourth statement refers to a file in the directory that's two up from the current directory.

As the table in this figure shows, the include_once and require_once functions work like the include and require functions, but they make sure that the file is only included once. Since this means that these functions need to check whether the file has already been included, they don't run as efficiently as the include and require functions.

Whenever possible, then, you should code your applications so they don't need to use the include_once and require_once functions. In chapter 5, you'll learn some techniques that will help you do that. If necessary, though, you can use the include_once and require_once functions to make sure that a file is only included once.

Built-in functions that you can use to pass control to another page

Name	Description
`include($path)`	Inserts and runs the specified file. However, if this function fails, it causes a warning that allows the script to continue. The parentheses are optional for this function.
`include_once($path)`	Same as include, but it makes sure that the file is included only once.
`require($path)`	Works the same as the include function. However, if this function fails, it causes a fatal error that stops the script.
`require_once($path)`	Same as require, but it makes sure that the file is only required once.
`exit([$status])`	Exits the current PHP script. If $status isn't supplied, the parentheses are optional. If $status is supplied, this function sends the $status string to the browser before it exits.
`die([$status])`	Works the same as the exit function.

The include function

```
include 'index.php';            // parentheses are optional
include('index.php');           // index.php in the current directory
```

The require function

```
require('index.php');           // index.php in the current directory
```

The exit function

```
exit;                           // parentheses are optional
exit();
exit('Unable to connect to DB.');  // passes a message to the browser
```

How to pass control to another PHP file in the current directory

```
if ($is_valid) {                // if $is_valid is true
    include('process_data.php');
    exit();
}
```

How to navigate up and down directories

```
include('view/header.php');     // navigate down one directory
include('./error.php');         // in the current directory
include('../error.php');        // navigate up one directory
include('../../error.php');     // navigate up two directories
```

Description

- You can use the include and require functions to pass control to another web page. When that page finishes, control returns to the statement after the include or require function.
- You can use the exit or die function to exit from the PHP script that is running.

Figure 2-16   How to pass control to another page

The Future Value application

At this point, you have learned a complete set of PHP skills that you can use to build applications of your own. To give you a better idea of how to do that, this chapter ends by presenting the Future Value application.

The user interface

The user interface for the Future Value application is shown in figure 2-17. The first page of this application asks the user for three numbers that are needed for calculating the future value of a one-time investment. The user types these values into the first three text boxes and clicks the Calculate button.

When the user clicks on the Calculate button, the data is submitted to the web server in an HTTP request for the second page. The application then does some data validation. If the data is valid, the application does the calculation and displays the results on a new page. As this figure shows, an investment of $10,000 at 7.5% for 25 years becomes $60,983.40

However, if the data that the user enters isn't valid, the application displays the first page again with an appropriate error message. For instance, the error message in the third browser window of this figure says: "Investment must be a valid number." In this example, the investment amount is invalid because the entry includes a $ sign and a comma, both of which are invalid in a numeric entry.

The first page

The second page

The first page with an error message

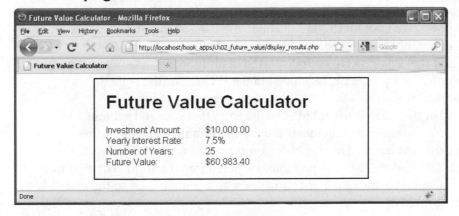

Figure 2-17   The user interface

The code for the index.php file

Figure 2-18 shows the code for the first page of this application. Unlike the Product Discount application, this is a PHP page named index.php, not an HTML page. In practice, most PHP applications start with an index.php file so some processing can be done before the first page of the application is displayed.

In the body of the HTML for this page, you can see a PHP tag that contains an if statement. This statement uses the built-in empty function to test whether the $error_message isn't empty (see the NOT operator). This function tests whether the variable hasn't been set, contains a null, or contains an empty string. The first time this page is requested, the error message will be empty, so this if statement won't do anything.

However, if the error message isn't empty the next time it's requested, this if statement issues an echo statement within a <p> tag to display the error message. Note here that a class attribute of "error" is set for this tag. Then, that class can be used by CSS to give the error message special formatting. Later, when you check the CSS for this application, you can see that this message is displayed in red, boldfaced type.

Note also that this <p> tag isn't displayed at all if $error_message is empty. In other words, the <p> tag isn't included in the HTML for the page that is returned to the browser unless there is an error message.

The rest of this page is the HTML for the form that gets and submits the data. But in this form, echo statements are used within the value attributes of the tags for the text boxes. These echo statements display the variables that contain the data that the user has previously entered into the form. The first time this page is displayed, though, these variables won't contain data so the text boxes will be empty.

The index.php file

```
<!DOCTYPE html PUBLIC "-//W3C//DTD XHTML 1.0 Transitional//EN"
    "http://www.w3.org/TR/xhtml1/DTD/xhtml1-transitional.dtd">
<html xmlns="http://www.w3.org/1999/xhtml">
<head>
    <title>Future Value Calculator</title>
    <link rel="stylesheet" type="text/css" href="main.css"/>
</head>

<body>
    <div id="content">
    <h1>Future Value Calculator</h1>
    <?php if (!empty($error_message)) { ?>
        <p class="error"><?php echo $error_message; ?></p>
    <?php } ?>
    <form action="display_results.php" method="post">

        <div id="data">
            <label>Investment Amount:</label>
            <input type="text" name="investment"
                value="<?php echo $investment; ?>"/><br />

            <label>Yearly Interest Rate:</label>
            <input type="text" name="interest_rate"
                value="<?php echo $interest_rate; ?>"/><br />

            <label>Number of Years:</label>
            <input type="text" name="years"
                value="<?php echo $years; ?>"/><br />
        </div>

        <div id="buttons">
            <label> </label>
            <input type="submit" value="Calculate"/><br />
        </div>

    </form>
    </div>
</body>
</html>
```

Figure 2-18   The code for the index.php file

The code for the display_results.php file

When the user clicks on the Calculate button on the first page, the data is submitted to the display_results.php file via the POST method. This file is presented in figure 2-19.

This file starts with a PHP tag that is divided into five parts. The first part gets the data from the form using the $_POST array.

The second part uses one long if statement to validate the entries for the investment amount and the interest rate. To make this statement easier to follow, it is divided into three parts by comments. First, the if clause and the two else if clauses that follow test whether the investment variable is empty, isn't numeric, or is less than or equal to zero. Then, the next three else if clauses test whether the interest rate variable is empty, isn't numeric, or is less than or equal to zero. If one of the conditions for these clauses is true, $error_message is set to an appropriate message. Otherwise, the else clause sets $error_message to an empty string. This type of checking is commonly referred to as *data validation*.

Note here that only the first error will be caught by this if statement because the statement ends when the condition in any clause is TRUE. This is okay for a simple application like this, but some applications try to catch all of the entry errors the first time and display appropriate messages for all of them. Note too that this application doesn't test the years entry for validity, which isn't okay for a production application.

The third part of the code checks whether $error_message is *not* empty. If it isn't, one of the entries wasn't valid so the if statement includes the index.php page and exits. That passes control back to the first page of this application. This time, though, that page will display an error message along with the values that the user entered into the text boxes.

The fourth part is executed if the investment entry is valid. Then, a for loop is used to calculate the future value of the investment. Note in the calculation that interest rate is multiplied by .01 to convert the interest rate to a decimal. Thus, an entry of 7.5 percent becomes .075.

The fifth part of this PHP code formats the investment amount, interest rate, and future value. This code uses the number_format function and concatenation just as the Product Discount application did. That ends the PHP and the HTML for the page begins.

The display_results.php file

```php
<?php
    // get the data from the form
    $investment = $_POST['investment'];
    $interest_rate = $_POST['interest_rate'];
    $years = $_POST['years'];

    // validate investment entry
    if ( empty($investment) ) {
        $error_message = 'Investment is a required field.';
    } else if ( !is_numeric($investment) )  {
        $error_message = 'Investment must be a valid number.';
    } else if ( $investment <= 0 ) {
        $error_message = 'Investment must be greater than zero.';
    // validate interest rate entry
    } else if ( empty($interest_rate) ) {
        $error_message = 'Interest rate is a required field.';
    } else if ( !is_numeric($interest_rate) )  {
        $error_message = 'Interest rate must be a valid number.';
    } else if ( $interest_rate <= 0 ) {
        $error_message = 'Interest rate must be greater than zero.';
    // set error message to empty string if no invalid entries
    } else {
        $error_message = '';
    }

    // if an error message exists, go to the index page
    if ($error_message != '') {
        include('index.php');
        exit(); }

    // calculate the future value
    $future_value = $investment;
    for ($i = 1; $i <= $years; $i++) {
        $future_value =
            ($future_value + ($future_value * $interest_rate * .01));
    }

    // apply currency and percent formatting
    $investment_f = '$'.number_format($investment, 2);
    $yearly_rate_f = $interest_rate.'%';
    $future_value_f = '$'.number_format($future_value, 2);
?>
```

Figure 2-19   The code for the display_results.php file (part 1 of 2)

The HTML code for this file just uses echo statements to display the formatted user entries and the future value within <span> tags.

Now, if you understand the PHP and HTML for this file, you're ready to write some applications of your own. However, you should be aware that this application can be improved in several ways that would make it more realistic.

First, this application should check all three user entries for validity, not just the investment amount and interest rate. Second, this application should check to make sure that the entries are not only valid, but also reasonable. For instance, you could check to make sure that the interest rate is less than 15 and that the number of years is less than 50. This type of data validation is common to all production applications.

Beyond that, you could add features that would make the application easier to use. For instance, you could add a Return button or link to the second page that would make it easier to get back to the first page. As it is, the user has to click on the Back button to do that. The good news is that you already have the skills for making enhancements like this.

The display_results.php file (continued)

```php
<!DOCTYPE html PUBLIC "-//W3C//DTD XHTML 1.0 Transitional//EN"
    "http://www.w3.org/TR/xhtml1/DTD/xhtml1-transitional.dtd">
<html xmlns="http://www.w3.org/1999/xhtml">
<head>
    <title>Future Value Calculator</title>
    <link rel="stylesheet" type="text/css" href="main.css"/>
</head>
<body>
    <div id="content">
        <h1>Future Value Calculator</h1>
        <label>Investment Amount:</label>
        <span><?php echo $investment_f; ?></span><br />
        <label>Yearly Interest Rate:</label>
        <span><?php echo $yearly_rate_f; ?></span><br />
        <label>Number of Years:</label>
        <span><?php echo $years; ?></span><br />
        <label>Future Value:</label>
        <span><?php echo $future_value_f; ?></span><br />
    </div>
</body>
</html>
```

Figure 2-19   The code for the display_results.php file (part 2 of 2)

How to use the PHP documentation

Whenever you learn a new language, it's good to have access to its documentation. Then, if you encounter a problem that you can't figure out based on what you already know, you can consult the documentation for more information.

How to access the PHP manual

Figure 2-20 shows how to access the PHP documentation from it's official web site. When you get to the URL for the starting page, you click on the name of the language (like English) that you want the documentation in. That displays the starting page for the PHP manual.

How to find the documentation you need

When the PHP manual is open, you have two ways to find the documentation that you need. First, you can click through the links in the manual to navigate to the information that you need. Second, you can enter a function name in the Search For text box to find the documentation for a specific function, but only if you know the name of the function.

To illustrate, the sidebar of the browser in this figure shows the structure of the links in the PHP manual that the user has clicked to get to the documentation for the isset function. Then, the main portion of the browser shows the documentation for that function. In this case, you can get that documentation either by drilling down through the links for the PHP manual or by searching for the isset function.

If you read the documentation for that function, you can see that it goes beyond what is presented in figure 2-10, although the syntax is the same as in this book. In both cases, italics are used to mark the code that you need to enter and brackets are used to mark optional entries.

Often, the official documentation is more than you need to know, especially when you're learning. For instance, the syntax and description for the isset function show that you can code it with more than one argument. In that case, this function returns TRUE only if all of the variables in the argument list are set. Because you typically don't need to check multiple values, this extra information just makes the documentation harder to use.

Eventually, though, you will find that the documentation can be useful. Sometimes, you'll use it to clarify the way something works. Other times, you'll use it to see if you can find a built-in function that does exactly what you're trying to do.

The URL for the PHP documentation

```
http://php.net/docs.php
```

Documentation for the if statement

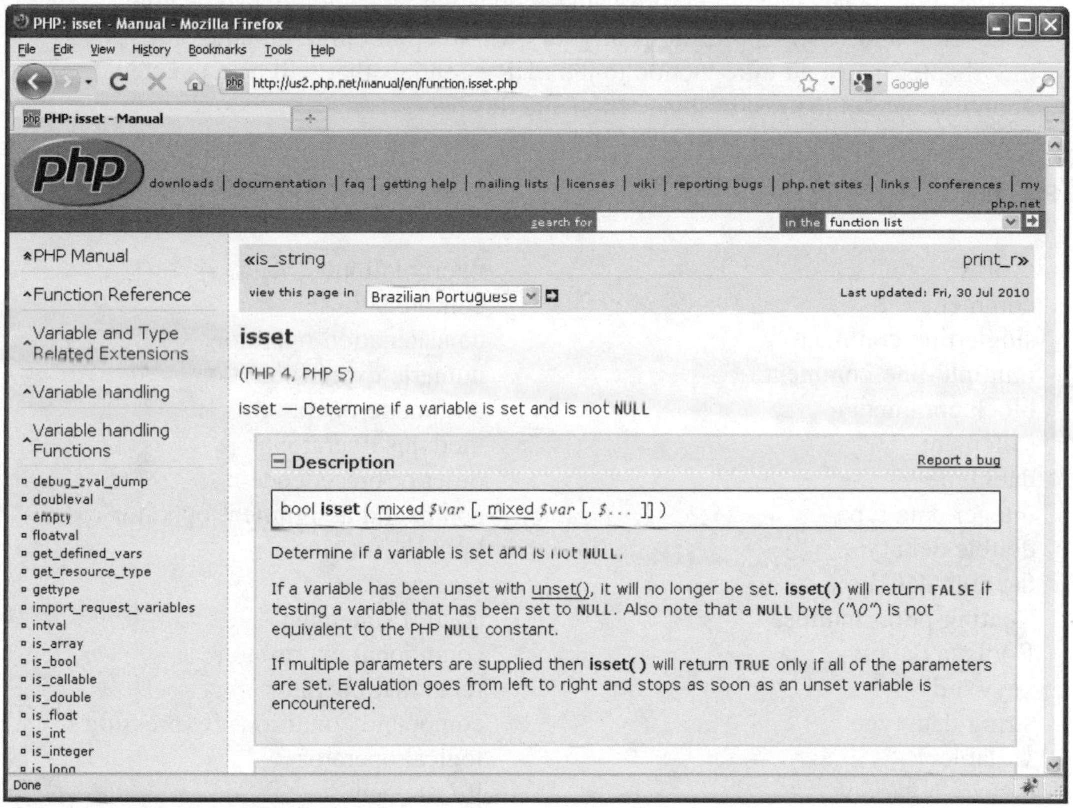

How to access the PHP manual

- On the first page of the web site, click on the name of the language that you want to use. That will access the first page of the PHP manual.

How to use the PHP manual

- Click on PHP Manual in the left pane of the window to display the contents for the manual in the main pane.
- Scroll down the contents until you find the link you're looking for, click on it, and continue this process until the right information is displayed.

How to find the documentation for a function when you know its name

- Type the function name in the Search For text box and press the Enter key.

Description

- When you're getting started with PHP, the PHP documentation is hard to read and understand, but it becomes more valuable as you become more experienced.

Figure 2-20   How to use the PHP documentation

Perspective

The goal of this chapter has been to get you off to a fast start with PHP. Now, if you understand the Future Value application, you should also be able to develop basic PHP applications of your own. Keep in mind, though, that this chapter is just an introduction to the PHP essentials that will be expanded upon throughout the rest of this section and this book.

Terms

syntax	interpolation
comment	concatenate
single-line comment	concatenation operator
multiple-line comment	numeric expression
block comment	arithmetic operator
statement	modulus operator
data type	order of precedence
integer data type	compound assignment operator
double data type	built-in function
decimal data type	argument
floating-point number	control statement
Boolean data type	conditional expression
keyword	relational operator
string data type	compound conditional expression
variable	logical operator
declare a variable	if statement
assignment operator	if clause
literal value	else if clause
numeric literal	else clause
string literal	nested if statements
Boolean literal	while statement
camel casing	while loop
constant	for statement
built-in array	for loop
expression	forward a request
string expression	conditional include
empty string	data validation
null value	

Summary

- When you use PHP, *statements* do the operations of the application, while *comments* can be used to document what the code does.

- PHP provides six *data types* including *integer*, *double*, *Boolean*, and *string* that are designed for storing those types of data.

- To *declare* a *variable* and *assign* a value to it, code a variable name, the equals sign, and an expression that contains a value. That value determines the data type that is used for the variable.

- You can code *literals* for numeric, string, and Boolean values, and you can use these literals in the expressions that you code.

- A *keyword* is a PHP word like true, false, if, and else that shouldn't be used for other purposes.

- To get the data from a form that has been submitted to the server, you use the *built-in arrays* named $_GET or $_POST, depending on whether the form is submitted with the GET or POST method.

- When you code string values, you should use single quotes to improve PHP efficiency, unless you're inserting a variable into a string. To *concatenate* two strings, you use the *concatenation operator*.

- To code an *arithmetic expression*, you use the *arithmetic operators*. To both assign and do an operation with a single operator, you can use the *compound assignment operators*.

- PHP provides many *built-in functions* for doing common tasks like formatting numbers, getting the current date, and checking variable values to see whether they're set, empty, or numeric.

- To code a *conditional expression*, you use *relational operators* and *logical operators*. Conditional expressions always return Boolean values.

- *If statements* provide the logic of an application. They consist of *if*, *else if*, and *else clauses*. When one if statement is coded within another, they're referred to as *nested if statements*.

- A *while loop* executes a block of code as long as a condition is TRUE. A *for loop* executes a block of code a specific number of times.

- The built-in include, require, and exit functions can be used to pass control from one PHP page to another.

- *Data validation* refers to the thorough checking that should be done to make sure each user entry is valid.

- The official PHP documentation that's available from the Internet provides detailed information about the PHP language and its built-in functions.

Before you do the exercises for this chapter

If you haven't already done so, you should install the software and the source code for this book as described in the appendix. Then, if you're new to programming, you should do exercise 2-1. But if you have some programming experience, you can start with exercise 2-2.

Exercise 2-1   Build the Product Discount application

This exercise steps you through the process of building the Product Discount application.

Open the files for the Product Discount application

1. Make sure the Apache server is running. Then, start your browser and run the application in this directory:

    `xampp/htdocs/ex_starts/ch02_ex1`

    copy ex-starts to MAmp/htdocs directory

    To do that, you can use the index of exercise starts that you bookmarked in exercise 1-2 or you can use this URL:

    `http://localhost/ex_starts/ch02_ex1`

2. Enter valid data in the three text boxes, and click the Calculate button. Note that the resulting web page indicates that it is under construction.

3. Use your IDE or text editor to open the display_discount.php file for this application. It is in the same folder as the index.html file. Then, note that this file doesn't contain the PHP statements that this application needs.

4. Use your IDE or text editor to open the index.html file for this application. Then, note the name attributes for the three text boxes.

Add the PHP statements

5. Switch to the display_discount.php file and add statements that use the $_POST array to get the product description, list price, and discount percent from the form. Then, modify the first three echo statements so they display this data, save the file, and run the application again. This should display unformatted versions of the data that you enter.

6. Switch to the display_discount.php file and add statements that calculate the discount amount and discount price. Then, modify the last two echo statements so they display this data, save the file, and run the application. This time, the application should display unformatted versions of the calculated data.

7. Switch to the display_discount.php file and add statements that format the numeric variables with the currency and percentage formats. Then, modify the last four echo statements so they display the formatted data, save the file, and run the application. Now, the application should display the formatted data.

8. Fix the heading for the display_discount.php file so it says "Product Discount Calculator". Then, test this change, and close the files.

Exercise 2-2   Enhance the Future Value application

In this exercise, you'll enhance the Future Value application by applying some of the skills that you've just learned.

Test the Future Value application

1. Make sure the Apache server is running. Then, start your browser and run the application in this directory:

    `xampp/htdocs/ex_starts/ch02_ex2`

    To do that, you can use the index of exercise starts that you bookmarked in exercise 1-2 or you can use this URL:

    `http://localhost/ex_starts/ch02_ex2/`

2. Enter valid numbers in all three text boxes. For the first test run, keep these values simple like 100 for investment amount, 5 for yearly interest rate, and 10 for number of years. Then, click the Calculate button to display the results.

3. Click the Back button to return to the first page, enter invalid values in the first two text boxes, and click the Calculate button. Then, respond to the error message that's displayed by entering valid data for the investment amount and clicking the Calculate button. This time, you need to respond to the error message for the invalid interest rate entry.

Enhance the validity checking

4. Use your IDE or text editor to open the display_results.php and index.php files. Then, review the code for these files.

5. Switch to the display_results.php file and enhance the code so it tests the interest rate entry to make sure it is also less than or equal to 15. To do that, use an OR operator. If the rate isn't valid, display an appropriate error message like:

    `Rate must be greater than zero and less than or equal to 15.`

    Then, save your changes, and test this enhancement.

6. Switch back to the display_results.php file and modify the code so it tests the years entry to make sure it is a valid number that's greater than zero and less than or equal to 50. If it isn't, display an appropriate error message like the one for the interest rate. Then, save your changes, and test this enhancement.

Add the date to the web page

7. Modify the display_results.php file so it uses embedded PHP to display the current date at the bottom of the web page like this:

    `This calculation was done on 11/25/2010.`

    To do this, use the date function in figure 2-10. Then, test this change. When you've got it working right, close the files.

<P> This Calculation was done
on<?php echo date date
('m/d/y'); ?></p>

3

Introduction to relational databases and MySQL

Before you can use PHP to work with a MySQL database, you need to be familiar with the concepts and terms that apply to database systems. You should also be able to review the structure and data in any of the databases that you'll be working with. So that's what you'll learn in this chapter. After you learn the concepts and terms, you'll learn how to use a web application called phpMyAdmin to work with a MySQL database.

An introduction to relational databases **94**
How a database table is organized 94
How the tables in a relational database are related 96
How the columns in a table are defined 98

The SQL statements for data manipulation **100**
How to select data from a single table 100
How to select data from multiple tables 102
How to insert, update, and delete data 104

An introduction to MySQL **106**
What MySQL provides 106
Two ways to work with MySQL 108

How to use phpMyAdmin **110**
How to start phpMyAdmin 110
How to log in, log out, and change your password 110
How to import and run a SQL script that creates a database 112
How to review the data and structure of a table 114
How to run SQL statements 116
How to create users with limited privileges 118

Perspective **120**

An introduction to relational databases

In 1970, Dr. E. F. Codd developed a model for a new type of database called a *relational database.* This type of database eliminated some of the problems that were associated with standard files and other database designs. By using the relational model, you can reduce data redundancy, which saves disk storage and leads to efficient data retrieval. You can also view and manipulate data in a way that is both intuitive and efficient. Today, relational databases are the de facto standard for database applications.

How a database table is organized

In a relational database, data is stored in one or more *tables* that consist of *rows* and *columns.* This is illustrated by the relational table in figure 3-1. Each row in this table contains information about a single product. A value that is stored at the intersection of each row and column is sometimes called a *cell.*

In general, each table is modeled after a real-word entity such as a product or a customer. Then, the columns of the table represent the attributes of the entity such as product code, name, and price for a product. And each row of the table represents one instance of the entity like one product.

If a table contains one or more columns that uniquely identify each row in the table, you can define these columns as the *primary key* of the table. For instance, the primary key of the products table in this figure is the productID column. In this example, the primary key consists of a single column, but a primary key can also consist of two or more columns.

In addition to primary keys, most database management systems let you define additional keys that uniquely identify each row in a table. If, for example, the productCode column in a products table contains unique data, it can be defined as a *non-primary key.* In MySQL, this is called a *unique key.*

Indexes provide an efficient way of accessing the rows in a table based on the values in one or more columns. Because applications typically access the rows in a table by referring to their key values, an index is automatically created for each primary and non-primary key. However, you can define indexes for other columns as well. If, for example, you frequently need to sort the rows in a customer table by zip code, you can set up an index for that column. Like a key, an index can include one or more columns.

A products table

productID	categoryID	productCode	productName	listPrice
1	1	strat	Fender Stratocaster	699.00
2	1	les_paul	Gibson Les Paul	1199.00
3	1	sg	Gibson SG	2517.00
4	1	fg700s	Yamaha FG700S	489.99
5	1	washburn	Washburn D10S	299.00
6	1	rodriguez	Rodriguez Caballero 11	415.00
7	2	precision	Fender Precision	799.99
8	2	hofner	Hofner Icon	499.99
9	3	ludwig	Ludwig 5-piece Drum Set with Cymbals	699.99
10	3	tama	Tama 5-Piece Drum Set with Cymbals	799.99

Primary key · *Columns* · *Rows*

Concepts

- A *relational database* consists of *tables*. Tables consist of *rows* and *columns*, which can also be referred to as *records* and *fields*.

- A table is typically modeled after a real-world entity, such as a product or customer.

- A column represents some attribute of the entity, such as the list price of a product or a customer's email address.

- A row contains a set of values for one instance of the entity, such as one product or one customer.

- The intersection of a row and a column is sometimes called a *cell*. A cell stores a single value.

- Most tables have a *primary key* that uniquely identifies each row in the table.

- The primary key is usually a single column, but it can also consist of two or more columns.

- In addition to primary keys, most database management systems let you define one or more *non-primary keys*. In MySQL, these keys are called *unique keys*. Like a primary key, a non-primary key uniquely identifies each row in the table.

- A table can also be defined with one or more *indexes*. An index provides an efficient way to access data from a table based on the values in specific columns. An index is automatically created for a table's primary and non-primary keys.

Figure 3-1   How a database table is organized

How the tables in a relational database are related

The tables in a relational database can be related to other tables by values in specific columns. The two tables shown in figure 3-2 illustrate this concept. Here, each row in the categories table is related to one or more rows in the products table. This is called a *one-to-many relationship*.

Typically, relationships exist between the primary key in one table and the *foreign key* in another table. The foreign key is simply one or more columns in a table that refer to a primary key in another table.

Although one-to-many relationships are the most common, two tables can also have a one-to-one or many-to-many relationship. If a table has a *one-to-one relationship* with another table, the data in the two tables could be stored in a single table. Because of that, one-to-one relationships are used infrequently.

In contrast, a *many-to-many relationship* is usually implemented by using an intermediate table that has a one-to-many relationship with the two tables in the many-to-many relationship. In other words, a many-to-many relationship can usually be broken down into two one-to-many relationships.

The relationship between two tables in a database

Primary key

categoryID	categoryName
1	Guitars
2	Basses
3	Drums

productID	categoryID	productCode	productName	listPrice
1	1	strat	Fender Stratocaster	699.00
2	1	les_paul	Gibson Les Paul	1199.00
3	1	sg	Gibson SG	2517.00
4	1	fg700s	Yamaha FG700S	489.99
5	1	washburn	Washburn D10S	299.00
6	1	rodriguez	Rodriguez Caballero 11	415.00
7	2	precision	Fender Precision	799.99
8	2	hofner	Hofner Icon	499.99
9	3	ludwig	Ludwig 5-piece Drum Set with Cymbals	699.99
10	3	tama	Tama 5-Piece Drum Set with Cymbals	799.99

Foreign key

Concepts

- The tables in a relational database are related to each other through their key columns. For example, the categoryID column is used to relate the categories and products tables above.

- The categoryID column in the products table is called a *foreign key* because it identifies a related row in the categories table. A table may contain one or more foreign keys.

- When you define a foreign key, you can't add rows to the table with the foreign key unless there's a matching primary key in the related table.

- The relationships between the tables in a database correspond to the relationships between the entities they represent. The most common type of relationship is a *one-to-many relationship* as illustrated by the categories and products table.

- A table can also have a *one-to-one relationship* or a *many-to-many relationship* with another table.

Figure 3-2   How the tables in a relational database are related

How the columns in a table are defined

When you define a column in a table, you assign properties to it as indicated by the design of the products table in figure 3-3. The most critical property for a column is its data type, which determines the type of information that can be stored in the column. With MySQL, you typically use the *data types* that are summarized in this figure. As you define each column in a table, you generally try to assign the data type that will minimize the use of disk storage because that will improve the performance of the queries later.

In addition to choosing a data type, you must identify whether the column can store a *null value*. A null represents a value that's unknown, unavailable, or not applicable. If you don't allow null values, then you must provide a value for the column or you can't store the row in the table.

You can also assign a *default value* to each column. Then, that value is assigned to the column if another value isn't provided when a row is added to a table.

Each table can also contain a numeric column whose value is generated automatically by the DBMS. In MySQL, a column like this is called an *auto-incremented column*. As this figure shows, the productID column in the products table is an auto-incremented column.

In chapter 17, you'll learn the details for defining the columns of a table. So at this point, you just need a general idea of how the columns in a table are defined and how the data is stored in a table.

The columns of the products table

Field	Type	Collation	Attributes	Null	Default	Extra
productID	int(11)			No	*None*	auto_increment
categoryID	int(11)			No	*None*	
productCode	varchar(10)	latin1_swedish_ci		No	*None*	
productName	varchar(255)	latin1_swedish_ci		No	*None*	
listPrice	decimal(10,2)			No	*None*	

Common MySQL data types

Type	Description
CHAR	A fixed-length string of charcters in the ASCII character set.
VARCHAR	A variable-length string of characters in the ASCII character set.
INT	Integer values of various sizes.
DECIMAL	Decimal values that can contain an integer portion and a decimal portion.
DATE, TIME, DATETIME	A date, time, or date and time.

Description

- The *data type* that's assigned to a column determines the type and size of the information that can be stored in the column.
- Each column definition also indicates whether or not it can contain *null values*. A null value indicates that the value of the column is unknown.
- A column can also be defined with a *default value*. Then, that value is used if another value isn't provided when a row is added to the table.
- A column can also be defined as an *auto-increment column*. An auto-increment column is a numeric column whose value is generated automatically when a row is added to the table.
- For more information on the MySQL data types, see chapter 17.

Figure 3-3   How the columns in a table are defined

The SQL statements for data manipulation

Structured Query Language, or *SQL*, is a standard language for working with databases. In conversation, SQL is referred to as S-Q-L or as sequel.

The SELECT, INSERT, UPDATE, and DELETE statements that you'll learn about next make up SQL's *Data Manipulation Language* (*DML*). These statements work with the data in a database and are the statements that programmers use everyday in their applications.

In contrast, statements like the CREATE DATABASE, DROP DATABASE, and CREATE TABLE statements are part of SQL's *Data Definition Language* (*DDL*). In chapter 17, you'll learn to use these statements to create a database.

How to select data from a single table

The SELECT statement is the most commonly used *SQL statement*. It can be used to retrieve data from one or more tables in a database. When you run a SELECT statement, it is commonly referred to as a *query* (although the execution of any SQL statement can also be referred to as a query). The result of this query is a table known as a *result set*, or a *result table*.

In figure 3-4, you can see the syntax for SELECT statements that get all of the columns of a table or just selected columns. In the syntax summaries that we use for SQL statements, the capitalized words are the required SQL words, and the lowercase words are the ones that you supply. Also, the brackets indicate optional components of a statement, and the bar (|) indicates a choice between two options.

The first example in this figure shows how the first syntax is used to retrieve selected rows and all columns from the products table. Here, the SELECT clause uses the asterisk (*) wildcard to indicate that all of the columns in the table should be retrieved, and the FROM clause identifies the products table. Then, the WHERE clause says to select only those rows in which the categoryID column is equal to 2. As a result, this query returns just two rows and five columns.

The second example shows how the second syntax is used to retrieve two columns and four rows from the products table. This time, the SELECT clause identifies the two columns, and the FROM clause identifies the table. Then, the WHERE clause limits the number of rows that are retrieved by specifying that the statement should only retrieve rows where the value in the listPrice column is less than 500. Last, the ORDER BY clause indicates that the retrieved rows should be sorted in ascending order by the listPrice column.

As you might guess, queries can have a significant effect on the performance of a database application. In general, the more columns and rows that a query returns, the more traffic the network has to bear. As a result, when you design queries, you should try to keep the number of columns and rows to a minimum.

The syntax for a SELECT statement that gets all columns

```
SELECT *
FROM table-1
[WHERE selection-criteria]
[ORDER BY column-1 [ASC|DESC] [, column-2 [ASC|DESC] ...]]
```

A SELECT statement that gets all columns

```
SELECT * FROM products
WHERE categoryID = 2
```

* All of columns should be retrieved

productID	categoryID	productCode	productName	listPrice
7	2	precision	Fender Precision	799.99
8	2	hofner	Hofner Icon	499.99

The syntax for a SELECT statement that gets selected columns

```
SELECT column-1 [, column-2] ...
FROM table-1
[WHERE selection-criteria]
[ORDER BY column-1 [ASC|DESC] [, column-2 [ASC|DESC] ...]]
```

A SELECT statement that gets selected columns and rows

```
SELECT productName, listPrice
FROM products
WHERE listPrice < 500
ORDER BY listPrice ASC
```

productName	listPrice ▲
Washburn D10S	299.00
Rodriguez Caballero 11	415.00
Yamaha FG700S	489.99
Hofner Icon	499.99

Description

- A SELECT statement is a SQL statement that returns a *result set* (or *result table*) that consists of the specified rows and columns.
- To specify the columns, you use the SELECT clause.
- To specify the table that the data should be retrieved from, you use the FROM clause.
- To specify rows, you use the WHERE clause.
- To specify how the result set should be sorted, you use the ORDER BY clause.

Figure 3-4   How to select data from a single table

How to select data from multiple tables

Figure 3-5 shows how to use the SELECT statement to retrieve data from two tables. This is commonly known as a *join*. The result of any join is a single result table.

An *inner join* is the most common type of join. When you use one, the data from the rows in the two tables are included in the result set only if their related columns match. In this figure, for example, the SELECT statement joins the data from the rows in the products and categories tables only if the value of the categoryID column in the products table is equal to the categoryID column in the categories table. In other words, if there isn't any data in the products table for a category, that category won't be added to the result set.

To code an inner join, you use the JOIN clause to specify the second table and the ON clause to specify the columns to be used for the join. If a column in one table has the same name as a column in the other table, you can code the table name, a dot, and the column name to specify the column that you want to use. This is illustrated by the ON clause in this figure.

Although this figure only shows how to join data from two tables, you can extend this syntax to join data from additional tables. For example, let's say you want to create a result set that includes data from three tables named categories, products, and orderitems. In that case, you can code the FROM clause of the SELECT statement like this:

```
FROM categories
    INNER JOIN products
        ON categories.categoryID = products.categoryID
    INNER JOIN orderitems
        ON products.productID = orderitems.productID
```

Then, you can include any of the columns from the three tables in the column list of the SELECT statement.

Another type of join is an *outer join*. With this type of join, all of the rows in one of the tables are included in the result set whether or not there are matching rows in the other table. In a *left outer join*, all of the rows in the first table (the one on the left) are included in the result set. In a *right outer join*, all of the rows in the second table are included.

To illustrate, suppose that a SELECT statement uses a left outer join to join the rows in a categories table with the rows in a products table. In that case, all of the rows in the categories table would be included in the result set…even if some of the rows in the categories table don't have any matching rows in the products table.

The syntax for a SELECT statement that joins two tables

```
SELECT column-1 [, column-2] ...
FROM table-1
    {INNER | LEFT OUTER | RIGHT OUTER} JOIN table-2
    ON table-1.column-1 {=|<|>|<=|>=|<>} table-2.column-2
[WHERE selection-criteria]
[ORDER BY column-1 [ASC|DESC] [, column-2 [ASC|DESC] ...]]
```

A statement that gets data from two related tables

```
SELECT categoryName, productName, listPrice
FROM categories
    INNER JOIN products
    ON categories.categoryID = products.categoryID
WHERE listPrice > 800
ORDER BY listPrice ASC
```

categoryName	productName	listPrice
Guitars	Gibson Les Paul	1199.00
Guitars	Gibson SG	2517.00

Description

- To return a result set that contains data from two tables, you *join* the tables. To do that, you can use a JOIN clause.

- Most of the time, you'll want to code an *inner join* so that rows are only included when the key of a row in the first table is equal to (matches) the key of a row in the second table.

- An *outer join* returns rows from one table in the join even if the other table doesn't contain a matching row.

- In a *left outer join*, the data for all of the rows in the first table (the one on the left) are included in the table, but only the data for matching rows in the second table are included. In a *right outer join*, the reverse is true.

Figure 3-5   How to select data from multiple tables

How to insert, update, and delete data

Figure 3-6 shows how to use the INSERT, UPDATE, and DELETE statements to add, update, or delete one or more rows in a database. Because these statements modify the data in a database, they are sometimes referred to as *action queries*.

The syntax and examples for the INSERT statement show how to use this statement to add one row to a database. To do that, the statement supplies the names of the columns that are going to receive values in the new row, followed by the values for those columns. Here, the first example inserts one row into the products table. The second example also inserts one row into the orders table, but it uses the NOW function provided by MySQL to automatically insert the current date and time into the orderDate column.

When you code an INSERT statement, you don't need to include values for any columns whose values are automatically generated. In this figure, for instance, the first example doesn't include a value for the productID column because the value for that column is automatically generated by MySQL. Similarly, you don't need to include values for any columns that provide a default value or for any columns that allow NULL values. However, since the products table in this chapter doesn't allow NULL values or provide default values, you must supply the four columns that are shown.

The syntax for the INSERT statement shows that the column list is optional. In other words, you don't need to supply the list of column names after the table name. However, if you don't supply a list of column names, you must code the values in the order that the columns are defined for the table.

Similarly, the syntax and examples for the UPDATE statement show how to update rows. In the first update example, the UPDATE statement updates the productName column in the row where the productCode is equal to "ludwig". In the second update example, the listPrice column is updated to 299 in all of the rows where the categoryID is equal to 1.

Last, the syntax and examples for the DELETE statement show how to delete rows. Here, the first delete example deletes the row from the products table where the productID equals 1. Since each row contains a unique value in the productID column, this only deletes a single row. However, in the second delete example, multiple rows in the products table may have a listPrice that's greater than 200. As a result, this statement deletes all rows that satisfy this condition.

When you specify a value within an INSERT, UPDATE, or DELETE statement, you must enclose any string or date values in single quotes, but you usually don't enclose numbers in quotes. Nevertheless, MySQL lets you code single quotes around numbers.

The syntax for the INSERT statement

```
INSERT INTO table-name [(column-list)]
VALUES (value-list)
```

A statement that adds one row to a table

```
INSERT INTO products
    (categoryID, productCode, productName, listPrice)
VALUES
    (1, 'tele', 'Fender Telecaster', 599.00)
```

A statement that uses the MySQL NOW function to get the current date

```
INSERT INTO orders (customerID, orderDate)
VALUES (1, NOW())
```

The syntax for the UPDATE statement

```
UPDATE table-name
SET expression-1 [, expression-2] ...
WHERE selection-criteria
```

A statement that updates a column in one row

```
UPDATE products
SET productName = 'Ludwig 5-Piece Kit with Zildjian Cymbals'
WHERE productCode = 'ludwig'
```

A statement that updates a column in multiple rows

```
UPDATE products
SET listPrice = 299
WHERE categoryID = 1
```

The syntax for the DELETE statement

```
DELETE FROM table-name
WHERE selection-criteria
```

A statement that deletes one row from a table

```
DELETE FROM products
WHERE productID = 1
```

A statement that deletes multiple rows from a table

```
DELETE FROM products
WHERE listPrice > 200
```

Description

- Since the INSERT, UPDATE, and DELETE statements modify the data that's stored in a database, they're sometimes referred to as *action queries*. These statements don't return a result set. Instead, they return the number of rows that were affected by the query.

Figure 3-6   How to insert, update, and delete data

An introduction to MySQL

MySQL is an open-source database management system (DBMS) that you can download for free from the MySQL web site (www.mysql.com). As you may remember, MySQL is also part of the XAMPP package (it's the M in XAMPP). Finally, MySQL is often available as part of the hosting packages from many Internet Service Providers (ISPs).

What MySQL provides

Figure 3-7 lists some of the reasons why MySQL enjoys such popularity among web developers. To start, it's inexpensive and easy to use when compared with products like Oracle Database or Microsoft SQL Server. It runs fast when compared to those products, especially when you consider the costs. And it runs on most modern operating systems, while Microsoft SQL Server runs only on Windows.

Even though it's free for most uses, MySQL provides most of the features that you would expect from a modern relational database management system. In particular, it provides support for SQL, which is the industry standard. It provides support for multiple clients. And it provides for connectivity and security.

For web applications, that means you can write PHP applications that use SQL statements to access and update the data in a MySQL database. You can connect a PHP web application to a MySQL database that's running on an intranet or the Internet. And you can secure your data by restricting access to it.

In the past, MySQL didn't provide some of the features that are typically provided by a relational database. In particular, MySQL didn't provide referential integrity or transaction processing. As a result, referential integrity and transaction processing needed to be implemented on the front end by the application that was using MySQL, which was fine for many types of web applications.

As of release 5.0, however, MySQL supports referential integrity and transaction processing. When *referential integrity* is enforced by a database, you can't delete a row in one table that is related to a row in another table. When *transaction processing* is used, a series of related statements can be processed as a group, so all of the statements can be rolled back if one of the statements fails. If, for example, processing an invoice requires additions to both an invoices table and an invoiceLineItems table, none of the statements will be committed unless all of the statements are successful. With these additions, MySQL became a database management system that had the best features of commercial products like Oracle and SQL Server.

MySQL is...

- **Inexpensive.** MySQL is free for most uses and relatively inexpensive for other uses.

- **Fast.** By many accounts, MySQL is one of the fastest relational databases currently available.

- **Easy to use.** Compared to other database management systems, MySQL is easy to install and use.

- **Portable.** MySQL runs on most modern operating systems including Windows, Unix, Solaris, and OS/2.

MySQL provides...

- **Support for SQL.** Like any modern database product, MySQL supports SQL, which is the standard language for working with data that's stored in relational databases.

- **Support for multiple clients.** MySQL supports access from multiple clients from a variety of interfaces and programming languages including Java, Perl, PHP, Python, and C.

- **Connectivity.** MySQL can provide access to data via an intranet or the Internet.

- **Security.** MySQL can protect access to your data so only authorized users can view the data.

- **Referential integrity.** If you use the InnoDB tables option, MySQL provides support for referential integrity just like commercial databases such as Oracle Database or Microsoft SQL Server.

- **Transaction processing.** With version 5.0, MySQL provides support for transaction processing just like commercial databases such as Oracle Database or Microsoft SQL Server.

Description

- MySQL is an open-source database management system that is part of XAMPP. It can be downloaded as a separate product from the MySQL web site. And many Internet Service Providers include MySQL in their packages.

- *Referential integrity* refers to keeping the relationships between tables intact. That means, for example, that you can't delete a row in one table that has a primary key that is referred to by a foreign key in another table.

- *Transaction processing* refers to processing a series of related SQL statements as a group. Then, if one of the statements fails, the processing that's been done by the other statements can be rolled back so the database isn't compromised.

Figure 3-7   An introduction to MySQL

Two ways to work with MySQL

Figure 3-8 shows two ways that you can work with MySQL. One way is to use a *command-line client*. A client like this is installed when you install MySQL. Although this figure shows the command-line client for the Windows operating system, MySQL's command-line client works similarly on all operating systems. In this example, the user has started the command-line tool, logged into a database named my_guitar_shop1, and displayed all of the columns and rows in the categories table.

The other way to work with MySQL is to use a program that has a graphic interface like the one in this figure. This is a *web-based client* known as phpMyAdmin that gets installed along with XAMPP. This figure shows its Home page. Because it's easier to use a web-based client than a command-line client, this chapter shows you how to use phpMyAdmin for working with MySQL.

When you work with MySQL, you may notice that the terms *database* and *schema* are often used interchangeably. For example, the my_guitar_shop1 database may sometimes be referred to as the my_guitar_shop1 schema.

A command-line client

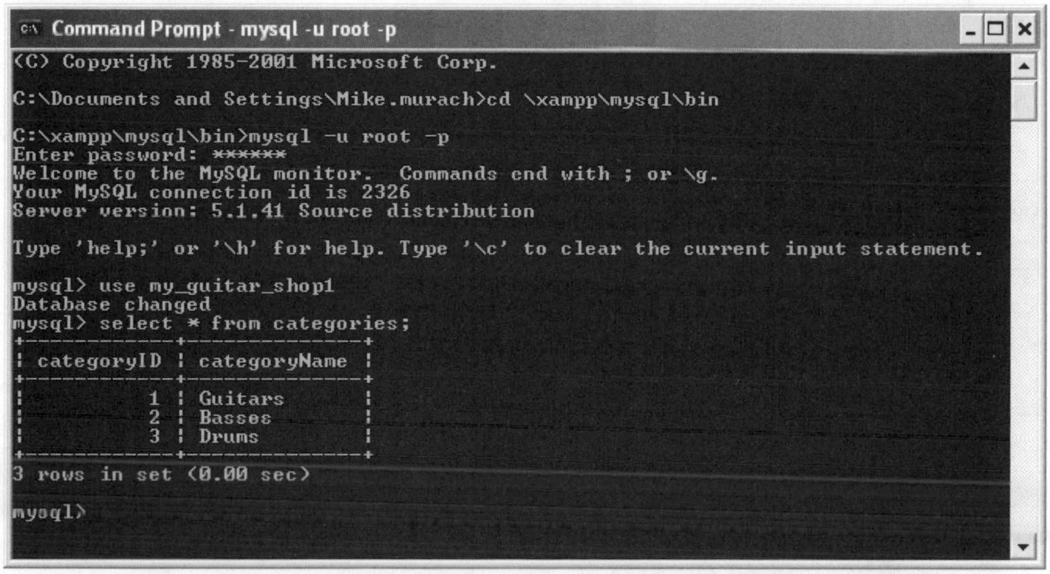

A web-based client

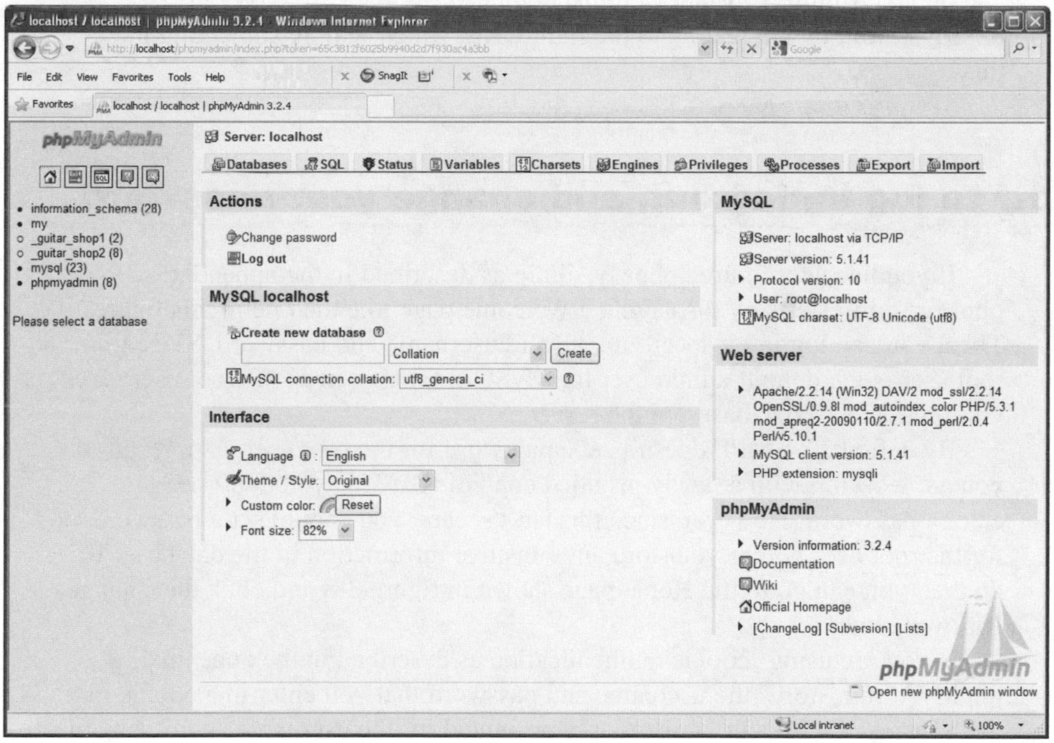

Figure 3-8   Two ways to work with MySQL

How to use phpMyAdmin

The topics that follow show you how to use phpMyAdmin. This client tool will let you review the structure and data of a database, and it will also let you test your SQL statements before you use them in your PHP applications.

How to start phpMyAdmin

Figure 3-9 shows how to start phpMyAdmin. To do that, you can start the XAMPP Control Panel and click the Admin button for MySQL. Remember, though, that phpMyAdmin is a web-based tool that requires the web server to be running for it to work. As a result, you must start the Apache web server before you start phpMyAdmin. Of course, you must also start the MySQL server.

Another way to start phpMyAdmin on a local system is to use your browser to navigate to this URL:

```
http://localhost/phpmyadmin
```

This approach also works if the MySQL server is located on a remote computer and phpMyAdmin is installed on that computer. In that case, you can start phpMyAdmin by navigating to the right URL, which will be something like this:

```
https://www.example.com/phpmyadmin
```

How to log in, log out, and change your password

If you have configured phpMyAdmin as described in the appendix, phpMyAdmin starts by displaying a Welcome page like the one in this figure. Then, you can log in by specifying a valid username and password. Since the root user is the default admin user for MySQL, logging in as the root user gives you access to all databases on the server.

By default, XAMPP doesn't set a password for the root user. As a result, if you are working with a newly installed copy of XAMPP, you don't need to enter a password. However, since this isn't secure, you should set a password for the root user before you store any sensitive information in the database. To do that, you can go to the Home page shown in figure 3-8 and click the Change Password link.

If you are using 'cookie' authentication as described in the appendix, phpMyAdmin stores the username and password that you enter in a cookie in the browser. As a result, you are only prompted for the username and password when you start phpMyAdmin for the first time. On subsequent starts, phpMyAdmin uses the cookie to log in automatically, skips the Welcome page, and displays the Home page. That is usually what you want.

The Welcome page

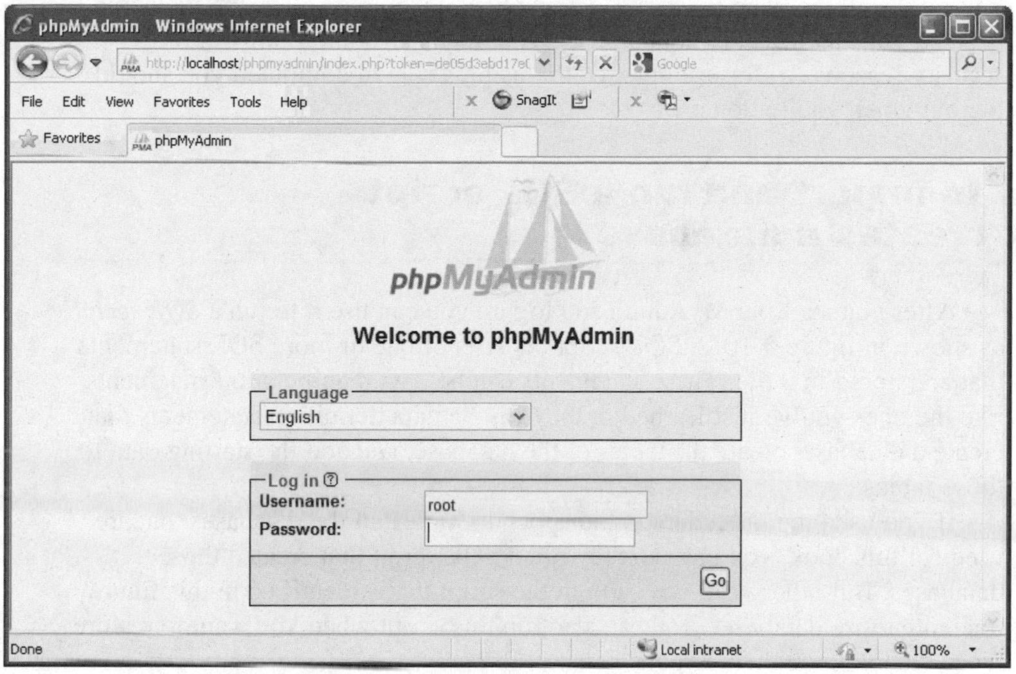

How to start phpMyAdmin on a local computer and log in

1. Start the XAMPP Control Panel as shown in figure 1-11 of chapter 1, and start the Apache and MySQL servers if they aren't already running.

2. Click the Admin button for the MySQL module to start the phpMyAdmin tool in your default web browser.

3. Enter your username and password.

How to log out and return to the Welcome page

- Click the Log out toolbar button (the Exit sign) that's in the sidebar of most pages. Or, go the Home page by clicking on the Home button, and then click the Log out link.

How to change your password

- Go to the Home page by clicking on the Home button. Then, click the Change Password link.

- On the Change Password page, enter and re-enter your new password, and click the Go button.

Description

- The Welcome page is only displayed if you have configured phpMyAdmin as shown in the appendix and your username and password isn't already stored in a cookie.

Figure 3-9   How to start phpMyAdmin, log in, log out, and change your password

However, if you want to log in as another user, you can use the "Log out" link on the Home page to log out. Then, phpMyAdmin displays the Welcome page so you can log in as another user. You may also want to log out for security reasons. If, for example, you're using a shared computer, you should log out when you're done.

How to import and run a SQL script that creates a database

After you start phpMyAdmin and log in, you can use it to run a *SQL script* as shown in figure 3-10. A SQL script consists of one or more SQL statements that are stored in a file. These statements can be data manipulation statements like the ones you've just learned or they can be data definition statements that create a database, create the tables of the database, and add the starting data to those tables.

If you used the procedure in the appendix to install the databases that are used for this book, you have already run a SQL script that created those databases. But otherwise, you can run the script that's identified in this figure to create those databases. You can also run this script when you want to restore those databases to their original data.

To run a script, you use the Import tab that's shown in this figure. Then, you use the File to Import section to browse to the file that contains the script that you want to import. Last, you click the Go button in the bottom right corner of this interface. That imports the script, runs it, displays the script in the top part of the interface, and shows the results of running the script. In this case, the message above the imported script says that the script ran successfully.

When you run SQL scripts, you sometimes need to select the database before you run the script. That's because the script has been designed to run against a particular database. However, the third statement in the script that's executed in this figure includes a USE command that selects the my_guitar_shop1 database. As a result, there's no need to use phpMyAdmin to select a database.

In contrast, suppose you run a script that consists of a SELECT statement that gets data from the my_guitar_shop1 database. Then, you need to select that database before you run the script. Also, when you import this statement, it will show both the statement and the result set that's returned by the statement.

An Import tab that imports and runs a SQL script that creates a database

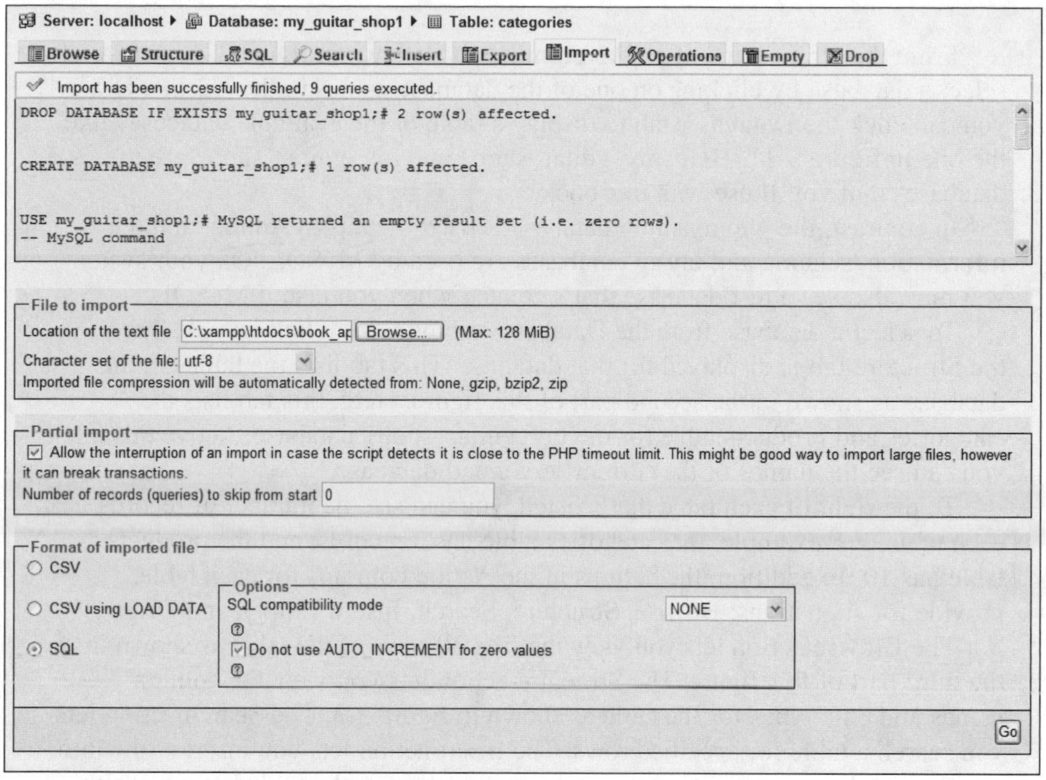

How to import and run a SQL script

1. Click the Import tab, go to the "File to Import" section, click the Browse button, and select the file that contains the script.

2. Click the Go button. This runs the script that's in the file.

The script for creating the databases used by this book

```
\xampp\htdocs\book_apps\_create_db\create_db.sql
```

Description

- A *SQL script* consists of one or more SQL statements that are stored in a file.

- A SQL script can include all of the SQL statements for creating a database, creating its tables, and adding data to those tables.

- To install the databases that are used by the downloadable applications and exercises for this book, import and run the script that's shown above.

Figure 3-10   How to import and run a SQL script that creates a database

How to review the data and structure of a table

From the Home page of phpMyAdmin that's shown in figure 3-8, you can select a database by clicking on one of the database names in the sidebar. Or, you can click the Databases tab to display a table of the available databases like the one in figure 3-11. Here, my_guitar_shop1 and my_guitar_shop2 are the databases that you'll use with this book.

In contrast, the phpmyadmin database is used by phpMyAdmin, and the information_schema and mysql databases are used by MySQL. On your system, you may also see a test database that's created when you install MySQL.

To select a database from the Databases tab, you just click its link. Then, the Structure tab is displayed for that database. This tab lists the tables in the database as shown in the second part of this figure. Here, this tab lists the categories and products table for the my_guitar_shop1 database. Above this tab, you can see the names of the current server and database.

To the right of each table that's listed, you can see the number of records in each table. For example, the categories table has 3 records, and the products table has 10. In addition, the buttons in the Action columns for each table, provide for six actions: Browse, Structure, Search, Insert, Empty, and Drop.

The Browse action lets you view the first 30 rows of the table as shown in the third part of this figure. The Structure action lets you view the column names and data types for the table as shown in figure 3-3. The Search action lets you search a table for specified rows. The Insert action lets you insert a row into a table. The Empty action lets you delete all rows from the table but retain the table's structure. And the Drop action lets you drop the table from the database, which deletes both the structure and the data for the table.

In the Browse tab, you can see the data for the table as shown in this figure. Then, you can click the Edit icon (the pencil) to edit a row. Or, you can click the Delete icon (the X) to delete a row.

By default, the Browse tab shows just the first 30 rows of a table. That's to prevent an accidental display of the hundreds of rows that a products or customers table might contain in a real-world database. To show more rows or to start at a row other than zero, though, you can change the variables above the table and click the Show button.

If you experiment with these tabs, you'll see how you can use them to analyze the structure and data of the database tables that your applications will be using. You can also experiment with the other phpMyAdmin tabs to see what they let you do.

The Databases tab

Server: localhost
Databases SQL Status Variables Charsets Engines Privileges Processes Export Import

Databases

	Database ▲	
☐	information_schema	
☐	mysql	
☐	my_guitar_shop1	
☐	my_guitar_shop2	
☐	phpmyadmin	
	Total: 5	

↰__ Check All / Uncheck All *With selected:* ✖

The Structure tab for the my_guitar_shop1 database

Server: localhost ▶ Database: my_guitar_shop1

Structure SQL Search Query Export Import Designer Operations Privileges Drop

	Table ▲	Action						Records[1]	Type	Collation	Size	Overhead
☐	categories						✕	3	MyISAM	latin1_swedish_ci	2.1 KiB	–
☐	products						✕	10	MyISAM	latin1_swedish_ci	3.4 KiB	–
	2 table(s)	**Sum**						**13**	**MyISAM**	**latin1_swedish_ci**	**5.5 KiB**	**0 B**

↰__ Check All / Uncheck All   With selected: ▾

The Browse tab for the categories table

Server: localhost ▶ Database: my_guitar_shop1 ▶ Table: categories

Browse Structure SQL Search Insert Export Import Operations Empty Drop

✔ Showing rows 0 - 2 (3 total, Query took 0.0009 sec)

```
SELECT *
FROM `categories`
LIMIT 0 , 30
```

☐ Profiling [Edit] [Explain SQL] [Create PHP Code] [Refresh]

Show : 30   row(s) starting from record # 0

in horizontal ▾ mode and repeat headers after 100 cells

Sort by key: None ▾

+ Options

			categoryID	categoryName
☐	✎	✕	1	Guitars
☐	✎	✕	2	Basses
☐	✎	✕	3	Drums

↰__ Check All / Uncheck All *With selected:* ✎ ✕ ▦

Show : 30   row(s) starting from record # 0

in horizontal ▾ mode and repeat headers after 100 cells

Description

- To select a database from the Database tab, click on its name.
- To look at the data in a table, click the table's Browse button in the Structure tab. To see the structure of the columns in a table, click the table's Structure button.
- MySQL uses the information_schema and mysql databases to manage its own operations.

Figure 3-11   How to review the data and structure of a table

How to run SQL statements

After you select a database, you can click the SQL tab to run SQL statements against that database. That way, you can test the SQL statements that your PHP applications are going to use before you code them in your applications. Because it's easier to correct a SQL statement before you include it in your PHP, this helps you work more efficiently.

Figure 3-12 shows how to run a SQL statement from the SQL tab of phpMyAdmin. After you enter a SQL statement, you click the Go button. Then, phpMyAdmin displays an appropriate response. In this figure, for example, a SELECT statement has run successfully so a result table is displayed.

However, if the SQL statement isn't valid, phpMyAdmin displays an error message that helps you find and fix the problem. Or, if the SQL statement performs an action such as inserting multiple rows into a table, phpMyAdmin displays a message that indicates the number of rows that were added to the table.

If you want to run a single SQL statement as shown in this figure, you just enter the SQL statement and click the Go button. However, if you want to enter a SQL script that contains multiple SQL statements, you need to code a semicolon (;) at the end of each statement.

To make it easy to identify the keywords in a SQL statement, the keywords are usually capitalized in this book as in this example:

```
SELECT productID, productName FROM products
```

Although this makes SQL statements easier to read, this capitalization is optional. If, for example, you want to use all lowercase letters for your statements because they're easier to type, you can do that. The one exception is if you're using a database that's running on a Unix server. Then, the column and table names are case-sensitive.

The SQL tab with a SQL statement that's ready to be executed

Server: localhost ▸ Database: my_guitar_shop1

Structure · SQL · Search · Query · Export · Import · Designer · Operations · Privileges · Drop

Run SQL query/queries on database **my_guitar_shop1**: ⓘ

```
SELECT categoryName, productName, listPrice
FROM categories
INNER JOIN products ON categories.categoryID = products.categoryID
WHERE listPrice > 800
ORDER BY listPrice ASC
```

Bookmark this SQL query: [ ]   ☐ Let every user access this bookmark   ☐ Replace existing bookmark of same name

[Delimiter ;] ☑ Show this query here again   [Go]

Open new phpMyAdmin window

The SQL tab after a SQL statement has been executed

Server: localhost ▸ Database: my_guitar_shop1 ▸ Table: categories

Browse · Structure · SQL · Search · Insert · Export · Import · Operations · Empty · Drop

✔ Showing rows 0 - 1 (2 total, Query took 0.0421 sec)

```
SELECT categoryName, productName, listPrice
FROM categories
INNER JOIN products ON categories.categoryID = products.categoryID
WHERE listPrice >800
ORDER BY listPrice ASC
LIMIT 0 , 30
```

☐ Profiling [Edit] [Explain SQL] [Create PHP Code] [Refresh]

[Show : 30] row(s) starting from record # 0

in [horizontal] mode and repeat headers after 100 cells

+ Options

categoryName	productName	listPrice
Guitars	Gibson Les Paul	1199.00
Guitars	Gibson SG	2517.00

[Show : 30] row(s) starting from record # 0

in [horizontal] mode and repeat headers after 100 cells

Query results operations
Print view · Print view (with full texts) · Export · CREATE VIEW

Bookmark this SQL query
Label: [ ]   ☐ Let every user access this bookmark

[Bookmark this SQL query]

Description

- To execute a SQL statement, select a database and click the SQL tab. Then, enter the SQL statement and click the Go button.
- To execute multiple SQL statements, include a semicolon (;) at the end of each SQL statement.
- On Unix systems, the column and table names are case-sensitive.

Figure 3-12   How to run SQL statements

How to create users with limited privileges

So far, you have been working with MySQL as the root user. This user is automatically created when you install MySQL, and it represents an administrative user who has all of the privileges to perform any operation on any database on the server. This means that this user can create and drop entire databases or tables.

To prevent users from doing this, either accidentally or intentionally, you can create other users who have fewer privileges than the root user. To do that, you use the SQL GRANT statement as shown in figure 3-13. Here, the first GRANT statement creates a user named mgs_tester on the host named localhost with "pa55word" as the password. This user only has the privilege to execute SELECT statements on the products table in the my_guitar_shop1 database. As a result, this user can't change the data in the products table or view or alter any of the data in any other tables.

The second user is named mgs_user with the same password. This user is also on the host named localhost, but it has privileges to execute SELECT, INSERT, UPDATE, and DELETE statements on all tables in the my_guitar_shop1 database. However, this user can't create or delete tables or work with other databases.

To test the privileges for a user, you can use phpMyAdmin to log in as that user. Then, you can execute SQL statements that test the user's privileges. In this figure, for example, I logged in as mgs_tester, selected the my_guitar_shop1 database, and attempted to run an UPDATE statement that modifies a row in the products table. However, as the warning message shows, this statement fails because that user doesn't have the privileges for updating the products table.

As you will see in the next chapter, a PHP application connects to a server with a username and password that is appropriate for the requirements of the application. As a result, most of the applications in this book attach to the server as mgs_user, and that user is created by the script that creates the databases for this book. That means that the applications can run SELECT, INSERT, UPDATE, and DELETE statements against the database.

How to create a user with limited privileges on a single table

```
GRANT SELECT
ON my_guitar_shop1.products
TO mgs_tester@localhost
IDENTIFIED BY 'pa55word'
```

How to create a user with limited privileges on all tables in a database

```
GRANT SELECT, INSERT, DELETE, UPDATE
ON my_guitar_shop1.*
TO mgs_user@localhost
IDENTIFIED BY 'pa55word'
```

Common privileges

Privilege	Description
SELECT	Lets the user select data.
UPDATE	Lets the user update data.
INSERT	Lets the user insert data.
DELETE	Lets the user delete data.
CREATE TABLE	Lets the user create a table.
DROP TABLE	Lets the user drop a table.

The SQL tab for mgs_tester after an UPDATE statement failed

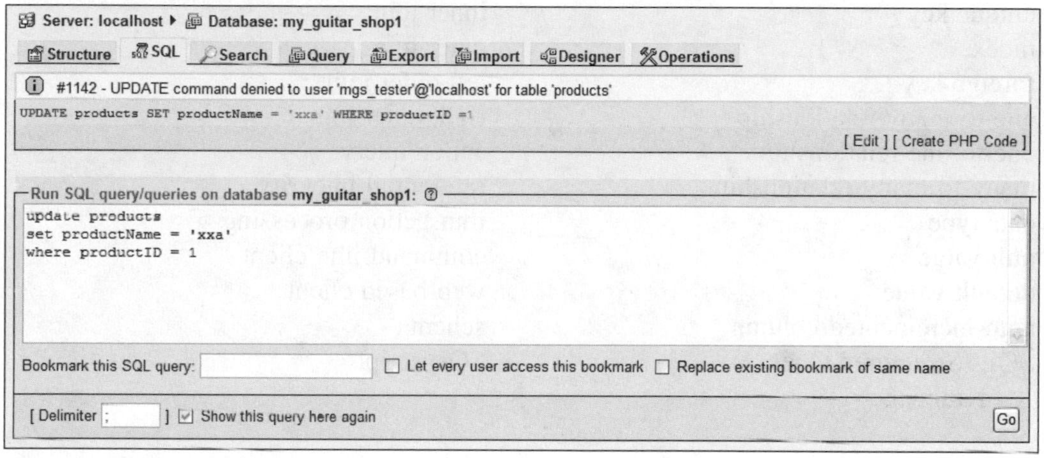

Description

- You should restrict the privileges for most users of a database to prevent the user from accidentally or intentionally damaging the database.
- You can use the GRANT statement to create a user, specify a password for that user, and grant privileges to the user.
- For more on creating users and granting privileges, see chapter 17.

Figure 3-13   How to create users with limited privileges

Perspective

The goal of this chapter is to prepare you for developing PHP applications that use a MySQL database. To that end, this chapter has introduced you to the SELECT, INSERT, UPDATE, and DELETE statements that you'll use in your PHP applications. This chapter has also shown you how to use phpMyAdmin to test SQL statements before you use them in your PHP applications.

Keep in mind, though, that this chapter has presented just a subset of MySQL skills. In particular, it has presented the MySQL skills that you need for developing PHP applications like those that are presented in the next two chapters. Then, in section 3, you can learn more about MySQL.

Terms

relational database	Data Manipulation Language (DML)
table	Data Definition Language (DDL)
row	SQL statement
column	query
cell	result set
primary key	result table
non-primary key	join
unique key	inner join
index	outer join
foreign key	left outer join
one-to-many relationship	right outer join
one-to-one relationship	action query
many-to-many relationship	referential integrity
data type	transaction processing
null value	command-line client
default value	web-based client
auto-incremented column	schema
SQL (Structured Query Language)	SQL script

Summary

- A *relational database* consists of *tables* that store data in *rows* and *columns*. A *primary key* is used to identify each row in a table.

- The tables in a relational database are related by *foreign keys* in one table that have the same values as primary keys in another table. Usually, these tables have a *one-to-many* relationship.

- Each column in a database table is defined with a *data type* that determines what can be stored in that column. In addition, the column definition specifies whether the column allows *null values* or has a *default value*.

- To work with the data in a database, you use *SQL* (*Structured Query Language*). To access and update the data in a database, you use these *SQL statements*: SELECT, INSERT, UPDATE, and DELETE.

- The SELECT statement returns data from one or more tables in a *result set*. To return data from two or more tables, you *join* the tables based on the data in related fields. An *inner join* returns a result set that includes data only if the related fields match.

- To update the data in a database, you use the INSERT, UPDATE, and DELETE statements. These statements are sometimes called *action queries*.

- To review the structure and data of a database and to run SQL statements against the database, you can use a web-based application known as phpMyAdmin. This is included with the XAMPP download.

- To create a database including its tables and data, you can use phpMyAdmin to run a *SQL script*. That's how the databases for this book are created. You can also use phpMyAdmin to import and run SQL scripts for SELECT, INSERT, UPDATE, and DELETE statements.

- Before you use SQL statements in your PHP applications, you should test them with phpMyAdmin. Later, when you copy them into your PHP applications, you'll know that the statements work.

- To create database users with limited privileges, you can use phpMyAdmin to run GRANT statements. Then, each of your PHP applications can connect to a database as a specific user that has the privileges that the application requires.

Exercise 3-1   Use phpMyAdmin with a database

This application will give you a chance to use phpMyAdmin to review the databases that are used with this book and to test the types of SQL statements that you will use in your PHP applications.

If necessary, set a password for the root user

1. Start Apache, MySQL, and phpMyAdmin as shown in figure 3-9. Then, log in as the root user.

2. *If you haven't already set a password for the root user*, use phpMyAdmin to do that. If you're only using MySQL for working with the applications in this book, use a password like "sesame" so it's easy to remember. Otherwise, use a more secure password.

3. Click the "Log out" button (the Exit sign) to log out. This should take you back to the Welcome page. Then, log in as the root user with the new password. That will take you to the Home page.

Run the script for creating the book databases

4. On the Home page, review the list of databases that are available in the sidebar. Then, click the Databases tab to see the same databases. Note that these databases include the databases that MySQL and phpMyAdmin use to manage their own operations. Are the my_guitar_shop1 and my_guitar_shop2 databases both available?

5. Use the procedure in figure 3-10 to import and run the script that creates the databases for this book. This will create or recreate the two databases for this book. As a result, the my_guitar_shop1 and my_guitar_shop2 databases will both be shown in the sidebar and in the Databases tab.

Review the my_guitar_shop1 database

6. Select the my_guitar_shop1 database to display the tables for this database, and click the Browse button to view the data for the products table.

7. Click the Structure tab to view the column definitions for the products table. Note that none of the columns allows nulls or provides default values.

Run SQL statements against the my_guitar_shop1 database

8. Use the SQL tab to run the first query in figure 3-4. Then, run the second query.

9. Run the query in figure 3-5. Then, modify the list price value in the query so it only selects products with a price that's less than 400, and run the query again.

10. Run the first query in figure 3-6 to add a row to the products table. Then, browse the products table to view the new row. Last, run a DELETE statement to delete the new row.

11. Continue to experiment until you're sure that you know how to code the SQL queries that your PHP applications will use.

Log in as a different user and check that user's privileges

12. Log out of phpMyAdmin, and log back in as mgs_tester with pa55word as the password. This user was created by the SQL script that you ran in step 5 of this exercise.

13. Use the SQL tab to run this SELECT statement:

```
SELECT * FROM categories
```

This statement should be refused because mgs_tester can only run statements against the products table.

Experiment

14. Continue to experiment until you're confident that you understand the use of phpMyAdmin and the types of SQL statements that you'll use in your PHP applications.

4

How to use PHP with a MySQL database

Now that you know how to work with a MySQL database, this chapter shows you how to use PHP to get data from a MySQL database. It also shows how to use PHP to insert, update, or delete rows in a MySQL database. To help you master these skills, this chapter ends by presenting two complete, database-driven applications.

PHP for working with MySQL **124**
How to connect to a MySQL database 124
How to execute SELECT statements 126
How to execute INSERT, UPDATE, and DELETE statements 128
How to use a try/catch statement to handle exceptions 130

How to get data from a result set **132**
How to work with arrays 132
How to get the data from the first row of a result set 134
How to get the data from all the rows of a result set 136

The Product Viewer application **138**
The user interface 138
The code 140

The Product Manager application **146**
The user interface 146
The code 148

Perspective **156**

PHP for working with MySQL

This topic shows you how to use *PDO* (*PHP Data Objects*) to work with a database. PDO is relatively new to PHP, and it supports most popular databases. Because it defines a consistent interface for accessing databases, the same PHP code can be used with more than one type of database.

PDO is included with PHP 5.1 and is available as a PECL extension for PHP 5.0. However, PDO doesn't work with earlier versions of PHP. As a result, if you need to maintain legacy code, you may need to use the older techniques that are presented in chapter 19. For new development, though, we recommend PDO.

How to connect to a MySQL database

As you develop PHP applications, you may need to create *objects* from *classes*. To do that, you use syntax shown in the first syntax summary of figure 4-1. This shows that you code the *new* keyword, the name of the class that you want to create the object from, a set of parentheses, and a list of the required *arguments* within the parentheses.

The second syntax summary shows how to create a *PDO object* from the PDO class. In this case, three arguments are required: one for the *Data Source Name* (*DSN*), one for the username, and one for the password.

The third syntax summary shows how to code a DSN for a MySQL database. A DSN identifies the host computer and the database to be used. Here again, the italicized words are the ones that you need to provide. Note, however, that this syntax is for a MySQL database. To use another type of database, you'll need to look up the appropriate DSN syntax on the Internet.

The first example shows the code that creates a PDO object. First, the $dsn variable is assigned a DSN that specifies a MySQL database named my_guitar_shop1 that's running on the same computer as the PHP interpreter (localhost). Then, the $username and $password variables are assigned values. Last, these variables are used as the arguments for creating a new PDO object that's assigned to the variable named $db.

Please note that the names of the arguments for creating the new PDO object don't have to be the same as the names of the arguments in the syntax summary. For instance, you could use $data_source_name instead of $dsn. If you use the same names, though, it's easy to remember what the names refer to.

The syntax for creating an object from any class

```
new ClassName(arguments);
```

The syntax for creating a database object from the PDO class

```
new PDO($dsn, $username, $password);
```

The syntax for a DSN (Data Source Name) for a MySQL database

```
mysql:host=host_address;dbname=database_name
```

How to connect to a MySQL database named my_guitar_shop1

```
$dsn = 'mysql:host=localhost;dbname=my_guitar_shop1';
$username = 'mgs_user';
$password = 'pa55word';

$db = new PDO($dsn, $username, $password);  // creates PDO object
```

Description

- To create an *object* from a *class*, you code the *new* keyword, followed by the name of the class, followed by a set of parentheses. Within the parentheses, you code the *arguments* that are required by the class, separating multiple arguments with commas.

- To create a *PDO object* that connects to a MySQL database, you use the PDO class with the three arguments shown above: *DSN* (*Data Source Name*), username, and password.

- The DSN for a MySQL connection specifies the host computer for the MySQL database and the name of the database. If the MySQL database is running on the same server as PHP, you can use the localhost keyword to specify the host computer.

- The *PDO* (*PHP Data Objects*) extension to PHP defines a consistent interface for accessing databases. Since PDO supports most popular databases, this lets you write PHP code that can be used for more than one type of database.

- PDO is included with PHP 5.1 and is available as a PECL extension for PHP 5.0. However, PDO doesn't work with earlier versions of PHP. For those versions, you must use the skills that are presented in chapter 19.

Figure 4-1   How to connect to a MySQL database

How to execute SELECT statements

Once you've created a PDO object, you can use its *methods* to execute SQL statements. To execute a SELECT statement, for example, you use the query method of the PDO object.

To execute a method of any object, you use the syntax in the first summary in figure 4-2. This means you code the object name, followed by ->, followed by the method name, followed by a set of parentheses that contains the arguments required by the method.

The second syntax summary in this figure shows how this works with the query method of a PDO object. Here, you code the name of the PDO object, ->, the word *query*, and a SELECT statement within a set of parentheses. When this method is executed, it returns the result set for the SELECT statement.

The first example shows how this works with the query method of a PDO object. Here, the first statement assigns a SELECT statement to a variable named $query. Then, the second statement calls the query method of the PDO object. This returns the result set for the SELECT statement and stores it in the variable named $products.

The second example shows that you don't have to use a variable as the argument for the query method. In this case, the argument is a string literal that contains a SELECT statement.

As you learned in the last chapter, the result set for a SELECT statement consists of columns and rows. When this result set is stored in a PHP variable, it is stored as a *PDOStatement object*. In other words, the query method of the PDO object creates another object. In figures 4-6 and 4-7, you'll learn how to get the result set data from the PDOStatement object by using one of its methods.

A method of the PDO class for executing a SELECT statement

Method	Description
query(*$select_statement*)	Executes the specified SQL SELECT statement and returns a PDOStatement object that contains the result set. If no result set is returned, this method returns a FALSE value.

The syntax for executing a method of any object

```
$objectName->methodName(argumentList)
```

The syntax for executing the query method of the database object

```
$PDO_object->query($select_statement)
```

A query method with the SELECT statement coded in a variable

```
$query = 'SELECT * FROM products
          WHERE categoryID = 1
          ORDER BY productID';
$products = $db->query($query);     // $products contains the result set
```

A query method with the SELECT statement coded as the argument

```
$products = $db->query('SELECT * FROM products');
```

Description

- To call a *method* from any object, you code the name of the object, followed by ->, followed by the name of the method, followed by a set of parentheses. Within the parentheses, you code the arguments that are required by the method, separating multiple arguments with commas.

- To execute a SELECT statement, you use the query method of the PDO object. It requires just one argument, which is the SELECT statement to be executed. This argument can be a variable that contains the SELECT statement or the statement itself.

- If the SELECT statement returns a result set, the query method returns the result set in a *PDOStatement object*. Then, you can get the data from the result set by using the techniques in figures 4-6 and 4-7.

Figure 4-2   How to execute SELECT statements

How to execute INSERT, UPDATE, and DELETE statements

Figure 4-3 shows how to execute INSERT, UPDATE, and DELETE statements. To do that, you use the exec method of the PDO object with the SQL statement as the argument. When this method is executed, it returns the number of rows that were affected by the statement. Then, you can store this value in a variable and use it in your application.

This is illustrated by the examples in this figure. Here, the first example executes an INSERT statement that should insert 1 row into the database. If this method is successful, it returns a value of 1. Similarly, the second and third examples should only affect 1 row, so they should return a value of 1 if they execute successfully.

However, INSERT, UPDATE, and DELETE statements can also affect more than one row. For example, to update the price for all products in category 1, you could use an UPDATE statement like this one:

```
UPDATE products
SET listPrice = 799.99
WHERE categoryID = 1
```

In this case, the number of rows that are affected depends on the number of rows that have a categoryID value of 1.

The last set of examples in this figure shows how you can use echo statements to display the row counts within paragraph tags. You can of course use the counts for other purposes too.

A method of the PDO class for modifying the database

Method	Description
exec(*$sql_statement*)	Executes the specified SQL statement and returns the number of affected rows. If no rows were affected, the method returns zero.

How to execute an INSERT statement

```
$category_id = 1;
$code = 'strat';
$name = 'Fender Stratocaster';
$price = 699.99;

$query = "INSERT INTO products
            (categoryID, productCode, productName, listPrice)
          VALUES
            ($category_id, '$code', '$name', $price)";

$insert_count = $db->exec($query);
```

How to execute an UPDATE statement

```
$product_id = 4;
$price = 599.99;

$query = "UPDATE products
          SET listPrice = $price
          WHERE productID = $product_id";

$update_count = $db->exec($query);
```

How to execute a DELETE statement

```
$product_id = 4;

$query = "DELETE FROM products
          WHERE productID = $product_id";

$delete_count = $db->exec($query);
```

How to display the row counts

```
<p>Insert count: <?php echo $insert_count; ?></p>
<p>Update count: <?php echo $update_count; ?></p>
<p>Delete count: <?php echo $delete_count; ?></p>
```

Description

- To execute an INSERT, UPDATE, or DELETE statement, you use the exec method of the PDO object with the SQL statement as the argument.
- Each of these methods returns a value that represents the number of rows that were affected, and this value can be assigned to a variable.

Figure 4-3   How to execute INSERT, UPDATE, and DELETE statements

How to use a try/catch statement to handle exceptions

Sometimes, when you try to create a PDO object from the PDO class, the PDO class can't create the object. In that case, the class *throws* an *exception*. An exception is an object that contains information about the error that occurred. Then, if the exception isn't handled, the application ends.

To handle an exception, you use a *try/catch statement* as shown in figure 4-4. To use this statement, you begin by coding a *try block* around any statement or statements that may throw an exception. Then, you code a *catch block* that contains the statements that will be executed if an exception is thrown by any statement in the try block. Note that the statements in both blocks are coded within braces.

Before the braces in the catch block, you code a set of parentheses. Within these parentheses, you code the name of an Exception class followed by a space and the variable name that you want to use for the Exception object that is thrown. Then, you can use the getMessage method of the Exception object to get the error message that is stored in the Exception object. This works like the method of any other object.

The first example shows how *exception handling* can be done for database exceptions. Here, the first statement in the try block attempts to create the PDO object. If this statement executes successfully, the second statement displays a message that indicates that you are connected to the database, and the try/catch statement ends.

However, if any statement in the try block throws an exception, the PHP interpreter skips the rest of the statements in the try block and executes the statements in the catch block. If, for example, the first statement in the try block throws an exception, the interpreter skips the second statement in the try block and executes the statements in the catch block.

Within the catch block, the first statement calls the getMessage method of the PDOException object that's stored in the variable named $e, and it stores this message in the variable named $error_message. Then, the second statement displays a message that indicates that an error has occurred. This message includes the message in the $error_message variable.

When you code a catch block for the PDOException class, it only catches PDOException objects. Then, if necessary, you can code other catch blocks for other types of exceptions. Or, if you want to code one catch block that catches every type of exception, you can code a catch block for the Exception class. This class includes all other types of exceptions, and this is illustrated by the second example.

Why would a PDOException be thrown when the code tries to create a PDO object? Here are a few of the reasons. The database server might not be running. The username and password combination might not have permission to access the database. Or the DSN argument may be incorrect. No matter what, though, if you carefully read the error message, you usually get a good indication of what's causing the error, and you can usually use that information to fix the problem.

The syntax for a try/catch statement

```
try {
    // statements that might throw an exception
} catch (ExceptionClass $exception_name) {
    // statements that handle the exception
}
```

How to handle a PDO exception

```
try {
    $db = new PDO($dsn, $username, $password);
    echo '<p>You are connected to the database!</p>';
} catch (PDOException $e) {
    $error_message = $e->getMessage();
    echo "<p>An error occurred while connecting to
            the database: $error_message </p>";
}
```

How to handle any type of exception

```
try {
    // statements that might throw an exception
} catch (Exception $e) {
    $error_message = $e->getMessage();
    echo "<p>Error message: $error_message </p>";
}
```

Description

- An *exception* is an object that contains information about an error that has occurred. Some PHP statements *throw* exceptions when they encounter an error. If an exception isn't handled, the application ends prematurely.

- To *handle exceptions*, you use a *try/catch statement*. First, you code a *try block* around any PHP statements that might *throw an exception*. Then, you code a *catch block* that *catches* the exception. This is known as *exception handling*.

- At the start of the catch block, you code a set of parentheses. Within these parentheses, you code the name of the class that defines the type of exception that the catch block should catch. After that, you code the name for the variable that the exception object will be stored in.

- The Exception class includes all types of exceptions, and all other exceptions are subclasses of the Exception class. The PDOException class is used for errors thrown by the PDO library.

- All Exception objects provide a getMessage method that lets you get the error message.

- If an exception is thrown in the try block, any remaining statements in the try block are skipped and the statements in the catch block are executed. If no exceptions are thrown in the try block, the catch block is skipped.

- For more on exception handling, please refer to chapter 15.

Figure 4-4   How to use a try/catch statement to handle exceptions

How to get data from a result set

When working with data from a database, it's helpful to understand how arrays work. That's why this topic begins by presenting an introduction to arrays. Then, it shows how to get the data from the result sets that are stored in PDOStatement objects.

How to work with arrays

An *array* can store one or more *elements*. To create an array, you can use the built-in array function that's summarized in figure 4-5. For instance, the first example in this figure shows how to use the array function to create a new array named $rates that doesn't contain any elements.

To refer to the elements in an array, you use an *index* that identifies the element that you want. This index can be a numeric or string value. This is illustrated by the two sets of examples in this figure.

The first numeric example shows how to set three values in the $rates array by using the index for the array. To use an index, you code a set of brackets ([ ]) after the name of the array. Then, you code the integer value for the index within the brackets. When you use numeric indexes, PHP uses 0 as the first element, 1 as the second element, and so on.

The second numeric example shows how to get a value from the $rates array. Here, the statement uses an index of 2 to get the value from the third element. When this statement is executed, the $rate variable gets a value of 15.95.

The third numeric example shows how to use a for loop to store all of the values for the $rates array in a variable named $message. To do that, the for loop uses the count function to get the number of elements in the array. It also uses $i as the index for the array. After this for loop is executed, the $message variable contains '5.95|10.95|15.95|'.

The fourth numeric example uses a *foreach loop* to accomplish the same task as the fourth example. The foreach loop is designed to work with each element of an array. As a result, this type of loop simplifies the code significantly when you need to process each element in an array.

The next set of examples shows how to set values in an array that uses string indexes. This type of array lets you use descriptive names for the indexes.

The first string example shows how to set three values in the $rates array using string indexes. Then, the next example shows how to get the value with 'Overnight' as the index and store it in a variable named $overnight. In this case, $overnight receives a value of 15.95.

The third string example shows how to use a foreach loop with an array that uses string indexes. Here, the loop specifies a name for the index ($index), followed by =>, followed by a name for the value ($rate). Within the loop, the statement appends the index, an equals sign, the value, and a pipe character to the $message variable. As a result, after this for loop executes, the $message variable is 'Ground=5.95 | 2nd Day=10.95 | Overnight=15.95 |'.

Two of the built-in functions for working with arrays

Name	Description
`array()`	Returns an array that doesn't include any elements.
`count($array_name)`	Returns the number of elements in the specified array.

How to create an array that doesn't contain any elements

```
$rates = array();
```

How to work with numeric indexes

How to set values

```
$rates[0] = 5.95;        // sets first element
$rates[1] = 10.95;       // sets second element
$rates[2] = 15.95;       // sets third element
```

How to get values

```
$rate = $rates[2];        // gets the value of the third element
```

How to loop through an array with a for loop

```
for ($i = 0; $i < count($rates); $i++) {
    $message .= $rates[$i] . '|';
}
```

How to loop through an array with a foreach loop

```
foreach ($rates as $rate) {    // $rate stores the value of each element
    $message .= $rate . '|';   // the loop executes once for each element
}
```

How to work with string indexes

How to set values

```
$rates['Ground'] = 5.95;
$rates['2nd Day'] = 10.95;
$rates['Overnight'] = 15.95;
```

How to get values

```
$overnight = $rates['Overnight'];
```

How to loop through an array with a foreach loop

```
foreach ($rates as $index=>$rate) {
    $message .= $index . '='. $rate . ' | ';
}
```

Description

- An *array* can store one or more *elements*.
- To refer to the elements in an array, you use an *index*. If you use numeric indexes, 0 refers to the first element, 1 to the second element, and so on.
- To loop through the elements in an array, you can use a *foreach statement* that defines a *foreach loop* that processes one element of the array each time through the loop.
- For more on arrays, please see chapter 11.

Figure 4-5   How to work with arrays

How to get the data from the first row of a result set

If a SELECT statement returns a result set that contains just one row, you can get that data by using the fetch method of the PDOStatement object. This method returns an array for the next row in the result set. This is illustrated in figure 4-6.

In the first example in this figure, the first statement defines a SELECT statement that returns a result set with a single row. Then, the second statement calls the query method of the PDO object to return a PDOStatement object for that result set, and it stores it in a variable named $products. Last, the third statement calls the fetch method of the PDOStatement object to get an array for the first (and only) row in the result set and stores it in a variable named $product.

When you use the fetch method to get an array for a row, the array contains string indexes for the names of the columns, and it contains numeric indexes for the position of the columns. As a result, you can get the data from the columns by using string indexes as shown in the second example. Or, you can get the data from the columns by using numeric indexes as shown in the third example. If you use numeric indexes, don't forget that you use an index of 0 for the first column, 1 for the second column, and so on.

As the description for the fetch method shows, this method actually returns the *next* row in a result set. So, if a result set contains more than one row, you can get one row at a time using this method. Normally, though, you use the foreach statement to get the rows in a result set that contains more than one row, as shown in the next figure.

A method of the PDOStatement class for getting an array for a row

Method	Description
fetch()	Returns an array for the next row in the result set. This array is indexed by both a string index for the column name and a numeric index for the column position. If no array is available, this method returns a FALSE value.

Code that returns a result set that contains one row

```
$query = 'SELECT productCode, productName, listPrice
        FROM products
        WHERE productID = $productID';
$products = $db->query($query);    // $products is a PDOStatement object
$product = $products->fetch();     // $product is an array for the first row
```

Code that uses a string index to access each column

```
$product_code = $product['productCode'];
$product_name = $product['productName'];
$product_list_price = $product['listPrice'];
```

Code that uses a numeric index to access each column

```
$product_code = $product[0];
$product_name = $product[1];
$product_list_price = $product[2];
```

Description

- You can use the fetch method of a PDOStatement object to get an array for the first row (or next row) of a result set. Then, you can use column names or numeric indexes to access the data that's stored in that row.

Figure 4-6   How to get the data from the first row of a result set

How to get the data from all the rows of a result set

To get the data from all of the rows of a result set, you can use the foreach statement as shown in figure 4-7. The first example in this figure returns a PDOStatement object for a multi-row result set. This object is stored in a variable named $products.

The second example shows how to use a foreach statement to get the data for all the rows of the result set, one row at a time. To do that, the foreach statement automatically uses the fetch method of the PDOStatement object.

The third example shows another syntax that you can use for foreach statements. In this case, you don't use an opening brace ({) to mark the beginning of the statements in the foreach loop or a closing brace (}) to mark the end of them. Instead, you use a colon (:) to mark the beginning of the statements in the loop and an endforeach statement to mark the end of them.

When you embed PHP within an HTML page, many programmers prefer the alternate foreach syntax that's shown in the third example. This syntax makes it easier to use the foreach statement with other control statements. Otherwise, if you code multiple control statements, you will have multiple PHP tags that only contain a closing brace (}), and that can lead to code that's difficult to read and maintain. By contrast, a PHP tag that contains an endforeach statement clearly marks the end of the foreach statement.

Although it isn't shown in this figure, you can use this alternate syntax with most control statements and clauses including if, else if, and else clauses, as well as while and for statements. To do that, you use a colon to mark the start of the block of statements to be executed and an appropriate end statement to mark the end of the clause or statement. To end an if clause, for example, you use an endif statement.

A query method that returns a result set of two or more rows

```
$query = 'SELECT productCode, productName, listPrice
          FROM products
          WHERE categoryID = 1;'
$products = $db->query($query);    // $products contains the result set
```

How to use a foreach statement to display the result set in an HTML table

```
<?php foreach ($products as $product) { ?>
<tr>
    <td><?php echo $product['productCode']; ?></td>
    <td><?php echo $product['productName']; ?></td>
    <td><?php echo $product['listPrice']; ?></td>
</tr>
<?php } ?>
```

Another syntax for the foreach statement that works better within PHP tags

```
<?php foreach ($products as $product) : ?>
<tr>
    <td><?php echo $product['productCode']; ?></td>
    <td><?php echo $product['productName']; ?></td>
    <td><?php echo $product['listPrice']; ?></td>
</tr>
<?php endforeach; ?>
```

Description

- When the query method of a database object is executed, it returns the result set in a PDOStatement object. Then, you can use a foreach statement to get the data from the result set for that object.

- The foreach statement calls the fetch method of the PDOStatement object automatically as it loops through the rows in the result set.

- The second syntax for the foreach statement makes it easier to use the foreach statement with other control statements because it doesn't require the use of braces.

- When you use the second syntax with other control statements, you code a colon after the clause that starts each control statement, and you end each control statement with an appropriate end statement, like endif for an if statement or endfor for a for statement.

Figure 4-7   How to get the data from all the rows of a result set

The Product Viewer application

Now that you know how to use PHP to work with MySQL, you're ready to see how database-driven PHP applications work. To start, figure 4-8 presents a simple Product Viewer application that lets you view product data by category. After you review this application, you'll study a more complicated application.

The user interface

The primary page of the Product Viewer application is divided into two parts. The sidebar on the left displays a list of category links that let the user select a category. The main portion of the page lists the products for that category in an HTML table.

When the application starts, this application displays the products in the category named Guitars. Then, if the user wants to view the products in another category, the user can click on the link for that category. If, for example, the user clicks on the Basses link, this application displays the products in that category. To facilitate that, the category_id field is sent with the HTTP request for the same page. This is illustrated by the URL for the second screen in this figure, which requests the default page in the ch04_product_viewer directory.

To make it easy to identify columns and rows for the product data, this application uses CSS to format the HTML table. This formatting adds a solid border around the outside of the table and a dashed border between the columns and rows.

The user interface

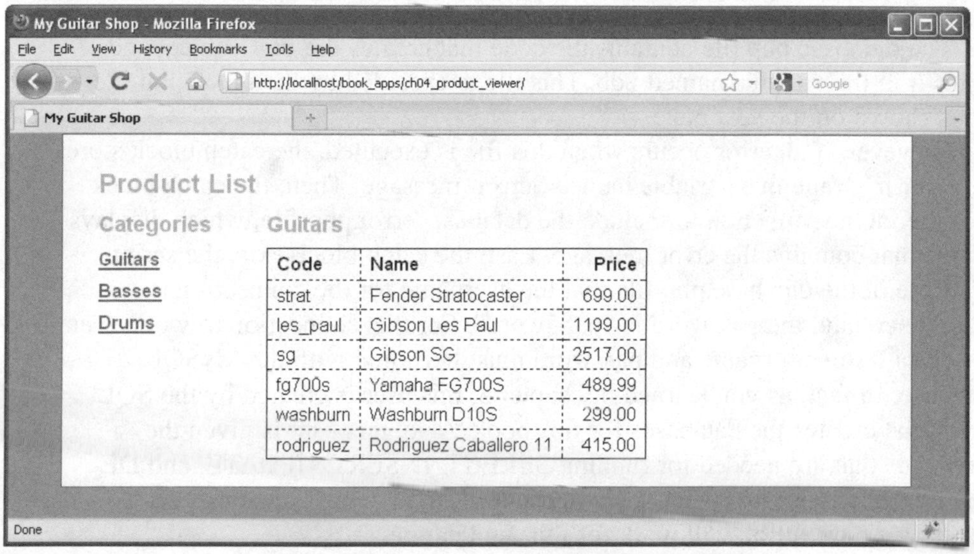

The user interface after the user selects a new category

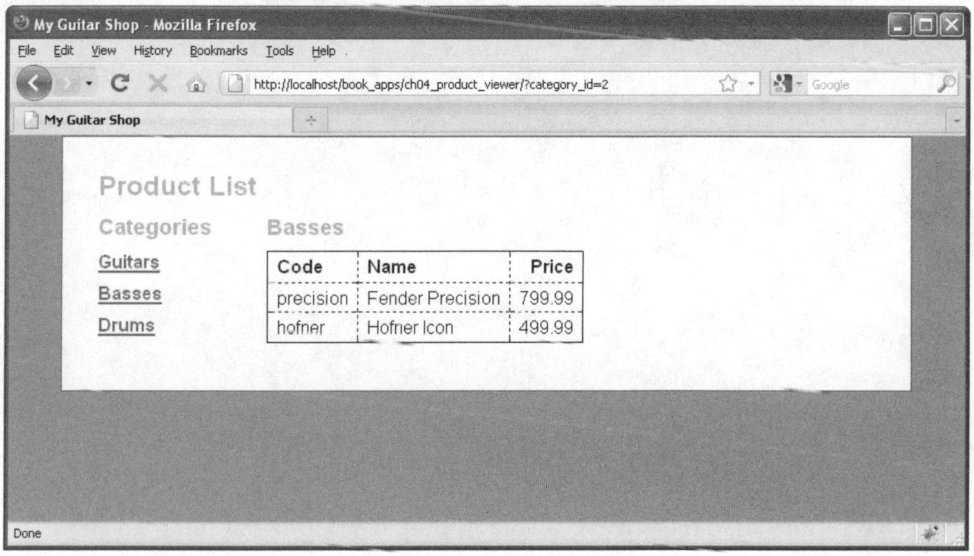

Figure 4-8   The Product Viewer application (part 1 of 4)

The code

The database.php file contains the code that creates the PDO object and stores it in the variable named $db. This file is executed by the index.php file that's shown on the next page.

However, if an error occurs when this file is executed, the catch block stores the error message in a variable named $error_message. Then, the catch block uses the include function to include the database_error.php file, which displays a page that contains the error message. Last, the catch block exits the script.

Note in the database.php file that the username for the connection is "mgs_user" and the password is "pa55word". For this connection to work, then, a user with this username and password must be stored with the MySQL database. In fact, as you learned in chapter 3, this user is created by the SQL script that creates the databases for this book. Also, this user is given the privileges that are needed for running SELECT, INSERT, UPDATE, and DE-LETE statements against any table in the my_guitar_shop1 database. As a result, this connection will work for this application

The database.php file

```php
<?php
    $dsn = 'mysql:host=localhost;dbname=my_guitar_shop1';
    $username = 'mgs_user';
    $password = 'pa55word';

    try {
        $db = new PDO($dsn, $username, $password);
    } catch (PDOException $e) {
        $error_message = $e->getMessage();
        include('database_error.php');
        exit();
    }
?>
```

The database_error.php file

```php
<!DOCTYPE html PUBLIC "-//W3C//DTD XHTML 1.0 Transitional//EN"
    "http://www.w3.org/TR/xhtml1/DTD/xhtml1-transitional.dtd">
<html xmlns="http://www.w3.org/1999/xhtml">
    <!-- the head section -->
    <head>
        <title>My Guitar Shop</title>
        <link rel="stylesheet" type="text/css" href="main.css" />
    </head>

    <!-- the body section -->
    <body>
    <div id="page">
        <div id="main">
            <h1>Database Error</h1>
            <p>There was an error connecting to the database.</p>
            <p>The database must be installed as described in appendix A.</p>
            <p>The database must be running as described in chapter 1.</p>
            <p>Error message: <?php echo $error_message; ?></p>
        </div>
    </div><!-- end page -->
    </body>
</html>
```

Figure 4-8   The Product Viewer application (part 2 of 4)

The index.php file contains the code that displays the product data. Its first statement is a require statement that executes the code that's stored in the database.php file on the previous page. This sets up the $db variable so it's available for the other statements in this file.

After that, the first block of code gets the category ID for the category link that the user has clicked on. To do that, the first statement gets the category ID from the global $_GET array. However, when the application starts, the user hasn't yet clicked on a category ID. As a result, the category ID won't be set yet. In that case, the if statement sets the category ID to a default value of 1.

The second block of code gets the name for the current category. To do that, this code defines a SELECT statement that gets the row for the category with the specified ID. Next, it executes the SELECT statement, which creates a PDOStatement object. Then, it uses the fetch method of that object to create an array for the only row in the result set that's returned by the SELECT statement. Last, it gets the name of the category from that array.

The third block of code gets all categories and stores them in the $categories variable. Here, the first statement defines a SELECT statement that gets all columns and rows from the categories table. Then, the second statement executes the SELECT statement and stores the PDOStatement object for the result set in the $categories variable.

The fourth block of code works like the third block of code. However, the first statement in this block defines a SELECT statement that gets all columns and rows from the products table for the specified category ID. Then, the second statement executes the SELECT statement and stores the PDOStatement for the result set in the $products variable.

After the initial PHP script, the rest of the index.php file contains mostly HTML tags. If you're familiar with HTML, you shouldn't have any trouble understanding these tags.

The index.php file

```php
<?php
    require 'database.php';

    // Get category ID
    $category_id = $_GET['category_id'];
    if (!isset($category_id)) {
        $category_id = 1;
    }

    // Get name for current category
    $query = "SELECT * FROM categories
            WHERE categoryID = $category_id";
    $category = $db->query($query);
    $category = $category->fetch();
    $category_name = $category['categoryName'];

    // Get all categories
    $query = 'SELECT * FROM categories
            ORDER BY categoryID';
    $categories = $db->query($query);

    // Get products for selected category
    $query = "SELECT * FROM products
            WHERE categoryID = $category_id
            ORDER BY productID";
    $products = $db->query($query);
?>
<!DOCTYPE html PUBLIC "-//W3C//DTD XHTML 1.0 Transitional//EN"
    "http://www.w3.org/TR/xhtml1/DTD/xhtml1-transitional.dtd">
<html xmlns="http://www.w3.org/1999/xhtml">
    <!-- the head section -->
    <head>
        <title>My Guitar Shop</title>
        <link rel="stylesheet" type="text/css" href="main.css" />
    </head>

    <!-- the body section -->
    <body>
    <div id="page">
        <div id="main">

        <h1>Product List</h1>
```

Figure 4-8   The Product Viewer application (part 3 of 4)

The HTML for this file contains embedded PHP tags that display the variables that are defined by the PHP script at the beginning of the file. To start, the first foreach loop displays a list of links for each category. Here, the href attribute specifies a URL that includes the category ID, and the link displays the name for the category. As a result, if the user clicks on one of these links, this application uses the GET method to pass the category ID for the link to the index.php file. This returns a web page that shows the products for the new category.

Please note that these category links are stored within the <li> tags of an unordered list. However, the CSS for this application turns the bullets for this list off so the bullets aren't displayed. Although the CSS isn't shown for any of the applications in this book, it is available in the downloaded applications so you can review it to see how it works.

After the first foreach loop, this page displays the name of the current category above the table of products. Then, it uses a second foreach loop to display the products for the current category. This displays three of the five columns in the result set in an HTML table. Specifically, it displays the product's code in the first column, the name in the second column, and the price in the third column. However, it doesn't display the product ID or the category ID in this table.

As you review this code, note that both foreach loops use the alternate syntax described in figure 4-7. This makes your code easier to read because it makes it easy to see where each foreach loop ends. In addition, both loops use string indexes instead of numeric indexes to get the values from the array for the row. This makes your code easier to read because it makes it easy to see how the data in each column corresponds with the header for each column.

The index.php file (continued)

```php
        <div id="sidebar">
            <!-- display a list of categories -->
            <h2>Categories</h2>
            <ul class="nav">
            <?php foreach ($categories as $category) : ?>
                <li>
                <a href="?category_id=<?php echo $category['categoryID']; ?>">
                    <?php echo $category['categoryName']; ?>
                </a>
                </li>
            <?php endforeach; ?>
            </ul>
        </div>

        <div id="content">
            <!-- display a table of products -->
            <h2><?php echo $category_name; ?></h2>
            <table>
                <tr>
                    <th>Code</th>
                    <th>Name</th>
                    <th class="right">Price</th>
                </tr>
                <?php foreach ($products as $product) : ?>
                <tr>
                    <td><?php echo $product['productCode']; ?></td>
                    <td><?php echo $product['productName']; ?></td>
                    <td class="right"><?php echo $product['listPrice']; ?></td>
                </tr>
                <?php endforeach; ?>
            </table>
        </div>

    </div><!-- end main -->

    <div id="footer"></div>

</div><!-- end page -->
</body>
</html>
```

Figure 4-8   The Product Viewer application (part 4 of 4)

The Product Manager application

This chapter ends by presenting a more complicated database application called the Product Manager application. This application enhances the Product Viewer application in several ways. Most importantly, it lets the user add and delete products.

The user interface

Part 1 of figure 4-9 shows the primary pages of the user interface for the Product Manager application: the Product List page and the Add Product page. Both of these pages include the name of the application in the header, and both of these pages include a copyright notice in the footer. These pages also include borders that separate the header and footer from the body of the page.

The Product List page lets the user view and delete products. It displays a list of categories and a table of products for the current category. This is similar to the main page of the Product Viewer application. However, this list includes a Delete button for each product that lets the user delete the product. In addition, this page includes an Add Product link below the table that lets the user display the Add Product page.

The Add Product page lets the user add a new product. This page starts by displaying a combo box that lets the user select a category for the product. Then, it displays three text boxes that lets the user enter data for the product's code, name, and price. Next, it displays an Add Product button that lets the user submit the data for the product. Finally, this page displays a View Product List link that lets the user return to the Product List page without adding a product.

The Product List page

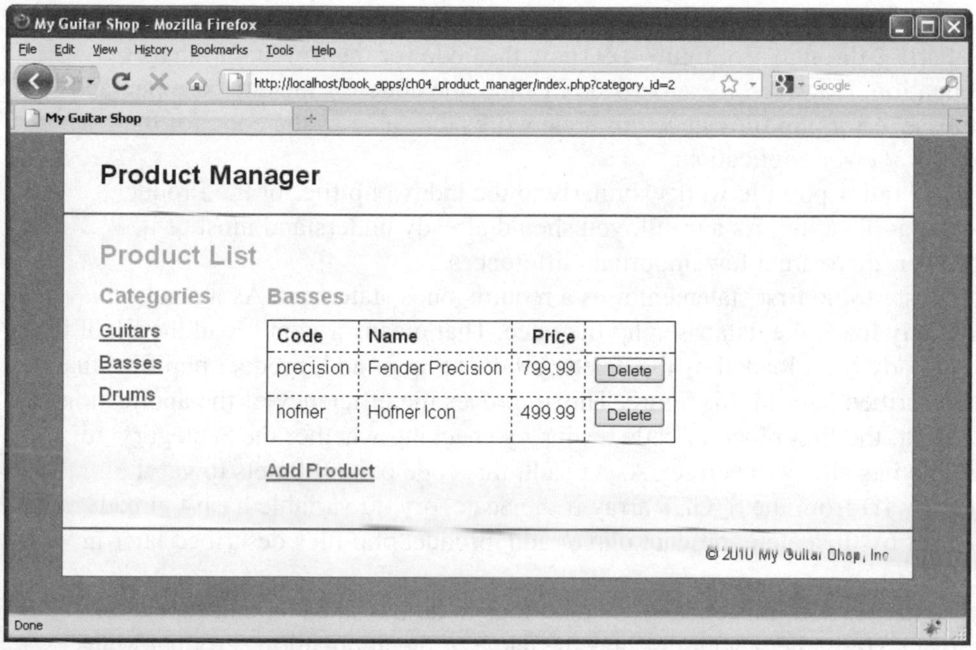

The Add Product page

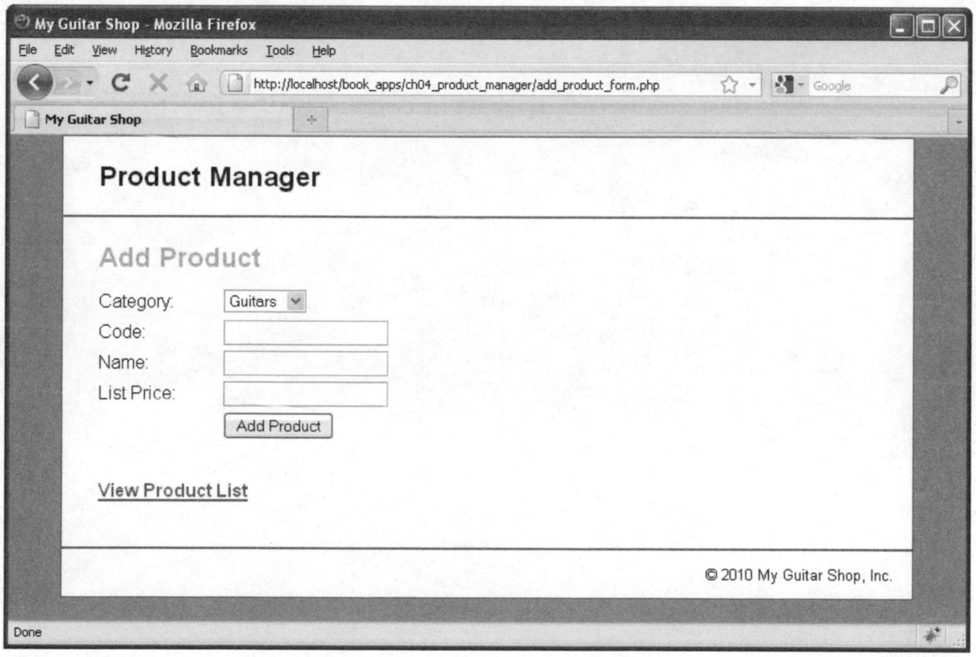

Figure 4-9   The Product Manager application (part 1 of 5)

The code

Parts 2 through 5 of figure 4-9 show the code for the Product Manager application. However, these parts don't show the code for the database.php and database_error.php files since this code works the same as the code for the Product Viewer application.

The index.php file works similarly to the index.php file for the Product Viewer application. As a result, you should already understand most of it. However, there are a few important differences.

To start, the first statement uses a require_once statement. As a result, this code only loads the database.php file once. That means it won't load the file if it has already been loaded by the delete_product.php or add_product.php files that are described later in this figure. This improves the efficiency of the application.

Next, the first block of code begins by checking whether the $category_id variable has already been set. As a result, this code only attempts to get the category ID from the $_GET array if the $category_id variable hasn't already been set by the delete_product.php or add_product.php files described later in this figure.

In the HTML, this code uses <div> tags to define a header and footer for the page. Here, the header displays the name of the application (Product Manager), and the footer displays a copyright notification for the application.

The index.php file

```php
<?php
    require_once('database.php');

    // Get category ID
    if(!isset($category_id)) {
        $category_id = $_GET['category_id'];
        if (!isset($category_id)) {
            $category_id = 1;
        }
    }

    // Get name for current category
    $query = "SELECT * FROM categories
            WHERE categoryID = $category_id";
    $category = $db->query($query);
    $category = $category->fetch();
    $category_name = $category['categoryName'];

    // Get all categories
    $query = 'SELECT * FROM categories
            ORDER BY categoryID';
    $categories = $db->query($query);

    // Get products for selected category
    $query = "SELECT * FROM products
            WHERE categoryID = $category_id
            ORDER BY productID";
    $products = $db->query($query);
?>
<!DOCTYPE html PUBLIC "-//W3C//DTD XHTML 1.0 Transitional//EN"
    "http://www.w3.org/TR/xhtml1/DTD/xhtml1-transitional.dtd">
<html xmlns="http://www.w3.org/1999/xhtml">

<!-- the head section -->
<head>
    <title>My Guitar Shop</title>
    <link rel="stylesheet" type="text/css" href="main.css" />
</head>

<!-- the body section -->
<body>
    <div id="page">

    <div id="header">
        <h1>Product Manager</h1>
    </div>

    <div id="main">

        <h1>Product List</h1>
```

Figure 4-9   The Product Manager application (part 2 of 5)

In the HTML table of products, the code displays four columns. Here, the fourth column contains a form that displays a Delete button that allows the user to delete the corresponding product. Note that this form uses the POST method to call the delete_product.php file, and it uses hidden fields to pass two variables to this file: product_id and category_id.

The index.php file (continued)

```php
        <div id="sidebar">
            <!— display a drop-down list of categories —>
            <h2>Categories</h2>
            <ul class="nav">
            <?php foreach ($categories as $category) : ?>
                <li>
                <a href="?category_id=<?php echo $category['categoryID']; ?>">
                    <?php echo $category['categoryName']; ?>
                </a>
                </li>
            <?php endforeach; ?>
            </ul>
        </div>

        <div id="content">
            <!— display a table of products —>
            <h2><?php echo $category_name; ?></h2>
            <table>
                <tr>
                    <th>Code</th>
                    <th>Name</th>
                    <th class="right">Price</th>
                    <th> </th>
                </tr>
                <?php foreach ($products as $product) : ?>
                <tr>
                    <td><?php echo $product['productCode']; ?></td>
                    <td><?php echo $product['productName']; ?></td>
                    <td class="right"><?php echo $product['listPrice']; ?></td>
                    <td><form action="delete_product.php" method="post"
                            id="delete_product_form">
                        <input type="hidden" name="product_id"
                                value="<?php echo $product['productID']; ?>" />
                        <input type="hidden" name="category_id"
                                value="<?php echo $product['categoryID']; ?>" />
                        <input type="submit" value="Delete" />
                    </form></td>
                </tr>
                <?php endforeach; ?>
            </table>
            <p><a href="add_product_form.php">Add Product</a></p>
        </div>
    </div>

    <div id="footer">
        <p>&copy; <?php echo date("Y"); ?> My Guitar Shop, Inc.</p>
    </div>

    </div><!— end page —>
</body>
</html>
```

Figure 4-9   The Product Manager application (part 3 of 5)

The delete_product.php file begins by getting the IDs for the product and category from the $_POST array. Then, it loads the database.php file to get a connection to the database. Next, it executes a DELETE statement that deletes the specified product. Finally, it runs the index.php file again. As a result, the index.php file can access the $category_id variable and use it to display a list of products for the current category.

The add_product_form.php file consists mostly of the HTML tags that display the Add Product page. However, this file begins by executing some PHP code that gets all categories from the database. Later, in the HTML for the page, a foreach loop uses these categories to create a drop-down list that lets the user select a category. Note that this drop-down list uses the category ID as the value for the option and that it displays the category name to the user. As a result, when the user selects the category name, the application gets the category ID that corresponds with that name.

The delete_product.php file

```php
<?php
// Get IDs
$product_id = $_POST['product_id'];
$category_id = $_POST['category_id'];

// Delete the product from the database
require_once('database.php');
$query = "DELETE FROM products
        WHERE productID = '$product_id'";
$db->exec($query);

// Display the Product List page
include('index.php');
?>
```

The add_product_form.php file

```php
<?php
require_once('database.php');
$query = 'SELECT *
        FROM categories
        ORDER BY categoryID';
$categories = $db->query($query);
?>
<!DOCTYPE html PUBLIC "-//W3C//DTD XHTML 1.0 Transitional//EN"
    "http://www.w3.org/TR/xhtml1/DTD/xhtml1-transitional.dtd">
<html xmlns="http://www.w3.org/1999/xhtml">

<!-- the head section -->
<head>
    <title>My Guitar Shop</title>
    <link rel="stylesheet" type="text/css" href="main.css" />
</head>

<!-- the body section -->
<body>
    <div id="page">
        <div id="header">
            <h1>Product Manager</h1>
        </div>

        <div id="main">
            <h1>Add Product</h1>
            <form action="add_product.php" method="post"
                id="add_product_form" >

                <label>Category:</label>
                <select name="category_id">
                <?php foreach ($categories as $category) : ?>
                    <option value="<?php echo $category['categoryID']; ?>">
                        <?php echo $category['categoryName']; ?>
                    </option>
                <?php endforeach; ?>
                </select>
                <br />
```

Figure 4-9   The Product Manager application (part 4 of 5)

When the user clicks on the Add Product button, the form uses the POST method to pass four product variables to the add_product.php file. This file begins by getting these four variable from the $_POST array. Then, it checks whether the user has left the code, name, or price variable empty. If so, this code defines an appropriate error message and uses a page named error.php to display this message.

Otherwise, this code uses an INSERT statement to add the product data to the products table. Then, it runs the index.php file again. This causes the index.php file to use the $category_id variable to display a list of products for the current category. As a result, if the user adds a product to the Drums category, the application displays the Product List page for the Drums category.

The add_product_form.php file (continued)

```
                <label>Code:</label>
                <input type="input" name="code" />
                <br />

                <label>Name:</label>
                <input type="input" name="name" />
                <br />

                <label>List Price:</label>
                <input type="input" name="price" />
                <br />

                <label> </label>
                <input type="submit" value="Add Product" />
                <br />
            </form>
            <p><a href="index.php">View Product List</a></p>
        </div><!-- end main -->

        <div id="footer">
            <p>&copy; <?php echo date("Y"); ?> My Guitar Shop, Inc.</p>
        </div>

    </div><!-- end page -->
</body>
</html>
```

The add_product.php file

```
<?php
// Get the product data
$category_id = $_POST['category_id'];
$code = $_POST['code'];
$name = $_POST['name'];
$price = $_POST['price'];

// Validate inputs
if (empty($code) || empty($name) || empty($price) ) {
    $error = "Invalid product data. Check all fields and try again.";
    include('error.php');
} else {
    // If valid, add the product to the database
    require_once('database.php');
    $query = "INSERT INTO products
                (categoryID, productCode, productName, listPrice)
            VALUES
                ('$category_id', '$code', '$name', '$price')";
    $db->exec($query);

    // Display the Product List page
    include('index.php');
}
?>
```

Figure 4-9   The Product Manager application (part 5 of 5)

Perspective

If you understand the two applications presented in this chapter, you are well on your way to building database-driven web sites of your own. As you will see in the next chapter, though, the code for these applications isn't structured well. As a result, this coding style isn't appropriate for large applications.

That's why the next chapter shows how to use the MVC pattern to structure a web application. This pattern makes it easier to build large applications that are easier to code, test, debug, and maintain.

Terms

PDO (PHP Data Objects)	exception handling
object	try/catch statement
class	try block
argument	catch block
PDO object	array
DSN (Data Source Name)	element
method	index
PDOStatement object	foreach statement
exception	foreach loop
throw an exception	

Summary

- The *PDO* (*PHP Data Objects*) extension to PHP defines an interface for accessing databases.

- To create an *object* from a *class*, you code the *new* keyword, followed by the name of the class, followed by a set of parentheses. Within the parentheses, you code the *arguments* that are required by the class, separating multiple arguments with commas.

- The *DSN* (*Data Source Name*) for a MySQL connection specifies the host computer for the MySQL database and the name of the database.

- To create a *PDO object* that connects to a MySQL database, you use the PDO class with three arguments: DSN, username, and password.

- To call a *method* from any object, you code the name of the object, followed by ->, followed by the name of the method, followed by a set of parentheses. Within the parentheses, you code the arguments that are required by the method, separating multiple arguments with commas.

- To execute a SELECT statement, you can use the query method of a PDO object. This returns a *PDOStatement object* that represents the result set.

- To execute an INSERT, UPDATE, or DELETE statement, you can use the exec method of a PDO object.

- An *exception* is an object that contains information about an error. Some PHP statements *throw* exceptions when they encounter an error.

- To handle exceptions, you use a *try/catch statement*. First, you code a *try block* around any PHP statements that might *throw an exception*. Then, you code a *catch block* that *catches* the exception. This is known as *exception handling*.

- An *array* can store one or more *elements*. To refer to the elements in an array, you use a string *index* or a numeric index. If you use numeric indexes, 0 refers to the first element, 1 to the second element, and so on.

- To get an array for the first row in a result set, you can call the fetch method of the PDOStatement object for the result set. Then, you can access one column at a time by using a string or numeric index.

- To get the data for each row in a result set, you can use a *foreach statement* to loop through the rows in the PDOStatement object for the result set. This automatically calls the fetch method for each row.

Exercise 4-1   Enhance the Product Manager application

This exercise has you enhance the Product Manager application by adding a page that lets you add and delete categories.

Test the Product Manager application

1. Start the Firefox browser and run the application in the ex_starts/ch04_ex1 directory. To do that, you can use this URL:

   `http://localhost/ex_starts/ch04_ex1/`

   This should display the products for the first category in the database named my_guitar_shop1.

2. View the products in each of the categories.

3. Add a new product to the database. When you add this product, make sure to enter valid values for a product. Then, delete the product you just added from the database.

4. Click on the List Categories link at the bottom of the page. Note that this link leads to a page that's under construction. However, the link back to the Product List page does work.

Add a Category Manager page

In the rest of this exercise, you'll add a page that looks like this:

5. Open the category_list.php file that's in the directory for this application. It contains some of the headings that you'll need for this page, and a link back to the Product List page.

6. Create an add_category.php file that adds a category to the database and a delete_category.php file that deletes a category from the database. These files should display the Category List page after they add or delete a category.

7. In the category_list.php file, write the code that creates the category table shown above with all of the category names in the first column and Delete buttons in the second column. Then, test that this table is displayed correctly.

8. In the category_list.php file, write the code that lets the user add a category to the database. This code should consist of a form that accepts the name for a new category followed by a Submit button that displays "Add".

9. Test the application by adding two categories. Then, navigate to the Add Product page and note that the drop-down list includes the new categories.

10. Test the application by deleting the categories that you just added. However, don't delete any of the existing categories because that will lead to products without categories. If necessary, though, you can restore the database by running the create_db.sql script again as described in the appendix.

5

How to use
the MVC pattern
to organize your code

As your applications grow larger, you'll find that it's more difficult to keep your code organized and more difficult to maintain that code later on. That's why you should learn the right way to organize your code early in your training. In this chapter, you'll learn how to use the MVC pattern to organize your code.

How to use the MVC pattern **160**
An introduction to the MVC pattern 160
How to code functions 162
How to redirect requests 164
The Product Manager application **166**
The user interface 166
The model 168
The controller 170
The view 172
The Product Catalog application **178**
The user interface 178
The model 180
The controller 180
The view 182
Perspective **186**

How to use the MVC pattern

The Product Manager application of the last chapter mixes the PHP code that accesses the database with the HTML code that defines the web page and with the PHP code that controls the flow of the application from one page to another. Unfortunately, this approach makes it difficult to code, test, debug, and maintain large applications. To fix this problem, professional web developers commonly use a programming pattern known as the *MVC (Model-View-Controller) pattern*.

An introduction to the MVC pattern

Figure 5-1 presents a diagram that shows how the MVC pattern works for the Product Manager application. To start, the *model* consists of the PHP files that represent the data of the application. In this diagram, the model includes three files: a database.php file that gets a connection to the database; a category_db.php file that works with the category data in the database; and a product_db.php file that works with the product data in the database. As a general rule, the model files don't contain any HTML.

The *view* consists of the HTML and PHP files that represent the user interface of the application. For a web application, the user interface consists of one or more web pages. In this diagram, the view consists of three files: the products_list.php file displays the page that lets the user view and delete products; the product_add.php file displays the page that lets the user add a product; and the database_error.php file displays a page that displays an error message if the application isn't able to connect to the database. As a general rule, the view files contain the HTML tags for the application with some embedded PHP tags that display the dynamic data that's returned from the database.

The *controller* consists of the PHP files that receive HTTP requests from browsers, get the appropriate data from the model, and return the appropriate views to the browsers. In this diagram, the controller consists of just one file: the index.php file. This file is the default file for the application's directory. As a result, this is the file that's called when the user starts the application.

When you use the MVC pattern, you try to construct each layer so it's as independent as possible. Then, if you need to make changes to one layer, any changes to the other layers are minimized. In addition, if you store the HTML tags for the application in the view, web designers who don't know much about PHP can work on the user interface without help from PHP programmers. This division of labor is especially important for large web sites that have multiple web designers and PHP programmers.

The diagram in this figure assumes that the application isn't using custom objects such as a Product object. However, if your application does use custom objects, they are included as part of the model. For more information about working with custom objects with the MVC pattern, see chapter 14.

The MVC pattern

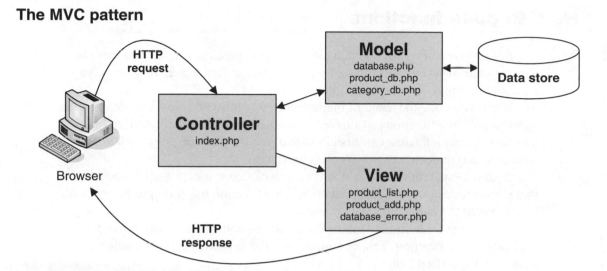

Description

- The *MVC* (*Model-View-Controller*) *pattern* is commonly used to structure web applications that have significant processing requirements. That makes them easier to code and maintain.

- The *model* consists of the PHP files that represent the data of the application.

- The *view* consists of the HTML and PHP files that represent the user interface of the application.

- The *controller* consists of the PHP files that receive requests from users, get the appropriate data from the model, and return the appropriate views to the users.

Figure 5-1   An introduction to the MVC pattern

How to code functions

Before you can write code that uses the MVC pattern, you need to learn how to code your own (custom) functions as described in figure 5-2. To do that, you can use the syntax shown in this figure.

When you code the name of the function, you must choose a unique name. In other words, one function can't have the same name as another function. In addition, a function name can't begin with a number and can only contain letters, numbers, and underscores (no special characters).

Within the parentheses of a function, you can code an optional *parameter list* that contains one or more *parameters*. When a function has multiple parameters, you separate the parameters with commas.

If you want a function to return data, you can code a *return statement* within the body of the function. This statement ends the execution of the function and returns the specified value.

The first example in this figure defines a function named get_products that doesn't have any parameters. However, it returns a PDOStatement object for the result set. To do that, the first statement uses the *global* keyword to make the $db variable (the PDO object) available within this function. This is necessary because the $db variable is declared outside of the get_products function. After that, this function uses the database techniques of chapter 4 to execute a SELECT statement and store the PDOStatement object for the result set in the $products variable. Then, the return statement returns this variable.

The second and third examples in this figure are similar. However, they execute DELETE and INSERT statements, and they return a count of the number of rows that have been affected by the statements. Here, the second example requires just one parameter, and the third example requires four parameters.

To *call* a function, you code the function name followed by a set of parentheses that contains the *arguments* that are required by the function. This works the same as when you call a built-in function. When you code these arguments, they must be in the same order as the parameters in the parameter list that's defined by the function and they must have compatible data types. Note, however, that the arguments don't have to have the same names as the parameters, although that's a common coding practice.

The examples of function calls illustrate how this works. Here, the first statement calls the get_products function with no arguments and stores the PDOStatement object that's returned in a variable named $products. The second statement calls the delete_product function with one argument and stores the row count that's returned in a variable named $row_count. And the third statement calls the add_product function with four arguments and also stores the row count that's returned.

In these examples, all of the function calls store the returned data in variables that have the same names as in the return statements of the functions. Although this is a common coding practice that makes it easy to remember variable names, this isn't required. For example, you could store the value that's returned by the delete_product function in a variable named $count.

How to code a function

The syntax

```
function function_name([parameter_list]) {
    // statements that are executed by the function
}
```

A function with no parameters that returns a PDOStatement object

```
function get_products() {
    global $db;
    $query = 'SELECT * FROM products';
    $products = $db->query($query);
    return $products;
}
```

A function with one parameter that deletes a product row and returns a count

```
function delete_product($product_id) {
    global $db;
    $query = "DELETE FROM products
            WHERE productID = '$product_id'";
    $row_count = $db->exec($query);
    return $row_count;
}
```

A function with four parameters that adds a product to a database table

```
function add_product($category_id, $name, $description, $price) {
    global $db;
    $query = "INSERT INTO products
                (categoryID, productCode, productName, listPrice)
            VALUES
                ('$category_id', '$code', '$name', '$price')";
    $row_count = $db->exec($query);
    return $row_count;
}
```

How to call a function

A function call with no arguments and a returned PDOStatement object

```
$products = get_products();
```

A function call with one argument and a returned row count

```
$row_count = delete_product($product_id);
```

A function call with four arguments and a returned row count

```
$row_count = add_product($category_id, $name, $description, $price);
```

Description

- When you create a function, you can code a *parameter list* within parentheses. A parameter list contains one or more *parameters*.

- To return data from a function, you code a *return statement* in the body of the function. This statement ends the execution of the function and returns the specified value.

- A variable that's declared outside of a function isn't available within the function. To make the variable available, you can use the *global* keyword to identify the variable.

Figure 5-2   How to code functions

How to redirect requests

In figure 2-16 of chapter 2, you learned how to use the include function to *forward* a request from one PHP file to another. When you forward a request, all of the processing takes place on the server. After the browser makes a request, the server forwards the request to another PHP file on the server, eventually returning a response to the browser. In other words, there is only one round trip to the server.

When you use the MVC pattern, you may occasionally need to *redirect* a request instead of forwarding it. To do that, you can use the header function as described in figure 5-3. You can use this function to return an HTTP response to the browser that contains a Location header. This header causes the browser to request the specified URL. In other words, this causes a second round trip to the server.

Since forwarding a request doesn't require a second trip to the server, it usually runs faster than redirecting a request. As a result, you should forward requests whenever possible. However, in some cases, you won't be able to forward a request. In those cases, you can use a redirect. For example, if a PHP file needs to run itself again, you can't use the include function to forward the request. Instead, you can use the header function to redirect the request to the same file. That way, the browser requests the file a second time.

The first set of examples shows how to use the header function to redirect a request to the specified URL. To do that, you send a Location header to the browser. This header consists of the name of the header, followed by a colon (:), followed by the value of the header. To redirect to another page, you can set the value of this header to a relative URL or to an absolute URL.

To redirect to the current directory, you code a single dot (.). To navigate up one directory, you code two dots (..). To navigate down one or more directories, you code a single dot followed by a directory path. To redirect to a file that's in the same directory as the current file, you can specify the filename. To redirect to a different web server, you can code an absolute URL.

The first redirect example shows how to redirect a request to the current directory. Here, the if statement checks the value of the $action variable. For a value of "delete", this statement gets the product ID from the $_POST array. Then, it calls a function that deletes a product from the database. Finally, it uses the header function to redirect to the default file for the current directory.

The second redirect example works like the first one, but it appends a parameter to the end of the URL. More specifically, it appends a parameter with a name of category_id and a value that's stored in the $category_id variable. To do that, it codes a question mark (?), followed by the parameter name, followed by an equals sign (=), followed by the parameter value.

Note that the second redirect example uses double quotes for the string so it can insert the value for the $category_id variable into the string. Conversely, the first redirect example uses single quotes since it doesn't need to insert a variable.

A built-in function that you can use to redirect a request

Name	Description
header(*$header*)	Sends an HTTP header to the browser. For example, you can use this function to send an HTTP Location header to the browser to redirect the browser to another URL.

The header function

```
header('Location: .');              // the current directory
header('Location: ..');             // navigate up one directory
header('Location: ./admin');        // navigate down one directory
header('Location: error.php');
header('Location: http://www.murach.com/');
```

How to redirect a request

```
if ($action == 'delete') {
    $product_id = $_POST['product_id'];
    delete_product($product_id);
    header('Location: .');
}
```

How to redirect a request that includes a parameter

```
if ($action == 'delete') {
    $product_id = $_POST['product_id'];
    $category_id = $_POST['category_id'];

    delete_product($product_id);

    header("Location: .?category_id=$category_id");
}
```

Description

- In figure 2-16 of chapter 2, you learned how to use the include function to *forward* a request from one PHP file to another. When you forward a request, all processing takes place on the server.

- You can use the header function to *redirect* a request to another URL. When you redirect a request, you return a response to the browser that has a Location header that specifies a page. This header causes the browser to make a new request for the specified URL.

Figure 5-3   How to redirect requests

The Product Manager application

To show how the MVC pattern works, this chapter now presents the Product Manager application of the last chapter after it has been modified to implement the MVC pattern. In programming jargon, modifying an application in this way is sometimes referred to as *refactoring*.

Since the MVC version of this application has been split into more files, it may at first seem to be harder to understand than the original version of the application. However, once you understand how the pieces fit together, I think you'll agree that the MVC version is easier to understand, and also that it will be easier to code, debug, maintain, and enhance.

The user interface

Part 1 of figure 5-4 shows the two main pages of the user interface for the Product Manager application. These pages work the same way they did in the Product Manager application of chapter 4. The Product List page lets the user view and delete products, and the Add Product page lets the user add a new product.

The Product List page

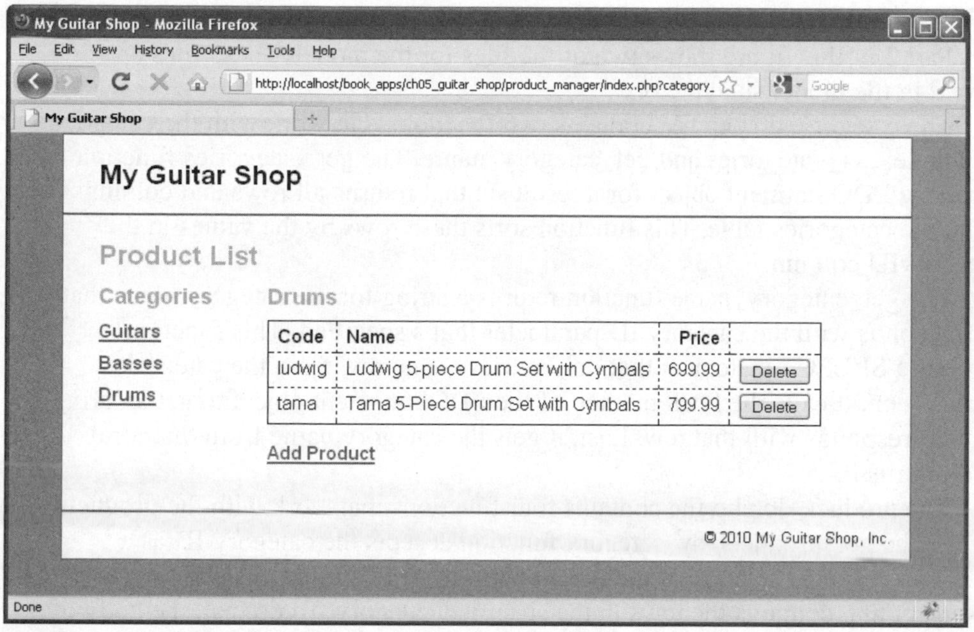

The Add Product page

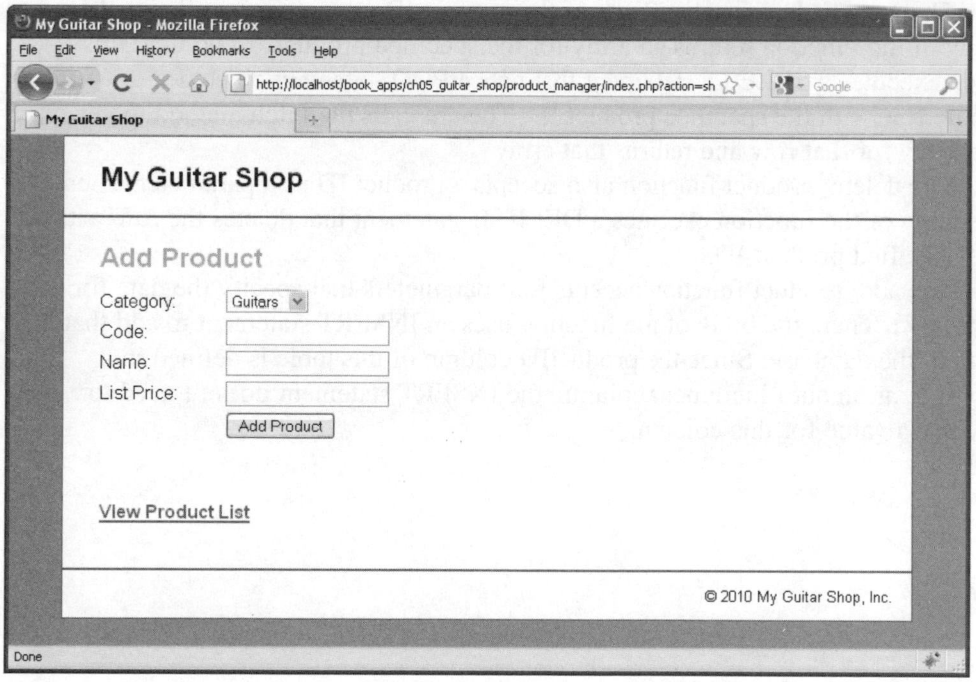

Figure 5-4   The Product Manager application (part 1 of 6)

The model

Part 2 of this figure shows two of the files for the model. These files are stored in the model subdirectory.

The category_db.php file contains two functions that work with the categories table: get_categories and get_category_name. The get_categories function returns a PDOStatment object for a result set that returns all rows and columns from the categories table. This function sorts these rows by the values in the categoryID column.

The get_category_name function returns a string for the category name that corresponds with the category ID parameter that's specified. This function defines a SELECT statement that only retrieves one row from the categories table. Then, it calls the fetch method of the PDOStatement object to get an array that corresponds with that row. Last, it gets the category name from that array and returns it.

The product_db.php file contains four functions that work with the products table. The get_products_by_category function accepts the category ID as a parameter. Then, the body of the function returns a PDOStatement object for a result set that contains the rows in the specified category. To do that, the body of this function executes a SELECT statement that gets all rows that have the specified category ID.

The get_product function accepts the product ID as a parameter. Then, the body of the function returns an array for the specified product. To do that, this code executes a SELECT statement that gets a PDOStatement object for a single row with the specified product ID. Then, it calls the fetch method to get the array for that row and returns that array.

The delete_product function also accepts a product ID as a parameter. Then, the body of the function executes a DELETE statement that deletes the row with the specified product ID.

The add_product function accepts four parameters that specify the data for a product. Then, the body of the function uses an INSERT statement to add that data to the database. Since the productID column of this table is defined in MySQL as an auto-increment column, the INSERT statement doesn't need to specify a value for this column.

The model/category_db.php file

```php
<?php
function get_categories() {
    global $db;
    $query = 'SELECT * FROM categories ORDER BY categoryID';
    $result = $db->query($query);
    return $result;
}

function get_category_name($category_id) {
    global $db;
    $query = "SELECT * FROM categories WHERE categoryID = $category_id";
    $category = $db->query($query);
    $category = $category->fetch();
    $category_name = $category['categoryName'];
    return $category_name;
}
?>
```

The model/product_db.php file

```php
<?php
function get_products_by_category($category_id) {
    global $db;
    $query = "SELECT * FROM products
              WHERE products.categoryID = '$category_id'
              ORDER BY productID";
    $products = $db->query($query);
    return $products;
}

function get_product($product_id) {
    global $db;
    $query = "SELECT * FROM products
              WHERE productID = '$product_id'";
    $product = $db->query($query);
    $product = $product->fetch();
    return $product;
}

function delete_product($product_id) {
    global $db;
    $query = "DELETE FROM products
              WHERE productID = '$product_id'";
    $db->exec($query);
}

function add_product($category_id, $code, $name, $price) {
    global $db;
    $query = "INSERT INTO products
                (categoryID, productCode, productName, listPrice)
              VALUES
                ('$category_id', '$code', '$name', '$price')";
    $db->exec($query);
}
?>
```

Figure 5-4   The Product Manager application (part 2 of 6)

The controller

Part 3 shows the code for the controller for the application: the index.php file. This file is stored in the product_manager directory. It begins by using three require statements to import the three files from the model. These files are necessary to connect to the database and to work with the products and categories tables. Although the database.php file isn't shown in this figure, it is the same as the one in the Product Manager application of chapter 4.

After importing these three files, this code uses an if statement to get the action parameter from the GET or POST request and to set the $action variable appropriately. If the action parameter doesn't exist in either the GET or POST request, this code sets the $action variable to a value of "list_products". This is the default action for the application, and it displays the Product List page.

After setting the value of the $action variable, this code uses a second if statement to execute the appropriate code depending on the value of the $action variable. This code provides for four actions: list_products, delete_product, show_add_form, and add_product.

For the list_products action, this code gets the current category ID from the $_GET array. Or, if the category ID hasn't been set, it sets the category ID to a default value of 1. After that, this code calls three functions from the model to get the data that's necessary to display the Product List page. Then, it displays the Product List page. To do that, this code uses an include statement to include the product_list.php file.

For the delete_product action, this code gets the ID of the product to delete and the ID of the current category from the $_POST array. Then, it deletes the product by passing the product ID to the delete_product function. Finally, it displays the Product List page for the current category. To do that, this code uses the header function to redirect the browser to the current directory. In addition, it passes a parameter named category_id that includes the category ID for the current category. This executes the index.php file again without an action parameter. As a result, the index.php file uses the default action and displays the Product List page for the current category.

For the show_add_form action, this code calls the get_categories function to get the categories that are needed by the Add Product page. Then, this code displays the Add Product page.

For the add_product action, this code gets product data from the four controls on the form. Then, it uses an if statement to check whether the user left any of the three text boxes empty. If so, it stores an error message in a variable named $error, and it displays the error.php page. Although the error.php file isn't shown in this figure, it's a simple page that's designed to display the message that's stored in the variable named $error.

On the other hand, if the user enters text for all three text boxes, the add_product action uses the add_product function to add the product to the database. Then, it displays the Product List page for the current category. This works similarly to the delete_product action.

The product_manager/index.php file (the controller)

```php
<?php
require('../model/database.php');
require('../model/product_db.php');
require('../model/category_db.php');

if (isset($_POST['action'])) {
    $action = $_POST['action'];
} else if (isset($_GET['action'])) {
    $action = $_GET['action'];
} else {
    $action = 'list_products';
}

if ($action == 'list_products') {
    // Get the current category ID
    $category_id = $_GET['category_id'];
    if (!isset($category_id)) {
        $category_id = 1;
    }

    // Get the product and category data
    $category_name = get_category_name($category_id);
    $categories = get_categories();
    $products = get_products_by_category($category_id);

    // Display the product list
    include('product_list.php');
} else if ($action == 'delete_product') {
    // Get the IDs and delete the product
    $product_id = $_POST['product_id'];
    $category_id = $_POST['category_id'];
    delete_product($product_id);

    // Display the Product List page for the current category
    header("Location: .?category_id=$category_id");
} else if ($action == 'show_add_form') {
    $categories = get_categories();
    include('product_add.php');
} else if ($action == 'add_product') {
    $category_id = $_POST['category_id'];
    $code = $_POST['code'];
    $name = $_POST['name'];
    $price = $_POST['price'];

    if (empty($code) || empty($name) || empty($price)) {
        $error = "Invalid product data. Check all fields and try again.";
        include('../errors/error.php');
    } else {
        add_product($category_id, $code, $name, $price);

        // Display the Product List page for the current category
        header("Location: .?category_id=$category_id");
    }
}
?>
```

Figure 5-4   The Product Manager application (part 3 of 6)

Of course, with minimal validation checking like this, the user can enter values that aren't valid. If, for example, the user doesn't enter a valid number for the price, this application won't work correctly. In a real-world application, then, you would need to add complete data validation. That's why you're going to learn sophisticated techniques for doing that as you progress through this book.

The view

Part 4 shows the code for the header and footer files for the application. These files are helper files that are used by all of the pages in the application, and they are stored in the view subdirectory.

The header file includes all of the tags for starting the web pages in the application. This includes a <link> tag that specifies the CSS file that's used throughout the application. To allow the CSS file to be called from any directory in the application, the href attribute specifies the path relative to the document root (which is usually the htdocs directory). In addition, the header file includes a <div> tag that defines the header section. This section includes an <h1> tag that displays the name of the application: My Guitar Shop.

The footer file includes a <div> tag that defines the footer section. This section includes a <p> tag that includes a copyright notice. This copyright notice includes a PHP tag that returns the current year. To accomplish this task, this PHP tag passed a value of "Y" to the date function to return a string that contains the four digits of the current year.

Although it isn't shown in this figure, the CSS file for this application applies formatting to the <div> tags for the header and footer sections. This formatting adds a bottom border to the header section, and it adds a top border to the footer section. This visually separates the header and footer sections from the main section that presents the unique parts of the interface for each page.

Although the header and footer files aren't strictly a part of the MVC pattern, using files like those is a common technique that reduces code duplication. This adheres to the *DRY (Don't Repeat Yourself) principle* that most programmers try to follow, and it makes the files in the view easier to maintain. For example, to change the title for every page of this web site, you only need to change the <title> tag in the header.php file. Or, to change the copyright notice at the bottom of every page in the web site, you only need to change the HTML and PHP in the footer.php file.

In this application, the header and footer files are short. As a result, using them doesn't yield a big reduction in code. However, header and footer files can be much longer. In that case, using header and footer files can yield a dramatic reduction in the code that needs to be maintained.

The view/header.php file

```
<!DOCTYPE html PUBLIC "-//W3C//DTD XHTML 1.0 Transitional//EN"
    "http://www.w3.org/TR/xhtml1/DTD/xhtml1-transitional.dtd">
<html xmlns="http://www.w3.org/1999/xhtml">
    <!-- the head section -->
    <head>
        <title>My Guitar Shop</title>
        <link rel="stylesheet" type="text/css"
            href="/book_apps/ch05_guitar_shop/main.css" />
    </head>

    <!-- the body section -->
    <body>
    <div id="page">
        <div id="header">
            <h1>My Guitar Shop</h1>
        </div>
```

The view/footer.php file

```
        <div id="footer">
            <p>
                &copy; <?php echo date("Y"); ?> My Guitar Shop, Inc.
            </p>
        </div>
    </div><!-- end page -->
    </body>
</html>
```

Figure 5-4   The Product Manager application (part 4 of 6)

Part 5 shows the product_list.php file that's stored in the product_manager subdirectory. This file defines the Product List page. This file starts by including the header.php file that defines the tags for the header of every page in the application, and it ends by including the footer.php file that defines the footer for every page in the application.

In the sidebar of this page, this code displays a list of category links for the categories stored in the $categories variable. To do that, it uses a foreach loop to display the category names in link tags within an unordered list. Then, the CSS for this application turns the bullets for this list off.

In the content portion of this page, the code displays the category name stored in the $category_name variable in an <h2> tag. Then, it uses an HTML table to display the product data that's stored in the $products variable. Here, the first three columns of this table display the data for each product, and the fourth column displays a Delete button that allows the user to delete the corresponding product row from the database. This column consists of a <form> tag that uses the POST method to submit its data to the controller.

Within the <form> tag, this code uses three hidden fields to store parameters. The first one stores a parameter with a name of "action" and a value of "delete_product". The second one stores a parameter with a name of "product_id" and a value that contains the product_id for the product to be deleted. The third hidden field stores a parameter with a name of "category_id" and a value that contains the category_id for the current category. Finally, this form contains a submit button with a value of "Delete". When the user clicks on this button, the form submits the three parameters to the index.php file, which causes the appropriate product to be deleted.

After the table, this code uses an <a> tag to code a link that displays the Add Product page. To accomplish this task, the href attribute passes a parameter with a name of "action" and a value of "show_add_form" to the index.php file. As a result, the index.php file displays the Add Product page.

At this point, you might be wondering why this code didn't use an <a> tag to code a link directly to the add_product.php file. The reason is that the add_product.php file expects the $categories variable to contain the PDOStatement object for the result set that contains the category IDs and names. As a result, you must use the index.php file to display the add_product.php file if you want the Add Product page to display correctly. That way, the index.php file can set up the $categories variable before it displays the Add Product page. This also means that the index.php file controls the logic of the application, which is what the controller is supposed to do.

The product_manager/product_list.php file (a view)

```php
<?php include '../view/header.php'; ?>
<div id="main">

    <h1>Product List</h1>

    <div id="sidebar">
        <!-- display a list of categories -->
        <h2>Categories</h2>
        <ul class="nav">
        <?php foreach ($categories as $category) : ?>
            <li>
            <a href="?category_id=<?php echo $category['categoryID']; ?>">
                <?php echo $category['categoryName']; ?>
            </a>
            </li>
        <?php endforeach; ?>
        </ul>
    </div>

    <div id="content">
        <!-- display a table of products -->
        <h2><?php echo $category_name; ?></h2>
        <table>
            <tr>
                <th>Code</th>
                <th>Name</th>
                <th class="right">Price</th>
                <th> </th>
            </tr>
            <?php foreach ($products as $product) : ?>
            <tr>
                <td><?php echo $product['productCode']; ?></td>
                <td><?php echo $product['productName']; ?></td>
                <td class="right"><?php echo $product['listPrice']; ?></td>
                <td><form action="." method="post">
                    <input type="hidden" name="action"
                        value="delete_product" />
                    <input type="hidden" name="product_id"
                        value="<?php echo $product['productID']; ?>" />
                    <input type="hidden" name="category_id"
                        value="<?php echo $product['categoryID']; ?>" />
                    <input type="submit" value="Delete" />
                    </form></td>
            </tr>
            <?php endforeach; ?>
        </table>
        <p><a href="?action=show_add_form">Add Product</a></p>
    </div>

</div>
<?php include '../view/footer.php'; ?>
```

Figure 5-4   The Product Manager application (part 5 of 6)

Part 6 shows the product_add.php file that's stored in the product_manager directory. This file defines the Add Product page. Like the Product List page, the Add Product page uses the header.php and footer.php files to define the header and footer of the page.

Most of the code for the Add Product page is coded within a <form> tag. This <form> tag uses the POST method to submit its data to the controller (the index.php file). It also includes an id attribute to make it easy to use CSS to format this form.

The first control on this form is a hidden field that specifies a parameter with a name of "action" and a value of "add_product".

After the hidden field, this code uses a <select> tag to allow the user to select a category from a drop-down list. This <select> tag has a name of "category_id". Within the <select> tag, this code uses a PHP foreach loop to display one <option> tag for each category that's stored in the $categories variable. This code uses the ID for each category as the value. Then, it inserts the name for each category between the opening and closing <option> tags. As a result, the category name is displayed to the user, and the category ID is submitted to the index.php file as the value.

After the <select> tag, this form contains three text boxes for the code, name, and price of the product. Finally, this form contains a submit button that submits the form data.

After the form, this code uses an <a> tag to code a link that displays the Product List page. To do that, the href attribute passes a parameter with a name of "action" and a value of "list_products" to the index.php file. As a result, the index.php file displays the Product List page.

As you review the code for the MVC version of the Product Manager application, take a moment to consider the benefits. To start, by removing most of the PHP code from the view, it's easier for HTML programmers who don't understand PHP to work on the view. This allows for a division of labor that's helpful for large applications. Second, by reducing code duplication, it's easier to test, debug, and maintain the application. Third, by providing a known structure to the application, you can more easily expand and enhance the application.

Incidentally, the design of the web pages in the applications throughout this book is minimal. That's because the purpose of this book is to teach you web programming, not HTML, CSS, or graphics. In practice, after the web programmer finishes the programming that provides the functionality for a web site, the web designer can enhance the design so it is appropriate for the users of the web site. This division of labor makes sense even if you are both the web programmer and the web designer.

The product_manager/product_add.php file (another view)

```php
<?php include '../view/header.php'; ?>
<div id="main">
    <h1>Add Product</h1>
    <form action="index.php" method="post" id="add_product_form">
        <input type="hidden" name="action" value="add_product" />

        <label>Category:</label>
        <select name="category_id">
        <?php foreach ( $categories as $category ) : ?>
            <option value="<?php echo $category['categoryID']; ?>">
                <?php echo $category['categoryName']; ?>
            </option>
        <?php endforeach; ?>
        </select>
        <br />

        <label>Code:</label>
        <input type="input" name="code" />
        <br />

        <label>Name:</label>
        <input type="input" name="name" />
        <br />

        <label>List Price:</label>
        <input type="input" name="price" />
        <br />

        <label> </label>
        <input type="submit" value="Add Product" />
        <br />
    </form>
    <p><a href="index.php?action=list_products">View Product List</a></p>

</div>
<?php include '../view/footer.php'; ?>
```

Figure 5-4   The Product Manager application (part 6 of 6)

The Product Catalog application

To illustrate some of the benefits of the MVC pattern, this chapter now presents a Product Catalog application. This application is the second application in the web site that contains the Product Manager application.

The difference between these two applications is that the Product Manager application is designed for the administrative users of a web site. These users are the employees who run the site. In contrast, the Product Catalog application is designed for the end users of the web site. These users are the customers who visit the site.

Since these applications present different views of the same data, they can both use the same model. In addition, since both applications are part of the same web site, they can use the same header and footer files. Reusing this code makes it easier to develop the Product Catalog application.

The user interface

Part 1 of figure 5-5 presents the user interface for the Product Catalog application. Here, the first page of the application lets the user select a category and a product within that category. When the user selects a product, this application displays a Product page that gets its product data from a MySQL database. It also uses this data to get an image for the product.

For now, the Product page only displays a minimal amount of data about each product. However, once you understand the principles for displaying this data, you can use the same techniques to display more data. In chapter 20, you'll also learn some advanced techniques that will help you display long product descriptions.

The Product List page

The Product page

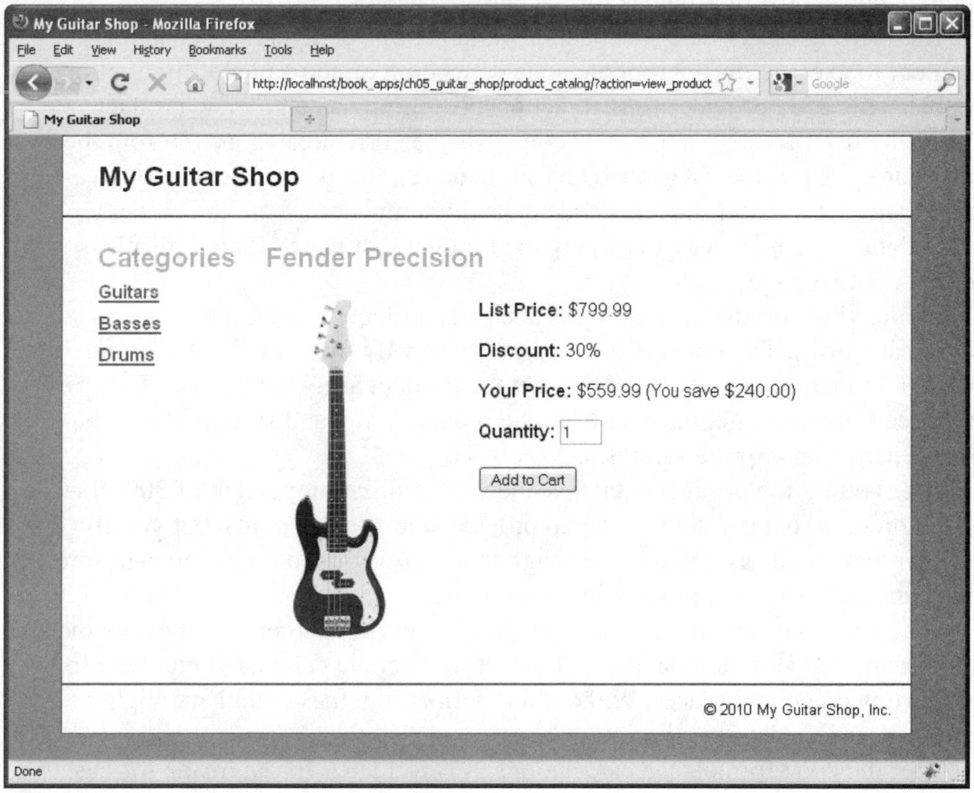

Figure 5-5   The Product Catalog application (part 1 of 4)

The model

Since the Product Catalog application uses the same model as the Product Manager application, the code for the model isn't shown in this figure. If you would like to review that code, you can refer to the category_db.php and product_db.php files in part 2 of figure 5-4.

The controller

Part 2 of this figure shows the code for the controller for the application: the index.php file. This file is stored in the product_catalog subdirectory. It begins by using three require statements to import the three files from the model. These are the same three files that are used by the Product Manager application.

After importing these files, this code uses an if statement to set the $action variable. If the action parameter doesn't exist in either the GET or POST request, this code sets the $action variable to a value of "list_products". This is the default action for the application, and it displays the Product List page, which displays a list of products for the current category.

After setting the value of the $action variable, this code uses a second if statement to execute the appropriate code depending on the value of the $action variable. This code provides for two actions: list_products and view_product.

For the list_products action, this code gets the current category ID from the $_GET array. Or, if the category ID hasn't been set, it sets the category ID to a default value of 1. After that, this code calls three functions from the model to get the data that's necessary to display the Product List page. Then, it displays the Product List page.

For the view_product action, this code calls a function from the model to get the categories. Then, it gets the current product ID from the $_GET array and uses a function from the model to get the product array for that ID. The next three statements get the data from the product array and store it in the $code, $name, and $price variables.

After getting the product data, this code sets a discount percent of 30% for all web orders. This is a simple way to provide web site discounts, but you'll see other techniques as you move through this book. For example, you can store a discount price for each product in the database.

After this code sets the discount percent, it uses that percent to calculate the discount amount and the final price. Then, it formats the calculated numbers so they have two decimal places. Without this formatting, these numbers might have more or less than two decimal places.

After the code formats the calculations, it gets a URL for an image for the product. This code assumes that the images for the web site have been stored in the images subdirectory, that the filename for each image is the same as the product code, and that the images are in PNG format with an extension of PNG. Then, this code creates a value for the alt attribute of the <img> tag. Finally, this code uses an include statement to display the page that's stored in the product_view.php file.

The product_catalog/index.php file (the controller)

```php
<?php
require('../model/database.php');
require('../model/product_db.php');
require('../model/category_db.php');

if (isset($_POST['action'])) {
    $action = $_POST['action'];
} else if (isset($_GET['action'])) {
    $action = $_GET['action'];
} else {
    $action = 'list_products';
}

if ($action == 'list_products') {
    $category_id = $_GET['category_id'];
    if (empty($category_id)) {
        $category_id = 1;
    }

    $categories = get_categories();
    $category_name = get_category_name($category_id);
    $products = get_products_by_category($category_id);

    include('product_list.php');
} else if ($action == 'view_product') {
    $categories = get_categories();

    $product_id = $_GET['product_id'];
    $product = get_product($product_id);

    // Get product data
    $code = $product['productCode'];
    $name = $product['productName'];
    $list_price = $product['listPrice'];

    // Set the discount percent (for all web orders)
    $discount_percent = 30;

    // Calculate discounts
    $discount_amount = round($list_price * ($discount_percent / 100.0), 2);
    $unit_price = $list_price - $discount_amount;

    // Format the calculations
    $discount_amount = number_format($discount_amount, 2);
    $unit_price = number_format($unit_price, 2);

    // Get image URL and alternate text
    $image_filename = '../images/' . $code . '.png';
    $image_alt = 'Image: ' . $code . '.png';

    include('product_view.php');
}
?>
```

Figure 5-5   The Product Catalog application (part 2 of 4)

The view

Part 3 shows the product_list.php file that's stored in the product_catalog subdirectory. This file defines the Product List page. In the sidebar of this page, this code displays a list of category links for the categories stored in the $categories variable.

In the content part of the page, this code displays the name stored in the $category_name variable in an <h1> tag. Then, it displays one link for each product that's stored in the $products variable. To do that, this code creates an <a> tag that displays each product name. This tag includes an href attribute that passes two parameters to the controller PHP file. First, it passes a parameter named "action" with a value of "view_product". Then, it passes a parameter named "product_id" that contains the ID for the product. As a result, if the user clicks on this link, the controller displays the product in the Product page.

Here again, these <a> tags are coded within an unordered list. Then, the CSS sets the bullet style to "none" so the bullets aren't displayed.

The product_catalog/product_list.php file (a view)

```php
<?php include '../view/header.php'; ?>
<div id="main">
    <div id="sidebar">
        <h1>Categories</h1>
        <ul class="nav">
            <!-- display links for all categories -->
            <?php foreach($categories as $category) : ?>
            <li>
                <a href="?category_id=<?php echo $category['categoryID']; ?>">
                    <?php echo $category['categoryName']; ?>
                </a>
            </li>
            <?php endforeach; ?>
        </ul>
    </div>
    <div id="content">
        <h1><?php echo $category_name; ?></h1>
        <ul class="nav">
            <?php foreach ($products as $product) : ?>
            <li>
                <a href="?action=view_product&product_id=
                    <?php echo $product['productID']; ?>">
                    <?php echo $product['productName']; ?>
                </a>
            </li>
            <?php endforeach; ?>
        </ul>
    </div>
</div>
<?php include '../view/footer.php'; ?>
```

Figure 5-5   The Product Catalog application (part 3 of 4)

Part 4 shows the product_view.php file that's stored in the product_catalog subdirectory. This file defines the Product page. In the sidebar, this code displays a list of category links for the categories stored in the $categories variable.

Note that this sidebar code is exactly the same as the code for the sidebar in the Product List page. Although this violates the DRY principle, I decided to leave this code as it is because it is only repeated once. However, if this code were repeated in more places, it would make sense to move the code for the sidebar into its own file. Then, it could be included in all the pages that use it. That way, the code for the sidebar would only be stored in one place.

In the content part of the page, this code displays the product name that's in the $name variable in an <h1> tag. Then, it uses <div> tags to divide the right side of the page into two columns. Here, the left column displays the image for the product, and the right column displays the data for the product. This column also displays a form that adds the product to a shopping cart by submitting the data to the default file in the cart subdirectory.

As you progress through this book, you'll learn how to code shopping cart applications. For now, though, you can focus on the two applications presented in this chapter.

The product_catalog/product_view.php file (another view)

```php
<?php include '../view/header.php'; ?>
<div id="main">
    <div id="sidebar">
        <h1>Categories</h1>
        <ul class="nav">
            <!-- display links for all categories -->
            <?php foreach($categories as $category) : ?>
            <li>
                <a href="?category_id=<?php echo $category['categoryID']; ?>">
                    <?php echo $category['categoryName']; ?>
                </a>
            </li>
            <?php endforeach; ?>
        </ul>
    </div>
    <div id="content">
        <h1><?php echo $name; ?></h1>
        <div id="left_column">
            <p>
                <img src="<?php echo $image_filename; ?>"
                    alt="Image: <?php echo $image_alt; ?>" />
            </p>
        </div>

        <div id="right_column">
            <p><b>List Price:</b> $<?php echo $list_price; ?></p>
            <p><b>Discount:</b> <?php echo $discount_percent; ?>%</p>
            <p><b>Your Price:</b> $<?php echo $unit_price; ?>
                (You save $<?php echo $discount_amount; ?>)</p>
            <form action="<?php echo '../cart' ?>" method="post">
                <input type="hidden" name="action" value="add" />
                <input type="hidden" name="product_id"
                        value="<?php echo $product_id; ?>" />
                <b>Quantity:</b>
                <input type="text" name="quantity" value="1" size="2" />
                <input type="submit" value="Add to Cart" />
            </form>
        </div>
    </div>
</div>
<?php include '../view/footer.php'; ?>
```

Figure 5-5   The Product Catalog application (part 4 of 4)

Perspective

If you understand how the applications in this chapter work, you are well on your way to building database-driven applications that are easy to code, test, debug, and maintain. Then, you can add to your PHP and MySQL skills by reading the other sections of this book. But first, chapter 6 presents the testing and debugging skills that you will need as you develop your own applications.

Terms

MVC (Model-View-Controller) pattern	global keyword
model	call a function
view	argument
controller	forward a request
parameter	redirect a request
parameter list	refactoring
return statement	DRY (Don't Repeat Yourself) principle

Summary

- The *MVC* (*Model-View-Controller*) *pattern* is commonly used to structure web applications that have significant processing requirements.

- The *model* in the MVC pattern consists of the PHP files that represent the data of the application. The *view* consists of the HTML and PHP files that represent the user interface of the application.

- The *controller* in the MVC pattern consists of the PHP files that get requests from users, get the appropriate data from the model, and return the appropriate views to the users.

- When you create a function, you can code a *parameter list* within parentheses. A parameter list contains one or more *parameters*. To return data from a function, you code a *return statement* in the body of the function.

- A variable that's declared outside of a function isn't available within the function. To make the variable available, you can use the *global* keyword to identify the variable.

- When you call a function, the *arguments* in the *argument list* must be in the same order as the *parameters* in the *parameter list*, and they must have compatible data types.

- You can use the include function to *forward* a request from one PHP file to another. When you forward a request, all processing takes place on the server.

- You can use the header function to *redirect* a request to another URL. When you redirect a request, the server returns a response that tells the browser to request another URL.

- In programming, modifying the organization or structure of an application is sometimes referred to as *refactoring*.

- It's generally considered a best practice to avoid duplicating code in multiple parts of an application. This is sometimes referred to as the *DRY (Don't Repeat Yourself) principle*.

Exercise 5-1   Enhance the Guitar Shop application

This exercise has you enhance the Guitar Shop application. That will give you a chance to use some of the skills that were presented in this chapter.

Test the Guitar Shop application

1. Start the Firefox browser and run the application in the ex_starts/ch05_ex1 directory. This should display a menu that lets you navigate to the Product Manager application or the Product Catalog application.

2. Use the Product Manager application to add a new product to the database with Guitars as the category, test1 as the code, Test Product 2211 as the name, and 550.00 as the list price.

3. Go to the Product Catalog application. To do that, you can use the Back button or run the application again. Then, view the product that you just added. Note that it doesn't display an image for the product. To fix that, go to the images directory and change the name of the test.png file to test1.png.

4. Go to the Product Manager application again. Then, click on the List Categories link at the bottom of the page. Note that this link doesn't display a page, even though it is coded correctly. You'll fix this later when you enhance the index.php page for this application. Now, click the Back button.

Enhance the Product Manager application

Now, you'll add a page to the Product Manager application that lets you add or delete categories. This is similar to what you did in exercise 4-1, but using the MVC pattern. The new page should look like this:

5. Open the category_list.php file in the product_manager directory. It contains some of the headings that you'll need for this page, and a link back to the Product List page.

6. Open the model/category_db.php file and add two functions to it that add and delete categories.

7. Open the index.php file in the product_manager directory and add three new actions to it. The first action should display the Category List page. This will fix the problem with the List Categories link. The second action should add a category to the database. And the third action should delete a category from the database.

   Tip: To return to the Category List page after adding or deleting a category, you can pass an action to the controller with a statement like this:

   ```
   header('Location: .?action=list_categories');
   ```

8. In the category_list.php file, write the code that creates the category table shown above with all of the category names in the first column and Delete buttons in the second column. Then, test that this table is displayed correctly.

9. In the category_list.php file, write the code that lets the user add a category to the database. This code should consist of a form that accepts the name for a new category followed by a Submit button that displays "Add".

10. Test the application by adding two categories. Then, navigate to the Add Product page and note that the drop-down list includes the new categories.

11. Test the application by deleting the categories that you just added. However, don't delete any of the existing categories because that will lead to products without categories. If necessary, though, you can restore the database by running the create_db.sql script again as described in the appendix.

12. If the formatting of your page isn't exactly like the one above, don't worry about that. The focus here is on web programming, not HTML and CSS.

Refactor the Product Catalog application

13. Open the product_list.php and product_view.php files in the product_catalog directory. Note that these files use the same code in the <div> tag for the sidebar.

14. Create a file named sidebar.php in the view directory, and copy all the code for the sidebar <div> tag from the product_list.php file to the sidebar.php file. Then, replace the code for the sidebar <div> tag in the product_list.php and product_view.php files with the appropriate include statements.

15. Test these changes to make sure your refactoring works.

6

How to test and debug a PHP application

As you build a PHP application, you need to test it to make sure that it performs as expected. Then, if there are any problems, you need to debug your application to correct any problems. This chapter shows you how to do that using just a text editor and your browser. But it also shows how using an IDE like NetBeans can make debugging easier.

An introduction to testing and debugging **190**
Typical test phases for a PHP application 190
The three types of errors that can occur 190
Common PHP errors 192
An easy way to trace the execution of your PHP code 194
How to debug with xDebug and NetBeans **196**
How to set and remove breakpoints 196
How to step through code 198
How to inspect variables 198
How to inspect the stack trace 200
Perspective **202**

An introduction to testing and debugging

When you *test* an application, you run it to make sure that it works correctly. As you test the application, you try every possible combination of input data and user actions to be certain that the application works in every case. In other words, the goal of testing is to make an application *fail*.

When you *debug* an application, you fix the errors (*bugs*) that you discover during testing. Each time you fix a bug, you test again to make sure that the change that you made didn't affect any other aspect of the application.

Typical test phases for a PHP application

When you test an application, you typically do so in phases, like the three that are summarized in figure 6-1.

In the first phase, as you test the user interface, you should visually check the controls to make sure they're displayed properly with the correct text. Then, you should make sure that all the keys and controls work correctly. For instance, you should test the Tab key and Enter key as well as the operation of check boxes and drop-down lists.

In the second phase, you should test the application with valid data. To start, you can enter data that you would expect a user to enter. Before you're done, though, you should enter valid data that tests all of the limits of the application.

In the third phase, you go all out to make the application fail by testing every combination of invalid data and user action that you can think of. That should include random actions like pressing the Enter key or clicking the mouse at the wrong time.

The three types of errors that can occur

As you test an application, there are three types of errors that can occur. These errors are described in figure 6-1.

Since *syntax errors* prevent your application from running, they are the easiest to find and fix. If you're using an IDE, it often identifies these types of errors before you run the application. Otherwise, the PHP interpreter isn't able to parse the script, so it displays an appropriate error message.

Runtime errors don't violate the syntax rules, but they cause the PHP interpreter to display errors. These errors may be warnings that don't stop execution of the script, or they may be fatal errors that stop the execution of the script. Either way, the error message that's displayed usually can help you to find and fix the error.

Logic errors can come from many places, and they are often the most difficult to find and fix. A mistake in a calculation or incorrect handling of a user action are just two of the ways that logic errors can creep into your applications. For instance, the Product Discount application in this figure has a logic error. Can you tell what it is?

The Product Discount application with a logic error

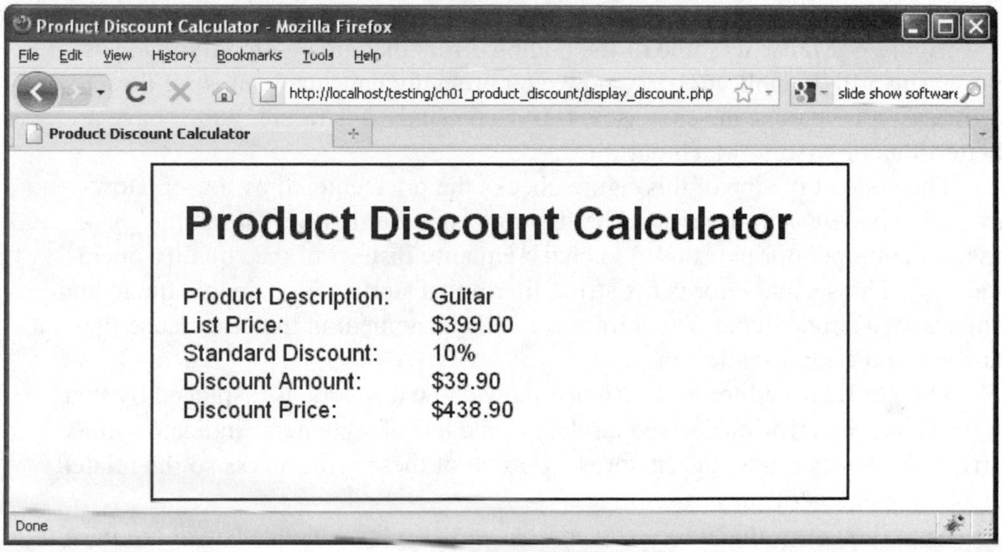

The goal of testing

- To find all errors before the application is put into production.

The goal of debugging

- To fix all errors before the application is put into production.

Three test phases

- Check the user interface to make sure that it works correctly.
- Test the application with valid input data to make sure the results are correct.
- Test the application with invalid data or unexpected user actions. Try everything you can think of to make the application fail.

The three types of errors that can occur

- *Syntax errors* violate the rules for how PHP statements must be written. These errors cause the PHP interpreter to display an error and to stop execution of the script.
- *Runtime errors* don't violate the syntax rules, but they cause the PHP interpreter to display an error that may or may not stop execution of the script.
- *Logic errors* are statements that don't cause syntax or runtime errors, but produce the wrong results.

Description

- To *test* a PHP application, you run it to make sure that it works properly no matter what combinations of valid or invalid data you enter or what sequence of controls you use.
- When you *debug* an application, you find and fix all of the errors (*bugs*) that you find when you test the application.

Figure 6-1 An introduction to testing and debugging

Common PHP errors

Figure 6-2 presents some of the coding errors that are commonly made as you write a PHP application. By now, you probably have made most of these errors as you've done the exercises. But if you study this figure, you'll have a better idea of what to watch out for.

The code at the top of this figure checks the price entered by a user. However, this code has three errors. The first one is in the first line. Here, the assignment operator (=) is used to check equality instead of the equality operator (==). The second error is the string literal that starts with a double quote and ends with a single quote. The third error is the statement in the else clause that doesn't end with a semicolon.

The NetBeans editor in this figure shows how this code is displayed by that IDE. Here, the error marks (red circles) to the left of statements indicate syntax errors. In this example, the cursor is over one of these error marks so the related error message is displayed.

Note, however, that these error marks aren't on the statements that are in error. This shows that some errors aren't correctly identified by NetBeans. In that case, you need to look at the statements above the error marks to see what code might be causing the errors. As you fix those errors, the error marks on the statements below will disappear. In most cases, though, NetBeans will mark your errors as you enter a statement so you can correct them right away.

PHP code that contains errors

```php
// validate the list price entry
if ( $list_price = '' ) {
    $error = "List price is a required field.';
} else if ( !is_numeric($list_price) )  {
    $error = 'List price must be a valid number.';
} else {
    $error = ''
}
```

The PHP code that contains errors in NetBeans

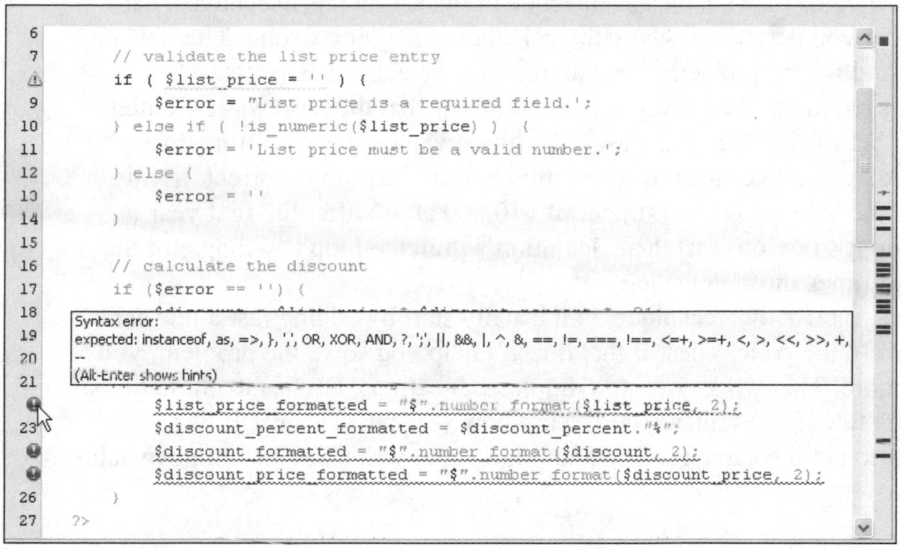

Common syntax errors

- Misspelling keywords.
- Forgetting an opening or closing parenthesis, bracket, brace, or comment character.
- Forgetting to end a PHP statement with a semicolon.
- Forgetting an opening or closing quotation mark.
- Not using the same opening and closing quotation mark.

Problems with variable names

- Misspelling or incorrectly capitalizing a variable name.
- Using a keyword as a variable name.

Problems with values

- Not checking that a value is the right data type before processing it. For example, you expect the user to enter a number, but the user enters a name instead.
- Using one equal sign instead of two when testing for equality.

Figure 6-2   Common PHP errors

An easy way to trace the execution of your PHP code

When you *trace* the execution of an application, you add statements to your code that display messages or variable values at key points in the code. This is typically done to help you find the cause of a logic error.

If, for example, you can't figure out why the future value that's calculated by the Future Value application is incorrect, you can insert echo statements into the code for the application as shown in figure 6-3. These statements display the values for two of the variables as the code in the for loop is executed. That should help you determine where the calculation is going wrong. Then, when you find and fix the problem, you can remove the echo statements.

In this example, the tracing statements show that the loop was executed the right number of times. It also shows the future value after each time through the loop so you can make sure the calculation within the loop is correct. In this example, the value of an investment of $10,000 at 5% after the first year is $60,000 so it's obvious that the calculation within the loop is wrong, not the number of times through the loop.

When you use this technique, you usually start by adding just a few echo statements to the code. Then, if that doesn't help you solve the problem, you can add more. This works well for simple applications, but has its limitations. In the next few figures, then, you'll learn how you can use an IDE like NetBeans to get the same result without having to write and then remove echo statements.

PHP with echo statements that trace the execution of the code

```
// calculate the future value
$future_value = $investment;
echo '$future_value: ' . $future_value . '<br />';
echo '$interest_rate: ' . $interest_rate . '<br />';
echo '$years: ' . $years . '<br />';
echo 'For loop for calculating future value is starting...<br /><br />';
for ($i = 1; $i <= $years; $i++) {
    $future_value = ($future_value + ($future_value * $interest_rate));
    echo '$i: ' . $i . '<br />';
    echo '$future_value: ' . $future_value . '<br />';
}
```

The data displayed in a browser

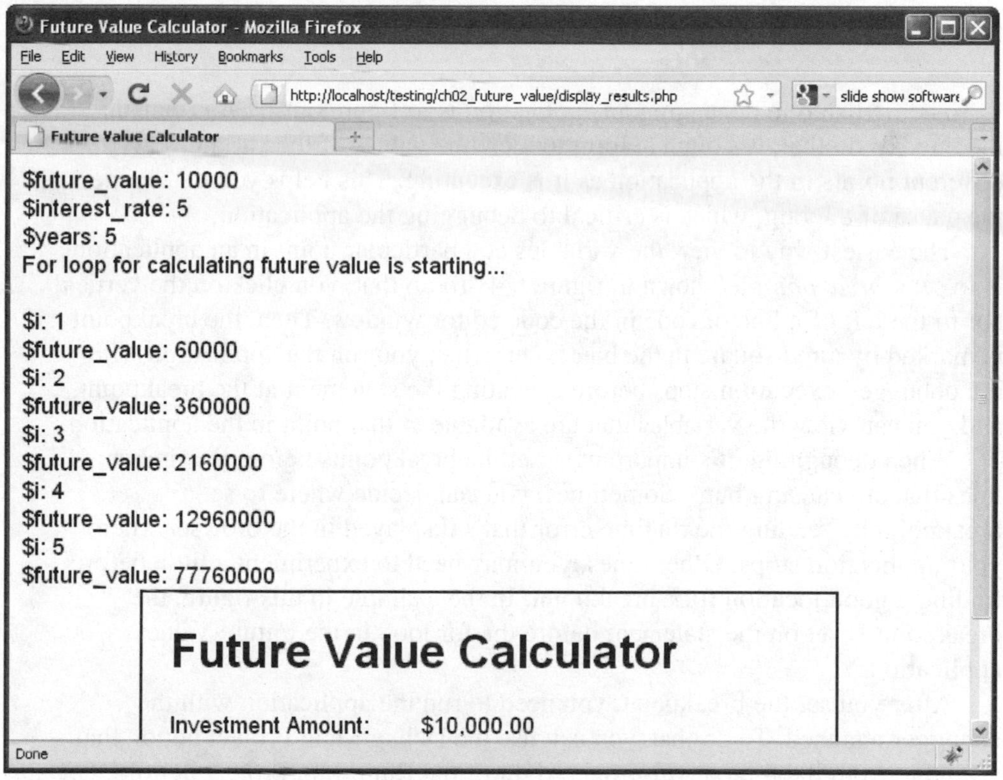

Description

- An easy way to *trace* the execution of a PHP application is to insert echo statements at key points in the code.

- The echo statements can display the values of variables or display messages that indicate what portion of the code is being executed.

- When you see an incorrect value displayed, there is a good chance that you have a logic error between the current echo statement and the previous one.

Figure 6-3   An easy way to trace the execution of your PHP code

How to debug with xDebug and NetBeans

XAMPP includes a powerful debugging tool, or *debugger*, named xDebug that you can use with an IDE such as NetBeans. Before you can use xDebug with NetBeans, however, you must configure xDebug as described in the appendix.

The topics that follow show you how to use this debugger with NetBeans. If you aren't using NetBeans, you can of course skip these topics. But if you're interested in what an IDE can do, you may want to read them anyway.

How to set and remove breakpoints

The first step in debugging an application is to figure out what is causing the bug. To do that, it's often helpful to view the values of the variables at different points in the application as it is executing. This helps you determine the cause of the bug, which is critical to debugging the application.

The easiest way to view the variables at a particular point in an application is to set a *breakpoint* as shown in figure 6-4. To do that, you click on the vertical bar to the left of a line of code in the code editor window. Then, the breakpoint is marked by a red square in the bar. Later, when you run the application with the debugger, execution stops before executing the statement at the breakpoint, and you can view the variables that are available at that point in the application.

When debugging, it's important to set the breakpoints before the line or lines that are causing bugs. Sometimes, you can decide where to set a breakpoint by reading the runtime error that's displayed in the browser when your application stops. Other times, you may need to experiment a little before finding a good location for a breakpoint. In the example in this figure, the breakpoint is set on the statement before the for loop in the Future Value application.

After you set the breakpoint, you need to run the application with the debugger attached. To do that, you can use the Debug Main Project button that's available from the toolbar (just to the right of the Run Main Project button). Or, if you want to debug a project that isn't the main project, you can right-click on the project folder in the Projects tab and select the Debug command.

When you run an application with the debugger, NetBeans displays the debugging windows and buttons that are shown in the next figure. After you run the application with the debugger, the breakpoints remain where you set them. If you want to remove a breakpoint, you can do that by clicking on the red square for the breakpoint.

A code editor window with a breakpoint

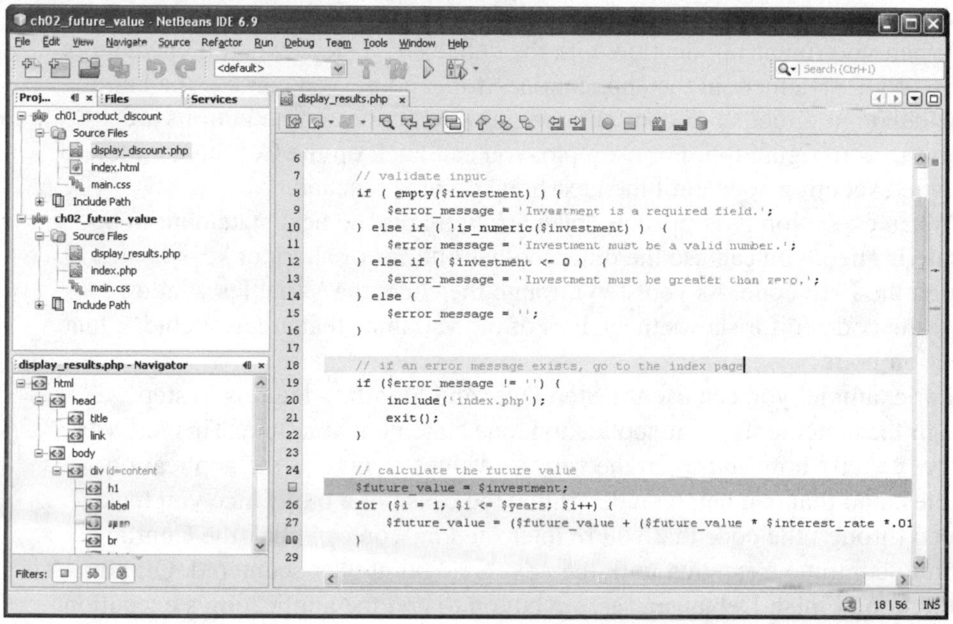

Description

- A *breakpoint* is indicated by a small red square that's placed in the bar to the left of the line of code.

- To set a breakpoint, open the file and click on the vertical bar to the left of the line that contains a statement.

- To remove a breakpoint, click on it.

- Once you set a breakpoint, you can use the Debug Main Project button on the toolbar to begin debugging. This works much like the Run Main Project button, except that it allows you to debug the application.

- To debug a project that isn't the main project, right-click on the project and select the Debug command.

- When you begin debugging, NetBeans may display a dialog box that asks you what you want to debug. If so, you can debug your PHP code by selecting the "Server side PHP" option and clicking the Debug button.

Figure 6-4   How to set and remove breakpoints

How to step through code

When you run an application with the debugger, it stops when it encounters the first PHP statement in the application. At this point, you can use the buttons in the debugging toolbar to continue program execution. These buttons are summarized in figure 6-5. For example, you can click on the Continue button to continue executing code until the next breakpoint is reached.

When execution is stopped, a green arrow marks the next statement to be executed. Then, you can use the other toolbar buttons or shortcut keys to step through the PHP code. As you step through the code, the Variables window below the code editor shows the values of the variables that are available at that execution point.

For example, you can use the Step Over and Step Into buttons to step through the statements in an application, one statement at a time. This lets you observe exactly how and when the variable values change as the application executes, and that can help you determine the cause of a bug. Once you have stepped through the code that you're interested in, you can click the Continue button to continue execution until the next breakpoint is encountered. Or, you can click the Finish Debugger Session button to end the application's execution.

As you step through a program, you will need to switch to the browser whenever the browser requires user entries. Then, after you make those entries and click the appropriate link or button, you will need to switch back to NetBeans to continue stepping through the code.

How to inspect variables

When you set breakpoints and step through code, the Variables window automatically displays the variables that are available. In the example in this figure, the execution point is in the display_results.php file. As a result, all of the variables for this file are available.

Whenever the Variables window is open, you can also view the superglobal variables because they're always available. To do that, you can expand the variable named Superglobals by clicking on the plus sign to its left. Then, you can view a list of the superglobal variables including the $_GET and $_POST arrays, and you can expand these variables to view the values that they contain.

A debugging session with variables displayed

The toolbar buttons and shortcut keys for stepping through the code

Button	Shortcut key	Description
Debug Main Project	Ctrl+F5	Start the debugger for the main project.
Continue	F5	Run until the next breakpoint is reached.
Step Into	F7	Step through the code, one statement at a time.
Step Over	F8	Same as Step Into, but doesn't step through functions.
Step Out	Ctrl+F7	Step out of a function that you've stepped into.
Stop Debugger Function	Shift+F5	Stop the debugger.

Description

- When you begin a debugging session, NetBeans stops on the first PHP statement that it encounters. At this point, you can use the buttons in the debugging toolbar to continue program execution.

- When the browser for the application requires user actions or entries, you need to switch to the browser, do the action or make the entries, and switch back to NetBeans.

- When a breakpoint is reached, program execution is stopped before the line is executed.

- In the code editor window, the arrow shows the line that will be executed next.

- The Variables window shows the values of the variables that are currently available.

- If a variable like the Superglobals variable contains other variables, you can view the values within that variable by clicking its plus sign.

Figure 6-5   How to step through code and inspect variables

How to inspect the stack trace

When you're debugging, it's sometimes helpful to view the *stack trace*, which is a list of functions in the reverse order in which they were called. To do that with NetBeans, you can use the Call Stack window as shown in figure 6-6.

When you display this window, you can click on any of the functions in the call stack to display the function and highlight the line of code that called the next function. This opens a new code editor window if necessary. Although this isn't of much use in a small application that doesn't use many functions, this can be useful when you're debugging a large application.

A debugging session with a stack trace displayed

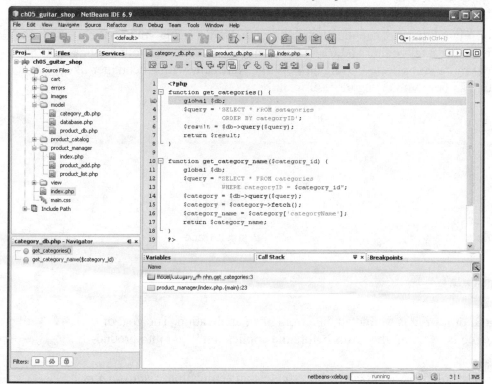

Description

- The Call Stack window shows the *stack trace*, which is a list of functions in the reverse order in which they were called.

- You can click on any of these functions to display the code for the function in a code editor window and to display the variables for that function in the Variables window.

Figure 6-6   How to inspect the stack trace

Perspective

For relatively simple applications, you can test and debug your applications by using a text editor and tracing statements. However, as your applications get more complicated, using an IDE like NetBeans with a debugger like xDebug can help you debug more efficiently.

Terms

test	logic error
debug	trace
bug	debugger
syntax error	breakpoint
runtime error	stack trace

Summary

- The goal of *testing* is to find all the errors in an application. The goal of *debugging* is to fix all the errors before the application is put into production.

- Three types of errors can occur when you test an application: *syntax errors*, *runtime errors*, and *logic errors*.

- You can *trace* the execution of an application by inserting echo statements at appropriate points. These statements can display messages that indicate what's happening or the values of variables.

- XAMPP includes a *debugger* known as xDebug that can be used with an IDE like NetBeans.

- When you use a debugger, you can set *breakpoints*, step through the code one statement at a time, and inspect the values of the variables that are available at each step.

- When you use a debugger, you can get a *stack trace* that lists the functions in the reverse order in which they were called.

Exercise 6-1   Trace with echo statements

In this exercise, you'll use echo statements to trace the execution of the Future Value application.

1. Open the display_results.php file for the Future Value application that's stored in the ex_starts/ch06_ex1 directory.

2. Add echo statements like those in figure 6-3 to trace the execution of the code. Then, run the application to see how the echo statements work.

Exercise 6-2   Use NetBeans to step through the Future Value application

In this exercise, you'll use NetBeans with xDebug to set a breakpoint and step through the Future Value application of chapter 2. Before you do that, though, be sure you have configured xDebug to work with NetBeans as described in the appendix.

1. Start NetBeans and open the ch06_ex2 application in the ex_starts directory. Then, open the display_results.php file in the editor.

2. Set a breakpoint in the display_results.php file on the statement before the for loop that calculates the future value.

3. Right-click on the project and select the Debug command to begin debugging. This should stop the application at the first PHP statement it encounters. Then, click on the Step Into button repeatedly to step through the code until the first web page is displayed.

4. Switch to the browser to view the first page. Then, enter valid values and click on the Calculate button. The application should stop at the next PHP statement it encounters.

5. Switch to NetBeans and click on the Step Into button to execute three statements. Then, click on the Variables tab to display the current variables.

6. Click on the plus sign of the Superglobal variable in the Variables tab, and then on the plus sign for the _POST array. That will display the values of the three user entries that were passed to the server.

7. Click on the Continue button to continue to the breakpoint that you set. Then, use the Step Into button to execute the loop. Note how the variables in the Variables tab change as you execute the loop.

8. Click on the Continue button to finish the calculation and display the next web page. To view this page, switch to your browser.

9. Run the application again and experiment with the Step Into, Step Over, and Step Out buttons as you step through the code of the application. At each step, notice the values that are displayed in the Variables tab.

10. When you're through experimenting, remove the breakpoint, click on the Finish Debugger Session button, and close the project.

Exercise 6-3 Use NetBeans to step through the Guitar Shop application

In this exercise, you'll use NetBeans with xDebug to set a breakpoint and step through the Guitar Shop application of chapter 5. This will help you understand the flow of control in an MVC application.

1. Start NetBeans, and open the ch06_ex3 application that's in the ex_starts directory.

2. Open the index.php file in the product_manager directory. Then, set a break point on its first statement.

3. Run the debugger and step through the application. Note how the required files are opened in the text editor as you do that.

4. When you're through experimenting, end the debugging session, remove the breakpoint, and close the project.

Section 2

Master PHP programming

Most of the chapters in this section expand upon the basic PHP skills that you learned in section 1. In chapter 7, for example, you'll learn more about getting input from the user and displaying output. In chapter 8, you'll learn more about coding control statements like if, while, and for statements. In chapter 11, you'll learn more about working with arrays. And so on. These chapters should answer any questions you have about the PHP basics.

In addition, some of the chapters in this section present new skills. In chapter 12, for example, you'll learn how to work with sessions and cookies. In chapter 14, you'll learn how to create and use your own objects. And in chapter 15, you'll learn how to use regular expressions, handle exceptions, and validate the data that's entered into a form.

When you finish the chapters in this section, you'll have all the PHP programming skills that you'll need on the job. Then, section 3 will show you the MySQL skills that you'll need on the job, including two ways to use PHP to work with a MySQL database.

7

How to work with form data

In chapter 2, you learned simple techniques for getting data from a form and for displaying data on a web page. Now, this chapter reviews these techniques. It also presents some new techniques for getting data from the controls on a form and for displaying data on a web page.

How to get data from a form **208**
How to get data from text boxes, password boxes, and hidden fields 208
How to get data from a radio button 210
How to get data from a check box 212
How to get data from an array of check boxes 214
How to get data from a drop-down list 216
How to get data from a list box 218
How to get data from a text area 220

How to display data on a web page **222**
How to format special characters 222
How to format line breaks 224
How to display data with echo and print statements 226

Perspective **228**

How to get data from a form

An HTML form can contain several types of controls such as text boxes, radio buttons, check boxes, drop-down lists, and text areas. As you learned in chapter 2, when a form that contains these controls is submitted to the server, the data in the controls is passed to the server as an array of name/value pairs. The topics that follow show how to use these controls in your web applications.

How to get data from text boxes, password boxes, and hidden fields

Figure 7-1 shows you how use three types of controls to get text input. These controls are all created using the HTML <input> tag.

Text boxes, also known as *text fields*, are the most common type of control for a form. Names, addresses, and phone numbers are just a few of the types of data you can collect with a text field.

Password boxes, also known as a *password fields*, are similar to text fields except that the text isn't displayed on the screen as the user types. Instead, a bullet character is displayed for each character. This type of field is useful for entering sensitive data such as passwords and PIN numbers.

Hidden fields are text fields that are not displayed on the web page. This type of field allows programmers to add hard-coded values to a form. In addition, programmers often use hidden fields to pass data from one web page to another.

When you code the name attribute for a control, you must follow the rules for naming PHP variables except for the initial dollar sign. In this figure, for example, the User Name text box has a name attribute of user_name, and its data gets stored in a variable named $user_name. Although you don't have to use the same name for the variable as for the control, it's considered a good coding practice.

For a text field, you can use the value attribute to provide a default value for the field. Since you usually don't want to supply default values for password fields, this attribute typically isn't used with password fields. However, the value attribute is necessary for hidden fields since the user can't type a value into this type of field.

This figure shows how to get the data from the form using the GET and POST methods. Since the only difference in the code is changing the name of the array from $_GET to $_POST, the rest of the figures in this chapter only show the POST method.

If the form uses the GET method, the browser displays the data for the controls in its URL. Since this isn't secure, you typically use the POST method if the form contains password fields or other sensitive data that you don't want to display in the URL.

Attributes of the HTML <input> tag for getting text input

Attribute	Description
type	Set to "text" to for a text field, "password" for a password field, or "hidden" for a hidden field. The default is "text".
name	The name for the field when the form is submitted.
value	The value for the field. For hidden fields, this attribute must be set for the field to work correctly.

The HTML for three types of fields

```
<input type="text" name="user_name" value="rharris">
<input type="password" name="password">
<input type="hidden" name="action" value="login">
```

The text and password fields in the browser

```
User Name: rharris

Password: ••••••••
```

The URL when using the GET method

```
process_data.php?user_name=rharris&password=s3cr3t72&action=login
```

The PHP for the GET method

```php
<?php
    $user_name = $_GET['user_name'];
    $password = $_GET['password'];
    $action = $_GET['action'];
?>
```

The URL when using the POST method

```
process_data.php
```

The PHP for the POST method

```php
<?php
    $user_name = $_POST['user_name'];
    $password = $_POST['password'];
    $action = $_POST['action'];
?>
```

Description

- A *text box* allows the user to type data into the box.
- A *password box* allows the user to type data into the box, but it obscures the characters typed by the user. This prevents sensitive data from being displayed on the screen.
- A *hidden field* allows the programmer to add additional name/value pairs to the form.
- When specifying the name attribute for controls, follow the PHP rules for naming variables, but don't code a dollar sign at the beginning of the name.
- If the form uses the GET method, the data for the fields is displayed in the URL.

Figure 7-1   How to get data from text boxes, password boxes, and hidden fields

How to get data from a radio button

Radio buttons let the user select one option from a group of options. To create a radio button, you use the <input> tag as shown in figure 7-2.

The HTML in this figure displays a group of three radio buttons. This code uses the same name for all three radio buttons. That way, all three radio buttons are in the same group, and the user can only select one of these buttons at a time. In addition, this code sets the checked attribute for the first button to a value of "checked". That way, the first button is selected by default when the browser loads the web page.

Since this HTML sets a default button for the group, one button is always selected, and the name/value pair for the group is always submitted to the server. As a result, you don't need to use the isset function to check whether this name/value pair has been set. In other words, you can use the first PHP example to get the selected value from the radio button group and store that value in a variable named $card_type.

However, if the group doesn't have a default button and the user doesn't select a button, the name/value pair for the group isn't submitted to the server. In that case, you need to use the isset function to check whether the name/value pair has been set. To do that, you can use the second PHP example to get the data from the radio button group.

This example begins by using an if statement with the isset function to check whether the name/value pair for the radio button group has been set in the $_POST array. If so, this code gets the selected value from the radio button group and stores that value in the $card_type variable. Otherwise, it sets the $card_type variable to a value of "unknown".

Attributes of the HTML <input> tag for radio buttons

Attribute	Description
type	Set to "radio" for a radio button.
name	The same name must be used for all radio buttons in a group.
value	The value for a radio button. This attribute is necessary for a radio button to work correctly.
checked	This optional attribute selects the default radio button.

The HTML for three radio buttons in a group

```
<input type="radio" name="card_type" value="visa" checked="checked">
     Visa<br>
<input type="radio" name="card_type" value="mastercard"> MasterCard<br>
<input type="radio" name="card_type" value="discover"> Discover
```

The radio buttons in the browser

The PHP to access a radio button group that has a default button

```
<?php
    $card_type = $_POST['card_type'];
?>
```

The PHP to access a radio button group that doesn't have a default button

```
<?php
    if (isset($_POST['card_type'])) {
        $card_type = $_POST['card_type'];
    } else {
        $card_type = "unknown";
    }
?>
```

Description

- A *radio button* allows the user to select one option from a group of options.
- If none of the radio buttons in the group are selected, the name/value pair for the group is not submitted to the server as part of the form.
- If you code the checked attribute for more than one radio button, the browser selects the last radio button when the page loads.

Figure 7-2   How to get data from a radio button

How to get data from a check box

A *check box* lets the user select an option. To create a check box, you use the <input> tag as shown in figure 7-3.

The HTML in this figure displays three check boxes. Unlike radio buttons, check boxes have different values for the name attribute, and you don't have to set the value attribute. In this figure, the first check box has its checked attribute set so it is checked by default when the web page loads.

In many cases, you don't want to check a check box by default. For instance, you shouldn't check a box indicating that the user wants to be added to a mailing list. That way, if this check box is checked, you're sure that the user checked the box and wants to be added to the mailing list.

The PHP in this figure shows how to process the data for a check box. For each check box, it uses the isset function to return a Boolean value that indicates whether the name/value pair is set in the $_POST array. If the check box has been selected, it is set in the array. As a result, a TRUE value is stored in the variable. Otherwise, a FALSE value is stored in the variable.

Attributes of the HTML <input> tag for check boxes

Attribute	Description
type	Set to "checkbox" for a check box.
name	Different names must be used for each check box. However, if you want to define an array of check boxes, you can use the same name as shown in the next figure.
value	Text used when the check box is selected. This attribute is only necessary if you are working with an array of check boxes as described in the next figure.
checked	This optional attribute selects the check box.

The HTML for three check boxes

```
<input type="checkbox" name="pep" checked="checked"> Pepperoni<br>
<input type="checkbox" name="msh"> Mushrooms<br>
<input type="checkbox" name="olv"> Olives
```

The check boxes in the browser

The PHP to access the check box data

```
<?php
    $pepperoni = isset($_POST['pep']);
    $mushrooms = isset($_POST['msh']);
    $olives = isset($_POST['olv']);
?>
```

Description

- A *check box* allows the user to select an option.
- The isset function returns TRUE if the check box is selected and FALSE if it isn't.

Figure 7-3   How to get data from a check box

How to get data from an array of check boxes

In the last figure, the three check boxes had unique names and were processed separately. However, since these check boxes represented different toppings for a pizza, they are actually related. Also, if the number of toppings grew, it would become cumbersome to process each check box separately.

Fortunately, PHP provides a mechanism that lets you combine the values of multiple check boxes into one array. This lets you use a loop to process related check boxes, which makes your code easier to extend and maintain.

Figure 7-4 shows how to combine the values of several check boxes into an array. To do that, this code uses the same name for all related check boxes. However, it adds an empty pair of brackets to the end of the name to indicate that these check boxes should be stored in an array.

When the data is submitted, PHP creates the array when it reads the first check box name that ends with square brackets. Then, it adds the value for the check box to the array. When it reads another check box with that name, it appends that value to the array as well. When the processing is done, PHP nests the array within the $_GET or $_POST array.

The HTML for this figure shows the three check boxes from the previous figure rewritten as an array of check boxes. Unlike the previous figure, this code includes values for these check boxes. PHP uses these values to identify the check box and indicate that it is checked. Often, this value corresponds to the primary key in a database table. That way, the value can be used to look up more information about the selected check box.

The first PHP example in this figure shows how to access the array. Here, the first statement gets the array named top from the $_POST array and stores it in a variable named $toppings. Then, the next three statements access the first three values in this array. In this figure, only two check boxes have been selected so the array only contains the two values that correspond with those check boxes.

The second PHP example uses a foreach loop to process the check boxes. To start, this code uses an if statement to check whether the array named top has been set in the $_POST array. If so, the top array contains at least one item. As a result, this code gets the array named top from the $_POST array and stores it in the variable named $toppings. Then, this code uses a foreach loop to process each item in the array. Here, this code sends the key and value for each item to the browser. However, any type of processing could be performed here. For example, this code could update the total price of the pizza depending on the selected toppings.

The HTML that stores three related check boxes in an array

```
<input type="checkbox" name="top[]" value="pep"> Pepperoni<br>
<input type="checkbox" name="top[]" value="msh"> Mushrooms<br>
<input type="checkbox" name="top[]" value="olv"> Olives
```

The check boxes in the browser

PHP that accesses the array and its values

```
$toppings = $_POST['top'];     // get the toppings array
$top1 = $toppings[0];          // $top1 is pep
$top2 = $toppings[1];          // $top2 is olv
$top3 = $toppings[2];          // $top3 is not set
```

PHP that uses a loop to process the array

```php
<?php
    if (isset($_POST['top'])) {
        $toppings = $_POST['top'];
        foreach($toppings as $key => $value) {
            echo $key. ' = ' . $value . '<br>';
        }
    } else {
        echo 'No toppings selected.';
    }
?>
```

The message displayed by the browser

```
0 = pep
1 = olv
```

Description

- If a check box name ends with [], PHP adds the check box to an array that's nested in the $_GET or $_POST array. This allows multiple values to be submitted with the same name.

- If none of the check boxes in an array of check boxes is selected, the array name won't be set in the $_GET or $_POST array.

Figure 7-4   How to get data from an array of check boxes

How to get data from a drop-down list

A *drop-down list*, also known as a *single-selection list*, forces the user to select one option from a list. To create a drop-down list, you use the <select> and <option> tags as shown in figure 7-5.

The HTML in this figure creates a drop-down list that lets the user select one of three credit card options. Here, the <select> tag specifies the name of the list. Then, within the <select> tag, the three <option> tags define the options. When the page is rendered by the browser, the code between the opening and closing <option> tags is displayed. When the page is submitted to the server, the value attribute specifies the value that's submitted to the server. For instance, the first option in this figure displays "Visa" in the list and submits "visa" to the server.

The PHP in this figure shows how to get the value of the selected option. Since a drop-down list forces the user to select an option, you don't need to use the isset function to check if the drop-down list has been submitted to the server. As a result, it only takes one statement to get the value for the selected option.

If you don't code the selected attribute for any of the options, the first option is selected by default when the page loads. However, if you want to set a different default option, you can code the selected attribute for that option. For example, to make MasterCard the default option, you could code its <option> tag like this:

```
<option value="mastercard"
        selected="selected">MasterCard<option>
```

For a drop-down list, you should only code the selected attribute for one option. If you do select more than one option, the browser selects the last option that has a selected attribute.

Attributes of the HTML <select> tag for drop-down lists

Attribute	Description
name	The name for the drop-down list.

Attributes of the HTML <option> tag

Attribute	Description
value	The value for the option.
selected	This optional attribute selects the option.

The HTML for a drop-down list

```
<select name="card_type">
    <option value="visa">Visa</option>
    <option value="mastercard">MasterCard</option>
    <option value="discover">Discover</option>
</select>
```

The drop-down list in a browser

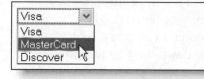

The PHP to access the drop-down list data

```
<?php
    $card_type = $_POST['card_type'];
?>
```

Description

- A *drop-down list* lets the user select one option from a group of options.
- If the selected attribute isn't coded, the first option in the drop-down list is selected by default.

Figure 7-5   How to get data from a drop-down list

How to get data from a list box

A *list box* works similarly to a drop-down list. However, you set the size attribute of the <select> tag to the number of options that you want displayed in the list box. In figure 7-6, for example, the size attribute has been set to 3 for both list boxes so both of these list boxes display three options. Then, if more options are coded, scroll bars are added to the list box so the user can scroll to the other others.

The first HTML example in this figure creates a list box that only allows the user to select one option. This works much like a drop-down list. However, since this list box doesn't specify a default option, the user might not select any option from the list. In that case, the list box isn't submitted as part of the form, and your PHP code should use the isset function to check whether the user has selected an option. Alternately, the HTML can use the selected attribute to set a default option for the list box. Then, the list box is always submitted as part of the form, and you can use the PHP shown in the last figure to get its value.

The second HTML example creates a list box that lets the user select multiple options. To start, the <select> tag includes the multiple attribute. In addition, the name attribute ends with a pair of square brackets ([]). These brackets indicate that the selected values should be stored in an array. As a result, the user can select multiple options by holding down the Ctrl or Shift keys while clicking on the options.

The PHP example in this figure shows how to get the data from a list box that lets the user select multiple items. This code is the same as the code presented in figure 7-4 that processes an array of check boxes.

When you design web forms, you often need to decide what type of control to use. In this figure, for example, the first list box could be used instead of the drop-down list presented in the previous figure. Similarly, the second list box could be used instead of the check boxes presented earlier in this chapter. In the end, you need to choose the approach that you think will work best for the user.

Attributes of the HTML <select> tag for list boxes

Attribute	Description
size	When set to 1 or omitted, a drop-down list displays the options. When set to 2 or more, a list box displays the specified number of options.
multiple	This optional attribute allows the user to select multiple options in the list box. It should only be used if the size attribute has been set to a value of 2 or more.

The HTML for a list box that doesn't allow multiple options

```
<select name="card_type" size="3">
    <option value="visa">Visa</option>
    <option value="mastercard">MasterCard</option>
    <option value="discover">Discover</option>
</select>
```

A list box that doesn't allow multiple options to be selected

The HTML for a list box that allows multiple options to be selected

```
<select name="top[]" size="3" multiple="multiple">
    <option value="pep" selected="selected">Pepperoni</option>
    <option value="msh">Mushrooms</option>
    <option value="olv">Olives</option>
</select>
```

A list box that allows multiple options to be selected

The PHP for a list box that allows multiple options to be selected

```php
<?php
    if (isset($_POST['top'])) {
        $toppings = $_POST['top'];
        foreach ($toppings as $key => $value) {
            echo $key. ' = ' . $value . '<br>'; // '0 = pep' and '1 = msh'
        }
    } else {
        echo 'No toppings selected.';
    }
?>
```

Description

- A *list box* allows the user to select zero or more options from a group of options.
- If a list box allows multiple options to be selected, the list box name must end with [].

Figure 7-6   How to get data from a list box

How to get data from a text area

A *text area* lets the user enter multiple lines of text. To create a text box, you use the <textarea> tag as shown in figure 7-7.

To set the approximate size of the area, you can use the rows and cols attributes. In this figure, for example, the text area is approximately 50 characters wide and 4 lines tall.

To display default text in the text area, you can place the text between the opening and closing <textarea> tags. In this figure, for example, the text area includes default text of "Welcome to PHP and MySQL!"

The PHP example in this figure shows how to get the data from a text area. Since a text area always submits a name/value pair to the server, even if the value is an empty string, you don't need to use the isset function to test for the presence of the name/value pair. As a result, you only need to code a single statement to get the data from a text area.

When the user types in the text area, there are two ways for the user to start a new line. First, if the user types past the end of one line, a *soft return* occurs and the cursor automatically moves to the next line. Second, the user can press the Enter or Return key to insert a *hard return* and move the cursor to the next line.

When the value for the text area is submitted to the server, no special characters are used to identify soft returns. However, special characters are used to identify hard returns. In particular, to identify a hard return, the submitted value may include a carriage return ("\r" in a string or %0D in a URL), a new line ("\n" in a string or %0A in a URL), or both depending on the operating system. In figure 7-9, you'll learn how to use a built-in function to handle hard returns.

Attributes of an HTML <textarea> tag

Attribute	Description
name	The name for the text area.
rows	The approximate number of lines for the text area.
cols	The approximate number of characters for each line in the text area.

The HTML for a text area

```
<textarea name="comment" rows="4" cols="50">Welcome to PHP and MySQL!
</textarea>
```

A text area in the browser

```
Welcome to PHP and MySQL!
```

The URL when using the GET method

When the user includes spaces in the text area

```
process_data.php?comment=Welcome+to+PHP+and+MySQL!
```

When the user presses the Enter or Return key to start a new line

```
process_data.php?comment=Welcome+to%0D%0APHP+and+MySQL!
```

When the user doesn't enter any text

```
process_data.php?comment=
```

The PHP to get the data from the text area

```php
<?php
    $comment = $_POST['comment'];
?>
```

Description

- A *text area* allows the user to enter multiple lines of text.
- To set the default text for a text area, code the default text between the opening and closing <textarea> tags.
- If the user types past the end of the line, a text area uses a *soft return* to start a new line. If the users presses the Enter or Return key, a text area uses a *hard return* to start a new line.
- If the user doesn't enter any text, the name/value pair for the text area is submitted to the server with an empty string for the value.

Figure 7-7   How to get data from a text area

How to display data on a web page

When you use HTML controls such as text boxes and text areas, you can never be sure what the user will enter into these controls. That's why this topic begins by looking at two formatting issues that arise when working with text that was entered by a user. Then, this topic describes two statements that you can use to send data to the browser.

How to format special characters

If you are familiar with HTML, you should know that you can't type every character into a web page. For example, the less than sign (<) and the greater than sign (>) are used to mark the start and end of HTML tags. As a result, to display these characters on a web page, you have to use the *HTML character entities* for these characters.

Some of these character entities are summarized in the second table in figure 7-8. For example, to display the less than sign (<), you have to code its HTML character entity (<). Otherwise, the browser interprets the less than sign as the beginning of an HTML tag.

So, what happens if the user enters special HTML characters in a control on a form? For example, what happens if the user enters "Welcome to <i> PHP</i> and MySQL" in a text area?

Well, there are two ways to handle this situation. First, you can let the browser italicize the text within the <i> tag. In this case, the <i> tags aren't displayed in the browser. Second, you can display the text exactly as it was entered by the user. In this case, the browser displays the <i> tags instead of italicizing the text. As a web developer, you have to decide how you want to handle this type of problem.

If you want to convert special characters to their HTML character entities, you can use the htmlspecialchars function that's shown in this figure. As the syntax summary shows, this function provides for four parameters. Of these parameters, the first parameter is required, and the other three are optional.

The first three parameters are relatively easy to understand. They provide the name of the string to be processed, a constant that specifies how quotation marks should be handled, and a code that specifies the character set to be used. However, the fourth parameter, the double_encode parameter, is more difficult to understand.

This parameter lets you determine if you want to double encode the ampersands in HTML entities. Let's say, for example, that the user has entered "Apples < Oranges". By default, the htmlspecialchars function encodes the ampersand in the HTML character entity. As a result, this string becomes "Apples &lt; Oranges" and this character entity (<) is displayed in the browser. However, if you set the double_encode parameter to FALSE, the ampersand isn't double encoded, and the character represented by the character entity (<) is displayed in the browser.

Syntax of the htmlspecialchars function

```
htmlspecialchars($string[, $quote_style[, $charset[, $double_encode]]])
```

Parameters of the htmlspecialchars function

Parameter	Description
$string	The string to convert. This parameter is required.
$quote_style	Specifies how to convert single and double quotes to their HTML entities. The ENT_COMPAT constant, which is the default, only converts double quotes. The ENT_QUOTES constant converts single and double quotes. The ENT_NOQUOTES constant doesn't convert single or double quotes.
$charset	Specifies the character set of the $string parameter. The default is "ISO-8859-1".
$double_encode	A Boolean value that specifies whether to double encode character entities. The default is TRUE. As a result, by default, character entities are double encoded.

Common HTML character entities

Character	Character entity	Character	Character entity
&	&amp;	"	&quot;
<	&lt;	'	&#039;
>	&gt;	Non-breaking space	

A double-encoded less than entity

```
&amp;lt;
```

The text entered by the user

```
Welcome to <i>PHP</i> and MySQL!
```

PHP that converts special characters to character entities

```php
<?php
    $comment = $_POST['comment'];
    $comment = htmlspecialchars($comment, ENT_COMPAT, 'ISO-8859-1', false);
?>
<p><?php echo $comment; ?></p>
```

The data displayed in the browser

Welcome to <i>PHP</i> and MySQL!

Description

- An HTML *character entity* lets you display some special characters on a web page.
- The htmlspecialchars function converts some special characters into character entities.

Figure 7-8   How to format special characters

How to format line breaks

When a user enters hard returns in a text area, you may want to render those hard returns in the browser. To do that, you can use the nl2br function as shown in figure 7-9. This function converts new line characters to HTML line breaks.

By default, this function insert line breaks that use the XHTML syntax (<br />). As a result, if you don't supply the optional second parameter, this function uses the XHTML syntax. If you want to insert line breaks that use the HTML syntax (<br>), though, you can specify FALSE as the second parameter.

Syntax of the nl2br function

```
nl2br($string[, $is_xhtml])
```

Parameters of the nl2br function

Parameter	Description
$string	The string to convert. This parameter is required.
$is_xhtml	A Boolean value that indicates whether to use the XHTML syntax ( ) or the HTML syntax ( ) for a line break. The default is TRUE.

The text entered into the text area

Welcome to
PHP and MySQL!

PHP that converts line break characters to HTML line break tags

```php
<?php
    $comment = $_POST['comment'];
    $comment = nl2br($comment, false);    // use <br> tags, not <br /> tags
?>
<p><?php echo $comment; ?></p>
```

The data displayed in the browser

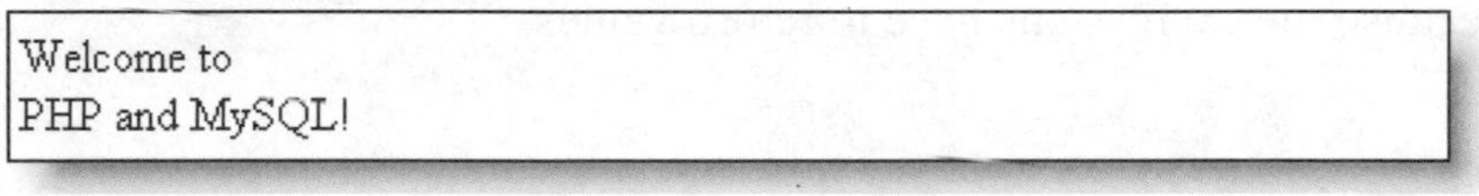

Welcome to
PHP and MySQL!

Description

- The nl2br function converts new line characters in a string to HTML <br> tags.
  This lets you display the line breaks on a web page.

Figure 7-9   How to format line breaks

How to display data with echo and print statements

In chapter 2, you learned how to use the echo statement to send data to the web browser. Now, figure 7-10 shows the full syntax of the echo statement. In addition, it shows how to use the print statement, which works similarly to the echo statement. If you compare the echo and print statements, you'll notice some advantages to each statement.

The advantage of the echo statement is that it accepts multiple parameters. To work with multiple parameters, you separate the parameters with commas. However, if you use multiple parameters, you can't use parentheses.

The advantage of the print statement is that it always returns a value of 1. As a result, you can use it as part of an expression. This is illustrated by the two print statements that are embedded in the last example. In this case, the parentheses are still optional, but it's considered a good practice to include them since they usually make your code more readable.

If the last example is confusing, that's because it uses the conditional operator, which isn't presented until the next chapter. This statement begins by evaluating the conditional expression that's in the first set of parentheses. If this expression is TRUE, the code evaluates the expression that's coded between the ? and : operators. This prints some data to the browser and returns a value of 1. Otherwise, this expression evaluates the expression that's coded after the : operator. Again, this prints some data to the browser and returns a value of 1. If these print statements were replaced with echo statements, this code would cause an error because the expressions have to return values.

The echo statement

Syntax
```
echo $var1
echo($var1)
echo $var1 [, $var2 ...]
```

Examples
```
echo 'Welcome to PHP and MySQL!';
echo 'Name: ' . $name;
echo('Name: ' . $name);
echo 'Cost: $', $cost;
```

The print statement

Syntax
```
print $var1
print($var1)
```

Examples
```
print 'Welcome to PHP and MySQL!';
print 'Name: ' . $name;
print('Name: ' . $name);
```

Using print in an expression
```
<?php
    ($age >= 18) ? print('Can vote.') : print('Cannot vote.');
?>
```

Description

- The echo and print statements send strings to the web page. Non-string values are converted to strings before they are sent to the web page.

- The echo statement can accept one or more string values, but the print statement can only accept one value.

- The parentheses are optional for both the echo and print statements. However, if you are providing multiple values to the echo statement, you must omit the parentheses.

- The echo statement doesn't return a value and cannot be used as part of an expression. However, the print statement returns a value of 1 so it can be used as part of an expression.

- The echo and print statements aren't functions. They are part of the PHP language definition.

Figure 7-10   How to display data with echo and print statements

Perspective

Now that you've finished this chapter, you should understand how to get the data from the controls on a form. Since this data is always submitted to the server as string data, chapter 9 presents more details about processing strings. But first, chapter 8 presents all of the essential skills for coding control structures.

Terms

text box	drop-down list
text field	single-selection list
password box	list box
password field	text area
hidden field	soft return
radio button	hard return
check box	HTML character entity

Summary

- The data that has been entered into the controls of a form is sent to the server as string data in an array of name/value pairs.

- *Text boxes* are used to get simple user entries. *Password boxes* are used to get entries that are displayed as bullets. And *hidden fields* are used to pass data to the server that the user hasn't entered.

- *Radio buttons* let the user select only one option from a group of options, while *check boxes* let the user select independent options. To get data from several related check boxes, you can set them up so the data is returned in an array.

- A *drop-down list* lets the user select one option from a group of options. A *list box* lets the user select one or more options from a group of options.

- A *text area* lets the user enter multiple lines of text that can include *hard returns* and *soft returns*.

- You can use the htmlspecialchars function to control the way special characters that were entered by the user are displayed in the browser. You can use the nl2br function to convert new line characters to <br> tags in either HTML or XHTML format.

- You can use either the PHP echo or print statements to send data to the browser.

Exercise 7-1   Get input and display output

In this exercise, you will write the PHP code that gets input from a form and displays output.

Open and test the application

1. Start the Firefox browser and run the application in the ex_starts/ch07_ex1 directory. To do that, you can use this URL:

   `http://localhost/ex_starts/ch07_ex1/`

   This should display a form that has a variety of controls.

2. Enter some data and click on the Submit button. Note that this only displays the data that you entered for the email address.

Write the code that gets and displays the data entered by the user

3. Open the index.php file for this application and review the code. Note the names that are used for the various input controls.

4. Open the display_results.php file for this application and review the code. Note that most of the code that gets data from the controls and displays it is missing.

5. Add the code that gets the data from the controls on the first page and displays this data on the second page.

6. For the radio buttons, display a value of "Unknown" if the user doesn't select a radio button.

7. For the check box, display a value of "Yes" or "No" depending on whether the user has selected the check box.

8. For all fields that allow the user to type text into the field, make sure to convert special characters into HTML entities before displaying that data on the second page as described in figure 7-8.

9. For the comment field, make sure to convert new line characters to <br /> tags so the web page can display new line characters correctly.

10. Test the application to make sure it works correctly. To do that, you can test text fields with special characters such as the ampersand (&), and you can press the Enter key in the comments field to enter a new line character.

Exercise 7-2 Enhance the Future Value application

In this exercise, you will enhance the Future Value application of chapter 2 so it uses drop-down lists instead of text boxes.

Open and test the application

1. Start the Firefox browser and run the application in the ex_starts/ch07_ex2 directory. This should display the first page of Future Value application that's similar to the one presented in chapter 2. Note that this page displays three default values in the three text boxes.

2. Click the Calculate button to perform the calculation. Note that this displays the correct future value calculation on the second page.

Write the code that gets and displays the data entered by the user

3. Open the index.php file for this application and review the code. Note the names that are used for the three text boxes.

4. Modify the code so it uses drop-down lists instead of text boxes for the first two entries.

5. For the investment amount, the drop-down list should display values from 10,000 to 50,000 incremented by 10,000. To do this, you can use a for loop that creates the HTML for the drop-down list.

   If you have any trouble with this, you may want to look ahead to the last example in figure 8-11 of the next chapter. Or, you can come back to this after you read chapter 8.

6. For the yearly interest rate, the drop-down list should display values from 4 to 12 incremented by .5.

7. Test the application to make sure it works correctly.

8

How to code control statements

In chapter 2, you were introduced to the if, while, and for statements. Now, you'll learn more about coding these control statements. This should clear up any questions you have about using these statements. You'll also learn how to code switch, do-while, break, and continue statements.

How to code conditional expressions **232**
How to use the equality and identity operators 232
How to use the relational operators 234
How to use the logical operators 236
How to code the selection structures **238**
How to code if statements with else clauses 238
How to code if statements with else if clauses 240
How to use the conditional operator 242
How to code switch statements 244
How to use a switch statement in the controller 246
How to code the iteration structures **248**
How to code while loops 248
How to code do-while loops 250
How to code for loops 252
How to use the break and continue statements 254
Perspective **256**

How to code conditional expressions

In chapter 2, you learned the basics of writing conditional expressions. In this topic, you'll learn more about using the equality, relational, and logical operators.

How to use the equality and identity operators

Figure 8-1 summarizes the use of the equality and identity operators in conditional expressions. For simple comparisons, the two *equality operators* are sufficient. If, for example, you want to test whether a numeric variable contains a certain number, the equal operator works just fine.

When the tests are more complex, however, unexpected results may occur when you use the equality operators. To illustrate, this figure lists several equality expressions that don't produce the results you might expect.

The problem is that the equality operators perform *type coercion*. This means that if different types of data are being compared, the values are converted to the same data type before the comparison takes place. For example, in the test 3 == "3", the string "3" is converted to the number 3 and then the comparison is done so the result is TRUE.

The figure shows the rules that PHP uses when performing type coercion. There are additional rules that apply when one of the operands is an array or an object, but these rules are covered in the appropriate chapters later on.

These problems can be avoided by using the *identity operators*, because the identity operators don't perform type coercion. Then, if two values of different types are compared, the result is always FALSE. In fact, if you were to replace all of the equality operators in the table of unusual results with identity operators, all of the results would be FALSE.

When you use the equality operators, it's usually best to perform your own data conversions before you do the comparisons. That way, you're sure that you're comparing values of the same type.

The equality operators

Operator	Description	Example
==	Equal	`$last_name == 'Harris'`
!=	Not equal	`$months != 0`
<>	Not equal	`$months <> 0`

PHP Type Coercion Rules

Operand 1	Operand 2	Action
NULL	String	Convert NULL to an empty string and compare as two strings.
Boolean or NULL	Not a string	Convert both to Boolean and compare.
String	Number	Convert string to a number and compare as two numbers.
Numeric string	Numeric string	Convert strings to numbers and compare as two numbers.
Text string	Text string	Compare strings as if using the strcmp function.

Unusual results with the equality operator

Expression	Result	Description
`null == ''`	true	NULL is converted to the empty string.
`null == false`	true	NULL is converted to FALSE.
`null == 0`	true	NULL is equal to any value that evaluates to FALSE.
`false == '0'`	true	Empty strings and "0" are converted to FALSE.
`true == 'false'`	true	All other strings are converted to true.
`3.5 == "\t3.5 mi"`	true	The string is converted to a number and then compared.
`INF == 'INF'`	false	The string "INF" is converted to 0.
`0 == ''`	true	The empty string is converted to 0.
`0 == 'harris'`	true	Any string that is not numeric is converted to 0.

The identity operators

Operator	Description	Example
===	Equal	`$last_name === 'Harris'`
!==	Not equal	`$months !== 0`

Description

- The *equality operators* perform *type coercion*. Type coercion converts data from one type to another. PHP follows the rules shown above when performing type coercion.

- When converting to the Boolean type, the following values are equivalent to FALSE: NULL, 0, 0.0, "0", an empty string, and an empty array. All other values are equivalent to TRUE.

- The *identity operators* do not perform type coercion. If the two operands are of different types, the result is always FALSE. As a result, all of the expressions listed above for the equality operator would return FALSE for the identity operator.

Figure 8-1   How to use the equality and identity operators

How to use the relational operators

Figure 8-2 summarizes the relational operators that were briefly introduced in chapter 3. Like the equality operators, the *relational operators* perform type coercion when the two values are of different types. For instance, when you compare strings and numbers, the string value is converted to a numerical value before the comparison takes place. This is illustrated by the second table in this figure. As a result, you often need to make sure that you're comparing two values of the same type before you use these operators.

When you use these operators to compare two strings, the strings are compared using the same rules as the strcmp function described in the next chapter. That is, the comparison is case-sensitive and uppercase letters come before lowercase letters so "Orange" comes before (is less than) "apple". Since that usually isn't what you want, you should normally use the string comparison functions instead of the relational operators when you're comparing string values.

Finally, this figure shows some unusual results that you get when you use the relational operators. Here again, the results are unusual because of the type coercion done by the relational operators.

The relational operators

Operator	Description	Example
<	Less than	`$age < 18`
<=	Less than or equal	`$investment <= 0`
>	Greater than	`$test_score > 100`
>=	Greater than or equal	`$rate / 100 >= 0.1`

Comparing strings to numbers with the relational operators

Expression	Result	Description
`1 < '3'`	true	The string "3" is converted to the number 3.
`'10' < 3`	false	The string "10" is converted to the number 10.

Comparing strings with the relational operators

Expression	Result	Description
`'apple' < 'orange'`	true	An earlier letter is less than a later letter.
`'apple' < 'appletree'`	true	When characters are the same, shorter strings are less than longer strings.
`'Orange' < 'apple'`	true	A capital letter is less than a lowercase letter.
`'@' < '$'`	false	Other characters are compared using their ASCII value.

Unusual results with the relational operators

Expression	Result	Description
`0 <= 'test'`	true	The string "test" is converted to 0.
`'' < 5`	true	The empty string is converted to 0.
`false < true`	true	FALSE is considered less than TRUE.
`null < true`	true	NULL is converted to FALSE.

Description

- When you use the relational operators, the operands are converted to the same types as described in the previous figure.
- When both operands are strings, they are compared character by character from the start of the strings based on the ASCII value of each character.

Figure 8-2   How to use the relational operators

How to use the logical operators

The first table in figure 8-3 lists the three *logical operators* that you learned about in chapter 2. This table is followed by three examples that use these operators in a *compound conditional expression*. Since these expressions use just one of the logical operators, this type of expression is relatively easy to evaluate.

In the first example, the NOT operator reverses the Boolean value that's returned by the is_numeric function. As a result, this expression is TRUE when the value of the variable named $number is not a number. In the second example, the AND operator is used to return TRUE only when the age is 18 or higher and the score is 680 or higher.

In the third example, the OR operator is used to return TRUE if the state is either CA or NC. A common mistake when using the OR operator is to write an expression like this:

```
$state == 'CA' || 'NC'
```

In this case, the string 'NC' is converted to a Boolean TRUE value and the result of the comparison is always TRUE, which isn't what you want.

The second table in this figure shows the order of precedence for conditional expressions. For instance, this table shows that relational operations are done before equality and identity operations, and AND operations are done before OR operations. This table is followed by three examples that use these operators in *complex conditional expressions*. Since these expressions use two or more of the logical operators, these expressions are more difficult to evaluate.

In the first example, the AND and OR operators are used in the conditional expression. Because the AND operator is evaluated first, this expression returns TRUE if the age is 18 or more *and* the score is 680 or more regardless of the state. This expression also returns TRUE if the state is NC regardless of the age and score.

In the second example, the AND, OR, and NOT operators are used in one expression. This expression returns TRUE if $old_customer is FALSE. It also returns TRUE if the loan amount is greater than or equal to 10000 *and* the score is less than the minimum score plus 200. Note that this expression uses an arithmetic operator, which is evaluated before the relational operators.

In the third example, parentheses change the order of precedence of the operators that are in the fifth example. This time, the OR operation is coded inside a set of parentheses. As a result, this expression returns TRUE if $old_customer is FALSE *and* the score is less than the minimum score plus 200. It also returns TRUE if the loan amount is greater than or equal to 10000 *and* the score is less than the minimum score plus 200.

As I think these examples illustrate, complex conditional expressions are hard to code. That's why you should use parentheses to clarify the order of evaluation whenever you are in doubt. But even then, you need to carefully test these expressions with all of the possible combinations of data to make sure they work correctly.

The logical operators

Operator	Name	Description
!	NOT	Returns the opposite Boolean value of its expression.
&&	AND	Returns TRUE only when the expressions on both sides are TRUE.
||	OR	Returns TRUE when the expression on either side or both sides is TRUE.

The logical operators in compound conditional expressions

The NOT operator
```
!is_numeric($number)
```

The AND operator
```
$age >= 18 && $score >= 680
```

The OR operator
```
$state == 'CA' || $state == 'NC'
```

The order of precedence for operators in conditional expressions

Order	Operators	Description
1	!	The NOT operator
2	<, <=, >, >=, <>	Relational operators
3	==, !=, ===, !==	Equality and identity operators
4	&&	The AND operator
5	||	The OR operator

The logical operators in complex conditional expressions

AND and OR operators
```
$age >= 18 && $score >= 680 || $state == 'NC'
```

AND, OR, and NOT operators
```
!$old_customer || $loan_amount >= 10000 && $score < $min_score + 200
```

How parentheses can change the evaluation
```
(!$old_customer || $loan_amount >= 10000) && $score < $min_score + 200
```

Description

- Parentheses have the highest order of precedence so the operations within parentheses are done first, working from the innermost sets of parentheses to the outermost sets.

- To clarify the way an expression is evaluated, you should use parentheses.

- You can use arithmetic expressions within a conditional expression. In the order of precedence, the arithmetic operators come between the NOT operator and the relational operators.

Figure 8-3   How to use the logical operators

How to code the selection structures

Chapter 2 introduced the if statement. Now, this topic expands upon that coverage. It also presents the switch statement and the conditional operator. These statements are often referred to as *selection structures*.

How to code if statements with else clauses

Figure 8-4 presents the details for coding the if and else clauses of an if statement. To start, you don't have to use braces to enclose the statements in these clauses if each clause consists of just one statement. This is illustrated by the first example. When you omit the braces, it's best to place the entire if statement on one line to make it clear that the if clause executes only one statement.

The second example is like the first example, but braces are used even though they're not required. If you write your code this way, it's easy to see which statements are part of the if clause. It's also easy to add more statements to the if clause if you need to do that as you develop your application.

The third example shows an if statement that has just one statement in both the if and the else clauses and no braces are used. Here, although the braces aren't required for either clause, it's best to use braces for both of them. The reason for this is shown in the fourth example.

In the fourth example, a statement is added after the statement in the else clause of the third example. The intent is to have it be executed as part of the else clause. But when you don't use braces for the else clause, only the first statement is part of that clause, no matter how it's indented. As a result, the last statement in this example is always executed.

The fifth example is similar to the third example, but braces are coded around the if and else clauses even though they consist of only one line. Here the extent of the if statement is well defined and you are less likely to introduce errors if you enhance this code later.

The last example illustrates an if statement that's nested three layers deep. Here, the use of braces and indentation help make the code easier to read. To understand this code, though, you need to know that a leap year isn't just a year that is divisible by 4. If a year is divisible by 100, it must also be divisible by 400 to be a leap year. That's why 2000 was a leap year but 2100 won't be.

An if clause with one statement and no braces

```
if (!isset($rate)) $rate = 0.075;
```

An if clause with one statement and braces

```
if ($qualified) { // This expression is equivalent to $qualified == true.
    echo 'You qualify for enrollment.';
}
```

If and else clauses with one statement each and no braces

```
if ($age >= 18)
    echo 'You may vote.';
else
    echo 'You may not vote.';
```

Why you should always use braces with else clauses

```
if ($age >= 18)
    echo 'You may vote.';
else
    echo 'You may not vote.';
    $may_vote = false;    // This statement isn't a part of the else clause.
```

Braces make your code easier to modify or enhance

```
if ($score >= 680) {
    echo 'Your loan is approved.';
} else {
    echo 'Your loan is not approved.';
}
```

A nested if statement to determine if a year is a leap year

```
$is_leap_year = false;
if ($year % 4 == 0) {
    if ($year % 100 == 0) {
        if ($year % 400 == 0) {
            $is_leap_year = true;       // divisible by 4, 100, and 400
        } else {
            $is_leap_year = false;      // divisible by 4 and 100, but not 400
        }
    } else {
        $is_leap_year = true;           // divisible by 4, but not 100
    }
} else {
    $is_leap_year = false;              // not divisible by 4
}
```

Description

- If you only have one statement after an if statement or an else clause, you don't have to put braces around that statement.

- You can *nest* an if statement within the if, else if, or else clause of another if statement. This nesting can continue many layers deep, and it is easier to read when braces and indentation are used.

Figure 8-4   How to code if statements with else clauses

How to code if statements with else if clauses

Figure 8-5 presents four examples of if statements that use else if clauses. In the first example, for instance, if the age is less than 18, the if clause displays a message. However, if the age is 18 or more, PHP evaluates the else if clause. Then, if the score is less than 680, the else if clause displays a message.

The second example shows that the else if clause can also be coded with the elseif keyword (no space between the else and if keywords). In this book, we typically include a space between the keywords, but you can use either style, though you should try to be consistent with the style that you choose.

The third example shows how to use else if clauses to validate the value in the variable named $rate. Before the if statement starts, a Boolean variable named $rate_is_valid is set to FALSE. Then, the if statement uses a series of tests to determine the validity of the $rate variable, starting with the worst case first (is not a number). If any of the tests fails, an appropriate message is displayed. But if the variable passes all of the tests, the $rate_is_valid variable is set to TRUE.

The fourth example also shows the use of multiple else if clauses. This code tests the value of the variable named $average in order to set the value of the variable named $grade. Note that these values must be tested from the high end of the range to the low. If, for example, you code the first test like this

```
$average >= 69.5
```

it won't work for the A and B ranges. To fix this problem, you can code the first test like this

```
$average >= 69.5 && $average < 79.5
```

However, that would mean extra code. Also, this would make the code harder to read and maintain. In general, then, it's best to test for a range of values in sequence.

Incidentally, these examples illustrate a coding style that I often use. Here, I code the else if or else keywords on the same line that contains the closing brace for the previous clause. This helps keep the code compact yet readable.

If you work with PHP code, you may see other styles. For example, some programmers prefer to code each brace on its own line. This approach also works and is easy to read, but it takes more vertical space.

An if statement with one else if clause

```
if ($age < 18) {
    echo "You're too young for a loan.";
} else if ($score < 680) {
    echo "Your credit score is too low for a loan.";
}
```

An if statement with an else if and an else clause

```
if ($age < 18) {
    echo "You're too young for a loan.";
} elseif ($score < 680) {
    echo "Your credit score is too low for a loan.";
} else {
    echo "You're approved for your loan.";
}
```

An if statement with two else if clauses and an else clause

```
$rate_is_valid = false;
if (!is_numeric($rate)) {
    echo 'Rate is not a number.';
} else if ($rate < 0) {
    echo 'Rate cannot be less than zero.';
} else if ($rate > 0.2) {
    echo 'Rate cannot be greater than 20%.';
} else {
    $rate_is_valid = true;
}
```

An if statement to determine a student's letter grade

```
if ($average >= 89.5) {
    $grade = 'A';
} else if ($average >= 79.5) {
    $grade = 'B';
} else if ($average >= 69.5) {
    $grade = 'C';
} else if ($average >= 64.5) {
    $grade = 'D';
} else {
    $grade = 'F';
}
```

Description

- When coding an else if clause, you can code the else and if keywords (with a space), or you can use the elseif keyword (no space).

Figure 8-5   How to code if statements with else if clauses

How to use the conditional operator

The *conditional operator* is PHP's only *ternary operator*. This means it has three operands. In contrast, a *unary operator* such as ++ has one operand while a *binary operator* such as * has two operands.

Since the conditional operator has three operands, it needs two symbols to separate them. In this case, the question mark and the colon are used as the operand separators. This is shown by the syntax in figure 8-6.

The first example in this figure shows how to use the conditional operator to set a variable to one of two values based on a comparison. If the age is 18 or more, the message is set to "Can vote". Otherwise, the message is set to "Cannot vote".

The second example shows how to use a mathematical expression in one of the operands. If $hours is over 40, $overtime contains 1.5 times the pay rate for the number of hours over 40. Otherwise, it is set to 0.

The third example shows how to select between a singular or plural ending for use in a message to the user. If $error_count is 1, the ending is empty. Otherwise, "s" is used for the ending.

The fourth example shows how to add one to a value or set it back to 1, depending on whether the value is at its maximum. For example, if $max_value is 10 and $value is 6, the test is FALSE and 1 is added to $value. However, when $value reaches 10, it is set to 1 instead.

If you need to perform this kind of rollover with a variable, but the starting value is 0 instead of 1, you don't have to use the conditional operator. Instead, you can use the % operator. For example, in the statement

```
$value = ($value + 1) % ($max_value + 1);
```

if $max_value is 9, $value ranges from 0 to 9 and then back to 0.

The fifth example shows how to combine the conditional operator with the return keyword so the result is returned by a function. Here, if $number is greater than $highest, $highest is returned. Otherwise, $number is returned.

The last example shows how to keep a value within a fixed range. It uses a nested conditional operator to do this. If $value is greater than $max, $value is set to $max. If $value is not greater than $max, the second conditional operator is evaluated. Here, if $value is less than $min, $value is set to $min. If $value is not less than $min, $value is set to $value leaving it unchanged.

The last two examples rewrite the first and sixth examples so they use if statements instead of the conditional operator. These statements show that if statements are easier to read than statements that use the conditional operator. As a result, if you want your code to be as easy to read as possible, you should avoid the conditional operator.

Nevertheless, many programmers like to use the conditional operator because it takes fewer lines of code. As a result, even if you don't use the conditional operator in your code, you still need to understand how it works, so you can understand code that has been written by other programmers.

Syntax of the conditional operator

```
(conditional_expression) ? value_if_true : value_if_false
```

Examples of using the conditional operator

Set a string based on a comparison
```
$message = ($age >= 18) ? 'Can vote' : 'Cannot vote';
```

Calculate overtime pay
```
$overtime = ($hours > 40) ? ($hours - 40) * $rate * 1.5 : 0;
```

Select a singular or plural ending based on a value
```
$ending = ($error_count == 1) ? '' : 's'.
$message = 'Found ' . $error_count . ' error' . $ending . '.';
```

Set a value to 1 if it's at a maximum value when adding 1
```
$value = ($value >= $max_value) ? 1 : $value + 1;
```

Return one of two values based on a comparison
```
return ($number > $highest) ? $highest : $number;
```

Bound a value within a fixed range
```
$value = ($value > $max) ? $max : (($value < $min) ? $min : $value);
```

The first example rewritten with an if statement
```
if ($age >= 18) {
    $message = 'Can vote';
} else {
    $message = 'Cannot vote';
}
```

The last example rewritten with an if statement
```
if ($value > $max) {
    $value = $max;
} else if ($value < $min) {
    $value = $min;
}
```

Description

- A *ternary operator* has three operands. The *conditional operator* is the only ternary operator available from PHP. This operator provides a compact way to code an if statement.

- The conditional operator begins by evaluating the conditional expression. Then, if the conditional expression is TRUE, the value that results from the middle expression is returned. Otherwise, the value that results from the last expression is returned.

Figure 8-6   How to use the conditional operator

How to code switch statements

A *switch statement* is a convenient way to express a certain form of if statement. Specifically, it can be used in place of an if statement with multiple else if clauses in which one expression is tested for equality with several values. This is illustrated by the statements in figure 8-7. The switch statement implements a control structure that is often referred to as the *case structure*.

The switch statement starts with the word switch followed by a *switch expression* inside of parentheses. This expression is *not* a conditional expression. It is an expression that returns a single value that's used to determine which *case* to execute. The expression is often as simple as a single variable as shown in the first example in this figure. But it can also be a more complex expression that results in a number or string value.

Once the value for the expression is found, the switch statement checks each of the values in the *case labels*. Then, it begins executing the code that follows the first case label that is equal to the result of the expression. It continues executing until it reaches either a break statement or the end of the switch statement.

If no case labels match the value in the switch expression, the switch statement starts executing the code that follows the default label. But this default case is optional. If it's omitted and no case labels match the expression, the switch statement won't execute any code.

In the first example in this figure, the expression is just a variable named $letter_grade that should contain a letter. Then, each case label is checked against the value of this variable. If, for example, $letter_grade is "B", the switch statement starts executing the code after the label for that case and sets the $message variable to "above average". It then encounters a break statement and no further code is executed by the switch statement. If $letter_grade had been "Z", however, the code after the default label would have been executed and the message would have been set to "invalid grade".

In the second example, the case labels are coded in a way that provides "fall through." This occurs when code starts executing at one case label but doesn't encounter a break statement, so it passes another case label and keeps executing. Although this is often discouraged because it can be confusing, this example shows one case where fall through is useful.

In this instance, the same code should be executed when $letter_grade is "A" or "B". Instead of repeating the code, two case labels are placed before the code. Then, if $letter_grade is "A", the switch statement falls through and executes the code after the case for "B". Likewise, if $letter_grade is "D", the switch statement falls through and executes the code after the case for "F". Except for clear cases like this, though, you should avoid using fall through in your switch statements because that can lead to unexpected errors and be hard to debug.

When you use a switch statement, you can nest if statements within the cases. You can also nest one switch statement within a case of another switch statement.

A switch statement with a default case

```
switch ($letter_grade) {
    case 'A':
        $message = 'well above average';
        break;
    case 'B':
        $message = 'above average';
        break;
    case 'C':
        $message = 'average';
        break;
    case 'D':
        $message = 'below average';
        break;
    case 'F':
        $message = 'failing';
        break;
    default:
        $message = 'invalid grade';
        break;
}
```

A switch statement with fall through

```
switch ($letter_grade) {
    case 'A':
    case 'B':
        $message = 'Scholarship approved.';
        break;
    case 'C':
        $message = 'Application requires review.';
        break;
    case 'D':
    case 'F':
        $message = 'Scholarship not approved.';
        break;
}
```

Description

- The *switch statement* starts by evaluating the *switch expression* in the parentheses.
- After evaluating the expression, the switch statement transfers control to the *case label* that has the value that matches the value of the expression. Then, it executes the statements for that *case*. It stops executing when it reaches a break statement or the end of the switch statement.
- The default case is optional and may be omitted. If included, you can only have one default case. It is usually the last case in the switch statement, but it can be anywhere.
- The values in the case label may be literal values or they may be expressions.
- If a case doesn't contain a break statement, execution "falls through" to the next label.
- You can nest if statements or other switch statements within the cases of a switch statement.

Figure 8-7   How to code switch statements

How to use a switch statement in the controller

The switch statement is often useful in the controller of an application that uses the MVC pattern. This is illustrated by figure 8-8. This is the critical portion of the controller code for the Product Manager application of chapter 5. This works because all of the actions are determined by the value of the $action variable.

This code starts by using an if statement to determine whether the $action variable is set. If it isn't, this variable is set to "list_products". Then, a switch statement provides for the four cases that the action variable calls for. If you compare this code to the code in part 3 of figure 5-4, I think you'll agree that the switch statement is easier to follow.

A switch statement in the controller for the Product Manager application

```php
if (isset($_POST['action'])) {
    $action = $_POST['action'];
} else if (isset($_GET['action'])) {
    $action = $_GET['action'];
} else {
    $action = 'list_products';
}
switch ($action) {
    case 'list_products':
        // Get the current category ID
        $category_id = $_GET['category_id'];
        if (!isset($category_id)) {
            $category_id = 1;
        }
        // Get product and category data
        $category_name = get_category_name($category_id);
        $categories = get_categories();
        $products = get_products_by_category($category_id);

        // Display the product list
        include('product_list.php');
        break;
    case 'delete_product':
        // Get the IDs
        $product_id = $_POST['product_id'];
        $category_id = $_POST['category_id'];

        // Delete the product
        delete_product($product_id);

        // Display the Product List page for the current category
        header("Location: .?category_id=$category_id");
        break;
    case 'show_add_form':
        $categories = get_categories();
        include('product_add.php');
        break;
    case 'add_product':
        $category_id = $_POST['category_id'];
        $code = $_POST['code'];
        $name = $_POST['name'];
        $price = $_POST['price'];

        // Validate the inputs
        if (empty($code) || empty($name) || empty($price)) {
            $error = "Invalid product data. Check all fields and try again.";
            include('../errors/error.php');
        } else {
            add_product($category_id, $code, $name, $price);

            // Display the Product List page for the current category
            header("Location: .?category_id=$category_id");
        }
        break;
}
```

Figure 8-8   How to use a switch statement in the controller

How to code the iteration structures

In chapter 2, you learned how to use while statements and for statements. Now, you'll learn more about coding those statements, and you'll learn how to code the do-while, break, and continue statements. These statements implement structures that are often referred to as the *iteration structures*.

How to code while loops

As you saw in chapter 2, a *while loop* executes a block of code as long as its conditional expression is TRUE. If the conditional expression starts off as FALSE, the code isn't executed at all. If the conditional expression never becomes FALSE, the while loop becomes an *infinite loop*. An infinite loop usually results from a coding error, and it can usually be fixed by modifying the code.

Figure 8-9 shows three examples that should give you some ideas for what you can do with while loops. In the first example, the while loop finds the average of 100 random numbers. The $total variable stores the total of the random numbers, the $count variable stores a count of the numbers average, and the while loop stops executing when $count becomes 100.

Note here that this loop uses the mt_rand function to get the random numbers. This is a function that you'll learn about in the next chapter. For now, you just need to know that it generates a random number each time it is executed that ranges from the value of the first argument to the value of the second argument.

In the second example, this function is used to generate random numbers between 1 and 6, thus simulating the roll of one die. The loop ends when the random number is 6, and the loop counts the number of times the die needed to be rolled to get that 6. Since the first roll of the die takes place in the while loop's expression, the increment statement in the loop won't be executed if the first roll is a 6. That's why the value for rolls is initially set to 1.

In the third example, the while loop from example 2 is nested inside another while loop that is executed 10,000 times. Each time the inner loop rolls a 6, the number of rolls to get that 6 is added to the variable named $total. In addition, the value of the variable named $max is changed if the number of rolls is greater than the current value of $max. To make that comparison, the max function is used to return the larger of the two values that are represented by its arguments. Here again, you'll learn more about this function in the next chapter.

Since the value of $max starts at –INF (minus infinity), any number of rolls the first time through the inner loop is greater than that and the starting value of $max is changed to the value of the number of tries to get a 6. Then, when the outer loop finishes, the average number of tries to get a 6 is calculated and the average and maximum values are displayed.

A while loop that finds the average of 100 random numbers

```
$total = 0;
$count = 0;
while ($count < 100) {
    $number = mt_rand(0, 100);     // get a random number from 0 to 100
    $total += $number;
    $count++;
}
$average = $total / $count;
echo 'The average is: ' . $average;
```

A while loop that counts dice rolls until a six is rolled

```
$rolls = 1;
while (mt_rand(1,6) != 6) {        // get a random number from 1 to 6
    $rolls++;
}
echo 'Number of times to roll a six: ' . $rolls;
```

Nested while loops that get the average and maximum rolls for a six

```
$total = 0;
$count = 0;
$max = -INF;

while ($count < 10000) {
    $rolls = 1;
    while (mt_rand(1, 6) != 6) {  // get a random number from 1 to 6
        $rolls++;
    }
    $total += $rolls;
    $count++;
    $max = max($rolls, $max);     // get the value of the larger argument
}
$average = $total / $count;
echo 'Average: ' . $average . ' Max: ' . $max;
```

Description

- The *while statement* executes the block of statements within its braces as long as its conditional expression is TRUE.

- When you use a while statement, the condition is tested before the *while loop* is executed.

Note

- These examples use the mt_rand and max functions, which are presented in the next chapter. The mt_rand function gets a random number in the range specified by its arguments. The max function gets the larger of the two values that are passed to it as arguments.

Figure 8-9   How to code while loops

How to code do-while loops

The *do-while loop* is similar to the while loop except that the conditional expression is tested at the end of the loop. As a result, the code inside the loop is always executed at least once.

The first example in figure 8-10 counts the number of rolls that it takes to get a 6. This is similar to the second example in figure 8-9, but here, the variable named $rolls is initialized to zero since it is incremented at least once inside the loop.

The second example uses a do-while loop to generate 10 random numbers between 0 and 100. It then displays the minimum and maximum values that were generated. To do that, it uses the min function, which is the opposite of the max function. Since the value of $max starts at –INF, the first random number is always greater than that. Likewise, since the value of $min starts a INF, the first random number is always less than that.

A do-while loop that counts dice rolls until a six is rolled

```
$rolls = 0;
do {
    $rolls++;
} while (mt_rand(1,6) != 6);        // get a random number from 1 to 6

echo 'Number of times to roll a six: ' . $rolls;
```

A do-while loop to find the max and min of 10 random values

```
$max = -INF;
$min = INF;
$count = 0;
do {
    $number = mt_rand(0, 100);      // get a random number from 0 to 100
    $max = max($max, $number);      // get the larger of the two arguments
    $min = min($min, $number);      // get the smaller of the two arguments
    $count++;
} while ($count < 10);

echo 'Max: ' . $max . ' Min: ' . $min;
```

Description

- The *do-while statement* executes the block of statements within its braces as long as its conditional expression is TRUE.

- When you use a do-while statement, the condition is tested at the end of the *do-while loop*. This means the code is always executed at least once.

Note

- These examples use the mt_rand, min, and max functions, which are presented in the next chapter. The mt_rand function gets a random number in the range specified by its arguments. The min function gets the smaller of the two values that are passed to it. And the max function gets the larger of the two values that are passed to it as arguments.

Figure 8-10   How to code do-while loops

How to code for loops

A *for loop* provides a convenient way to code a loop that requires a counter variable. This is illustrated by the for and while loops at the start of figure 8-11. Here, the first line of the for statement initializes the counter variable, provides the condition that ends the loop, and provides the code for incrementing the counter variable. In the while loop, these tasks are coded on three separate lines.

The first example in this figure shows that you can start and increment the counter variable with values other than 1. Here, the statement initializes the counter to 2 and increments the counter by 2. As a result, the loop displays the even numbers from 2 through 10. You can also increment a counter by negative values (which in effect decrements the value), which is useful in some situations.

The second example displays all the factors of a number. A *factor* is any number that can be divided into the number with a remainder of zero, so 1, 2, 3, 6, and 9 are factors of 18. This time, the counter starts at 1 and is incremented by 1, and the loop continues as long as the counter is less than the original number. Inside the loop, a message is displayed if the original number divided by the current value of the counter has a remainder of zero.

Incidentally, this example uses $i as the variable name for the counter. This is a common practice. And when one loop is nested within another loop, $j is often used as the counter name for the inner loop.

The third example shows the alternate syntax for a for loop that you were introduced to in chapter 4. Note here that the statements in the loop are coded after the colon (:), not within braces. Note too that this statement is ended by the endfor keyword.

This alternate syntax is useful when you're generating HTML code that will be rendered by a browser. The code in this example generates eight <option> tags for a drop-down list with values that range 5 through 12.

The for statement compared to the while statement

The for statement

```php
for ($count = 1; $count <= 10; $count++) {
    echo $count . '<br />';
}
```

The while statement

```php
$count = 1;
while ($count <= 10) {
    echo $count . '<br />';
    $count++;
}
```

A for loop to display even numbers from 2 to 10

```php
for ($number = 2; $number <= 10; $number += 2) {
    echo $number . '<br />';
}
```

A for loop to display all the factors of a number

```php
$number = 18;
for ($i = 1; $i < $number; $i++) {
    if ($number % $i == 0) {
        echo $i . ' is a factor of ' . $number . '<br />';
    }
}
```

A for loop that uses the alternate syntax to display a drop-down list

```php
<label>Interest Rate:</label>
<select name="rate">
<?php for ($v = 5; $v <= 12; $v++) : ?>
    <option value="<?php echo $v; ?>">
        <?php echo $v; ?>
    </option>
<?php endfor; ?>
</select><br />
```

Description

- The *for statement* is useful when you need to increment or decrement a counter that determines how many times the *for loop* is executed.

- Within the parentheses of a for statement, you code an expression that assigns a starting value to a counter variable, a conditional expression that determines when the loop ends, and an increment expression that indicates how the counter should be incremented or decremented each time through the loop.

- When you use the alternate for statement syntax, you end the statement with the endfor keyword.

Figure 8-11   How to code for loops

How to use the break and continue statements

The break and continue statements give you additional control over loops. The *break statement* causes the loop to end immediately. The *continue statement* causes the loop to skip the remaining code in the loop and start back at the beginning of the loop.

The first example in figure 8-12 shows the break statement inside a while loop. Here, the while loop is intentionally coded as an infinite loop. However, if the conditional expression in the if statement is TRUE, the break statement executes and that ends the while loop. This occurs when the random number that's generated by the mt_rand function is even.

The second example shows the break statement in a for loop. Here, the loop determines whether the value in the $number variable is prime. Once one factor is found, though, the number isn't prime so the code sets the value of the $prime variable to FALSE and issues the break statement. If, for example, the value of $number is 42, the loop ends as soon as 2 is found to be a factor so the loop won't check the values from 3 to 41.

The third example shows the continue statement used in a for loop. Here, when the number to be displayed is a multiple of 3, the continue statement skips the remainder of the loop and starts the loop again after the counter is incremented. As a result, only numbers that are not multiples of 3 are displayed by the loop.

The fourth example shows the continue statement used in a while loop. Here, the while loop is based on the for loop from the previous example. The $number++ statement had to be added both at the end of the while loop and before the continue statement inside the if statement. Had this increment statement not been added to the if statement, the loop would have become an infinite loop as soon as $number became 3. After that, the continue statement would cause the loop to repeat but the $number variable would never be incremented so the loop would never end.

When you use break and continue statements within nested loops, you need to know that the break or continue statement applies only to the innermost loop. If, for example, you code the break statement within an inner loop, it skips to the end of that loop, not the end of the outer loop. Although you can get around this limitation by using a numeric argument with the break or continue statement to indicate how many nested loops to apply the statement to, that isn't illustrated in this book.

The break statement in a while loop

```
while (true) {
    $number = mt_rand(1,10);
    if ($number % 2 == 0) {
        break;
    }
}
echo $number; // $number is between 1 and 10 and even
```

The break statement in a for loop

```
$number = 13;
$prime = true;
for ($i = 2; $i < $number; $i++) {
    if ($number % $i == 0) {
        $prime = false;
        break;
    }
}
$result = ($prime) ? ' is ' : ' is not ';
echo $number . $result . 'prime.';
```

The continue statement in a for loop

```
for ($number = 1; $number <= 10; $number++) {
    if ($number % 3 == 0) {
        continue;
    }
    echo $number . '<br>';
}
// Only displays 1, 2, 4, 5, 7, 8, and 10
```

The continue statement in a while loop

```
$number = 1;
while ($number <= 10) {
    if ($number % 3 == 0) {
        $number++;
        continue;
    }
    echo $number . '<br>';
    $number++;
}
// Only displays 1, 2, 4, 5, 7, 8, and 10
```

Description

- The *break statement* ends a loop. In other words, it jumps out of the loop.
- The *continue statement* ends the current iteration of a for or while loop, but allows the next iteration to proceed. In other words, it jumps to the start of the loop.
- When you're working with nested loops, the break and continue statements apply only to the loop that they're in.

Figure 8-12   How to use the break and continue statements

Perspective

Now that you've finished this chapter, you should know how to code all of the control statements. These are the PHP statements that implement the selection, case, and iteration structures that provide the logic of an application. As you progress through this book, you'll see many examples of the use of these statements that will help you use them effectively.

Terms

equality operator	case
type coercion	case label
identity operator	flag
relational operator	switch
logical operator	iteration structure
compound conditional expression	while statement
complex conditional expression	while loop
selection structure	do-while statement
conditional operator	do-while loop
ternary operator	for statement
switch statement	for loop
case structure	break statement
switch expression	continue statement

Summary

- The *equality operators* use *type coercion*. The *identity operators* don't use type coercion.

- To create a conditional expression, you can use equality operators, identify operators, *relational operators*, *logical operators*, and arithmetic operators.

- In the *order of precedence* for a conditional expression, the arithmetic operators come between the NOT logical operator and the relational operators. To override the order of precedence, you can use parentheses.

- The if statement is used to implement the *selection structure*, and the switch statement is used to implement the *case structure*. The case structure is often useful for the controller of an application that uses the MVC pattern.

- The *iteration structure* is implemented by *while loops*, *do-while loops*, and *for loops*. A for loop is useful when you need to increment or decrement a counter that determines how many times the loop is executed.

- The alternate syntax for a for loop is useful when you're generating HTML code. This syntax starts the loop with a colon, and ends it with the endfor keyword.

- The *break* and *continue statements* are used to exit from a loop or to restart one.

Exercise 8-1   Use if and switch statements

This exercise gives you a chance to experiment with nested if and switch statements.

Open and test the application

1. Run the application in the ex_starts/ch08_ex1 directory. Then, test this application by entering either "R" or "C" in the Customer Type box and a value from 0 to 500 in the Invoice Subtotal box. When you click on the Calculate button, you can see that the discount percent is based on both the customer type and subtotal amount.

2. Open the index.php and invoice_total.php files for this application and review the code. Note that this code uses nested if statements to determine the discount percent.

Change the code that determines the discount percent

3. Change the if statement so customers of type R with a subtotal that's greater than or equal to $250 but less than $500 get a 25% discount and those with a subtotal of $500 or more get a 30% discount. Next, change the if statement so customers of type C always get a 20% discount. Then, test these changes.

4. Add another type to the if statement so customers of type T get a 40% discount for subtotals of less than $500, and a 50% discount for subtotals of $500 or more. Also, make sure that customer types that aren't R, C, or T get a 10% discount. Then, test these changes.

5. Test the application again, but use lowercase letters for the customer types. Note that these letters aren't evaluated as capital letters.

6. Modify the code so the users can enter either capital or lowercase letters for the customer types. To do that, use logical operators. Then, test this change.

Use a switch statement with nested if statements to get the same results

7. Code a switch statement right before the if statement. This statement should provide the structure for handling the three cases for customer types: R, C, and T. Then, within each of these cases, you can copy the related code from the if statement below to provide for the discounts that are based on subtotal variations. In other words, you can nest the if statements within the switch cases.

8. Comment out the entire if statement that's above the switch statement. Then, test to make sure the switch statement works correctly.

9. If you haven't done so already, modify the switch statement so it works for both lowercase and uppercase entries of the three customer types. To do that, use the strtoupper function to convert the customer type to uppercase before it's evaluated. Then, test that change.

Exercise 8-2 Use loops

This exercise gives you some practice using loops.

Test the application

1. Run the application in the ex_starts/ch08_ex2 directory.

2. Click on the Process Scores button and note that it only displays the scores and doesn't calculate the total or the average.

3. Click on the Process Rolls button and note that it displays the maximum and average number of rolls that it took to roll the specified number.

4. Open the index.php and loop_tester.php files for this application and review the code.

Implement the score processing

5. In the index.php file, add code that calculates the score total. When you're done, clicking the Process Scores button should display the correct total and average.

6. In the index.php file, use a for loop to validate the user entries instead of using multiple conditions in a hard-coded if statement.

7. Test your changes to make sure they work correctly.

Modify the roll processing

8. In the index.php file, modify the code that processes the rolls so it uses a for loop as the outer loop instead of a while loop.

9. In the loop_tester.php file, use a for loop to display the <option> tags for the drop-down list instead of hard-coding six <option> tags.

10. Test your changes to make sure they work correctly.

9

How to work with strings and numbers

In chapter 2, you learned the basic skills for working with strings and numbers. Now, you'll learn the other essential skills for working with strings and numbers in your web applications.

How to work with strings **260**
How to create strings 260
How to use escape sequences 262
How to work with string length and substrings 264
How to search a string 266
How to replace part of a string 266
How to modify strings 268
How to convert strings to and from arrays 270
How to convert strings to and from ASCII values 270
How to compare strings 272

How to work with numbers **274**
How to assign integers 274
How to assign floating-point values 276
How to use the math functions 278
How to generate random numbers 280

Other skills for working with strings and numbers **282**
How to use the sprintf function to format strings and numbers 282
How to convert strings to numbers 286

Perspective **288**

How to work with strings

When you use an HTML form to get data from a user, the data in the form is initially submitted to the server as a string. As a result, working with strings is an important part of most PHP applications.

How to create strings

Figure 9-1 shows four ways to create a string. The first example shows how to create strings with single quotes. Here, the first statement stores a value of "PHP" in the variable named $language. Then, the second statement appends the $language variable to a string literal of "Welcome to " and stores the resulting string in the variable named $message. Finally, the third statement shows how to code a string across multiple lines. In this string, the $query variable includes a new line character and the spaces that indent the second line.

The second example shows how to create strings with double quotes. When you use double quotes, the PHP engine performs *variable substitution*, which is also known as *interpolation*. This means that the PHP engine searches the string for variables. If the PHP engine finds a variable inside the string, it replaces its name with its value. For example, the second statement in the second example, substitutes a value of "PHP" for the $language variable.

When using variable substitution, you may need to separate the variable name from the surrounding text with braces. In this figure, for example, the statement that assigns a value to variable named $message1 doesn't work correctly since PHP is trying to access the $items variable instead of the $item variable. To fix this problem, you can use braces to clearly identify the variable name. To do that, code the opening brace immediately after the dollar sign that begins the name, and code the closing brace at the end of the name.

The third example shows how to use a *heredoc* to create a string. To start a heredoc, code three less than (<) signs followed by a name for the heredoc. This name follows the same rules for naming PHP variables, but it's typically coded in all caps. In this figure, for example, the heredoc has a name of MESSAGE. This name must be followed immediately by a new line. In other words, it can't have any extra spaces at the end of the line.

To end a heredoc, code its name on a line followed by a semicolon. When you do this, you can't include any spaces or tabs between the start of the line and the heredoc name, and you can't include any characters after the semicolon.

Within a heredoc, all the new line characters, tabs, and spaces are included as part of the string, except the new line character just before the heredoc terminator. In addition, PHP performs variable substitution within a heredoc.

The fourth example shows how to use a *nowdoc* to create a string. Creating a nowdoc is similar to creating a heredoc, but you enclose the name for the nowdoc in single quotes. In addition, like a string created with single quotes, a nowdoc doesn't perform variable substitution.

Assign strings with single quotes

```
$language = 'PHP';
$message = 'Welcome to ' . $language;        // 'Welcome to PHP'

$query = 'SELECT firstName, lastName
          FROM Users';                       // Spans multiple lines
```

Assign strings with double quotes

Using variable substitution

```
$language = "PHP";
$message = "Welcome to $language";           // 'Welcome to PHP'
```

Using braces with variable substitution

```
$count = 12;
$item = "flower";
$message1 = "You bought $count $items.";     // 'You bought 12 .'
$message2 = "You bought $count ${item}s.";   // 'You bought 12 flowers.'
```

Assign a string with a heredoc

```
$language = 'PHP';
$message = <<<MESSAGE
The heredoc syntax allows you to build multi-line
strings in $language. Inside, it acts like a double-quoted
string and performs variable substitution.
MESSAGE;
```

Assign a string with a nowdoc

```
$message = <<<'MESSAGE'
The nowdoc syntax also allows you to build multi-line
strings in PHP. However, no variable substitution takes place
inside the nowdoc string. This is similar to single-quoted strings.
MESSAGE;
```

Description

- There are four ways to create strings. You can use single quotes, double quotes, the *heredoc* syntax, or the *nowdoc* syntax.

- When you create a string using double quotes or the heredoc syntax, the PHP engine performs *variable substitution*. Variable substitution replaces the variable name in the string with its value. If necessary, this process converts the variable's value to a string. This is also known as *interpolation*.

- When working with variable substitution, if the variable name is adjacent to text that's interpreted as part of the variable name, the variable substitution won't work correctly. In that case, you can clarify the variable name by enclosing the name, not including the dollar sign, inside braces.

- When you create a heredoc or a nowdoc, the identifier must be immediately followed by a new line. Similarly, the closing identifier must be on a line by itself, and it can't begin with any spaces or tabs. After the closing identifier, the only character that's allowed is the semicolon that ends the statement. Otherwise, a syntax error occurs.

Figure 9-1   How to create strings

How to use escape sequences

Figure 9-2 shows how to use *escape sequences* to include special characters in strings. The escape sequences that you can use depend on how you create the string.

The first table shows three escape sequences that only work in some strings. For example, you can use the first escape sequence to include a backslash in any type of string except a nowdoc. To include a backslash in a nowdoc, you don't need to use the escape sequence. Instead, you can just type a single backslash.

Similarly, you can use the second sequence to include a single quote in a single-quoted string, but you don't need to use it to include single quotes in other types of strings. And you can use the third sequence to include a double quote in a double-quoted string, but you don't need it to include double quotes in other types of strings.

The second table shows escape sequences that you can use in both double-quoted strings and heredocs. However, you can't use them in single-quoted strings or nowdocs. In this figure, for example, the statement that assigns a value to the $comment2 variable doesn't work correctly because it uses the escape sequence for a new line in a single-quoted string. Since single-quoted strings don't recognize this escape sequence, this string stores the two characters for the escape sequence instead of storing the new line character.

The escape sequences for octal and hexadecimal values let you use any ASCII character in a string. However, web browsers aren't always able to display all characters correctly. For example, many web browsers don't display the copyright character correctly. To fix this problem, you must convert the copyright character to its HTML entity (©). To do this, you can use the htmlentities function. This function parses a string and returns a new string with any special characters converted to the corresponding HTML entity.

The second example shows how the htmlentities function works. To start, the statement that creates the $copyright1 variable uses the escape sequence for hex value xa9 to include a character for the copyright symbol. However, since this statement doesn't use the htmlentities function, the browser isn't able to display this character correctly.

In contrast, the statement that creates the $copyright2 variable uses the htmlentities function. As a result, this statement converts the character for the copyright symbol to the corresponding HTML entity, and the browser displays the copyright symbol correctly.

By default, the htmlentities function converts a double quote to its HTML entity ("), but it doesn't convert a single quote to an HTML entity. To change this behavior, you can specify a second parameter. If you set this parameter to ENT_NOQUOTES, this function doesn't convert single or double quotes to HTML entities. However, if you set the second parameter to ENT_QUOTES, this function converts both types of quotes.

Escape sequences only used in some strings

Sequence	Description	Used in...
\\	Backslash	All strings except nowdocs
\'	Single quote	Single-quoted strings
\"	Double quote	Double-quoted strings

Escape sequences used in double-quoted strings and heredocs

Sequence	Description
\$	Dollar sign
\n	New line
\t	Tab
\r	Carriage return
\f	Form feed
\v	Vertical tab
\ooo	Character with the specified octal value
\xhh	Character with the specified hexadecimal value

Examples of escape sequences with single quotes

```
$dir = 'C:\\xampp\\php';                      // C:\xampp\php
$name = 'Mike\'s Music Store';                // Mike's Music Store
$quote = "He said, \"It costs \$12.\"";       // He said, "It costs $12."
$comment1 = "This is a\nmulti-line string.";  // This is a
                                              // multi-line string.
$comment2 = 'Not a\nmulti-line string.';      // Not a\nmulti-line string
```

The htmlentities function

Function	Description
htmlentities($str [, $quotes])	Returns a string with all special HTML characters converted to the HTML entity. You can use the $quotes parameter to control how single and double quotes are converted.

Examples of the htmlentities function

An example that doesn't use the htmlentities function
```
$copyright1 = "\xa9 2010";             // Result is '© 2010'
echo $copyright1;                      // Displays  2010
```

An example that uses the htmlentities function
```
$copyright2 = htmlentities("\xa9 2010");  // Result is '&copy; 2010'
echo $copyright2;                         // Displays © 2010
```

Description

- *Escape sequences* provide a way to insert special characters into text strings. These escape sequences work differently depending on the type of the string.

Figure 9-2   How to use escape sequences

How to work with string length and substrings

The next few figures are going to show how to use some of the most common functions for working with strings. However, there are many more string functions available in PHP. To learn more about these functions, you can visit the URL that's shown at the top of figure 9-3.

The table in this figure presents three functions that you can use to work with string length and substrings. The *length* of a string is the number of characters in a string. For example, a string of "Ray Harris" has a length of 10, with 9 characters for letters and 1 character for the space. A *substring* is part of a string. For example, "Ray" is a substring of "Ray Harris."

The first example uses the empty function to check whether the variable named $first_name is empty. If so, this code stores a message in the variable named $message that indicates that you must enter a first name. This code is executed if the $first_name variable hasn't been set, or if the variable contains a NULL value, an empty string (""), or a string of "0".

The second example shows how to use the strlen and substr functions. To start, the first statement stores a string of "Ray Harris" in the $name variable. Then, the second statement uses the strlen function to get an integer value for the length. Next, the third and fourth statements use the substr function to get substrings for the first and last name.

When working with strings, you often need to specify the *position* of a character within a string. To do that, you use a value of 0 for the first character, 1 for the second character, and so on. In this figure, for example, the third statement gets a substring that starts at the first character (position 0) and has a length of three characters. As a result, it returns a value of "Ray". The fourth statement, on the other hand, gets a string that starts at the fifth character (position 4) and goes to the end of the string. As a result, it returns a value of "Harris".

When using the substr function, you can also specify a negative value for the second parameter to indicate a starting position relative to a string's end instead of its start. For example, the fifth statement in the second example specifies a value of -6 so the substring starts six characters from the end of the string. As a result, it returns a value of "Harris".

The third example shows how to format a phone number. To start, the first statement stores the phone number as a string that contains numbers with no formatting characters. Then, the next three statements use the substr function to extract the three parts of the phone number. Finally, the fifth and sixth statements join these three parts together into two different formats.

The fourth example shows how to use a for loop to process each character in a string separately. This loop increments a counter from 0 to one less than the length of the string. Within the loop, the first statement uses the substr function to extract the character at the current position in the string and store it in a variable named $vert_str. Then, the second statement appends a <br /> tag to that string. As a result, when the browser displays this string, it displays each character on its own line.

A URL for a list of all PHP string functions

```
http://www.php.net/manual/en/ref.strings.php
```

Functions for working with string length and substrings

Function	Description
empty(*$str*)	Returns TRUE if $str is the empty string (""), a NULL value, or "0" (0 as a string). This function also returns TRUE if $str isn't set.
strlen(*$str*)	Returns the length of the string.
substr(*$str*, *$i*[, *$len*])	Returns a substring of $str starting at the position specified by $i and containing the number of characters specified by $len. If $len is omitted, the function returns the substring from $i to the end of the string.

Code that checks a string to determine if a string is empty

```php
if (empty($first_name)) {
    $message = 'You must enter the first name.';
}
```

Code that gets the length of a string and two substrings

```php
$name = 'Ray Harris';
$length = strlen($name);              // $length is 10
$first_name = substr($name, 0, 3);    // $first_name is 'Ray'
$last_name = substr($name, 4);        // $last_name is 'Harris'
$last_name = substr($name, -6);       // $last_name is 'Harris'
```

Code that formats a phone number in two ways

```php
$phone = '5545556624';
$part1 = substr($phone, 0, 3);
$part2 = substr($phone, 3, 3);
$part3 = substr($phone, 6);
$format_1 = $part1 . '-' . $part2 . '-' . $part3;            // 554-555-6624
$format_2 = '(' . $part1 . ') ' . $part2 . '-' . $part3;  // (554) 555-6624
```

Code that displays each letter in a string on a separate line

```php
$input = 'JAN';
for ($i = 0; $i < strlen($input); $i++) {
    $vert_str .= substr($input, $i, 1);
    $vert_str .= '<br />';
}
```

Description

- The *length* of a string is the number of characters in the string.
- A *substring* is a part of another string.
- To specify the *position* of a character from the left side of a string, use a positive integer value where 0 is the first character, 1 is the second character, and so on. To specify a position from the right side, use a negative integer value.

Figure 9-3   How to work with string length and substrings

How to search a string

Figure 9-4 shows how to use four functions to search a string. If these functions find the search string, they return an integer value that indicates the position where the string was found. But if the string isn't found, these functions return a Boolean value of FALSE. As a result, if you want to code a conditional expression to test for a FALSE value, you must use the identity operator (===), which you learned about in the last chapter, rather than the equality operator (==). Otherwise, your conditional expression converts integer values of 0 to FALSE values and doesn't evaluate correctly.

The strpos and stripos functions search the string in a forward direction, from the start of the string towards the end. The strrpos and strripos functions reverse the direction of the search. As a result, they search from the end of the string towards the start.

The first example shows how to use the strpos and strrpos functions to search a string for spaces. Here, the first statement defines a string of "Martin Van Buren". Then, the second statement uses the strpos function to find the position of the first space in the string. Here, the seventh character is a space, which corresponds with a position of 6. Next, the third statement begins searching at position 7. As a result, it finds the position of the second space in the string. Finally, the fourth statement uses the strrpos to search from the end of the string to the start. This also finds the second space in the string.

The second example shows how to search a string for a substring. Here, the second statement uses the strpos function to search the string for a substring of "Van". Since this substring starts at position 7, this function returns a value of 7. Then, the third statement shows that the strpos function is case-sensitive. Since this statement doesn't find a substring of "van", it returns a Boolean value of FALSE. Next, the fourth statement shows how to use the stripos function to perform a search that's case-insensitive. Finally, the fifth statement uses the strripos function to perform a reverse search that's also case-insensitive.

The third example shows how to use the result of a search to work with a string. Here, the first statement uses the strpos function to search the string for a space. Then, this code checks if the result is FALSE. If so, this code stores a message that the string doesn't contain spaces. Otherwise, this code splits the string into two strings based on the position of the space.

How to replace part of a string

This figure also shows how to use the str_replace and str_ireplace functions to replace part of a string. Here, the first example after the table for these functions shows how to replace periods in a phone number with dashes. Then, the second example uses the str_ireplace function to perform a case-insensitive operation that successfully replaces "Hello" with "Hi" even though the search string was "hello".

Functions that search a string

Function	Description
`strpos($str1, $str2[, $offset])`	Searches $str1 for an occurrence of $str2. If $str2 is found, returns an integer value for the position. If $str2 isn't found, returns FALSE. By default, the search starts at position 0, but you can use $offset to specify the start position.
`stripos($str1, $str2[, $offset])`	A version of strpos that's case-insensitive.
`strrpos($str1, $str2[, $offset])`	A version of strpos that searches in reverse, from the end of the string to the start.
`strripos($str1, $str2[, $offset])`	A version of strrpos that's case-insensitive.

Code that searches a string for spaces

```
$name = 'Martin Van Buren';
$i = strpos($name, ' ');          // $i is 6
$i = strpos($name, ' ', 7);       // $i is 10 - use offset to find second space
$i = strrpos($name, ' ');         // $i is 10 - search string in reverse
```

Code that searches a string for a substring

```
$name = 'Martin Van Buren';
$i = strpos($name, 'Van');        // $i is 7
$i = strpos($name, 'van');        // $i is FALSE - case-sensitive
$i = stripos($name, 'van');       // $i is 7      - case-insensitve
$i = strripos($name, 'A');        // $i is 8      - reverse + case-insensitve
```

Code that splits a string into two substrings

```
$name = 'Ray Harris';
$i = strpos($name, ' ');
if ($i === false) {
    $message = 'No spaces were found in the name.';
} else {
    $first_name = substr($name, 0, $i);     // $first_name = Ray
    $last_name = substr($name, $i+1);       // $last_name = Harris
}
```

Functions that replace part of a string

Function	Description
`str_replace($str1, $new, $str2)`	Returns a new string with all occurrences of $str1 in $str2 replaced with $new. It is case sensitive.
`str_ireplace($str1, $new, $str2)`	A version of str_replace that's case-insensitive.

Code that replaces periods with dashes in a phone number

```
$phone = '554.555.6624';
$phone = str_replace('.', '-', $phone);     // $phone is '554-555-6624'
```

Code that replaces one string with another string

```
$message = 'Hello Ray';
$message = str_ireplace('hello', 'Hi', $message);   // $message is 'Hi Ray'
```

Figure 9-4   How to search strings and replace parts of strings

How to modify strings

Figure 9-5 shows how to use functions that return a modified version of the original string. To start, you can use the ltrim, rtrim, and trim functions to remove, or *trim*, unwanted characters from the start or end of a string. In this figure, the first example shows how to trim spaces from a string.

You can use the str_pad function to add characters to the start or end of a string. This is known as *padding* a string. This is often useful if you need to use spaces to align columns of data. In this figure, the first example shows how to pad a string with spaces. Here, the first str_pad function specifies a width of 13. At this point, the string is only 10 characters wide. As a result, this adds three spaces to the right side of the string. Then, the second str_pad function specifies a width of 16, and it specifies that the left side of the string should be padded with the space character. At this point, the string has a width of 13. As a result, this adds three spaces to the left side of the string. Together these two statements, center the text in the string.

You can use the lcfirst, ucfirst, and ucwords functions to convert some characters in a string to lowercase or uppercase. In addition, you can use the strtolower and strtoupper functions to convert the entire string to lowercase or uppercase. The second example shows how these functions work.

You can use the strrev and str_shuffle functions to change the sequence of the characters in a string. In particular, the strrev function reverses the characters in the string, and the str_shuffle function randomly shuffles the characters in the string. The third example shows how these functions work.

You can use the str_repeat function to repeat a string a certain number of times. This is sometimes useful for creating strings. For instance, the fourth example in this figure repeats the asterisk character 10 times and stores the resulting string in a variable named $sep.

Functions that modify strings

Function	Description
ltrim(*$str*)	Returns a new string with white space trimmed from the left side of the string.
rtrim(*$str*)	Returns a new string with white space trimmed from the right side of the string.
trim(*$str*)	Returns a new string with white space trimmed from both sides of the string.
str_pad(*$str*, *$len* [, *$pad*[, *$type*]])	Returns a new string with $str padded on the right with spaces until it is $len characters long. By default, the pad character is a space, but you can use the optional $pad parameter to specify a different padding character. By default, padding is added to the right, but you can use the optional $type parameter to add padding to the left, right, or both. To do that, you can use these constants: STR_PAD_RIGHT, STR_PAD_LEFT, and STR_PAD_BOTH.
lcfirst(*$str*)	Returns a new string with the first character converted to lowercase.
ucfirst(*$str*)	Returns a new string with the first character converted to uppercase.
ucwords(*$str*)	Returns a new string with the first letter of each word in uppercase.
strtolower(*$str*)	Returns a new string with all letters in lowercase.
strtoupper(*$str*)	Returns a new string with all letters in uppercase.
strrev(*$str*)	Returns a new string with the sequence of characters in reverse.
str_shuffle(*$str*)	Returns a new string with the characters in $str randomly shuffled.
str_repeat(*$str*, *$i*)	Returns a new string with $str repeated $i times.

Code that trims and pads a string

```
$name = '   ray harris    ';
$name = ltrim($name);          // $name is 'ray harris    '
$name = rtrim($name);          // $name is 'ray harris'

$name = str_pad($name, 13);    // $name is 'ray harris    '
$name = str_pad($name, 16,
         ' ', STR_PAD_LEFT);   // $name is '    ray harris   '

$name = trim($name);           // $name is 'ray harris'
```

Code that works with capitalization

```
$name = ucfirst($name);        // $name is 'Ray harris'
$name = lcfirst($name);        // $name is 'ray harris'
$name = ucwords($name);        // $name is 'Ray Harris'
$name = strtolower($name);     // $name is 'ray harris'
$name = strtoupper($name);     // $name is 'RAY HARRIS'
```

Code that changes the sequence of the characters

```
$name = strrev($name);         // $name is 'SIRRAH YAR'
$name = str_shuffle($name);    // $name is 'SHYIRRR AA' (for example)
```

Code that repeats a string

```
$sep = str_repeat('*', 10);    // $sep is '**********'
```

Figure 9-5   How to modify strings

How to convert strings to and from arrays

Figure 9-6 shows how to convert strings to and from arrays. This is often useful when working with strings.

To convert a string to an array of substrings, you can use the explode function as shown in the first example. Here, the first statement creates a $names variable that contains four names that are delimited by a pipe character (|). Then, the second statement uses the explode function to convert the $names variable from a string to an array. Finally, the third and fourth statements show that you can use an index to access the elements in the array. Note that the values that are stored in the array don't include the delimiter character.

Conversely, to convert an array to a string, you can use the implode function as shown in the second example. Here, the first statement specifies a delimiter of the pipe character (|). As a result, this function inserts this delimiter between the strings.

When working with these functions, you can specify a delimiter of any length, including empty. If you specify an empty string as the delimiter for the explode function, it returns FALSE. If you specify an empty string as the delimiter for the implode function, it returns all of the substrings joined together without a delimiter.

A string that is separated by tabs is known as *tab-delimited data*. To work with this type of data, you can use a tab character as the delimiter. To specify a tab character, you can use the \t escape sequence. This is illustrated by the third example.

How to convert strings to and from ASCII values

The *ASCII character set* is a set of characters that provides for most characters, numbers, and symbols in the English language. This character set is commonly used, and it provides an integer value that corresponds with each character. If necessary, you can convert characters within strings to and from their ASCII integer values.

To convert an integer value to an ASCII character, you can use the chr function. In this figure, the first example after the table for these functions converts integer values of 65 and 66 to strings of "A" and "B".

To convert a character to an integer value, you can use the ord function. In this figure, the next example converts strings of "A" and "B" to integer values of 65 and 66. Note, however, that this function is designed to work with a string that contains a single string character such as "B". If you pass this function a longer string such as "Bike", it only returns the integer value for the first character in the string.

Functions that convert between strings and arrays

Function	Description
explode(*$sep*, *$str*)	Returns an array of strings that are separated in $str by the string delimiter specified by $sep. This delimiter can be any length. If it is an empty string, this function returns FALSE.
implode(*$sep*, *$sa*)	Returns a string that results from joining the elements in the array $sa with the $sep string between them. The $sep parameter is required, but it may be an empty string.

How to convert a string to an array

```
$names = 'Mike|Anne|Joel|Ray';
$names = explode('|', $names);
$name1 = $names[0];      // $name1 is 'Mike'
$name2 = $names[1];      // $name2 is 'Anne'
```

How to convert an array to a string

```
$names = implode('|', $names);   // $names is 'Mike|Anne|Joel|Ray'
```

How to convert an array to a tab-delimited string

```
$names = implode('\t', $names);
```

Functions that convert between strings and ASCII integer values

Function	Description
chr(*$value*)	Returns a string with the character who's ASCII value is specified by $value.
ord(*$string*)	Returns an integer which is the ASCII value of the first character in $string.

How to convert an integer value to a character

```
$char = chr(65);      // $char is 'A'
$char = chr(66);      // $char is 'B'
```

How to convert a character to an integer value

```
$val = ord('A');      // $val is 65
$val = ord('B');      // $val is 66
$val = ord('Bike');   // $val is 66
```

Description

- The *ASCII character set* is a set of characters that provides for most characters, numbers, and symbols in the English language. This character set has an integer value that corresponds with each character.

Figure 9-6   How to convert strings to and from arrays and ASCII values

How to compare strings

Figure 9-7 shows four functions that you can use to determine the sequence of two strings. These functions return -1 if the first string comes before the second string; 1 if the first string comes after the second string; and zero if they're the same. Determining the sequence can be useful if you want to sort a series of string values.

The strcmp function is case-sensitive. As a result, "Orange" comes before "apple". Since this isn't usually what you want, it's common to use the strcasecmp function. This function ignores case when comparing strings. As a result, "apple" comes before "Orange", which is usually what you want.

If you are comparing strings that contain numbers, you may want to use the versions of these methods that use a "natural" comparison for numbers. For example, if you use the strcasecmp function, "img10" comes before "img6", which usually isn't what you want. However, with the strnatcasecmp function, "img6" comes before "img10", which is usually what you want.

The third example in this figure shows how to compare two strings. Here, the first statement uses the strnatcasecmp function to compare two strings. Then, this code uses an if statement to check whether the string is a negative number, zero, or a positive number. Finally, this statement uses an echo statement to display a message that's based on the result of the comparison.

Functions that compare two strings

Function	Description
strcmp(*$str1, $str2*)	Compares two strings and returns an integer value that indicates their sequence: -1 if $str1 comes before $str2, 1 if $str1 comes after $str2, or 0 if they're the same. This comparison is case-sensitive. As a result, upper-case comes before lowercase.
strcasecmp(*$str1, $str2*)	A version of the strcmp function that's case-insensitive.
strnatcmp(*$str1, $str2*)	A version of the strcmp function that uses a "natural" comparison for numbers within the string.
strnatcasecmp(*$str1, $str2*)	A version of the strcmp function that uses a "natural" comparison for numbers and is *not* case-sensitive.

How a case-sensitive comparison works

```
$result = strcmp('Anders', 'Zylka');      // $result is -1 (A before Z)
$result = strcmp('anders', 'Zylka');      // $result is 1  (Z before a)
$result = strcasecmp('anders', 'Zylka'); // $result is -25 (a before Z)
```

How a "natural" number comparison works

```
$result = strcmp('img06', 'img10');       // $result is -1 (img06 first)
$result = strcmp('img6', 'img10');        // $result is 1  (img10 first)
$result = strnatcmp('img6', 'img10');     // $result is -1 (img6 first)
```

How to compare two strings

```
$result = strnatcasecmp($name_1, $name_2);

if ($result < 0) {
    echo $name_1 . ' before ' . $name_2;
} else if ($result == 0) {
    echo $name_1 . ' matches ' . $name_2;
} else {
    echo $name_1 . ' after ' . $name_2;
}
```

Description

- You can use the compare functions to determine the sequence of two strings. This can be useful if you need to sort a series of string values.

Figure 9-7   How to compare strings

How to work with numbers

Chapter 2 presented the basic skills for working with numbers. This topic expands on those skills.

How to assign integers

As you learned in chapter 2, an *integer* is a number that doesn't have a fractional part. Integers are also known as *whole numbers*. An integer can be positive, negative, or zero.

Figure 9-8 shows how to assign an integer to a variable. Integers can be entered in three bases: *decimal* (base 10), *octal* (base 8), and *hexadecimal* (base 16). Most of the time, you use decimal values to work with integers. However, for the sake of completeness, this figure also shows how to work with octal and hexadecimal values.

The first example shows you how to assign decimal (base 10) values. Since you have been using base 10 values throughout this book, you shouldn't have any trouble understanding this example. If necessary, you can add a leading positive sign (+) or negative sign (-) to change the sign of the number. You can even use two negative signs to return a positive number if you code the inner number within parentheses. However, you can't use two negative signs (--) to return a positive value. If you attempt to do that, PHP interprets the two negative signs as the decrement operator.

The maximum positive integer value that can be represented by PHP is typically 2,147,483,647. PHP stores this value in the constant named PHP_INT_MAX. The second example shows how to use this constant to assign the maximum and minimum values for an integer to variables. If you attempt to assign an integer value that's outside this range, PHP automatically converts the integer to a floating-point number since floating-point numbers can store larger values.

The third example shows how to work with octal (base 8) values. Although you probably won't ever need to use octal values, it's important to know that PHP interprets integers that start with a leading zero as octal values. As a result, if you want to code a decimal value, you must *not* start the integer with a zero. If you do, PHP interprets the integer as an octal value, causing calculations with that number to be wrong and introducing a bug into your code that can be hard to find.

The fourth example shows you how to assign hexadecimal (base 16) values. A hexadecimal value begins with 0x or 0X, and the value isn't case-sensitive. If you have experience doing web development, you've probably used hexadecimal values when working with color values in your HTML and CSS code. However, you typically don't need to use hexadecimal values in your PHP code.

How to assign a decimal value (base 10)

```
$number_1 = 42;
$number_2 = +72;      // Positive numbers can have an optional plus sign
$number_3 = -13;      // Negative numbers must begin with a minus sign
$number_4 = -(-39);   // Same as 39 - two negatives make a positive
$number_5 = --39;     // Error - two minus signs are the decrement operator
```

How to find the maximum and minimum integer values (base 10)

```
$max_int = PHP_INT_MAX;
$min_int = -1 * (PHP_INT_MAX + 1);
```

How to assign an octal value (base 8)

```
$octal_1 = 0251;      // Must begin with 0 - 251 octal is 169 decimal
$octal_2 = -0262;     // An octal value can be negative
```

How to assign a hexadecimal value (base 16)

```
$hex_1 = 0X5F;        // Must begin with 0x or 0X - 5F hex is 95 decimal
$hex_2 = 0x4a3b;      // Upper and lower case letters are allowed
```

Description

- An *integer* is a number without a fractional part. Integers are also called *whole numbers*.

- An integer may be positive, negative, or zero.

- To assign an integer value, you can use *decimal* (base 10), *octal* (base 8), or *hexadecimal* (base 16) values.

- When assigning decimal values, do not begin the value with a zero. If you do, PHP interprets the value as an octal value.

- When assigning octal values, you must begin the value with a zero.

- When assigning hexadecimal values, you must begin the value with 0x or 0X. Then, you can specify the hexadecimal value.

- The constant named PHP_INT_MAX holds the largest positive integer that can be represented. This value is typically about 2 billion. If an integer value exceeds PHP_INT_MAX, PHP converts the value to a floating-point value.

Figure 9-8   How to assign integers

How to assign floating-point values

A *floating-point number* is a numerical value that has a fractional component. Floating-point numbers are also known as *floats*, *doubles*, or *real numbers*, and they always use base 10. When assigning a floating-point value, you can use normal notation or exponential notation as shown in figure 9-9.

The first example shows how to assign a floating-point value using normal notation. Note that you must include a decimal point in the number if you want it to be stored as a floating-point number. For example, PHP assigns a value of 1 to the integer data type, but it assigns a value of 1.0 to the floating-point data type.

The second example shows how to assign a floating-point value using *exponential notation*. This notation consists of a *mantissa*, the letter e, and an *exponent*. The mantissa can be a whole number or floating-point number in normal notation. The exponent is a whole number from -307 to 308. The exponential notation expands to m * 10^e. For example, 3.5e4 expands to 3.5 * 10^4 or 3500. Similarly, -1.25e-2 expands to -1.25 * 10^{-2} or -0.0125. Note that the sign of the mantissa determines if the overall number is positive or negative and the sign of the exponent determines if the number is larger or small than 1.

If a number is outside the range that can be represented by a floating-point value, it is converted to positive or negative infinity. Positive infinity is represented by the constant named INF while negative infinity is represented by the constant named –INF.

The third example shows operations that involve an infinite value. You can assign infinity directly to a variable or the result of an operation may be infinite. Most operations where one operand is infinity have an infinite result. The exception is that PHP returns a value of 0 if you divide by infinity. On a related note, PHP generates a warning if you divide by 0 even though some other languages, such as JavaScript, return an infinite value.

The fourth example shows how to use the is_infinite function to test if a value is infinite. Since the multiplication operation in the first line of code results in an infinite value, the if statement displays a message that indicates the result was out of range.

How to assign floating-point values

Using normal notation
```
$float_1 = 3.5;        // Must contain a decimal point
$float_2 = -6.0;       // May be negative
$float_3 = .125;       // Same as 0.125
$float_4 = 1.;         // Same as 1.0
```

Using exponential notation
```
$exp_1 = 9.451e15;     // Expands to 9.451 x 10¹⁵ - 9451000000000000
$exp_2 = 6.022e+23;    // Plus sign for exponent is optional
$exp_3 = 1.602e-19;    // Exponent may be negative
$exp_4 = 9.806e0;      // Exponent may be zero
$exp_5 = -1.759e11;    // Mantissa may be negative
$exp_6 = 3e9;          // Mantissa may be a whole number
```

Two functions for working with infinity

Function	Description
is_infinite($value)	Returns TRUE if $value is a positive or negative infinite value.
is_finite($value)	Returns TRUE if $value is a finite value.

Working with infinity

Getting an infinite value
```
$inf_x = INF;              // Positive infinity, case-sensitive
$inf_x = -INF;             // Negative infinity
$inf_x = 1e200 * 1e200;    // Result is INF
$inf_x = 1 + INF;          // Result is INF
$inf_x = 1 / INF;          // Result is 0
$inf_x = 1 / 0;            // Generates a warning
```

Testing for an infinite value
```
$result = 1e200 * 1e200;
if (is_infinite($result)) {
    echo('Result was out of range.');
} else {
    echo('Result is ' . $result);
}
```

Description

- A *floating-point number* is a number with a fractional part. Floating point numbers are also called *floats*, *doubles*, or *real numbers*.

- To store numbers that are extremely large or small, you can use *exponential notation*. A floating-point number has about 14 digits of precision and the exponent can typically range from -307 to 308.

- The constants named INF and –INF represent infinite values. INF represents numbers that are too large to store as floating-point numbers, and –INF represents numbers that are too small to store.

- Operations that involve an infinite value may return unexpected results.

- Dividing by zero generates a warning.

Figure 9-9   How to assign floating-point values

How to use the math functions

Figure 9-10 shows how to use some of the most common functions for performing math with numbers. However, if you need to perform another mathematical operation on a number, you should know that there are many more math functions available in PHP. To learn more about these functions, you can visit the URL that's shown at the top of this figure.

The functions described in this figure work with both integers and floating-point values. Most of these functions work as you would expect. However, the max and min functions take two or more values as parameters. In other words, you can code a variable number of arguments for these functions.

If you study the examples, you shouldn't have much trouble understanding how these functions work. To start, the first example shows how to use the round function to round a floating-point value. Then, the second example shows how to use the sqrt function to get the square root of a number. Next, the third example shows how to use the pow function to raise one number to a power.

The fourth example shows how to calculate the distance between two points. This calculation uses the sqrt and pow functions to implement the Pythagorean Theorem to find the distance between two points.

The fifth example shows how to place an upper bound on a number. It uses the min function to ensure that the value is no more than the maximum number allowed. In this case, that number is 10.

URL for a list of all PHP math functions

```
http://www.php.net/manual/en/ref.math.php
```

Common mathematical functions

Function	Description
abs(*$value*)	Returns the absolute value of a number.
ceil(*$value*)	Returns the value rounded up to the next highest whole number.
floor(*$value*)	Returns the value rounded down to the next lowest whole number.
max(*$n1, $n2*[, *$n3* ...])	Returns the value of the largest number provided.
min(*$n1, $n2*[, *$n3* ...])	Returns the value of the smallest number provided.
pi()	Returns the value of pi (approximately 3.141593).
pow(*$base, $exp*)	Returns the value of the calculation of $base to the power of $exp. Both parameters may be floating-point numbers.
round(*$value*[, *$precision*])	Returns the value that results from rounding $value to the number of decimal points specified by $precision. If $precision is omitted, its default is 0. If $precision is negative, this method rounds to a whole number. For example, -1 rounds to the nearest ten and -2 rounds to the nearest hundred.
sqrt(*$value*)	Returns the square root of $value.

How to round a number

```
$subtotal = 15.99;
$tax_rate = 0.08;
$tax = round($subtotal * $tax_rate, 2);   // 1.28 instead of 1.2792
```

How to get the square root of a number

```
$num1 = 4;
$root = sqrt($num1);          // 2
```

How to work with exponents

```
$num2 = 5;
$power = pow($num2, 2);       // 5 raised to the power of 2 = 25
```

How to calculate the distance between two points

```
$x1 = 5; $y1 = 4;
$x2 = 2; $y2 = 8;
$distance = sqrt(pow($x1 - $x2, 2) + pow($y1 - $y2, 2));   // 5
```

How to place a maximum bound on a number

```
$value = 15;
$max_value = 10;
$value = min($max_value, $value);   // 10
```

Figure 9-10   How to use the math functions

How to generate random numbers

Figure 9-11 shows how to use functions to generate random numbers. To start, this figure shows three standard functions for working with random numbers. Then, it shows the Mersenne Twister equivalents of these functions. Unless you have a compelling reason for doing otherwise, you should use the Mersenne Twister functions because these functions generate better random numbers than the standard functions.

The first example shows how to use the mt_rand function to simulate a dice roll. This code returns an integer from 1 to 6.

The second example shows how to generate a random floating-point value between 0 and 1 with 5 digits of precision. To start, the first statement initializes the number to zero. Within the for loop, the first statement generates a random number between 0 and 9 and adds it to the number. Then, the second statement shifts the decimal point to the left by dividing the number by 10. So, let's say the first three random numbers are 8, 3, and 6. In that case, the number is 0.8 after the first loop, 0.38 after the second loop, and 0.638 after the third loop. This process is repeated until the value is 5 digits long.

The third example shows how to generate a random password that includes one symbol, one number, one uppercase letter, and five lowercase letters. To start, the first statement defines a string of possible symbols to pick from. Then, it picks a position in this string at random using the strlen and mt_rand functions. Next, it uses the substr function to add the symbol to the password.

After adding a symbol, this code picks a random number and a random uppercase letter and adds them to the password. To understand this code, you need to know that numbers 0 through 9 have the values 48 to 57 in the ASCII character set. Similarly, the uppercase letters range from 65 to 90 in the ASCII character set.

After adding the number and uppercase letter, this code adds random lowercase letters until the password is the specified length. This time, the ASCII values range from 97 through 122. Then, the str_shuffle function is used to randomly shuffle the characters in the password.

Functions that generate random numbers

Function	Description
`getrandmax()`	Returns the largest integer the rand function can return. This may be a relatively small number (about 32000) on some systems.
`rand()`	Returns a random integer between 0 and getrandmax().
`rand($lo, $hi)`	Returns a random integer between $lo and $hi.
`mt_getrandmax()`	Returns the largest integer the mt_rand function can return. This number is typically PHP_INT_MAX.
`mt_rand()`	Returns a random integer between 0 and mt_getrandmax(). This function uses the Mersenne Twister algorithm which is faster and "more random" than the algorithm used by the rand function.
`mt_rand($lo, $hi)`	Returns a random integer between $lo and $hi using the Mersenne Twister algorithm.

How to simulate a random dice roll

```
$dice = mt_rand(1, 6);
```

How to generate a random value between 0 and 1 with 5 decimal places

```
$number = 0;
$places = 5;                    // Number of decimal places
for($i = 0; $i < $places; $i++) {
    $number += mt_rand(0,9);   // Add the random number
    $number /= 10;             // Increase the number of decimal places
}
echo $number;                  // For example 0.46073
```

How to generate a random password

```
$password_length = 8;

// Add a symbol to the password
$symbols  = '~!@#$%^&*()-_=+[]{};:,.<>?';    // Symbols to pick from
$symbol_count = strlen($symbols);
$index = mt_rand(0, $symbol_count - 1);      // Choose a random position
$password = substr($symbols, $index , 1);    // Add the symbol

$password .= chr(mt_rand(48, 57));           // Add a number
$password .= chr(mt_rand(65, 90));           // Add an uppercase letter

// Add lowercase letters to reach the specified length
while (strlen($password) < $password_length) {
    $password .= chr(mt_rand(97, 122));
}

$password = str_shuffle($password);          // Shuffle the characters
echo $password;                              // For example, 'd7kug-Hf'
```

Figure 9-11   How to generate random numbers

Other skills for working with strings and numbers

This topic presents some other skills that you can use for formatting strings and numbers as well as converting strings to numbers.

How to use the sprintf function to format strings and numbers

Part 1 of figure 9-12 shows how to use the sprintf function to format strings and numbers. You can use this function to code a single *format string* that formats multiple string and numeric values based on their corresponding *format codes*.

When you call the sprintf function, you pass the format string as the first parameter. Then, you pass the values to be formatted as the remaining parameters. The sequence of the parameters must match the sequence of their format codes in the format string.

The simplest format code consists of the percent sign (%) followed by one of the data type characters listed in this figure. For example, a code of %s formats the value as a string. Similarly, a code of %d formats the value as an integer.

The first example shows a sprintf function that formats two values. Here, the first parameter contains a format string that contains two format codes. Then, the next two parameters supply the values to be formatted. The first value is a string that's formatted as a string, and the second value is an integer that's formatted as an integer.

The second example shows how to use the sprintf function to format values as other data types. For example, the first statement formats an integer as a string. The second and third statements format floating-point numbers as strings. The fourth and fifth statements format floating-point numbers in exponential notation and in standard notation. The sixth statement formats an integer as an ASCII character. And the seventh and eighth statements format an integer as a hexadecimal value.

If you want to include a percent sign in the format string, you can code two percent signs. This indicates that you want to include a single percent sign instead of starting a new format code. In this figure, the format string for the variable named $s9 converts a floating-point number to a string and includes a percent sign after the number.

The sprintf function

Name	Description
sprintf($format, $val1[, val2 ...])	Returns a string that contains one or more values that are formatted as specified by the $format parameter.

Data type code

Character	Description
s	Formats the value as a string.
d	Formats the value as an integer.
f	Formats the value as a floating-point number.
e	Formats the value using exponential notation.
c	Formats an integer value as its corresponding ASCII character.
b	Formats an integer value as a binary number.
o	Formats an integer value as an octal number.
x	Formats an integer value as a hexadecimal number (lowercase).
X	Formats an integer value as a hexadecimal number (uppercase).

A sprintf function that formats two values

```
$message = sprintf('The book about %s has %d pages.', 'PHP', 800);
```

How to use sprintf to convert numbers to strings

```
$s1 = sprintf('It cost %s dollars', 12);        // It cost 12 dollars
$s2 = sprintf('%s', 4.5);                        // 4.5
$s3 = sprintf('%s', 9451000.000000);             // 9451000
$s4 = sprintf('%f', 9.451e6);                    // 9451000.000000
$s5 = sprintf('%e', 9451000.000000);             // 9.451000e+6
$s6 = sprintf('%c', 65);                         // A
$s7 = sprintf('%x', 15);                         // f
$s8 = sprintf('%X', 15);                         // F
$s9 = sprintf('%s%%', 4.5);                      // 4.5%
```

Description

- Within a sprintf function, the *format string* can contain one or more format codes.

- A *format code* always begins with the % sign and ends with a character that specifies the data type for the value.

- To code a percent sign (%) within a format string, code two percent signs.

Figure 9-12 How to use the sprintf function (part 1 of 2)

The table in part 2 of figure 9-12 shows all the parts of a format code. As you've learned, all format codes begin with a percent sign and end with a character that specifies the data type. However, between these required parts of a format code, you can use the optional specifiers shown in this figure.

The first example shows how to use the optional format specifiers. For instance, the first two statements use the plus sign (+) to include a positive or negative sign in the formatted value.

The next three statements format a string with a minimum width of 10 characters. Here, the third statement aligns the string to the right by padding it with spaces on the left. The fourth statement aligns the string to the left by padding it with spaces on the right. And the fifth statement aligns the string to the left by padding it with asterisks (*) on the right.

The next two statements format integer values with a width of 6 characters. Here, the sixth statement aligns the integer to the right by padding it with spaces on the left. The seventh statement also aligns the integer to the right, but pads the value with zeros.

The eighth statement contains three format codes that format a date. These three format codes format three integers by padding them with zeros on the left. Here, the first two format codes are two characters wide, and the third format code is four characters wide. Note that the dashes between the format codes are literal values that are displayed in the string that's returned by the sprintf function.

The ninth statement formats a floating-point value. This value is formatted so it is ten characters wide and has two decimal places. Note that the sprintf function rounds the value from 123.456 to 123.46 to get the correct number of decimal places.

The last example shows how to generate a random HTML color value. Here, the first statement stores a pound sign (#) in the $color variable. Then, this code executes a loop six times. Within the loop, there is a single statement that generates a random number between 0 and 15, uses the sprintf function to format the number as a hexadecimal digit, and appends the hexadecimal digit to the $color variable.

The parts of a format code

Specifier	Required?	Description
%	Required	A percent sign always starts the format code. To code a percent sign within a format code, you can code two percent signs in a row (%%).
Sign	Optional	By default, the negative sign is displayed for negative numbers but no sign is displayed for positive number. To always display a sign, code a plus (+) or minus (-) sign.
Alignment	Optional	By default, the value is right-aligned. To align on the left, code a dash (-) character.
Padding	Optional	By default, the padding character is a space. To specify a different padding character, code a zero or a single quote (') followed by the padding character.
Width	Optional	To specify a minimum width, code an integer.
Precision	Optional	To specify precision, code a period (.) followed by an integer value. For a number, this indicates the number of decimal points. For a string, this indicates the maximum characters. Longer strings are truncated.
Data Type	Required	A code that specifies the data type. These data types are described in part 1 of this figure.

How to use the optional specifiers

```
$s1 = sprintf("%+d", 42);                    // Returns '+42'
$s2 = sprintf("%+d", -42);                   // Returns '-42'
$s3 = sprintf("%10s", 'PHP');                // Returns '       PHP'
$s4 = sprintf("%-10s", 'PHP');               // Returns 'PHP       '
$s5 = sprintf("%-'*10s", 'PHP');             // Returns 'PHP*******'
$s6 = sprintf("%6d", 42);                    // Returns '    42'
$s7 = sprintf("%06d", 42);                   // Returns '000042'
$s8 = sprintf("%02d-%02d-%04d", 3, 5, 2010); // Returns '03-05-2010'
$s9 = sprintf("%010.2f", 123.456);           // Returns '0000123.46'
```

How to generate a random HTML color

```
$color = '#';
for($i = 0; $i < 6; $i++) {
    $color .= sprintf("%x", mt_rand(0,15) );
}
echo $color;    // For example '#984e1e'
```

Figure 9-12   How to use the sprintf function (part 2 of 2)

How to convert strings to numbers

Figure 9-13 shows how to convert strings to numbers. One way to do that is to use *type casting*. To cast a value from one type to another, code the data type in parentheses followed by the value to convert. In this figure, for example, the examples show how to cast a string to the integer (int) data type or the floating-point (float) data type.

The first example shows how to convert string values to integer values. Here, the second statement shows that floating-point values are truncated, not rounded. Then, the third and fourth statements show that the conversion process stops when any non-numeric text is encountered. The fifth and sixth statements show that the resulting value is 0 if the string doesn't begin with a number. The seventh statement shows that values that are too large to be stored as integers return a value of PHP_INT_MAX. And the last two statements show that only base 10 numbers can be converted correctly using type casting.

The second example shows how to use the intval function to convert a string to an integer. This function follows the same rules as type casting when performing the conversion.

The third example shows how to convert strings to floating-point values by using type casting. Here, the second statement shows that any non-numeric text stops the conversion process. The third statement shows that the resulting value is 0 if the string doesn't begin with or contain a number. The fourth statement shows that type casting can convert a value that uses exponential notation. And the fifth statement shows that the resulting value is INF if the value is too large to be represented as a floating-point value.

The fourth example shows how to use the floatval function to convert a string to a floating-point value. Like the intval function, this function follows the same rules as type casting when performing the conversion.

Two functions for converting strings to numbers

Function	Description
`intval($var)`	Returns an integer value for the $var parameter.
`floatval($var)`	Returns a floating-point value for the $var parameter.

How to convert a string to an integer

Using type casting

```
$value_1 = (int) '42';              // Result is 42
$value_2 = (int) '42.5';            // Result is 42
$value_3 = (int) '42 miles';        // Result is 42
$value_4 = (int) '2,500 feet';      // Result is 2
$value_5 = (int) 'miles: 42';       // Result is 0
$value_6 = (int) 'miles';           // Result is 0
$value_7 = (int) '10000000000';     // Result is PHP_INT_MAX
$value_8 = (int) '042';             // Result is 42
$value_9 = (int) '0x42';            // Result is 0
```

Using the intval function

```
$value = intval('42');              // Result is 42
```

How to convert a string to a floating-point number

Using type casting

```
$value_1 = (float) '4.2';           // Result is 4.2
$value_2 = (float) '4.2 gallons';   // Result is 4.2
$value_3 = (float) 'gallons';       // Result is 0
$value_4 = (float) '1.5e-3';        // Result is 0.0015
$value_5 = (float) '1e400';         // Result is INF
```

Using the floatval function

```
$value = floatval('4.2');           // Result is 4.2
```

Description

- You can use *type casting* to convert, or *cast*, a value from one type to another. To do that, code the data type within parentheses just before the value that you want to convert. Here, you can use the int keyword for the integer data type and the float keyword for the floating-point data type.

- You can also use the intval and floatval functions to convert a value from one type to another. The result is the same as it is with type casting.

- When converting strings to numbers, any text after the number is ignored.

- When converting strings to numbers, strings that don't start with a number are converted to a value of 0.

- When converting strings to floating-point values, the string can use exponential notation.

- If a value is too large to fit in its data type, PHP converts integer values to the PHP_INT_MAX constant and floating-point values to the INF constant.

Figure 9-13   How to convert strings to numbers

Perspective

In this chapter, you learned new ways to work with strings and numbers. When you combine these skills with those you learned in section 1, you have the skills that you need for working with strings and numbers. In the next chapter, you'll learn the skills for working with dates and times.

Although this chapter includes the essential functions for working with strings and numbers, PHP provides many more. As a result, if you find yourself faced with a task, and it seems like PHP might provide a function that can help you with that task, there's a good chance the function exists. So, before you write your own code, you should search the online PHP reference manual to see if you can find the function you need. If you can find it, you can save a lot of time and effort.

Terms

variable substitution	integer
interpolation	whole number
heredoc	floating-point number
nowdoc	float
escape sequence	double
length of a string	real number
substring	exponential notation
position in a string	mantissa
trim a string	exponent
pad a string	format string
tab-delimited data	format code
ASCII character set	type casting

Summary

- When you use PHP, you can create strings by using single quotes, double quotes with *variable substitution*, *heredoc* syntax, and *nowdoc* syntax.

- *Escape sequences* provide a way to insert special characters into text strings. The htmlentities function provides a way to convert escape sequences and HTML characters to HTML character entities that display properly in a browser.

- PHP provides many functions for working with strings, including functions for getting the *length* and *substrings* of a string; for searching and replacing strings; for *trimming*, *padding*, and modifying strings; for converting strings to and from arrays; for comparing two strings; and for formatting strings based on format codes.

- PHP provides functions for working with both *integer* and *floating-point numbers*. It also provides functions for generating random numbers.

- You can use *type casting* to convert a string to an integer or floating-point number. You can also use the intval and floatval functions for these conversions.

Exercise 9-1   Write code that works with strings

In this exercise, you will write the PHP code that works with strings.

Open and test the application

1. Start the Firefox browser and run the application in the ex_starts/ch09_ex1 directory. To do that, you can use this URL:

    `http://localhost/ex_starts/ch09_ex1/`

    This should display a page that allows you to submit a name, email address, and phone number.

2. Enter data into the controls and click on the Submit button. Note that this displays a message that indicates that this application is under construction.

Write the code that processes the data entered by the user

3. Open the index.php file for this application and review the code. Note that it doesn't process the data that's entered into the text boxes.

4. Open the string_tester.php file for this application and review the code. Note that the PHP code that displays the $message variable uses the nl2br function to convert new line characters to <br /> tags.

5. Add the code that uses the data that's entered into the text box controls to display a message that's formatted like this:

    `Hello Joel,`

    `Thank you for entering this data:`

    `Name: Joel Murach`
    `Email: joelmurach@yahoo.com`
    `Phone: 415-123-4567`

    When formatting this message, use escape sequences to insert new line characters.

6. Make sure the user enters a name, but only display the first name in the message. For both the complete name and the first name, capitalize the first letter of the name only.

7. Make sure the user enters an email address, and make sure that this address contains at least one @ sign and one dot character (.).

8. Make sure the phone number contains at least seven digits, not including formatting characters such as dashes, spaces, and parenthesis.

9. Test the application to make sure it works correctly.

Exercise 9-2 Write code that works with numbers

In this exercise, you can write some PHP code that works with numbers.

Open and test the application

1. Start the Firefox browser and run the application in the ex_starts/ch09_ex2 directory. This should display a page that allows you to enter three numbers and provides starting values for the three numbers.

2. Click on the Submit button. Note that this displays a message that includes the values of the three numbers but doesn't include the values for the rest of the message.

Write the code that processes the data entered by the user

3. Open the index.php file for this application and review the code. Note that it doesn't process the data. Instead, it just displays the data on the form.

4. Open the number_tester.php file for this application and review the code. Note that the PHP code that displays the $message variable uses the nl2br function to convert new line characters to <br /> tags.

5. Add the code that uses the data that's entered into the text box controls to display a message that's formatted like this:

```
Number 1: 78
Number 2: -105.33
Number 3: 0.0049

Number 2 ceiling: -105
Number 2 floor: -106
Number 3 rounded: 0.005

Min: -105.33
Max: 78

Random: 86
```

When formatting this message, use escape sequences to insert new line characters.

6. Make sure the user enters all three numbers and that these numbers are valid.

7. Make sure the rounded number is rounded to 3 decimal places.

8. Make sure the random number is a number between 1 and 100.

9. Test the application to make sure it works correctly with the default values and also with other values.

10

How to work with dates

In chapter 2, you were introduced to the date function. In this chapter, you'll learn the rest of the skills that you need for working with dates and times in PHP.

To start, this chapter shows how to use timestamps to work with dates and times. Timestamps were widely used before PHP 5.0, and you're likely to encounter them if you have to work with old PHP code. Then, this chapter shows the newer object-oriented approach that was introduced with PHP 5.0. This approach has several advantages over the timestamp approach and is recommended for new development.

Fortunately, many of the skills for working with timestamps also apply to the object-oriented approach. As a result, once you learn how to work with timestamps, you shouldn't have much trouble learning how to use the object-oriented approach.

How to use timestamps to work with dates 292
How to create and format timestamps 292
How to work with timestamps 294
How to use the strtotime function 296
Examples of working with timestamps 298
How to use objects to work with dates 300
How to use the DateTime class 300
How to use the DateInterval class 302
How to use the DateInterval and DateTime classes together 304
Examples of working with DateTime objects 306
Perspective 308

How to use timestamps to work with dates

A *timestamp* uses an integer to represent a date and time. This integer stores the number of seconds since midnight on January 1, 1970 GMT (Greenwich Mean Time). This point in time is known as the *Unix Epoch*.

Today, most systems store a timestamp as a 32-bit signed integer. As a result, timestamps on these systems can range from December 13, 1901 to January 19, 2038. When these systems reach the upper limit in 2038, the number of seconds "rolls over" to the lower limit in 1901. When this happens, this will cause bugs due to erroneous calculations, and it's known as the *year 2038 problem*. Since this problem is similar to the Y2K problem that affected many applications in the year 2000, the year 2038 problem is also known as the *Y2K38 problem*. One way to solve this problem is to use DateTime objects as described later in this chapter instead of using timestamps.

How to create and format timestamps

Figure 10-1 shows how to use the date function to create and format timestamps. In the first argument for this function, each format code represents one part of a date or time. For example, the 'm' character represents the month part of a date. Note, however, that many parts of a date or time have multiple representations. For example, the month can be represented as a number without a leading zero, as a number with a leading zero, as a three-letter abbreviation, or as multiple letters that spell out the full name.

The first six statements show how this works. Here, the first three statements format the current date three different ways. Then, the next two statements format the current time in two different ways. Finally, the sixth statement formats both the date and the time.

Any character in the format string that isn't a format code is displayed as itself. For example, the first five statements include slashes, dashes, commas, spaces, and colons in the format string. However, if you want to display a format code as itself in the format string, you must code a backslash before the format code. For example, the sixth statement uses the backslash to include the 'a' and 't' characters in the format string. This is necessary because both the 'a' and 't' character are format codes. In this figure, the 't' character isn't listed in the table of format codes, but it is a format code. For a complete list of format codes, look up the date function in the PHP documentation.

Although you usually use the date function to format the timestamp for the current date and time, you can also use it to format other timestamps. To do that, you supply the timestamp as the second parameter as shown in the seventh statement. Here, the timestamp is an integer value for March 15, 2012. In the next figure, though, you'll learn several other ways to create timestamps and store them in variables. Then, you can use the date function to format those variables.

The date function

Name	Description
date(*$format*[, *$ts*])	Returns a string formatted as a date as specified by the format string. By default, this function works with the current date and time. However, you can use the second parameter to specify a timestamp for any date or time.

Common format codes for the date function

Character	Description	From	To
D	Day of week – three letters	Mon	Sun
l (lowercase L)	Day of week – full name	Monday	Sunday
n	Month – no leading zero	1	12
m	Month – leading zero	01	12
M	Month – three letters	Jan	Dec
F	Month – full name	January	December
j	Day of month – no leading zero	1	31
d	Day of month – leading zero	01	31
Y	Year – four digits	2010	
L	Leap year (1) or not (0)	0	1
g	Hours – 12-hour format, no leading zero	1	12
h	Hours – 24-hour format, no leading zero	0	23
G	Hours – 12-hour format, leading zero	01	12
H	Hours – 24-hour format, leading zero	00	23
i	Minutes – leading zero	00	59
s	Seconds – leading zero	00	59
a	am/pm – lowercase	am	pm
A	AM/PM – uppercase	AM	PM
T	Time zone abbreviation	EST	
U	Seconds since Unix epoch	-2,147,483,648	2,147,483,647

How to format a timestamp

```
$date1 = date('n/j/Y');                  // 3/15/2011
$date2 = date('Y-m-d');                  // 2011-03-15
$date3 = date('l, F d, Y');              // Monday, March 15, 2011
$date4 = date('g:i a');                  // 1:30 pm
$date5 = date('H:i:s');                  // 13:30:00
$date6 = date('Y-m-d \a\t H:i:s');       // 2011-03-15 at 13:30:00
$date7 = date('Y-m-d', 1331843400);      // 2012-03-15
```

Description

- A *timestamp* is an integer that represents a date and time as the number of seconds since midnight, January 1, 1970 GMT. This date and time is known as the *Unix epoch*.

- To include a literal value for a format character in the format string, code a backslash before the character.

Figure 10-1   How to create and format timestamps

How to work with timestamps

Figure 10-2 shows how to use four functions to work with timestamps. However, you should know that PHP provides many more functions to work with timestamps. For a complete list or for more information about the functions described in this figure, you can visit the URL shown at the top of this figure.

To create a timestamp, you can use either the time or mktime functions. The time function creates a timestamp for the current date and time, and the mktime function creates a timestamp from the values you provide. These functions return an integer value for the timestamp. To format the timestamp so it shows a date and time, you can use date function shown in the previous figure.

When using the mktime function, the parameters are optional. As a result, you can omit parameters starting with the last parameter and working towards the first parameter. If you omit a parameter, the mktime function uses the value from the current date and time. For example, the last parameter specifies the year. So, if you omit this parameter, the mktime function uses the current year for the timestamp. Similarly, if you omit the last two parameters, the mktime function uses the current year and day for the timestamp.

The mktime function doesn't validate the values provided to it. If a value for a part of the date or time is out of range, the other parts are adjusted to account for the excess amount in the out-of-range value. For example, if you provide a minute value of 90, this function adds 1 hour to the hour part and 30 minutes to the minute part.

To validate a date before using it, you can use the checkdate function. This is illustrated by the second example in this figure. Here, the checkdate function returns a FALSE value because the specified date is November 31, which isn't valid because November only has 30 days.

Although PHP doesn't provide a built-in function to validate a time, you can create a checktime function like the one in the third example to validate a 24 hour time. This function checks to make sure the specified hour is from 0 to 23 and the specified minutes and seconds are from 0 to 59. If so, it returns a true value. Otherwise, it returns a false value.

To get the parts of a timestamp, you can use the getdate function. This function takes a timestamp and returns an associative array that contains the date and time parts. In the example in this figure, the code uses the mktime function to make a new timestamp and the getdate function to convert that timestamp to an array named $parts. Then, it copies each part of the date from the $parts array into a separate variable.

URL for a list of all PHP timestamp functions

```
http://www.php.net/manual/en/ref.datetime.php
```

Functions for working with timestamps

Name	Description
`time()`	Returns the current date and time as a timestamp.
`mktime([$h[, $m[, $s[,` `$M[, $D[, $Y]]]]]])`	Returns a timestamp based on the time and date given. Any parts omitted are set to the value from the current date and time.
`checkdate($M, $D, $Y)`	Returns true if the provided month, day, and year values are a valid date.
`getdate([$ts])`	Returns an array containing the parts of the specified timestamp. If you omit the parameter, this function uses the current date and time.

How to create a timestamp

```
$now = time();                                // for example, 1265656521
$expires = mktime(13, 30, 0, 3, 15, 2012);    // 3/15/2012 13:30:00
$expires = mktime(13, 30, 0, 3, 15);          // uses current year
$expires = mktime(13, 30, 0, 3);              // uses current year and day
```

How to validate a date

```
$valid_date = checkdate(11, 31, 2012);        // returns FALSE
```

How to validate a time

A custom function for validating time

```
function checktime($h, $m, $s) {
    return $h >= 0 && $h < 24 && $m >= 0 && $m < 60 && $s >= 0 && $s < 60;
}
```

A statement that calls the custom function

```
$valid_time = checktime(12, 30, 0);           // TRUE
```

How to get the parts of a timestamp

```
$expires = mktime(13, 30, 0, 3, 15, 2012);
$parts = getdate($expires);
$year    = $parts['year'];      // 2012
$mon     = $parts['mon'];       // Month number - 3
$month   = $parts['month'];     // Month name - 'March'
$mday    = $parts['mday'];      // Day of month - 15
$weekday = $parts['weekday'];   // Weekday - 'Monday'
$wday    = $parts['wday'];      // Weekday as number - 1
$hours   = $parts['hours'];     // Hours - 13
$minutes = $parts['minutes'];   // Minutes - 30
$seconds = $parts['seconds'];   // Seconds - 0
```

Figure 10-2   How to work with timestamps

How to use the strtotime function

The strtotime function presented in figure 10-3 is one of the most versatile date and time functions in just about any programming language. Fortunately, most of the skills for using it also apply to DateTime objects. As a result, it makes sense to learn how to use this function whether you're going to use timestamps or DateTime objects.

You can use the strtotime function to generate a timestamp for most strings that specify dates. To do that, you can pass this function a string that specifies a date, a time, or a date and a time. This works for strings that store dates and times in most common formats. These types of strings are known as *absolute templates*.

In the first example, for instance, the first three statements specify strings for dates. Since these statements don't set the time, the time is set to midnight. Similarly, since the third statement doesn't set the year, the year is set to the current year. The next two statements specify strings for times. Since these statements don't set the date, the date is set to the current date. Finally, the last statement specifies a string for a date and a time.

The second example shows how to specify a format string that gets a timestamp that's relative to current date and time. The part of a format string that specifies a date or time relative to another date or time is known as a *relative template*. In the second example, for instance, the first statement uses a relative template to add one hour. The second statement subtracts two days. The third statement sets the date to the next day. Note that this resets the time to midnight. The fourth statement uses the relative template of "tomorrow" to set the date to the next day and also uses an absolute template to set the time to 10:15 am.

The fifth statement specifies next Sunday. The sixth statement sets the date to the last day of the current month. The seventh statement sets the date to the first day of the next month.

The eighth statement sets the date to third Wednesday of the current month. The ninth statement uses an absolute template to set the month to November, uses a relative template to set the day to the second Tuesday of that month, and uses an absolute template to set the time to 8 am.

The templates in the format string are processed from left to right. Most relative templates are cumulative and the changes are applied when the end of the format string is reached. Some relative templates reset the time to midnight. For these templates, you can specify time by coding an absolute time template after the relative template.

The third example shows how to use the strtotime function to modify a timestamp. To start, the first statement uses the mktime function to make a timestamp. Then, the second statement uses the strtotime function to get a timestamp that's three weeks later at 6 pm.

The strtotime function provides many more templates than we can cover in this chapter. Most of the time, these functions can convert your strings to timestamps. As a result, to get the most from this function, you may need to do some testing and experimentation.

The strtotime function

Name	Description
strtotime($str[, $ts])	Returns a timestamp for the specified string. By default, this function works relative to the current date and time. However, if you supply the $ts parameter, this function works relative to the specified timestamp. This function is able to parse most date and time formats and most relative time specifications.

Types of templates used in strtotime

Type	Description
Absolute	A format string that specifies a date or time. A date without a time sets the time to midnight. A partial date (for example, just month and day) leaves the unspecified date parts unchanged. A time without a date does not change the date. A partial time specification (for example, only hours and minutes) sets the unspecified time parts to zero.
Relative	An offset to be added to or subtracted from the base date and time. Some relative dates set the time to midnight.

How to generate a timestamp with an absolute template

```
// Examples assume a current time of Sun 04/08/2012 1:30:00 pm
$date1 = strtotime('2013-06-01');              // Sat 06/01/2013 00:00
$date2 = strtotime('6/1/2013');                // Sat 06/01/2013 00:00
$date3 = strtotime('Jun 1');                   // Fri 06/01/2012 00:00
$date4 = strtotime('8:45');                    // Sun 04/08/2012 08:45
$date5 = strtotime('8am');                     // Sun 04/08/2012 08:00
$date6 = strtotime('2013-02-29 8:45am');       // Fri 03/01/2013 08:45
```

How to generate a timestamp with a relative template

```
// Examples assume a current time of Sun 04/08/2012 1:30:00 pm
$date1 = strtotime('+1 hour');                 // Sun 04/08/2012 14:30
$date2 = strtotime('-2 days');                 // Sat 04/06/2012 13:30
$date3 = strtotime('tomorrow');                // Mon 04/09/2012 00:00
$date4 = strtotime('tomorrow 10:15am');        // Mon 04/09/2012 10:15
$date5 = strtotime('next sunday');             // Sun 04/15/2012 00:00
$date6 = strtotime('last day of');             // Mon 04/30/2012 13:30
$date7 = strtotime('first day of next month'); // Tue 05/01/2012 13:30
$date8 = strtotime('third wednesday of');      // Wed 04/18/2012 00:00
$date9 = strtotime('nov second tue of 8am');   // Tue 11/13/2012 08:00
```

How to modify a timestamp

```
$checkout = mktime(13, 30, 0, 4, 8, 2012);
$due_date = strtotime('+3 weeks 6pm', $checkout);
```

Description

- An *absolute template* specifies a specific date, time, or both.

- A *relative template* specifies an offset to the base date and time. To specify an offset, you can use most English descriptions of time and date offsets.

Figure 10-3   How to use the strtotime function

Examples of working with timestamps

To round out your skills for working with timestamps, figure 10-4 shows four examples of working with timestamps. The first example determines if a year is a leap year. To start, it defines a function named is_leapyear that takes a timestamp as its parameter. Within the function, the statement uses the date function with a format string of 'L' to check if the timestamp is a leap year. If the date function returns a string of "1", the year is a leap year and the is_leapyear function returns a true value. Otherwise, this function returns a FALSE value.

The second example compares two timestamps to determine which comes first. Since timestamps are stored as integers, you can use relational operators such as the less than sign to compare timestamps. To start, the variable named $now stores a timestamp for the current date and time. Then, the variable named $exp stores a timestamp for the expiration date of a credit card. This expiration date is set to the first day of the next month after April 2012. If $exp is less than $now, the current date has passed the expiration date. In other words, the card is current if the current date and time is before midnight of May 1, 2012. Otherwise, the card is expired.

The third example displays a more detailed message about the card expiration date. To start, this code gets the current time and stores the expiration date in the typical mm/yyyy format. However, the strtotime function needs a month and year in the yyyy-mm format. So, the code uses the substr function to extract the month and year and changes the format of the expiration date.

After changing the format of the expiration date, the code uses the strtotime function to calculate the expiration date and time (midnight of May 1, 2012). Then, the code calculates the number of days between the current time and the expiration date by subtracting the two timestamps, dividing by the number of seconds in a day (86400), and using the floor function to truncate the result. Finally, this code checks the number of days and displays an appropriate message that includes the number of days between the current date and the expiration date.

The fourth example displays a countdown until the New Year. To start, this code gets the current time. Then, it uses the strtotime function to get midnight on Jan 1 of the next year. Next, the code calculates the number of seconds between the two dates.

After getting the number of seconds, this code calculates the number of days remaining and subtracts that many seconds from the total number of seconds. It repeats this type of calculation to find the number of hours, minutes, and seconds remaining. Finally, it displays the number of days, hours, minutes, and seconds remaining until the New Year.

If the current date is before daylight savings time and the time is 12 noon, this code displays 13 hours. That's because timestamps take the change from daylight savings time to standard time into account. For a date after daylight savings time and a time of 12 noon, this code displays 12 hours.

Determine if a year is a leap year

```
function is_leapyear($ts) {
    return (date('L', $ts) == '1');
}
$year_2010 = is_leapyear(strtotime('2010-1-1'));    // FALSE
$year_2012 = is_leapyear(strtotime('2012-1-1'));    // TRUE
```

Display a simple message about an expiration date

```
$now = time();
$exp = strtotime('2012-4 first day of next month midnight');
if ($exp < $now) {
    echo 'Your card has expired.';
} else {
    echo 'Your card has not expired.';
}
```

Display a detailed message about an expiration date

```
$now = time();
$exp = '04/2012';      // Typical expiration date format

// Change exp format from mm/yyyy to yyyy-mm
$month = substr($exp, 0, 2);
$year  = substr($exp, 3, 4);
$exp = $year . '-' . $month;

// Set expiration date and calculate the number of days from current date
$exp = strtotime($exp . ' first day of next month midnight');
$days = floor(($exp - $now) / 86400);   // There are 86400 seconds/day

// Display a message
if ($days < 0) {
    echo 'Your card expired ' . abs($days) . ' days ago.';
} else if ($days > 0) {
    echo 'Your card expires in ' . $days . ' days.';
} else {
    echo 'Your card expires at midnight.';
}
```

Display a countdown until the New Year

```
$now = time();
$new_year = strtotime('next year Jan 1st', $now);

// Calculate the days, hours, minutes, and seconds
$seconds = $new_year - $now;
$days = floor($seconds / 86400);
$seconds -= $days * 86400;
$hours = floor($seconds / 3600);
$seconds -= $hours * 3600;
$minutes = floor($seconds / 60);
$seconds -= $minutes * 60;

// Display the countdown
echo "$days days and $hours:$minutes:$seconds remaining to the New Year.";
```

Figure 10-4   Examples of working with timestamps

How to use objects to work with dates

The DateTime class provides an object-oriented way to work with dates and times. Internally, each part of the date and time is stored as a separate 64-bit signed integer. As a result, there is no practical limit on the range of dates and times that can be stored in a DateTime object.

For new applications, then, you should use the DateTime class to work with dates and times. For existing applications, you should consider converting timestamps to DateTime objects whenever that's practical.

How to use the DateTime class

Figure 10-5 starts by showing how to create a DateTime object. In the first example, the statement doesn't include an argument so the DateTime object stores the current date and time.

The four statements in the second example create four DateTime objects. However, these statements include format strings in the parentheses after the DateTime class. These format strings follow the same templates as the strtotime function described in figure 10-3. Here, the first statement uses an absolute template to specify a date and time. The second and third statements use relative templates to specify dates. And the fourth statement uses relative and absolute templates to specify a date and time.

The table that follows describes six methods of a DateTime object. These methods let you manipulate and display the data of the DateTime object.

To copy a DateTime object, you use the clone keyword as shown in the first example after the table. Without the clone keyword, both the $invoice_date and $due_date variables would refer to the same DateTime object. As a result, modifying one object as shown in the second and third examples would also modify the other. With the clone keyword, you can modify the $due_date variable without changing the $invoice_date variable.

The second example after the table shows how to set the date and time of a DateTime object by using the setDate and setTime methods. If you pass a date or time part that's outside its range, the excess rolls over to the other parts of the date and time. As a result, you may want to validate the date and time parts before you pass them to these methods by using the checkdate and checktime functions of figure 10-2.

The third example after the table shows how to modify a DateTime object. Here, the modify method of the DateTime object uses a valid format string for the strtotime function to change the date and time that's stored in the object.

The fourth example shows how to use the format method to format a DateTime object. This method takes the same formatting codes as the date function in figure 10-1.

The last example shows how to convert a timestamp to a DateTime object. Here, the first statement creates the timestamp, and the second statement creates the DateTime object. Then, the third statement calls the setTimestamp method of the DateTime object to set it to the date and time of the timestamp.

How to create a DateTime object

Using the current date and time
```
$now = new DateTime();
```

Using a strtotime format string
```
$expires = new DateTime('2012-03-15 13:30:00');
$tomorrow = new DateTime('+1 day');
$due_date = new DateTime('+3 weeks');
$appointment = new DateTime('next Friday +1 week 13:30');
```

Methods of a DateTime object

Name	Description
format($format)	Returns a string with the date and time formatted as specified by the format string. This method uses the same formatting codes as the date function.
setTime($h, $m, $s)	Sets the time.
setDate($y, $m, $d)	Sets the date.
modify($str)	Modifies the date and time based on a format string. This works similarly to the strtotime function for a relative date or time.
getTimestamp()	Gets the time and date as a timestamp.
setTimestamp($ts)	Sets the time and date using a timestamp.

How to use the methods of a DateTime object

How to copy a DateTime object
```
$invoice_date = new DateTime('2012-03-15 13:30:00');
$due_date = clone $invoice_date;
```

How to set the time and date of a DateTime object
```
$due_date->setTime(22, 30, 0);      // 10:30 pm
$due_date->setDate(2012, 3, 15);    // 3/15/2012
```

How to modify a DateTime object
```
$due_date->modify('+3 weeks');
```

How to display a DateTime object
```
echo 'Payment Due: ' . $due_date->format('M. j, Y \a\t g:i a');
```

How to convert a timestamp to a DateTime object
```
$tomorrow = strtotime('tomorrow 8am');
$nextday = new DateTime();
$nextday->setTimestamp($tomorrow);
```

Description

- The DateTime class provides an object-oriented way to work with dates and times.
- To create a DateTime object, you can pass any string to its constructor that's accepted by the strtotime function.
- To copy an object such as a DateTime object, code the clone keyword before the object.

Figure 10-5   How to use the DateTime class

How to use the DateInterval class

A *date interval* represents a span of time, or a period of time, rather than a point in time. Figure 10-6 shows how to create and display DateInterval objects that represent data intervals. To start, the first example shows how to use the new keyword to create a DateInteval object from the DateInterval class. To do that, you must include a string in the parentheses after the DateInterval class, and that string must specify the interval.

To specify a string for an interval, you begin by coding a P (for period). Then, you can a code positive integer and the letter that corresponds to the date or time part. The date and time parts must be in the order shown in this figure. If the string includes time parts, they must be preceded with a T (for time) even if there aren't any date parts. Since the DateInterval class converts weeks into days, you can't specify both days (D) and weeks (W) in the same interval string.

The second example shows how interval strings work. Here, the first statement creates an interval of 1 year, 2 months, and 10 days. Since this statement doesn't specify a time, it doesn't include a T in the string. The second statement creates an interval of 1 hour, 2 minutes, and 3 seconds. Since this statement specifies a time, it includes a T in the string. And the third statement combines the date and time intervals from the previous two statements.

To display an interval, you can use the format method of the DateInterval object. When you call this method, you must pass a format string that specifies the format of the interval. To do that, you can use the format codes shown in this figure.

The third example shows how these format codes work. All of these statements work with the DateInterval object named $interval_1 that was created earlier in this figure. Note that this object only contains year, month, and day values. In other words, it doesn't contain any time values. Here, the first statement uses the %m and %d codes to display the months and days in the DateInterval object named $interval_1.

When formatting intervals, the format method sets any parts that are not present to zero. For example, the last two statements set the time parts of the interval to zero. If necessary, you can use an uppercase format code to display date and time parts with a leading zero. For example, the second statement uses the %M code to display the month part of the interval with a leading zero. Finally, you can use the %R code to display a sign that indicates whether the interval is positive or negative. For example, the last three statements use this code to include a sign.

How to create a DateInterval object

```
$interval = new DateInterval('P30D');    // 30 days
```

The parts of the interval string

Part	Description	Examples
P	Begins the interval code	
nY	Specifies the number of years	'P1Y'
nM	Specifies the number of months	'P2M', 'P1Y6M'
nW	Specifies the number of weeks	'P3W', 'P1M2W'
nD	Specifies the number of days	'P4D', 'P1Y6M4D'
T	Starts the time portion of the interval code	
nH	Specifies the number of hours	'PT3H', 'P3DT12H'
nM	Specifies the number of minutes	'PT10M', 'P1MT4H30M'
nS	Specifies the number of seconds	'PT30S', 'P1Y1MT1M10S'

How to use interval strings

```
$interval_1 = new DateInterval('P1Y2M10D');    // 1 year, 2 months, 10 days
$interval_2 = new DateInterval('PT1H2M3S');    // 1 hour, 2 minutes, 3 seconds
$interval_3 = new DateInterval('P1Y2M3DT1H2M3S');
```

The format method of a DateInterval object

Name	Description
format($format)	Returns a string formatted as specified by the format string.

Format codes for the DateInterval format method

Code	Description
%R	Sign of the interval, "+" for positive and "-" for negative
%y	Years
%m	Months
%d	Days
%h	Hours
%i	Minutes
%s	Seconds

How to display a date interval

```
echo $interval_1->format('%m months, %d days');       // '2 months, 10 days'
echo $interval_1->format('%R %M months');             // '+ 02 months'
echo $interval_1->format('%R %y %m %d %h %i %s');     // '+ 1 2 10 0 0 0'
echo $interval_1->format('%R%yy %mm %dd %H:%I:%S');   // '+1y 2m 10d 00:00:00'
```

Description

- You can use a DateInterval object to represent a time span called a *date interval*.

- To display a date part with a leading zero, change its format code to uppercase.

Figure 10-6   How to use the DateInterval class

How to use the DateInterval and DateTime classes together

Figure 10-7 shows three more methods of a DateTime object. The add method modifies a DateTime object by adding the amount of time in the specified DateInterval object. Conversely, the sub method modifies a DateTime object by subtracting the amount of time in the specified DateInterval object.

The diff method determines the amount of time between the current DateTime object and the specified DateTime object. Then, it returns that time span as a DateInterval object. If the specified DateTime object is earlier than the current DateTime object, this method returns a negative DateInterval object.

The first example shows how to use the add method to modify a DateTime object. To start, the first statement creates a DateInterval object that represents 3 weeks, and the second statement creates a new DateTime object for the current date and time. Then, the third statement adds the DateInterval object to the DateTime object.

The second example shows how to use the sub method to modify a DateTime object. To start, the first statement creates a DateInterval object that represents 18 years, and the second statement creates a DateTime object for the current date and time. Then, the third statement subtracts the DateInterval object from the DateTime object to determine the latest date of birth that would allow someone to vote. Finally, the fourth statement displays a message that includes the modified DateTime object.

The third example shows how to use the diff method to determine the amount of time between two dates. This example starts by creating two DateTime objects named $now and $due. Here, the $due variable is earlier than the $now variable. When the third statement calculates the difference between these dates, $now is subtracted from $due. Because $due is earlier than $now, this returns a negative interval. This indicates that the due date has passed. Finally, the fourth statement displays the interval. This message indicates that the due date has passed by 15 days, 12 hours, and 45 minutes.

Methods of a DateTime object that use DateInterval objects

Name	Description
add(*$interval*)	Adds the amount of time specified by the DateInterval object.
sub(*$interval*)	Subtracts the amount of time specified by the DateInterval object.
diff(*$date*)	Returns a DateInterval object that represents the amount of time between the current DateTime object and the specified DateTime object. If the specified DateTime object is earlier, this function returns a negative DateInterval object.

How to add a DateInterval object to a DateTime object

```
$checkout_length = new DateInterval('P3W');
$due_date = new DateTime();
$due_date->add($checkout_length);
```

How to subtract a DateInterval object from a DateTime object

```
$voting_age = new DateInterval('P18Y');
$dob = new DateTime();
$dob->sub($voting_age);
echo 'You can vote if you were born on or before ' .
    $dob->format('n/j/Y');
```

How to determine the amount of time between two dates

```
$now = new DateTime('2012-05-15 12:45:00');
$due = new DateTime('2012-04 last day of midnight');
$time_span = $now->diff($due);
echo $time_span->format('%R%dd %H:%I:%Sh');        // '-15d 12:45:00h'
```

Figure 10-7   How to use DateInterval and DateTime classes together

Examples of working with DateTime objects

Figure 10-8 shows how you can combine the methods of a DateTime object with other functions to perform more complex tasks. These examples are similar to the examples in figure 10-4 except that they use DateTime objects instead of timestamps.

The first example determines if a year is a leap year. It defines a function named is_leapyear that takes a DateTime object as its parameter. Within the function, the statement uses the date function with a format string of 'L' to check if the timestamp is a leap year. If the date function returns a string of "1", the year is a leap year and the is_leapyear function returns a true value. Otherwise, this function returns a false value.

The second example compares two DateTime objects to determine which comes first. To do that, this example uses the less than (<) operator to compare the two dates. To start, the variable named $now stores a DateTime object for the current date and time. Then, the variable named $exp stores a DateTime object for the expiration date of a credit card. This expiration date is set to the first day of the next month after April 2012. If $exp is less than $now, the card is expired.

The third example displays a more detailed message about the card expiration date. To start, it gets the current date and time and stores the expiration date in the typical mm/yyyy format. However, the DateTime constructor method needs a month and year in the yyyy-mm format. So, the code uses the substr function to extract the month and year and changes the format of the expiration date.

After changing the format of the expiration date, the code creates a DateTime objection that represents the expiration date. Then, this code uses the diff method to get the DateInterval object for the time span between the current time and the expiration date. Next, this code uses the format method to format the interval as a string that includes the numbers of years, months, and days. Finally, this code checks whether the sign of the interval is negative. If so, the card has expired. Otherwise, the card has not expired. Either way, this code displays an appropriate message that includes the formatted string for the interval.

The fourth example displays a countdown until the New Year. To start, this code gets the current time. Then, it creates a DateTime object for the point in time when the next New Year starts. This works because setting the date to "Jan 1st" in the DateTime constructor method resets the time to midnight. Next, the code calculates and formats the time span remaining until the New Year. To do that, this code stores the formatted months and days in one variable and the formatted hours, minutes, and seconds in another.

After formatting the time until the New Year, this code uses an if statement to check whether the current date is Jan 1 (01/01). If so, this code displays a message that says "Happy New Year!" If the current date is Dec 31 (12/31), the code displays the hours, minutes, and seconds remaining. Otherwise, the code displays the months, days, hours, minutes, and seconds remaining.

Determine if a year is a leap year

```
function is_leap($date) {
    return ($date->format('L') == '1');
}
$year_2010 = is_leap(new DateTime('2010-1-1'));   // false
$year_2012 = is_leap(new DateTime('2012-1-1'));   // true
```

Display a simple message about an expiration date

```
$now = new DateTime();
$exp = new DateTime('2012-4 first day of next month midnight');
if ($exp < $now) {
    echo 'Your card has expired.';
} else {
    echo 'Your card has not expired.';
}
```

Display a detailed message about an expiration date

```
$now = new DateTime();
$exp = '04/2012';       // Typical expiration date format

// Change exp from mm/yyyy to yyyy-mm
$month = substr($exp, 0, 2);
$year  = substr($exp, 3, 4);
$exp = $year . '-' . $month;

// Set expiration date and calculate the interval from current date
$exp = new DateTime($exp . ' first day of next month midnight');
$span = $now->diff($exp);

// Display a message
$span_text  = $span->format('%y years, %m months, and %d days');
if ($span->format('%R') == '-') {
    echo 'Your card expired ' . $span_text . ' ago.';
} else {
    echo 'Your card expires in ' . $span_text . '.';
}
```

Display a countdown until the New Year

```
$now = new DateTime();
$new_year = new DateTime('next year Jan 1st');

// Calculate and format the time left until the new year
$span = $now->diff($new_year);
$md_left = $span->format('%m months, %d days');
$hms_left = $span->format('%h:%I:%S');

// Display a message
if ($now->format('MD') == '0101') {
    echo 'Happy New Year!';
} else if ($now->format('MD') == '1231') {
    echo "$hms_left remaining to the New Year.";
} else {
    echo "$md_left, and $hms_left remaining to the New Year.";
}
```

Figure 10-8   Examples of working with DateTime objects

Perspective

Now that you've completed this chapter, you have all the skills you need to work with dates and times in most PHP applications. For new applications, you should use DateTime objects instead of timestamps. In addition, you should convert any existing applications from timestamps to DateTime objects before they encounter the year 2038 problem.

Although the year 2038 may seem distant now, applications that calculate dates in the future may encounter the year 2038 problem much sooner than the year 2038. For example, an application that needs to work with dates up to 20 years in advance should be converted by 2017.

Terms

timestamp
Unix Epoch
year 2038 problem
Y2K38 problem

absolute template
relative template
date interval

Summary

- A *timestamp* is an integer that represents a date and time as the number of seconds since midnight, January 1, 1970 GMT.

- On most systems, the upper limit of a timestamp is January 19, 2038. As a result, dates after that will lead to bugs that will need to be fixed. This is known as the *year 2038 problem* or the *Y2K38 problem*, but this can be avoided by using DateTime objects instead of timestamps.

- To create and format timestamps, you can use functions. You can also use functions to validate a date and to store the parts of a date in an array.

- The DateTime class provides an object-oriented way to work with dates and times. After you create a DateTime object, you can use its methods to set or modify the date and to convert a timestamp to a DateTime object.

- A *date interval* is a span of time, not a point in time, that can be stored in a DateInterval object. Then, you can use the methods of a DateTime object to add date intervals, subtract date invervals, or create a DateInterval object that represents the interval between two dates.

Exercise 10-1 Write code that works with dates

In this exercise, you can write the PHP code that works with dates.

Open and test the application

1. Start the Firefox browser and run the application in the ex_starts/ch10_ex1 directory. To do that, you can use this URL:

   `http://localhost/ex_starts/ch10_ex1/`

   This should display a page that allows you to enter an invoice date and a due date. Note that this page displays two default dates in a standard date format.

2. Click on the Submit button. Note that this displays some labels, but doesn't display any dates or times.

Write the code that processes the data entered by the user

3. Open the index.php file for this application and review the code. Note that it displays a starting invoice date that's one month before the current date and a starting due date that's two months after the current date. However, this code doesn't process the dates that are entered into the text boxes.

4. Open the date_tester.php file for this application and review the code. Note that this code uses an if statement to display an error message or a table of date and time data.

5. In the index.php file, add the code that uses the two dates that are entered into the text box controls to display a table of data that calculates dates and times and formats them like this:

   ```
   Invoice date:     March 3, 2011
   Due date:         June 6, 2011
   Current date:     May 4, 2011
   Current time:     11:27:46 am
   Due date message: This invoice is due in 0 years, 1 months, and
                     2 days.
   ```

   If the current date is after the due date, the due date message should be in this format:

   ```
   Due date message: This invoice is 0 years, 2 months, and 25 days
                     overdue.
   ```

6. Make sure the user enters both dates.

7. Allow the user to enter a date in any format that can be parsed by the constructor of the DateTime class. This includes all of the most common date formats.

8. Make sure the user enters dates in a valid date format. To do that, you can use a try/catch statement to catch an exception that's thrown if the constructor of the DateTime class can't parse the date. For a review of the try/catch statement, you can refer to chapter 4.

9. Make sure the user enters a due date that's later than the invoice date.

10. Test the application to make sure it works correctly.

11

How to create
and use arrays

In chapter 4, you were introduced to arrays. Now, in this chapter, you'll learn more about creating and using arrays, which are important in a variety of PHP applications. For example, you can use an array to store the items in a shopping cart. Then, you can work with the array to update and display those items.

How to create and use an array **312**
How to create an array 312
How to add and delete elements 314
How to work with variable substitution 314
How to use for loops to work with arrays 316

How to create and use an associative array **318**
How to create an associative array 318
How to add and delete elements 320
How to work with variable substitution 320
How to use foreach loops to work with arrays 322

How to use functions to work with arrays **324**
How to fill, merge, slice, and splice arrays 324
How to work with queues and stacks 326
How to get the sum and product of elements 328
How to search arrays 328
How to sort arrays 330
How to modify arrays 332

How to work with arrays of arrays **334**
Understanding an array of arrays 334
How to create and use an array of arrays 336

The Task List Manager application **338**
The user interface 338
The code for the controller 338
The code for the view 340

Perspective **344**

How to create and use an array

In PHP, the most common type of array uses integers as index values. In this topic, you'll learn how to create and use this type of array.

How to create an array

An *array* is a data type that contains one or more items called *elements*. Each element stores a *value* that you can refer to with an *index*. The *length* of an array indicates the number of elements that it contains.

Figure 11-1 shows how to create an array. To start, the first example shows two ways to create an array of names. Here, the first technique uses a single statement to create an array that contains three values. To do that, this statement uses the array keyword followed by a set of parentheses. Within the parentheses, this statement includes the initial values for the array separated by commas.

By default, the first element in an array has an index of 0, the second has an index of 1, and so on. As a result, the 3 elements in this array have indexes that range from 0 to 2.

The second technique shows how to code the same array using four statements. Here, the first statement creates an empty array by coding an empty set of parentheses after the array keyword. Then, the next three statements assign values to the first three elements of the array. To do that, these statements refer to the element by specifying the name of the array followed by a set of brackets that include the index of the element. In this figure, for instance, the three names are added to the elements with indexes of 0, 1, and 2.

The second example shows two ways to create an array that stores four discount amounts. Here, the first technique uses a single statement to specify the four values. As a result, these values have indexes of 0, 1, 2, and 3. Then, the second technique creates the same array using five statements. Here, the last four statements assign a value to the specified index.

The syntax for creating an array

```
$array_name = array([value1[, value2, ... ]])
```

The syntax for referring to an element an array

```
$array_name[index];
```

How to create an array of names

With one statement

```
$names = array('Ted Lewis', 'Sue Jones', 'Ray Thomas');
```

With multiple statements

```
$names = array();              // create an empty array
$names[0] = 'Ted Lewis';       // set three values in the array
$names[1] = 'Sue Jones';
$names[2] = 'Ray Thomas';
```

How to create an array of discounts

With one statement

```
$discounts = array(0, 5, 10, 15);    // create an array with four elements
```

With multiple statements

```
$discounts = array();          // create an empty array
$discounts[0] = 0;             // set four values in the array
$discounts[1] = 5;
$discounts[2] = 10;
$discounts[3] = 15;
```

Description

- An *array* can store one or more *elements*. Each element consists of an *index* and a *value*. An index can be either an integer or a string. A value can be any PHP data type.

- By default, PHP uses integer indexes where 0 is the first element, 1 is the second element, and so on.

Figure 11-1   How to create an array

How to add and delete elements

Because PHP arrays are dynamic, you can change the length of an array by adding or removing elements from the array as shown in figure 11-2. To add an element to the end of an array, you can leave the index out of the brackets when assigning a value to the array. Then, PHP takes the highest index, adds one to it, and uses that value as the index for the new element.

You can set an element anywhere in an array by specifying the index when assigning a value to the array as shown in the second example. If you use an index that already has a value, you replace the old value with the new value. If you use an index that is past the end of the array, you'll leave gaps in the array that contain NULL values. Since this makes the array harder to use, it's generally a good idea to avoid gaps whenever possible.

You can get an element from an array by specifying the index as shown in the third example. If you try to access an element that hasn't been assigned a value, the NULL value is returned.

When you need to delete a value from an element in an array, you can use the unset function as shown in the fourth example. Note that this leaves a gap in the array. You can also delete all the values from an array by passing the name of the array (omitting the index) to the unset function. This deletes the entire array and its elements.

To close up any gaps in an array, you can use the array_values function as shown in the fifth example. This function takes an array as its parameter and returns a new array with any gaps in the array removed. The elements in the new array are numbered sequentially from zero to one less than the length of the array.

How to work with variable substitution

You can also use array values in variable substitution as shown in the last example in this figure. When you code a reference to an array element inside a double-quoted string, PHP replaces the reference to the array element with the value of the array element. The index for the array can be either a literal number or a number stored in a variable. If necessary, you can enclose the array reference in braces to separate it from other text. When you use braces, the dollar sign at the start of the array name must be inside the braces.

The syntax for adding an element to the end of an array

```
$array_name[] = $value;
```

Functions for removing the values from elements in an array

Function	Description
unset($var1[, $var2 ...])	Deletes the value in the specified array element or deletes the entire array by setting it to a NULL value.
array_values($array)	Returns all values from the specified array after any NULL values have been removed and the array has been reindexed.

How to add a value to the end of an array

```
$letters = array('a', 'b', 'c', 'd');      // array is a, b, c, d
$letters[] = 'e';                          // array is a, b, c, d, e
```

How to set a value at a specific index

```
$letters = array('a', 'b', 'c', 'd');      // array is a, b, c, d
$letters[0] = 'e';                         // array is e, b, c, d
$letters[3] = 'f';                         // array is e, b, c, f
$letters[5] = 'g';                         // array is e, b, c, f, NULL, g
```

How to get values from an array

```
$letters = array('a', 'b', 'c', 'd');      // array is a, b, c, d
$letter1 = $letters[0];                    // $letter1 is 'a'
$letter2 = $letters[1];                    // $letter2 is 'b'
$letter4 = $letters[4];                    // $letter4 is NULL
```

How to delete values from an array

```
$letters = array('a', 'b', 'c', 'd');      // array is a, b, c, d
unset($letters[2]);                        // array is a, b, NULL, d
unset($letters);                           // $letters is NULL
```

How to remove elements that contain NULL values and reindex an array

```
$letters = array('a', 'b', 'c', 'd');      // array is a, b, c, d
unset($letters[2]);                        // array is a, b, NULL, d
$letters = array_values($letters);         // array is a, b, d
```

How to use array elements with variable substitution

```
$name = array ('Ray', 'Harris');
echo "First Name: $name[0]";               // First Name: Ray
echo "First Name: {$name[0]}";             // First Name: Ray
```

Description

- You can set and get elements from an array by coding the index for the element between brackets.

- When you add or delete elements from an array, you may leave gaps in the array that contain NULL values.

- You can access array elements using variable substitution in a double-quoted string. If necessary, you can place braces around the array name and index to separate the array element from the rest of the text in the string.

Figure 11-2   How to work with array elements

How to use for loops to work with arrays

The primary benefit of using an array is the ability to use a loop to perform a task with each element in the array. Figure 11-3 shows you how to use a for loop to work with all of the elements in an array.

The first example shows how to use a for loop to fill an array with 10 random numbers. To start, the first statement creates an empty array. Then, a for loop fills this array with 10 random numbers that range from 1 to 100. To do that, this code doesn't specify an index. As a result, this code adds each new value to the end of the array.

The second example displays the array that was created by the first example. To start, the first statement creates an empty string to store the values of the array. Then, this code uses a for loop to add the numbers stored in the array to the string. To do that, this code uses a counter variable named $i for the loop and as the index for the array. The loop continues executing as long as the counter variable is less than the length of the array. To get the length of the array, this code uses the count function. This function takes an array as its parameter and returns the number of elements in the array.

Within the for loop, this code uses the counter variable to access an element in the array. Then, it appends the value for the element and a space to the end of the text string. After the loop, an echo statement displays the numbers that are stored in the string.

The third example computes the sum and average of an array of prices. Here, the first statement creates an array that stores four prices, and the second statement creates a variable to store the sum of the prices. Then, a for loop gets each price from the array and adds it to the sum. After this loop is finished, the last statement computes the average by dividing the sum of the prices by the count.

In most cases, arrays don't contain gaps in them. As a result, you can use a for loop to work with the array as shown in the first three examples. But if an array contains gaps, it becomes more difficult to use a for loop to work with it. Often, the easiest solution is to use a foreach loop to loop through each element in the array as described in figure 11-6. However, if a foreach loop doesn't give you the control you need, you can use the techniques described in the fourth example to work with an array.

The fourth example begins by creating an array and removing the values from two elements. This creates two gaps in the array. Then, the third statement uses the end function to move the pointer to the last element in the array. Next, the fourth statement uses the key function to retrieve the index value of the last element. After that, the for loop uses this index to determine how many times to execute the loop. Inside the loop, an if statement uses the isset function to test each element. If the element has a value, this code retrieves the value and adds it to the display string. Otherwise, the element isn't added to the string.

Functions for loops that work with arrays

Function	Description
count(*$array*)	Returns the number of elements in an array. This function doesn't count gaps in the array.
end(*$array*)	Moves the cursor for the array to the last element in the array.
key(*$array*)	Returns the index of the array element that the cursor is on.
isset(*$var*)	Returns a TRUE value if the specified variable or array element contains a value. Otherwise, it returns a FALSE value.

Code that stores 10 random numbers in an array

```
$numbers = array();
for ($i = 0; $i < 10; $i++) {
    $numbers[] = mt_rand(1, 100);
}
```

Code that displays the elements of an array

```
$numbers_string = '';
for ($i = 0; $i < count($numbers); $i++) {
    $numbers_string .= $numbers[$i] . ' ';
}
echo $numbers_string;
```

Code that computes the sum and average of an array of prices

```
$prices = array(141.95, 212.95, 411, 10.95);
$sum = 0;
for ($i = 0; $i < count($prices); $i++) {
    $sum += $prices[$i];
}
$average = $sum / count($prices);
```

How to skip gaps in an array

```
$numbers = array(1, 2, 3, 4, 5, 6, 7, 8, 9, 10);
unset($numbers[2], $numbers[6]);
end($numbers);
$last = key($numbers);
$numbers_string = '';
for($i = 0; $i <= $last; $i++) {
    if (isset($numbers[$i])) {
        $numbers_string .= $numbers[$i] . ' ';
    }
}
echo $numbers_string;                    // Displays: 1 2 4 5 6 8 9 10
```

Description

- For loops are commonly used to process the data in arrays. In this case, the counter for the loop is used as the index for each element in the array

---

Figure 11-3   How to use for loops to work with arrays

How to create and use an associative array

In PHP, you can also use strings as index values. When an array uses strings for its indexes, the array is known as an *associative array*. The indexes in an associative array are often called *keys*.

How to create an associative array

Figure 11-4 shows two ways to create an associative array. For instance, the first example shows two techniques for creating an associative array of tax rates for various states. Here, the first technique uses a single statement to create the array and to store three key/value pairs in it. To do that, this code uses the array keyword followed by a set of parentheses. Within the parentheses, this code uses an arrow (=>) to specify the key/value pairs, and it separates each pair with a comma.

Then, the second technique uses four statements to create the same array. To do that, the first statement creates an empty array. Then, the next three statements specify the key/value pairs. Here, the key is a string and the value is an integer.

The two techniques in the second example works much like those in the first example. However, they use a string for the key and a string for the value.

The third example shows that a numerical array with numerous gaps can be considered an associative array. Here, the code uses an integer as the key and a string as the value.

In PHP, it's possible to mix integer and string indexes in the same array as shown in the fourth example. In general, this isn't considered a good practice, so you should avoid this whenever possible.

The syntax for creating an associative array

```
array([key1 => value1, key2 => value2, ... ])
```

How to create an associative array of state tax rates

With one statement

```
$tax_rates = array('NC' => 7.75, 'CA' => 8.25, 'NY' => 8.875);
```

With multiple statements

```
$tax_rates = array();
$tax_rates['NC'] = 7.75;
$tax_rates['CA'] = 8.25;
$tax_rates['NY'] = 8.875;
```

How to create an associative array of country codes

With one statement

```
$country_codes = array('DEU' => 'Germany', 'JPN' => 'Japan',
                       'ARG' => 'Argentina', 'USA' => 'United States');
```

With multiple statements

```
$country_codes = array();
$country_codes['DEU'] = 'Germany';
$country_codes['JPN'] = 'Japan';
$country_codes['ARG'] = 'Argentina';
$country_codes['USA'] = 'United States';
```

How to create an associative array of telephone extensions

```
$ext = array();
$ext[10] = 'Sales';
$ext[13] = 'Customer Service';
$ext[16] = 'Returns';
$ext[18] = 'Warehouse';
```

How to create an array that contains integer and string indexes

```
$employees = array();
$employees[0] = 'Mike';
$employees[1] = 'Anne';
$employees[2] = 'Judy';
$employees['senior'] = 'Mike';
$employees['newest'] = 'Pren';
```

Description

- An *associative array* uses a string as the index for the value that's stored in the array. When using an associative array, the index is commonly called a *key*.

- An array with integer keys that have gaps between them can also be thought of as an associative array.

- Although it's generally not considered a good practice, a single array can have both integer and string indexes.

Figure 11-4   How to create an associative array

How to add and delete elements

Once you've created an associative array, you can modify it by adding and deleting elements as shown in figure 11-5. To add an element, you usually specify the key as shown in the first example. If a value already exists at that key, the old value is replaced with the new value. Otherwise, the new element is added to the array.

If you omit the key when setting a value in an associative array, PHP uses an integer index. In the second example, for instance, the array doesn't contain any integer indexes in the array, so PHP uses zero as the index. However, if the array already had an integer index, PHP would take the highest integer index, add one to it, and use that value as the index. Since this usually isn't what you want, you typically specify a key when working with associative arrays.

You can get an element from an array by specifying the index as shown in the third example. Here, the second statement gets the first name, and the third statement gets the last name.

When you need to delete the value from one or more elements in an associative array, you can use the unset function just as you do for regular arrays. This is illustrated by the fourth example. You can also use this function to delete the entire array.

How to work with variable substitution

You can also use array values in string substitution as shown by the last example in this figure. This works as you would expect. However, if the key is a string literal and it isn't coded inside braces, you can't use quotes around the key. If you do, you'll get a syntax error. To fix this error, you can either omit the quotes, or you can enclose the element in braces. In that case, you also need to include the quotes.

How to set a value with a specific key

```
$name = array('first' => 'Ray', 'last' => 'Harris');
$name['middle'] = 'Thomas';
```

What happens when you omit the key when adding a value

```
$name = array('first' => 'Ray', 'last' => 'Harris');
$name[] = 'Thomas';                    // key is 0
```

How to get a value at a specified key

```
$name = array('first' => 'Ray', 'last' => 'Harris');
$first_name = $name['first'];
$last_name = $name['last'];
```

How to delete values from an array

```
$name = array('first' => 'Ray', 'last' => 'Harris');
unset($name['first']);               // delete the value from an element
unset($name);                        // delete all elements
```

How to use variable substitution with array elements

```
$name = array('first' => 'Ray', 'last' => 'Harris');
echo "First Name: $name['first']";        // Generates a parse error
echo "First Name: $name[first]";          // First Name: Ray
echo "First Name: {$name['first']}";      // First Name: Ray
```

Description

- To set or get a value in an associative array, specify the key for the value within the brackets.

- If you use an empty pair of brackets to add an element to an array, PHP uses an integer key for the element, which usually isn't what you want for an associative array.

- You can access array elements using variable substitution in a double-quoted string. To do that for a string key, you don't need to code quotes around the key. However, if you place braces around the element to separate it from other text in the string, you must include quotes around the key.

Figure 11-5   How to work with array elements

How to use foreach loops to work with arrays

The *foreach loop* is commonly used to work with associative arrays. Figure 11-6 shows how this type of loop works.

As the syntax at the top of this figure shows, the foreach loop doesn't require separate expressions that initialize, test, and increment an index counter like a for loop does. Instead, you declare a variable that stores the value from each element in the array. In addition, you can optionally declare a variable that stores the key from each element. Then, within the loop, you can use these variables to work with each element in the array.

The first example displays the values in an associative array. Here, the first statement creates an associative array that stores state tax rates. Then, the code uses a foreach loop to display the values for all three elements as list items in an unordered list.

The second example works much like the first example. However, it displays both the keys and values of the associative array. To do that, the foreach loop uses the arrow operator (=>) to declare variables for the key and the value. Within the loop, the code uses these variables to display the key and value.

The third example shows how to use a foreach loop to process all elements in a regular array that has gaps. This accomplishes the same task as the fourth example in figure 11-3. However, if you compare the code for these two examples, I think you'll agree that the foreach loop works better than the for loop for this task.

The syntax of a foreach loop

```
foreach ($array_name as [ $key => ] $value) {
    // Statements that use $key and $value
}
```

A foreach loop that displays the values in an associative array

```
$tax_rates = array('NC' => 7.75, 'CA' => 8.25, 'NY' => 8.875);
echo '<ul>';
foreach ($tax_rates as $rate) {
    echo "<li>$rate</li>";
}
echo '</ul>';
```

The result displayed in a browser

- 7.75
- 8.25
- 8.875

A foreach loop that displays the keys and values

```
$tax_rates = array('NC' => 7.75, 'CA' => 8.25, 'NY' => 8.875);
echo '<ul>';
foreach ($tax_rates as $state => $rate) {
    echo "<li>$state ($rate)</li>";
}
echo '</ul>';
```

The result displayed in a browser

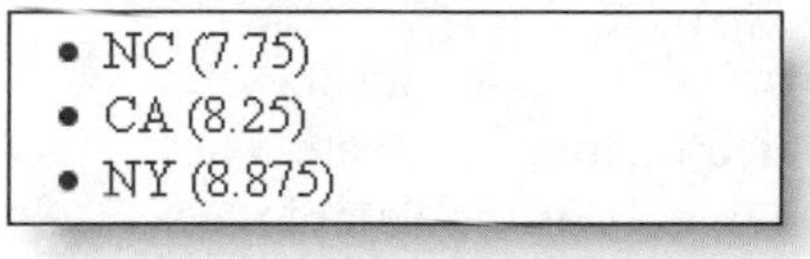

- NC (7.75)
- CA (8.25)
- NY (8.875)

A foreach loop that displays the values in a regular array

```
$numbers = array(1, 2, 3, 4, 5, 6, 7, 8, 9, 10);
unset($numbers[2], $numbers[6]);
$numbers_string = '';
foreach($numbers as $number) {
    $numbers_string .= $number . ' ';
}
echo $numbers_string;                 // Displays: 1 2 4 5 6 8 9 10
```

Description

- You can use a *foreach statement* to create a *foreach loop* that accesses only those elements in an array that are defined.

Figure 11-6   How to use foreach loops to work with arrays

How to use functions to work with arrays

To make it easier to work with arrays, PHP provides many functions that operate on arrays. This topic presents some of the most useful of these functions.

How to fill, merge, slice, and splice arrays

Figure 11-7 shows some functions that are useful for creating arrays from scratch or from existing arrays. The first example shows how to use the range function to fill an array with a list of numbers. Here, the first statement creates an array with a range of values that are incremented by a value of 1. Then, the second statement uses the optional third parameter to create a range of values that are incremented by a value of 4.

The second example shows how to fill and pad an array. Here, the first statement uses the array_fill function to create an array that consists of five elements that contain the value 1. Then, the second statement uses the array_pad function to pad that array with elements that contain the value 0 until the array contains 10 elements.

The third example shows how to merge two arrays into one array. Here, the first two statements create two arrays. Then, the third statement uses the array_merge function to merge the two arrays into one array. Although this example only merges two arrays, you can use the array_merge function to merge more than two arrays. The last statement in this example uses the implode function to extract the values from the array.

The fourth example shows how to create a new array by taking a slice of another array. Here, the second statement uses the slice method to create a new array named $new_hires that contains the last two elements of the $employees array. Since this code doesn't use the optional fourth parameter, the values in the $new_hires array are reindexed starting at 0. As a result, these values have indexes of 0 and 1. However, if this code specified a TRUE value for the fourth parameter, the values in the $new_hires array would retain their original indexes of 2 and 3.

The fifth example shows how to use the array_splice function. This function lets you insert one array into another, possibly replacing elements in the process. In this example, the third statement inserts the names in the $new_hires array into the $employees array. This inserts both names in the $new_hires array starting at the second element in the $employees array. As a result, it replaces the second and third elements in the $employees array.

Note that the array_splice function works a little differently than the other functions in this figure since it doesn't return an array. Instead, it modifies the array that's passed as the first parameter. From a coding point of view, this means that you don't code an assignment statement when you work with the array_splice function. However, you do code assignment statements when you work with the other functions.

Functions for creating arrays

Function	Description
range(*$lo*, *$hi* [, *$step*])	Returns an array filled with values from $lo to $hi with $step added to get the next value. If omitted, $step defaults to 1.
array_fill(*$start*, *$count*, *$value*)	Returns an array filled with $count $values starting at index $start.
array_pad(*$array*, *$size*, *$value*)	Returns an array with $value added to the end of $array until it contains $size elements. If $size is negative, the value is added to the start of the array.
array_merge(*$array1*, *$array2*, ...)	Returns an array with the elements of two or more arrays in one array. String keys in $array2 overwrite string keys in $array1 but numerical keys are appended.
array_slice(*$array*, *$index* [, *$len* [, *$keys*]])	Returns part of an array starting from $index and containing $len elements. If $len is omitted, it returns the elements to the end of the array. If $keys is TRUE, the original keys are used. Otherwise, the slice is reindexed starting at 0.
array_splice(*$array*, *$index* [, *$len* [, *$new*]])	Modifies $array by replacing its elements with the elements in $new starting at $index and replacing $len elements. The array is reindexed. Note that this function doesn't return an array, it modifies the elements in the $array parameter.

How to create an array that has a range of values

```
$numbers = range(1, 4);              // 1, 2, 3, 4
$numbers = range(10, 22, 4);         // 10, 14, 18, 22
```

How to fill and pad an array

```
$numbers = array_fill(0, 5, 1);         // 1, 1, 1, 1, 1
$numbers = array_pad($numbers, 10, 0);  // 1, 1, 1, 1, 1, 0, 0, 0, 0, 0
```

How to merge two arrays

```
$employees = array('Mike', 'Anne');
$new_hires = array('Ray', 'Pren');
$employees = array_merge($employees, $new_hires);
echo implode(', ', $employees);          // Mike, Anne, Ray, Pren
```

How to slice one array from another

```
$employees = array('Mike', 'Anne', 'Ray', 'Pren');
$new_hires = array_slice($employees, 2);
echo implode(', ', $new_hires);          // Ray, Pren
```

How to splice two arrays together

```
$employees = array('Mike', 'Anne', 'Joel');
$new_hires = array('Ray', 'Pren');
array_splice($employees, 1, 2, $new_hires);
echo implode(', ', $employees);          // Mike, Ray, Pren
```

Figure 11-7   How to fill, merge, slice, and splice arrays

How to work with queues and stacks

Figure 11-8 shows four functions that you can use to work with two special types of arrays known as queues and stacks. A *stack* implements a *last-in, first-out (LIFO)* collection of values. You can think of a stack as a stack of dishes. The last dish you put on the stack is the first dish you must take off the stack.

The first example shows how to use a stack. Here, the first statement creates an array. Then, the second statement uses the array_push function to put a new value on the stack. Next, the third statement uses the array_pop function to take the value off the stack. Finally, the fourth statement displays the value that has just been taken off the stack.

A *queue*, on the other hand, implements a *first-in, first-out (FIFO)* collection of values. You can think of a queue as a single line of people waiting at a bank. The first person in the line is the first person to be served and get out of the line.

The second example shows how to use a queue. Here, the first statement creates an array. Then, the second statement uses the array_push function to push a new value onto the end of the queue. Next, the third statement uses the array_shift function to remove the value from the front of the queue and shift the rest of the queue over to take its spot. Finally, the fourth statement displays the value that has just been removed from the queue.

When you work with stacks, it doesn't matter which side of the array you add and remove values from as long as you always work with the same side of the array. The example in this figure uses the array_push and array_pop functions to work with the end of an array. However, you can also implement a stack by using the array_unshift and array_shift functions to work with the front of an array.

Similarly, when working with a queue, you always add values to one side of the array and remove them from the other side. As a result, you can use the array_push and array_shift functions to create a queue. Or, you can use the array_unshift and array_pop functions to create a queue.

As you review the functions in this figure, note that they modify the array that's passed to the function. In other words, they don't return a new array.

Functions for working with queues and stacks

Function	Description
array_push($array, $value)	Adds $value to the end of $array.
array_pop($array)	Removes and returns the last value in $array.
array_unshift($array, $value)	Adds $value to the start of $array.
array_shift($array)	Removes and returns the first value in $array.

How to work with a stack

```
$names = array('Mike', 'Joel', 'Anne');
array_push($names, 'Ray');              // $names is Mike, Joel, Anne, Ray
$next = array_pop($names);              // $names is Mike, Joel, Anne
echo $next;                             // displays Ray
```

How to work with a queue

```
$names = array('Mike', 'Anne', 'Joel');
array_push($names, 'Ray');              // $names is Mike, Anne, Joel, Ray
$next = array_shift($names);            // $names is Anne, Joel, Ray
echo $next;                             // displays Mike
```

Description

- A *stack* is a special type of array that implements a *last-in, first-out* (*LIFO*) collection of values. You can use the array_push and array_pop functions to add and remove elements in a stack.

- A *queue* is a special type of array that implements a *first-in, first-out* (*FIFO*) collection of values. You can use the array_push and array_shift functions to add and remove elements in a queue.

- The functions in this figure modify the array that's passed to the function. In other words, they don't return a new array.

Figure 11-8   How to work with queues and stacks

How to get the sum and product of elements

Figure 11-9 shows how to use the array_sum function to add the elements in an array together. In the first example, the first statement creates an array that contains four prices, and the second statement uses the array_sum function to add all four prices together. This accomplishes the same task as the third example in figure 11-3 with less code.

This figure doesn't show an example of the array_product function. However, this function works similarly to the array_sum function, except that it multiplies the values together instead of adding them.

How to search arrays

The second table in this figure summarizes the functions for searching arrays. Then, the first search example shows how to use three functions to search an array. The first statement creates an associative array that contains three elements that have keys and values. Then, the second statement uses the in_array function to search the array to check whether it includes a value of 7.75.

The third statement searches the array for a string value of '7.75'. By default, the in_array function uses the equality operator for this comparison. As a result, it converts the values to the same data type before comparing them and yields a TRUE value.

The fourth statement performs the same comparison as the third statement, but it specifies a TRUE value for the third parameter. As a result, this statement uses the identity operator to perform a strict comparison. Since this comparison doesn't convert the data types before comparing them, it yields a FALSE value.

The fifth statement uses the array_key_exists function to check if a key exists in an array. Here, the key of 'CA' exists in the array, so the statement returns a TRUE value.

The sixth statement uses the array_search function to search the array for a value of 7.75. If this value isn't found in the array, this function returns a FALSE value. However, if this value is found, this function returns the key for the value. By comparison, the in_array function returns a TRUE value if it finds the value.

The second search example shows how to use the array_count_values function to count the number of times each value is used in an array. Here, the first statement creates an array that has six values, but only three unique values. Then, the second statement uses the array_count_values function to return an associative array that counts the number of occurrences for each value in the original array. This is shown by the last three statements in this figure.

Functions for performing mathematical calculations on arrays

Function	Description
array_sum(*$array*)	Returns the sum of the elements in $array.
array_product(*$array*)	Returns the product of the elements in $array.

How to add all values in an array

```
$prices = array(141.95, 212.95, 411, 10.95);
$sum = array_sum($prices);                          // 776.85
```

Functions for searching arrays

Function	Description
in_array(*$value, $array* [, *$strict*])	Returns TRUE if $value is in $array. If $strict is TRUE, the comparison only returns TRUE if the data type also matches.
array_key_exists(*$key, $array*)	Returns TRUE if $key is used as a key in $array.
array_search(*$value, $array* [, *$strict*])	Returns the key if $value is in $array or FALSE if it isn't. found. The $strict parameter works the same as in the in_array function.
array_count_values(*$array*)	Counts the number of times each value in $array is used. Returns a new array where the value is used as the key and the value is the number of times the value is used.

How to search an array

```
$tax_rates = array('NC' => 7.75, 'CA' => 8.25, 'NY' => 8.875);
$is_found = in_array(7.75, $tax_rates);             // TRUE
$is_found = in_array('7.75', $tax_rates);           // TRUE
$is_found = in_array('7.75', $tax_rates, true);     // FALSE
$key_exists = array_key_exists('CA', $tax_rates);   // TRUE
$key = array_search(7.75, $tax_rates);              // 'NC'
```

How to count the number of occurrences of a value in an array

```
$names = array('Mike', 'Mike', 'Mike', 'Anne', 'Joel', 'Joel');
$occurences = array_count_values($names );
echo $occurences['Mike'];                           // 3
echo $occurences['Anne'];                           // 1
echo $occurences['Joel'];                           // 2
```

Figure 11-9   How to search arrays and get the sum or product of its elements

How to sort arrays

Figure 11-10 shows how to use functions to sort arrays. The functions for sorting arrays differ depending on whether they sort ascending or descending, whether they preserve keys or reindex the array, and whether they sort by values or by keys. However, all of the sorting functions modify the original array.

The sorting functions also use three constants to let you control how the comparisons are performed during the sort. By default, the SORT_REGULAR constant uses the regular type casting rules of the relational operators to perform the sort. Most of the time, this constant works the way you want. However, if it doesn't, you can use the SORT_STRING constant to cast each value to a string before comparing them. Or, you can use the SORT_NUMERIC constant to cast each value to a number before comparing them.

The sort function sorts an array in ascending order by value and reindexes the array. The rsort function sorts an array in descending order by value and reindexes the array. These functions are typically used on arrays with integer indexes as shown in the first three examples.

The asort function sorts an array in ascending order by value and preserves element keys. The arsort function sorts an array in descending order by value and preserves element keys. These functions are typically used on associative arrays as shown in the fourth example.

The ksort function sorts an array in ascending order by key. The krsort functions sorts an array in descending order by key. They both keep the keys and values together as the array is sorted. These functions are typically used on associative arrays as shown in the fourth example.

Functions for sorting arrays

Function	Description
sort(*$array*[, *$compare*])	Sorts the values in an array in ascending order and reindexes the array. If $compare is SORT_REGULAR, the default, each element is compared using the relational operators. If $compare is SORT_STRING, each element is converted to a string before the comparison. If $compare is SORT_NUMERIC, each element is converted to a number before the comparison.
rsort(*$array*[, *$compare*])	Sorts the values in an array in descending order and reindexes the array.
asort(*$array*[, *$compare*])	Sorts the values in an array in ascending order and keeps the keys with the values.
arsort(*$array*[, *$compare*])	Sorts the values in an array in descending order and keeps the keys with the values.
ksort(*$array*[, *$compare*])	Sorts the keys in an array in ascending order and keeps the values with the keys.
krsort(*$array*[, *$compare*])	Sorts the keys in an array in descending order and keeps the values with the keys.

How to sort strings in ascending order

```
$names = array('Mike', 'Anne', 'Joel', 'Ray', 'Pren');
sort($names);                       // Anne, Joel, Mike, Pren, Ray
```

How to sort numbers in ascending order

```
$numbers = array(520, '33', 9, '199');
sort($numbers, SORT_NUMERIC);       // 9, 33, 199, 520
```

How to sort in descending order

```
$names = array('Mike', 'Anne', 'Joel', 'Ray', 'Pren');
rsort($names);                      // Ray, Pren, Mike, Joel, Anne
```

How to sort an associative array

```
$tax_rates = array('NC' => 7.75, 'NY' => 8.875, 'CA' => 8.25);
asort($tax_rates);                  // sorts by value (ascending)
ksort($tax_rates);                  // sorts by key (ascending)
arsort($tax_rates);                 // sorts by value (descending)
krsort($tax_rates);                 // sorts by key (descending)
```

Description

- The sorting functions don't return an array. Instead, they modify the array that's passed to them.
- The $compare parameter works the same for all sorting functions.

Figure 11-10   How to sort arrays

How to modify arrays

Figure 11-11 shows how to modify arrays. To start, the first example uses the array_unique function to return a new array with duplicate values removed from the array. It uses the same comparison constants that the sorting functions use, but the default is SORT_STRING instead of SORT_REGULAR.

The first example also shows how to use the array_reverse function to reverse the order of the elements in the array. In addition, it shows how to use the shuffle function to shuffle the elements in the array randomly. Note that the shuffle function modifies the $array parameter directly instead of returning an array. As a result, you don't need to code an assignment statement when you use this function.

If you use the array_reverse or shuffle functions to modify an associative array, you usually want to keep the keys and the values together. To do that, you can set the $keys parameter to TRUE as shown in the second example.

The third example shows how to use the array_rand function to select a random element from the array and return its key. If the $count parameter is greater than one, it returns an array of random keys. These keys don't contain duplicates and are sorted in ascending order. However, the $count parameter can't be greater than the number of elements in the array or PHP issues a runtime error.

The fourth example shows how to create a deck of cards, shuffle the deck, and deal a hand of cards from the deck. To create the deck of cards, this example begins by creating two arrays to hold the face and suit values. Then, this code creates an empty array to hold the deck. Next, it uses two nested foreach loops to loop through the face and suit values, and it joins each combination of face and suit values and adds it to the deck of cards. This array starts with '2h', '2d', '2c', '2s' and ends with 'Ah', 'Ad', 'Ac', 'As'.

After this code creates the deck of cards, it uses the shuffle function to shuffle the deck. Then, it creates new array to hold a hand of cards, uses a for loop to deal five cards from the deck, and adds these cards to the hand. The last statement uses the implode function to display the hand.

Functions for modifying arrays

Function	Description
array_unique($array[, $compare])	Returns $array with duplicate values removed. The $compare property works the same as it does for the sort function except that SORT_STRING is the default.
array_reverse($array [, $keys])	Returns $array with the elements in the reverse order. If keys is TRUE, the original keys are used. Otherwise, the elements are reindexed.
shuffle($array [, $keys])	Shuffles the values in $array in a random order. The array is reindexed.
array_rand($array [, $count])	Returns a random key from $array. If $count is greater than one, it returns an array of $count random keys from $array.

How to modify an array

```
$names = array('Mike', 'Mike', 'Mike', 'Anne', 'Joel', 'Joel');
$names = array_unique($names);          // Mike, Anne, Joel
$names = array_reverse($names);         // Joel, Anne, Mike
shuffle($names);                        // Mike, Joel, Anne (for example)
```

How to modify an associative array

```
$tax_rates = array('NC' => 7.75, 'NY' => 8.875, 'CA' => 8.25);
$tax_rates = array_reverse($tax_rates, true);
```

How to get random keys from an array

```
$names = array('Mike', 'Anne', 'Joel', 'Ray', 'Pren');
$key = array_rand($names);              // 2        (for example)
$names_rand = array_rand($names, 3);    // 0, 1, 3 (for example)
```

How to shuffle and deal a deck of cards

```
// Create the deck of cards
$faces = array('2', '3', '4', '5', '6', '7', '8',
               '9', 'T', 'J', 'Q', 'K', 'A');
$suits = array('h', 'd', 'c', 's');
$cards = array();
foreach($faces as $face) {
    foreach($suits as $suit) {
        $cards[] = $face . $suit;
    }
}

// Shuffle the deck and deal the cards
shuffle($cards);
$hand = array();
for ($i = 0; $i < 5; $i++) {
    $hand[] = array_pop($cards);
}
echo implode(', ', $hand);              // 3c, Js, Qs, Jc, Qc (for example)
```

Figure 11-11   How to modify arrays

How to work with arrays of arrays

An *array of arrays*, or *two-dimensional array*, is an array where each element of the array is another array.

Understanding an array of arrays

Figure 11-12 presents three diagrams to help you understand and visualize how an array of arrays works. The first diagram illustrates a simple array with integer indexes. This is the type of array you've worked with so far in this chapter. Each element is shown as an index in brackets above a value in a shaded box. In this array, the value for each element is a string.

The second diagram illustrates a type of two-dimensional array called a *rectangular array*. In this case, the nested arrays are all the same length. The outer array across the top of the diagram uses integer indexes. The nested arrays use string indexes. You can use a rectangular array like this to store tabular data. Here, for example, the rectangular array stores the data for five people.

The third diagram illustrates another type of two-dimensional array called a *jagged array*. In this case, the nested arrays are of different lengths. The outer array in this diagram uses string indexes while the nested arrays use integer indexes. Although jagged arrays aren't used as often as rectangular arrays, you may need to use them in some situations.

Although this figure doesn't show them, PHP also allows you to create *multi-dimensional arrays* that nest arrays three or more levels deep. PHP doesn't have a technical limit on how deeply arrays can be nested, but the logic of your application and the web server running your application place practical limits on the depth of nested arrays.

A simple array

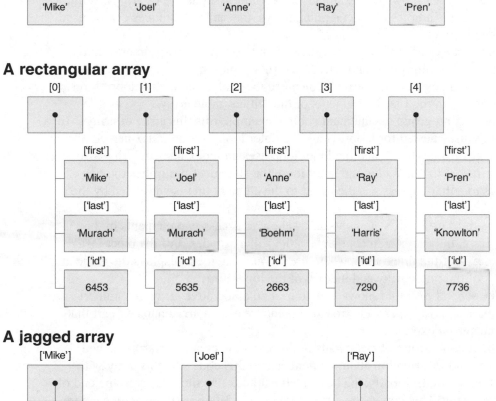

A rectangular array

A jagged array

Description

- An *array of arrays*, or *two-dimensional array*, is an array whose elements are also arrays.
- If the nested arrays within an array are the same size, the array is known as a *rectangular array*. If the nested arrays are different sizes, the array is known as a *jagged array*.

Figure 11-12   Understanding an array of arrays

How to create and use an array of arrays

Figure 11-13 shows two examples of working with arrays of arrays. While both of these examples use rectangular arrays, the same techniques can be used for jagged arrays.

The first example shows how to create and populate a two-dimensional array to hold a multiplication table. In the first group of statements, the first statement creates an empty array named $times_table. Then, a for loop stores empty arrays in the first 13 elements of the $times_table array.

The second group of statements in this example fills this array of arrays. To do that, it uses nested for loops. Here, the outer loop uses an index named $i that ranges from 0 to 12, and the inner loop uses an index named $j that also ranges from 0 to 12. Within the inner loop, the statement multiplies the two indexes together and assigns the result to the element that is addressed by the two indexes.

The third group of statements shows how to access two elements in this array. Here, the first statement displays the value at index 3 of the outer array and index 4 of the inner array. Then, the second statement displays the value at index 7 of the outer array and index 6 of the inner array.

The second example shows how to nest an associative array in a numerically indexed array. Here, the first statement creates an array named $cart that uses integer indexes.

The second group of statements in this example creates an array named $item to hold information about an item. Then, this code fills this array with data about an item. Finally, the last statement adds the $item array to the end of the $cart array. This copies the array stored in the $item variable to an element in the $cart array. As a result, the variable named $item can be reused later.

The third group of statements creates a new empty array and stores it in the $item variable. This replaces the original array stored in the $item variable. Then, this code fills the new array with data about an item. Finally, the last statement adds the $item array to the end of the $cart array.

The final group of statements shows how to access the elements in this array. Here, the first statement displays the code of the first item in the cart. Then, the second statement displays the name of the second item in the cart. If you want to display the data for each item in the cart, you can do that by nesting a foreach loop within a for loop.

How to create and use an array of arrays

Code that creates an array of arrays

```
$times_table = array();              // create an empty array
for ($i = 0; $i <= 12; $i++) {       // add 13 elements to the array
    $times_table[$i] = array();      // that contain empty arrays
}
```

Code that adds values to the array of arrays

```
for ($i = 0; $i <= 12; $i++) {
    for ($j = 0; $j <= 12; $j++) {
        $times_table[$i][$j] = $i * $j;
    }
}
```

Code that refers to elements in the array of arrays

```
echo $times_table[4][3];             // displays 12
echo $times_table[7][6];             // displays 42
```

How to create and use an array of associative arrays

Code that creates a cart array

```
$cart = array();                     // create an empty cart array
```

Code that creates an associative array and adds it to the cart array

```
$item = array();                     // create an empty item array
$item['itemCode'] = 123;
$item['itemName'] = "Visual Basic 2010";
$item['itemCost'] = 52.5;
$item['itemQuantity'] = 5;
$cart[] = $item;                     // add item array to cart array
```

Code that creates and adds another associative array to the cart array

```
$item = array();                     // create an empty item array
$item["itemCode"] = 456;
$item["itemName"] = "C++ 2010";
$item["itemCost"] = 52.5;
$item["itemQuantity"] = 2;
$cart[]  = $item;                    // add item array to cart array
```

Code that refers to the elements in the array of associative arrays

```
echo $cart[0]["itemCode"];           // displays 123
echo $cart[1]["itemName"];           // displays C++ 2010
```

Description

- To refer to the elements in an array of arrays, you use two index values for each element. The first index is for an element in the outer array. The second index is for an element in the inner array.

Figure 11-13   How to create and use an array of arrays

The Task List Manager application

This chapter ends by showing how to use some of the skills you've just learned in an application. In particular, figure 11-14 shows how to use a Task List Manager application to work with a list of tasks. Because this application doesn't store these tasks in a database, the tasks are lost when the user closes the application. However, once you understand this application, it's easy to modify it so it stores the tasks in a database.

The user interface

The user interface for the Task List Manager shows the tasks at the top of the web page in a numbered list. The user interface also includes an add form that lets the user add a new task to the list, and it includes a delete form that lets the user delete a task from the list.

The code for the controller

When the user starts this application, the code in the controller file checks to see if an existing task list has been submitted as part of an add or delete operation. If so, this code gets the task list that's stored in the global $_POST variable and copies it in to the $task_list variable. Otherwise, the $task_list variable is initialized with an empty array. Then, this code creates an empty $errors array to store any errors that the application may encounter.

After setting up the $task_list and $errors arrays, this code uses a switch statement to check whether an "add" or "delete" action has been requested by the user interface. If the "add" action is requested, the new task is copied into the $new_task variable. Then, an if statement checks this variable to make sure it isn't empty. If the new task variable is empty, this statement adds an appropriate error message to the end of the $errors array. Otherwise, the new task is added to the end of the $task_list array. If the "delete" action is requested, this code copies the task ID into the $task_index variable. Then, this code deletes the task and reindexes the array.

Whatever happens, the last statement in the controller displays the view for the application by including the task_list.php file. Then, this file displays the data that's stored in the $task_list and $errors arrays.

The user interface for the Task List Manager application

The index.php file

```php
<?php
if (isset($_POST['tasklist'])) {
    $task_list = $_POST['tasklist'];
} else {
    $task_list = array();
}

$errors = array();

switch( $_POST['action'] ) {
    case 'add':
        $new_task = $_POST['newtask'];
        if (empty($new_task)) {
            $errors[] = 'The new task cannot be empty.';
        } else {
            $task_list[] = $new_task;
        }
        break;
    case 'delete':
        $task_index = $_POST['taskid'];
        unset($task_list[$task_index]);
        $task_list = array_values($task_list);
        break;
}

include('task_list.php');
?>
```

Figure 11-14   The Task List Manager application (part 1 of 3)

The code for the view

Part 2 of figure 11-14 shows the code for the view of the application. This code is a mix of PHP and HTML. The CSS code for this application isn't shown, but it's available in the download for the book. The four parts of the view are contained in the <div> element with an id of "main".

The first part displays any error messages in the $errors array. To start, this part uses the count function to determine whether there are error messages. If so, it uses a foreach loop to display each error message in an unordered list. For this application, the only possible error message occurs when a user doesn't enter a task. However, if this application was enhanced to provide for other types of errors, this part would display all errors in the $errors array.

The second part displays the tasks in the $task_list array. To start, this code uses the count function to determine whether there are any tasks. If not, it displays a paragraph that indicates that there aren't any tasks in the list. Otherwise, it uses a foreach loop to display each task in the list. When displaying the index number, the code adds one to the index before displaying it. This starts the task numbers at one instead of zero.

The third part displays a form to add a new task to the task list. Since the tasks aren't stored in a database, the existing tasks have to be submitted along with the new task. The foreach loop in the form adds each existing task as a hidden field with a name of "tasklist[]" in the form. Here, the name attribute of the <input> tag ends with brackets so that the tasks are combined into an array in the $_POST array. That way, the code at the beginning of the controller can get this array of tasks.

The hidden field named action has a value of "add" to trigger the correct section of code in the switch statement in the controller. The remaining code displays the text box and button that allow the user to enter a task and submit it to the controller.

The task_list.php file

```
<!DOCTYPE html PUBLIC "-//W3C//DTD XHTML 1.0 Transitional//EN"
    "http://www.w3.org/TR/xhtml1/DTD/xhtml1-transitional.dtd">
<html xmlns="http://www.w3.org/1999/xhtml">
<head>
    <title>Task List Manager</title>
    <link rel="stylesheet" type="text/css" href="main.css">
</head>
<body>
    <div id="page">
    <div id="header">
        <h1>Task List Manager</h1>
    </div>
    <div id="main">

    <!— part 1: the errors —>
    <?php if (count($errors) > 0) : ?>
    <h2>Errors</h2>
    <ul>
        <?php foreach($errors as $error) : ?>
            <li><?php echo $error; ?></li>
        <?php endforeach; ?>
    </ul>
    <?php endif; ?>

    <!— part 2: the tasks —>
    <h2>Tasks</h2>
    <?php if (count($task_list) == 0) : ?>
        <p>There are no tasks in the task list.</p>
    <?php else: ?>
        <ul id="task">
        <?php foreach( $task_list as $id => $task ) : ?>
            <li><?php echo $id + 1 . '. ' . $task; ?></li>
        <?php endforeach; ?>
        </ul>
    <?php endif; ?>

    <!— part 3: the add form —>
    <h2>Add Task</h2>
    <form action="." method="post" >
        <?php foreach( $task_list as $task ) : ?>
          <input type="hidden" name="tasklist[]" value="<?php echo $task; ?>">
        <?php endforeach; ?>
        <input type="hidden" name="action" value="add">
        <label>Task:</label>
        <input type="text" name="newtask" id="newtask"> <br />
        <label> </label>
        <input type="submit" value="Add Task"><br />
    </form>
```

Figure 11-14   The Task List Manager application (part 2 of 3)

The fourth part of the application displays a form to delete a task from the task list, but it only displays this form if there are any tasks in the task list. Again, the existing tasks have to be submitted along with the index of the task to delete. That's why the foreach loop in the form adds each existing task as a hidden field in the form.

The hidden field named action has a value of "delete" to trigger the correct section of code in the controller. After that, the code uses a foreach loop to display the tasks as a drop-down list. Here, the value attribute of the <option> tag is the key of the task element, and the text that's displayed in the drop-down list is the value of the task element.

The task_list.php file (continued)

```php
<!-- part 4: the delete form -->
<?php if (count($task_list) > 0) : ?>
<h2>Delete Task</h2>
<form action="." method="post" >
    <?php foreach( $task_list as $task ) : ?>
      <input type="hidden" name="tasklist[]" value="<?php echo $task; ?>">
    <?php endforeach; ?>
    <input type="hidden" name="action" value="delete">
    <label>Task:</label>
    <select name="taskid">
        <?php foreach( $task_list as $id => $task ) : ?>
            <option value="<?php echo $id; ?>">
                <?php echo $task; ?>
            </option>
        <?php endforeach; ?>
    </select>
    <br />
    <label> </label>
    <input type="submit" value="Delete Task">
</form>
<?php endif; ?>

    </div><!-- end main -->
    </div><!-- end page -->
</body>
</html>
```

Figure 11-14   The Task List Manager application (part 3 of 3)

Perspective

Arrays are an important part of many PHP applications, and PHP provides many functions for working with arrays. In the chapters that follow, you'll see other uses of arrays and other ways to work with them.

As you review other developer's PHP code, you may encounter code that uses operators such as the plus sign (+) to work with arrays. I didn't present these operators in this chapter because they don't always work the way you would expect. For example, you would expect to be able to use the plus sign to add one array to another. However, that's not what this operation does. As a result, I recommend using the array functions instead of the array operators. For example, to add one array to another, I recommend using the array_merge function as described in this chapter.

Terms

array	last-in, first-out
element	LIFO
value of an element	queue
index of an element	first-in, first-out
length of an array	FIFO
associative array	array of arrays
key	two-dimensional array
foreach statement	rectangular array
foreach loop	jagged array
stack	multi-dimensional array

Summary

- An *array* can contain one or more *elements* that are referred to by *indexes*. These indexes can be either integers or strings. The *length* of an array indicates the number of elements that it contains.

- PHP arrays are dynamic, which means that you can change the length of an array by adding or removing elements. You can also create empty elements within an array (gaps).

- An *associative array* is an array that has string values for its indexes. This type of index is commonly called a *key*, so an associative array can be thought of as a series of key/value pairs.

- A for loop is commonly used for processing arrays with integer indexes, and a foreach loop is commonly used for processing associative arrays.

- PHP provides many functions that make it easier to work with arrays. These include functions for creating, searching, sorting, and modifying arrays.

- A *stack* is a type of array that provides for *last in, first out (LIFO)* processing. A *queue* is a type of array that provides for *first in, first out (FIFO)* processing.

- An *array of arrays*, or a *two-dimensional array*, is an array with elements that contain other arrays. A two-dimensional array is usually *rectangular*, but it can also be *jagged*.

Exercise 11-1   Work with the arrays of the Task List Manager application

This exercise gives you a chance to experiment with arrays and array methods in the context of the Task List Manager application.

Open and test the application

1. Run the application in the ex_starts/ch11_ex1 directory. This is a modified version of the Task List Manager application that has a Modify Task button, a Promote Task button, and a Sort Tasks button.

2. Test this application by using the Add Task button to enter three tasks and the Delete Task button to delete one of the tasks. These buttons should work as described in the text. However, the other buttons shouldn't do anything.

3. Open the index.php and task_list.php files for this application. Note that these files use the name and value attributes of the submit buttons to get the action to be performed.

Modify and enhance the application

4. Modify the code for adding a task so it uses the array_push function to add a new task to the end of the task_list array. Then, test this change.

5. Add code that lets the user modify an existing task. If the user clicks on the Modify Task button, this code should hide the form that contains the Modify Task button, and it should display the form that's included in the task_list.php file. This form displays the current task in a text box and includes buttons that let users save or cancel their changes.

6. Add code that allows the user to promote a task. This code should move the selected task up one index in the array of tasks. If the user selects the first task, this code should display an error that indicates that you can't promote the first task.

7. Add code that lets the user sort all tasks alphabetically.

8. Don't forget to test your changes to make sure that they work correctly!

12

How to work with cookies and sessions

In all but the simplest of web applications, you need to keep track of your users as they move through an application. That's why this chapter shows how to use sessions to track users. But first, since sessions use cookies, this chapter begins by showing how to use cookies.

How to work with cookies **348**
An introduction to cookies 348
How to set and get a cookie 350
How to enable or disable cookies 352

How to work with sessions **354**
Why session tracking is difficult with HTTP 354
How session tracking works in PHP 354
How to start a session 356
How to set and get session variables 358
How to end a session 360
How to manage a session 362

The Shopping Cart application **364**
The user interface 364
The controller 366
The model 368
The Add Item view 370
The Cart view 372

Perspective **376**

How to work with cookies

Cookies provide a way for a web application to store information in the user's web browser and retrieve it every time the user requests a page. This concerns some web users because they've heard rumors that cookies can transmit viruses, steal passwords, and copy files from your hard drive.

Although these rumors aren't true, cookies are sometimes abused. For example, some advertisers use cookies to track the web sites you've visited. These cookies are called *third-party cookies* because they are sent from the advertisers, not from the web sites you visit. To combat this abuse, modern web browsers let you block third-party cookies by changing browser options.

An introduction to cookies

Figure 12-1 introduces you to some basic information about cookies. To start, it shows that a cookie is a text string stored by the browser as a name/value pair. When a browser requests a web page, the server can create a cookie and return it to the browser as part of the response. Then, the browser sends the cookie back to the server every time it requests a web page from that server. This allows the server to access the data in the cookie and to use that data to control how the web application behaves.

Examples of cookies

```
PHPSESSID=D1F15245171203E8670487F020544490
user_id=87
email=jsmith@hotmail.com
userName=jsmith
passwordCookie=opensesame
```

How cookies work

- A *cookie* is a name/value pair that is stored in a browser.

- On the server, a web application creates a cookie and sends it to the browser. On the client, the browser saves the cookie and sends it back to the server every time it accesses a page from that server.

- By default, cookies only last until the user closes his or her web browser. However, cookies can be set to persist in the user's browser for up to three years.

- Some users disable cookies in their browsers. As a result, you can't always count on all users having their cookies enabled.

- Browsers generally accept only 20 cookies from each site and 300 cookies total. In addition, they can limit each cookie to 4 kilobytes.

- A cookie can be associated with one or more subdomain names.

Typical uses for cookies

- **To allow users to skip login and registration forms** that gather data like username, password, address, or credit card data.

- **To customize pages** that display information like weather reports, sports scores, and stock quotations.

- **To focus advertising** like banner ads that target the user's interests.

Description

- A common misconception is that cookies are harmful. Since cookies consist only of plain text, they cannot directly modify a user's computer, create pop-up ads, generate spam, or steal files.

Figure 12-1   An introduction to cookies

How to set and get a cookie

Figure 12-2 shows you how to set a cookie in the user's browser and how to get data from that cookie. To create a cookie and set it in the browser, you can use the setcookie function. To get the value of a cookie, you can use the autoglobal $_COOKIE variable. This variable is an associative array.

When using the setcookie function, the $name parameter is the only required parameter. However, in most cases, you need to provide values for the first four parameters. That way, you can use the $name and $value parameters to specify the name/value pair for the cookie, you can use the $expire parameter to specify an expiration date for the cookie, and you can use the $path parameter to make the cookie available to all pages for the current web application.

If you set the $expire parameter to 0, the cookie only exists until the user closes the browser. This is called a *per-session cookie*. However, if you want, you can set the $expire parameter to a date up to three years from the current date. In that case, the cookie stays in the browser until the expiration date. This is called a *persistent cookie*.

The $path parameter should almost always be set to the root of your web site. That way, every page in your application can access the cookie. If you use the default value of the current directory, a cookie created here:

```
http://www.example.com/login/index.php
```

isn't available here:

```
http://www.example.com/checkout/index.php.
```

The first example shows how to create a cookie with a name of "userid" and a value of "rharris". This cookie expires after one year and is available to any page in any directory on the web server. To create the timestamp for the expiration date, this code uses the strtotime function to get a timestamp that's one year from the current date.

The second example uses the $_COOKIE variable to get the value of the cookie named userid. As a result, if the browser has a cookie named userid, this code returns the value. Otherwise, it returns a NULL value. If necessary, you can use the isset function to determine if the cookie's value is in the array before retrieving it.

The third example shows how to delete a cookie. To do that, you can use the setcookie function to set the $expire parameter of the cookie to a date in the past. Here, the code sets the $expire parameter to one year in the past. In addition, you must set the $value parameter to an empty string, and you must set all remaining parameters to the same values that were used when the cookie was created.

The syntax of the setcookie function

```
setcookie($name, $value, $expire, $path, $domain, $secure, $httponly)
```

The parameters of the setcookie function

Parameter	Description
$name	The name of the cookie.
$value	The value of the cookie. The default is the empty string.
$expire	The expiration date of the cookie as a timestamp. If set to 0, the cookie expires when the user closes the browser. The default is 0.
$path	The path on the server that the cookie is available to. If set to '/', the cookie is available to all directories on the current server. The default is the directory of the PHP file that's setting the cookie.
$domain	The domain that the cookie is available to. The default is the name of the server that's setting the cookie.
$secure	If TRUE, the cookie is available only if it is sent using HTTPS. The default is FALSE.
$httponly	If TRUE, the cookie is only made available through the HTTP protocol and not through client-side scripting languages such as JavaScript. The default is FALSE.

Set a cookie in the browser

```
$name = 'userid';
$value = 'rharris';
$expire = strtotime('+1 year');
$path = '/';
setcookie($name, $value, $expire, $path);
```

Gets the value of a cookie from the browser

```
$userid = $_COOKIE['userid'];        // $userid is 'rharris'
```

Delete a cookie from the browser

```
$expire = strtotime('-1 year');
setcookie('userid', '', $expire, '/');
```

Description

- To set a cookie in the user's browser, you can use the setcookie function. This function must be called before any HTML output is sent from your application.

- A *per-session cookie* expires when the user closers the browser. A *persistent cookie* doesn't expire until the specified expiration date.

- Once a cookie has been set, you can get it the next time the browser requests a page. To do that, you can use the superglobal $_COOKIE variable. This variable is an associative array where the cookie name is the key and the cookie value is the value.

- To delete a cookie from a browser, set the value to the empty string and the expiration date to a time in the past. Any remaining parameters must have the same values as when the cookie was originally created.

Figure 12-2   How to set and get a cookie

How to enable or disable cookies

Although most users have cookies enabled, it's generally considered a good practice to test your application with cookies disabled. That way, you can test your application for users who have disabled cookies. Then, you can modify your application so it handles this situation appropriately.

For example, you may want to display a message that indicates that cookies are required for the application to function properly. Once you're done with this testing, you can enable cookies again to continue testing the application for users who have cookies enabled.

Figure 12-3 shows how to enable and disable cookies in Firefox and Internet Explorer. With the Internet Explorer, you may have to reset the security settings to their default values to be able to block cookies from a development web server running on the same computer as Internet Explorer.

If you're using a web browser other than Firefox or IE or you're using older versions of these browsers, you can search the Internet or your browser's documentation to learn how to enable and disable cookies.

How to enable or disable cookies in Firefox 3.6

1. Open the Tools menu and select the Options command.
2. Click on the Privacy tab.
3. Use the "Accept cookies from sites" check box to enable or disable cookies.

How to enable or disable cookies in Internet Explorer 8

1. Open the Tools menu and select the Internet Options command.
2. Click the Privacy tab.
3. Use the slider control to enable or disable cookies. To disable cookies, set the security level to "Block All Cookies". To enable cookies, click the Default button to return to default privacy settings.

How to reset default security settings in Internet Explorer 8

1. Open the Tools menu and select the Internet Options command.
2. Click the Security tab.
3. If not disabled, click the "Reset all zones to default level" button.

Description

- To test how your application behaves if a user has cookies disabled, you can disable cookies in your browser.
- To test how your application behaves under normal circumstances, you can enable cookies in your browser.
- In IE 8, you may need to reset the security settings to their default levels to block cookies from the web server running on your computer.
- For other web browsers, use the browser's documentation or search the Internet to find instructions for enabling and disabling cookies.

Figure 12-3   How to enable or disable cookies

How to work with sessions

Keeping track of users as they move around a web site is known as *session tracking*. In this topic, you'll learn why session tracking is important and how to use PHP's built-in support for session tracking.

Why session tracking is difficult with HTTP

Figure 12-4 shows why session tracking is more difficult for web applications that use HTTP than it is for other types of applications. To start, a browser on a client requests a page from a web server. After the web server returns the page, it closes the connection. When the browser makes a subsequent request, the web server has no way to associate the current request with the previous request. Since HTTP doesn't maintain state, it is known as a *stateless protocol*.

How session tracking works in PHP

This figure also shows how PHP keeps track of sessions. To start, a browser on a client requests a PHP page from a web server. Then, PHP checks if the request includes a PHP session ID. If it doesn't, PHP creates a new *session* on the server and assigns it a unique session ID. At this point, the application can store data in the session. Then, the session ID is sent back to the browser as a cookie in the response.

When the browser makes a subsequent request, it includes the session ID cookie in the request. Again, PHP checks whether the request includes a PHP session ID. This time it does, so PHP uses the session ID to access the data for the session that's stored on the server. Then, the application can use that data, modify it, or add to it as needed.

By default, PHP 5.3 only uses cookies to work with the session ID. As a result, session tracking only works if the user has cookies enabled. For most web applications, that's what you want since the vast majority of web browsers have cookies enabled.

However, if you need your application to work correctly even for users who have cookies disabled, PHP can encode the session ID in the URL. This is sometimes called *URL encoding*, and you can configure your system so PHP transparently encodes the session ID in the URL. Unfortunately, this causes a problem with the way that your web pages appear in search engines. As a result, we don't recommend using transparent URL encoding, and we don't cover it in this chapter. If you need to use it, you can learn more by visiting these web pages:

`http://www.php.net/manual/en/session.idpassing.php`

`http://php.net/session.use-trans-sid`

Why session tracking is difficult with HTTP

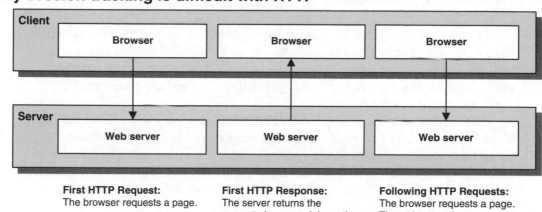

First HTTP Request:
The browser requests a page.

First HTTP Response:
The server returns the requested page and drops the connection.

Following HTTP Requests:
The browser requests a page. The web server has no way to associate the browser with its previous request.

How PHP keeps track of sessions

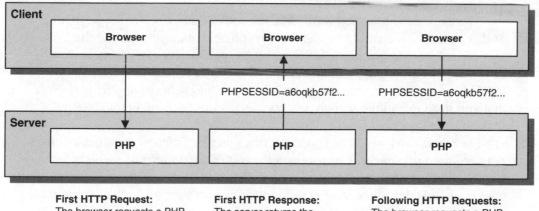

First HTTP Request:
The browser requests a PHP page. PHP creates a session and assigns it an ID.

First HTTP Response:
The server returns the requested page and the ID for the session as a cookie.

Following HTTP Requests:
The browser requests a PHP page and sends the session ID cookie. PHP uses the session ID to associate the browser with its session.

Description

- HTTP is a *stateless protocol*. Once a browser makes a request, it drops the connection to the server. To maintain *state*, a web application uses *session tracking*.

- By default, PHP uses a cookie to store a session ID in each browser. Then, the browser passes the cookie to the server with each request.

- To provide session tracking when cookies are disabled in the browser, you can use *URL encoding* to store the session ID in the URL for each page of an application. However, we don't recommend that.

Figure 12-4   An introduction to session tracking

How to start a session

Figure 12-5 shows how to start a session. Although session tracking is built-in to PHP, it isn't automatically available. To make it available, you can start a new session or resume a previous session by calling the session_start function at the beginning of each page in your application that needs to access the session data.

The session_start function prompts PHP to check for a session ID in the request and to create a new session ID and session cookie if one isn't found. Since the session_start function may set a cookie, it must be called before any HTML content is sent to the browser. By default, PHP uses a per-session cookie to store the session ID in the user's browser. As a result, when the user closes the browser, the session ends.

However, if you're using Firefox and you select the Save and Quit option (not the Quit option) when you close the browser, the session doesn't end. Instead, Firefox saves the per-session cookie and uses it the next time it restarts. As a result, to end a session with Firefox, you must use the Quit option (not the Save and Quit option) when you close the browser.

The cookie for a session works like the cookies described at the beginning of this chapter. To control how the session cookie works, you can use the session_set_cookie_params function to set the parameters of the session cookie. In this figure, the second example creates a session cookie that persists in the user's browser for one year and is available to all pages of the application. Note that you need to call the session_set_cookie_params function before the session_start function.

For the session_set_cookie_params function, the $lifetime parameter is the only required parameter. This parameter specifies the number of seconds for the session cookie to be stored in the browser. When PHP creates the session cookie, it adds this number of seconds to the current time to get the expiration date for the session cookie. However, you usually want to set the $path parameter to allow all pages in the application to access the session cookie. In addition, you may occasionally want to set one of the other four parameters described in this figure.

A function to start a session

Function	Description
`session_start()`	Starts a new session or resumes a previous session. Returns TRUE if successful and FALSE otherwise. This function must be called before the page sends any HTML output to your application.

Start a session with the default cookie parameters

```
session_start();
```

The syntax of the session_set_cookie_params function

```
session_set_cookie_params($lifetime, $path, $domain, $secure, $httponly)
```

The parameters of the session_set_cookie_params function

Parameter	Description
`$lifetime`	The lifetime of the session cookie in seconds. The default is 0.
`$path`	The path on the server the session cookie is available to. The default is the current directory of the script that is setting the cookie.
`$domain`	The domain that the cookie is available to. The default is the name of the server that is setting the cookie.
`$secure`	If TRUE, the cookie is available only if it is sent using a secure HTTP connection (an HTTPS connection). The default is FALSE.
`$httponly`	If TRUE, the cookie is only available through the HTTP protocol and not through client-side scripting languages such as JavaScript. The default is FALSE.

Start a session with custom cookie parameters

```
$lifetime = 60 * 60 * 24 * 365;   // 1 year in seconds
session_set_cookie_params($lifetime, '/');
session_start();
```

Description

- A *session* starts when a browser makes its first request to a page that includes the session_start function.

- By default, a session uses a per-session cookie to associate a browser with the data for its session. However, you can use the session_set_cookie_params function to customize the cookie for the session.

- In the session_set_cookie_params function, the $lifetime parameter is the only required parameter. The other parameters are optional.

- The session_set_cookie_params function must be called before the session_start function.

Figure 12-5   How to start a session

How to set and get session variables

Once you start a session, you can set and get session variables. To do that, you can use the global $_SESSION variable as shown in figure 12-6. This variable is an associative array that stores the data for the session. The first example shows how to set a scalar value in the $_SESSION array. Then, the second example show how to get that value from the $_SESSION array.

After showing how to work with scalar values in a session, this figure shows how to work with an array in a session. Here, the first example uses the isset function to check whether an element named cart has already been set in the $_SESSION array. If not, it sets that element to an empty array. Then, the second example sets two values in the cart array, and the third example gets the cart array and sends a list of its contents to the browser.

After showing how to store an array in a session, this figure shows how to remove elements from a session. Here, the first example shows how to use the unset function to remove an element from the $_SESSION array. Then, the second example shows how to remove all elements from the $_SESSION array by setting it to an empty array. When removing all elements from the $_SESSION array, don't use the unset function directly on the $_SESSION variable as this can cause unpredictable results in your application.

As your application runs, PHP stores the $_SESSION array in memory. When the session ends, PHP saves the contents of the $_SESSION array in a file on the web server. Finally, PHP deletes this session data when the session expires. By default, a session expires after 24 minutes of inactivity.

When working with sessions, it's safe to store strings, numbers, and Boolean values in the session. In addition, it's safe to store arrays of these types of values. However, it often isn't safe to store objects in a session. For more information about objects, please refer to chapter 14.

The problem is that PHP stores the session data in a file on the web server. To do this for an object, PHP has to be able to convert the object to a text representation for storage. Then, when PHP reloads the session, it has to convert the text representation back to an object. These processes are known respectively as *serialization* and *deserialization*.

As a result, before you store an object in a session, you should consider three issues. First, your code needs to load the class definition before it calls the session_start function. Second, objects that refer back to themselves can't be stored as text representations. Third, serialization is slow and takes up more storage space than the original object. For large scale web applications, there is a significant performance penalty for storing objects in a session.

Fortunately, an object often represents a row in a database. As a result, you can often store the primary key for the row in the session. Then, you can reload the data from the database into the object when the new page is loaded. This is typically faster than serializing and deserialization an object.

How to set and get scalar variables

Set a variable in a session
```
$_SESSION['product_code'] = 'MBT-1753';
```

Get a variable from a session
```
$product_code = $_SESSION['product_code'];
```

How to set and get arrays

Set an array in a session
```
if (!isset($_SESSION['cart'])) {
    $_SESSION['cart'] = array();
}
```

Add an element to an array that's stored in a session
```
$_SESSION['cart']['key1'] = 'value1';
$_SESSION['cart']['key2'] = 'value2';
```

Get and use an array that's stored in a session
```
$cart = $_SESSION['cart'];
foreach ($cart as $item) {
    echo '<li>' . $item . '</li>';
}
```

How to remove variables from a session

Remove a session variable
```
unset($_SESSION['cart']);
```

Remove all session variables
```
$_SESSION = array();
```

Description

- Once you start a session, you can use the autoglobal $_SESSION variable to set and get the user's data for a session. This variable is an associative array.

- If necessary, you can use the isset function to test if an element already exists in the $_SESSION array.

- You can use the unset function to remove an element from the $_SESSION array. However, don't use the unset function on the $_SESSION array itself as it can cause unpredictable results.

- You can set the $_SESSION array to an empty array to remove its contents.

Figure 12-6   How to set and get session variables

How to end a session

By default, a session ends after 24 minutes without a request. As a result, you often don't need to write any code to end a session. However, in some cases, you may need to write code that ends a session. For example, if a user logs out of your application, you typically want to end the session.

The first example shows how to end a session. To start, the first statement removes all session variables from memory by setting the $_SESSION array to an empty array. Then, the second statement cleans up the session ID by calling the session_destroy function. However, this doesn't delete the session cookie from the user's browser.

As a result, if you want to completely remove the session data from both the client and the server, you need to delete the session cookie as shown in the second example. This code begins by using the session_name function to get the name of the session cookie. Then, it sets an expiration date of one year in the past. Next, it uses the session_get_cookie_params function to get an associative array of the values used when creating the session cookie, and it copies four elements from this array to individual variables. Finally, it calls the setcookie function with these values. Since this call uses an empty string for the $value parameter and a date in the past for the $expire parameter, this deletes the session cookie.

When you use the session_destroy function, you must call it after the session_start function. In addition, you shouldn't use it after the session_write_close function that's described in the next figure.

A function to end a session

Function	Description
`session_destroy()`	Ends a session. Returns TRUE if successful and FALSE otherwise.

End a session

```
$_SESSION = array();    // Clear session data from memory
session_destroy();      // Clean up the session ID
```

Delete the session cookie from the browser

```
$name = session_name();                     // Get name of session cookie
$expire = strtotime('-1 year');             // Create exp date in the past
$params = session_get_cookie_params();      // Get session params
$path = $params['path'];
$domain = $params['domain'];
$secure = $params['secure'];
$httponly = $params['httponly'];
setcookie($name, '', $expire, $path, $domain, $secure, $httponly);
```

Description

- A session ends when the user closes the browser, when a specified amount of time elapses without a request, or when the code calls the session_destroy function.

- To remove all data associated with the session from the client and the server, you can clear the session data from memory, call the session_destroy function, and use the setcookie function to delete the session cookie.

- The session_name function gets the name of the session cookie. By default, the session cookie has a name of "PHPSESSID".

- The session_get_cookie_params function gets an associative array that contains all of the parameters for the session cookie. For a list of these parameters, see figure 12-5.

Figure 12-7   How to end a session

How to manage a session

Figure 12-8 describes several functions you can use to manage a session. You typically won't need to use these functions, but they are useful in certain situations.

To start, you can use the session_name function to get the name of the session cookie as shown in the first example. By default, this cookie has a name of "PHPSESSID". In addition, you can use the session_id function to get or set the session ID. Here, the second example gets the session ID, and the third example sets the session ID.

Since the session cookie is often unencrypted, it's possible for an attacker on the network to view the session cookie and to use that data to impersonate the user. This is called *session hijacking*. To help prevent this, you can call the session_regenerate_id function at key points in your code to change the value of the session ID. For example, you may want to call this function after a user logs in or changes a password. Then, if someone has stolen an old session ID, that ID can't be used to impersonate the user.

In most cases, PHP automatically saves session data when the script ends. However, if you redirect the browser by using the header function followed by the exit function, PHP doesn't always save the session data. As a result, when using the header function to redirect users, you should call the session_write_close function to force PHP to save the session data.

Functions to manage sessions

Function	Description
`session_name()`	Gets the name of the session cookie. The default is PHPSESSID.
`session_id([$id])`	If the parameter isn't specified, this function gets the current session ID. If no session exists, this function gets the empty string. If the parameter is specified, this function sets the session ID to the specified value.
`session_write_close()`	Ends the current session and saves session data. This function is only needed in special cases like redirects.
`session_regenerate_id()`	Creates a new session ID for the current session. Returns TRUE if successful and FALSE otherwise. This function can be used to help prevent session hijacking.

Get the name of the session cookie

```
$name = session_name();    // By default, PHPSESSID
```

Get the value of the session ID

```
$id = session_id();        // For example, 11jef1foi1g8u6qnui4f8b6e14
```

Set the session ID

```
session_id('abc123');
```

Description

- The session_write_close function must be called before the session_destroy function.

Figure 12-8   How to manage a session

The Shopping Cart application

This topic presents an application that illustrates the use of session variables. Without session tracking, the code for this application would be much more complicated.

The user interface

Figure 12-9 shows the user interface for the Shopping Cart application. This application consists of two pages: the Add Item page and the Cart page.

The Add Item page allows the user to add an item to the cart. In addition, it includes a link that allows the user to view the cart without adding an item.

The Cart page displays all items in the user's cart along with a subtotal. From this page, the user can update the quantities for the items in the cart by changing the quantity and clicking the Update button. Or, the user can remove an item by changing the quantity to 0 and clicking the Update button. To add more items, the user can click on the Add Item link to return to the Add Item page. Or, to remove all items from the cart, the user can click on the Empty Cart link.

Since the point of this application is to illustrate the use of cookies and sessions, the user interface isn't at all realistic. Also, this application doesn't get the product data from a database or store the session in a database. These, of course, are improvements that you would make in a real-world applications.

The Add Item page

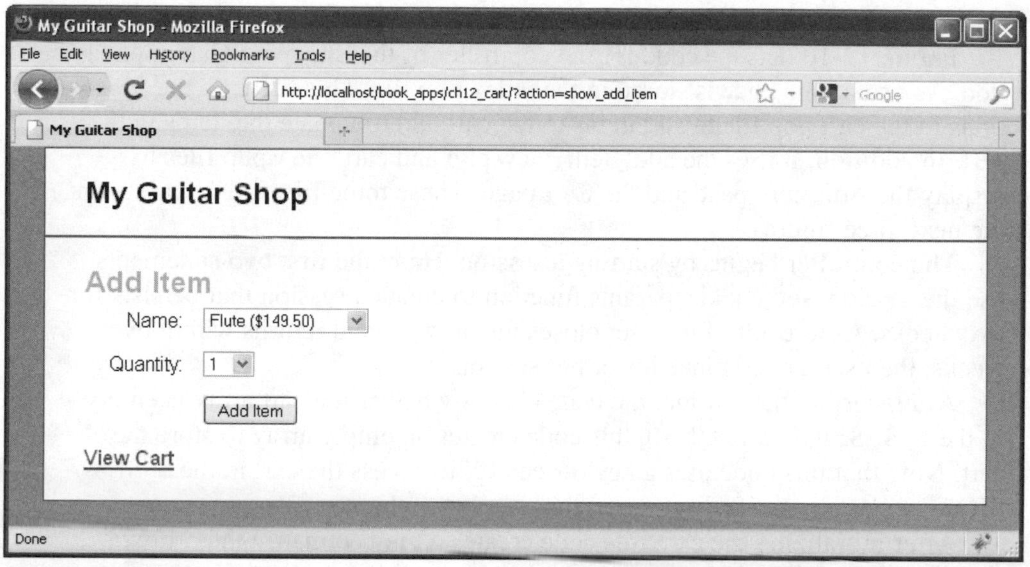

The Cart page

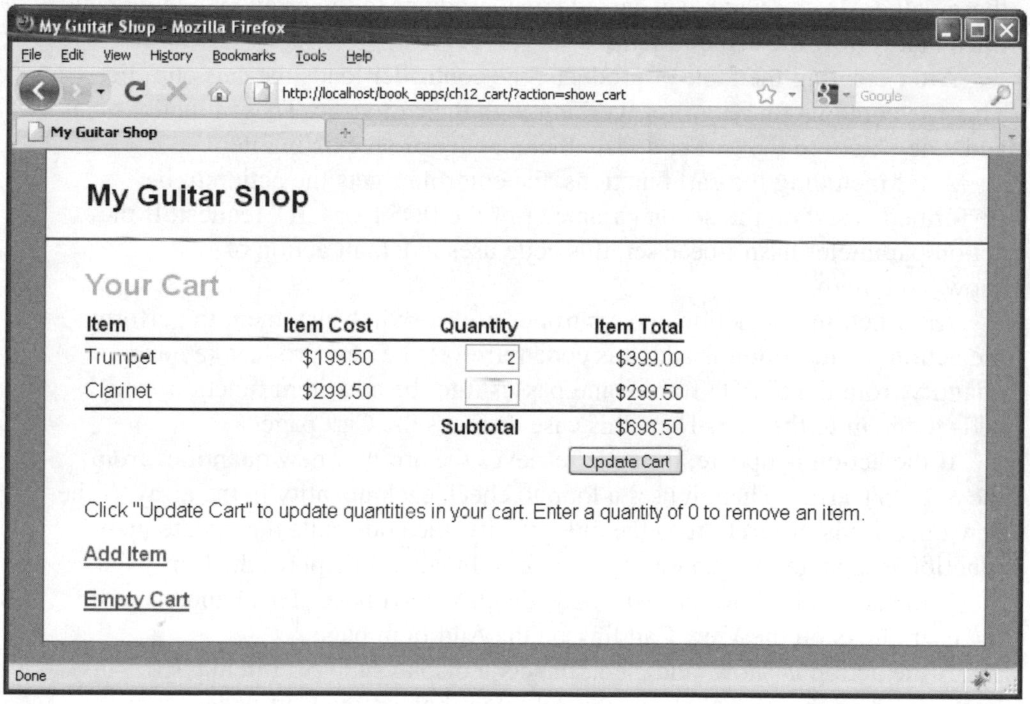

Figure 12-9   The Shopping Cart application

The controller

Figure 12-10 lists the code for the controller of the Shopping Cart application. As usual, this code is stored in the index.php file. This file uses the functions in the cart.php file to add items to the cart and to update the items in the cart. In addition, it uses the add_item_view.php and cart_view.php files to display the Add Item page and the Cart page. These three files are discussed in the next three figures.

The controller begins by starting a session. Here, the first two statements use the session_set_cookie_params function to create a session that persists for two weeks. As a result, if the user closes the browser and returns within two weeks, the user can continue his or her session.

After starting the session, the code checks whether the cart array is empty in the $_SESSION array. If so, this code creates an empty array to store the cart. Note that this code uses a key of 'cart12' to access the cart in the $_SESSION array. This key indicates that this cart is for chapter 12.

After initializing the cart, this code creates a multi-dimensional array of products. In a real-world application, this data would typically be read from a database. However, for the sake of simplicity, this application has hard-coded these values. If you want, you can add new products to the array by adding new lines that follow the same format.

After creating the table of products, the controller loads the cart.php file. This file contains functions for working with the cart array. These functions can add a new item to the cart or update the quantity of an existing item.

After including the cart functions, the controller gets the action to be performed based on the action parameter of the POST or GET request. If the action parameter hasn't been set, this code uses a default action of show_add_item.

After getting the action, the controller uses a switch statement to perform the action. If the action is add, this code retrieves the new product key and quantity from the $_POST array and passes it to the add_item function, which adds the item to the cart. Then, this case displays the Cart page.

If the action is update, the code retrieves the array of new quantities from the $_POST array. Then, it uses a loop to check each quantity in the array. If the new quantity is different than the old quantity, the code calls the update_item function to update the quantity for the item. Finally, it displays the Cart page.

If the action is show_cart, the code displays Cart page. This happens when the user clicks on the View Cart link on the Add Item page.

If the action is show_add_item, the code displays the Add Item page. This happens when the user clicks on the Add Item link on the Cart page.

If the action is empty_cart, the code uses the unset function to remove the cart from the $_SESSION variable. Then, it displays the Cart page. This happens when the user clicks on the Empty Cart link on the Cart page. Note that this code doesn't end the session for the user. However, it does unset the only session variable that's used by this application. From the user's point of view, this effectively ends the session.

The index.php file

```php
<?php
// Start session management with a persistent cookie
$lifetime = 60 * 60 * 24 * 14;     // 2 weeks in seconds
session_set_cookie_params($lifetime, '/');
session_start();

// Create a cart array if needed
if (empty($_SESSION['cart12'])) $_SESSION['cart12'] = array();

// Create a table of products
$products = array();
$products['MMS-1754'] = array('name' => 'Flute', 'cost' => '149.50');
$products['MMS-6289'] = array('name' => 'Trumpet', 'cost' => '199.50');
$products['MMS-3408'] = array('name' => 'Clarinet', 'cost' => '299.50');

// Include cart functions
require_once('cart.php');

// Get the action to perform
if (isset($_POST['action'])) {
    $action = $_POST['action'];
} else if (isset($_GET['action'])) {
    $action = $_GET['action'];
} else {
    $action = 'show_add_item';
}

// Add or update cart as needed
switch($action) {
    case 'add':
        add_item($_POST['productkey'], $_POST['itemqty']);
        include('cart_view.php');
        break;
    case 'update':
        $new_qty_list = $_POST['newqty'];
        foreach($new_qty_list as $key => $qty) {
            if ($_SESSION['cart12'][$key]['qty'] != $qty) {
                update_item($key, $qty);
            }
        }
        include('cart_view.php');
        break;
    case 'show_cart':
        include('cart_view.php');
        break;
    case 'show_add_item':
        include('add_item_view.php');
        break;
    case 'empty_cart':
        unset($_SESSION['cart12']);
        include('cart_view.php');
        break;
}
?>
```

Figure 12-10   The index.php file of the Shopping Cart application

The model

Figure 12-11 shows the code that models the behavior of the shopping cart. This code defines three functions. These functions let you add an item to the cart, update an item in the cart, and get the subtotal for the items in the cart.

The add_item function takes an item key and quantity as its parameters and uses them to add the specified item to the cart. To start, this code gets access to the global products array. Then, it checks if the quantity is less than 1. If so, this code exits the function.

If the item is already in the cart, the add_item function adds the existing quantity to the new quantity and calls the update_item function to update the quantity for the item. Then, it exits the function.

If the item isn't already in the cart, the add_item function gets the cost of the item from the products array and calculates the total for the item. Then, it creates an array that contains the item's name, cost, quantity, and total. Next, it stores the item array in the cart array using the item's key as the index.

The update_item function also takes an item key and quantity as its parameters and uses them to update the item's quantity and total. To start, this code gets the global products array.

If the item isn't in the cart, the update_item function doesn't execute any code. If the item is in the cart, this function checks if the quantity is less than or equal to zero. If so, this code uses the unset function to remove the item from the cart. Otherwise, this code stores the new quantity in the cart array. In addition, it calculates a new item total and stores it in the cart array.

The get_subtotal function adds the totals for each item in the cart and returns it as a formatted number. To start, it sets the subtotal to zero. Then, it loops over each item in the cart and adds its total to the subtotal. Finally, it returns the subtotal as a number with two digits after the decimal.

The cart.php file

```php
<?php
// Add an item to the cart
function add_item($key, $quantity) {
    global $products;
    if ($quantity < 1) return;

    // If item already exists in cart, update quantity
    if (isset($_SESSION['cart12'][$key])) {
        $quantity += $_SESSION['cart12'][$key]['qty'];
        update_item($key, $quantity);
        return;
    }

    // Add item
    $cost = $products[$key]['cost'];
    $total = $cost * $quantity;
    $item = array(
        'name' => $products[$key]['name'],
        'cost' => $cost,
        'qty'  => $quantity,
        'total' => $total
    );
    $_SESSION['cart12'][$key] = $item;
}

// Update an item in the cart
function update_item($key, $quantity) {
    global $products;
    $quantity = (int) $quantity;
    if (isset($_SESSION['cart12'][$key])) {
        if ($quantity <= 0) {
            unset($_SESSION['cart12'][$key]);
        } else {
            $_SESSION['cart12'][$key]['qty'] = $quantity;
            $total = $_SESSION['cart12'][$key]['cost'] *
                     $_SESSION['cart12'][$key]['qty'];
            $_SESSION['cart12'][$key]['total'] = $total;
        }
    }
}

// Get cart subtotal
function get_subtotal () {
    $subtotal = 0;
    foreach ($_SESSION['cart12'] as $item) {
        $subtotal += $item['total'];
    }
    $subtotal = number_format($subtotal, 2);
    return $subtotal;
}
?>
```

Figure 12-11   The cart.php file of the Shopping Cart application

The Add Item view

Figure 12-12 shows the code for the Add Item page. This page displays a form that lets the user add an item to the cart by selecting a product and a quantity for that item. In addition, this page displays a link that lets the user view the cart without adding an item.

The form uses the POST method to submit the data back to the index.php controller for processing. This form includes a hidden field with a name of "action" and a value of "add" to indicate that the controller should add the item to the cart.

The first <select> tag has a name of "productkey". This tag lets the user select a product from a drop-down list. Within this tag, the PHP code uses a foreach loop to generate the <option> tags for the drop-down list. To start, this code loops through each item in the products array. At the beginning of the loop, this code formats the cost of each item as a number with two digits, and it uses the item name and formatted cost to generate the text to display for the item.

Within the loop, this code sets the value of the <option> tag to the key for the product. As a result, the key for the selected product is submitted to the controller. This code sets the text for the <option> tag to a string that includes the name and cost of the product, so this text is displayed in the drop-down list.

The second <select> tag has a name of "itemqty". This tag lets the user select the quantity from a drop-down list. This code uses a for loop to generate the <option> tags for the drop-down list. These tags display values from 1 to 10. Here, the code uses the index of the loop as both the value that's submitted to the control and the text that's displayed in the drop-down list.

At the end of the page, the View Cart link lets the user go to the Cart view page without adding an item. Here, the href attribute of the <a> tag links to the controller and submits an action parameter of show_cart. In the controller, this parameter is in the $_GET array since it's in the URL. That's why the controller checks both the $_POST and $_GET arrays for the action to perform.

The add_item_view.php file

```
<!DOCTYPE html PUBLIC "-//W3C//DTD XHTML 1.0 Transitional//EN"
    "http://www.w3.org/TR/xhtml1/DTD/xhtml1-transitional.dtd">
<html xmlns="http://www.w3.org/1999/xhtml">
<head>
    <title>My Guitar Shop</title>
    <link rel="stylesheet" type="text/css" href="main.css">
</head>
<body>
    <div id="page">
        <div id="header">
            <h1>My Guitar Shop</h1>
        </div>
        <div id="main">

            <h1>Add Item</h1>
            <form action="." method="post">
                <input type="hidden" name="action" value="add">

                <label>Name:</label>
                <select name="productkey">
                <?php foreach($products as $key => $product) :
                    $cost = number_format($product['cost'], 2),
                    $name = $product['name'];
                    $item = $name . ' ($' . $cost . ')';
                ?>
                    <option value="<?php echo $key; ?>">
                        <?php echo $item; ?>
                    </option>
                <?php endforeach; ?>
                </select><br />

                <label>Quantity:</label>
                <select name="itemqty">
                <?php for($i = 1; $i <= 10; $i++) : ?>
                    <option value="<?php echo $i; ?>">
                        <?php echo $i; ?>
                    </option>
                <?php endfor; ?>
                </select><br />

                <label> </label>
                <input type="submit" value="Add Item">
            </form>
            <p><a href=".?action=show_cart">View Cart</a></p>

        </div><!-- end main -->
    </div><!-- end page -->
</body>
</html>
```

Figure 12-12   The add_item_view.php file of the Shopping Cart application

The Cart view

Figure 12-13 shows the code for the Cart page. Here, the first line of PHP code checks the number of items in the cart. If the number of items is 0, this code displays a message stating that there aren't any items in the cart. Otherwise, this code displays the contents of the cart in a table.

The cart table is contained within a form that lets the user update the quantity of each item in the cart. This form uses the POST method and submits the data to the index.php controller for processing. In addition, it contains a hidden field with a name of "action" and a value of "update". This tells the controller to update the quantities in the cart.

The cart table begins with a row that displays the headers for each of the columns in the table. Within this table, the <th> and <td> tags include class attributes. These attributes allow the CSS file for this application to control the alignment of the text in these columns.

This form uses a foreach loop to display each item in the cart. To start, the top of the loop formats the item's cost and total as a number with two digits after the decimal. Then, this code displays the item's name, cost, and total in a row. In addition, it displays the quantity. However, it displays the quantity within a text field so the user can update it. The tag for the text field has a name of "newqty" with the item key in brackets. This defines the newqty field as an array in the $_POST variable. In addition, this code defines the value of the text field as the item's quantity.

The cart_view.php file

```
<!DOCTYPE html PUBLIC "-//W3C//DTD XHTML 1.0 Transitional//EN"
    "http://www.w3.org/TR/xhtml1/DTD/xhtml1-transitional.dtd">
<html xmlns="http://www.w3.org/1999/xhtml">
<head>
    <title>My Guitar Shop</title>
    <link rel="stylesheet" type="text/css" href="main.css">
</head>
<body>
    <div id="page">
        <div id="header">
            <h1>My Guitar Shop</h1>
        </div>
        <div id="main">

            <h1>Your Cart</h1>
            <?php if (count($_SESSION['cart12']) == 0) : ?>
                <p>There are no items in your cart.</p>
            <?php else: ?>
                <form action="." method="post">
                <input type="hidden" name="action" value="update">
                <table>
                    <tr id="cart_header">
                        <th class="left">Item</th>
                        <th class="right">Item Cost</th>
                        <th class="right">Quantity</th>
                        <th class="right">Item Total</th>
                    </tr>
                    <?php foreach( $_SESSION['cart12'] as $key => $item ) :
                        $cost  = number_format($item['cost'],  2);
                        $total = number_format($item['total'], 2);
                    ?>
                        <tr>
                            <td>
                                <?php echo $item['name']; ?>
                            </td>
                            <td class="right">
                                $<?php echo $cost; ?>
                            </td>
                            <td class="right">
                                <input type="text" class="cart_qty"
                                    name="newqty[<?php echo $key; ?>]"
                                    value="<?php echo $item['qty']; ?>">
                            </td>
                            <td class="right">
                                $<?php echo $total; ?>
                            </td>
                        </tr>
                    <?php endforeach; ?>
```

Figure 12-13   The cart_view.php file of the Shopping Cart application (part 1 of 2)

After the item rows generated by the foreach loop, the table displays the cart subtotal in one row and a submit button in another. In addition, it displays instructions that explain how to update the items in the cart and how to remove items from the cart.

At the end of the page, the Add Item link lets the user return to the Add Item page. To do that, it sends an action of show_add_item to the controller. In addition, the Empty Cart link lets the user remove all items form the cart. To do that, it sends an action of empty_cart to the controller.

If you prefer, you can use buttons instead of the Add Item, View Cart, and Empty Cart links. To do that, you can code a form for each button instead of coding a link. Then, you can include a hidden field for the action parameter, and you can submit the form using either the GET or POST method. However, both techniques for passing an action are acceptable and there are advantages and disadvantages to each approach.

The cart_view.php file

```php
                    <tr id="cart_footer">
                        <td colspan="3"><b>Subtotal</b></td>
                    <td>$<?php echo get_subtotal(); ?></td>
                    </tr>
                    <tr>
                        <td colspan="4" class="right">
                            <input type="submit" value="Update Cart">
                        </td>
                    </tr>
                </table>
                <p>Click "Update Cart" to update quantities in your
                    cart. Enter a quantity of 0 to remove an item.
                </p>
                </form>
            <?php endif; ?>
            <p><a href=".?action=show_add_item">Add Item</a></p>
            <p><a href=".?action=empty_cart">Empty Cart</a></p>

        </div><!-- end main -->
    </div><!-- end page -->
</body>
</html>
```

Figure 12-13   The cart_view.php file of the Shopping Cart application (part 2 of 2)

Perspective

The goal of this chapter is to show you how to use PHP to track sessions and work with cookies. If you understand the Shopping Cart application presented at the end of this chapter, you're ready to develop web applications that use session tracking.

Terms

cookie	stateless protocol
third-party cookie	state
per-session cookie	URL encoding
persistent cookie	serialization
session tracking	deserialization
session	session hijacking

Summary

- A *cookie* is a name/value pair that is stored in the browser. A *per-session cookie* expires when the user closes the browser. A *persistent cookie* doesn't expire until the expiration date is reached.

- Although most browsers have cookies enabled, some browsers don't. As a result, your application may need to provide for those browsers that don't allow cookies.

- Because HTTP is a *stateless protocol*, most web applications need to use *session tracking* to track each user's *session*.

- By default, PHP provides for session tracking by storing a cookie on each user's browser with a unique session ID. Then, that ID can be used to access the data that's stored for a session.

- To set and get the data for a session, you use the autoglobal $_SESSION variable. This variable is an associative array.

- To start, end, and manage sessions, you can use PHP functions.

Exercise 12-1   Modify the Shopping Cart application

In this exercise, you can modify and enhance the Shopping Cart application.

Open and test the application

1. Run the application that's stored in the ex_starts/ch12_ex1 directory.

2. Test this application by adding several items to the cart. Then, exit the browser, restart it, and view the cart. Since this application uses a persistent session cookie, this should display any items that were previously in the cart.

3. Open the index.php file for this application and review the code. Note that this code configures the cookie for the session so it persists for 2 weeks.

Use a per-session cookie

4. Modify the code that configures the cookie for the session so the session uses a per-session cookie.

5. Test this change to make sure it works correctly. You should be able to remove all items from your cart by exiting the browser. (When you exit the browser, don't save any open tabs. Otherwise, your browser may remember the cookie for the session and the items won't be removed from the cart.)

Use a persistent cookie that lasts for 3 years

6. Modify the code that configures the cookie for the session so the session persists for 3 years.

7. Add code that displays the session ID on both pages of the application.

8. Test these changes. The session ID should remain the same even if you exit and restart the browser.

9. Add a link to the Cart page that says "End Session and Delete Cookie". Then, add code that processes this link by clearing all session data from memory, cleaning up the session ID, and deleting the cookie for the session.

10. Test this change. When you click the "Empty Cart" link, the items should be removed from the cart, but the session ID should stay the same. When you click the "End Session" link, the items should be removed from the cart, and the session ID should be cleared. Then, if you add an item to the cart, the Cart page should display a new session ID.

Exercise 12-2   Improve the Task List Manager application

In this exercise, you can modify the Task List Manager application of the last chapter so it uses sessions instead of hidden fields to store the array of tasks.

1. Open the index.php and task_list.php files in the ex_starts/ch12_ex2 directory and review the code. Note how each form in the task_list.php file includes a loop that outputs the task list as a series of hidden HTML fields.

2. Modify the index.php file so it starts a session that lasts for 1 year.

3. Modify the index.php file so it stores the array of tasks in the session.

4. Modify the task_list.php file so it does *not* store the array of tasks in hidden HTML fields.

5. Test this application. Make sure to exit and restart the browser to make sure the session is persistent.

13

How to create and use functions

In chapter 5, you learned how to write simple functions and you've been using them throughout section 2. Now, this chapter reviews the basic skills for working with functions and presents some additional skills for working with functions.

Basic skills for working with functions **380**
How to create and call a function 380
How to pass arguments by value and by reference 382
How variable scope works 384
How to provide default values for parameters 386
How to use variable-length parameter lists 388

How to create and use a library of functions **390**
A library of functions 390
How to set the include path 392
How function scope works 392
How to create and use namespaces 394

Advanced skills for working with functions **396**
How to work with variable functions and callbacks 396
How to work with anonymous functions 398
How to work with closures 400

The Shopping Cart application **402**
The user interface 402
The model 404
The controller 406
The view 406

Perspective **410**

Basic skills for working with functions

This topic reviews some of the basic skills you've already learned for working with functions, and it presents some new skills.

How to create and call a function

Figure 13-1 shows how to create and call a reusable block of code known as a *function*. You can create a function by coding the function keyword, the name of the function, a set of parentheses, and the statements for the function in braces. Within the parentheses of a function, you can code a *parameter list* that contains zero or more *parameters*.

When you code the name for the function, you must begin with a letter or underscore. Then, the rest of the name can contain letters, numbers, and underscores.

Within the braces of a function, you can code the statements for the function. These statements can include a *return statement*. When the function reaches a return statement, it stops executing and returns the value specified by the return statement. Or, if the return statement doesn't specify a value, the function returns a NULL value. Similarly, if you don't code a return statement, the function returns the NULL value.

The first example creates a function named coin_toss. This function uses an empty set of parentheses to indicate that it doesn't accept any parameters. Within the braces, the first statement randomly gets a string of "heads" or "tails" and stores it in the $coin variable. Then, the second statement returns that string.

The second example creates a function named display_error that has one parameter that accepts an error message. The only statement in this function puts a <p> tag around the error message and uses an echo statement to send the string to the browser.

The third example creates a function named avg_of_3 that returns the average of its three parameters. Here, the first statement calculates the average of three numbers. Then, the second statement returns the average.

When you call a function, the *arguments* in the *argument list* that are passed to the function must be in the same order as the parameters in the parameter list. The first two examples of function calls show that calling user-defined functions works like calling PHP's built-in functions.

In the first example, the first statement stores the result of the avg_of 3 function in a variable, and the second statement uses the result of the coin_toss function as the argument of the echo statement. In the second example, the statement calls a function that doesn't return a value.

The third example shows how to discard the value returned from a function. Here, the array_pop function that was presented in chapter 11 removes the last element in an array and returns that element. If you want to store this element, you can assign it to a variable as in the second statement. Or, you can discard this element by not assigning this value to a variable as in the third statement.

The syntax for a function

```
function function_name([$param_1, $param_2, ... , $param_n]) {
    // Code for function
    [return [value];]
}
```

How to define a function

A function with no parameters that returns a value

```
function coin_toss() {
    $coin = (mt_rand(0, 1) == 0) ? 'heads' : 'tails';
    return $coin;
}
```

A function with one parameter

```
function display_error($error) {
    echo '<p class="error">' . $error . '</p>';
}
```

A function with three parameters that returns a value

```
function avg_of_3($x, $y, $z) {
    $avg = ($x + $y + $z) / 3;
    return $avg;
}
```

How to call a function

Functions that return values

```
$average = avg_of_3(5, 2, 8);          // $average is 5
echo coin_toss();                      // Displays heads or tails
```

A function that doesn't return a value

```
display_error('Value out of range.');
```

Discarding the return value

```
$list = array('Apples', 'Oranges', 'Grapes');
$last = array_pop($list);    // Removes Grapes - stores return value
array_pop($list);            // Removes Oranges - discards return value
```

Description

- A *function* is a reusable block of code. To code a function, code the function keyword followed by the name of the function, followed by a set of parentheses.

- Within the parentheses of a function, you can code an optional *parameter list* that contains one or more *parameters*.

- To code a function that returns data, code a *return statement* in the body of the function. The return statement ends the execution of the function and returns the specified value. If you don't specify a value in the return statement, it returns the NULL value.

- To code a function that doesn't return data, don't include a return statement.

- When you call a function, the *arguments* in the *argument list* must be in the same order as the parameters in the parameter list defined by the function, and they must have compatible data types.

Figure 13-1   How to create and call a function

How to pass arguments by value and by reference

By default, all arguments are *passed by value* to the functions that are called. This means that PHP sends a copy of the argument to the function, not the argument itself. As a result, the function can't change the original argument.

The first example in figure 13-2 shows how this works. To start, this example creates a function that adds 3 to the argument and displays the result. Then, the code creates a $number variable that contains a value of 5 and passes this value to the function. This adds 3 to the parameter and displays it. Finally, the last statement displays the $number variable again. Since a copy of this variable was passed to the function, the function doesn't change the value stored in the original variable.

If you want an argument to be *passed by reference*, you can code an ampersand (&) in front of the parameter. This means that PHP sends a pointer to the original variable instead of sending a copy of the variable. As a result, if the function changes the value that's stored in the variable, it also changes the original variable.

The second example shows how this works. This example works the same as the first example, except that it accepts arguments that are passed by reference. As a result, the function in this example changes the value of the $number variable.

The third example shows a function named wrap_in_tag that accepts a text string that's passed by reference and a tag string that's passed by value. Then, this function modifies that text string passed to the function by wrapping it with the specified tag. Note that this function doesn't need to include a return statement since it modifies the value that's passed by reference.

The fourth example shows how passing by reference can allow you to return multiple values from a function call. Here, the array_analyze function needs to return three calculations that are performed on an array of numbers: the sum, the product, and the average. To accomplish this, this function passes the $sum, $product, and $average parameters by reference. Then, this function performs three calculations and stores the results in these three parameters. Note that the code that calls the array_analyze function doesn't initialize the $s, $p, and $a variables since these variables are only used to store the return values from the function.

Although you can use this technique to return multiple values from a function, you should use it sparingly. That's especially true if you need to return a large number of values. In that case, consider using an associative array as the return value.

An argument passed by value

```
function add_3_by_val($value) {
    $value += 3;
    echo '<p>Number: ' . $value . '</p>';
}

$number = 5;
add_3_by_val($number);                      // Displays 8
echo '<p>Number: ' . $number . '</p>';      // Displays 5
```

An argument passed by reference

```
function add_3_by_ref(&$value) {
    $value += 3;
    echo '<p>Number: ' . $value . '</p>';
}

$number = 5;
add_3_by_ref($number);                      // Displays 8
echo '<p>Number: ' . $number . '</p>';      // Displays 8
```

How to modify a string that's passed by reference

```
function wrap_in_tag(&$text, $tag) {
    $before = '<'  . $tag . '>';
    $after  = '</' . $tag . '>';
    $text = $before . $text . $after;
}

$message = 'Value out of range.';
wrap_in_tag($message, 'p');
echo $message;                              // <p>Value out of range.</p>
```

How to return multiple values

```
function array_analyze($array, &$sum, &$prod, &$avg) {
    $sum = array_sum($array);
    $prod = array_product($array);
    $avg = $sum / count($array);
}

$list = array(1, 4, 9, 16);
array_analyze($list, $s, $p, $a);
echo '<p>Sum: ' . $s . '<br />Product: ' . $p . '<br />Average ' . $a .
    '</p>';
```

Description

- By default, all function arguments are *passed by value*. This means that a copy of the argument is sent to the function. As a result, when the function changes a parameter, it changes a copy of the argument, not the original argument.

- To allow a function to modify the original argument instead of a copy, you can code an ampersand (&) in front of the parameter. In that case, the argument is *passed by reference*. This means that a reference to the original argument is sent to the function. Then, when the function changes the parameter, it's actually changing the original argument.

Figure 13-2   How to pass arguments by value and by reference

How variable scope works

In a programming language, *scope* refers to the visibility of variables and functions. In other words, scope determines what code can access the variables and functions that you've defined. If you're familiar with other languages, you may be surprised to find that scope works differently in PHP than in most languages.

Figure 13-3 presents four examples that show how scope works for variables. To start, you can create a *global variable* by declaring the variable outside a function. Or, you can create a *local variable* by declaring the variable inside a function.

By default, a function doesn't have access to global variables as shown by the first example. This example begins by creating a global variable named $a. Then, this example defines a function that attempts to access the global variable. However, since functions don't have access to global variables by default, this function isn't able to access the global variable.

To give a function access to a global variable, you can code a global statement inside the function as shown in the second example. This example works like the first example, except that it uses a global statement to indicate that this function should use the global variable named $b.

Most of the time, you can use the global statement to access global variables from within a function. However, if you need to access several global variables, you might want to use the $GLOBALS array as shown in the third example. This array is a predefined variable that works much like the $_POST and $_GET variables. Like those variables, the $GLOBALS array is an *autoglobal variable*. As a result, it's available anywhere in your code.

When you code a variable within a function as shown in the fourth example, that variable is a local variable and is only available within that function. In other words, it isn't available to statements that are coded at the global scope, and it isn't available to statements that are coded within other functions.

A variable with global scope

```
$a = 10;                    // $a has global scope
function show_a() {
    echo $a;                // Inside function, $a is NULL
}
show_a();                   // Displays nothing
```

How to access a global variable from within a function

```
$b = 10;                    // $b has global scope
function show_b() {
    global $b;              // $b now refers to the global variable named $b
    echo $b;
}
show_b();                   // Displays 10
```

Another way to access a global variable from within a function

```
$c = 10;                    // $c has global scope
function show_c() {
    $c = $GLOBALS['c'];     // $c now refers to global variable named $c
    echo $c;
}
show_c();                   // Displays 10
```

A variable with local scope

```
function show_d() {
    $d = 10;                // $d has local scope within show_d function
    echo $d;
}
echo $d;                    // Outside function, $d is NULL
```

Description

- The *scope* of a variable determines what code can access it. PHP only allows a variable to have a single scope. This means that a variable can only be used where it is defined.

- If a variable is defined inside a function, it has *local scope*. Then, the variable is only available to code that runs inside that function and is not available outside the function or to any other functions.

- If a variable is defined outside of a function, it has *global scope*. Then, by default, it is only available to code that runs at the global level and is not available within any functions.

- To access a global variable from within a function, you can use the global statement to import a variable from global scope to local scope.

- To get all variables that are stored in the global scope, you can use the built-in $GLOBALS array. This array is an autoglobal variable like the $_POST and $_GET arrays.

Figure 13-3   How variable scope works

How to provide default values for parameters

Figure 13-4 shows how to provide a default value for a parameter of a function. If you provide a default value, that parameter becomes optional. Then, if you don't pass the argument when the function is called, the function uses the default value for the parameter.

The first example adds a default value to a parameter. To do that, it adds an equal sign and the default value after the parameter in the parameter list. Here, the $type parameter has a default value of "coin". As a result, if you don't pass an argument to this parameter, the function uses the default value of "coin". Otherwise, the function uses the argument passed to the function.

When you code a default value, you must use a scalar value or an array of scalar values. A *scalar value* is a string literal, a numeric literal, a Boolean value, or the NULL value. In other words, you can't use an expression, a function call, or an object as a default value for a parameter.

If you need to provide a more complex default value, you can use the NULL value in the parameter list as a placeholder. Then, in the body of the function, you can use the isset function to test the parameter. If it isn't set, you can initialize the parameter using any expression.

The second example illustrates this technique. Here, the $date parameter in the is_leap_year function uses NULL for the default value. Then, within the function, the code checks whether the $date parameter is set. If not, the code initializes the parameter as a new DateTime object, which contains the current date and time. This is necessary because you can't use a new DateTime object as a default value for a parameter.

When you mix required parameters and default parameters, you must code the default parameters after any required parameters in the parameter list as shown by the third example. Here, the function has one required parameter and two default parameters. As a result, the code that calls this function can supply one, two, or three parameters.

When you call a function with default values, you can pass some or none of the optional parameters. This is illustrated by the next group of examples. Here, the first example shows how to call a function using its default values. To do that, these statements omit all optional parameters.

Then, the next example shows how to call a function and supply some or all of the optional parameters. Note that the call to the display_error function only provides a value for the first default parameter. As a result, this function still uses the default value for the $class parameter.

How to assign a default value to a parameter

A function with one default parameter

```
function get_rand_bool text($type = 'coin') {
    $rand = mt_rand(0, 1);
    switch ($type) {
        case 'coin':
            $result = ($rand == 1) ? 'heads' : 'tails';
            break;
        case 'switch':
            $result = ($rand == 1) ? 'on' : 'off';
            break;
    }
    return $result;
}
```

A function with an optional parameter

```
function is_leap_year($date = NULL) {
    if (!isset($date)) {
        $date = new DateTime();
    }
    if ($date->format('L') == '1') return true;
    else return false;
}
```

A function with one required and two default parameters

```
function display_error($error, $tag = 'p', $class = 'error') {
    $opentag  = '<'  . $tag . ' class="' . $class . '">';
    $closetag = '</' . $tag . '>';
    echo $opentag . $error . $closetag;
}
```

Calling a function with a default parameter value

Omitting optional parameters

```
echo get_rand_bool_text();               // Displays 'heads' or 'tails'
echo display_error('Out of range');      // 'p' tag with 'error' class
$is_leap_year = is_leap_year();          // true or false based on current date
```

Providing optional parameters

```
echo get_rand_bool_text('switch');        // Displays 'on' or 'off'
echo display_error('Out of range', 'li');
$is_leap_year = is_leap_year(new DateTime('March 15, 2015'));      // false
```

Description

- To supply a default value for a parameter, code the parameter name followed by the equals sign and the default value. The default value must be a scalar value, an array of scalar values, or the NULL value. A *scalar value* is a literal number, string, or Boolean value. A scalar value cannot contain operators, variables, or function calls.

- To code a function that sets a default value for a parameter, assign a NULL value to the parameter. Then, within the function, you can check whether the parameter contains a NULL value. If so, you can write the code that sets the default value for the parameter.

Figure 13-4   How to provide default values for parameters

How to use variable-length parameter lists

Occasionally, a function needs to be able to work with multiple parameters where the number of parameters might vary. To create a function that can work with a varying number of parameters, you can create a variable-length parameter list as shown in figure 13-5.

To start, this figure shows three built-in functions that you can use to get arguments that have been passed to a function. Here, the func_get_args function returns all of the arguments as an array with indexes that start at zero. As a result, you can use this function with a foreach loop to process each argument in the array. In contrast, the second function gets a count of the arguments, and the third function returns the argument at the specified index. As a result, you can also use these functions with a for loop to process each argument.

When you use these functions, any parameters that are coded in the parameter list are also included in the array that these functions use. For example, if you have two named parameters, those parameters are included in the array. As a result, you need to skip over those two arguments before you get to the unnamed arguments. To do that, you can use the array_shift function to remove elements from the start of the array, or you can start the counter variable in the for loop at a value greater than zero.

The first example in this figure shows how to use the func_get_args function. Here, the first statement in this function stores all arguments in the $numbers array. Then, the second statement initializes the $total variable to 0. Next, a foreach loop adds each number in the $numbers array to the total. Finally, the last statement returns the total.

The second example shows how to use the func_num_args and func_get_arg functions. Here, the first statement gets the number of arguments and stores that number in the $count variable. Then, the second statement initializes the $total variable to 0. Next, a for loop adds each parameter to the total. Finally, the last statement calculates the average and returns the result.

Note that the average function uses a single parameter named $x in its parameter list to force the user to provide at least one argument. Then, this function uses the func_get_arg function to access the value stored in that parameter. As a result, this function doesn't need to use the parameter name to access that parameter.

The third example shows how to create a function that mixes two required parameters with a variable number of optional parameters. Here, the $array parameter is required and stores a reference to the array that the function modifies, and the $x parameter is a placeholder that forces the user to enter at least one value to append. Within the function, the first statement stores the array of arguments in the $values variable. Since the $array parameter is the first element in that array, the second statement uses the array_shift function to remove that element from the $values array. That way, the function doesn't process the $array parameter in the foreach loop. Finally, the foreach loop appends the remaining values to the array.

Three functions for working with variable-length parameter lists

Function	Description
`func_get_args()`	Returns an array that contains the arguments passed to the function.
`func_num_args()`	Returns the number of arguments passed to the function.
`func_get_arg($i)`	Returns the argument at the specified index.

How to write a function with a variable parameter list

A function that adds a list of numbers

```
function add() {
    $numbers = func_get_args();
    $total = 0;
    foreach($numbers as $number) {
        $total += $number;
    }
    return $total;
}

$sum = add(5, 10, 15);                   // $sum is 30
```

A function that averages one or more numbers

```
function average($x) {       // $x is here to force at least one argument
    $count = func_num_args();
    $total = 0;
    for($i = 0; $i < $count; $i++) {
        $total += func_get_arg($i);
    }
    return $total / $count;
}

$avg = average(75, 95, 100);         // $avg is 90
```

Using required parameters with a variable parameter list

```
function array_append(&$array, $x) {
    $values = func_get_args();           // Also contains $array
    array_shift($values);                // Removes $array from front
    foreach($values as $value) {
        $array[] = $value;
    }
}

$data = array('apples', 'oranges');
array_append($data, 'grapes', 'pears');
```

Description

- A variable-length parameter list lets you create a function that works with a variable number of arguments.

- You can require a minimum number of arguments by using placeholder parameters in the parameter list.

Figure 13-5   How to use variable-length parameter lists

How to create and use a library of functions

Applications often have numerous functions. In that case, it usually helps to organize those functions in external libraries. This serves two purposes. First, you can use the libraries for more than one application. Second, you can have different developers working on different libraries to reduce the time it takes to build an application.

A library of functions

Figure 13-6 shows a library of three functions that lets the user work with a shopping cart in a web application. These functions begin with a prefix of "cart_" to show that they are all part of the same library.

To start, the cart_add_item function adds an item to the cart. Here, the $cart parameter is an array that stores the items of the cart. Then, the next three parameters specify the name, cost, and quantity of the item to add to the cart. Within the function, the first statement calculates the total for the item. Then, the next statement creates an associative array for the item. Finally, the last statement adds the item to the cart.

The cart_update_item function updates an item in the cart. Here, the $cart parameter stores the items for the cart, the $key parameter specifies the item to update, and the $quantity parameter specifies the new quantity for the item. Within the function, the code uses the key to check whether the item exists in the cart. If so, the code checks whether the quantity is less than or equal to zero. If so, this code removes the item from the cart. Otherwise, it updates the quantity for the item, calculates a new total for the item, and updates the total.

The cart_get_subtotal function gets the subtotal for the cart by adding the total for each item in the cart. Then, it rounds and formats the number so that it shows two decimal places. Finally, it returns the subtotal.

Once you have developed a library of functions, you can load that library into your application using one of these functions: include, include_once, require, or require_once. In most cases, I recommend using the require_once function as shown at the bottom of this figure. That way, if PHP can't find the library you need, the require_once function throws a fatal error and stops execution right away. On the other hand, if the library has already been loaded, this function prevents it from being loaded twice, which prevents a fatal error.

Once the code at the bottom of this figure loads the library, it creates an array to store the cart. Then, it calls all three functions of the library to add an item, to update that item, and to get the subtotal for the cart. Finally, this code displays the subtotal for the cart.

A library of functions (the cart.php file)

```php
<?php
    // Add an item to the cart
    function cart_add_item(&$cart, $name, $cost, $quantity) {
        $total = $cost * $quantity;
        $item = array(
            'name' => $name,
            'cost' => $cost,
            'qty'  => $quantity,
            'total' => $total
        );
        $cart[] = $item;
    }

    // Update an item in the cart
    function cart_update_item(&$cart, $key, $quantity) {
        if (isset($cart[$key])) {
            if ($quantity <= 0) {
                unset($cart[$key]);
            } else {
                $cart[$key]['qty'] = $quantity;
                $total = $cart[$key]['cost'] * $cart[$key]['qty'];
                $cart[$key]['total'] = $total;
            }
        }
    }

    // Get cart subtotal
    function cart_get_subtotal($cart) {
        $subtotal = 0;
        foreach ($cart as $item) {
            $subtotal += $item['total'];
        }
        $subtotal = round($subtotal, 2);
        $subtotal = number_format($subtotal, 2);
        return $subtotal;
    }
?>
```

Code that uses the library

```php
// load the library
require_once('cart.php');

// create an array to store the cart
$cart = array();

// call methods from the library
cart_add_item($cart, 'Flute', 149.95, 1);
cart_update_item($cart, 0, 2);   // update the first item (key of 0)
$subtotal = cart_get_subtotal($cart);

// display the result
echo 'This subtotal is $' . $subtotal;
```

Figure 13-6   A library of functions

How to set the include path

When you use a library, you may want to store it in its own directory so it can be accessed by multiple applications. Then, to make it easy to load the library, you can add its directory to the *include path*. This path is a list of directories that PHP searches for included files. For example, you may want to store the cart.php file in the book_apps\lib directory. Then, you can add the book_apps\lib directory to the include path as shown in figure 13-7.

If you installed XAMPP on your system as described in the appendix, the default include path specifies the current directory (a dot) followed by the php\PEAR directory. But note that this directory varies depending on the operating system. Then, to add a directory to the include path, you can use the get_include_path function to get the current include path, and you can use the set_include_path function to append the directory to the end of that include path.

How function scope works

The scope rules for functions in PHP are different than the scope rules for functions in most other programming languages. Put simply, all functions in PHP are global. Even if one function is defined inside another function, the inner function is global and can be used anywhere. Also, once a function is defined, it can't be defined again. If your application attempts to redefine a function, a runtime error occurs.

This can be an issue when developing a library of functions because PHP has over 1700 internal functions. As a result, many function names are already taken, and an application that uses multiple libraries may experience naming conflicts.

When you're developing a library that you plan on sharing with other developers, it's a good idea to make sure that functions avoid naming conflicts. The traditional way to do that in PHP is to use a unique prefix for all of the functions in the library. For example, all of the functions in PHP's mysqli library begin with a prefix of "mysqli_". As a result, it's unlikely that they will conflict with any other functions. Similarly, the functions in the cart.php file all begin with a prefix of "cart_" to avoid naming conflicts. However, if you think this prefix might lead to naming conflicts with other libraries, you can use a more unique prefix such as "mgs_cart_".

Functions for working with the include path

Function	Description
get_include_path()	Gets a string that contains the current include path.
set_include_path($path)	Sets the include path.

The default include path

Windows
```
.;C:\xampp\php\PEAR
```

Mac or Linux
```
.:/Applications/XAMPP/xamppfiles/lib/php/pear
```

How to get the include path
```
$include_path = get_include_path();
```

How to set the include path

Windows
```
set_include_path($include_path . ';C:\xampp\htdocs\book_apps\lib');
```

Mac or Linux
```
set_include_path($include_path .
              ':/Applications/XAMPP/htdocs/book_apps/lib');
```

How to include a file after the include path has been set
```
require_once cart.php;
```

Description

- The *include path* specifies the directories that are searched for included files. By default, the include path specifies the current directory (a dot), followed by any system specific directories (such as the PEAR libraries).

- If you want to add a directory to the include path, you can use the get_include_path and set_include_path functions. To separate the directories of the include path, you should use semicolons for Windows and colons for Mac and Linux.

Figure 13-7   How to set the include path

How to create and use namespaces

If you're careful, you can usually avoid naming conflicts for function names by using a unique prefix for all functions in the library. However, this technique is an older technique that requires the prefix to be hard-coded into all function names. As a result, this technique yields code that's inflexible and potentially difficult to maintain. To make your code flexible and easy to maintain, you can use a newer feature known as namespaces that was introduced with version 5.3 of PHP.

A *namespace* contains a group of names that isn't in the global scope. It lets you organize your functions and to use names that have already been used in the global namespace. You can think of a namespace as a directory on your computer. For example, you can have two files named report.txt as long as they're in different directories. Likewise, you can have two functions named show as long as they're in different namespaces.

Figure 13-8 shows how to create namespaces and use functions from a namespace. When you create a namespace, the namespace must be the first statement in the file. You can't include HTML or other PHP code before the namespace declaration. As a result, namespaces are primarily used within library files.

The first two examples show the two ways you can define a namespace. The first uses the namespace statement to create the namespace. This statement must be the first statement in the file. The second example uses the namespace keyword and a set of braces to declare the namespace. Again, this code must be at the beginning of the file. I prefer the brace syntax since it clearly shows that the statements are in the namespace.

The third example shows how to create nested namespaces. Here, a backslash is used to separate namespace names. In this example, the cart namespace is nested inside the murach namespace. This allows you to nest multiple namespaces within the murach namespace.

The next two examples show how to call the functions in a namespace. Here, the first example shows how to create a murach\errors namespace that contains a function named log. Since PHP already provides a function named log, you can't create a function named log unless you use a namespace.

The second example shows how to call the log function in the murach\errors namespace. Here, the first statement loads the errors.php file that defines the namespace. Then, the second statement calls the log function from that namespace. To do that, this statement specifies the namespace name, a backslash, and the function name.

Since nested namespaces can be fairly long, PHP lets you create an alias for a namespace as shown by the last two statements. Here, the use statement creates an alias of e for the murach\errors namespace. Then, you can use "e" instead of "murach\errors" to call functions from the namespace.

How to create a namespace in a file

Using the statement syntax

```
<?php
namespace cart;

// Functions in cart namespace
?>
```

Using the brace syntax

```
<?php
namespace cart {
    // Functions in cart namespace
}
?>
```

How to create nested namespaces

```
<?php
namespace murach\cart {
    // Functions in murach\cart namespace
}
?>
```

How to use the functions that are defined in a namespace

Create a file that contains a namespace with one function

```
<?php
namespace murach\errors {
    function log($error) {
        echo '<p class="error">' . $error . '</p>';
    }
}
?>
```

Call a function that is stored in the namespace

```
// load the file that stores the namespace
require_once 'errors.php';

// call the log function
murach\errors\log('Invalid value');

// create an alias and use it to call the log function
use murach\errors as e;     // Use 'e' instead of 'murach\errors'
e\log('Invalid value');
```

Description

- You can use a *namespace* to store functions in a namespace other than the global namespace. This helps you avoid name collisions.

- Within a namespace, you can include constants, functions, and classes. In the next chapter, you'll learn more about classes.

- To call a function in a namespace, code the namespace name, a backslash, and the function name.

- To create an alias for the namespace, code the use keyword, followed by the namespace name, followed by the as keyword, followed by the alias.

Figure 13-8   How to create and use namespaces

Advanced skills for working with functions

This topic presents three advanced features for working with functions. If you're new to programming, you might find it hard to understand these features at first. In that case, you might want to skip this topic and come back to it later. However, these features are all useful in some situations, and you can use them to solve some complex coding problems. In fact, the Shopping Cart application at the end of this chapter uses them.

How to work with variable functions and callbacks

A *variable function* is a function whose name is stored in a variable. Then, you can call the function by coding the variable name followed by the arguments to the function within a set of parentheses as shown in figure 13-9.

The first example in this figure shows a simple variable function. Here, the first statement randomly selects a function name of either "array_sum" or "array_product" and stores that name in a variable named $function. These functions are built-in functions that work on arrays as shown in chapter 11. Then, the third statement calls the function by coding the variable name followed by the argument list for the function.

Variable functions are useful when you don't know which function to use until runtime. In that case, you can use an if or switch statement to determine which function to call and store it in a variable name. Then, you can use the variable function throughout the application without having to execute an if or switch statement each time.

The second example shows a function that uses a callback. A *callback* occurs when one function is passed as an argument to a second function. Then, the second function calls the first function as part of its processing. In this example, the validate function actually uses an array of callbacks to call multiple functions passed in the $functions parameter. Here, the callbacks are functions that return a TRUE value if a value passes a test.

The validate function starts by assuming the data is valid. Then, it loops through the function names in the $functions array. Inside the loop, it calls the function stored in the $function variable. If the function returns a TRUE value and the $valid variable is also TRUE, the $valid variable is set to TRUE. Otherwise, the $valid variable is set to FALSE. As a result, the validate function only returns TRUE if all the functions in the $functions array return TRUE.

The next two functions validate a number. These functions are used as callbacks in the validate function.

After the functions, the $age variable is set to 25, the $functions variable is set to an array of function names, and the $is_valid_age function is set to the result of the validate function.

How to pass one function to another

A variable function

```
$function = (mt_rand(0,1) == 1) ? 'array_sum' : 'array_product';
$values = array(4, 9, 16);
$result = $function($values);     // 29 for array_sum, 576 for array_product
```

A function that uses a callback

```
function validate($data, $functions) {
    $valid = true;
    foreach ($functions as $function) {
        $valid = $valid && $function($data);
    }
    return $valid;
}

function is_at_least_18($number) {
    return $number >= 18;
}

function is_less_than_62($number) {
    return $number < 62;
}

$age = 25;
$functions = array('is_numeric', 'is_at_least_18', 'is_less_than_62');
$is_valid_age = validate($age, $functions);     // true
```

Language constructs that can't be used in variable functions

die	eval	list	print
echo	include	require	unset
empty	include_once	require_once	
exit	isset	return	

Description

- A *variable function* is a function name stored in a variable as a string. When PHP encounters a variable function, it evaluates the variable and attempts to call the function.

- To call a variable function, code the variable name followed by a set of parentheses. Within the parentheses, code the argument list for the function.

- You can use a variable function when the function isn't known until runtime.

- You can use a variable function in a function that uses a callback. A *callback* is a function that's passed as an argument to another function.

- You can't use the language constructs listed above with variable functions directly. However, you can use a wrapper function that calls one of these constructs in a variable function.

Figure 13-9   How to work with variable functions

The figure also lists several language constructs that you can't use directly with variable functions. However, you can use a wrapper function that calls one of these constructs in a variable function.

How to work with anonymous functions

Figure 13-10 shows how to work with anonymous functions. An *anonymous function* is a function that doesn't have a name. Anonymous functions were introduced with version 5.3 of PHP. As a result, they won't work with earlier versions of PHP.

Since you call anonymous functions the same way you call variable functions, you can pass an anonymous function to any function that uses a callback. The primary difference between a variable function and an anonymous function is that an anonymous function is never given a name in the global namespace. This helps reduce function name usage and eliminates the possibility of a naming conflict.

The usort function is a built-in PHP function that sorts an array using a user-defined comparison function. The usort function accepts two arguments. The first argument is the array to be sorted, and the second argument is the user-defined comparison function. To code a custom comparison function for the usort function, you must code a function that accepts two arguments. This function should return -1 if the arguments are in the correct order, 1 if they aren't in the correct order, and 0 if the two arguments are the same.

The first example shows how to define a comparison function for the usort function. This function is stored in a variable named $compare_function and has two parameters named $left and $right. Note that there isn't a function name between the function keyword and the parameter list. As a result, the function is an anonymous function. Also, note that there is a semicolon after the function definition. This semicolon ends the statement that assigns the anonymous function to the variable. Within the comparison function, the two parameters are converted to floating point values and the appropriate value is returned based on the comparison of the two numbers.

The second example tests the comparison function. Here, the third statement calls the anonymous function stored in the $compare_function variable. This compares the numbers 3 and 5 and returns a value of -1. This indicates that the two numbers are in order. However, if you used this function to compare 5 and 3, the function would return a value of 1 to indicate the two numbers were not in order.

The third example uses the usort function with the comparison function to sort the values in an array. Here, the first statement creates an array of numbers. Then, the second statement sorts the array by passing the array and the anonymous compare function to the usort function.

If necessary, anonymous functions can be returned as a result from another function. This allows you to create a function that creates other functions. However, since this use of anonymous functions is more commonly used with closures, it is presented in the next figure.

A function to sort an array with a custom comparison function

Function	Description
usort(*$array, $function*)	Sorts the specified array using the specified function. The specified function must compare two arguments and return -1 if the arguments are in the correct order, 0 if they're the same, or 1 if they're not in the correct order.

How to create and use an anonymous function

A custom sorting function

```
$compare_function = function($left, $right) {
    $l = (float) $left;
    $r = (float) $right;
    if ($l < $r) return -1;
    if ($l > $r) return 1;
    return 0;
};
```

Code that tests the custom sorting function

```
$a = 3;
$b = 5;
$result = $compare_function($a, $b);    // -1
```

Code that uses the custom sorting function

```
$values = array(5, 2, 4, 1, 3);
usort($values, $compare_function);       // 1, 2, 3, 4, 5
```

Description

- An *anonymous function* is a function that doesn't have a name. You can store an anonymous function in a variable and use it as a variable function.

Figure 13-10   How to work with anonymous functions

How to work with closures

A *closure* is a nested function that has access to the outer function's local variables. Like anonymous functions, closures were introduced with version 5.3 of PHP. Prior to version 5.3 of PHP, there wasn't a good way to sort an array of arrays based on the values in the nested arrays. However, closures provide an elegant way to solve this problem as shown in figure 13-11.

Under normal PHP scope rules, a function defined inside an outer function doesn't have access to the outer function's parameters and local variables. Closures circumvent this issue by allowing you to give an inner function access to the outer function's variables. To do that, the inner function definition includes a use clause.

The first example defines an array of arrays that contains data for five employees that you may want to sort it by name or id. To do that, you can use the usort function. However, you need to pass a comparison function as a callback and that function needs to know which key in the nested arrays to compare.

One way to solve this problem is to code a comparison function for each key. In this example, that would only require coding two functions. However, if the inner array had dozens of key fields, that would require coding dozens of functions.

To solve this problem, you can use a closure to generate an anonymous comparison function that knows which key to sort on. Then, you can send this anonymous function to the usort function as a callback.

The second example defines the array_compare_factory function. This function creates and returns a new anonymous comparison function. To do that, it uses a closure to generate the comparison function.

The array_compare_factory function has one parameter named $sort_key that specifies the key used to sort the nested arrays. Within the anonymous function definition, the use clause indicates that the anonymous function has access to the $sort_key parameter. As a result, the comparison function can return an appropriate value based on the comparison of the two keys in the $left and $right arrays.

The third example shows how to sort the array by name. Here, the first statement uses the array_compare_factory function to generate a custom comparison function that sorts by the name key. This statement also stores this anonymous function in a variable. Then, the second statement passes this function to the usort function as a callback.

The fourth example works the same as the third example, but it sorts the array by id. This shows that it's easy to sort the inner array by key once you have a function that can generate a compare function based on the key.

How to create a closure

An array of arrays

```
$employees = array (
    array('name' => 'Ray',  'id' => 5685),
    array('name' => 'Mike', 'id' => 4302),
    array('name' => 'Anne', 'id' => 3674),
    array('name' => 'Pren', 'id' => 1527),
    array('name' => 'Joel', 'id' => 6256)
);
```

A function to sort the array by any column

```
function array_compare_factory($sort_key) {
    return function ($left, $right) use ($sort_key) {
        if ($left[$sort_key] < $right[$sort_key]) {
            return -1;
        } else if ($left[$sort_key] > $right[$sort_key]) {
            return 1;
        } else {
            return 0;
        }
    };
}
```

Code that sorts the array by the name column

```
$sort_by_name = array_compare_factory('name');
usort($employees, $sort_by_name);
```

Code that sorts the array by the id column

```
$sort_by_id = array_compare_factory('id');
usort($employees, $sort_by_id);
```

Description

- A *closure* is an inner function that has access to the outer function's variables. To create a closure, code a use clause in the inner function.

- To allow the inner function to change the outer function's variable, use the reference operator (&) in the use clause.

- The outer function's variables are available after it has finished executing as long as there is a reference to the inner function.

- The inner function is an anonymous function that is returned by the outer function or stored in a parameter that was passed by reference. You can store it in a variable and call it as a variable function like you would an anonymous function.

Figure 13-11   How to work with closures

The Shopping Cart application

To illustrate the use of functions, figure 13-12 presents a Shopping Cart application that extends the Shopping Cart application presented in chapter 12. This version of the application uses namespaces to create a library of functions, and it uses closures to allow the user to sort the items in the cart.

The user interface

The Add Item page lets the user add items to the cart. Since this page works exactly the same as the Add Item page presented in chapter 12, this chapter doesn't present the code for this page.

The Cart page shows the current contents of the cart. Here, the user can update the quantity of an item or delete an item as described in chapter 12. In addition, the user can sort the items in the cart by the specified column. To do that, the user can select the radio button for the column and click the Update Cart button. In this figure, the user has sorted the cart by the total amount for each item.

Here again, the purpose of this application is to illustrate the use of functions. As a result, the interface is simplified and the data isn't stored in a database.

The Add Item page

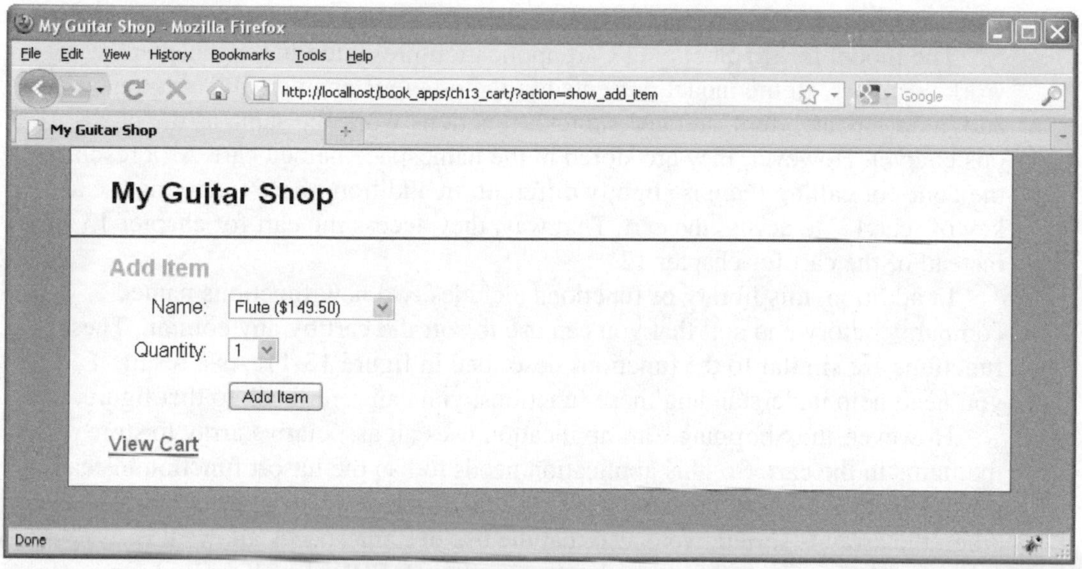

The Cart page

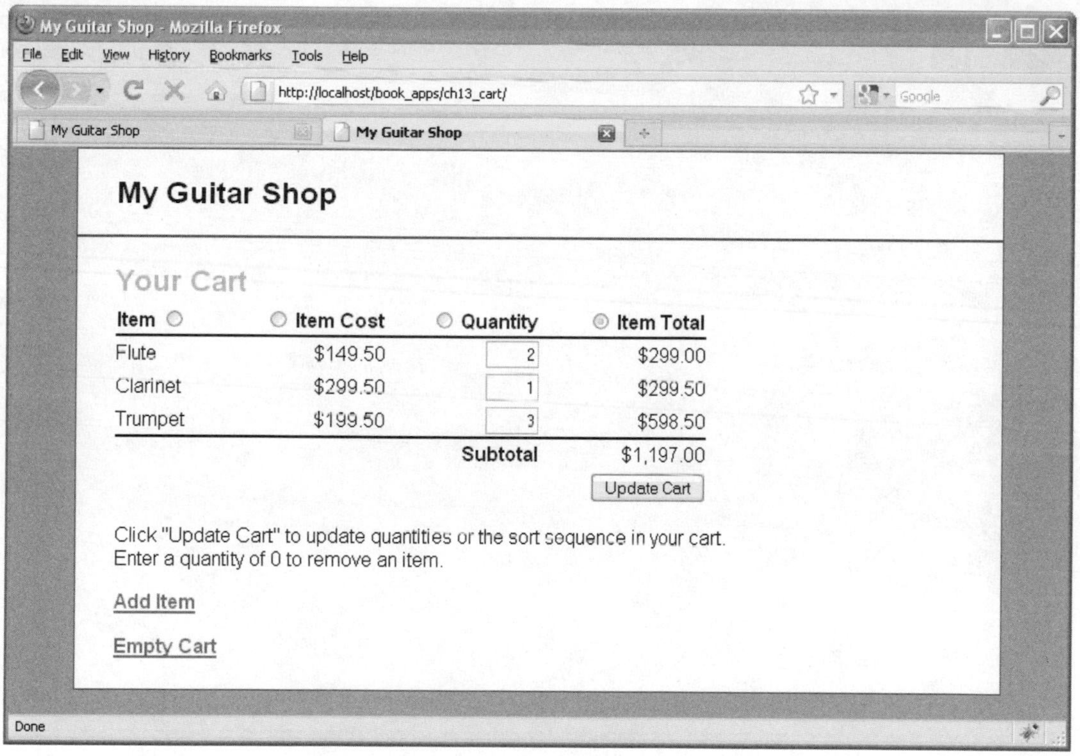

Figure 13-12   The Shopping Cart application (part 1 of 5)

The model

The model for the Shopping Cart application presented in this chapter works similarly to the model presented in the previous chapter. To start, the add_item, update_item, and get_subtotal functions work the same as the previous chapter. However, they are stored in the namespace named cart. As a result, the code for calling them is slightly different. In addition, these functions use a key of 'cart13' to access the cart. That way, they access the cart for chapter 13 instead of the cart for chapter 12.

In addition, this library of functions includes two new functions named compare_factory and sort that you can use to sort the cart by any column. These functions are similar to the functions described in figure 13-11. As a result, if you need help understanding these functions, you can refer back to that figure.

However, the Shopping Cart application uses an associative array to store the items in the cart. So, this application needs to use the uasort function instead of the usort function to prevent the keys in the associative array from being lost when the array is sorted. Note also that the use of namespaces allows this library to define a function named sort even though PHP already provides a function with that name.

The cart.php file

```php
<?php
namespace cart {

    // Add an item to the cart
    function add_item($key, $quantity) {
        // Same code as cart application for chapter 12
    }

    // Update an item in the cart
    function update_item($key, $quantity) {
        // Same code as cart application for chapter 12
    }

    // Get cart subtotal
    function get_subtotal () {
        // Same code as cart application for chapter 12
    }

    // Get a function for sorting the cart on the specified key
    function compare_factory($sort_key) {
        return function($left, $right) use ($sort_key) {
            if ($left[$sort_key] == $right[$sort_key]) {
                return 0;
            } else if ($left[$sort_key] < $right[$sort_key]) {
                return -1;
            } else {
                return 1;
            }
        };
    }

    // Sort the cart on the specified key
    function sort($sort_key) {
        $compare_function = compare_factory($sort_key);
        uasort($_SESSION['cart13'], $compare_function);
    }
}
?>
```

Figure 13-12   The Shopping Cart application (part 2 of 5)

The controller

The controller works like the controller presented in the previous chapter. The important differences are highlighted.

To start, this controller gets the sort key if one exists and sets a default value if one doesn't exist. Note that this code only checks the global $_POST array since the sort key can only be submitted using the POST method in this application.

In addition, this controller prefaces the function calls with the namespace for the function library. In particular, the calls to the add_item, update_item, and sort functions are all prefaced with the cart namespace.

Finally, this controller calls the sort function whenever the user updates or shows the cart. This call passes the sort key to the sort function.

The view

The Cart page works similarly to the Cart page presented in the previous chapter. However, the Cart page in this chapter displays a header row that has a radio button beside each column header. This allows the user to select the sort column. Note that this code uses an if statement to select the radio button that matches the current sort key.

The index.php file

```php
<?php
// Start session management
session_start();

// Create a cart array if needed
if (empty($_SESSION['cart13'])) $_SESSION['cart13'] = array();

// Create a table of products
$products = array();
$products['MMS-1754'] = array('name' => 'Flute', 'cost' => '149.50');
$products['MMS-6289'] = array('name' => 'Trumpet', 'cost' => '199.50');
$products['MMS-3408'] = array('name' => 'Clarinet', 'cost' => '299.50');

// Include cart functions
require_once('cart.php');

// Get the sort key
if (isset($_POST['sortkey'])) {
    $sort_key = $_POST['sortkey'];
} else {
    $sort_key = 'name';
}

// Get the action to perform
if (isset($_POST['action'])) {
    $action = $_POST['action'];
} else if (isset($_GET['action'])) {
    $action = $_GET['action'];
} else {
    $action = 'show_add_item';
}

// Add or update cart as needed
switch($action) {
    case 'add':
        cart\add_item($_POST['productkey'], $_POST['itemqty']);
        include('cart_view.php');
        break;
    case 'update':
        $new_qty_list = $_POST['newqty'];
        foreach($new_qty_list as $key => $qty) {
            if ($_SESSION['cart13'][$key]['qty'] != $qty) {
                cart\update_item($key, $qty);
            }
        }
        cart\sort($sort_key);
        include('cart_view.php');
        break;
    case 'show_cart':
        cart\sort($sort_key);
        include('cart_view.php');
        break;
```

Figure 13-12   The Shopping Cart application (part 3 of 5)

The index.php file (continued)

```php
        case 'show_add_item':
            include('add_item_view.php');
            break;
        case 'empty_cart':
            unset($_SESSION['cart13']);
            include('cart_view.php');
            break;
    }
?>
```

The cart_view.php file

```php
<!DOCTYPE html PUBLIC "-//W3C//DTD XHTML 1.0 Transitional//EN"
    "http://www.w3.org/TR/xhtml1/DTD/xhtml11-transitional.dtd">
<html xmlns="http://www.w3.org/1999/xhtml">
<head>
    <title>My Guitar Shop</title>
    <link rel="stylesheet" type="text/css" href="main.css">
</head>
<body>
<div id="page">
    <div id="header">
        <h1>My Guitar Shop</h1>
    </div>
    <div id="main">
    <h1>Your Cart</h1>
    <?php if (count($_SESSION['cart13']) == 0) : ?>
        <p>There are no items in your cart.</p>
    <?php else: ?>
        <form action="." method="post">
            <input type="hidden" name="action" value="update">
            <table>
                <tr id="cart_header">
                    <th class="left">
                        Item <input type="radio"
                        <?php if ($sort_key == 'name') : ?>
                            checked="checked"
                        <?php endif; ?>
                        name="sortkey" value="name"></th>
                    <th class="right">
                        <input type="radio"
                        <?php if ($sort_key == 'cost') : ?>
                            checked="checked"
                        <?php endif; ?>
                            name="sortkey" value="cost">
                        Item Cost</th>
                    <th class="right" >
                        <input type="radio"
                        <?php if ($sort_key == 'qty') : ?>
                            checked="checked"
                        <?php endif; ?>
                            name="sortkey" value="qty">
                        Quantity</th>
```

Figure 13-12   The Shopping Cart application (part 4 of 5)

The cart_view.php file (continued)

```php
                    <th class="right">
                        <input type="radio"
                        <?php if ($sort_key == 'total') : ?>
                            checked="checked"
                        <?php endif; ?>
                            name="sortkey" value="total">
                    Item Total</th>
                </tr>
                <?php foreach( $_SESSION['cart13'] as $key => $item ) :
                    $cost  = number_format($item['cost'],  2);
                    $total = number_format($item['total'], 2);
                ?>
                <tr>
                    <td>
                        <?php echo $item['name']; ?>
                    </td>
                    <td class="right">
                        $<?php echo $cost; ?>
                    </td>
                    <td class="right">
                        <input type="text" class="cart_qty"
                            name="newqty[<?php echo $key; ?>]"
                            value="<?php echo $item['qty']; ?>">
                    </td>
                    <td class="right">
                        $<?php echo $total; ?>
                    </td>
                </tr>
                <?php endforeach; ?>
                <tr id="cart_footer">
                    <td colspan="3"><b>Subtotal</b></td>
                    <td>$<?php echo cart\get_subtotal(); ?></td>
                </tr>
                <tr>
                    <td colspan="4" class="right">
                        <input type="submit" value="Update Cart"
                            id="update_button" >
                    </td>
                </tr>
            </table>
            <p>Click "Update Cart" to update quantities or the sort
                sequence in your cart.<br /> Enter a quantity of 0
                to remove an item.
            </p>
        </form>
    <?php endif; ?>
    <p><a href=".?action=show_add_item">Add Item</a></p>
    <p><a href=".?action=empty_cart">Empty Cart</a></p>

    </div><!-- end main -->
</div><!-- end page -->
</body>
</html>
```

Figure 13-12   The Shopping Cart application (part 5 of 5)

Perspective

If you understand everything in this chapter, you have all the skills you need to use functions effectively in your applications. In addition, you know how to use namespaces to organize functions, and how to use variable functions, callbacks, anonymous functions, and closures to write functions that generate other functions.

In the next chapter, you'll learn how to create and use objects. This allows you to further organize the variables and functions in your applications. Fortunately, many of the skills that you have learned for developing functions also apply to working with objects.

Terms

function	global variable
parameter	autoglobal variable
parameter list	scalar value
return statement	relative path
argument	absolute path
argument list	include path
passed by value	namespace
passed by reference	variable function
scope	callback
local scope	anonymous function
local variable	closure
global scope	

Summary

- A *function* is a reusable block of code. Within the parentheses of a function, you can code an optional *parameter list* that contains one or more *parameters*. Within the body of a function, you can code a *return statement* that ends the execution of the function and returns the specified value.

- When you call a function, the *arguments* in the *argument list* must be in the same order as the parameters in the parameter list defined by the function, and they must have compatible data types.

- By default, all function arguments are *passed by value*. This means that a copy of the argument is sent to the function. However, function arguments can also be *passed by reference*. This means that a reference to the original argument is sent to the function.

- The *scope* of a variable determines what code can access it. If a variable is defined inside a function, it has *local scope*. If a variable is defined outside of a function, it has *global scope*.

- A *scalar value* is a literal number, string, or Boolean value. A scalar value cannot contain operators, variables, or function calls.

- The *include path* specifies the directories to search for included files.

- In PHP, all functions are stored in the global namespace. As a result, you must be careful to avoid naming conflicts for function names. However, as of PHP 5.3, you can store functions in a *namespace* other than the global namespace. This provides a flexible way to avoid naming conflicts.

- A *variable function* is a function name stored in a variable as a string.

- A *callback* is a function that's passed as an argument to another function. You can use a variable function in a callback.

- An *anonymous function* is a function that doesn't have a name. You can store an anonymous function in a variable and use it as a variable function.

- A *closure* is an inner function that has access to the outer function's variables.

Exercise 13-1 Modify the Shopping Cart application

In this exercise, you can modify and enhance the library of functions for a simplified version of the Shopping Cart application.

Open and test the application

1. Run the application that's stored in the ex_starts\ch13_ex1 directory.

2. Test this application by adding items to the cart, by modifying items, and by emptying the cart.

3. Open the index.php and cart.php files for this application and review the code. Note that the code in the cart.php file uses the $_SESSION variable within the library of cart functions.

Pass the cart by value

4. Modify the parameters for the functions in the cart.php file so the first parameter for each function is a cart array that's passed by value like this:

```
function add_item($cart, $key, $quantity) {}
function update_item($cart, $key, $quantity) {}
function get_subtotal($cart) {}
```

5. Modify the code for the functions so they use the $cart parameter. To do that, you can use the $cart parameter instead of getting the cart array from the global $_SESSION array.

6. Modify the code in the index.php file so it uses these functions instead of getting the cart array from the global $_SESSION array. That way, you only need to get the cart array from the $_SESSION array at the beginning of the script. However, you need to set the cart array in the $_SESSION array each time you change the contents of the cart.

7. Modify the code in the cart_view.php file so the get_subtotal function works correctly.

Pass the cart by reference

8. Modify the parameters for the following functions so that the cart array is passed by reference like this:

```
function add_item(&$cart, $key, $quantity) {}
function update_item(&$cart, $key, $quantity) {}
```

9. Modify the code for these functions so they don't return the cart array.

10. Modify the statements in the index.php file that call these functions so they work correctly.

Store the library in a namespace

11. Modify the code in the cart.php file so it includes a namespace for the library. For the name of the namespace, use this format:

```
yourlastname\cart
```

12. Modify the code in the index.php and cart_view.php files so they call the functions in this namespace.

Use an optional parameter

13. Modify the code in the cart.php file so the get_subtotal function accepts an optional parameter that allows you to specify the number of decimal places for the subtotal like this:

```
function get_subtotal($cart, $decimals = 2) {}
```

14. Test this change to make sure it works correctly. To do that, modify the cart_view.php file so it displays 3 decimal places.

15. Modify this code so it uses the default value of 2 decimal places again.

14

How to create and use objects

So far in this book, you have learned how to create and use objects from the built-in classes that are provided by PHP. In this chapter, you'll learn how to define your own classes. Then, you can create and use objects from your own classes.

This is known as *object-oriented programming*, and it can speed the development of large applications and make your code more reusable. Object-oriented programming was introduced in PHP 3 and improved in PHP 4, but many of the features presented in this chapter weren't introduced until PHP 5.

How to create and use classes **414**
The code for the Category class 414
The code for the Product class 416
How to code properties 420
How to code constructors and destructors 422
How to code methods 424
How to create and use objects 426

How to code class constants, properties, and methods 428
How to code class constants 428
How to code static properties and methods 430

The object-oriented Product Manager application **432**
The user interface 432
The model 434
The controller 438
The view 440

Additional skills for working with objects **442**
How to loop through an object's properties 442
How to clone and compare objects 444
How to inspect an object 446

How to work with inheritance **448**
How to inherit a class 448
How to use the protected access modifier 450
How to create abstract classes and methods 452
How to create final classes and methods 454
How to work with interfaces 456

Perspective **458**

How to create and use classes

This section begins by presenting an overview of the code for two related classes: the Category class and the Product class. Then, this topic presents the details of writing code that creates and uses classes like these.

The code for the Category class

Figure 14-1 shows the code for the Category *class*. Here, the class definition starts with the class keyword followed by the name of the class and a block of code to define the class. Although you can use any PHP identifier for class names, it's a common convention to start class names with a capital letter.

The first two statements in the Category class declare two properties named ID and name. These *properties* are variables that store the data for a class. Since these properties begin with the private keyword, they are private properties that can only be accessed from within the class.

After the property declarations, the class defines the constructor method for the Category class. This *constructor method*, or just *constructor*, is automatically called whenever a Category object is created from the Category class. In this figure, the constructor takes two parameters to use as initial values for the two private properties. Since this method uses the public keyword, the constructor can be called by code outside the class.

After the constructor method, the class defines four public *methods*. These methods provide a way for code outside the class to get and set the private properties of the object. For example, the public setID method stores a new value in the private ID property, and the public getID method retrieves the current value of the private ID property.

This class illustrates the concept of *encapsulation*, which is a fundamental concept of object-oriented programming. Encapsulation provides a way to group related data and functionality. In this figure, for example, the properties store the data for a category, and the methods provide the functionality for a category. For now, these methods only get and set the value of the property. However, if necessary, you can enhance these methods later to provide additional functionality.

In other words, since other classes don't have direct access to the properties, you have the potential to change the way the methods get and set the properties. This is known as *information hiding*, and it is one of the main advantages of object-oriented programming. In the next chapter, for example, you'll learn techniques for data validation that you can use to add functionality to set methods.

The Category class

```
class Category {
    private $id;
    private $name;

    public function __construct($id, $name) {
        $this->id = $id;
        $this->name = $name;
    }

    public function getID() {
        return $this->id;
    }

    public function setID($value) {
        $this->id = $value;
    }

    public function getName() {
        return $this->name;
    }

    public function setName($value) {
        $this->name = $value;
    }
}
```

Description

- *Object-oriented programming* groups related variables and functions into data structures called *objects*.

- A *class* defines the *properties* and *methods* of a particular type of object. You can think of a class as a blueprint for an object.

Figure 14-1   The code for the Category class

The code for the Product class

Figure 14-2 shows the code for the Product class. This code is similar to the code for the Category class. To start, this code defines five private properties. Then, it defines a constructor method that sets four of these properties. Next, it defines get and set methods for all of the properties.

As you review this code, note that the getCategory and setCategory methods can get and set an object that's created from the Category class defined in figure 14-1. In other words, you can nest one class within another class. As you progress though this chapter, you'll learn more about how this works.

The getPriceFormatted method works a little differently than the previous get methods. This method uses the number_format method to convert the price to a string that has two digits and stores the string in a variable named $formatted_price. Then, the second statement returns the string for the formatted price. As a result, you can use the getPriceFormatted method to get a formatted string for the price, and you can use the getPrice method to get a numeric value for the price.

The Product class

```
class Product {
    private $category, $id, $code, $name, $price;

    public function __construct($category, $code, $name, $price) {
        $this->category = $category;
        $this->code = $code;
        $this->name = $name;
        $this->price = $price;
    }

    public function getCategory() {
        return $this->category;
    }

    public function setCategory($value) {
        $this->category = $value;
    }

    public function getID() {
        return $this->id;
    }

    public function setID($value) {
        $this->id = $value;
    }

    public function getCode() {
        return $this->code;
    }

    public function setCode($value) {
        $this->code = $value;
    }

    public function getName() {
        return $this->name;
    }

    public function setName($value) {
        $this->name = $value;
    }

    public function getPrice() {
        return $this->price;
    }

    public function getPriceFormatted() {
        $formatted_price = number_format($this->price, 2);
        return $formatted_price;
    }

    public function setPrice($value) {
        $this->price = $value;
    }
```

Figure 14-2   The code for the Product class (part 1 of 2)

Although most properties have get and set methods, you don't always have to provide both. In fact, you often only need to provide a get method. In this case, the property can be referred to as a *read-only property*.

For example, since there is no corresponding set method for the getDiscountPercent method, you can think of the discount percent as a read-only property. Similarly, since there is no set method for the rest of the methods in this class, you can think of those methods as providing access to read-only properties. Most of the return values for those methods are calculated from the data that's stored in other properties.

The getDiscountPercent method sets the discount percent for all products to 30%. In general, it isn't a good practice to hard-code a value that you might want to change such as the value for the discount percent. A better practice would be to store this value in a database. Then, you can read it from the database and store it in your objects, and you can change it easily enough by modifying the database. However, for the sake of simplicity, this object has a discount percent that's hard-coded.

The getDiscountAmount method gets the discount amount for the product. To do that, it begins by using the getDiscountPercent method to get the discount percent. Then, it multiplies the discount percent by the list price, rounds the result to 2 digits, and formats the result so it displays 2 digits. Next, it returns the discount amount.

The getDiscountPrice method gets the price that's available to the customer. To do that, it subtracts the discount amount from the full price. Note that this code uses the price property to get the full price, and it uses the getDiscountPercent method to get the discount percent.

The last three methods get strings that are used to work with images. First, the getImageFilename method gets a filename for the image by appending an extension of ".png" to the code for the product. Second, the getImagePath method gets a path to the image by appending the filename to a subdirectory named images. Third, the getImageAltText method gets a string you can use for the alt attribute of an <img> tag by appending the filename to a string literal of "Image:". Note that the getImagePath and getImageAltText methods both use the getImageFilename method.

The Product class (continued)

```php
    public function getDiscountPercent() {
        $discount_percent = 30;
        return $discount_percent;
    }

    public function getDiscountAmount() {
        $discount_percent = $this->getDiscountPercent() / 100;
        $discount_amount = $this->price * $discount_percent;
        $discount_amount = round($discount_amount, 2);
        $discount_amount = number_format($discount_amount, 2);
        return $discount_amount;
    }

    public function getDiscountPrice() {
        $discount_price = $this->price - $this->getDiscountAmount();
        $discount_price = number_format($discount_price, 2);
        return $discount_price;
    }

    public function getImageFilename() {
        $image_filename = $this->code . '.png';
        return $image_filename;
    }

    public function getImagePath() {
        $image_path = '../images/' . $this->getImageFilename();
        return $image_path;
    }

    public function getImageAltText() {
        $image_alt = 'Image: ' . $this->getImageFilename();
        return $image_alt;
    }
}
```

Figure 14-2   The code for the Product class (part 2 of 2)

How to code properties

Figure 14-3 shows how to code the properties of a class. To start, you code the access modifier followed by the property name and an optional initial value. The initial value must be a scalar value, an array of scalar values, or the NULL value. A *scalar value* is a literal number, string, or Boolean value.

When you declare a property, you begin by coding an access modifier to control its visibility. If you omit the access modifier, the property defaults to public. However, to make your code more readable, it's generally considered a good practice to always code the access modifier.

In most cases, you should use the private modifier for your properties as shown in the first example. That way, you create a *private property* that can't be directly accessed by code outside the class.

In some cases, you may want to use the public modifier as shown in the second example. That way, you create a *public property* that can be directly accessed by code outside the class. Note that this public property also includes a default value of an empty string.

In rare cases, you may want to use the protected modifier for your properties as shown in the third example. This creates a *protected property* that works similarly to a private property. You'll learn about the differences between private and protected properties later in this chapter in the topic on inheritance.

Although it's common to code each property on its own line, you can code multiple properties on the same line as shown in the fourth example. Here, five private properties are coded on the same line by separating each property name with a comma.

How to code a property

The syntax
```
[ public | protected | private ] $propertyName [ = initialValue ];
```

A private property
```
private $firstName;
```

A public property with a default value
```
public $comment = '';
```

A protected property
```
protected $counter;
```

Five properties on the same line
```
private $category, $id, $name, $description, $price;
```

Description

- A *public property* can be directly accessed by code outside of the class.
- *Private* and *protected properties* can't be directly accessed by code outside the class.
- By default, properties are public. As a result, if you omit the access modifier, the property is public.
- To code an initial value for a property, you must supply a scalar value, an array of scalar values, or a NULL value. A *scalar value* is a literal number, string, or Boolean value.
- To code multiple properties on the same line, you can separate the property names with commas.

Figure 14-3   How to code properties

How to code constructors and destructors

Figure 14-4 shows how to code a *constructor method*, or just *constructor*. A constructor is a special method that's automatically executed when a new object is created from a class. To code a constructor method, you code the public keyword and the function keyword followed by the special function name __construct (with two underscores), a set of parentheses, and a block of code. Within the parentheses, you can code the list of parameters for the method separating each parameter with a comma.

If you don't code a constructor method for a class, the class automatically provides a default constructor that doesn't include any parameters as shown in the first example. In that case, you can create an object from the class, but you can't pass any arguments to the class. As a result, you need to use the set methods of the class to set the object's properties.

When you code a constructor, it's a common practice to code parameters that supply the initial values for the properties of the object as shown in the second example. Here, the constructor for the Category class takes two parameters and uses them to initialize the properties of a new Category object.

A PHP class may only have one constructor method. As a result, if you need to pass a variable number of parameters to a constructor, you can use the techniques you learned in chapter 13 for working with variable-length parameter lists. In the third example, for instance, the constructor for the Category class provides default values for both parameters. As a result, the code that creates an object from the Category class can pass zero, one, or two arguments to the constructor. If the code doesn't pass any values, both properties are set to a NULL value.

Within a class, you can use the special variable named $this to refer to the current object. In addition, you can use the *object access operator* (->) to access the properties and methods of an object. In this figure, the second and third examples use the $this variable to access the ID and name properties of the current Category object, and the last example calls the close method of a database connection object.

A *destructor method*, or *destructor*, is automatically executed when an object is no longer available for use. This can occur when program execution reaches the end of a function or script. It can also occur when code uses the unset function to delete references to the object.

A destructor is typically used to release resources such as file handles and database connections before the object is deleted. However, this book shows how to use the PDO objects to connect to a database, and these objects have destructors that close the database connections. As a result, if you use PDO for your database connections, you won't need to code destructors for your data access objects.

If you need to code a destructor, the last example shows how. Here, the destructor calls the close method of a database connection object to close a database connection. Note that the syntax for a destructor is similar to the syntax for a constructor. However, you can't code any parameters for a destructor.

How to code a constructor method

The syntax
```
public function __construct([parameterList]) {
    // Statements to execute
}
```

The default constructor
```
public function __construct() { }
```

The constructor for the Category class
```
public function __construct($id, $name) {
    $this->id = $id;
    $this->name = $name;
}
```

The constructor for the Category class with default values
```
public function __construct($id = NULL, $name = NULL) {
    $this->id = $id;
    $this->name = $name;
}
```

How to code a destructor method

The syntax
```
public function __destruct() {
    // Statements to execute
}
```

A destructor for a database class
```
public function __destruct() {
    $this->dbConnection->close();
}
```

Description

- A *constructor method*, or just *constructor*, is a special method that is executed when a new object is created from the class. It often initializes the properties of the object.

- A *destructor method*, or just *destructor*, is a special method that's executed when an object is no longer available for use. In other words, it is executed when there are no variables that refer to the object.

- Within a class, the special variable named $this stores a reference to the current object. As a result, it allows you to access the properties and methods of the current object.

- The *object access operator* (->) provides access to an object's properties and methods. When you code the object access operator, you can't have a space between the two characters.

Figure 14-4   How to code constructors and destructors

How to code methods

Figure 14-5 shows how to code the methods of a class. When you declare a method, you typically begin by coding an access modifier to control its visibility. Other than that, the skills for coding a method work the same as the skills for coding a function as described in chapter 13.

The first example shows a public method that returns a summary that's a shortened version of the object's description property. To start, the first statement sets the maximum length for the summary to 25 characters. Then, the second statement gets the description property of the current object and stores it in a variable named $summary. Next, if the summary is longer than 25 characters, the code shortens the summary to 22 characters and appends 3 dot characters for a total of 25 characters. Finally, the last statement returns the summary.

The second example shows a private method with a default value for its $country parameter. This code uses a switch statement to check the $country parameter. Then, it returns the object's price property formatted as a currency string for the country specified by the $country parameter.

The third example shows how to code a method that accesses a property of the current object. In particular, it shows how to use the $this keyword to access the description property of the current object. Note that this works even if the property is private or protected.

The fourth example shows how to call a method of the current object. In particular, it shows how to use the variable named $this to call the private internationalizePrice method that's coded in the second example. This shows that you can use the variable named $this to access all methods of the current object including private and protected methods.

How to code a method

The syntax

```
[public | private | protected] function functionName ([parameterList]) {
    // Statements to execute
}
```

A public method

```
public function getSummary() {
    $maxLength = 25;
    $summary = $this->description;
    if (strlen($summary) > $maxLength) {
        $summary = substr($summary, 0, $maxLength - 3) . '...';
    }
    return $summary;
}
```

A private method

```
private function internationalizePrice($country = 'US') {
    switch ($country) {
        case 'US':
            return '$' . number_format($this->price, 2);
        case 'DE':
            return number_format($this->price, 2, ',' , '.') . ' DM';
        default:
            return number_format($this->price, 2);
    }
}
```

A method that accesses a property of the current object

```
public function showDescription() {
    echo $this->description;
}
```

A method that calls a method of the current object

```
public function showPrice($country = 'US') {
    echo $this->internationalizePrice($country);
}
```

Description

- To code a method in a class, you code one of the access modifier keywords followed by the function keyword, the name of the method, an optional parameter list in a set of parentheses, and a block of code to execute.

- By default, methods are public. As a result, if you omit the access modifier, the method is public. However, to make your code more consistent and readable, it's generally considered a good practice to code an access modifier for all methods.

Figure 14-5   How to code methods

How to create and use objects

Once you've created a class, you can create objects from that class and use them in your application. Figure 14-6 shows how to create objects and use their properties and methods.

You can create an object by coding the new keyword followed by the name of the class and a set of parentheses. Inside the parentheses, you code any arguments for the object's constructor separated by commas. Typically, you store the new object in a variable. However, you can also store a new object in an array, pass a new object as an argument to a function or method, or store the object in a property of another object.

The first example creates a new Category object and stores it in a variable. This code passes two arguments to the constructor for the Category object. These arguments specify the initial values for the properties of the Category object.

The second example creates a new Product object and stores it in a variable. This code passes four arguments to the constructor for the Product object. The first argument is the Category object from the first example. The rest of the arguments are the number and string values for the remaining properties.

Once you've created an object, you can use its properties and methods. If an object has public properties, you can get and set them. To do that, you code a reference to the object, typically a variable name, followed by the object access operator (->) and the name of the property. Note that you don't need to include a dollar sign between the access operator and the property name.

The examples that illustrate this assume that the Product class has a public property named comment. Here, the first example sets the comment property to a string value of "Discontinued". Then, the second example gets uses an echo statement to display the value of the comment property.

Although some objects provide public properties, it's more common for an object to provide public methods. Then, you can use these methods to work with the object. To do that, you code a reference to the object followed by the object access operator, the method name, and the method arguments in parentheses. This is illustrated by the next two examples.

The first example shows how to call a method that returns a value. Here, the code calls the getFormattedPrice method of the object, and it stores the returned value in a variable named $price.

The second example shows how to use *object chaining*. Here, the code calls the getCategory method of the Product object to return a reference to a Category object. However, the Category object isn't stored in a variable. Instead, this code calls the getName method directly from the getCategory method to get the name of the category. This makes it easy for you to access properties and methods of nested objects.

How to create an object

The syntax
```
$objectName = new ClassName(argumentList);
```

Create a Category object
```
$brass = new Category(4, 'Brass');
```

Create a Product object
```
$trumpet = new Product($brass, 'Getzen', 'Getzen 700SP Trumpet', 999.95);
```

How to access an object's properties

The syntax for setting a public property value
```
$objectName->propertyName = value;
```

The syntax for getting a public property value
```
$objectName->propertyName;
```

Set a property
```
$trumpet->comment = 'Discontinued';
```

Get a property
```
echo $trumpet->comment;
```

How to call an object's methods

The syntax
```
$objectName->methodName(argumentList);
```

Call the getFormattedPrice method
```
$price = $trumpet->getFormattedPrice();
```

Object chaining
```
echo $trumpet->getCategory()->getName();
```

Description

- An object is an *instance* of a class. In other words, you can create more than one object from a single class. The process of creating an object from a class is sometimes called *instantiation*.

- To create an object, you code the new keyword followed by name of the class and a set of parentheses. Inside the parentheses, you code the arguments for the constructor separated by commas.

- To access an object's property, you code a reference to the object followed by the object access operator (->) and the name of the property.

- To call an object's method, you code a reference to the object followed by the object access operator (->), the name of the method, and a set of parentheses. Inside the parentheses, you code the arguments for the method separated by commas.

- If a function or method returns an object, you can use the function or method call as a reference to the object and continue accessing the returned object's properties and methods. This is called *object chaining*.

Figure 14-6   How to create and use objects

How to code class constants, properties, and methods

So far, this chapter has shown how to define the properties and methods of an object that is created from a class. As a result, you must create an object from the class before you can access these properties and methods. Now, you'll learn how to define constants, properties, and methods that you can access directly from the class.

How to code class constants

Figure 14-7 shows how to create and use *class constants*. A class constant is a constant that is defined in a class. All class constants are public. As a result, they are available to code outside the class. In addition, class constants belong to the class, not the object. As a result, you can access class constants directly from the class without creating an object from the class first.

Class constants are often used to provide a set of fixed values for an option. In this figure, for example, the Person class defines two constants for gender: MALE and FEMALE. Using constants to define a set of fixed values helps eliminate errors by forcing the programmer to specify one of the fixed values. In this figure, for example, the setGender method only accepts the MALE and FEMALE constants.

To create a class constant, you code the const keyword followed by the constant name, an equals sign, and a scalar value. Then, to refer to the constant inside the class declaration, you code the self keyword followed by the double colon and the name of the constant. This keyword is a reference to the current class. To refer to the constant outside the class declaration, you code the name of the class followed by a double colon and the name of the constant.

The double colon is also known as the *scope resolution operator*. However, some error messages may refer to the double colon as *Paamayim Nekudotayim*, which means double colon in Hebrew. This term crept into the PHP error messages because the internal PHP code was developed in Israel.

Within the Person class, the setGender method checks whether the value of its parameter is one of the two accepted values. If so, the property is set. Otherwise, the method exits with an error message.

Outside the Person class, the second example begins by creating a Person object. Then, it calls the setGender method and passes one of the class constants as an argument to the method. Here, the string 'f' could also have been used, but if the value of the constant were changed later, the call to the setGender method would no longer work.

How to create a class constant

A class with two class constants

```
class Person {
    const MALE = 'm';
    const FEMALE = 'f';

    private $gender;

    public function getGender() {
        return $this->gender;
    }

    public function setGender($value) {
        if ($value == self::MALE || $value == self::FEMALE) {
            $this->gender = $value;
        } else {
            exit('Invalid Gender');
        }
    }
}
```

Use the constant outside the class

```
$person = new Person();
$person->setGender(Person::FEMALE);
```

Description

- A *class constant* is a constant value that belongs to the class, not objects created from the class.

- To access a constant that belongs to a class, you can code the name of the class followed by a double colon. This double colon is known as the *scope resolution operator*. It is also known as the *Paamayim Nekudotayim*, which means double colon in Hebrew.

- Inside a class, you can access a class constant by coding the self keyword followed by a double colon and the class constant name.

- Outside the class, you can access a class constant by coding the class name followed by a double colon and the class constant name.

- Class constants are always public. You can't use the public, private, or protected keywords with them.

- Class constants are typically used for defining a set of options that are passed to methods in the class.

Figure 14-7   How to code class constants

How to code static properties and methods

Figure 14-8 shows how to use *static properties* and *static methods*. Since static properties and methods belong to the class, not to an object, they are also known as *class properties* and *class methods*. In this sense, static properties and methods are similar to class constants.

There are two main differences between class constants and static properties and methods. First, when you declare a static property or method, you can use an access modifier such as public or private. Second, since a static method doesn't belong to an object, you can't use the $this variable inside a static method to get the current object. However, you can use the self keyword to access the current class. As a result, a static method can only work with other static methods, properties, and class constants.

The Category class in this figure begins by declaring a static property named $objectCount to count the number of objects created from this class. Here, the code uses the static keyword to specify that this property is static. In addition, the code initializes this property to a value of zero. This shows that you can specify an initial value for a static property. However, the initial value must follow the same rules as an initial value for an object property. In other words, it must be a scalar value, an array of scalar values, or a NULL value.

Within the constructor, the static $objectCount property is incremented by one. As a result, this property indicates how many objects have been created from the Category class.

The static method named getObjectCount returns a count of the objects created. This provides a public way to get the value stored in the private $objectCount property.

Inside a class, you can access a static property or method by coding the self keyword followed by a double colon and the name of the static property or method. Note, however, that static property names are preceded by a dollar sign and static methods are not.

Outside a class, you can access the public static properties and methods by coding the class name followed by a double colon and name of the static property or method. Again, static property names are preceded by a dollar sign and static methods are not.

When you call a static method from within a class, you can access all properties and methods even if they are private or protected. However, when you call a static method from outside a class, you can only access the public properties and methods.

The second example shows how to use a static method. Here, the first two statements create two objects from the Category class. Then, the third statement calls the static getObjectCount method to display the count. Finally, the last two statements create a third object and display the count again.

The third example shows how to call a public static object. For this call to work, however, the $objectCount property would need to be coded as public instead of private.

How to create static properties and methods

A class with a static property and method

```
class Category {
    private $id, $name;
    private static $objectCount = 0;    // declare a static property

    public function __construct($id, $name) {
        $this->id = $id;
        $this->name = $name;
        self::$objectCount++;                // update the static property
    }

    // A public method that gets the static property
    public static function getObjectCount(){
        return self::$objectCount;
    }

    // The rest of the methods for the Category class
}
```

Using a static method

```
$brass = new Category(1, 'Guitars');
$brass = new Category(2, 'Bass');
echo '<p>Object count: ' . Category::getObjectCount() . '</p>';    // 2

$brass = new Category(3, 'Drums');
echo '<p>Object count: ' . Category::getObjectCount() . '</p>';    // 3
```

Using a public static property

```
echo '<p>Object count: ' . Category::$objectCount . '</p>';
```

Description

- A *static property* or *static method* is a property or method that belongs to a class, not to objects created from the class. You use the static keyword to create these types of properties and methods, which are also referred to as *class properties* and *class methods*.

- Inside a class, you can access a static property or method by coding the self keyword followed by a double colon and the property or method name.

- Outside a class, you can access a static property or method that's public by coding the class name followed by a double colon and the static property or method name.

- When you access a static property, you must include the dollar sign at the beginning of the property's name.

- In a PHP application, the code space is separate for each user. As a result, static properties and methods aren't shared between multiple users.

Figure 14-8   How to code static properties and methods

The object-oriented Product Manager application

Chapter 5 presented a Guitar Shop web site that included a Product Manager application that used procedural techniques, not object-oriented techniques. Now, this topic presents that Product Manager application after it has been rewritten to use object-oriented programming techniques. For the sake of brevity, this topic doesn't show all of the code for the Product Manager application. However, it does present excerpts that show the key object-oriented techniques. As always, you can view the complete code for this application by downloading the source code for this book.

The user interface

To refresh your memory about this application, figure 14-9 starts by presenting the user interface. This administrative application lets the user view the products in each category using the Product List page. It also lets the user add a product to a category using the Add Product page.

The Product List page

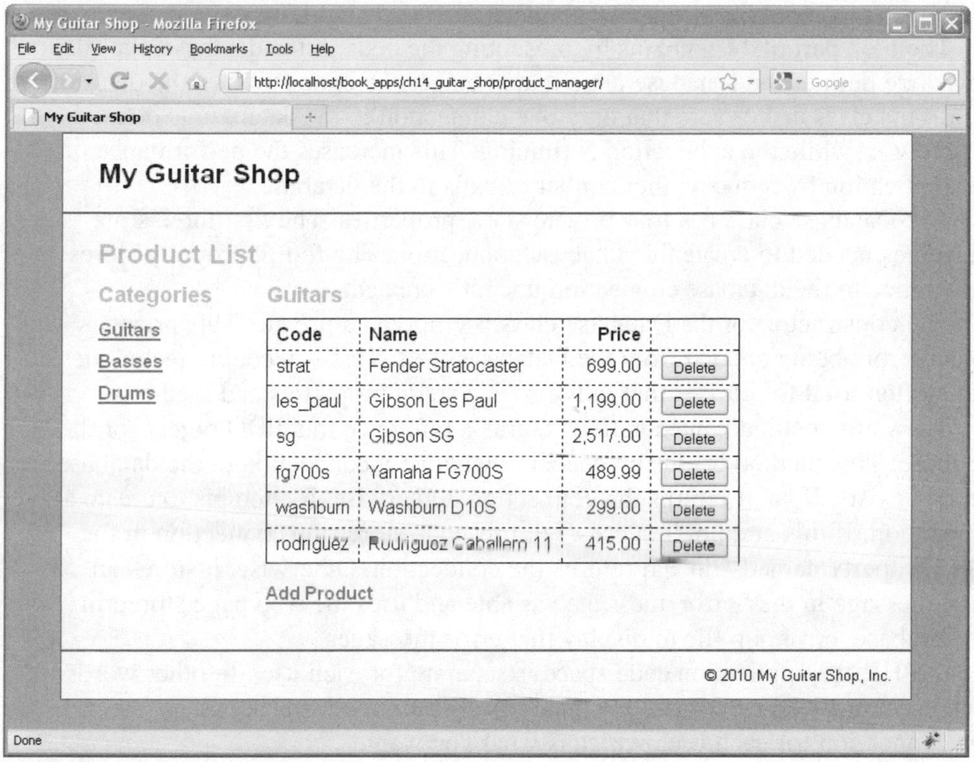

The Add Product page

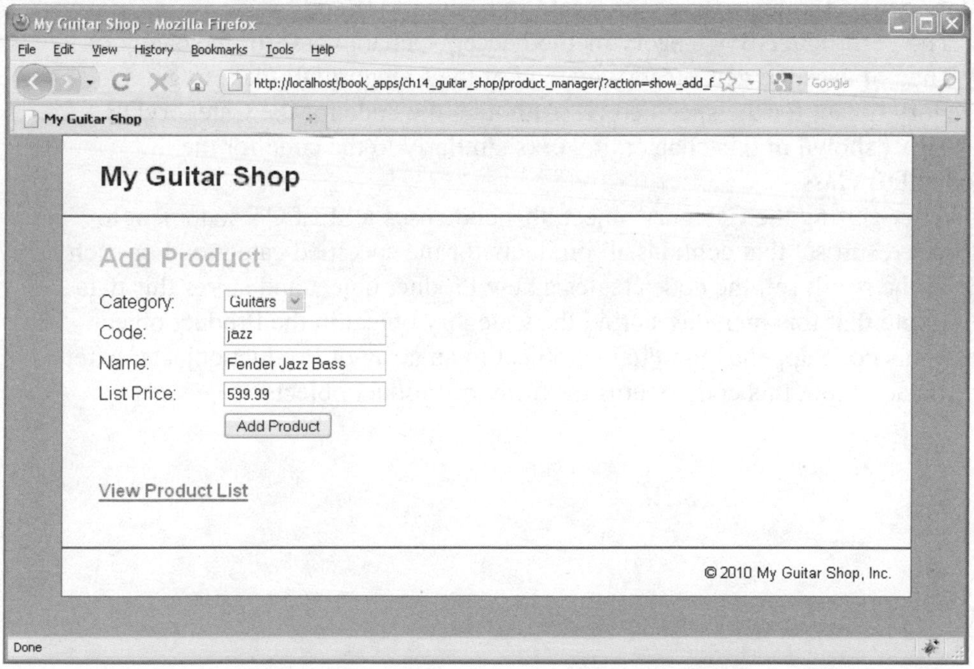

Figure 14-9   The object-oriented Product Manager application (part 1 of 5)

The model

The next part of 14-9 begins by presenting the code in the database.php file. This code defines the Database class that manages the connection to the database. This class makes sure that only one connection to the database is created per browser while the application is running. This increases the performance of the application by reducing the number of calls to the database.

The Database class has four private static properties. The first three store the values needed to create the database connection. The fourth property stores a reference to the database connection once it's created.

The constructor for the Database class is empty and private. This prevents objects from being created from the Database class. This is a coding technique that's often used for classes that only provide static properties and methods.

The static method named getDB returns a reference to a PDO object for the database. This method begins by checking whether a connection to the database already exists. If so, it returns the connection. Otherwise, it attempts to create a connection. If this attempt is successful, this code stores the connection in the static property named $db and returns the connection. Otherwise, it stores an error message in the $error_message variable and uses the web page stored in the database_error.php file to display that error message.

In PHP, the application code space is separate for each user. In other words, each user runs its own copy of the code. As a result, the Database class stores one connection for each user, which is what you want.

Next, this figure shows the code for the ProductDB class, which consists of four static methods that interact with the products table. These methods use the Category and Product classes presented in figures 14-1 and 14-2.

The getProductsByCategory method accepts a parameter for the category ID. Then, it uses the getCategory method of the CategoryDB class to get a Category object for the specified ID. Although the code for the CategoryDB class isn't shown in this chapter, it works similarly to the code for the ProductDB class.

After getting the Category object, this code uses a SELECT statement to return a result set that contains all products for the specified category. For each row in the result set, the code creates a new Product object and stores this data in it. Note that this includes storing the Category object in the Product object. Next, this code appends the Product object to an array of Product objects. After the foreach loop, this code returns the array of Product objects.

The database.php file

```php
<?php
class Database {
    private static $dsn = 'mysql:host=localhost;dbname=my_guitar_shop1';
    private static $username = 'mgs_user';
    private static $password = 'pa55word';
    private static $db;

    private function __construct() {}

    public static function getDB () {
        if (!isset(self::$db)) {
            try {
                self::$db = new PDO(self::$dsn,
                                    self::$username,
                                    self::$password);
            } catch (PDOException $e) {
                $error_message = $e->getMessage();
                include('../errors/database_error.php');
                exit();
            }
        }
        return self::$db;
    }
}
?>
```

The product_db.php file

```php
<?php
class ProductDB {
    public static function getProductsByCategory($category_id) {
        $db = Database::getDB();

        $category = CategoryDB::getCategory($category_id);

        $query = "SELECT * FROM products
                  WHERE categoryID = '$category_id'
                  ORDER BY productID";
        $result = $db->query($query);
        $products = array();
        foreach ($result as $row) {
            $product = new Product($category,
                                   $row['productCode'],
                                   $row['productName'],
                                   $row['listPrice']);
            $product->setID($row['productID']);
            $products[] = $product;
        }
        return $products;
    }
}
```

Figure 14-9   The object-oriented Product Manager application (part 2 of 5)

The getProduct method accepts the product ID as a parameter. Then, it uses a SELECT statement to return a result set that contains the row for the specified ID. Next, it uses the fetch method to convert the result set into an array, and it uses the getCategory method for the CategoryDB class to get a Category object for the category ID. Finally, it creates a Product object, stores this data in that object, and returns the object.

The deleteProduct method accepts a product ID as a parameter. Then, it uses a DELETE statement to delete the specified product from the database, and it returns the number of rows deleted by the statement. If the DELETE statement executes successfully, it deletes one row and returns a value of 1.

The addProduct method accepts a Product object as a parameter. Then, it gets the data that's needed by the INSERT statement from the Product object. Next, it uses the INSERT statement to add the new product to the products table, and it returns the number of rows added. If the INSERT statement executes successfully, this adds one row to the product table and returns a value of 1.

Note that all four of these methods call the getDB method of the Database class to get a reference to the database connection.

The product_db.php file (continued)

```php
    public static function getProduct($product_id) {
        $db = Database::getDB();
        $query = "SELECT * FROM products
                    WHERE productID = '$product_id'";
        $result = $db->query($query);
        $row = $result->fetch();
        $category = CategoryDB::getCategory($row['categoryID']);
        $product = new Product($category,
                                $row['productCode'],
                                $row['productName'],
                                $row['listPrice']);
        $product->setID($row['productID']);
        return $product;
    }

    public static function deleteProduct($product_id) {
        $db = Database::getDB();
        $query = "DELETE FROM products
                    WHERE productID = '$product_id'";
        $row_count = $db->exec($query);
        return $row_count;
    }

    public static function addProduct($product) {
        $db = Database::getDB();

        $category_id = $product->getCategory()->getID();
        $code = $product->getCode();
        $name = $product->getName();
        $price = $product->getPrice();

        $query =
            "INSERT INTO products
                    (categoryID, productCode, productName, listPrice)
                VALUES
                    ('$category_id', '$code', '$name', '$price')";

        $row_count = $db->exec($query);
        return $row_count;
    }
}
?>
```

Figure 14-9   The object-oriented Product Manager application (part 3 of 5)

The controller

The index.php file contains the code for the controller of the Product Manager application. The first five statements in this file use the require statement to load all of the files that define the model. Here, you must include the category.php and product.php files since they store the code that defines the Category and Product objects.

The rest of the code works similarly to the Product Manager application described in chapter 5. As a result, you shouldn't have much trouble understanding how it works. However, there are a few differences to notice.

The main difference is that this controller uses object-oriented techniques to work with the data that's in the database. To do that, it calls static methods from the CategoryDB and ProductDB classes. Of these methods, the ones that get data either return an object or an array of objects. For example, the getProduct method of the ProductsDB class returns a Product object for the specified category ID. Similarly, the getProductsByCategories method of the ProductsDB class returns an array of Product objects. As a result, the code that's in the view can call methods from these objects.

The index.php file

```php
<?php
require('../model/database.php');
require('../model/category.php');
require('../model/category_db.php');
require('../model/product.php');
require('../model/product_db.php');

if (isset($_POST['action'])) {
    $action = $_POST['action'];
} else if (isset($_GET['action'])) {
    $action = $_GET['action'];
} else {
    $action = 'list_products';
}

if ($action == 'list_products') {
    $category_id = $_GET['category_id'];
    if (!isset($category_id)) {
        $category_id = 1;
    }

    $current_category = CategoryDB::getCategory($category_id);
    $categories = CategoryDB::getCategories();
    $products = ProductDB::getProductsByCategory($category_id);

    include('product_list.php');
} else if ($action == 'delete_product') {
    $product_id = $_POST['product_id'];
    $category_id = $_POST['category_id'];

    ProductDB::deleteProduct($product_id);

    header("Location: .?category_id=$category_id");
} else if ($action == 'show_add_form') {
    $categories = CategoryDB::getCategories();
    include('product_add.php');
} else if ($action == 'add_product') {
    $category_id = $_POST['category_id'];
    $code = $_POST['code'];
    $name = $_POST['name'];
    $price = $_POST['price'];

    if (empty($code) || empty($name) || empty($price)) {
        $error = "Invalid product data. Check all fields and try again.";
        include('../errors/error.php');
    } else {
        $category = CategoryDB::getCategory($category_id);
        $product = new Product($category, $code, $name, $price);
        ProductDB::addProduct($product);

        header("Location: .?category_id=$category_id");
    }
}
?>
```

Figure 14-9   The object-oriented Product Manager application (part 4 of 5)

The view

The product_list.php file contains the code that displays the list of products. To display the category and product data, this code calls the methods from the variables that refer to the Category and Product objects. To make it easy for you to focus on these calls, they are highlighted in this figure.

To start, the code that displays the list of categories uses the getID and getName methods of the Category object to display the category ID and name. Then, the code that displays the name of the current category uses the getName method of the Category object for the current category. Finally, the code that displays the table of products uses the get methods of the Product object.

The product_list.php file

```php
<?php include '../view/header.php'; ?>
<div id="main">

    <h1>Product List</h1>

    <div id="sidebar">
        <!-- display a list of categories -->
        <h2>Categories</h2>
        <ul class="nav">
        <?php foreach ($categories as $category) : ?>
            <li>
            <a href="?category_id=<?php echo $category->getID(); ?>">
                <?php echo $category->getName(); ?>
            </a>
            </li>
        <?php endforeach; ?>
        </ul>
    </div>

    <div id="content">
        <!-- display a table of products -->
        <h2><?php echo $current_category->getName(); ?></h2>
        <table>
            <tr>
                <th>Code</th>
                <th>Name</th>
                <th class="right">Price</th>
                <th> </th>
            </tr>
            <?php foreach ($products as $product) : ?>
            <tr>
                <td><?php echo $product->getCode(); ?></td>
                <td><?php echo $product->getName(); ?></td>
                <td class="right"><?php echo $product->getPriceFormatted(); ?>
                </td>
                <td><form action="." method="post"
                        id="delete_product_form">
                    <input type="hidden" name="action"
                        value="delete_product" />
                    <input type="hidden" name="product_id"
                        value="<?php echo $product->getID(); ?>" />
                    <input type="hidden" name="category_id"
                        value="<?php echo $current_category->getID(); ?>"/>
                    <input type="submit" value="Delete" />
                </form></td>
            </tr>
            <?php endforeach; ?>
        </table>
        <p><a href="?action=show_add_form">Add Product</a></p>
    </div>

</div>
<?php include '../view/footer.php'; ?>
```

Figure 14-9   The object-oriented Product Manager application (part 5 of 5)

Additional skills for working with objects

Now that you've seen the basic skills for working with objects, you're ready to learn additional skills for working with objects. Although you won't need these for most applications, you may need them occasionally.

How to loop through an object's properties

Figure 14-10 shows how to use a foreach loop to loop through the properties of an object. Although the code in this figure just displays each property, you can perform any type of processing on each property of the object.

The foreach loop works differently depending on whether it's coded inside or outside of the class for the object. If you code a foreach loop within a method of a class, the foreach loop processes all properties whether they are public, protected, or private. If you code a foreach loop outside of a class, the loop only processes the public properties of the object.

Using a foreach loop to process an object's properties works much like using a foreach loop to process an associative array. To start, you code the foreach keyword followed by a set of parentheses and a block of code. Within the parentheses, you code a reference to the object followed by the as keyword, an optional variable to hold the property name, and a variable to hold the property value.

The first example in this figure defines an Employee class that contains both public and private properties. To save space, the get and set methods for the private properties aren't shown in this example. Within this class, the showAll method uses a foreach loop to display a list of all property names and values.

The second example creates an object from the Employee class and sets all four properties. Here, the constructor sets the two public properties, and methods set the two private properties.

The third example calls the showAll method of the Employee object to execute a foreach loop that's coded inside a class. As a result, this code displays all properties of the object including its private properties.

The fourth example codes a foreach loop outside the class declaration. As a result, it only displays the two public properties of the object.

How to loop through an object's properties

The syntax

```
foreach($objectName as [ $propertyName => ] $propertyValue) {
    // statements to execute
}
```

Define an Employee class

```
class Employee {
    public $firstName, $lastName;
    private $ssn, $dob;

    public function __construct($first, $last) {
        $this->firstName = $first;
        $this->lastName = $last;
    }

    // getSSN, setSSN, getDOB, setDOB methods not shown

    // Show all properties - private, protected, and public
    public function showAll() {
        echo '<ul>';
        foreach($this as $name => $value ) {
            echo "<li>$name = $value</li>";
        }
        echo '</ul>';
    }
}
```

Create an Employee object with four properties

```
$employee = new Employee('John', 'Doe');
$employee->setSSN('999-14-3456');
$employee->setDOB('3-15-1970');
```

Show all properties

```
$employee->showAll();
```

Show public properties only

```
echo '<ul>';
foreach($employee as $name => $value ) {
    echo "<li>$name = $value</li>";
}
echo '</ul>';
```

Description

- You can use a foreach loop to access each property in an object.
- A foreach loop coded inside a method of an object loops through the object's private, protected, and public properties.
- A foreach loop coded outside an object only loops through the object's public properties.

Figure 14-10   How to loop through an object's properties

How to clone and compare objects

When working with objects, you often need to make a copy, or *clone*, of an object. Figure 14-11 shows how to clone an object, and it shows how to compare objects.

The first example in this figure creates a Product object. Here, the first statement creates a new Category object for a category named Brass. Then, the second statement nests the Category object inside a Product object for a trumpet.

The second example attempts to copy the Product object by using the equals operator (=). However, this only creates a new reference to the same Product object. In other words, the $trumpet and $trombone variables both point to the same object. So, if you use one variable to set a property of the object, that modifies the property for the other variable too.

The third example uses the clone keyword to copy the object. This code stores the cloned object in a variable. However, a cloned object can also be passed as an argument to a function or method. In this example, the $trumpet and $trombone variables each refer to their own copy of the object. As a result, you can modify the properties in each object independently.

When PHP makes a copy of an object, it makes a *shallow copy* of an object. This means that nested objects are not copied. In the fourth example, for instance, the $trumpet and $trombone variable both point to the same Category object. To show this, the first statement uses the $trombone variable to get the Category object and set its name to Orchestral Brass. Then, the second statement uses the $trumpet variable to get the name from the Category object.

Occasionally, you may want to compare two variables to determine if they refer to the same object. To do that, you can use the identify operator (===). Or, you may want to compare variables to see if they are instances of the same class with the same values for every property. To do that, you can use the equality operator (==). This is illustrated by the compare examples.

The first compare example shows how to use the equality operator to test if two objects are equal. When the $trumpet and $trombone variables are compared, the result is FALSE. That's because these variables refer to objects that have different values for the price property. When the $trumpet and $flugelhorn variables are compared, the result is TRUE. That's because these variables refer to objects that have the same values for each property.

The second compare example shows how to use the identity operator to test if two variables refer to the same object. When the $trumpet and $flugelhorn variables are compared, the result is FALSE. That's because each variable refers to its own copy of the object. As a result, these objects don't have the same identity even though they currently store the same data. When the $trumpet and $trumpet_2 variables are compared the result is TRUE. That's because both variables refer to the same object.

When the result of the getCategory method of the $trumpet object is compared to the result of the getCategory method of the $trombone object, the result is TRUE. This again shows that a clone is a shallow copy. As a result, both of these Product objects refer to the same Category object.

How to clone an object

The syntax
```
clone $objectName
```

An object to clone
```
$brass = new Category(4, 'Brass');
$trumpet = new Product($brass, 'Getzen', 'Getzen 700SP Trumpet', 999.95);
```

Create a second reference to an object
```
$trombone = $trumpet;              // both variables refer to the same object
$trombone->setPrice(699.95);       // changes the price for both variables
```

Create a clone of an object
```
$trombone = clone $trumpet;        // copy the object
$trombone->setPrice(899.95);       // this only changes the price for trombone
```

The copies are shallow copies
```
$trombone->getCategory()->setName('Orchestral Brass');
echo $trumpet->getCategory()->getName();   // Displays 'Orchestral Brass'
```

How to compare two objects

Use the equality (==) operator
```
$result_1 = ($trumpet == $trombone);       // $result_1 is FALSE

$flugelhorn = clone $trumpet;
$result_2 = ($trumpet == $flugelhorn);     // $result_2 is TRUE
```

Use the identity (===) operator
```
$result_3 = ($trumpet === $flugelhorn);  // $result_3 is FALSE

$trumpet_2 = $trumpet;
$result_4 = ($trumpet === $trumpet_2);   // $result_4 is TRUE

$result_5 = ($trumpet->getCategory() === $trombone->getCategory());
                                         // $result_5 is TRUE
```

Description

- To create a second reference to an object, you can use the equals (=) operator. To create a copy, or *clone*, of an object, you must use the clone operator.

- When you create a copy of an object, PHP makes a *shallow copy* of the object. This means that PHP doesn't create copies of nested objects within the original object.

- You can use the equality operator (==) to check whether both objects are instances of the same class and have the same values for every property.

- You can use the identity operator (===) to check whether both object variables refer to the same instance of an object.

- You can also use the logical not versions of the equality (!=) and identity (!==) operators.

Figure 14-11   How to clone and compare objects

How to inspect an object

Figure 14-12 shows how to inspect an object. This is known as *introspection* or *reflection*. To start, this figure summarizes some of the methods that are used to inspect an object. These methods are often used in functions and methods to check if an object parameter is of the expected type. In addition, they can be used to make sure a property or method exists before it's called.

The first example shows how to use the is_a function. To start, an if statement checks whether the $trumpet object is an instance of the Product class. If so, this example executes code that works with a Product object.

The second example shows how to use the property_exists function. To start, an if statement checks whether the $trumpet object has a price property. If so, this example executes code that uses the price property.

The third example shows how to use the method_exists function. To start, an if statement checks whether the $trumpet object has a getPrice method. If so, this example executes code that uses the getPrice method.

When you use the property_exists and method_exists methods, you should be aware that they both return TRUE for properties and methods whether they are public, protected, or private. However, you may not be able to call properties and methods if they are protected or private, even though they exist.

The functions presented in this figure provide only a brief introduction to the reflection capabilities of PHP. Beyond this, PHP 5 provides comprehensive reflection capabilities that allow you to get any information you want about an object. However, this information is primarily used in debugging very large applications. To learn more about reflection, you can visit the URL shown at the top of this figure.

The URL for the reflection API

```
http://www.php.net/manual/en/book.reflection.php
```

Functions for inspecting an object

Function	Description
class_exists($class)	Returns TRUE if the specified class has been defined.
get_class($object)	Returns the class name of the specified object as a string.
is_a($object, $class)	Returns TRUE if the specified object is an instance of the specified class.
property_exists($object, $property)	Returns TRUE if the specified object has the specified property.
method_exists($object, $method)	Returns TRUE if the specified object has the specified method.

Determine if an object is an instance of a class

```
if (is_a($trumpet, 'Product')) {
    // Code to work with a Product object
}
```

Determine if an object has a property

```
if (property_exists($trumpet, 'price')) {
    // Code to work with the price property
}
```

Determine if an object has a method

```
if (method_exists($trumpet, 'getPrice')) {
    // Code to work with the getPrice method
}
```

Description

- Inspecting an object is known as *introspection* or *reflection*.

- When you specify the argument for the property_exists and method_exists functions, you can specify an object or the name of a class.

- The property_exists and method_exists functions return TRUE even if the property or method is private or protected.

- Version 5 of PHP introduced a reflection API that allows you to examine functions, classes, methods, and properties. To learn more about it, you can go to the URL at the top of this figure.

Figure 14-12   How to inspect an object

How to work with inheritance

Inheritance is a fundamental concept of object-oriented programming. Inheritance is the process of creating a new class by inheriting and extending the properties and methods of an existing class. Inheritance is used by the developers of large applications to develop a consistent set of classes.

How to inherit a class

Figure 14-13 shows the basic skills for working with inheritance. To start, this figure presents a class named Person that defines properties and methods that provide the basic functionality needed to represent a person. This class has four private properties, a public constructor method, and a public get and set method for each property.

Then, this figure presents a class named Employee that *inherits* the properties and methods of the Person class. The Employee class begins by using the extends keyword to indicate that it inherits the Person class. Then, the Employee class *extends* the Person class by adding properties and methods. Since the Employee class inherits from another class, it is often referred to as a *subclass*, *derived class*, or *child class*. Conversely, since the Person class is inherited by another class, it can be referred to as a *superclass*, *base class*, or *parent class*.

The Employee class defines two private properties, a constructor method, and four public get and set methods to work with the new properties. In addition, this class inherits the eight public get and set methods of the Person class. As a result, you can use the twelve methods of the Employee object to work with all six properties defined by the Person and Employee classes.

Because the four properties of the Person class are private, the Employee class doesn't inherit them. However, because the get and set methods in the Person class are public, the Employee class inherits these methods. As a result, the Employee class can use these methods to work with the private properties of the Person class.

The constructor method in the Employee class has the same name as the constructor method in the Person class. As a result, when you create a new Employee object, PHP uses the new constructor rather than the old one. In other words, the new method *overrides* the old method. For this to work, the constructor in the Employee class needs to call the constructor method in the Person class.

To call a method in the superclass, you can code the parent keyword followed by a double colon, the name of the method, and any arguments to the method in parentheses. Although this figure only shows how to override a constructor method, you can use the same technique to override other methods.

By using inheritance, you can modularize your code to speed development and reduce debugging time. If, for example, you need to code a class that defines a customer, you can start by coding a Customer class that inherits the Person class.

A superclass

```
class Person {
    private $firstName, $lastName, $phone, $email;

    public function __construct($first, $last) {
        $this->firstName = $first;
        $this->lastName  = $last;
    }

    public function getFirstName()        { return $this->firstName;    }
    public function setFirstName($value) { $this->firstName = $value; }
    public function getLastName()         { return $this->lastName;     }
    public function setLastName($value)  { $this->lastName = $value;  }
    public function getPhone()            { return $this->phone;       }
    public function setPhone($value)     { $this->phone = $value;     }
    public function getEmail()            { return $this->email;       }
    public function setEmail($value)     { $this->email = $value;     }
}
```

A subclass

```
class Employee extends Person {
    private $ssn, $hireDate;

    public function __construct($first, $last, $ssn, $hireDate) {
        $this->ssn = $ssn;
        $this->hireDate = $hireDate;

        // Call Person constructor to finish initialization
        parent::__construct($first, $last);
    }

    public function getSSN()              { return $this->ssn;      }
    public function setSSN($value)       { $this->ssn = $value;   }
    public function getHireDate()         { return $this->hireDate;  }
    public function setHireDate($value)  { $this->hireDate = $value; }
}
```

Code that uses the subclass

```
$emp = new Employee('John', 'Doe', '999-14-3456', '8-25-1996');
$emp->setPhone('919-555-4321');  // Inherited from Person Class
```

Description

- *Inheritance* provides a way to create a new class based on an existing class. The new class *inherits* the properties and methods of the existing class.

- A class that inherits from a class is called a *subclass*, *derived class*, or *child class*. A class that is inherited by another class is called a *superclass*, *base class*, or *parent class*.

- A subclass can *extend* the superclass by adding new properties and methods. It can also *override* a method from the superclass with its own version of the method.

- A subclass can call a method from the superclass by prefixing the method name with the parent keyword and a double colon. The parent keyword is a reference to the superclass.

Figure 14-13   How to inherit a class

How to use the protected access modifier

So far, this chapter has used public and private access modifiers to control the visibility of properties and methods. When you use inheritance, you can also use the protected modifier to control when a property is inherited.

Figure 14-14 shows a table that summarizes how the three keywords work. For each keyword, there are two questions that must be answered. First, does the keyword allow the property or method to be accessed outside of the class? Second, does the keyword allow the property or method to be accessed by a subclass?

The answers to these questions show that a public property or method can always be accessed outside the current class. Conversely, a private property or method can never be accessed outside the current class. In contrast, a protected property or method can't be accessed outside the current class, but it can be accessed by subclasses.

To show how the protected modifier works, two classes are defined in this figure. The first class is the Person class. This class is similar to the Person class in the previous figure, except that the firstName and lastName properties are protected instead of private.

In the Person class, this change has no practical difference. When a subclass inherits from the Person class, however, the two protected properties are accessible within the subclass declaration. As a result, the getFullName method in the Employee class can access both of these protected properties as if they were defined in the Employee class.

If the firstName and lastName properties were defined as private in the Person class, the getFullName method in the Employee class would have to use the inherited getFirstName and getLastName methods to access the values in these properties. To see an example of this, you can look ahead to the next figure.

When you design your classes, you should be as restrictive as possible when choosing your access modifiers. If you initially give too much access to a property, you can't restrict the property later without breaking your application. For example, if you start with a public property and later change it to protected or private, any code outside the class declaration that relies on the public property no longer works and needs to be rewritten to use a get or set method instead. If, however, you start with a private property and later change it to protected or public, any code that uses get and set methods to access the private property still works.

How the access modifiers work

Modifier	Access outside class?	Access from subclass?
public	Yes	Yes
protected	No	Yes
private	No	No

A superclass

```
class Person {
    protected $firstName, $lastName;
    private   $phone, $email;

    // The constructor and the get and set methods are the same
    // as the Person class in figure 14-13
}
```

A subclass

```
class Employee extends Person {
    private $ssn, $hireDate;

    // The constructor and the get and set methods are the same
    // as the Employee class in figure 14-13

    // This method uses the protected properties from the Person class
    public function getFullName() {
        return $this->lastName . ', ' . $this->firstName;
    }
}
```

Description

- Public and protected properties and methods are inherited by the subclass.
- Private properties and methods are not inherited by the subclass.

Figure 14-14   How to use the protected access modifier

How to create abstract classes and methods

An *abstract class* is a class that can't be used to create an object. However, abstract classes are useful when you want to provide a superclass that other classes can inherit, but you don't want objects to be created from the superclass. Then, you can code a subclass that inherits the abstract class, and you can create objects from that subclass.

Figure 14-15 shows how to work with abstract classes. To declare an abstract class, you include the abstract keyword in the class declaration as shown in the Person class.

Within an abstract class, you can use the abstract keyword to create abstract methods. An *abstract method* is a method that does not have any code to execute. It forces the subclass to implement the method, but it leaves all of the details of the implementation to the subclass. In this figure, for example, the Person class includes an abstract method named getFullName.

You can declare an abstract method by coding the abstract keyword followed by an access modifier, the function keyword, the method name, and the method parameters in parentheses. Note that an abstract method does *not* include a set of braces or any statements within those braces.

The first example in this figure defines an abstract class named Person that can be used as a superclass for other classes such as the Customer and Employee classes. This superclass defines an abstract method named getFullName that must be implemented by any subclasses.

The second example defines a Customer class that inherits the Person class. Since this subclass isn't declared as abstract, it's known as a *concrete class*. Note that this subclass provides an implementation of the abstract getFullName method. If this class didn't implement this method, PHP would issue a fatal error.

The third example attempts to create an object from the abstract Person class. This code generates a fatal error. Instead, you must create an object from the concrete Customer class as shown in the fourth example.

An abstract class with an abstract method

```
abstract class Person {
    private $firstName, $lastName, $phone, $email;

    // The constructor and the get and set methods are the same
    // as the Person class in figure 14-13

    // An abstract method
    abstract public function getFullName();
}
```

A concrete class that implements an abstract class

```
class Customer extends Person {
    private $cardNumber, $cardType;

    public function __construct($first, $last, $phone, $email) {
        $this->setPhone($phone);
        $this->setEmail($email);
        parent::__construct($first, $last);
    }

    public function getCardNumber()           { return $this->cardNumber;       }
    public function setCardNumber($value) { $this->cardNumber = $value; }
    public function getCardType()              { return $this->cardType;        }
    public function setCardType($value)    { $this->cardType = $value;   }

    // Concrete implementation of the abstract method
    public function getFullName() {
        return $this->getFirstName() . ' ' . $this->getLastName();
    }
}
```

Code that attempts to create an object from the abstract class

```
$customer = new Person('John', 'Doe');    // Fatal error
```

Code that creates and uses an object from the concrete class

```
$customer = new Customer('John', 'Doe', '919-555-4321', 'jdoe@example.com');
echo '<p>' . $customer->getFullName() . '</p>';
```

Description

- An *abstract class* is a class that can't be used to create an object. It's useful as a superclass for other classes.

- An *abstract method* is a method that specifies the name and parameters for the method but doesn't provide a code block that implements the method.

- An abstract method can only be coded in an abstract class. However, an abstract class isn't required to have an abstract method.

- A *concrete class* is a class that can be used to create an object. A concrete subclass of an abstract class must provide an implementation for all abstract methods in the abstract class. Otherwise, PHP issues a fatal error.

Figure 14-15   How to create abstract classes and methods

How to create final classes and methods

Occasionally, you may need to make sure that a method doesn't get overridden by a method in a subclass. To do that, you can use the final keyword to create a *final method* as shown in figure 14-16. You may also need to make sure that a class doesn't get extended by a subclass. To do that, you can use the final keyword to create a *final class*.

The first example shows how to declare a final method. Here, the code declares the getFirstName method in the Person class as final. As a result, when the Employee class in the second example attempts to override the getFirstName method, it generates a fatal error.

The third example shows how to declare a final class. Here, the code declares the Employee class as final. Then, when the PartTime class in the fourth example attempts to inherit the Employee class, it generates a fatal error.

How to prevent a method from being overridden

A class with a final method

```
class Person {
    // Other properties and methods not shown here

    final public function getFirstName() {
        return $this->firstName;
    }
}
```

A subclass that attempts to override a final method leading to a fatal error

```
class Employee extends Person {
    // Other properties and methods not shown here

    // This method attempts to override a final method - fatal error
    public function getFirstName() {
        return ucwords($this->firstName);
    }
}
```

How to prevent a class from being inherited

A final class

```
final class Employee extends Person {
    // Properties and methods for class
}
```

A class that attempts to inherit a final class leading to a fatal error

```
class PartTime extends Employee {
    // Properties and methods for class
}
```

Description

- A *final method* cannot be overridden by a method in a subclass. As a result, all subclasses must use the final version of the method.
- A *final class* cannot be inherited by a subclass.

Figure 14-16   How to create final classes and methods

How to work with interfaces

In some languages such as C++, a class can inherit multiple classes. This is known as *multiple inheritance*. In PHP, a class can only inherit from one other class. However, a class can *implement* multiple *interfaces*. An interface defines a set of public methods that can be implemented by a class.

Figure 14-17 shows how to create and use interfaces. To create an interface, you code the interface keyword followed by the name of the interface and a set of braces. Within the braces, an interface can contain two types of statements. First, an interface can contain statements that define class constants. Second, an interface can contain statements that define methods. These methods must be public and can't contain a block of code. That's because these methods are abstract methods that must be implemented by the class that implements the interface.

Note that you can't declare properties in an interface. It's up to the class that implements the interface to determine what properties it needs to implement the methods in the interface.

The first example defines an interface named Showable. This interface specifies a single method named show that doesn't take any parameters.

The second example defines an interface named Testable. This interface specifies two methods named test1 and test2. Here, the test1 method accepts one parameter, and the test2 method accepts two parameters.

The third example defines an interface named Gender. This interface defines two constants named MALE and FEMALE.

The last example shows an Employee class that extends the Person class and implements the Showable interface. Since the Employee class implements the Showable interface, it must implement the show method defined by that interface. If it doesn't, PHP generates a fatal error. In this example, the Employee class implements the show method by using four echo statements to send some of the object's data to the web browser.

The fifth example shows the declaration for a Customer class that inherits the Person class and implements three interfaces: the Showable, Testable, and Gender interfaces. As a result, this class can use both of the constants defined by the Gender interface, and it must implement all methods specified by the Showable and Testable interfaces.

How to create an interface

The syntax

```
interface interfaceName {
    const contantName = contantValue;
    public function methodName( parameterList );
}
```

An interface to show an object

```
interface Showable {
    public function show();
}
```

An interface to require two test methods

```
interface Testable {
    public function test1($value1);
    public function test2($value1, $value2);
}
```

An interface that provides two constants

```
interface Gender {
    const MALE = 'm';
    const FEMALE = 'f';
}
```

A class that inherits a class and implements an interface

```
class Employee extends Person implements Showable {
    // The constructor and the get and set methods are the same
    // as the Person class in figure 14-13

    // Implement the Showable interface
    public function show() {
        echo 'First Name: ' . $this->getFirstName() . '<br />';
        echo 'Last Name: ' . $this->getLastName() . '<br />';
        echo 'SSN: ' . $this->ssn . '<br />';
        echo 'Hire Date: ' . $this->hireDate . '<br />';
    }
}
```

A class declaration that implements three interfaces

```
class Customer extends Person implements Showable, Testable, Gender { ... }
```

Description

- An *interface* defines a set of public methods that can be *implemented* by a class. The interface doesn't provide any code to implement the methods, but it provides the method names and parameter lists.

- All methods in an interface must be public and cannot be static.

- A class that implements an interface must provide an implementation for each method defined by the interface.

- An interface can define class constants that are available to any class that implements the interface.

- Although a class can only inherit one class, it can implement multiple interfaces.

Figure 14-17   How to work with interfaces

Perspective

Object-oriented programming provides many benefits. It promotes code reuse and makes it easier to test, debug, and maintain your code. These benefits can speed development time, especially for large projects. Also, since object-oriented techniques allow you to organize your code in multiple classes that function as independent modules, it makes it easier for multiple programmers to work on the same project.

Terms

object-oriented programming	static method
class	class method
object	clone an object
property	shallow copy
method	introspection
encapsulation	reflection
data hiding	inheritance
scalar value	subclass
public property	derived class
private property	child class
protected property	superclass
constructor method	base class
constructor	parent class
destructor method	inherit a class
destructor	extend a class
object access operator	override a method
instance	abstract class
instantiation	abstract method
object chaining	concrete class
class constant	final method
scope resolution operator	final class
Paamayim Nekudotayim	multiple inheritance
static property	interface
class property	

Summary

- When you use *object-oriented programming*, a *class* defines the *properties* and *methods* of each type of *object*. Then, you can create an object with those properties and methods from the class.

- A *constructor method*, or just *constructor*, is a special method within a class that is used to create an object from the class. A *destructor method* is a special method that's executed when an object is no longer available for use.

- An object is an *instance* of a class. The process of creating an object from a class is sometimes called *instantiation*.

- A *public property* can be directly accessed by code outside of the class. *Private* and *protected properties* can't be directly accessed by code outside the class.

- A *method* is a function that's coded within a class. It can be accessed from the object.

- The *object access operator* (->) provides access to an object's properties and methods.

- A *class constant* is a constant value that belongs to the class, not to objects that are created from the class. To access a class constant, you can code the name of the class followed by a double colon, which is known as the *scope resolution operator*.

- A *static property* or *static method* is a property or method that belongs to a class, not to objects created from the class. As a result, these properties and methods are also referred to as *class properties* and *class methods*.

- To create a second reference to an object, you can use the equals (=) operator. To create a copy, or *clone*, of an object, you must use the clone operator.

- When you create a copy of an object, PHP makes a *shallow copy* of the object. This means that PHP doesn't create copies of nested objects within the original object.

- Writing code that inspects an object is known as *introspection* or *reflection*.

- *Inheritance* provides a way to create a new class based on an existing class. The new class *inherits* the properties and methods of the existing class.

- A class that inherits from a class is called a *subclass*, *derived class*, or *child class*. A class that is inherited by another class is called a *superclass*, *base class*, or *parent class*.

- A subclass can *extend* the superclass by adding new properties and methods. It can also *override* a method from the superclass with its own version of the method.

- An *abstract class* is a class that can't be used to create an object. An *abstract method* is a method that specifies the name and parameters for the method but doesn't provide a block of code that implements the method.

- A *concrete class* is a class that can be used to create an object.

- A *final method* can't be overridden by a method in a subclass. A *final class* can't be inherited by a subclass.

- An *interface* defines a set of public methods that can be *implemented* by a class. The interface doesn't provide any code to implement the methods, but it provides the method names and parameter lists.

Exercise 14-1   Modify the Product Manager application

In this exercise, you will modify and enhance the Product Manager application described in this chapter. In addition, you will modify and enhance the Product Catalog application that uses the same model as the Product Manager application.

Open and test the application

1. Run the application that's stored in the ex_starts/ch14_ex1 directory.

2. Test this application by adding and deleting a product.

3. Open the product_manager/index.php file for this application and review the code. Then, open the model/category.php and model/product.php file for this application and review the code.

Use set methods to set data in the objects

4. Modify the constructor for the Category class so that it has zero parameters and sets the properties to default values.

5. Modify all code in the application that creates a Category object so it uses the set methods to set the data in the object.

6. Modify the constructor for the Product class so it has zero parameters and sets all properties to default values.

7. Modify all code in the application that creates a Product object so it uses the set methods to set the data in the object.

8. Test this application by adding and deleting a product.

Use regular methods instead of static methods

9. Modify the CategoryDB class so it uses regular methods instead of static methods.

10. Modify all code that uses the CategoryDB class so it creates a CategoryDB object and calls regular methods from that object.

11. Modify the ProductDB class so it uses regular methods instead of static methods.

12. Modify all code that uses the ProductDB class so it creates a ProductDB object and calls regular methods from that object.

13. Test this application by adding and deleting a product.

Modify the Product Catalog application

14. Open the product_catalog/index.php file for this application and review its code.

15. Modify all of this code so it works correctly with the new model.

16. Test this application by viewing at least one product in each category.

15

How to use regular expressions, handle exceptions, and validate data

In this chapter, you'll learn how to create regular expressions and use them to validate the data that's submitted in a form. You'll also learn how exceptions work and how to use them to handle errors in your code. After you study the code for the Registration application at the end of this chapter, you'll be able to develop applications that provide complete data validation.

How to use regular expressions **462**
How to create and use regular expressions 462
How to match characters 464
How to use the character class 466
How to create complex patterns 468
How to use look-ahead assertions 470
How to use a multiline regular expression 472
How to use a global regular expression 472
How to replace a regular expression with a string 474
How to split a string on a regular expression 474
Regular expressions for data validation 476

How to handle exceptions **478**
How to create and throw exceptions 478
How to use the try-catch statement 480

The Registration application **482**
The user interface 482
The file structure 482
The model 484
The controller 492
The view 494
A long version of the Registration application 496

Perspective **498**

How to use regular expressions

Regular expressions are coded patterns that you can use to search for matching patterns in text strings. These expressions are commonly used to validate the data that users enter in web forms.

How to create and use regular expressions

Figure 15-1 shows how regular expressions work. To start, you create a string that holds the regular expression pattern inside a pair of forward slashes. In this figure, the first pattern simply matches the text "Harris".

Once you've created the regular expression, you can use the preg_match function to determine if a match is found in a string. In the first example in this figure, the first preg_match function searches for the pattern "Harris" in the $author string. Since that string contains the pattern, the function returns 1. Then, the second preg_match function searches for the pattern in the $editor string. Since that string doesn't contain the pattern, the function returns 0.

If there is an error in the regular expression, the preg_match returns FALSE. Since FALSE and 0 are treated as equal when you use the equality operator (==), you need to test for FALSE with the identity operator (===) before testing if the result is 1 or 0.

By default, the search that's done is case-sensitive. However, you can change that to case-insensitive as shown in the last example. To do this, you code a lowercase i after the closing slash in the regular expression. In this example, the case-insensitive pattern "murach" matches "Murach" in the $editor string.

A function to match a regular expression in a string

Function	Description
`preg_match($pattern, $string)`	Searches the specified string for a match to the specified regular expression. It returns 1 if the pattern is found and 0 if it's not found. If there is an error in the pattern, it returns FALSE.

How to use the preg_match function

How to create a regular expression

```
$pattern = '/Harris/';
```

Two strings to test

```
$author = 'Ray Harris';
$editor = 'Joel Murach';
```

How to use the preg_match method to search for the pattern

```
$author_match = preg_match($pattern, $author);   // $author_match is 1
$editor_match = preg_match($pattern, $editor);   // $author_match is 0
```

How to test for errors in a regular expression

```
if ($author_match === false) {
    echo 'Error testing author name.';
} else if ($author_match === 0) {
    echo 'Author name does not contain Harris.';
} else {
    echo 'Author name contains Harris.';
}
```

A case-insensitive regular expression

A case-insensitive regular expression

```
$pattern = '/murach/i';
```

How to use a case-insensitive regular expression

```
$editor_match = preg_match($pattern, $editor);   // $editor_match is 1
```

Description

- A *regular expression* defines a pattern that can be searched for in a string. The pattern is case sensitive and enclosed in forward slashes in a text string.

- To create a case-insensitive regular expression, add an i modifier to the end of the regular expression. Then, the case is ignored in both the pattern and string.

Figure 15-1   How to create and use a regular expression

How to match characters

In a regular expression, letters and numbers stand for themselves. Matching other characters, however, can become quite complex. Figure 15-2 shows how to match other characters in a pattern.

The first table in this figure shows how to include special characters in a pattern. To do that, you start with the *escape character*, which is the backslash. For instance, \\ is equivalent to one backslash, \/ is equivalent to one forward slash, and \n matches a new line character. You can also match characters by their Latin-1 code using the \x sequence followed by the Latin-1 code in hexadecimal. For example, \xA9 matches the © character.

When using the sequence \\ to match a single backslash, you have to use the sequence \\\\ to get the desired result. That's because both single and double-quoted PHP strings convert the \\ pair to a single backslash. As a result, the string "/\\/" would become the pattern /\/ which would cause an error. Instead, you have to enter the string "/\\\\/" for it to become the pattern /\\/ which then tests for a single backslash.

The second table shows how to match types of characters instead of specific characters. For example, if the pattern is /MB\d/, it matches the letters MB followed by any digit. If the pattern is /MB.../, it matches the letters MB followed by any three characters.

When a character, such as the backslash, has a special meaning in a pattern, it's called a *metacharacter*. The purpose of the backslash is to toggle a character between a regular character and a metacharacter.

Some characters (typically punctuation) start as metacharacters and the backslash turns off their special meaning. For example, the period starts as a metacharacter that matches any character. To match a period, you must use the backslash to turn the period from a metacharacter into a regular character.

Other characters (typically letters and digits) start as regular characters and the backslash turns on their special meaning. For example, the letter d starts as a regular character. The sequence \d, however, turns on the special meaning and that sequence matches any digit.

When working with regular expressions, one of the most common mistakes is to forget when a character is a regular character and when it's a metacharacter. So, as you read through the next few figures, notice which characters start as metacharacters and which start as regular characters. So far, the metacharacters you've encountered are the forward slash, backslash, and period. Other common ones are: [ ] $ ^ ( ) | { } ? + *

Also, some characters have different meanings depending on their context. For example, the – is normally a regular character, but when it's inside brackets, it becomes a metacharacter as shown in the next figure.

How to match special characters

Pattern	Matches
\\	Backslash character
\/	Forward slash
\t	Tab
\n	New line
\r	Carriage return
\f	Form feed
\xhh	The Latin-1 character whose value is the two hexadecimal digits

Special characters

```
$string = "© 2010 Mike's Music. \ All rights reserved (5/2010).";
preg_match('/\xA9/', $string)          // Matches © and returns 1
preg_match('///', $string)             // Returns FALSE and issues a warning
preg_match('/\//', $string)            // Matches / and returns 1
preg_match('/\\\\/', $string)          // Matches \ and returns 1
```

How to match types of characters

Pattern	Matches
.	Any single character except a new line character (use \. to match a period)
\w	Any letter, number, or the underscore
\W	Any character that's not a letter, number or the underscore
\d	Any digit
\D	Any character that's not a digit
\s	Any whitespace character (space, tab, new line, carriage return, form feed, or vertical tab)
\S	Any character that's not whitespace

Types of characters

```
$string = 'The product code is MBT-3461.';
preg_match('/MB./', $string)           // Matches MBT and returns 1
preg_match('/MB\d/', $string)          // Matches nothing and returns 0
preg_match('/MBT-\d/', $string)        // Matches MBT-3 and returns 1
```

Description

- The backslash is the *escape character* in regular expressions. It gives special meaning to some characters and removes the special meaning from others.

- Since the backslash is the escape character in patterns, any backslash in your pattern must be preceded by another backslash. Then, since the backslash is also the escape character in PHP strings, each backslash must be preceded by another backslash.

- When a character has a special meaning in a pattern, it's called a *metacharacter*.

Figure 15-2   How to match characters

How to use the character class

The *character class* lets you build a list of characters to match against a single character. Figure 15-3 shows how to create and use a character class in a regular expression. To do that, you code an opening bracket followed by the characters you want to match and a closing bracket.

In the first example, the first character class matches either an uppercase T or F. The second character class matches a period. This is similar to the sequence \. outside of a character class. And the third character class matches any odd digit.

Most metacharacters lose their special meaning inside a character class. However, there are two metacharacters that work inside a character class.

The first metacharacter inside a character class is the caret. When used as the first character in the character class, the entire character class is negated. That is, it matches any character *except* the characters listed in the class.

The second metacharacter inside a character class is the dash. When used between two characters, it represents the range of characters between them. If you want to use the dash as a regular character in a character class, just place it at the end of the list of characters.

In the second example, the first character class matches any character except a T or F. The second matches any character except a caret. The third matches the digits 1 through 5. The fourth matches an underscore, asterisk, or dash.

You can also use *bracket expressions* in a character class. A bracket expression is a named range of characters. For example, the [:lower:] expression is equivalent to the range a-z. The [:alnum:] expression is equivalent to the ranges a-zA-Z0-9. Although bracket expressions don't provide any new functionality, you can use them to make your regular expressions easier to read.

The third example shows how to use bracket expressions. Note that the bracket expressions must be inside a character class.

You can use multiple bracket expression in a single character class. You can also use other characters, the dash, and the caret along with bracket expressions. For example, this character class

```
[^[:lower:]1-5AEIOU]
```

matches any character except a lowercase letter, a digit 1 through 5, or an uppercase vowel.

How to use the character class

Pattern	Matches
[*chars*]	A single character that is listed inside the brackets (use \[or \] to match a bracket)

The character class

```
$string = 'The product code is MBT-3461.';
preg_match('/MB[TF]/', $string)          // Matches MBT and returns 1
preg_match('/[.]/', $string)             // Matches . and returns 1
preg_match('/[13579]/', $string)         // Matches 3 and returns 1
```

Metacharacters inside a character class

Character	Example	Meaning
^	[^aeiou]	Negates the list of characters inside the character class
-	[a-z]	Creates a range of characters based on their Latin-1 character set values

Metacharacters

```
preg_match('/MB[^TF]/', $string)         // Matches nothing and returns 0
preg_match('/MBT[^^]/', $string)         // Matches MBT- and returns 1
preg_match('/MBT-[1-5]/', $string)       // Matches MBT-3 and returns 1
preg_match('/MBT[_*-]/', $string)        // Matches MBT- and returns 1
```

How to use bracket expressions in a character class

Pattern	Matches
[:digit:]	Digits (same as \d)
[:lower:]	Lower case letters
[:upper:]	Upper case letters
[:letter:]	Upper and lower case letters
[:alnum:]	Upper and lower case letters and digits
[:word:]	Upper and lower case letters, digits, and the underscores (same as \w)
[:print:]	All printable characters including the space
[:graph:]	All printable characters excluding the space
[:punct:]	All printable characters excluding letters and digits

Bracket expressions

```
preg_match('/MBT[[:punct:]]/', $string)  // Matches MBT- and returns 1
preg_match('/MBT[[:digit:]]/', $string)  // Matches nothing and returns 0
preg_match('/MB[[:upper:]]/', $string)   // Matches MBT and returns 1
```

Description

- A *character class* lets you match a single character from a list of possible characters.

- Most characters with a special meaning lose it inside the brackets. The caret and dash are the only characters that retain their special meanings, and they are position dependent.

- You can use a *bracket expression* inside a character class for several predefined character ranges, and you can combine several bracket expressions in one character class.

Figure 15-3   How to use the character class

How to create complex patterns

The techniques you've learned so far allow you to write some interesting regular expressions. When you add positional indicators and subpattern repetition as shown in figure 15-4, you can create complex patterns that can be used to validate almost any type of form data.

The first table describes the position indicator characters. Of these characters, the caret and dollar sign are commonly used to validate form data. When you use the two together together, you can indicate a pattern that the entire string must match.

The second table describes how to group part of a pattern into a subpattern. Here, the parentheses are used to create a numbered subpattern. You can then match the same pattern again later in the string using the \n sequence. You can also create an unnumbered subpattern by following the opening parenthesis with the ?: sequence.

In the examples, the first pattern matches the name Rob or Bob at the start of the string. The \b makes sure that the last letter of the name is the end of the name.

The second pattern matches three word characters at the start of the string followed by a space and the same three characters again. When the subpattern in parentheses is matched (to "Rob" in this example), the \1 sequence now stands for those three exact characters, not just the general pattern of three characters. As a result, this pattern will also match the string "Bob Bobbins" but not "Bob Robertson".

The third table describes how to match a repeating subpattern. The last three characters (?, +, and *) are convenient shortcuts for subpatterns that you can create using braces.

In the examples, the first pattern matches numbers in the format 559-555-1234. That is, three digits, a dash, three digits, a dash, and four digits.

The second pattern matches numbers in the format (559) 555-1234 with the space after the area code being optional. The pattern is a left parenthesis, three digits, a right parenthesis, an optional space, three digits, a dash, and four digits. Since this pattern uses the parentheses as regular characters rather than grouping metacharacters, they must be preceded by a backslash.

The third pattern combines the two previous patterns. For an area code, it matches three characters followed by a dash. Or, it matches a left parenthesis, three digits, a right parenthesis, and an optional space. Then, the rest of the pattern matches three digits, a dash, and four digits.

How to match string positions

Pattern	Matches
^	The beginning of the string (use \^ to match a caret)
$	The end of the string (use \$ to match a dollar sign)
\b	The beginning or end of a word (must not be inside brackets)
\B	A position other than the beginning or end of a word

String positions

```
$author = 'Ray Harris';
preg_match('/^Ray/', $author)                    // Returns 1
preg_match('/Harris$/', $author)                 // Returns 1
preg_match('/^Harris/', $author)                 // Returns 0

$editor = 'Anne Bohme';
preg_match('/Ann/', $editor)                      // Returns 1
preg_match('/Ann\b/', $editor)                    // Returns 0
```

How to group and match subpatterns

Pattern	Matches
(*subpattern*)	Creates a numbered subpattern group (use \(and \) to match a parenthesis)
(?:*subpattern*)	Creates an unnumbered subpattern group
|	Matches either the left or right subpattern
\n	Matches a numbered subpattern group

Subpatterns

```
$name = 'Rob Robertson';
preg_match('/^(Rob)|(Bob)\b/', $name)            // Returns 1
preg_match('/^(\w\w\w) \1/', $name)              // Returns 1
```

How to match a repeating pattern

Pattern	Matches
{*n*}	Pattern must repeat exactly *n* times (use \{ and \} to match a brace)
{*n*,}	Pattern must repeat *n* or more times
{*n*,*m*}	Subpattern must repeat from *n* to *m* times
?	Zero or one of the previous subpattern (same as {0,1})
+	One or more of the previous subpattern (same as {1,})
*	Zero or more of the previous subpattern (same as {0,})

Repeating patterns

```
$phone = '559-555-6627';
preg_match('/^\d{3}-\d{3}-\d{4}$/', $phone)        // Returns 1

$fax = '(559) 555-6635';
preg_match('/^\(\d{3}\) ?\d{3}-\d{4}$/', $fax)   // Returns 1

$phone_pattern = '/^(\d{3}-)|(\(\d{3}\) ?)\d{3}-\d{4}$/';
preg_match($phone_pattern, $phone)                 // Returns 1
preg_match($phone_pattern, $fax)                   // Returns 1
```

Figure 15-4   How to create complex patterns

How to use look-ahead assertions

In a regular expression, an *assertion* is a fact about the pattern that must be true. For example, you can use the ^ and $ metacharacters to make an assertion about the position of the pattern in the string.

Figure 15-5 shows how to use another type of assertion called a *look-ahead assertion* that places a condition on the characters that follow the assertion. This allows you to specify an additional pattern for a regular expression. Look-ahead assertions are position dependent. In other words, the pattern in the assertion must be matched starting at the current location in the string. To create a look-ahead assertion, you code an opening parenthesis followed by a question mark, an equal sign, the pattern for the assertion to test, and a closing parenthesis.

The first example shows how to use a look-ahead assertion. Without the assertion, the pattern matches a string that consists of six alphanumeric characters. However, the assertion places a further restriction on those six characters that at least one of them must be a digit. To do that, the assertion states that zero or more characters (.*) must be followed by a digit.

A *negative look-ahead assertion* is similar to a look-ahead assertion except that it checks to make sure its pattern is *not* matched. To create a negative look-ahead assertion, you can code an opening parenthesis followed by a question mark, an exclamation mark, the pattern for the assertion to test, and a closing parenthesis.

This figure also shows how to use a negative look-ahead assertion. Without the assertion, the pattern matches the digits 0 through 3 followed by any other digit. The negative look-ahead assertion excludes the numbers 32 to 39. It states that if the next digit is a 3 followed by a 2 through 9, the regular expression does not match the pattern.

You could also use a regular expression without the negative look-ahead assertion to perform the same test on the string like this:

```
/^([0-2][[:digit:]])|(3[0-1])$/
```

For a simple pattern, either form works equally well. When you have a more complex pattern, however, using an assertion often yields code that's shorter and easier to understand.

The second example shows a pattern that you can use to validate passwords. This example begins by showing the full pattern. Then, it explains the parts of the pattern. In short, the pattern ensures that a password consists of six or more characters with at least one digit and one punctuation character. Finally, the last two statements use the pattern to test two passwords. The first does not match the pattern, but the second does.

If necessary, you can modify this pattern to add, remove, or change some of its restrictions. For example, you can add another assertion that requires an uppercase letter.

How to match assertions

Pattern	Meaning
`(?=assertion)`	Creates a look-ahead assertion
`(?!assertion)`	Creates a negative look-ahead assertion

Two subpatterns for look-ahead assertions

```
(?=[[:digit:]])        // The next character in the pattern must be a digit
(?=.*[[:digit:]])      // The pattern must contain at least one digit
```

How to create a look-ahead assertion

A look-ahead assertion

```
$pattern = '/^(?=.*[[:digit:]])[[:alnum:]]{6}$/';
preg_match($pattern, 'Harris')      // Assertion fails and returns 0
preg_match($pattern, 'Harri5')      // Matches and returns 1
```

A negative look-ahead assertion

```
$pattern = '/^(?![3[2-9])[0-3][[:digit:]]$/';
preg_match($pattern, '32')          // Assertion fails and returns 0
preg_match($pattern, '31')          // Matches and returns 1
```

A pattern to enforce password complexity

The full pattern

```
$pw_pattern = '/^(?=.*[[:digit:]])(?=.*[[:punct:]])[[:print:]]{6,}$/';
```

The parts of the pattern

```
^                      // From the start of the string
(?=.*[[:digit:]])      // Must contain at least one digit
(?=.*[[:punct:]])      // Must contain at least one punctuation character
[[:print:]]{6,}        // Must contain six or more printable characters
$                      // With nothing else until the end of the string
```

Using the pattern

```
$password1 = 'sup3rsecret';
$password2 = 'sup3rse(ret';
preg_match($pw_pattern, $password1)      // Assertion fails and returns 0
preg_match($pw_pattern, $password2)      // Matches and returns 1
```

Description

- A *look-ahead assertion* is special type of subpattern that must be matched for the overall pattern to be matched.

- A look-ahead assertion must be matched starting immediately after the position of the assertion in the pattern.

- A *negative look-ahead assertion* is similar to a look-ahead assertion except that its pattern must *not* be matched.

Figure 15-5   How to use look-ahead assertions

How to use a multiline regular expression

A *multiline regular expression* allows the ^ and $ metacharacters to work with new line characters in the string in addition to the beginning and end of the string. You can create a multiline regular expression by coding an m at the end of the regular expression after the closing forward slash.

The example in figure 15-6 shows how to use a multiline regular expression. To start, this example creates a string that contains a new line character. As a result, the string contains two lines. Then, this example creates two similar patterns. The first one is not a multiline pattern, and the second one is a multiline pattern.

When the first pattern is tested, the dollar sign only matches the end of the string. Since the matched text occurs in the middle of the string, this pattern fails to match. When the second pattern is tested, the dollar sign also matches the end of a line in addition to the end of the string. Since the matched text occurs just before the new line character, this pattern matches the string.

How to use a global regular expression

A *global regular expression* allows you to find multiple matches of a pattern in a string. In PHP, you can use the preg_match_all function to return the substrings that match a pattern in an array.

The preg_match_all function has three parameters: a pattern, a string, and an array to store the matches to the pattern. This function returns the number of matches found, and it stores the matches in the third parameter, the $matches array. This array is a multi-dimensional array where the $matches[0] array stores all matches to the full pattern. The remaining arrays in the $matches array correspond to each of the numbered subgroups in the pattern. For example, $matches[1] contains the matches for the first numbered subgroup in the pattern.

The example shows how to use the preg_match_all function. To start, the function finds two matches of the pattern in the string. As a result, it returns a value of 2 and stores the matches in element 0 of the $matches array. Then, a foreach loop displays both of these matches.

How to work with a multiline regular expression

```
$string   = "Ray Harris\nAuthor";    // A multiline string

$pattern1 = '/Harris$/';              // A non-multiline regular expression
preg_match($pattern1, $string);       // Does not match Harris and returns 0

$pattern2 = '/Harris$/m';             // A multiline regular expression
preg_match($pattern2, $string);       // Matches Harris and returns 1
```

A function to find multiple matches in a string

Function	Description
preg_match_all(*$pattern*, *$string*, *$matches*)	Returns a count of the number of matches or FALSE if there is an error in the pattern.
	Also, stores all matched substrings as a multi-dimensional array in the $matches parameter. The first element ($matches[0]) is an array of the matched substrings. If your pattern contains numbered subpatterns, element 1 contains matches for the first subpattern, element 2 for the second, and so on.

How to work with a global regular expression

```
$string  = 'MBT-6745 MBT-5712';
$pattern = '/MBT-[[:digit:]]{4}/';

$count = preg_match_all($pattern, $string, $matches);   // Count is 2

foreach ($matches[0] as $match) {
    echo '<div>' . $match . '</div>';   // Displays MBT-6745 and MBT-5712
}
```

Description

- In a *multiline regular expression*, the ^ pattern matches the beginning of a line and the $ pattern matches the end of a line.

- In a *global regular expression*, the pattern finds multiple matches in the string.

Figure 15-6   How to use multiline and global regular expressions

How to replace a regular expression with a string

Figure 15-7 starts by showing how to use the preg_replace function to replace text that matches a pattern. This works similarly to the str_replace and stri_replace functions for working with strings described in chapter 9. However, the preg_replace function allows you to replace any text that can be specified with a regular expression.

The example replaces any text in the string that matches MBT or MBS with ITEM. Note that the function returns the modified string. As a result, you typically store the modified string in a variable. In this example, the code replaces the original string by storing the modified string in the same variable as the original string. However, you can also store the modified string in another variable.

How to split a string on a regular expression

Figure 15-7 also shows how to use the preg_split function to split a string on a regular expression. This works similarly to the explode function for working with strings that was described in chapter 9. However, the preg_split function allows you to use a regular expression to split the string. As a result, this function is useful when the delimiter is not as simple as one or two characters.

The example splits the string on a regular expression that matches one or more spaces and commas followed by an optional "and" with zero or more spaces. When this pattern is matched, the preg_split function splits the string. In this example, a poorly formatted list of item numbers is correctly split into an array.

Two more functions for working with regular expressions

Function	Description
preg_replace(*$pattern*, *$new*, *$string*)	Returns a string that's created by replacing the specified pattern in the specified string with a new substring.
preg_split(*$pattern*, *$string*)	Returns an array of strings that's created by splitting the specified string on the specified pattern.

How to use the preg_replace function to replace a pattern with a string

```
$items = 'MBT-6745 MBS-5729';
$items = preg_replace('/MB[ST]/', 'ITEM', $items);

echo $items;          // Displays ITEM-6745 ITEM-5729
```

How to use the preg_split function to split a string on a pattern

```
$items = 'MBT-6745 MBS-5729, MBT-6824, and MBS-5214';
$pattern = '/[, ]+(and[ ]*)?/';
$items = preg_split($pattern, $items);

// $items contains: 'MBT-6745', 'MBS-5729', 'MBT-6824', 'MBS-5214'

foreach ($items as $item) {
    echo '<li>' . $item . '</li>';
}
```

Description

- To replace a simple pattern in a string, you can also use the str_replace and stri_replace functions described in chapter 9.
- To split a string on a simple pattern, you can also use the explode function described in chapter 9.

Figure 15-7   Two more functions for working with regular expressions

Regular expressions for data validation

Figure 15-8 starts with some patterns that are commonly used for data validation. The first pattern is for phone numbers so it matches 3 digits at the start of the string, a hyphen, 3 more digits, another hyphen, and 4 digits at the end of the string. Similarly, the second pattern is for credit card numbers so it matches 4 digits followed by three repetitions of a hyphen and 4 digits.

The third pattern is for 5- or 9-digit ZIP codes. It requires 5 digits at the start of the string. Then, it uses the ? metacharacter with a subpattern that contains a hyphen followed by four digits. As a result, this subpattern is optional.

The fourth pattern is for dates in the mm/dd/yyyy format. For the month, this pattern accepts either a digit 1 through 9 with an optional leading zero or a 1 followed by a digit 0 through 2. For the date, this pattern accepts either a digit 1 through 9 with an optional leading zero, a 1 or 2 followed by any digit, or a 3 followed by a 0 or 1. For the year, this pattern accepts any 4 digits. Despite the complexity of this pattern, it still matches some invalid dates such as 04/31/2011. As a result, when you use this pattern, you still need to provide some additional validation.

The examples that follow the patterns show how they can be used in your code. The first example uses the phone number pattern with the preg_match function to validate a phone number. Since the phone number is valid, the function returns a 1 indicating a match was found.

The second example works the same, but it uses the date pattern. Since the year in this example only contains three digits, the function returns a 0 indicating a match wasn't found.

The third example shows a function named valid_email that validates an email address based on the Simple Mail Transport Protocol (SMTP) specification for how an email address may be formed. This specification calls the part before the @ symbol the local part and the part after the @ symbol the domain part.

In brief, this function splits the email into its two parts before and after the @ symbol. If there aren't two parts or the parts are too long, it returns FALSE. It then builds a regular expression to test the local part and returns FALSE if the test fails. Likewise, it builds a regular expression to test the domain part and returns FALSE if this test fails.

Of course, it's the patterns in this function that are the most difficult to understand. For instance, the [^\\\\"] pattern matches any character that's not a backslash or a double quote. And the (\\\\[\\\\"]) pattern matches either \\ or \" in a string. An expanded version of this function, including the patterns, is more fully explained in the application at the end of this chapter.

Regular expressions for testing validity

Phone numbers in this format: 999-999-9999

```
/^[[:digit:]]{3}-[[:digit:]]{3}-[[:digit:]]{4}$/
```

Credit card numbers in this format: 9999-9999-9999-9999

```
/^[[:digit:]]{4}(-[[:digit:]]{4}){3}$/
```

Zip codes in either of these formats: 99999 or 99999-9999

```
/^[[:digit:]]{5}(-[[:digit:]]{4})?$/
```

Dates in this format: mm/dd/yyyy

```
/^(0?[1-9]|1[0-2])\/(0?[1-9]|[12][[:digit:]]|3[01])\/[[:digit:]]{4}$/
```

Test a phone number for validity

```
$phone = '559-555-6624';                        // Valid phone number
$phone_pattern = '/^[[:digit:]]{3}-[[:digit:]]{3}-[[:digit:]]{4}$/';
$match = preg_match($phone_pattern, $phone);  // Returns 1
```

Test a date for a valid format, but not for a valid month, day, and year

```
$date = '8/10/209';                             // Invalid date
$date_pattern = '/^(0?[1-9]|1[0-2])\/'
              . '(0?[1-9]|[12][[:digit:]]|3[01])\/'
              . '[[:digit:]]{4}$/';
$match = preg_match($date_pattern, $date);      // Returns 0
```

A function that does complete validation of an email address

```
function valid_email ($email) {
    $parts = explode("@", $email);
    if (count($parts) != 2 ) return false;
    if (strlen($parts[0]) > 64) return false;
    if (strlen($parts[1]) > 255) return false;

    $atom = '[[:alnum:]_!#$%&\'*+\/=?^`{|}~-]+';
    $dotatom = '(\.' . $atom . ')*';
    $address = '(^' . $atom . $dotatom . '$)';
    $char = '([^\\\\"])';
    $esc  = '(\\\\[\\\\"])';
    $text = '(' . $char . '|' . $esc . ')+';
    $quoted = '(^"' . $text . '"$)';
    $local_part = '/' . $address . '|' . $quoted . '/';
    $local_match = preg_match($local_part, $parts[0]);
    if ($local_match === false || $local_match != 1) return false;

    $hostname = '([[:alnum:]]([-[:alnum:]]{0,62}[[:alnum:]])?)';
    $hostnames = '(' . $hostname . '(\.' . $hostname . ')*)';
    $top = '\.[[:alnum:]]{2,6}';
    $domain_part = '/^' . $hostnames . $top . '$/';
    $domain_match = preg_match($domain_part, $parts[1]);
    if ($domain_match === false || $domain_match != 1) return false;

    return true;
}
```

Figure 15-8   Regular expressions for data validation

How to handle exceptions

To prevent your applications from crashing due to runtime errors, you can write code that handles any *exceptions*. Exceptions are runtime errors that occur due to unexpected error conditions. You can also *throw* your own exceptions and then write code that handles them.

How to create and throw exceptions

Figure 15-9 shows how to create and throw an exception. To do that, you can create a new Exception object and use a *throw statement* to throw it.

To create a new Exception object, you call the Exception constructor and pass an argument to it that specifies the error message. In addition, you can pass an optional second argument that specifies an error code. Although you can store the exception object in a variable and then throw the variable, you typically create and throw the Exception object in the same statement.

The calculate_future_value function in this figure throws an exception when a parameter is invalid. If, for example, you pass 0 years to the function, it throws an exception that has an appropriate error message. When the exception is thrown, the function ends and control is passed back to the code that called it. Then, that code can catch the exception and display the error message as shown in the next figure.

The Exception object provides methods that you can use to get the error message, error code, and other information about the point in the code where the exception was thrown. This figure summarizes six of the most common methods available from the Exception object. In this next figure, you'll see how to use the getMessage method to display the error message.

The syntax for creating a new Exceptions

```
new Exception($message [, $code])
```

The syntax for the throw statement

```
throw $exception;
```

A function that may throw an Exception

```
function calculate_future_value($investment, $interest_rate, $years) {
    if ($investment <= 0 || $interest_rate <= 0 || $years <= 0 ) {
        throw new Exception("Please check your entries for validity.");
    }

    $future_value = $investment;
    for ($i = 1; $i <= $years; $i++) {
        $future_value =
            ($future_value + ($future_value * $interest_rate * .01));
    }
    return round($futureValue, 2);
}
```

A statement that causes an exception to be thrown

```
$futureValue = calculate_future_value(10000, 0.06, 0);  // Throws exception
```

Methods of Exception objects

Method	Description
getMessage()	Returns the message set in the Exception object
getCode()	Returns the code set in the Exception object
getFile()	Returns the file in which the Exception object was thrown
getLine()	Returns the line number at which the Exception object was thrown
getTrace()	Returns an array containing a stack trace for the Exception object
getTraceAsString()	Returns a string containing a stack trace for the Exception object

Description

- You can create an Exception object by using the syntax above. If the $message parameter isn't a string, it's converted to one. If the $code parameter isn't supplied, it's set to zero.

- You can use the *throw statement* to *throw* an Exception object. This triggers a runtime error called an *exception*. The throw statement can throw a new or existing Exception object.

- You can use the methods of an Exception object to find out more about the exception.

- A *stack trace* is a list of functions or methods in the reverse order in which they were called when the exception was thrown.

Figure 15-9   How to create and throw exceptions

How to use the try-catch statement

When an Exception object is thrown, your application needs to *catch* it and handle it. Otherwise, your application ends with a runtime error.

To catch exceptions, you use a *try-catch statement* as shown in figure 15-10. First, you code a *try block* around the statement or statements that may throw an exception. Then, you code a *catch block* that contains the statements that are executed if an exception is thrown by any statement in the try block. This is known as *exception handling*.

The first example shows how to use a try-catch statement to catch the exception thrown by the calculate_future_value function. Here, the first statement in the try block calls the calculate_future_value function. Since this function call contains an invalid third argument, it throws an exception. As a result, when the exception is thrown, control jumps over the rest of the statements in the try block and goes to the catch block. Within the catch block, the Exception object is stored in a variable named $e. Here, the first and only statement uses the getMessage method of the Exception object to display the error message in the browser.

In some cases, you may want to use a catch block to re-throw an exception as illustrated by the second example. Then, the catch block can execute some code before it re-throws the exception to the code that called it. This gives the catch block an opportunity to perform any cleaning up it may need to do before the exception is re-thrown.

In addition, there are times when you may want to code multiple catch blocks as illustrated by the third example. This allows you to handle multiple types of exceptions with a single try-catch statement. To understand how this works, you need to know that the Exception class represents the most general type of exception and its subclasses represent more specific types of errors. For example, the PDOException class is a subclass of the Exception class that represents a specific type of exception.

If you have multiple catch blocks, the first catch block that matches the class of the exception catches and handles the exception. Since all exceptions are subclasses of the Exception class, you can use the Exception class to catch all exceptions. As a result, if you want to catch more specific types of exceptions, you need to code the most specific exception classes first and end with the Exception class. In general, it's considered a good practice to end with a catch block for the Exception class since it catches any exceptions that don't match the preceding catch blocks. This is analogous to the default case in a switch statement.

Most of the time, you only need to use the Exception class and other built-in exceptions such as the PDOException class. However, if necessary, you can create your own custom exception classes that inherit the Exception class. To do that, you can use the skills for working with inheritance that were described in chapter 14.

The syntax for a try-catch statement

```
try { statements }
catch (ExceptionClass $exceptionName) { statements }
[ catch (ExceptionClass $exceptionName) { statements } ]
```

A try-catch statement that catches an Exception object

```
try {
    $fv = calculate_future_value(10000, 0.06, 0); // Throws error
    echo 'Future value was calculated successfully.';
} catch (Exception $e) {
    echo 'Error: ' . $e->getMessage();
}
```

A try-catch statement that re-throws an Exception object

```
try {
    $fv = calculate_future_value($investment, $annual_rate, $years);
} catch (Exception $e) {
    // if needed, do something before re-throwing the exception
    throw $e;
}
```

A try-catch statement that catches two types of exceptions

```
try {
    $db = new PDO($dsn, 'mmuser', 'pa55word', $options);
    // other statements
} catch (PDOException $e) {
    echo 'PDOException: ' . $e->getMessage();
} catch (Exception $e) {
    echo 'Exception: ' . $e->getMessage();
}
```

Description

- You can use a *try-catch statement* to *catch* any exceptions that are *thrown*.
- In a try-catch statement, you code a *try block* that contains the statements that may throw exceptions. Then, you code at least one *catch block* that contains the statements to execute when an exception is thrown in the try block.
- At the beginning of the catch block, you code the name of the class that defines the exception followed by a variable that allows you to access the exception object.
- If necessary, you can code a throw statement inside a catch block to *re-throw* the exception.
- The Exception class represents the most general type of exception and its subclasses represent more specific types of errors. For example, the PDOException class is a subclass of the Exception class that represents a specific type of exception.
- If you code multiple catch blocks, you should code the most specific Exception classes first and end with the Exception class.
- You can create a custom Exception object by inheriting the Exception class.

Figure 15-10   How to use the try-catch statement

The Registration application

To show you how to validate data in a real-world application, figure 15-11 presents a simple Registration application. This application validates the data that the user enters into the four fields of the form before processing that data.

Although the validation requirements for this form are limited, this application uses a highly structured, object-oriented approach to data validation that can be used to validate the data in any form. After you review this code, you'll be introduced to a longer version of this application that validates the data in several different types of fields. The code for that application is available in one of the downloadable applications for this chapter so you can re-use it in your own applications.

The user interface

Part 1 of figure 15-11 shows the user interface for the Registration application. Here, the user has submitted invalid data, and the form has been redisplayed with error messages next to the invalid data. Once the user submits valid data, the application can process the data and display the next page.

The file structure

Part 1 also shows the file structure for the Registration application. This application uses the Model-View-Controller pattern. To clearly show that pattern, this application stores its classes in the model directory, it stores most of its HTML in the view directory, and it stores the controller in the index.php file of the root directory.

The next four figures present the four highlighted files. The rest of the files aren't explained in this chapter because you shouldn't have any trouble understanding them by now. If you want to view them, they are available in the download for the book.

The user interface

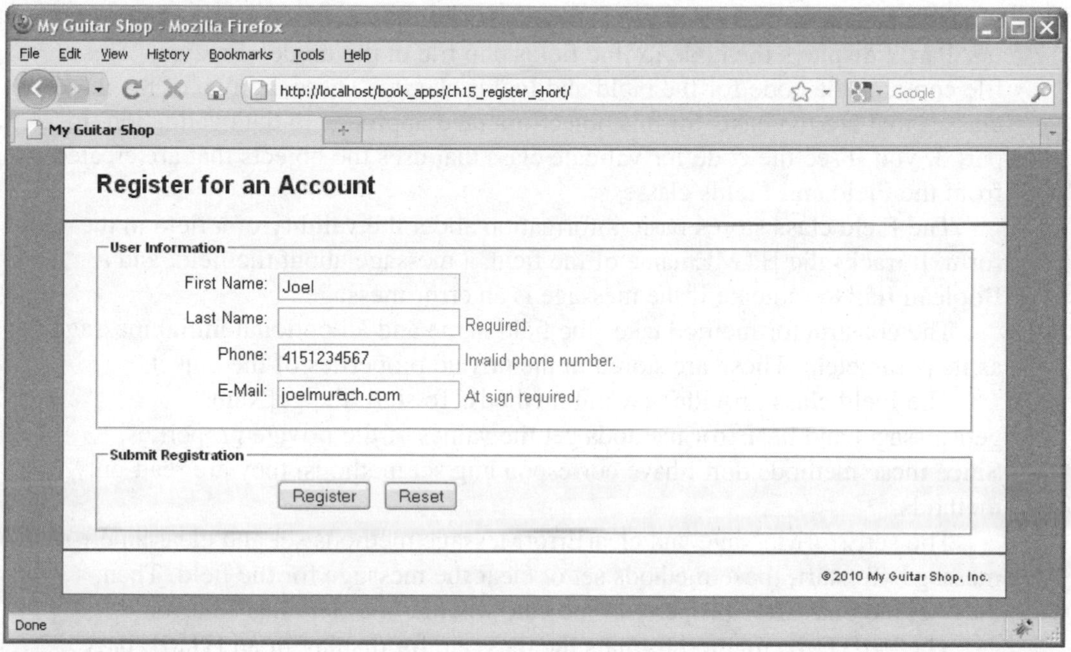

The file structure

app_root/
   model/
     fields.php   The Field and Fields classes
     validate.php   The Validate class
   view/
     header.php   The HTML and PHP for the header
     register.php   The HTML and PHP for the form view
     success.php   The HTML and PHP for the success view
     footer.php   The HTML and PHP for the footer
  index.php   The PHP for the controller
  main.css   The CSS for the application

Description

- This application uses a highly structured, object-oriented approach to data validation.
- The download for this book contains the complete code for this application.
- The next four figures present the four highlighted files.

Figure 15-11   The Registration application (part 1 of 7)

The model

Part 2 displays the code for the fields.php file in the model directory. This file contains the code for the Field and Fields classes. These are two of the three classes that are the basis for this object-oriented approach to data validation. In part 3, you'll see the code for Validate class that uses the objects that are created from the Field and Fields classes.

The Field class stores basic information about the validity of a field in the form. It tracks the HTML name of the field, a message about the field, and a Boolean flag to indicate if the message is an error message.

The constructor method takes the field name and an optional initial message as its parameters. These are stored in the private properties of the object.

The Field class provides several methods. To start, the getName, getMessage, and hasError methods get the values of the private properties. Since these methods don't have corresponding set methods, they are read-only methods.

The setErrorMessage and clearErrorMessage methods set and clear an error message. To start, these methods set or clear the message for the field. Then, they set the $hasError property to indicate whether the field has an error.

The getHTML method formats the message for display in an HTML page. First, it first uses the htmlspecialchars function to convert special characters such as ampersands to their HTML entity equivalent. Then, it returns the message wrapped in a <span> tag. If the field is an error, this code adds a class attribute with a value of "error" so the CSS for the application can format the <span> tag appropriately.

The Fields class stores Field objects in a private associative array. Since there's no work for the constructor method to do, it's omitted.

The addField method takes a field name and optional message as its parameters. Then, it creates a Field object and stores it the array using the field name as the key. Conversely, the getField method takes a field name and returns the appropriate Field object from the array.

The hasErrors method returns TRUE if any of the individual fields has an error. It uses a foreach loop to check the hasError method of each field object and returns TRUE if one is found to have an error. If none of the fields have an error, the method returns FALSE.

The Field and Fields classes (model/fields.php)

```php
<?php
class Field {
    private $name;
    private $message = '';
    private $hasError = false;

    public function __construct($name, $message = '') {
        $this->name = $name;
        $this->message = $message;
    }
    public function getName()    { return $this->name; }
    public function getMessage() { return $this->message; }
    public function hasError()   { return $this->hasError; }

    public function setErrorMessage($message) {
        $this->message = $message;
        $this->hasError = true;
    }
    public function clearErrorMessage() {
        $this->message = '';
        $this->hasError = false;
    }

    public function getHTML() {
        $message = htmlspecialchars($this->message);
        if ($this->hasError()) {
            return '<span class="error">' . $message . '</span>';
        } else {
            return '<span>' . $message . '</span>';
        }
    }
}

class Fields {
    private $fields = array();

    public function addField($name, $message = '') {
        $field = new Field($name, $message);
        $this->fields[$field->getName()] = $field;
    }

    public function getField($name) {
        return $this->fields[$name];
    }

    public function hasErrors() {
        foreach ($this->fields as $field) {
            if ($field->hasError()) return true;
        }
        return false;
    }
}
?>
```

Figure 15-11   The Registration application (part 2 of 7)

Parts 3 through 5 display the code for the validate.php file in the model directory. This file contains the code for the Validate class.

The Validate class has a Fields object as a private property. The constructor method initializes this object, and the getFields method returns a reference to it.

The text method validates the text in a field such as an address field. It takes the field name and value as required parameters. In addition, it takes three optional parameters that control whether the field is required, its minimum length, and its maximum length.

Within the test method, the first statement gets the Field object that corresponds with the name parameter. Then, an if statement checks whether the field is not required and empty. If so, the code clears the error message from the field and exits the method. Otherwise, the code checks whether the field is valid. If the field is not valid, the code uses the setErrorMessage method of the field to set its message and error flag. If the field is valid, the code uses the clearErrorMessage method of the field to clear its message and error flag.

The Validate class (model/validate.php)   **Page 1**

```php
<?php
class Validate {
    private $fields;

    public function __construct() {
        $this->fields = new Fields();
    }

    public function getFields() {
        return $this->fields;
    }

    // Validate a generic text field
    public function text($name, $value,
            $required = true, $min = 1, $max = 255) {

        // Get Field object
        $field = $this->fields->getField($name);

        // If field is not required and empty, remove errors and exit
        if (!$required && empty($value)) {
            $field->clearErrorMessage();
            return;
        }

        // Check field and set or clear error message
        if ($required && empty($value)) {
            $field->setErrorMessage('Required.');
        } else if (strlen($value) < $min) {
            $field->setErrorMessage('Too short.');
        } else if (strlen($value) > $max) {
            $field->setErrorMessage('Too long.');
        } else {
            $field->clearErrorMessage();
        }
    }
}
```

Figure 15-11   The Registration application (part 3 of 7)

The pattern method validates a value based on a regular exception such as a zip code field. It takes the field name, value, the pattern, and a message as its required parameters. In addition, it takes an optional fifth parameter that controls whether the field is required.

Within the pattern method, the first statement gets the Field object that corresponds with the name parameter. Then, an if statement checks whether the field is not required and is empty. If so, the code clears the error message and exits. Otherwise, it tests the value using the preg_match function. If there's an error in the pattern or if the pattern doesn't match the value, this code sets an appropriate error message in the field. If the pattern matches the value, this code clears the error message.

The phone method validates a phone number in a field. It takes the field name and value as required parameters. In addition, it takes an optional third parameter that controls whether the field is required.

Within the phone method, the first statement gets the Field object. Then, the second statement calls the text method and passes the three parameter values to it. If this method sets an error message in the Field object, the third statement exits the method. This code makes sure that the phone number field is a valid text object.

After making sure the phone number is a valid text field, this code calls the pattern method to make sure the phone number matches a pattern for a phone number. To start, the $pattern variable stores a regular expression for a phone number. Then, the $message variable stores an error message that's used if the phone number doesn't match the regular expression. Finally, this code passes these variables to the pattern method. In addition, this code passes the $name, $value, and $required parameters of the phone method to the pattern method. This makes sure that the phone number field matches the pattern.

The email method validates an email address in a field. It takes the field name and value as required parameters and a required flag as an optional parameter. Like the previous three methods, the email method begins by getting the Field object. Then, it exits if the field is empty and is not required. In addition, it checks whether the field is a valid text field and exits if it is not.

The Validate class (model/validate.php)   Page 2

```php
    // Validate a field with a generic pattern
    public function pattern($name, $value, $pattern, $message,
            $required = true) {

        // Get Field object
        $field = $this->fields->getField($name);

        // If field is not required and empty, remove errors and exit
        if (!$required && empty($value)) {
            $field->clearErrorMessage();
            return;
        }

        // Check field and set or clear error message
        $match = preg_match($pattern, $value);
        if ($match === false) {
            $field->setErrorMessage('Error testing field.');
        } else if ( $match != 1 ) {
            $field->setErrorMessage($message);
        } else {
            $field->clearErrorMessage();
        }
    }

    public function phone($name, $value, $required = false) {
        $field = $this->fields->getField($name);

        // Call the text method and exit if it yields an error
        $this->text($name, $value, $required);
        if ($field->hasError()) { return; }

        // Call the pattern method to validate a phone number
        $pattern = '/^[[:digit:]]{3}-[[:digit:]]{3}-[[:digit:]]{4}$/';
        $message = 'Invalid phone number.';
        $this->pattern($name, $value, $pattern, $message, $required);
    }

    public function email($name, $value, $required = true) {
        $field = $this->fields->getField($name);

        // If field is not required and empty, remove errors and exit
        if (!$required && empty($value)) {
            $field->clearErrorMessage();
            return;
        }

        // Call the text method and exit if it yields an error
        $this->text($name, $value, $required);
        if ($field->hasError()) { return; }
```

Figure 15-11   The Registration application (part 4 of 7)

After doing the preliminary field checks, this code splits the email address into its *local* and *domain* parts. If there are not two parts or either of the parts is too long, it sets an appropriate error message in the Field object. Otherwise, it uses regular expressions to test each part for validity.

According to the SMTP specification, the local part of an email address can be in one of two formats: an *address format* or a *quoted text format*. Of these two formats, the address format is the format that's almost always used. Although the quoted text format is rarely if ever used, it is still potentially valid. As a result, you should validate it or you run the risk of blocking a valid email address.

The address format starts with an *atom*, which is a letter, number, or one of 19 symbols (_!#$%&'*+/=?^'{|}~-). After that, an atom may be followed by other atoms. Or, an atom may be followed by zero or more atoms that are preceded by a dot. In other words, the address format can contain letters, numbers, and some symbols. However, it can't begin or end with a dot or have two consecutive dots. For example, "ray.harris" would be valid, but "ray..harris" or "ray." would not be valid.

The quoted text format contains text surrounded by double quotes. The text can contain any characters, but the double quote and backslash must be preceded by a backslash. For example, "Ray Harris" and "Ray\\Harris" are valid but "Ray\Harris" is invalid. In this code, the $char pattern matches any character that is not a backslash or double quote, and the $esc pattern matches either the \\ or \" escaped characters. As a result, the $text pattern matches any character or the escaped backslash or double quote, and the $quoted pattern is the $text pattern surrounded by double quotes.

The final pattern for the local part is a choice of either the address format or the quoted text format. Next, this code uses the pattern method to validate the local part of the email address against the pattern. If the local part is not valid, it sets an appropriate error message in the Field object and exits the method.

The domain part consists of one or more *host names* followed by a *top level domain*. A host name can have up to 64 letters, numbers, or hyphens, but can't start or end with a hyphen. The $hostname pattern matches a beginning alphanumeric character followed by an optional subpattern of up to 62 hyphens and alphanumeric characters with an ending alphanumeric character. This gives a total possible range of 1 to 64 characters.

When an email address has multiple host names, they must be separated by a dot. That's why the $hostnames pattern matches a $hostname pattern followed by zero or more host names that are preceded by a dot. Finally, the top level domain can have two to six letters or numbers and must be preceded by a dot.

The final pattern for the domain part is one or more hostnames followed by a top level domain. Next, this code uses the pattern method to validate the domain part of the email address. If the domain part is not valid, the pattern method sets an appropriate error message in the Field object. However, if the domain part is valid, the pattern method clears the error message from the Field object. As a result, the email address for the field is valid.

The Validate class (model/validate.php)   **Page 3**

```php
        // Split email address on @ sign and check parts
        $parts = explode('@', $value);
        if (count($parts) < 2) {
            $field->setErrorMessage('At sign required.');
            return;
        }
        if (count($parts) > 2) {
            $field->setErrorMessage('Only one at sign allowed.');
            return;
        }
        $local = $parts[0];
        $domain = $parts[1];

        // Check lengths of local and domain parts
        if (strlen($local) > 64) {
            $field->setErrorMessage('Username part too long.');
            return;
        }
        if (strlen($domain) > 255) {
            $field->setErrorMessage('Domain name part too long.');
            return;
        }

        // Patterns for address formatted local part
        $atom = '[[:alnum:]_!#$%&\'*+\/=?^`{|}~-]+';
        $dotatom = '(\.' . $atom . ')*';
        $address = '(^' . $atom . $dotatom . '$)';

        // Patterns for quoted text formatted local part
        $char = '([^\\\\"])';
        $esc  = '(\\\\[\\\\"])';
        $text = '(' . $char . '|' . $esc . ')+';
        $quoted = '(^"' . $text . '"$)';

        // Combined pattern for testing local part
        $localPattern = '/' . $address . '|' . $quoted . '/';

        // Call the pattern method and exit if it yields an error
        $this->pattern($name, $local, $localPattern,
                'Invalid username part.');
        if ($field->hasError()) { return; }

        // Patterns for domain part
        $hostname = '([[:alnum:]]([-[:alnum:]]{0,62}[[:alnum:]])?)';
        $hostnames = '(' . $hostname . '(\.' . $hostname . ')*)';
        $top = '\.[[:alnum:]]{2,6}';
        $domainPattern = '/^' . $hostnames . $top . '$/';

        // Call the pattern method
        $this->pattern($name, $domain, $domainPattern,
                'Invalid domain name part.');
    }
}
?>
```

Figure 15-11   The Registration application (part 5 of 7)

The controller

Part 6 presents the controller for the Registration application that's stored in the index.php file. This code checks all data entered on the registration page to see if it's valid.

The code for the controller begins by loading the fields.php and validate.php files that contain the classes. Then, it creates a new Validate object and stores it in the $validate variable. Next, it stores a reference to the Fields object in the $fields variable.

After getting the Fields object from the Validate object, this code uses the addField method to add a field for each of the fields in the form. This code gives a default message to the phone and email fields. As a result, when the browser loads the form for the first time, these messages are displayed to the user.

After the setting up the fields, the code checks whether a field named action exists in the global $_POST array. If so, this code copies the action to a local variable named $action. Otherwise, it sets the $action variable to a default value of "reset".

After getting the action, this code uses a switch statement to execute the appropriate code based on the current action. But first, it uses the strtolower function to convert the action string to all lowercase letters. Then, if the action is reset, this code displays the registration page using the default values for the fields and the controller ends.

If the action is register, the code copies the data for the form fields to local variables using the trim function to remove any leading or trailing spaces. Then, it uses the text, phone, and email methods of the Validate object to validate each of the form fields.

After validation, this code uses the hasErrors method of the Validate object to check whether any of the fields has an error. If so, it displays the registration page. Otherwise, it displays a page that indicates that the data was successfully entered.

Note that the calls to the text, email, and phone methods don't provide a value for the optional third argument that specifies whether the field is required. As a result, these fields use the default values provided by the methods. This means that the phone number field isn't required, but the other three fields are required. If you want to change the default value, of course, you can specify the third argument. For example, to require the phone number field, you can specify the third parameter like this:

```
$validate->phone('phone', $phone, true);  // require phone field
```

The controller (index.php)

```php
<?php
require_once('model/fields.php');
require_once('model/validate.php');

// Add fields with optional initial message
$validate = new Validate();
$fields = $validate->getFields();
$fields->addField('first_name');
$fields->addField('last_name');
$fields->addField('phone', 'Use 888-555-1234 format.');
$fields->addField('email', 'Must be a valid email address.');

if (isset($_POST['action'])) {
    $action =  $_POST['action'];
} else {
    $action =  'reset';
}

$action = strtolower($action);
switch ($action) {
    case 'reset':
        include 'view/register.php';
        break;
    case 'register':
        // Copy form values to local variables
        $first_name = trim($_POST['first_name']);
        $last_name = trim($_POST['last_name']);
        $phone = trim($_POST['phone']);
        $email = trim($_POST['email']);

        // Validate form data
        $validate->text('first_name', $first_name);
        $validate->text('last_name', $last_name);
        $validate->phone('phone', $phone);
        $validate->email('email', $email);

        // Load appropriate view based on hasErrors
        if ($fields->hasErrors()) {
            include 'view/register.php';
        } else {
            include 'view/success.php';
        }
        break;
}
?>
```

Figure 15-11   The Registration application (part 6 of 7)

The view

Part 7 presents the code for the first page of the Registration application. This code is stored in the register.php file in the view directory. Before PHP displays this page, it includes the header.php file. Similarly, PHP includes the the footer.php file after the form is displayed. These files display some boilerplate code for the header and footer for all pages of the application.

The <form> tag for this code submits the data to the controller using the post method. This tag has a class attribute of "alignedForm" to allow the CSS file for the application to control the layout of the form elements.

The next four <input> tags define text fields. The value of each text field corresponds with a PHP variable in the controller and is formatted with the htmlspecialchars function. When the form is displayed for the first time, these variables are empty and so are the text boxes. If the user enters invalid data, however, these variables contain data. This allows the application to redisplay the original data so the user doesn't have to retype it.

After each of these text fields, the PHP code gets the Field object that corresponds with the field. Then, it displays that field's message by calling the getHTML method of the Field object.

The form ends with two submit buttons. These buttons have a name of "action" and a value of "Register" or "Reset". As a result, clicking on these buttons submits the action that's triggered in the controller. This means that these buttons allow the user to submit the form data to the controller or to reset the form fields back to their original values.

The view (view/register.php)

```php
<?php include 'header.php'; ?>
<div id="content">
    <form action="." method="post">
    <fieldset>
        <legend>User Information</legend>
            <label>First Name:</label>
                <input type="text" name="first_name"
                    value="<?php echo htmlspecialchars($first_name);?>">
                <?php echo $fields->getField('first_name')->getHTML(); ?>
                <br>
            <label>Last Name:</label>
                <input type="text" name="last_name"
                    value="<?php echo htmlspecialchars($last_name);?>">
                <?php echo $fields->getField('last_name')->getHTML(); ?>
                <br>
            <label>Phone:</label>
                <input type="text" name="phone"
                    value="<?php echo htmlspecialchars($phone);?>">
                <?php echo $fields->getField('phone')->getHTML(); ?>
                <br>
            <label>E-Mail:</label>
                <input type="text" name="email"
                    value="<?php echo htmlspecialchars($email);?>">
                <?php echo $fields->getField('email')->getHTML(); ?>
                <br>
    </fieldset>
    <fieldset>
        <legend>Submit Registration</legend>
            <label> </label>
                <input type="submit" name="action" value="Register">
                <input type="submit" name="action" value="Reset" />
                <br>
    </fieldset>
    </form>
</div>
<?php include 'footer.php'; ?>
```

Figure 15-11   The Registration application (part 7 of 7)

A long version of the Registration application

Figure 15-12 shows the user interface for the long version of the Registration application. This version of the application validates most of the fields that web applications commonly need to validate. Although the code for this application isn't shown in this chapter, it is available in the download for the book. Once you understand the code for the short version, you shouldn't have much trouble understanding the code for the long version.

If you compare the code for the long version of the application with the code for the short version, you'll see that the long version uses the same Field and Fields classes as the short version. In addition, the long version uses a Validate class that's similar to the one that's used in the short version. As a result, most of the additional code is in the view for the application, not in the Validate class or the controller. This shows that it's easy to modify this structured approach to data validation so it can be used to validate the fields on most forms.

A long version of the Registration application

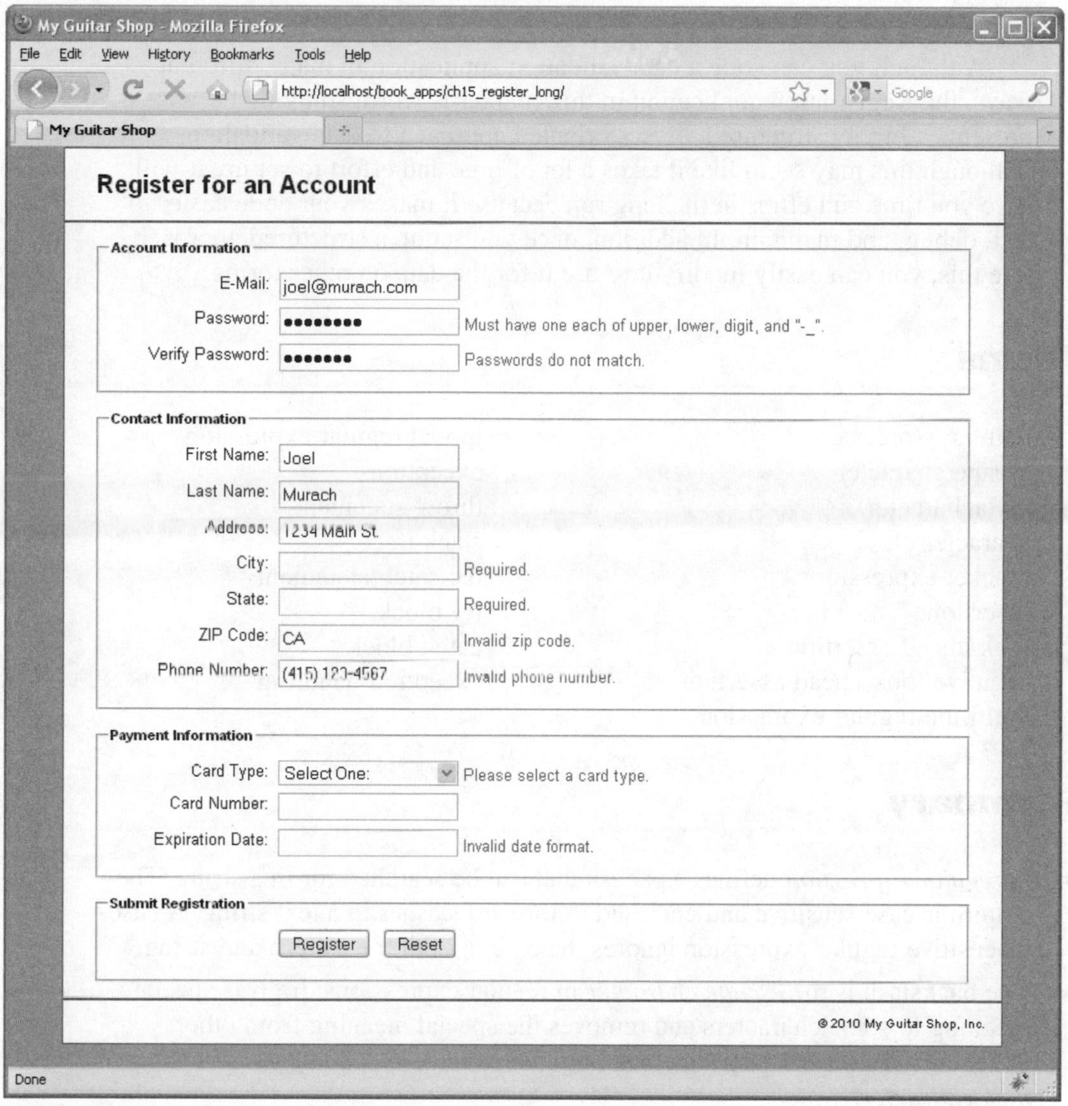

Description

- This long version of the application is like the short version, but it provides methods for validating most types of user entries.
- The download for this book contains the complete code for this application.

Figure 15-12   A long version of the Registration application

Perspective

Although you can code a data validation application in many different ways, the Registration application in this chapter is worth studying because it presents a highly structured, object-oriented approach to data validation. Although this may seem like it takes a lot of time and effort to set up, it will save you time and effort in the long run because it makes your code easier to test, debug, and maintain. In addition, once you set up a structured approach like this, you can easily modify it to use it for the data on other forms.

Terms

regular expression	global regular expression
escape character	exception
metacharacter	throw statement
character class	stack trace
bracket expression	try-catch statement
assertion	try block
look-ahead assertion	catch block
negative look-ahead assertion	exception handling
multiline regular expression	

Summary

- A *regular expression* defines a pattern that can be searched for in a string. The pattern is case sensitive and enclosed in forward slashes in a text string. A case-insensitive regular expression ignores the case in both the pattern and string.

- The backslash is the *escape character* in regular expressions. It gives special meaning to some characters and removes the special meaning from others. When a character has a special meaning in a pattern, it's called a *metacharacter*.

- A *character class* lets you match a single character from a list of possible characters. You can use a *bracket expression* inside a character class for several predefined character ranges, and you can combine several bracket expressions in one character class.

- A *look-ahead assertion* is special type of subpattern that must be matched for the overall pattern to be matched. A *negative look-ahead assertion* is similar to a look-ahead assertion except that its pattern must *not* be matched.

- In a *multiline regular expression*, the ^ pattern matches the beginning of a line and the $ pattern matches the end of a line. In a *global regular expression*, the pattern finds multiple matches in the string.

- You can use the *throw statement* to *throw* an Exception object. That will trigger a runtime error called an *exception*. Then, you can use the methods of the object to get more information about the exception.

- A *stack trace* is a list of functions or methods in the reverse order in which they were called when the exception was thrown.

- You can use a *try-catch statement* to *catch* any exceptions that are *thrown*. In a try-catch statement, you code a *try block* that contains the statements that may throw exceptions. Then, you code at least one *catch block* that contains the statements to execute when an exception is thrown in the try block.

- According to the SMTP specification, an email address has a *local* part and a *domain* part. The local part of an email address can be in one of two formats: an *address format* or a *quoted text format*. The domain part consists of one or more *host names* followed by a *top level domain*.

Exercise 15-1   Modify the long version of the Registration application

In this exercise, you can modify and enhance the Registration application.

Open and test the application

1. Run the application that's stored in the ex_starts/ch15_ex1 directory.

2. Test this application by entering valid and invalid data. To test the credit card fields with valid data, you can use a Visa card with a number of 4111111111111111.

3. Open the index.php, validate.php, and register.php files for this application and review the code. Note that this code works like the short Registration application except that it gets more data from the user.

Modify the code

4. In the phone and zip methods of the Validate class, use the \d pattern instead of the [[:digit:]] pattern.

5. In the password method of the Validate class, modify the code so the password must be at least 8 characters long with at least one uppercase letter and one number. But don't require a lowercase letter or a special character.

6. Modify the index.php file so that the Address, City, State, and Zip fields are optional. To do that, you can pass a third argument to the text method of the Validate class.

7. Add a Birthdate field after the Phone number field that requires the user to enter a birthdate in this format: mm/dd/yyyy. To get this to work properly, add a birthdate method to the Validate class. This method should make sure that the birthdate isn't a date in the future.

Exercise 15-2   Modify the Product Manager application

In this exercise, you can modify and enhance the Product Manager application so it uses the validation techniques described in this chapter.

Open and test the application

1. Run the application that's stored in the ex_starts/ch15_ex2 directory.

2. Use the Product Manager application to add a new product. Test this application by entering valid and invalid data. Note that it doesn't handle all types of invalid data such as entering "xx" for the price. Note also that it doesn't display error messages on the Add Product page. Instead, it displays errors on a separate errors page.

3. Open the index.php file for the Product Manager application and review the code. Note that this code uses an if statement to make sure that none of the text boxes are empty.

Modify the code

4. Open the fields.php and validate.php files in the model directory. These are the files for the short form of the Registration application in figure 15-11.

5. Open the index.php file for the Product Manager application and modify it so it uses the fields.php and validate.php files to validate the product code and name. Both of these fields are required. In addition, the product code must be less than 11 characters.

6. In the validate.php file, add a function named number that validates numeric entries.

7. In the index.php file for the Product Manager application, modify the code so it uses the fields.php and validate.php files to validate the product price. This field is required and it can contain any valid number.

Section 3

Master MySQL programming

In section 1, you learned the basic skills for developing a database-driven web application. Now, this section will expand on those skills. When you're through with this section, you'll have all the skills that you need for developing database-driven web applications.

To start, you need to learn how to design the tables and indexes of a database, so that's what you'll learn in chapter 16. Then, in chapter 17, you'll learn how to use SQL's Data Definition Language (DDL) to create and maintain those tables and indexes. And in chapter 18, you'll learn how to use SQL's Data Manipulation Language (DML) to work with the data that's stored in the database.

Then, chapters 19 and 20 present the rest of the PHP skills that you need for developing database-driven applications. In chapter 19, you'll learn three ways to use PHP to work with MySQL and how to use prepared statements to improve the efficiency of your database operations. In chapter 20, you'll learn how to apply your PHP skills to a database application that uses large text columns in the context of a content management system.

16

How to design a database

In this chapter, you'll learn how to design a new database. To illustrate this process, this chapter uses an accounts payable (AP) database. This database keeps track of the invoices that a company receives from its vendors.

How to design a data structure **504**
The basic steps for designing a data structure 504
How to identify the data elements 506
How to subdivide the data elements 508
How to identify the tables and assign columns 510
How to identify the primary and foreign keys 512
How to enforce the relationships between tables 514
How normalization works 516
How to identify the columns to be indexed 518

How to normalize a data structure **520**
The seven normal forms 520
How to apply the first normal form 522
How to apply the second normal form 524
How to apply the third normal form 526
When and how to denormalize a data structure 528

A database design tool **530**
An introduction to MySQL Workbench 530
How to use MySQL Workbench to create database diagrams 532

Perspective **534**

How to design a data structure

Databases are often designed by *database administrators* (*DBAs*) or design specialists. This is especially true for large databases that have thousands of users. However, for small- and medium-sized web sites, the database for the web site is often designed by the web programmer.

How well a database is designed affects your ability to use SQL to work with the database. In general, a well-designed database is easy to understand and query, while a poorly-designed database is difficult to work with.

The topics that follow teach a basic approach for designing a *data structure*. We use that term to refer to a model of the database rather than the database itself. Once you design the data structure, you can use the techniques presented in the next chapter to create a database with that design.

The basic steps for designing a data structure

In many cases, you can design a data structure based on an existing real-world system. The illustration at the top of figure 16-1 presents a conceptual view of how this works. Here, all of the information about the people, documents, and facilities within a real-world system is mapped to the tables, columns, and rows of a database system.

As you design a data structure, each table represents one object, or *entity*, in the real-world system. Then, within each table, each column stores one item of information, or *attribute*, for the entity, and each row stores one occurrence, or *instance*, of the entity.

This figure also presents the six steps you can follow to design a data structure. You'll learn more about each of these steps in the topics that follow. In general, though, step 1 is to identify all the data elements that need to be stored in the database. Step 2 is to break complex elements down into smaller components. Step 3 is to identify the tables that will make up the system and to determine which data elements are assigned as columns in each table. Step 4 is to define the relationships between the tables by identifying the primary and foreign keys. Step 5 is to normalize the database to reduce data redundancy. And step 6 is to identify the indexes that are needed for each table.

To model a database system after a real-world system, you can use a technique called *entity-relationship (ER) modeling*. Because this is a complex subject of its own, I won't present it in this book. However, I have applied some of the basic elements of this technique to the design diagrams presented in this chapter. In effect, then, you'll be learning some of the basics of this modeling technique.

A database system is modeled after a real-world system

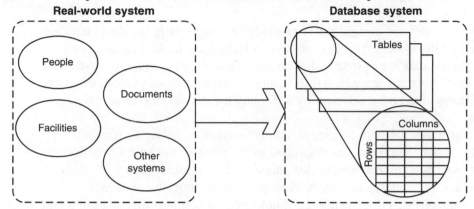

The six basic steps for designing a data structure

Step 1:   Identify the data elements

Step 2:   Subdivide each element into its smallest useful components

Step 3:   Identify the tables and assign columns

Step 4:   Identify the primary and foreign keys

Step 5:   Review whether the data structure is normalized

Step 6:   Identify the indexes

Description

- A relational database system should model the real-world environment where it's used. The job of the designer is to analyze the real-world system and then map it onto a relational database system.

- A table in a relational database typically represents an object, or *entity*, in the real world. Each column of a table is used to store an *attribute* associated with the entity, and each row represents one *instance* of the entity.

- To model a database and the relationships between its tables after a real-world system, you can use a technique called *entity-relationship (ER) modeling*. Some of the diagrams you'll see in this chapter apply the basic elements of ER modeling.

Figure 16-1   The basic steps for designing a data structure

How to identify the data elements

The first step for designing a data structure is to identify the data elements required by the system. You can use several techniques to do that, including analyzing the existing system if there is one, evaluating comparable systems, and interviewing anyone who will be using the system. Also, you can often get good information about a system by analyzing the documents for an existing system.

Figure 16-2, for example, shows an invoice that's used by an accounts payable system. We'll use this document as the main source of information for the database design presented in this chapter. Keep in mind, though, that you'll want to use all available resources when you design your own database.

If you study this document, you'll notice that it contains information about three different entities: vendors, invoices, and line items. First, the form itself has preprinted information about the vendor who issued the invoice, such as the vendor's name and address. If this vendor were to issue another invoice, this information wouldn't change.

This document also contains specific information about the invoice. Some of this information, such as the invoice number, invoice date, and invoice total, is general in nature. Although the actual information varies from one invoice to the next, each invoice includes this information. In addition to this general information, each invoice includes information about the items that were purchased. Although each line item contains similar information, each invoice can contain a different number of line items.

One of the things you need to consider as you review a document like this is how much information your system needs to track. For an accounts payable system, for example, you may not need to store detailed data such as the information about each line item. Instead, you may just need to store summary data like the invoice total. As you think about what data elements to include in the database, then, you should have an idea of what information you'll need to get back out of the system.

An invoice that can be used to identify data elements

Acme Fabrication, Inc.					
Custom Contraptions, Contrivances and Confabulations			Invoice Number:		I01-1088
1234 West Industrial Way East Los Angeles California 90022			Invoice Date:		10/05/10
800.555.1212 fax 562.555.1213 www.acmefabrication.com			Terms:		Net 30

Part No.	Qty.	Description	Unit Price	Extension
CUST345	12	Design service, hr	100.00	1200.00
457332	7	Baling wire, 25x3ft roll	79.90	559.30
50173	4375	Duct tape, black, yd	1.09	4768.75
328771	2	Rubber tubing, 100ft roll	4.79	9.58
CUST281	7	Assembly, hr	75.00	525.00
CUST917	2	Testing, hr	125.00	250.00
		Sales Tax		245.20

Your salesperson:	Ruben Goldberg, ext 4512	$7,557.83
Accounts receivable:	Inigo Jones, ext 4901	PLEASE PAY THIS AMOUNT

Thanks for your business!

The data elements identified on the invoice document

Vendor name	Invoice date	Item extension
Vendor address	Invoice terms	Vendor sales contact name
Vendor phone number	Item part number	Vendor sales contact extension
Vendor fax number	Item quantity	Vendor AR contact name
Vendor web address	Item description	Vendor AR contact extension
Invoice number	Item unit price	Invoice total

Description

- Depending on the nature of the system, you can identify data elements in a variety of ways, including interviewing users, analyzing existing systems, and evaluating comparable systems.

- The documents used by a real-world system, such as the invoice shown above, can often help you identify the data elements of the system.

- As you identify the data elements of a system, you should begin thinking about the entities that those elements are associated with. That will help you identify the tables of the database later on.

Figure 16-2   How to identify the data elements

How to subdivide the data elements

Some of the data elements you identify in step 1 of the design procedure will consist of multiple components. The next step, then, is to divide these elements into their smallest useful values. Figure 16-3 shows how you can do that.

The first example in this figure shows how you can divide the name of the sales contact for a vendor. Here, the name is divided into two elements: a first name and a last name. When you divide a name like this, you can easily perform operations like sorting by last name and using the first name in a salutation, such as "Dear Ruben." In contrast, if the full name is stored in a single column, you have to use the string functions to extract the component you need. However, that can lead to inefficient and complicated code. In general, then, you should separate a name like this whenever you'll need to use the name components separately. Later, when you need to use the full name, you can combine the first and last names using concatenation.

The second example shows how you typically divide an address. Notice in this example that the street number and street name are stored in a single column. Although you could store these components in separate columns, that usually doesn't make sense since these values are typically used together. That's what I mean when I say the data elements should be divided into their smallest *useful* values.

With that guideline in mind, you might even need to divide a single string into two or more components. A bulk mail system, for example, might require a separate column for the first three digits of the zip code. And a telephone number could require as many as four columns: one for the area code, one for the three-digit prefix, one for the four-digit number, and one for the extension.

As in the previous step, knowledge of the real-world system and of the information that will be extracted from the database is critical. In some circumstances, it may be okay to store data elements with multiple components in a single column. That can simplify your design and reduce the overall number of columns. In general, though, most designers divide data elements as much as possible. That way, it's easy to accommodate almost any query, and you don't have to change the database design later on when you realize that you need to use just part of a column value.

A name that's divided into first and last names

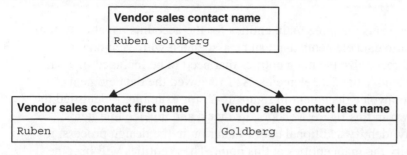

An address that's divided into street address, city, state, and zip code

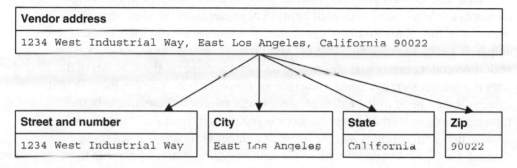

Description

- If a data element contains two or more components, you should consider subdividing the element into those components. That way, you won't need to parse the element each time you use it.

- The extent to which you subdivide a data element depends on how it will be used. Because it's difficult to predict all future uses for the data, most designers subdivide data elements as much as possible.

- When you subdivide a data element, you can easily rebuild it when necessary by concatenating the individual components.

Figure 16-3   How to subdivide the data elements

How to identify the tables and assign columns

Figure 16-4 presents the three main entities for the accounts payable system and lists the possible data elements that can be associated with each one. In most cases, you'll recognize the main entities that need to be included in a data structure as you identify the data elements. As I reviewed the data elements represented on the invoice document in figure 16-2, for example, I identified the three entities shown in this figure: vendors, invoices, and invoice line items. Although you may identify additional entities later on in the design process, it's sufficient to identity the main entities at this point. These entities will become the tables of the database.

After you identify the main entities, you need to determine which data elements are associated with each entity. These elements will become the columns of the tables. In many cases, the associations are obvious. For example, it's easy to determine that the vendor name and address are associated with the vendors entity and the invoice date and invoice total are associated with the invoices entity. Some associations, however, aren't so obvious. In that case, you may need to list a data element under two or more entities. In this figure, for example, the invoice number is included in both the invoices and invoice line items entities and the account number is included in all three entities. Later, when you normalize the data structure, you may be able to remove these repeated elements. For now, though, it's okay to include them.

Before I go on, I want to point out the notation that's used in this figure. To start, any data elements that weren't identified in previous steps are shown in italics. Although you should be able to identify most of the data elements in the first two steps of the design process, you'll occasionally think of additional elements during the third step.

Similarly, you may decide during this step that you don't need some of the data elements you've identified. For example, I decided that I didn't need the fax number or web address of each vendor. So I applied the strikethrough effect to indicate that these data elements should not be included.

Finally, I identified the data elements that are included in two or more tables by coding an asterisk after them. Although you can use any notation you like for this step of the design process, you typically want to document your design decisions. For a complicated design, you will probably want to use a *CASE (computer-aided software engineering)* tool such as the MySQL Work-bench tool that's described at the end of this chapter.

By the way, a couple of the new data elements that I added may not be clear to you if you haven't worked with a corporate accounts payable system before. "Terms" refers to the payment terms that the vendor offers. For example, the terms might be net 30 (the invoice must be paid in 30 days) or might include a discount for early payment. "Account number" refers to the general ledger accounts that a company uses to track its expenses. For example, one account number might be assigned for advertising expenses, while another might be for office supplies. Each invoice that's paid is assigned to an account, and in some cases, different line items on an invoice are assigned to different accounts.

Possible tables and columns for an accounts payable system

Vendors	Invoices	Invoice line items
Vendor name	Invoice number*	Invoice number*
Vendor address	Invoice date	~~Item part number~~
Vendor city	Terms*	Item quantity
Vendor state	Invoice total	Item description
Vendor zip code	*Payment date*	Item unit price
Vendor phone number	*Payment total*	Item extension
~~Vendor fax number~~	*Invoice due date*	*Account number**
~~Vendor web address~~	*Credit total*	*Sequence number*
Vendor contact first name	*Account number**	
Vendor contact last name		
~~Vendor contact phone~~		
~~Vendor AR first name~~		
~~Vendor AR last name~~		
~~Vendor AR phone~~		
*Terms**		
*Account number**		

Description

- After you identify and subdivide all of the data elements for a database, you should group them by the entities with which they're associated. These entities will later become the tables of the database, and the elements will become the columns.
- If a data element relates to more than one entity, you can include it under all of the entities it relates to. Then, when you normalize the database, you may be able to remove the duplicate elements.
- As you assign the elements to entities, you should omit elements that aren't needed, and you should add any additional elements that are needed.

The notation used in this figure

- Data elements that were previously identified but aren't needed are crossed out.
- Data elements that were added are displayed in italics.
- Data elements that are related to two or more entities are followed by an asterisk.
- You can use a similar notation or develop one of your own. You can also use a *CASE (Computer-Aided Software Engineering) tool* if one is available to you.

Figure 16-4   How to identify the tables and assign columns

How to identify the primary and foreign keys

Once you identify the entities and data elements of a system, the next step is to identify the relationships between the tables. To do that, you need to identify the primary and foreign keys as shown in figure 16-5.

As you know, a *primary key* is used to uniquely identify each row in a table. In some cases, you can use an existing column as the primary key. For example, you might consider using the vendorName column as the primary key of the vendors table. Because the values for this column can be long, however, and because it would be easy to enter a value like that incorrectly, that's not a good candidate for a primary key. Instead, you should use an ID column like vendorID that's incremented by one for each new record.

Similarly, you might consider using the invoiceNumber column as the primary key of the invoices table. However, it's possible for different vendors to use the same invoice number, so this value isn't necessarily unique. Because of that, another ID column like invoiceID can be used as the primary key.

To uniquely identify the rows in the invoiceLineItems table, this design uses a *composite key*. This composite key uses two columns to identify each row. The first column is the invoiceID column from the invoices table, and the second column is the invoiceSequence column. This is necessary because this table may contain more than one row (line item) for each invoice. And that means that the invoiceID value by itself may not be unique.

After you identify the primary key of each table, you need to identify the relationships between the tables and add *foreign key* columns as necessary. In most cases, two tables have a *one-to-many relationship* with each other. For example, each vendor can have many invoices, and each invoice can have many line items. To identify the vendor that each invoice is associated with, a vendorID column is included in the invoices table. Because the invoiceLineItems table already contains an invoiceID column, it isn't necessary to add another column to this table.

The diagram at the top of this figure illustrates the relationships I identified between the tables in the accounts payable system. Here, the primary keys are displayed in bold. Then, the lines between the tables indicate how the primary key in one table is related to the foreign key in another table. Here, a small, round connector indicates the one side of the relationship, and the connector with three lines indicates the many side of the relationship.

In addition to the one-to-many relationships shown in this diagram, you can also use many-to-many relationships and one-to-one relationships. The second diagram in this figure, for example, shows a *many-to-many relationship* between an employees table and a committees table. This type of relationship can be implemented by creating a *linking table*. This table contains the primary key columns from the two tables. Then, each table has a one-to-many relationship with the linking table. Notice that the linking table doesn't have its own primary key. Because this table doesn't correspond to an entity and because it's used only in conjunction with the employees and committees tables, a primary key isn't needed.

The relationships between the tables in the accounts payable system

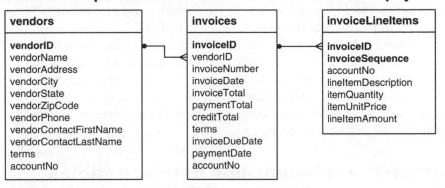

Two tables with a many-to-many relationship

Linking table

Two tables with a one-to-one relationship

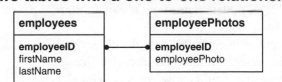

Description

- Each table should have a *primary key* that uniquely identifies each row. If possible, you should use an existing column for the primary key.

- The values of the primary keys should seldom, if ever, change. The values should also be short and easy to enter correctly.

- If a suitable column doesn't exist for a primary key, you can create an ID column that is incremented by one for each new row as the primary key.

- If two tables have a *one-to-many relationship*, you may need to add a *foreign key* column to the table on the "many" side. The foreign key column must have the same data type as the primary key column it's related to.

- If two tables have a *many-to-many relationship*, you can define a *linking table* to relate them. Then, each of the tables in the many-to-many relationship will have a one-to-many relationship with the linking table. The linking table doesn't usually have a primary key.

- If two tables have a *one-to-one relationship*, they should be related by their primary keys. This type of relationship is typically used to improve performance. Then, columns with large amounts of data can be stored in a separate table.

Figure 16-5   How to identify the primary and foreign keys

The third example illustrates two tables that have a *one-to-one relationship*. With this type of relationship, both tables have the same primary key, which means that the information could be stored in a single table. This type of relationship is often used when a table contains one or more columns with large amounts of data. In this case, the employeePhotos table contains a large binary column with a photo of each employee. Because this column is used infrequently, storing it in a separate table makes operations on the employees table more efficient. Then, when this column is needed, it can be combined with the columns in the employees table using a join.

How to enforce the relationships between tables

Although the primary keys and foreign keys indicate how the tables in a database are related, MySQL doesn't enforce those relationships by default. As a result, any of the operations shown in the table at the top of figure 16-6 would violate the *referential integrity* of the tables. If you deleted a row from a primary key table, for example, and the foreign key table included rows related to that primary key, the referential integrity of the two tables would be destroyed. In that case, the rows in the foreign key table that no longer have a related row in the primary key table would be *orphaned*. Similar problems can occur when you insert a row into the foreign key table or update a primary key or foreign value.

Since MySQL doesn't enforce referential integrity by default, it's up to the web programmer to write PHP code that enforces referential integrity. For example, if a user attempts to delete a row that would cause rows in related tables to be orphaned, the web application should either prevent the user from deleting this row, or it should delete the corresponding rows in the related tables.

However, if you want MySQL to enforce referential integrity, you can switch from MyISAM tables (the default) to InnoDB tables. Then, the InnoDB tables can maintain the referential integrity of the tables. This is known as *declarative referential integrity* (*DRI*). To use it, you define *foreign key constraints* that indicate how the referential integrity between the tables is enforced. These constraints can prevent all of the operations listed in this figure that violate referential integrity.

The advantage of using DRI is that the database makes sure that referential integrity is enforced even if the application that's using the database attempts to violate referential integrity. However, most well-coded applications prevent their users from violating referential integrity, so this often isn't an issue.

There are a few disadvantages to DRI. To start, it requires some additional setup since you must declare how the database should enforce referential integrity when you create the database. In addition, enforcing referential integrity can slow the performance of a database. As a result, it's up to the database designer to decide whether or not to use DRI.

Operations that can violate referential integrity

This operation...	Violates referential integrity if...
Delete a row from the primary key table	The foreign key table contains one or more rows related to the deleted row
Insert a row in the foreign key table	The foreign key value doesn't have a matching primary key value in the related table
Update the value of a foreign key	The new foreign key value doesn't have a matching primary key value in the related table
Update the value of a primary key	The foreign key table contains one or more rows related to the row that's changed

Description

- *Referential integrity* means that the relationships between tables are maintained correctly. That means that a table with a foreign key doesn't have rows with foreign key values that don't have matching primary key values in the related table.

- By default, MySQL uses MyISAM tables that don't enforce referential integrity. As a result, referential integrity must be enforced by the PHP code of the web application.

- If you want MySQL to enforce referential integrity, you can use InnoDB tables. InnoDB tables provide for *declarative referential integrity (DRI)*. To use declarative referential integrity, you define *foreign key constraints*.

- When you define foreign key constraints, you can specify how referential integrity is enforced when a row is deleted from the primary key table. The options are to return an error or to delete the related rows in the foreign key table.

- You can also specify how referential integrity is enforced when the primary key of a row is changed and foreign key constraints are in effect. The options are to return an error or to change the foreign keys of all the related rows to the new value.

- If referential integrity isn't enforced and a row is deleted from the primary key table that has related rows in the foreign key table, the rows in the foreign key table are said to be *orphaned*.

Figure 16-6   How to enforce the relationships between tables

How normalization works

The next step in the design process is to review whether the data structure is *normalized*. To do that, you look at how the data is separated into related tables. If you follow the first four steps for designing a database that are presented in this chapter, your database will already be partially normalized when you get to this step. However, almost every design can be normalized further.

Figure 16-7 illustrates how *normalization* works. The first two tables in this figure show some of the problems caused by an *unnormalized* data structure. In the first table, each row represents an invoice. Because an invoice can have one or more line items, however, the itemDescription column must be repeated to provide for the maximum number of line items. But since most invoices have fewer line items than the maximum, this can waste storage space.

In the second table, each line item is stored in a separate row. That eliminates the problem caused by repeating the itemDescription column, but it introduces a new problem: the invoice number must be repeated in each row. This, too, can cause storage problems, particularly if the repeated column is large. In addition, it can cause maintenance problems if the column contains a value that's likely to change. Then, when the value changes, each row that contains the value must be updated. And if a repeated value must be reentered for each new row, it would be easy for the value to vary from one row to another.

To eliminate the problems caused by *data redundancy*, you can normalize the data structure. To do that, you apply the *normal forms* you'll learn about later in this chapter. As you'll see, there are a total of seven normal forms. However, it's common to apply only the first three. The diagram in this figure, for example, shows the accounts payable system in third normal form. Although it may not be obvious at this point how this reduces data redundancy, that will become clearer as you learn about the different normal forms.

A table that contains repeating columns

vendorName	invoiceNumber	itemDescription_1	itemDescription_2	itemDescription_3
Cahners Publishing	112897	VB ad	SQL ad	Library directory
Zylka design	97/552	Catalogs	SQL flyer	*NULL*
Zylka design	97/553B	Card revision	*NULL*	*NULL*

A table that contains redundant data

vendorName	invoiceNumber	itemDescription
Cahners Publishing	112897	VB ad
Cahners Publishing	112897	SQL ad
Cahners Publishing	97/533B	Card revisions
Zylka design	112897	Library directory
Zylka design	97/522	Catalogs
Zylka design	97/522	SQL flyer

The accounts payable system in third normal form

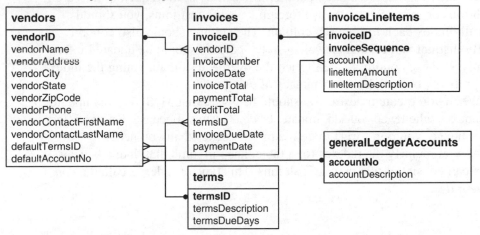

Description

- *Normalization* is a formal process that you can use to separate the data in a data structure into related tables. Normalization reduces *data redundancy*, which can cause storage and maintenance problems.

- In an *unnormalized data structure*, a table can contain information about two or more entities. It can also contain repeating columns, columns that contain repeating values, and data that's repeated in two or more rows.

- In a *normalized data structure*, each table contains information about a single entity, and each piece of information is stored in exactly one place.

- To normalize a data structure, you apply the *normal forms* in sequence. Although there are a total of seven normal forms, a data structure is typically considered normalized if the first three normal forms are applied.

Figure 16-7   How normalization works

How to identify the columns to be indexed

The last step in the design process is to identify the columns that should be indexed. An *index* is a structure that provides for locating one or more rows directly. Without an index, a database management system has to perform a *table scan*, which involves searching through the entire table.

Just as the index of a book has page numbers that direct you to a specific subject, a database index has pointers that direct the system to a specific row. This can speed performance not only when you're searching for rows based on a search condition, but also when you're joining data from tables. If a join is done based on a primary key to foreign key relationship, for example, and an index is defined for the foreign key column, the database management system can use that index to locate the rows for each primary key value.

When you use MySQL, an index is automatically created for the primary key in each table that you create. But you should consider creating indexes for other columns in some of the tables based on the guidelines at the top of figure 16-8.

To start, you should index a column if it will be used frequently in search conditions or joins. Since you use foreign keys in most joins, you should typically index each foreign key column. The column should also contain mostly distinct values, and the values in the column should be updated infrequently. If these conditions aren't met, the overhead of maintaining the index will probably outweigh the advantages of using it.

When you create indexes, you should be aware that MySQL must update the indexes whenever you add, update, or delete rows. Because that can affect performance, you don't want to define more indexes than you need.

As you identify the indexes for a table, keep in mind that, like a key, an index can consist of two or more columns. This type of index is called a *composite index*.

When to create an index

- When the column is a foreign key
- When the column is used frequently in search conditions or joins
- When the column contains a large number of distinct values
- When the column is updated infrequently

Description

- MySQL automatically creates an index for a primary key.
- An *index* provides a way for a database management system to locate information more quickly. When it uses an index, the database management system can go directly to a specific row rather than having to search through all the rows until it finds it.
- Indexes speed performance when searching and joining tables.
- You can create *composite indexes* that include two or more columns. You should use this type of index when the columns in the index are updated infrequently or when the index will cover almost every search condition on the table.
- Because indexes must be updated each time you add, update, or delete a row, you shouldn't create more indexes than you need.

Figure 16-8   How to identify the columns to be indexed

How to normalize a data structure

The topics that follow describe the seven normal forms and teach you how to apply the first three. As I said earlier, you apply these three forms to some extent in the first four database design steps, but these topics will give you more insight into the process. Then, the last topic explains when and how to denormalize a data structure. When you finish these topics, you'll have the basic skills for designing databases that are efficient and easy to use.

The seven normal forms

Figure 16-9 summarizes the seven normal forms. Each normal form assumes that the previous forms have already been applied. Before you can apply the third normal form, for example, the design must already be in the second normal form.

Strictly speaking, a data structure isn't normalized until it's in the fifth or sixth normal form. However, the normal forms past the third normal form are applied infrequently. Because of that, I won't present those forms in detail here. Instead, I'll just describe them briefly so you'll have an idea of how to apply them if you need to.

The *Boyce-Codd normal form* can be used to eliminate *transitive dependencies*. With this type of dependency, one column depends on another column, which depends on a third column. To illustrate, consider the city, state, and zip code columns in the vendors table. Here, a zip code identifies a city and state, which means that the city and state are dependent on the zip code. The zip code, in turn, is dependent on the vendorID column. To eliminate this dependency, you could store the city and state values in a separate table that uses zip code as its primary key.

The fourth normal form can be used to eliminate multiple *multivalued dependencies* from a table. A multivalued dependency is one where a primary key column has a one-to-many relationship with a non-key column. To illustrate, consider the vendor contact phone number in the vendors table. If you wanted to accommodate alternate phone numbers, such as a cell or home phone, you could add extra columns for each type of number. However, this creates a multivalued dependency between the phone numbers and the vendorID. To be in fourth normal form, therefore, you'd need to store phone numbers in a separate table that uses vendorID as a foreign key.

To apply the fifth normal form, you continue to divide the tables of the data structure into smaller tables until all redundancy has been removed. When further splitting would result in tables that couldn't be used to reconstruct the original table, the data structure is in fifth normal form. In this form, most tables consist of little more than key columns with one or two data elements.

The *domain-key normal form*, sometimes called the sixth normal form, is only of academic interest since no database system has implemented a way to apply it. For this reason, even normalization purists might consider a database to be normalized in fifth normal form.

The seven normal forms

Normal form	Description
First (1NF)	The value stored at the intersection of each row and column must be a scalar value, and a table must not contain any repeating columns.
Second (2NF)	Every non-key column must depend on the entire primary key.
Third (3NF)	Every non-key column must depend only on the primary key.
Boyce-Codd (BCNF)	A non-key column can't be dependent on another non-key column. This prevents *transitive dependencies*, where column A depends on column C and column B depends on column C. Since both A and B depend on C, A and B should be moved into another table with C as the key.
Fourth (4NF)	A table must not have more than one *multivalued dependency*, where the primary key has a one-to-many relationship to non-key columns. This form gets rid of misleading many-to-many relationships.
Fifth (5NF)	The data structure is split into smaller and smaller tables until all redundancy has been eliminated. If further splitting would result in tables that couldn't be joined to recreate the original table, the structure is in fifth normal form.
Domain-key (DKNF) or (6NF)	Every constraint on the relationship is dependent only on key constraints and domain constraints, where a *domain* is the set of allowable values Sixth for a column. This form prevents the insertion of any unacceptable data by enforcing constraints at the level of a relationship, rather than at the table or column level. DKNF is less a design model than an abstract "ultimate" normal form.

The benefits of normalization

- Since a normalized database has more tables than an unnormalized database, and since each table has an index on its primary key, the database has more indexes. That makes data retrieval more efficient.

- Since each table contains information about a single entity, each index has fewer columns (usually one) and fewer rows. That makes data retrieval and insert, update, and delete operations more efficient.

- Each table has fewer indexes, which makes insert, update, and delete operations more efficient.

- Data redundancy is minimized, which simplifies maintenance and reduces storage.

Description

- Each normal form assumes that the design is already in the previous normal form.

- A database is typically considered to be normalized if it is in third normal form. The other four forms are not commonly used and are not covered in detail in this book.

Figure 16-9   The seven normal forms

Figure 16-9 also lists the benefits of normalizing a data structure. To summarize, normalization produces smaller, more efficient tables. In addition, it reduces data redundancy, which makes the data easier to maintain and reduces the amount of storage needed for the database. Because of these benefits, you should always consider normalizing your data structures.

You should also be aware that the subject of normalization is a contentious one in the database community. In the academic study of computer science, normalization is considered a form of design perfection that should always be strived for. In practice, though, database designers and DBAs tend to use normalization as a flexible design guideline.

How to apply the first normal form

Figure 16-10 illustrates how you apply the first normal form to an unnormalized invoice data structure consisting of the data elements that are shown in figure 16-2. The first two tables in this figure illustrate structures that aren't in first normal form. Both of these tables contain a single row for each invoice. Because each invoice can contain one or more line items, however, the first table allows for repeating values in the itemDescription column. The second table is similar, except it includes a separate column for each line item description. Neither of these structures is acceptable in first normal form.

The third table in this figure has eliminated the repeating values and columns. To do that, it includes one row for each line item. Notice, however, that this has increased the data redundancy. Specifically, the vendor name and invoice number are now repeated for each line item. This problem can be solved by applying the second normal form.

Before I describe the second normal form, I want you to realize that I intentionally omitted many of the columns in the invoice data structure from the examples in this figure and the next figure. In addition to the columns shown here, for example, each of these tables would also contain the vendor address, invoice date, invoice total, etc. I eliminated these columns to make it easier for you to focus on the columns that are affected by applying the normal forms.

The invoice data with a column that contains repeating values

vendorName	invoiceNumber	itemDescription
Cahners Publishing	112897	VB ad, SQL ad, Library directory
Zylka design	97/522	Catalogs, SQL Flyer
Zylka design	97/533B	Card revision

The invoice data with repeating columns

vendorName	invoiceNumber	itemDescription_1	itemDescription_2	itemDescription_3
Cahners Publishing	112897	VB ad	SQL ad	Library directory
Zylka design	97/552	Catalogs	SQL flyer	NULL
Zylka design	97/553B	Card revision	NULL	NULL

The invoice data in first normal form

vendorName	invoiceNumber	itemDescription
Cahners Publishing	112897	VB ad
Cahners Publishing	112897	SQL ad
Cahners Publishing	97/533B	Card revisions
Zylka design	112897	Library directory
Zylka design	97/522	Catalogs
Zylka design	97/522	SQL flyer

Description

- For a table to be in first normal form, its columns must not contain repeating values. Instead, each column must contain a single, scalar value. In addition, the table must not contain repeating columns that represent a set of values.
- A table in first normal form often has repeating values in its rows. This can be resolved by applying the second normal form.

Figure 16-10   How to apply the first normal form

How to apply the second normal form

Figure 16-11 shows how to apply the second normal form. To be in second normal form, every column in a table that isn't a key column must be dependent on the entire primary key. This form only applies to tables that have composite primary keys, which is often the case when you start with data that is completely unnormalized. The table at the top of this figure, for example, shows the invoice data in first normal form after key columns have been added. In this case, the primary key consists of the invoiceID and invoiceSequence columns. The invoiceSequence column is needed to uniquely identify each line item for an invoice.

Now, consider the three non-key columns shown in this table. Of these three, only one, itemDescription, depends on the entire primary key. The other two, vendorName and invoiceNumber, depend only on the invoiceID column. Because of that, these columns should be moved to another table. The result is a data structure like the second one shown in this figure. Here, all of the information related to an invoice is stored in the invoices table, and all of the information related to an individual line item is stored in the invoiceLineItems table.

Notice that the relationship between these tables is based on the invoiceID column. This column is the primary key of the invoices table, and it's the foreign key in the invoiceLineItems table that relates the rows in that table to the rows in the invoices table. This column is also part of the primary key of the invoiceLineItems table.

When you apply second normal form to a data structure, it eliminates some of the redundant row data in the tables. In this figure, for example, the invoice number and vendor name are now included only once for each invoice. In first normal form, this information was included for each line item.

The invoice data in first normal form with keys added

invoiceID	vendorName	invoiceNumber	invoiceSequence	itemDescription
1	Cahners Publishing	112897	1	VB ad
1	Cahners Publishing	112897	2	SQL ad
1	Cahners Publishing	112897	3	Library directory
2	Zylka design	97/522	1	Catalogs
2	Zylka design	97/522	2	SQL flyer
3	Zylka design	97/533B	1	Card revision

The invoice data in second normal form

invoiceNumber	vendorName	invoiceID
11287	Cahners Publishing	1
97/522	Zylka design	2
97/533B	Zylka design	3

invoiceID	invoiceSequence	itemDescription
1	1	VB ad
1	2	SQL ad
1	3	Library directory
2	1	Catalogs
2	2	SQL flyer
3	1	Card revision

Description

- For a table to be in second normal form, every non-key column must depend on the entire primary key. If a column doesn't depend on the entire key, it indicates that the table contains information for more than one entity. This is reflected by the table's composite key.

- To apply second normal form, you move columns that don't depend on the entire primary key to another table and then establish a relationship between the two tables.

- Second normal form helps remove redundant row data, which can save storage space, make maintenance easier, and reduce the chance of storing inconsistent data.

Figure 16-11   How to apply the second normal form

How to apply the third normal form

To apply the third normal form, you make sure that every non-key column depends *only* on the primary key. Figure 16-12 illustrates how you can apply this form to the data structure for the accounts payable system. The top of this figure shows all of the columns in the invoices and invoiceLineItems tables in second normal form. Then, this figure presents a list of questions that you might ask about some of the columns in these tables when you apply third normal form.

First, does the vendor information depend only on the invoiceID column? Another way to phrase this question is, "Will the information for the same vendor change from one invoice to another?" If the answer is no, the vendor information should be stored in a separate table. That way, you can be sure that the vendor information for each invoice for a vendor is the same. In addition, you can reduce the redundancy of the data in the invoices table. This is illustrated by the diagram in this figure that shows the accounts payable system in third normal form. Here, a vendors table has been added to store the information for each vendor. This table is related to the invoices table by the vendorID column, which has been added as a foreign key to the invoices table.

Second, does the terms column depend only on the invoiceID column? The answer to that question depends on how this column is used. In this case, I'll assume that this column is used not only to specify the terms for each invoice, but also to specify the default terms for a vendor. Because of that, the terms information could be stored in both the vendors and the invoices tables. To avoid redundancy, however, the information related to different terms can be stored in a separate table, as illustrated by the terms table in this figure. Here, the primary key is an identity column named termsID. Then, a foreign key column named defaultTermsID has been added to the vendors table, and a foreign key column named termsID has been added to the invoices table.

Third, does the accountNo column depend only on the invoiceID column? Again, that depends on how this column is used. In this case, it's used to specify the general ledger account number for each line item, so it depends on the invoiceID and the invoiceSequence columns. In other words, this column should be stored in the invoiceLineItems table. In addition, each vendor has a default account number, which should be stored in the vendors table. Because of that, another table named generalLedgerAccounts has been added to store the account numbers and account descriptions. Then, foreign key columns have been added to the vendors and invoiceLineItems tables to relate them to this table.

Fourth, can the invoiceDueDate column in the invoices table and the lineItemAmount column in the invoiceLineItems table be derived from other data in the database? If so, they depend on the columns that contain that data rather than on the primary key columns. In this case, the value of the lineItemAmount column can always be calculated from the itemQuantity and itemUnitPrice columns. Because of that, this column could be omitted. Alternatively, you could omit the itemQuantity and itemUnitPrice columns and keep just the lineItemAmount column. That's what I did in the data structure shown in this figure. The solution you choose, however, depends on how the data will be used.

The accounts payable system in second normal form

invoices	
invoiceID	
vendorName	invoiceDate
vendorAddress	invoiceTotal
vendorCity	paymentTotal
vendorState	creditTotal
vendorZipCode	terms
vendorPhone	invoiceDueDate
vendorContactFirstName	paymentDate
vendorContactLastName	accountNo
InvoiceNumber	

invoiceLineItems
invoiceID
invoiceSequence
accountNo
invoiceLineItemDescription
itemQuantity
itemUnitPrice
lineItemAmount

Questions about the structure

1. Does the vendor information (vendor_name, vendor_address, etc.) depend only on the invoice_id column?
2. Does the terms column depend only on the invoice_id column?
3. Does the account_no column depend only on the invoice_id column?
4. Can the invoice_due_date and line_item_amount columns be derived from other data?

The accounts payable system in third normal form

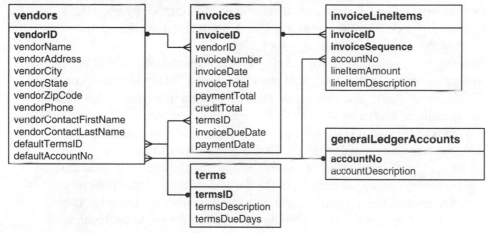

Description

- For a table to be in third normal form, every non-key column must depend *only* on the primary key.
- If a column doesn't depend only on the primary key, it implies that the column is assigned to the wrong table or that it can be computed from other columns in the table. A column that can be computed from other columns contains *derived data*.

Figure 16-12   How to apply the third normal form

In contrast, although the invoiceDueDate column could be calculated from the invoiceDate column in the invoices table and the termsDueDays column in the related row of the terms table, the system also allows this date to be overridden. Because of that, the invoiceDueDate column should not be omitted. If the system didn't allow this value to be overridden, however, this column could be safely omitted.

When and how to denormalize a data structure

Denormalization is the deliberate deviation from the normal forms. Most denormalization occurs beyond the third normal form. In contrast, the first three normal forms are almost universally applied.

To illustrate when and how to denormalize a data structure, figure 16-13 presents the design of the accounts payable system in fifth normal form. Here, the vendor zip codes are stored in a separate table that contains the city and state for each zip code. In addition, the area codes are stored in a separate table. Because of that, a query that retrieves vendor addresses and phone numbers would require two joins. In contrast, if you left the city, state, and area code information in the vendors table, no joins would be required, but the vendors table would be larger. In general, you should denormalize based on the way the data will be used. In this case, we'll seldom need to query phone numbers without the area code. Likewise, we'll seldom need to query city and state without the zip code. For these reasons, I've denormalized my design by eliminating the zipCodes and areaCodes tables.

You might also consider denormalizing a table if the data it contains is updated infrequently. In that case, redundant data isn't as likely to cause problems.

Finally, you should consider including derived data in a table if that data is used frequently in search conditions. For example, if you frequently query the invoices table based on invoice balances, you might consider including a column that contains the balance due. That way, you won't have to calculate this value each time it's queried. Keep in mind, though, that if you store derived data, it's possible for it to deviate from the derived value. For this reason, you may need to protect the derived column so it can't be updated directly. Alternatively, you could update the table periodically to reset the value of the derived column.

Because normalization eliminates the possibility of data redundancy errors and optimizes the use of storage, you should carefully consider when and how to denormalize a data structure. In general, you should denormalize only when the increased efficiency outweighs the potential for redundancy errors and storage problems. Of course, your decision to denormalize should also be based on your knowledge of the real-world environment in which the system will be used. If you've carefully analyzed the real-world environment as outlined in this chapter, you'll have a good basis for making that decision.

The accounts payable system in fifth normal form

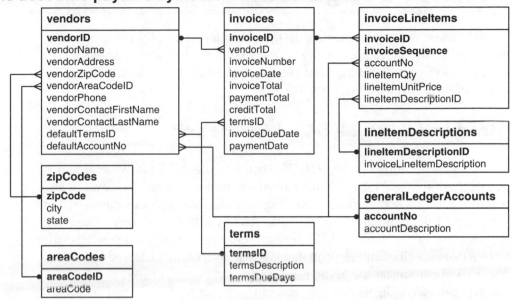

When to denormalize

- When a column from a joined table is used repeatedly in search criteria, you should consider moving that column to the primary key table if it will eliminate the need for a join.

- If a table is updated infrequently, you should consider denormalizing it to improve efficiency. Because the data remains relatively constant, you don't have to worry about data redundancy errors once the initial data is entered and verified.

- Include columns with derived values when those values are used frequently in search conditions. If you do that, you need to be sure that the column value is always synchronized with the value of the columns it's derived from.

Description

- Data structures that are normalized to the fourth normal form and beyond typically require more joins than tables normalized to the third normal form and can therefore be less efficient.

- SQL statements that work with tables that are normalized to the fourth normal form and beyond are typically more difficult to code and debug.

- Most designers *denormalize* data structures to some extent, usually to the third normal form.

- *Denormalization* can result in larger tables, redundant data, and reduced performance.

- Only denormalize when necessary. It is better to adhere to the normal forms unless it is clear that performance will be improved by denormalizing.

Figure 16-13   When and how to denormalize a data structure

A database design tool

When you're ready to create a database diagram, it usually makes sense to use a design tool that's specifically for creating those diagrams. Fortunately, dozens of tools for designing databases are available. This topic introduces you to one of them: MySQL Workbench.

An introduction to MySQL Workbench

We chose to introduce MySQL Workbench in this book partly because it's available for free and runs on most modern operating systems. However, it also makes it easy to create visually appealing database diagrams as summarized in figure 16-14. In addition, it provides functionality that allows you to generate a diagram from an existing MySQL creation script or to generate a creation script from a database diagram. Beyond that, MySQL Workbench lets you run SQL queries and administer the MySQL server.

To install MySQL Workbench, you can go to the MySQL Workbench web site and follow the instructions there. This is similar to installing other programs for your operating system. Then, when you start MySQL Workbench, it displays the Home page that's shown in this figure. To work with database diagrams (also known as models), you click on the one of the options in the middle panel.

The MySQL Workbench web site

`http://wb.mysql.com/`

The Home page

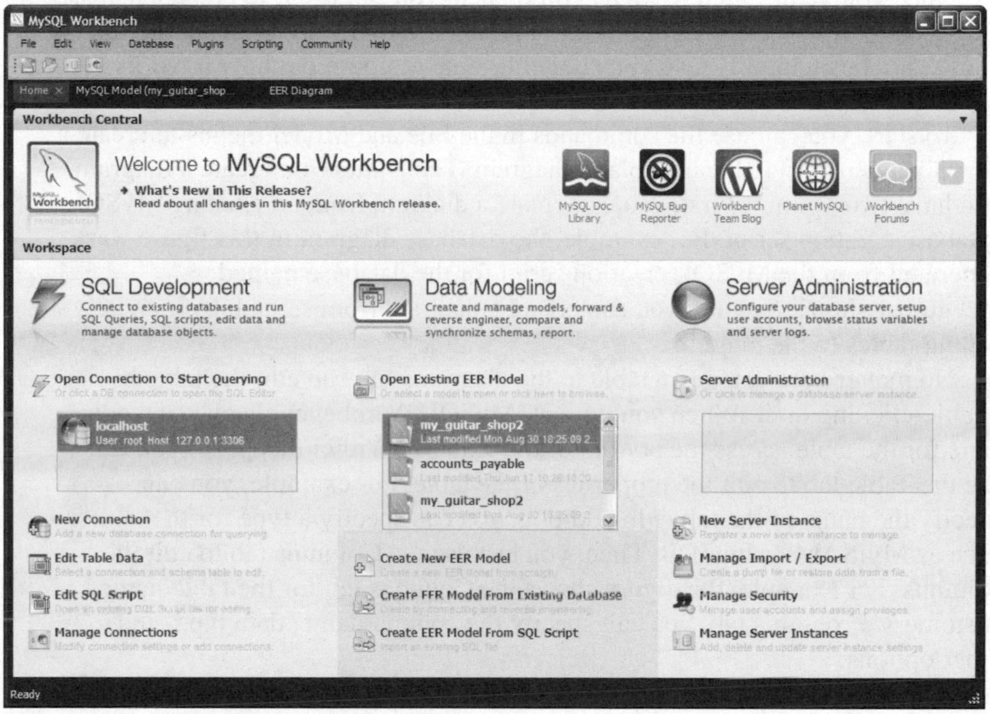

MySQL Workbench...

- Lets you create and edit diagrams.
- Lets you define the tables, columns, and indexes for a database.
- Lets you define the relationships between the tables in a database.
- Lets you generate a diagram from a SQL creation script.
- Lets you generate a SQL creation script from a diagram.

How to install MySQL Workbench

1. Go to the MySQL Workbench web site shown above.
2. Download the version for your system.
3. Run the installer or setup file and respond to the prompts.

Description

- MySQL Workbench is a database design tool that's available for free and runs on most modern operating systems.

Figure 16-14   An introduction to MySQL Workbench

How to use MySQL Workbench to create database diagrams

Once you've installed MySQL Workbench, you can use it to create database diagrams as described in figure 16-15. Although MySQL Workbench has some quirks, it's fairly intuitive, so you should be able to figure out how it works by experimenting with it.

To start, you can use the commands in the File and Model menus to create a new document and to create a blank diagram. Then, after you create a diagram, you have two options. First, you can create a diagram from an existing MySQL database creation script. For example, the database diagram in this figure was generated from the MySQL creation script for the database named my_guitar_shop2. Second, you can create a diagram from scratch by manually adding tables to the diagram.

No matter how you add a table to the diagram, you can edit the table by double-clicking on it. When you do that, MySQL Workbench displays an edit pane for the table across the bottom of the window. Within this pane, you can use the Table tab to edit the properties of the table. For example, you can specify the name of the table. In addition, you can specify a type for the table such as MyISAM or InnoDB. Then, you can use the Columns tab to edit its columns. For example, this figure shows the Columns tab for the table named customers. From this tab, you can specify the column name, data type, and other options.

After you have added some tables to a diagram, you can define the relationships between the tables. To do that, you can use the relationship buttons in the toolbar. The first few buttons generate foreign keys for the table so you can use these buttons when the column for a foreign key doesn't exist yet. However, you can use the last relationship button if the foreign key columns already exist in your diagram. For example, to create a relationship between the customers and orders tables, I clicked on the "Place a Relationship Using Existing Columns" button. Then, I clicked on the customerID column in the orders table to identify the foreign key, and I clicked on the customerID column in the customers table to identify the primary key.

When you're done creating your database diagram, you can create a MySQL database creation script from the diagram. To do that, you can select the Forward Engineer MySQL Create Script command from the File menu. Then, you can create the database by using a different tool such as phpMyAdmin to run the script.

In the next chapter, you'll learn more about the SQL statements that are generated by a tool like this. This will help you understand how to use MySQL Workbench, and it will allow you to edit the SQL statements that are generated by your database design tools.

MySQL Workbench

Description

- To create a new model, select the File→New Model command.

- To create a new diagram, select the Model→Add Diagram command.

- To import tables from an existing creation script, select the File→Import→Reverse Engineer MySQL Create Script command.

- To export a database creation script from the diagram, select the File→Export→Forward Engineer MySQL Create Script command.

- To add a table to a diagram, click the Place New Table button in the toolbar. Then, click on the diagram where you want to add the table.

- To edit a table, double-click on the table. Then, use the pane that appears across the bottom of the window to modify the properties of the table, its columns, its indexes, and its foreign keys.

- To define the relationships between tables, click one of the relationship buttons in the toolbar. Then, click on the tables. To edit or delete a relationship, right-click on the relationship icon and select the appropriate command.

Figure 16-15   How to use MySQL Workbench

Perspective

Database design is a complicated subject. Because of that, it's impossible to teach you everything you need to know in a single chapter. With the skills you've learned in this chapter, however, you should be able to design databases of your own.

One aspect of database design that isn't covered in this chapter is designing the security of the database. Among other things, that involves creating database users and assigning permissions for each user. In the next chapter, you'll learn how to get started with database security.

Terms

database administrator (DBA)	linking table
data structure	one-to-one relationship
entity	referential integrity
attribute	orphaned row
instance	declarative referential integrity (DRI)
entity-relationship (ER) modeling	foreign key constraint
Computer-Aided Software Engineering	normalization
(CASE)	data redundancy
primary key	normal forms
composite key	index
foreign key	composite index
one-to-many relationship	derived data
many-to-many relationships	denormalization

Summary

- Databases are often designed and maintained by *database administrators* (*DBAs*).

- A table in a relational database typically represents an object, or *entity*, in the real world. Each column of a table is used to store an *attribute* associated with the entity, and each row represents one *instance* of the entity.

- To model a database and the relationships between its tables after a real-world system, you can use a technique called *entity-relationship (ER) modeling*.

- You can use a *CASE (Computer-Aided Software Engineering) tool* to help you design a database.

- Each table should have a *primary key* that uniquely identifies each row. If two tables have a *one-to-many relationship*, you may need to add a *foreign key* column to the table on the "many" side.

- If two tables have a *many-to-many relationship*, you can define a *linking table* to relate them. Then, each of the tables in the many-to-many relationship will have a one-to-many relationship with the linking table. The linking table doesn't usually have a primary key.

- If two tables have a *one-to-one relationship*, they should be related by their primary keys.

- *Referential integrity* means that the relationships between tables are maintained correctly. If referential integrity isn't enforced, it's possible for rows in a related table to be *orphaned*.

- Using a database to enforce referential integrity is known as *declarative referential integrity (DRI)*. To use declarative referential integrity, you define *foreign key constraints*.

- *Normalization* is a formal process you can use to separate the data in a data structure into related tables. Normalization reduces *data redundancy*, which can cause storage and maintenance problems.

- In a *normalized* data structure, each table contains information about a single entity, and each piece of information is stored in exactly one place. In an unnormalized data structure, a table can contain information about two or more entities. It can also contain repeating columns, columns that contain repeating values, and data that's repeated in two or more rows.

- To normalize a data structure, you apply the *normal forms* in sequence. Although there are a total of seven normal forms, a data structure is typically considered normalized if the first three normal forms are applied.

- An *index* provides a way for a database management system to locate information more quickly. If necessary, you can create *composite indexes* that include two or more columns.

- A column that can be computed from other columns contains *derived data*.

- Most designers *denormalize* data structures to some extent, usually to the third normal form. However, denormalization can result in larger tables, redundant data, and reduced performance.

Exercise 16-1   Create a database diagram from a SQL script

In this exercise, you can use MySQL Workbench to create a database diagram for the my_guitar_shop2 database.

1. If necessary, install MySQL Workbench.
2. Start MySQL Workbench.
3. Start a new model and a new diagram within that model.

4. Use the Reverse Engineer MySQL Create Script command to reverse engineer a diagram from this SQL script file:

```
htdocs/book_apps/_create_db/my_guitar_shop2.sql
```

5. Look on the left side of the window until you find the seven tables that were created. Drag all seven tables from the catalog tree to the diagram.

6. Double-click the Products table to display a pane across the bottom of the window. Click the Columns tab to review the column definitions for that table. Then, click the close button on the Products tab to close the pane.

7. Add the arrows that show the relationships between these tables. To do that, click the "Place a relationship using existing columns" link, click the column for the foreign key, and click the column for the primary key. Note how this identifies the foreign keys in the tables. If you make a mistake, you can right-click on the relationship arrow to delete it.

8. Save the diagram with a name of my_guitar_shop3.mwb.

9. When you're done, review the diagram. There should be a one-to-many relationship between six of the tables. However, the administrators table is a supporting table that isn't related to any of the other tables.

Exercise 16-2 Create some simple database designs

In this exercise, you can use your preferred database design tool. If you don't already have a preference, we recommend using MySQL Workbench.

1. Create a diagram for a database of music albums created by music artists. Each artist may have one or more albums, and each album may have one or more tracks. Keep track of this data: artist name, album name, album release date, track name, and track time.

2. Create a diagram for a database of members of groups within an association. Assume that each member can belong to any number of groups and that each group can have any number of members. Keep track of this data: member name, member email address, member phone number, group name, and group description.

17

How to use SQL
to create a database

Now that you've learned how to design a database, you're ready to learn how to implement your design. To do that, you use the set of SQL statements that are known as the data definition language (DDL). In this chapter, you'll learn how to use the DDL statements that work with tables and indexes. You'll also learn how to use the DDL statements that work with users and privileges.

If you use MySQL Workbench to design your database, you can generate a SQL script that contains the DDL statements needed to create the database. Then, you can run that script to create the database. However, it's still important to understand DDL statements for several reasons. First, understanding DDL statements helps you understand how to use MySQL Workbench. Second, you may need to edit the DDL statements in a generated script. Third, you may need to write DDL statements on your own to modify a database that already exists.

How to work with databases **538**
How to create a database 538
How to select a database 538
How to drop a database 538

How to work with tables **540**
An introduction to MySQL data types 540
How to create a table 542
How to code a primary key 544
How to alter a table 546
How to drop a table 548

How to work with indexes **550**
How to create an index 550
How to drop an index 550

How to work with users and privileges **552**
A summary of privileges 552
How to create, rename, and drop users 554
How to grant privileges 556
How to revoke privileges 558
How to view privileges 560

Other skills for creating a database **562**
How to load data from text files 562
How to dump a database to a SQL script 564

The script for the Guitar Shop database **566**

Perspective **570**

How to work with databases

Before you can begin creating the tables of a database, you must create the database. Then, since multiple databases may be running on a single MySQL server, you usually select the database before you begin working with it. Of course, if you decide that you no longer need a database, you can drop it, which causes it to be deleted.

If you're working on a large web site, you probably won't need to code DDL statements like these because that will be handled by a database administrator (DBA). For small- and medium-sized web sites, though, the web programmer may often have to serve as the DBA too. And even when working on a large web site, the web programmer often needs to use DDL to create smaller databases that are needed for testing.

How to create a database

The first example in figure 17-1 uses the CREATE DATABASE statement to create a database named my_guitar_shop2. If a database already exists with that name, this statement generates an error and doesn't execute. Also, if this statement is part of a script, this error stops the execution of the rest of the script. To prevent this, you can add the IF NOT EXISTS keywords to the CREATE DATABASE statement as shown in the second example. Then, the statement only executes if the database doesn't already exist.

How to select a database

The third example uses the USE statement to select the database that was created by the first example. Although the USE statement isn't a standard SQL statement, it's a MySQL extension that's commonly used when working with MySQL databases.

How to drop a database

The fourth example uses the DROP DATABASE statement to delete the database named my_guitar_shop2 that was created in the first example. This permanently deletes everything in the entire database, so use it with caution! If the specified database doesn't exist, this statement generates an error that stops the execution of any script. To prevent this, you can add the IF EXISTS keywords to the statement as shown in the fifth example. Then, the statement only drops the database if it exists.

How to create a database

```
CREATE DATABASE my_guitar_shop2;
```

How to create a database only if it does not exist

```
CREATE DATABASE IF NOT EXISTS my_guitar_shop2;
```

How to select a database

```
USE my_guitar_shop2;
```

How to drop a database

```
DROP DATABASE my_guitar_shop2;
```

How to drop a database only if it exists

```
DROP DATABASE IF EXISTS my_guitar_shop2;
```

Description

- You can use the CREATE DATABASE statement to create a database.
- You can use the USE statement to select a database.
- You can use the DROP DATABASE statement to drop a database.

Warning

- You should never drop a production database without first consulting the DBA. In most cases, though, you won't have the privilege to do that (see figure 17-10).

Figure 17-1   How to create, select, and drop a database

How to work with tables

This topic shows how to code the DDL statements that work with the tables of a database. But first, it presents an introduction to the MySQL data types.

An introduction to MySQL data types

Figure 17-2 shows nine of the most common MySQL data types. This figure divides these data types into three groups: numeric, string, and date/time.

Of the three numeric types, the first two are for storing integers. Here, the INT type can store more integer values than the TINYINT type. So, why should you ever use the TINYINT type? The answer is because each INT value takes 4 bytes of storage while each TINYINT type only takes 1 byte of storage. As a result, if you know that a column will only store integer values between -127 and 128, you should use the TINYINT type to save storage space. If, for example, you want to store a Boolean value in a column, you can use the TINYINT type to store the value as a 0 or a 1. When you define an integer type, the data type controls the amount of storage space that's used, and the optional size parameter specifies the maximum width that's used to display the number.

The DECIMAL type stores an exact value that has a fixed number of decimal places. This data type is commonly used for storing monetary values. The *precision* of a DECIMAL type indicates the total number of digits that can be stored in the data type. The *scale* indicates the number of decimal digits that can be stored to the right of the decimal point.

Of the three string types, the first two are used for storing short string values such as names, addresses, and so on. So, which one should you use? If you know that the values for a column will usually have the same number of characters, you should use the CHAR type because it requires less storage for this type of data. However, if the values in a column will usually have a varying number of characters, you should use the VARCHAR type because it requires less storage for this type of data.

When you define a CHAR or VARCHAR type, the size refers to the number of characters, not the number of bytes. By default, MySQL uses the *Latin-1 character set* that's designed for storing characters from most Western European languages. This character set uses 1 byte per character. As a result, it takes 20 bytes to store 20 characters. However, if you need to store characters from other languages from around the world, you can use the *Unicode character set*. This character set typically uses 2 bytes per character. As a result, it typically takes 40 bytes to store 20 characters.

The TEXT type is designed for storing extremely long string values such as paragraphs or pages of text. In general, the TEXT type works like the VARCHAR type. However, the maximum number of characters is limited only by the maximum number of bytes that can be stored in a row. By default, this allows you to store 65,535 characters, but this may vary depending on how MySQL is configured on your system.

Common numeric data types

Type	Description
INT[(size)]	An integer between -2,147,483,648 and 2,147,483,647 where size is the maximum display size. Default size is 11.
TINYINT[(size)]	An integer between -127 and 128 where size is the maximum display size. Default size is 4.
DECIMAL[(p[,s])]	Decimal numbers with fixed precision (p) and scale (s). The maximum precision is 65 and the default is 10. The maximum scale is 30 and the default is 0.

Common string data types

Type	Description
VARCHAR(size)	Variable-length characters where size is the maximum number of characters. The size argument is required. The maximum size is 65,535
CHAR[(size)]	Fixed-length characters where size is the number of characters. The default size is 1. The maximum size is 255.
TEXT	Variable-length characters up to a maximum size of 65,535 bytes.

Common date and time data types

Type	Description
DATE	Dates from January 1, 1000 through December 31, 9999. The default format for entry and display is "yyyy-mm-dd".
TIME	Times in the range -838:59:59 through 838:59:59. The default format for display and entry is "hh:mi:ss".
DATETIME	Date and time from January 1, 1970 through December 31, 9999. The default format for display and entry is "yyyy-mm-dd hh:mi:ss".

Description

- By default, MySQL uses the *Latin-1 character set*, which provides for 256 characters with 1 byte per character.
- The *Unicode character set* provides for over 65,000 characters, usually with 2 bytes per character.
- The CHAR data type is typically used for *fixed-length strings*. This data type uses the same amount of storage regardless of the actual length of the string. If you insert a value that's shorter than the specified type, the end of the value will be padded with spaces.
- The VARCHAR data type is typically used for *variable-length strings*. This data type uses only the amount of storage needed for a given string.
- The *precision* of a DECIMAL type indicates the total number of digits that can be stored in the data type. The *scale* indicates the number of decimal digits that can be stored to the right of the decimal point. The decimal point and minus sign for the number aren't counted in the precision.

Figure 17-2   An introduction to MySQL data types

Of the date and time types, the DATE type is designed to store a date when you don't need to store the time, the TIME type is designed to store a time when you don't need to store a date, and the DATETIME type is designed for storing both the date and the time. MySQL also provides a TIMESTAMP type, but it isn't described here because it can't store dates past the year 2038.

Before you go on, you should know that this chapter only presents some of the most common MySQL data types. However, MySQL provides many other data types. For example, MySQL provides data types for storing very large and small floating-point numbers, binary large objects (BLOBs), enumerations, and sets. So, if the data types in this figure aren't what you need, please refer to the online MySQL Reference Manual for more information. To get started, you can search for "data type" or "data type overview".

How to create a table

Figure 17-3 presents a simplified syntax for the CREATE TABLE statement. Because the syntax for this statement and other statements presented in this chapter is complex, this chapter doesn't present complete syntax diagrams. Instead, it presents simplified diagrams that illustrate how the common clauses are used. To view the complete syntax of any statement, you can look up the statement in the MySQL Reference Manual that's available online.

By default, the CREATE TABLE statement creates a new table in the current database. As a result, you must make sure to select the correct database before executing this statement.

In its simplest form, the CREATE TABLE statement consists of the name of the new table followed by the names and data types of its columns. This is illustrated by the first example in this figure. However, in most cases, you'll code one or more *attributes* for each column as illustrated by the second example. For instance, to indicate that a column doesn't accept NULL values, you can code the NOT NULL attribute. If you omit this attribute, the column will allow NULL values.

To indicate that each row in a column must contain a unique value, you can code the UNIQUE attribute. Since two NULL values aren't considered to be the same, a unique column can contain NULL values. However, it's common to use the NOT NULL and UNIQUE attributes to define a column that can't contain NULL values and where each value in the column must be unique.

To specify a default value for a column, you can use the DEFAULT attribute. This value is used if another value isn't specified when a row is added to the database. The default value you specify must correspond to the data type for the column. For example, the default value for the paymentTotal column is set to zero.

Before I continue, you should realize that if you run the statements shown in this figure against the my_guitar_shop2 database, the statements will fail. That's because the my_guitar_shop2 database already contains tables named customers and orders. As a result, if you want to test these statements, you need to create another database and run them against that database.

The syntax of the CREATE TABLE statement

```
CREATE TABLE [IF NOT EXISTS] tableName
(
      columnName1   dataType   [columnAttributes][,
      columnName2   dataType   [columnAttributes]][,
      columnName3   dataType   [columnAttributes]]...
)
```

Three common column attributes

Attribute	Description
UNIQUE	Specifies that each value stored in the column must be unique, but allows the column to store NULL values.
NOT NULL	Indicates that the column doesn't accept NULL values. If omitted, the column can accept NULL values.
DEFAULT default_value	Specifies a default value for the column.

A table without column attributes

```
CREATE TABLE customers
(
    customerID   INT,
    firstName    VARCHAR(60),
    lastName     VARCHAR(60)
);
```

A table with column attributes

```
CREATE TABLE customers
(
    customerID   INT           NOT NULL    UNIQUE,
    firstName    VARCHAR(60)   NOT NULL,
    lastName     VARCHAR(60)   NOT NULL
);
```

Another table with column attributes

```
CREATE TABLE orders
(
    orderID       INT            NOT NULL    UNIQUE,
    customerID    INT            NOT NULL,
    orderNumber   VARCHAR(50)    NOT NULL,
    orderDate     DATE           NOT NULL,
    orderTotal    DECIMAL(9,2)   NOT NULL,
    paymentTotal  DECIMAL(9,2)               DEFAULT 0
);
```

Description

- The CREATE TABLE statement creates a table based on the column definitions and column *attributes* you specify.

- Since the NOT NULL and UNIQUE attributes limit the type of data that a column can store, they are known as *constraints*.

- To review the complete syntax of the CREATE TABLE statement, you can search the MySQL Reference Manual, which is available online.

Figure 17-3   How to create a table

How to code a primary key

Whether you realize it or not, the NOT NULL and UNIQUE keywords are examples of constraints. A *constraint* restricts the type of data that can be stored in a column. For example, the NOT NULL keyword prevents NULL values from being stored in a column, and the UNIQUE keyword only allows unique values.

Now, figure 17-4 shows how to code another type of constraint that's known as a *primary key*. In addition, it shows how to code the AUTO_INCREMENT attribute that's commonly used with a primary key.

The easiest way to define a primary key is to code the PRIMARY KEY keywords after the data type for the column as shown in the first example. Then, if you want MySQL to automatically generate a value for the primary key, you can also code the AUTO_INCREMENT keyword for that column.

When you identify a column as the primary key, two of the column's attributes are changed automatically. First, the column is forced to be NOT NULL. Second, the column is forced to contain a unique value for each row. In addition, an index is automatically created based on the column.

In the first example, the primary key is coded after the column name. As a result, it is known as a *column-level primary key*. However, you can also code a primary key at the table level as shown in the second example. Then, the primary key is known as a *table-level primary key*. In this figure, the primary key for the first two examples works the same. As a result, where you decide to code the primary key is largely a matter of personal preference.

However, a table-level primary key does provide one capability that isn't available from a column-level primary key: it can refer to multiple columns in the table. As a result, if you need to refer to multiple columns, you must use a table-level primary key. In the third example, the primary key for the orderItems table refers to the orderID column and the productID column.

When you code a primary key at the table level, you must code a comma at the end of the preceding column definition. If you don't, you will get an error when you try to run the statement.

Two column attributes for working with a primary key

Attribute	Description
PRIMARY KEY	Specifies that the column is the primary key for the table.
AUTO_INCREMENT	Automatically generates an integer value for the column. By default, this value starts at 0 and increments by a value of 1.

A table with a column-level primary key

```
CREATE TABLE customers (
  customerID     INT             NOT NULL   PRIMARY KEY   AUTO_INCREMENT,
  emailAddress   VARCHAR(255)    NOT NULL   UNIQUE
);
```

A table with a table-level primary key

```
CREATE TABLE customers (
  customerID     INT             NOT NULL   AUTO_INCREMENT,
  emailAddress   VARCHAR(255)    NOT NULL   UNIQUE,

  PRIMARY KEY (customerID)
);
```

A table with a two-column primary key

```
CREATE TABLE orderItems (
  orderID          INT             NOT NULL,
  productID        INT             NOT NULL,
  itemPrice        DECIMAL(10,2)   NOT NULL,
  discountAmount   DECIMAL(10,2)   NOT NULL,
  quantity         INT             NOT NULL,

  PRIMARY KEY (orderID, productID)
);
```

Description

- A *primary key* requires that each row has unique values for the column or columns that are used for the primary key, and it does not allow NULL values.

- You code a *column-level primary key* as part of the definition of the column definition. You code a *table-level primary key* as if it is a separate column definition, and you name its column or columns within that definition.

Figure 17-4   How to code a primary key

How to alter a table

After you create tables, you may need to modify the table. To do that, you can use the ALTER TABLE statement as shown in figure 17-5.

To start, the first example in this figure shows how to rename an existing table. Here, the statement changes the name of the products table to product. This is useful if you want to change the name of a table without modifying its column definitions or the data that's stored in the table.

The second example shows how to add a new column to a table at the end of the list of columns. To do that, you code the column definition the same way you do when you create a new table. To start, you specify the column name. Then, you code the data type and its attributes. In this example, the statement adds a column of the DATE type named lastTransactionDate.

The third example shows how to add a new column after a specified column. To do that, you can include an optional AFTER clause that specifies where to add the column. In this example, the statement adds the new column after the column named emailAddress.

The fourth example shows how to drop an existing column. This example drops the column named lastTransactionDate that was created by the code in the second example.

The fifth example shows how to rename an existing column. In this case, the code changes the name of the column from emailAddress to email. Note that you must include the data type and all of the attributes for the column when you rename it.

The sixth example shows how to change the definition of an existing column by modifying the length of the data type for that column. In this case, a column that was defined as VARCHAR(60) is changed to VARCHAR(100). Since the new data type is bigger than the old data type, you can be sure that the existing data will still fit.

The seventh example shows how to change the data type to a different data type. In this case, a column that was defined as VARCHAR(100) is changed to CHAR(100). Since these data types both store the same type of characters, you can be sure that no data will be lost.

The eighth example shows how to change the data type to a different data type that may result in lost data. If, for example, the firstName column contains one or more values that has more than 8 characters, this may result in lost data. On most systems, MySQL will truncate this data. As a result, a name of "Alexandra" will be truncated to "Alexandr".

The ninth example shows how to change the default value for a column. Here, the statement assigns a default value of an empty string to the firstName column. However, since the firstName column is of the VARCHAR type, you could assign any string literal or a NULL value as the default value.

The tenth example shows how to drop the default value from a column. In this example, the statement drops the default value that was set in the previous example.

A statement that renames a table

```
ALTER TABLE products RENAME TO product;
```

A statement that adds a new column at the end of the table

```
ALTER TABLE customers ADD lastTransactionDate DATE;
```

A statement that adds a new column after a specified column

```
ALTER TABLE customers ADD lastTransactionDate DATE
AFTER emailAddress;
```

A statement that drops a column

```
ALTER TABLE customers DROP lastTransactionDate;
```

A statement that renames a column

```
ALTER TABLE customers
CHANGE emailAddress email VARCHAR(255) NOT NULL UNIQUE;
```

A statement that changes the definition of a column

```
ALTER TABLE customers MODIFY firstName VARCHAR(100) NOT NULL;
```

A statement that changes the data type of a column

```
ALTER TABLE customers MODIFY firstName CHAR(100) NOT NULL;
```

A statement that may cause data to be lost

```
ALTER TABLE customers MODIFY firstName VARCHAR(8);
```

A statement that sets the default value of a column

```
ALTER TABLE customers ALTER firstName SET DEFAULT '';
```

A statement that drops the default value of a column

```
ALTER TABLE customers ALTER firstName DROP DEFAULT;
```

Description

- You can use the ALTER TABLE statement to modify the columns of an existing table.

Warning

- You should never alter a table or other database object in a production database without first consulting the DBA, but you probably won't have the privileges for doing that.

Figure 17-5   How to alter a table

How to drop a table

Figure 17-6 shows how to use the DROP TABLE statement. When you use this statement, use it cautiously, especially when you're working on a production database.

You can use the DROP TABLE statement to delete the definition of a table. In addition, the DROP TABLE statement deletes all data that's stored in the table. In this figure, for instance, the first example drops the customers table. However, if the customers table doesn't exist, this generates an error that stops a SQL script from continuing. To prevent this error, you can add the IF EXISTS keywords to the DROP TABLE statement as shown in the second statement.

By default, MySQL doesn't use foreign keys to enforce referential integrity. As a result, you can drop any table in the database even if other tables depend on that table. However, if you have configured MySQL to enforce referential integrity for your database, MySQL checks whether other tables depend on the table you're trying to drop. If so, MySQL won't allow you to drop the table. For example, you can't delete the customers table if a foreign key in the orders table refers to the customers table. In that case, you must drop the orders table before you can drop the customers table.

When you drop a table, MySQL also drops any indexes that have been defined for that table. In the next figure, you'll learn how to work with the indexes of a table.

A statement that drops a table

```
DROP TABLE customers;
```

A statement that drops a table if it exists

```
DROP TABLE IF EXISTS customers;
```

Description

- You can use the DROP TABLE statement to delete a table.
- If you drop a table, MySQL deletes its definition (including its indexes) and its data.

Warning

- You should never drop a table in a production database without first consulting the DBA, but you probably won't have the privileges for doing that.

Figure 17-6   How to drop a table

How to work with indexes

An *index* speeds joins and searches by providing a way for a database management system to go directly to a row rather than having to search through all the rows until it finds the one you want. By default, MySQL creates indexes for the primary keys and unique constraints of a table, which is usually what you want. In addition, you may want to create indexes for foreign keys and other columns that are used frequently in search conditions or joins. However, you'll want to avoid creating indexes on columns that are updated frequently since this slows insert, update, and delete operations.

How to create an index

Figure 17-7 presents the basic syntax of the CREATE INDEX statement, which creates an index based on one or more columns of a table. This syntax omits some of the optional clauses that you can use for tuning the indexes for better performance. This tuning is typically done by DBAs working with large databases, but usually isn't necessary for smaller databases.

To create an index, you use the ON clause to specify the name of the table and the column or columns for the index. In this figure, the first two examples create an index based on a single column, and the third example creates an index based on two columns. For each column, you can use the UNIQUE keyword to specify that an index contains only unique values. In addition, you can specify the ASC or DESC keyword to indicate whether you want the index sorted in ascending or descending sequence.

In these examples, the index names follow a standard naming convention. Here, the index name is the same as the name of the column or columns for the index. For instance, the first example creates an index named customerID for the customerID column of the customers table, and the third example creates an index named customerIDorderNumber for the customerID and orderNumber columns of the orders table.

Although you can use the CREATE INDEX statement to add indexes to an existing table, you can use the CREATE TABLE statement to create indexes for a new table. In this figure, the fifth example creates a customers table that has the same indexes that were created by the first two examples. Note that the syntax is slightly different, but you still need to specify the name of the index before the parentheses, and you need to specify the column or columns for the index within the parentheses.

How to drop an index

The sixth example shows how to use the DROP INDEX statement to drop an index. You may want to drop an index if you suspect that it isn't speeding up your joins and searches and that it may be slowing down your insert, update, and delete operations.

The syntax of the CREATE INDEX statement

```
CREATE [UNIQUE] INDEX|KEY indexName
ON tableName (columnName1 [ASC|DESC] [, columnName2 [ASC|DESC]]...)
```

A statement that creates an index based on a single column

```
CREATE INDEX customerID
ON orders (customerID);
```

A statement that creates a unique index

```
CREATE UNIQUE INDEX emailAddress
ON customers (emailAddress);
```

A statement that creates an index based on two columns

```
CREATE UNIQUE INDEX customerIDorderNumber
ON orders (customerID, orderNumber);
```

A statement that creates an index that's sorted in descending order

```
CREATE INDEX orderTotal
ON orders (orderTotal DESC);
```

A CREATE TABLE statement that also creates indexes

```
CREATE TABLE customers (
    customerID     INT           NOT NULL    AUTO_INCREMENT,
    emailAddress   VARCHAR(255)  NOT NULL,
    firstName      VARCHAR(60)   NOT NULL,

    PRIMARY KEY (customerID),
    UNIQUE INDEX emailAddress (emailAddress),
    INDEX firstName (firstName)
);
```

A DROP INDEX statement that drops an index

```
DROP INDEX firstName ON customers;
```

Description

- An *index* improves performance when MySQL searches for rows in the table.
- MySQL automatically creates an index for primary keys and for unique constraints.
- You can use the CREATE TABLE statement to create indexes for a table.
- You can use the CREATE INDEX statement to add an index to a table.
- You can use the DROP INDEX statement to drop an index.

Figure 17-7   How to create and drop an index

How to work with users and privileges

Now that you know how to create databases and tables, you're ready to learn how to create users and grant them privileges to work with those databases and tables. You'll also learn how to revoke privileges from those users or drop them entirely whenever that's necessary.

A summary of privileges

Figure 17-8 summarizes some of the common *privileges* that a database user can have. To start, a user can have privileges to work with the data that's stored in the database. These privileges allow a user to execute DML statements such as the SELECT, UPDATE, INSERT, and DELETE statements. These privileges are the most common types of privileges since most users need to be able to work with the data that's stored in a database.

A user can also have privileges to modify the definition of the database. These privileges allow a user to execute DDL statements such as the CREATE TABLE, ALTER TABLE, DROP TABLE, CREATE INDEX, and DROP INDEX statements. These privileges are common for administrative users of a database such as database administrators or programmers, but they aren't commonly granted to the end users of a database.

The ALL privilege lets the user grant all privileges available at the current level except the GRANT OPTION privilege. In general, you only grant this privilege to users like database administrators or programmers. In some cases, you may also want to grant these users the GRANT OPTION privilege as described in the next figure. If you do, they can grant privileges to other users.

The USAGE privilege doesn't grant any privileges. If you grant this privilege to a new user, the user will have no privileges. Then, you can grant other privileges to the user later. If you grant this privilege to an existing user, it doesn't change the privileges for that account. This can be useful for modifying other attributes of the account such as the password for the account.

To understand how privileges work, you need to understand that MySQL assigns them at four different levels: global, database, table, and column. In this figure, you can see examples of the four levels. Note that the asterisk (*) is a wildcard character that can be used to indicate all databases or all tables. Note also that the column or columns for a table are enclosed in parentheses. For more complete examples of these four levels, please see figure 17-10.

Before you go on, you should know that this figure only presents some of the most common MySQL privileges. However, MySQL provides many others. For example, MySQL provides an EXECUTE privilege that allows you to execute stored procedures and user-defined functions. As a result, if the privileges presented in this chapter aren't adequate for your security needs, please refer to the online MySQL Reference Manual for more information. To get started, you can search for "privileges provided" or "privileges".

Privileges for working with data

Privilege	Description
SELECT	Select data from a table.
INSERT	Insert data into a table.
UPDATE	Update data in a table.
DELETE	Delete data from a table.

Privileges for modifying the database structure

Privilege	Description
CREATE	Create a database or a table.
ALTER	Alter a table.
DROP	Drop a database or a table.
INDEX	Create or drop an index.

Other privileges

Privilege	Description
ALL [PRIVILEGES]	All privileges available at the current level except the GRANT OPTION privilege.
GRANT OPTION	Allows a user to grant his or her privileges to other users.
USAGE	No privileges. It can be used to modify existing accounts without changing privileges for that account.

The four privilege levels

Level	Example	Description
Global	*.*	All databases and all tables.
Database	music_db.*	All tables on the specified database.
Table	music_db.products	All columns on the specified table.
Column	(listPrice) music_db.products	Only the specified column or columns.

Description

- The first group of privileges allows the user to work with the data that's stored in the tables of the database.
- The second group of privileges allows the user to modify the structure of the database.
- MySQL makes it possible to specify privileges at the global level, the database level, the table level, and the column level.
- For a complete list of privileges, search for "privileges provided" in the MySQL Reference Manual that's available online.

Figure 17-8   A summary of privileges

How to create, rename, and drop users

Figure 17-9 shows how to work with users. To start, when you use the CREATE USER statement, you typically specify the name of the user, followed by an @ sign, followed by the name of the host, followed by the password for the user. In the first example, for instance, the CREATE USER statement creates a user named joel on the host named localhost with a password of sesame.

If you don't use the @ sign to specify a host, MySQL uses a percent sign (%) as the name of the host. This indicates that the user can be from any host. In the second example, for instance, the CREATE USER statement creates a user named dba on any host with a password of sesame. If you don't include the host name, you might not be able to connect to the database as that user on some operating systems. As a result, we recommend that you specify the host name in most cases.

Once you use the CREATE USER statement to create a user, the user has no privileges. However, you can use the GRANT statement to assign privileges to the user as shown in the next figure.

The third example uses the RENAME USER statement to change the name of the user from joel@localhost to joelmurach@localhost. If this user has privileges, the privileges are transferred to the new name.

The fourth example shows how to change the password for the user named joelmurach@localhost. To do that, you can use the GRANT statement to grant the USAGE privilege for all databases and tables to the user. Then, you can use the IDENTIFIED BY keywords to specify a new password for the user. This grants all of the user's current privileges to the same user, but it changes the password for that user.

The fifth and sixth examples use the DROP USER statement to drop the users named joelmurach@localhost and dba@%. This deletes these user accounts from the internal database that MySQL uses to keep track of users, and it revokes all privileges from those users.

How to create a user from a specific host

```
CREATE USER joel@localhost IDENTIFIED BY 'sesame';
```

How to create a user from any host

```
CREATE USER dba IDENTIFIED BY 'sesame';    -- creates 'dba@%'
```

How to rename a user from a specific host

```
RENAME USER joel@localhost TO joelmurach@localhost;
```

How to change a user's password

```
GRANT USAGE ON *.*
TO joelmurach@localhost
IDENTIFIED BY 'newpassword';
```

How to drop a user from a specific host

```
DROP USER joelmurach@localhost;
```

How to drop a user from any host

```
DROP USER dba;                             -- drops 'dba@%'
```

Description

- You use the CREATE USER statement to create a user that has no privileges.
- If you want to specify the host for a user, you can code the username, followed by the @ character, followed by the hostname.
- If you specify a user without specifying a hostname, MySQL uses a percentage sign (%) as a wildcard character to indicate that the user can be from any host.
- You can use the RENAME USER statement change the name of a user.
- You can use the GRANT statement to change a user's password.
- You can use the DROP USER statement to drop a user.

Figure 17-9   How to create, rename, and drop users

How to grant privileges

In general, it's a good practice to use the CREATE USER statement to create users and the GRANT statement to grant privileges. However, MySQL allows you to use the GRANT statement to create users and grant privileges in a single statement as shown in the first three examples of figure 17-10.

The first statement creates a user that has no privileges. This user has a name of joel, a host of localhost, and a password of sesame.

The second statement creates a user named mgs_user@localhost and grants the SELECT, INSERT, UPDATE, and DELETE privileges on all tables in the my_guitar_shop2 database to that user. To do that, this statement specifies the name of the database, followed by a dot, followed by the asterisk character (*) to specify all tables. As a result, the user named mgs_user@localhost can work with data from all of the tables in the specified database.

The third statement creates a user named dba@% and grants all privileges on all databases to that user. To do that, this statement uses the ALL keyword to specify all privileges at the current level except the GRANT OPTION privilege. Then, it uses the asterisk character (*) in the ON clause to specify the global level. In addition, this statement includes the WITH GRANT OPTION clause. This grants the GRANT OPTION privilege to the user. As a result, the dba user can grant privileges to other users.

The advantage of using the ALL keyword is that you write less code to grant all privileges to a user. The disadvantage is that you may accidentally grant more privileges than the user needs, which could open a hole in the security of your database. In general, it's a good practice to only grant the user the privileges that he or she needs.

Before you can grant privileges, you must connect as an appropriate user. In this figure, the examples assume that you are connected as the root user because this user has the necessary privileges to grant all privileges to other users. If you are connected as another user that has the GRANT OPTION privilege, you can still use the ALL keyword, but it only grants all of the privileges for that user.

The fourth statement shows that you can grant multiple privileges by separating the privileges with commas. This statement grants the SELECT, INSERT, and UPDATE privileges on the products table in the my_guitar_shop2 database to an existing user named joel@localhost. The fifth statement works similarly, but it grants these privileges on all tables in the database. And the sixth statement works similarly, but it grants these privileges to all tables of all databases.

The seventh statement grants privileges to specific columns of a table. This statement grants the SELECT privilege on three columns of the products table, but it only grants the UPDATE privilege on one column. Most of the time, you won't need to get down to the column level, but you can do it if necessary.

The eighth statement assumes that the my_guitar_shop2 database is selected. As a result, this statement doesn't specify the database name. Since this makes it easier to work with the privileges of the database, it often makes sense to select the database before working with the privileges of its users.

The syntax of the GRANT statement

```
GRANT privilegeList
ON [dbName.]table
TO userName1 [IDENTIFIED BY 'password1'][,
    userName2 [IDENTIFIED BY 'password2']...]
[WITH GRANT OPTION]
```

A statement that creates a user with no privileges

```
GRANT USAGE
ON *.*
TO joel@localhost IDENTIFIED BY 'sesame';
```

A statement that creates a user with database privileges

```
GRANT SELECT, INSERT, UPDATE, DELETE
ON my_guitar_shop2.*
TO mgs_user@localhost IDENTIFIED BY 'pa55word';
```

A statement that creates a user with global privileges

```
GRANT ALL
ON *.*
TO dba IDENTIFIED BY 'supersecret'
WITH GRANT OPTION;
```

A statement that grants table privileges to a user

```
GRANT SELECT, INSERT, UPDATE
ON my_guitar_shop2.products TO joel@localhost;
```

A statement that grants database privileges to a user

```
GRANT SELECT, INSERT, UPDATE
ON my_guitar_shop2.* TO joel@localhost;
```

A statement that grants global privileges to a user

```
GRANT SELECT, INSERT, UPDATE
ON *.* TO joel@localhost;
```

A statement that grants column privileges to a user

```
GRANT SELECT (productCode, productName, listPrice), UPDATE (description)
ON my_guitar_shop2.products TO joel@localhost
```

A statement that uses the current database

```
GRANT SELECT, INSERT, UPDATE, DELETE
ON customers TO joel@localhost;
```

Description

- The WITH GRANT OPTION clause allows the user to grant the privileges for that user to other users.
- You can use the asterisk (*) to specify all databases or all tables.
- If you don't specify a database, MySQL uses the current database.

Figure 17-10   How to grant privileges

How to revoke privileges

After you've created users and granted privileges to them, you may need to revoke privileges from a user. For example, if a user abuses his or her privileges, you may need to revoke some or all of them. To do that, you can use the REVOKE statement as shown in figure 17-11. Since this statement works similarly to the GRANT statement, you shouldn't have much trouble using the REVOKE statement once you understand the GRANT statement.

Here, the first statement shows how to revoke all privileges from a user named dba@%. To do that, you can code a REVOKE statement that uses the ALL keyword to revoke all privileges. In addition, you must specify GRANT OPTION to revoke the GRANT OPTION privilege. This revokes all privileges from a user on all databases. To be able to use this syntax, you must be logged in as a user that has the CREATE USER privilege. Otherwise, you won't have the privileges you need to execute the REVOKE statement.

The second statement works like the first statement. However, it revokes all privileges from two users. To do that, this statement separates the user names in the FROM clause with a comma.

The third statement revokes specific privileges from a user. This statement shows that you can revoke multiple privileges by separating each privilege with a comma. For example, this statement revokes the UPDATE and DELETE privileges on the customers table in the my_guitar_shop2 database from the user named joel@localhost. To be able to use this syntax, you must be logged in as a user that has the GRANT OPTION privilege and the privilege that you're revoking. Otherwise, you won't have the privileges you need to execute the REVOKE statement.

The REVOKE statement removes privileges, but doesn't remove the user from the database that MySQL uses to keep track of users. To remove a user account entirely, use the DROP USER statement described in figure 17-9.

The syntax of the REVOKE statement for all privileges

```
REVOKE ALL[ PRIVILEGES], GRANT OPTION
FROM user [, user]
```

A statement that revokes all privileges from a user

```
REVOKE ALL, GRANT OPTION
FROM dba;
```

A statement that revokes all privileges from multiple users

```
REVOKE ALL, GRANT OPTION
FROM dba, joel@localhost;
```

The syntax of the REVOKE statement for specific privileges

```
REVOKE privilegeList
ON [dbName.]table
FROM user [, user]
```

A statement that revokes specific privileges from a user

```
REVOKE UPDATE, DELETE
ON my_guitar_shop2.customers FROM joel@localhost
```

Description

- You can use the REVOKE statement to revoke privileges from a user.
- To revoke all privileges, you must have the global CREATE USER privilege.
- To revoke specific privileges, you must have the GRANT OPTION privilege and you must have the privileges that you are revoking.
- To delete a user account, use the DROP USER statement described in figure 17-9.

Figure 17-11   How to revoke privileges

How to view privileges

When you're done granting or revoking privileges, you may want to view the privileges that have been granted to make sure that you have granted the correct privileges to each user. To do that, you can use the techniques described in figure 17-12.

To start, if you want to get a list of users for the current server, you can use a SELECT statement like the one shown in the first example to query the table named user of the database named mysql. This statement allows you to view the User and Host columns of the user table.

In this figure, the MySQL server has six users. I created the first four, and the last two were created when I installed the XAMPP package. Here, the root user is the admin user for MySQL, and the pma user stores the privileges for the phpMyAdmin application. Note that the Host column for these users specifies localhost. Similarly, the users named joel, mgs_user, and mgs_tester have a Host column of localhost. In contrast, the user named dba has a Host column of %.

Once you know the name of the user and the host, you can use the SHOW GRANTS statement to view the privileges for that user. For instance, the second example shows how to view the privileges for a user from any host. In particular, it shows how to view the privileges for the user named dba@%. The result set for this user shows that it has all privileges including the GRANT OPTION privilege for all tables and databases on the server.

The third example shows how to view the privileges for a user from a specific host. In particular, it shows how to view the privileges for the user named mgs_user@localhost. Here, the result set shows that this user has a global USAGE privilege (*.*). By itself, this privilege only allows the user to view the mysql database, but it doesn't allow the user to be able to view or work with any other databases. However, this user also has SELECT, INSERT, UPDATE, and DELETE privileges for all tables on the databases named my_guitar_shop1 and my_guitar_shop2. As a result, it can work with the data in those databases.

The fourth example shows how to view the privileges for the current user. To do that, you can execute a SHOW GRANTS statement without a FOR clause. For example, if you are logged in as the root user, you can use the SHOW GRANTS keywords to show the privileges for that user. In that case, you'll get a result set similar to the one for the user named dba@%.

A statement that lists all users

```
SELECT User, Host from mysql.user;
```

The result set

User	Host
dba	%
joel	localhost
mgs_tester	localhost
mgs_user	localhost
pma	localhost
root	localhost

The syntax of the SHOW GRANTS statement

```
SHOW GRANTS [FOR user]
```

A statement that shows the privileges for a user from any host

```
SHOW GRANTS FOR dba;
```

The result set

Grants for dba@%
GRANT ALL PRIVILEGES ON *.* TO 'dba'@'%' IDENTIFIED BY PASSWORD '*90BA3AC0BFDE07AE334CA523CB27167AE33825B9' WITH GRANT OPTION

A statement that shows the privileges for a user with a specific host

```
SHOW GRANTS FOR mgs_user@localhost;
```

The result set

Grants for mgs_user@localhost
GRANT USAGE ON *.* TO 'mgs_user'@'localhost' IDENTIFIED BY PASSWORD '*F71B0AF6B232C58021B6AC63A29FCF13A4E46E59'
GRANT SELECT, INSERT, UPDATE, DELETE ON `my_guitar_shop2`.* TO 'mgs_user'@'localhost'
GRANT SELECT, INSERT, UPDATE, DELETE ON `my_guitar_shop1`.* TO 'mgs_user'@'localhost'

A statement that shows the privileges for the current user

```
SHOW GRANTS;
```

Description

- MySQL uses an internal database named mysql to keep track of its users. Within that database, MySQL uses a table named users to keep track of its users. You can query that table to get a list of users for the current MySQL server.
- You can use the SHOW GRANTS statement to show the privileges for a user.

Figure 17-12   How to view privileges

Other skills for creating a database

This topic describes two more skills that you may need to create a database. To start, you may want to load data that's stored in text files into a database. In addition, you may want to dump a database and its data to a SQL script file. Then, you can create the same database on another computer by running that script.

How to load data from text files

After you've created a table, you can fill the table with data. There are two ways to do that. First, you can use the INSERT statement to insert one or more rows into a table as described in the next chapter. Second, you can load data from text files into a table as described in figure 17-13.

If you have a tab-delimited text file like the one shown in this figure, you can load the data in that file into a table. However, for this to work, the file must provide for all of the columns that are defined for the table. For example, a table for this text file would need to have four columns like this: userID, firstName, lastName, emailAddress.

The easiest way to load data from text files into MySQL is to use phpMyAdmin. To do that, you start phpMyAdmin, select the database, select the table, and click the Import tab. In this figure, for example, I have selected the database named my_guitar_shop2 and the table named products. Then, you select the file to import. Although you can't see it in this figure, I have selected the file named products.txt that's in the ch17_db_scripts directory. Next, you select the option that you want to use for importing. For this import, I have selected the "CSV using LOAD DATA" option, and I have set the field terminator to a tab character (\t), but I have left the rest of the options at their default settings. (Here, CSV stands for comma-separated values, even though this import uses tab-separated values.)

If you don't have access to phpMyAdmin, you can use the command prompt to load data. To do that on a Windows system, you can use commands like the ones in this figure. To start, you use the mysql command to connect to the MySQL server. Then, you use the USE command to select the database. Finally, you use the LOAD command to load the data from the text file into the specified table. In this example, the LOAD command loads data from a local file named products.txt into the products table.

If you aren't using a Windows system, the commands in this procedure will vary somewhat. Similarly, if you're loading data into a table on a remote web server, this procedure will vary depending on how your web server is configured. As a result, you may need to check with your Internet service provider for details about connecting to the server and for the correct path to your files.

The Import tab for the table named products

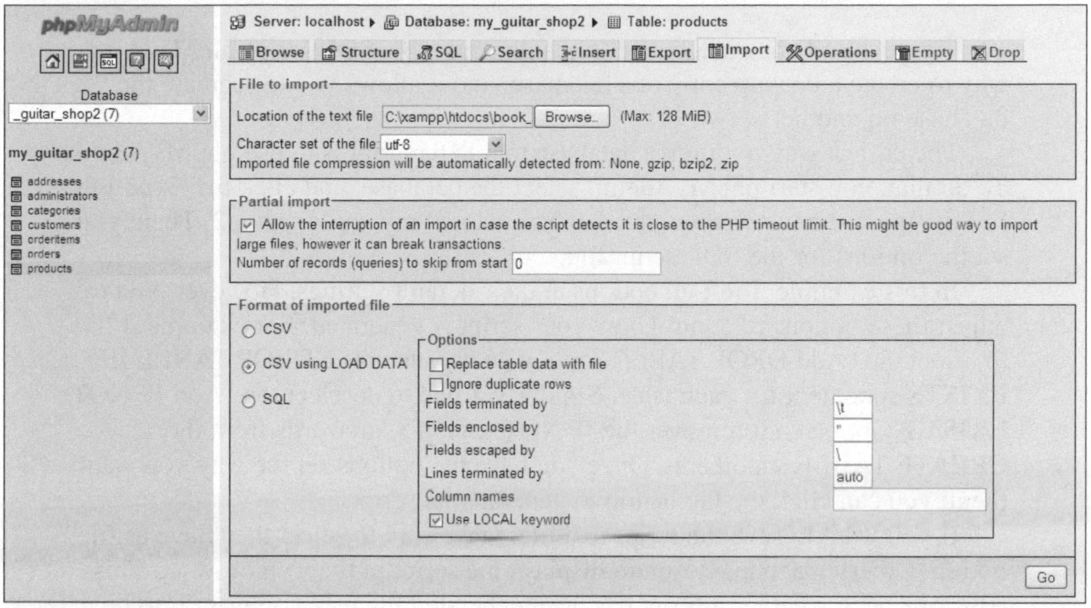

A tab-delimited text file that's stored in users.txt

```
1       John        Smith        jsmith@gmail.com
2       Andrea      Steelman     andi@murach.com
3       Joel        Murach       joelmurach@yahoo.com
```

How to use phpMyAdmin to load data from a text file

1. Start phpMyAdmin, select the database, select the table, and click on the Import tab.

2. Select the file to import.

3. Set the options for the import and click the Go button. If you get an error, you can modify the import options and try again.

How to use the Windows command prompt to load data from a text file

```
cd \xampp\mysql\bin
mysql -u root -p
Enter password: ******
use my_guitar_shop2;
load data local infile "c:/murach/products.txt" into table products;
exit;
```

Description

- You can use phpMyAdmin or the LOAD command to load data into a MySQL database from a text file.

Figure 17-13   How to load data from text files

How to dump a database to a SQL script

Figure 17-14 shows how to dump a database to a SQL script file. This is a way to create a backup copy of a database, and it allows you to recreate the database on another server.

The easiest way to dump a database to a SQL script is to use phpMyAdmin. To do that, you start phpMyAdmin, select the database, and click the Export tab. In this figure, I have selected the database named my_guitar_shop2. Then, you set the options for the SQL script file.

In this example, I left all options at their default settings. However, you can adjust these options to control how your script is generated. For example, I like to select the "Add DROP TABLE" option so it generates a DROP TABLE IF EXISTS statement for each table. Similarly, I like to deselect the "Add IF NOT EXISTS" option so it removes the IF NOT EXISTS keywords from the CREATE TABLE statements. Once you have the options set the way you want them, you can click the Go button to generate the script.

If you want to save the script to a file, make sure to select the "Save as file" option. Otherwise, phpMyAdmin displays the script in the web browser. This lets you check whether a script has been generated the way you want it to be.

By default, phpMyAdmin also generates the INSERT statements that insert the data for the database into the tables. As a result, if you only want the structure of the database, not the data, you can deselect the options that generate the INSERT statements. You'll learn more about INSERT statements in the next chapter.

If you don't have access to phpMyAdmin, you can use the command prompt to dump a database to a SQL script. To do that, you can use the mysqldump command. To illustrate, this figure shows how this works on a Windows system.

To start, you use the mysqldump command to specify the username, the database, and the name of the script file. After you execute this command, you enter the password for the specified user. Then, by default, MySQL writes this file to its bin directory. In this example, the file named my_guitar_shop2.sql should be stored in MySQL's bin directory.

If you aren't using a Windows system, this procedure will vary somewhat. Similarly, if you're dumping a database on a remote web server, this procedure will vary depending on how your web server is configured. As a result, you may need to check with your Internet service provider for details about connecting to the server and for the correct path to your files.

The Export tab for the database named my_guitar_shop2

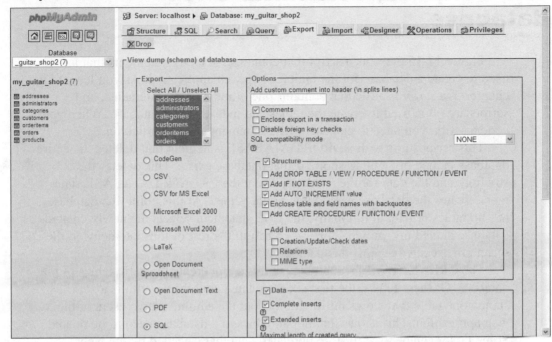

How to use phpMyAdmin to dump a database to a SQL script

1. Start phpMyAdmin, select the database, and click on the Export tab.
2. Set the options for the SQL script file.
3. Click on the Go button and save the file.

How to use the Windows command prompt to dump a database to a SQL script

```
cd \xampp\mysql\bin
mysqldump -u root -p my_guitar_shop2 > my_guitar_shop2.sql
Enter password: ******
```

Description

- You can use phpMyAdmin or the mysqldump command to generate a SQL script that includes all of the CREATE and INSERT statements needed to create a copy of the database.

Figure 17-14   How to dump a database to a SQL script

The script for the Guitar Shop database

Figure 17-15 presents a script that contains the DDL statements that are used to create a database for the Guitar Shop web application. As you learned in chapter 3, a *script* is a file that contains one or more SQL statements, and scripts are often used to create the tables and indexes for a database. When you code a script, you need to end each SQL statement with a semicolon.

This script starts with a DROP DATABASE statement that deletes the entire database named my_guitar_shop2 if that database exists. This deletes the structure and the data for the database. Then, the CREATE DATABASE statement creates the database named my_guitar_shop2. At this point, the database has no tables or data in it. Finally, the USE statement selects the newly created database named my_guitar_shop2. As a result, the rest of the statements in the script are executed against this database.

The CREATE TABLE statements in this script create the eight tables of the database. Of these tables, the first six are related, and the seventh is a standalone table that stores information about the administrative users of the web application. This shows that not all tables in a database need to be related. Some tables can be used to store unrelated data that's needed by the web application.

Each CREATE TABLE statement begins with its primary key column (or columns) first, followed by its foreign key columns. Although this isn't required, it's a good programming practice. Since the order in which you declare the columns defines the default order for the columns, this script defines these columns in a logical order. That way, when you use a SELECT * statement to retrieve all of the columns, they're returned in this order.

For most of the columns in these tables, this script includes a NOT NULL constraint or a DEFAULT attribute. In general, it's a good practice to only allow a column to accept NULL values when you want to allow for unknown values. If, for example, a customer doesn't supply the second line of an address, the second line of the address is unknown. In that case, you can store a NULL value in the line2 column.

Another option is to store an empty string for this column. To do that, you can define the address columns like this:

```
line2    VARCHAR(60)    DEFAULT '',
```

In this case, empty strings are stored for this column unless other values are assigned to it.

In practice, a NULL value is a more intuitive representation of an unknown value than an empty string. In other words, an empty string typically indicates that the value is known and is empty. Although how you use NULL values and empty strings is largely a matter of personal preference, it does affect the way you query a table.

For the sake of consistency, this script codes all primary key constraints, unique constraints, and indexes at the end of the CREATE TABLE statement. In

The SQL script that creates the my_guitar_shop2 database   Page 1

```sql
-- create and select the database
DROP DATABASE IF EXISTS my_guitar_shop2;
CREATE DATABASE my_guitar_shop2;
USE my_guitar_shop2;

-- create the tables for the database
CREATE TABLE customers (
    customerID          INT                     NOT NULL    AUTO_INCREMENT,
    emailAddress        VARCHAR(255)            NOT NULL,
    password            VARCHAR(60)             NOT NULL,
    firstName           VARCHAR(60)             NOT NULL,
    lastName            VARCHAR(60)             NOT NULL,
    shipAddressID       INT                                 DEFAULT NULL,
    billingAddressID    INT                                 DEFAULT NULL,
    PRIMARY KEY (customerID),
    UNIQUE INDEX emailAddress (emailAddress)
);

CREATE TABLE addresses (
    addressID           INT                     NOT NULL    AUTO_INCREMENT,
    customerID          INT                     NOT NULL,
    line1               VARCHAR(60)             NOT NULL,
    line2               VARCHAR(60)                         DEFAULT NULL,
    city                VARCHAR(40)             NOT NULL,
    state               VARCHAR(2)              NOT NULL,
    zipCode             VARCHAR(10)             NOT NULL,
    phone               VARCHAR(12)             NOT NULL,
    disabled            TINYINT(1)              NOT NULL    DEFAULT 0,
    PRIMARY KEY (addressID),
    INDEX customerID (customerID)
);

CREATE TABLE orders (
    orderID             INT         NOT NULL    AUTO_INCREMENT,
    customerID          INT         NOT NULL,
    orderDate           DATETIME    NOT NULL,
    shipAmount          DECIMAL(10,2) NOT NULL,
    taxAmount           DECIMAL(10,2) NOT NULL,
    shipDate            DATETIME                DEFAULT NULL,
    shipAddressID       INT         NOT NULL,
    cardType            INT         NOT NULL,
    cardNumber          CHAR(16)    NOT NULL,
    cardExpires         CHAR(7)     NOT NULL,
    billingAddressID    INT         NOT NULL,
    PRIMARY KEY (orderID),
    INDEX customerID (customerID)
);
```

Figure 17-15   The script for the Guitar Shop database (part 1 of 2)

addition, this script follows a strict convention for naming these constraints where each constraint name is the same as the name of the column (or columns) of the constraint.

As you review this script, note that most of the indexes for the database are based on the foreign keys of each table. For example, since the categoryID column in the products table refers to the categoryID column in the categories table, this script creates an index on categoryID in the products table.

The GRANT statement at the end of the script creates a user named mgs_user with a password of pa55word. In addition, it grants this user the SELECT, INSERT, UPDATE, and DELETE privileges on all tables in the current database. As a result, if you connect to MySQL as mgs_user, you can work with any of the data that's stored in the database named my_guitar_shop2. However, you can't change the structure of this database.

A script like this one often contains multiple INSERT statements that insert starting data into the database. For example, even a new database should contain some products and categories. In addition, it often makes sense to add some customers and orders for testing purposes. In the next chapter, you'll learn how to code the INSERT statements to do that. Then, if you want, you can add those INSERT statements to the end of a script like this one.

To make it easy for you to read, this script uses all caps for all SQL keywords, data types, and column attributes. In addition, it uses spaces to align the data types and column attributes. That way, it's easy for you to identify the data type and attributes for a column. However, SQL is not a case sensitive language. As a result, you can use any capitalization convention you want for the SQL keywords, data types, and attributes.

The SQL script that creates the my_guitar_shop2 database   Page 2

```
CREATE TABLE orderItems (
    itemID              INT             NOT NULL    AUTO_INCREMENT,
    orderID             INT             NOT NULL,
    productID           INT             NOT NULL,
    itemPrice           DECIMAL(10,2)   NOT NULL,
    discountAmount      DECIMAL(10,2)   NOT NULL,
    quantity            INT NOT NULL,
    PRIMARY KEY (itemID),
    INDEX orderID (orderID),
    INDEX productID (productID)
);

CREATE TABLE products (
    productID           INT             NOT NULL    AUTO_INCREMENT,
    categoryID          INT             NOT NULL,
    productCode         VARCHAR(10)     NOT NULL,
    productName         VARCHAR(255)    NOT NULL,
    description         TEXT            NOT NULL,
    listPrice           DECIMAL(10,2)   NOT NULL,
    discountPercent     DECIMAL(10,2)   NOT NULL    DEFAULT 0.00,
    dateAdded           DATETIME        NOT NULL,
    PRIMARY KEY (productID),
    INDEX categoryID (categoryID),
    UNIQUE INDEX productCode (productCode)
);

CREATE TABLE categories (
    categoryID          INT             NOT NULL    AUTO_INCREMENT,
    categoryName        VARCHAR(255)    NOT NULL,
    PRIMARY KEY (categoryID)
);

CREATE TABLE administrators (
    adminID             INT             NOT NULL    AUTO_INCREMENT,
    emailAddress        VARCHAR(255)    NOT NULL,
    password            VARCHAR(255)    NOT NULL,
    firstName           VARCHAR(255)    NOT NULL,
    lastName            VARCHAR(255)    NOT NULL,
    PRIMARY KEY (adminID)
);

-- Create a user and grant privileges to that user
GRANT SELECT, INSERT, UPDATE, DELETE
ON *
TO mgs_user@localhost
IDENTIFIED BY 'pa55word';
```

Figure 17-15   The script for the Guitar Shop database (part 2 of 2)

Perspective

Now that you've completed this chapter, you should be able to create and modify the tables and indexes of a database by coding DDL statements. You should be able to create users for a database and manage their privileges. And you should be able to code a script that creates a database. Those are the skills you need to create a database that's suitable for most web sites.

You should realize, though, that MySQL offers many other features and capabilities. For example, you can have MySQL enforce referential integrity. You can have MySQL support transactions. And you can have MySQL use the Unicode character set instead of the Latin-1 character set. To learn more about those skills, you can check the online MySQL Reference Manual or you can get a book that's dedicated to MySQL.

Terms

Latin-1 character set	constraint
Unicode character set	primary key
fixed-length string	column-level primary key
variable-length string	table-level primary key
precision	index
scale	privilege
attribute	script

Summary

- By default, MySQL uses the *Latin-1 character set*, which provides for 256 characters with 1 byte per character. However, MySQL also supports the *Unicode character set*, which provides for over 65,000 characters, usually with 2 bytes per character.

- The CHAR data type is typically used for *fixed-length strings*. The VARCHAR data type is typically used for *variable-length strings*.

- The *precision* of a DECIMAL type indicates the total number of digits that can be stored in the data type. The *scale* indicates the number of decimal digits that can be stored to the right of the decimal point.

- The CREATE TABLE statement creates a table based on the column definitions and column *attributes* you specify. Since the NOT NULL and UNIQUE attributes limit the type of data that a column can store, they are known as *constraints*.

- A *primary key* requires that each row has a unique value for the column or columns for the primary key, and it doesn't allow NULL values.

- You code a *column-level primary key* as part of the definition of the column definition. You code a *table-level primary key* as if it is a separate column definition, and you name the column or columns it works with within that definition.

- An *index* improves performance when MySQL searches for rows in the table.

- A *user* can be granted *privileges* for working with different parts of the database.

- A *script* is a file that contains one or more SQL statements. Scripts are often used to create the tables and indexes for a database.

Exercise 17-1   Create a database and alter it

In this exercise, you will run a script that creates a database named my_guitar_shop2. Then, you will create your own script that contains some statements that alter that database.

Create a database by executing an existing script

1. Use a text editor to open the script named my_guitar_shop2.sql that's stored in the book_apps/_create_db directory.

2. Review the code and note how it creates the database named my_guitar_shop2.

3. Use phpMyAdmin to execute this script as shown in chapter 3. Then, view the structure of the database.

Create a script that alters the database

4. Use your text editor to create a file named customers_alter.sql that you'll use for storing a script.

5. Write an ALTER TABLE statement that adds a column named middleInitials to the customers table. This column should store up to 3 characters, allow NULL values, and be added after the firstName column.

6. Write an ALTER TABLE statement that modifies the customers table so the lastName column can store up to 100 characters.

7. Use phpMyAdmin to test this script. Then, use phpMyAdmin to view the structure of the database. Check to make sure the middleInitials column has been added and that the data type for the lastName column has been changed.

Exercise 17-2   Create a simple databse

In this exercise, you will write a script that creates a simple Accounts Payable (AP) database.

Write a script that creates a database and its tables

1. Start your text editor and create a file named ap.sql that you'll use for storing a script.

2.   Write the CREATE DATABASE statement needed to create a database named ap. If the database already exists, drop it.

3.   Use phpMyAdmin to test these statements by cutting and pasting them into phpMyAdmin.

4.   Write the USE statement that selects the database.

5.   Write CREATE TABLE statements to create the following tables in the ap database:

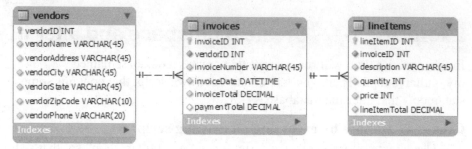

When you create these tables, be sure to use the correct data types and to identify the primary key for each table. Also, make sure to automatically generate a value for each primary key. For each column, include any UNIQUE, NOT NULL, or DEFAULT attributes you think are necessary.

6.   Use phpMyAdmin to run the script. Then, view the structure of the database.

Add statements to the script to create some indexes and a user

7.   Add CREATE INDEX statements to the end of the script to create indexes for the foreign keys of the invoices and lineItems tables. Also, write a CREATE INDEX statement to create an index for the invoiceNumber column.

8.   Add a GRANT statement to the end of the script that creates a user named ap_user with a password of "sesame" and grants this user privileges to select, insert, or update data from any table in the database. However, don't allow this user to delete any data from the database.

9.   Test the entire ap.sql script to make sure it runs correctly.

18

How to use SQL to work with a database

This chapter presents the essential SQL statements for working with the data in a MySQL database. To start, it shows you how to code SELECT statements to get data from a single table or from multiple tables. Then, it shows you how to work with summary queries and subqueries. Finally, it shows how to use the INSERT, UPDATE, and DELETE statements to add new rows to a table, to modify existing rows in a table, and to remove rows from a table.

How to select data from a single table **574**
How to select columns from a table 574
How to use an alias for a column 576
How to select rows with a LIMIT clause 578
How to select rows with a WHERE clause 580
How to use the logical operators 582
How to use the IS NULL operator 584
How to use the LIKE operator 586
How to sort rows with an ORDER BY clause 588

How to select data from multiple tables **590**
How to code an inner join 590
When and how to use table aliases 592

How to code summary queries **594**
How to code aggregate functions 594
How to group queries by column 596

How to code subqueries **598**
Where to use subqueries 598
How to code correlated subqueries 600

How to insert, update, and delete rows **602**
How to insert rows 602
How to update rows 604
How to delete rows 606

Perspective **608**

How to select data from a single table

To start, you need to learn how to code SELECT statements that retrieve data from a single table. Once you learn these skills, you can apply them to multiple tables and more complex queries.

How to select columns from a table

Figure 18-1 presents the basic syntax of the SELECT statement. Here, the capitalized words are keywords that you must spell exactly as shown, though you can use whatever capitalization you prefer.

This syntax summary has been simplified so that you can focus on the four main clauses of the SELECT statement: the SELECT clause, the FROM clause, the WHERE clause, and the ORDER BY clause. Here, the SELECT clause specifies the columns to retrieve. The FROM clause specifies the *base table* or tables to retrieve the data from. The WHERE clause specifies the rows to retrieve. And the ORDER BY clause specifies how to sort the rows.

The first SELECT statement in this figure retrieves all of the rows and columns from the products table. This statement uses the asterisk (*) wildcard character to indicate that all of the columns should be retrieved, and the WHERE clause is omitted so there are no conditions on the rows that are retrieved. This figure shows the result set for this statement as it's displayed by phpMyAdmin. However, to save space, this figure only shows the first three rows out of the ten rows that are retrieved by the statement.

Note that this statement doesn't include an ORDER BY clause. Without an ORDER BY clause, you can't be sure of the sequence in which the rows are presented. They might be in the sequence you expect, or they might not. As a result, if the sequence matters to you, you should include an ORDER BY clause.

The second statement retrieves selected columns from the products table. To do that, this statement uses the SELECT clause to specify the columns. Like the first statement, this statement doesn't include a WHERE clause, so all the rows are retrieved. However, this statement does include an ORDER BY clause. This clause sorts the rows by the listPrice column in ascending sequence.

The third statement works similarly to the second statement. However, the third statement uses a WHERE clause to only retrieve products that have a list price of less than 450.

The fourth statement shows another variation of the WHERE clause. In this case, this statement only retrieves products with a list price less than 10. Since none of the rows in the products table have a price this low, the result set is empty.

The simplified syntax of the SELECT statement

```
SELECT select_list
FROM table_source
[WHERE search_condition]
[ORDER BY order_by_list]
```

Retrieve all rows and columns from a table

```
SELECT * FROM products
```

productID	categoryID	productCode	productName	description	listPrice	discountPercent	dateAdded
1	1	strat	Fender Stratocaster	The Fender Stratocaster is the electric guitar des...	699.00	30.00	2009-10-30 09:32:40
2	1	les_paul	Gibson Les Paul	This Les Paul guitar offers a carved top and humbu...	1199.00	30.00	2009-12-05 16:33:13
3	1	sg	Gibson SG	This Gibson SG electric guitar takes the best of t...	2517.00	52.00	2010-02-04 11:04:31

```
(3 rows of 10)
```

Retrieve three columns and sort them by price

```
SELECT productID, productName, listPrice
FROM products
ORDER BY listPrice
```

productID	productName	listPrice ▲
5	Washburn D10S	299.00
6	Rodriguez Caballero 11	415.00
4	Yamaha FG700S	489.99
8	Hofner Icon	499.99
1	Fender Stratocaster	699.00
9	Ludwig 5-piece Drum Set with Cymbals	699.99
7	Fender Precision	799.99
10	Tama 5-Piece Drum Set with Cymbals	799.99
2	Gibson Les Paul	1199.00
3	Gibson SG	2517.00

Retrieve rows in the specified price range

```
SELECT productID, productName, listPrice
FROM products
WHERE listPrice < 450
ORDER BY listPrice
```

productID	productName	listPrice ▲
5	Washburn D10S	299.00
6	Rodriguez Caballero 11	415.00

Retrieve an empty result set

```
SELECT productID, productName, listPrice
FROM products
WHERE listPrice < 10
```

Figure 18-1   How to select columns from tables

How to use an alias for a column

By default, MySQL gives a column in a result set the same name as the column in the base table. You can specify a different name, however, whenever necessary. When you do that, the new column name is known as a *column alias*. Figure 18-2 presents two techniques for creating column aliases.

The first technique is to code the column specification followed by the AS keyword and the column alias. This is the coding technique specified by the American National Standards Institute (ANSI, pronounced 'ann-see'), and it's illustrated by the first example in this figure.

The second technique is to code the column specification followed by a space and the column alias, as illustrated by the second example. However, it's better to use the first technique since the AS keyword makes it easier to identify the alias for the column, which makes your SQL statement easier to read and maintain.

When you code an alias, you must enclose the alias in double quotes if the alias contains a space or is a keyword that's reserved by MySQL. In this figure, the third example specifies an alias for the listPrice column that uses two words with a space between them.

When you specify an alias, the result set uses the exact capitalization that you specify. As a result, you should be sure to specify the capitalization that you want.

When you code a column that contains a calculated value, it's a good practice to specify an alias for the calculated column. If you don't, MySQL assigns the entire calculation as the name, which can be unwieldy. You'll learn more about calculated values later in this chapter.

Use the AS keyword to specify an alias

```
SELECT productID, productName AS name, listPrice AS price
FROM products
WHERE listPrice < 450
ORDER BY listPrice
```

productID	name	price ▲
5	Washburn D10S	299.00
6	Rodriguez Caballero 11	415.00

Omit the AS keyword

```
SELECT productID, productName name, listPrice price
FROM products
WHERE listPrice < 450
ORDER BY listPrice
```

productID	name	price ▲
5	Washburn D10S	299.00
6	Rodriguez Caballero 11	415.00

Use quotes to include spaces

```
SELECT productID AS "ID", productName AS "Product Name",
       listPrice AS "Price"
FROM products
WHERE listPrice < 450
ORDER BY listPrice
```

ID	Product Name	Price ▲
5	Washburn D10S	299.00
6	Rodriguez Caballero 11	415.00

Description

- By default, a column in the result set is given the same name as the column in the base table. If that's not what you want, you can specify a *column alias* for the column.

- One way to name a column is to use the AS keyword as shown in the first example above. Although the AS keyword is optional, it enhances readability.

- When you enclose an alias in quotes, you can use spaces within the column name.

Figure 18-2   How to use an alias for a column

How to select rows with a LIMIT clause

In the database for this chapter, each table has a small number of rows. As a result, you don't need to limit the number of rows that your SELECT statements retrieve from this database. With a production database, however, it's common for a table to have thousands or even millions of rows. Then, you don't want to accidentally retrieve hundreds or thousands of rows.

One way to limit the number of rows that a SELECT statement retrieves is to code a LIMIT clause at the end of the statement as shown in figure 18-3. The easiest way to do that is to code the LIMIT keyword followed by the number of rows as shown in the first example. This retrieves the same rows as coding the LIMIT keyword followed by a row offset of 0, a comma, and the number of rows to retrieve as shown in the second example.

However, if you don't want to begin retrieving rows starting at the first row, you can specify another offset. In this figure, for example, the third statement specifies an offset of 1 to begin retrieving rows at the second row. To begin retrieving rows at the third row, specify an offset of 2. To begin at the fourth row, specify an offset of 3. And so on.

By default, phpMyAdmin automatically adds a LIMIT clause to most SELECT statements so they only retrieve the first 30 rows of a table. This is usually what you want since it prevents you from accidentally retrieving thousands of rows from a database. However, if you want to use phpMyAdmin to view more than 30 rows, you can override this default setting by coding your own LIMIT clause.

The syntax of the LIMIT clause

```
LIMIT [rowOffset, ] maxRows
```

Retrieve the first three rows of the result set

```
SELECT productID, productName
FROM products
LIMIT 3
```

productID	productName
1	Fender Stratocaster
2	Gibson Les Paul
3	Gibson SG

Another way to retrieve the first three rows

```
SELECT productID, productName
FROM products
LIMIT 0, 3
```

productID	productName
1	Fender Stratocaster
2	Gibson Les Paul
3	Gibson SG

Retrieve three rows starting at the second row

```
SELECT productID, productName
FROM products
LIMIT 1, 3
```

productID	productName
2	Gibson Les Paul
3	Gibson SG
4	Yamaha FG700S

Description

- You can use the LIMIT clause to limit the number of rows that are included in the result set.

Figure 18-3   How to select rows with a LIMIT clause

How to select rows with a WHERE clause

Another way to limit the number of rows that a SELECT statement retrieves is to code a WHERE clause. When you do that, you often use the comparison operators shown in figure 18-4. If the result of the comparison is TRUE for a row, MySQL includes the row in the result set.

The examples in this figure show how to use some of the comparison operators. For instance, the first WHERE clause uses the equal operator (=) to retrieve only those rows with a categoryID column that has a value of 2. Since the category ID is a numeric literal, it doesn't need to be enclosed in quotes, although it's okay to enclose it in quotes. In contrast, a string literal like the one in the second WHERE clause must be enclosed in quotes.

The third WHERE clause uses the less than (<) operator to retrieve only those rows that have a list price that's less than 499.99. Then, the fourth example uses the greater than or equal to (>=) operator to retrieve those rows that have a list price that's greater than or equal to 499.99.

The fifth WHERE clause illustrates how you can use comparison operators other than the equal operator with string data. In this example, the less than (<) operator is used to compare the value of the productName column to a string literal that has the letter G in the first position. That causes the query to return all product names that begin with the letters A through F.

You can also use the comparison operators with date literals, as illustrated by the sixth and seventh clauses. The sixth clause retrieves rows that were added before January 31, 2010, and the seventh clause retrieves rows that were added on or after January 31, 2010. Like string literals, date literals must be enclosed in single quotes. MySQL also expects date literals to use this format: yyyy-mm-dd.

When you code a date literal, MySQL adds a default time of 00:00:00, which is the start of the day. As a result, if you're working with a date/time value that includes a time component, you need to take this into account. If necessary, you can code a date literal that includes a time component. For example, you can code a time component for 4:30pm and 10 seconds like this:

```
'2010-10-30 16:30:10'
```

Note that the time component uses a 24 hour clock where 16 hours is 4pm.

The eighth WHERE clause shows how you can test for a *not equal* condition. To do that, you code a less than (<) sign followed by a greater than (>) sign. In this example, the WHERE clause only retrieves rows with a discount percent that's not equal to 30.

Whenever possible, you should compare expressions that have similar data types. If you attempt to compare expressions that have different data types, MySQL may implicitly convert the data types for you. Although implicit conversions are often acceptable, they occasionally yield unexpected results.

The syntax of the WHERE clause with comparison operators

```
WHERE expression_1 operator expression_2
```

The comparison operators

=	Equal
>	Greater than
<	Less than
<=	Less than or equal to
>=	Greater than or equal to
<>	Not equal

A WHERE clause that selects products where the product...

Is in the specified category
```
WHERE categoryID = 2
```

Has the specified name
```
WHERE productName = 'Gibson Les Paul'
```

Has a list price less than the specified price
```
WHERE listPrice < 499.99
```

Has a list price greater than or equal to the specified price
```
WHERE listPrice >= 499.99
```

Has a name that starts with the letters A to F
```
WHERE productName < 'G'
```

Was added before the specified date
```
WHERE dateAdded < '2010-01-31'
```

Was added on or after the specified date
```
WHERE dateAdded >= '2010-01-31'
```

Has a discount percent that does not equal the specified amount
```
WHERE discountPercent <> 30
```

Description

- If the result of a comparison results in a TRUE value, the row being tested is included in the result set. If it's FALSE or unknown, the row isn't included.

- To use a string literal or a date literal in a comparison, enclose it in single quotes. To use a numeric literal, the single quotes are optional.

- Character comparisons are not case-sensitive.

- You can use a comparison operator to compare any two expressions that result in like data types. Although unlike data types may be converted to data types that can be compared, the comparison may produce unexpected results.

Figure 18-4   How to select rows with a WHERE clause

How to use the logical operators

Figure 18-5 shows how to use *logical operators* in a WHERE clause. You can use the AND and OR operators to combine two or more search conditions into a *compound condition*. And you can use the NOT operator to negate a search condition.

The first two examples illustrate the difference between the AND and OR operators. When you use the AND operator, both conditions must be TRUE. So, the first example only retrieves products with a category ID of 1 and a discount percent of 30. When you use the OR operator, though, only one of the conditions must be TRUE. So, the second example retrieves all products with a category ID of 1 *and* all the products with a discount percent of 30.

The third example shows a WHERE clause that uses the NOT operator. Note, however, that the NOT operator makes this clause more difficult to understand than necessary. Because of that, you should avoid using this operator. You can usually do that by rewriting the WHERE clause as shown in the fourth example. As a result, the condition in the fourth example is easier to understand.

The last two examples show how the order of precedence for the logical operators works. By default, MySQL evaluates the NOT operator first, followed by the AND operator and then the OR operator. So, in the fifth example, MySQL first evaluates the two conditions connected by the AND operator. Then, it evaluates the conditions connected by the OR operator.

However, if the default order of precedence doesn't work the way you want, you can use parentheses to override it. In the sixth example, for instance, the statement uses parentheses so the two conditions connected by the OR operator are evaluated first.

In practice, using logical operators can be confusing. With a little experimentation, though, you should be able to code compound conditions that retrieve just the rows that you want.

The syntax of the WHERE clause with logical operators

```
WHERE [NOT] search_condition_1 {AND|OR} [NOT] search_condition_2 ...
```

A search condition that uses the AND operator

```
WHERE categoryID = 1 AND discountPercent = 30
```

A search condition that uses the OR operator

```
WHERE categoryID = 1 OR discountPercent = 30
```

A search condition that uses the NOT operator

```
WHERE NOT listPrice >= 500
```

The same condition rephrased to eliminate the NOT operator

```
WHERE listPrice < 500
```

A compound condition without parentheses

```
SELECT productName, listPrice, discountPercent, dateAdded
FROM products
WHERE dateAdded > '2010-07-01' OR listPrice < 500
AND discountPercent > 25
```

productName	listPrice	discountPercent	dateAdded
Yamaha FG700S	489.99	38.00	2010-06-01 11:12:59
Washburn D10S	299.00	0.00	2010-07-30 13:58:35
Rodriguez Caballero 11	415.00	39.00	2010-07-30 14:12:41
Hofner Icon	499.99	25.00	2010-07-30 14:18:33
Ludwig 5-piece Drum Set with Cymbals	699.99	30.00	2010-07-30 12:46:40
Tama 5-Piece Drum Set with Cymbals	799.99	15.00	2010-07-30 13:14:15

The same compound condition with parentheses

```
SELECT productName, listPrice, discountPercent, dateAdded
FROM products
WHERE (dateAdded > '2010-07-01' OR listPrice < 500)
AND discountPercent > 25
```

productName	listPrice	discountPercent	dateAdded
Yamaha FG700S	489.99	38.00	2010-06-01 11:12:59
Rodriguez Caballero 11	415.00	39.00	2010-07-30 14:12:41
Ludwig 5-piece Drum Set with Cymbals	699.99	30.00	2010-07-30 12:46:40

Description

- You can use the AND and OR *logical operators* to create *compound conditions* that consist of two or more conditions. You use the AND operator to specify that the search must satisfy both of the conditions, and you use the OR operator to specify that the search must satisfy at least one of the conditions.

- You can use the NOT operator to negate a condition.

- When MySQL evaluates a compound condition, it evaluates the operators in this sequence: (1) NOT, (2) AND, and (3) OR. You can use parentheses to override this order of precedence or to clarify the sequence in which the operations will be evaluated.

Figure 18-5   How to use the logical operators

How to use the IS NULL operator

In the last chapter, you learned that a column can contain a *NULL value*. Remember, though, that a NULL value isn't the same as zero, a blank string that contains one or more spaces (' '), or an empty string that doesn't contain any spaces (''). Instead, a NULL value indicates that the data is not applicable, not available, or unknown.

When a database allows NULL values in one or more columns, you need to know how to test for them in search conditions. To do that, you can use the IS NULL operator, as shown in figure 18-6.

This figure uses the table named orders to illustrate how to search for NULL values because it allows NULL values in its shipDate column. The first example selects three columns and all rows from this table. The result set shows that two of the three rows have NULL values in the shipDate column.

The second example shows how you can use the IS NULL operator to retrieve all rows that have a NULL value in its shipDate column. Similarly, you can use the NOT operator within the IS NULL operator as illustrated in the third example. Then, all the rows that don't contain NULL values are included in the query results.

The syntax of the WHERE clause with the IS NULL operator

```
WHERE expression IS [NOT] NULL
```

Retrieve all rows

```
SELECT orderID, orderDate, shipDate
FROM orders
```

orderID	orderDate	shipDate
1	2010-05-30 09:40:28	2010-06-01 09:43:13
2	2010-06-01 11:23:20	NULL
3	2010-06-03 09:44:58	NULL

Retrieve rows for orders that haven't been shipped

```
SELECT orderID, orderDate, shipDate
FROM orders
WHERE shipDate IS NULL
```

orderID	orderDate	shipDate
2	2010-06-01 11:23:20	NULL
3	2010-06-03 09:44:58	NULL

Retrieve rows for orders that have been shipped

```
SELECT orderID, orderDate, shipDate
FROM orders
WHERE shipDate IS NOT NULL
```

orderID	orderDate	shipDate
1	2010-05-30 09:40:28	2010-06-01 09:43:13

Description

- If the database allows NULL values in a column, you can use the IS NULL operator to select rows that have or don't have NULL values in that column.

Figure 18-6   How to use the IS NULL operator

How to use the LIKE operator

Another operator you can use in a WHERE clause is the LIKE operator, as shown in figure 18-7. This operator provides a powerful technique for finding information in a database that can't be found using any other technique. To use it, you can code the LIKE operator along with the *wildcards* shown at the top of this figure to specify the *string pattern*, or *mask*, that you want to match.

In the first example, the LIKE phrase specifies that all products that have a name that starts with the letters FENDER should be included in the query results. Here, the percent (%) sign indicates that any characters can follow these three letters. This includes "Fender Precision" and "Fender Stratocaster" in the results.

The second example selects all products that have the letters "cast" anywhere in the name. This includes "Fender Stratocaster" in the results.

The third example uses the underscore (_) to select all rows where the zip code begins with 076 followed by any two characters. This includes zip codes such as 07652, but it doesn't include zip codes such as 07652-1938.

The fourth example selects all orders that have a date in June of 2010. Note that this works because the example uses two underscore wildcards for the day portion of the date and a percent wildcard to allow for any time of day.

The syntax of the WHERE clause with the LIKE operator

```
WHERE match_expression [NOT] LIKE pattern
```

Wildcard symbols

Symbol	Description
%	Matches any string of zero or more characters.
_	Matches any single character.

WHERE clauses that use the LIKE operator

Example	Results that match the mask
`WHERE productName LIKE 'Fender%'`	All rows that have a name that starts with "Fender". For example, "Fender Stratocaster" and "Fender Precision".
`WHERE productName LIKE '%cast%'`	All rows that have a name that includes the "cast" string. For example, "Fender Stratocaster",
`WHERE zipCode LIKE '076__'`	All rows that have a zip code that begins with 076, followed by any two characters. For example, "07652" and "07677", but not "07652-4455".
`WHERE orderDate LIKE '2010-06-__%'`	All rows that have an order date in June of 2010.

Description

- You use the LIKE operator to retrieve rows that match a *string pattern*, called a *mask*. Within the mask, you can use special characters, called *wildcard* characters, that determine which values in the column satisfy the condition.

- You can use the NOT operator before the LIKE operator. Then, only those rows with values that don't match the string pattern are included in the result set.

Figure 18-7   How to use the LIKE operator

How to sort rows with an ORDER BY clause

The ORDER BY clause specifies the sort order for the rows in a result set. In most cases, you can use a single column name from the base table to sort the rows by that column in ascending order. However, you can also use other techniques to sort the rows in a result set, as described in figure 18-8.

To start, this figure presents the expanded syntax of the ORDER BY clause. This shows that you can sort by one or more expressions in either ascending or descending sequence.

The first two examples show how to sort the rows in a result set by a single column. In the first example, the rows in the products table are sorted in ascending sequence by the productName column. Since ascending is the default sequence, the ASC keyword is omitted. In the second example, the rows in the products table are sorted by the listPrice column in descending sequence. Here, the DESC keyword is necessary.

To sort by more then one column, you list the column names in the ORDER BY clause separated by commas as shown in the third example. Here, the rows in the products table are first sorted by the discountPercent column in ascending sequence. Then, within each discountPercent grouping, the rows are sorted by the listPrice column in descending sequence. This can be referred to as a *nested sort* because one sort is nested within another.

The syntax of the ORDER BY clause

```
ORDER BY expression [ASC|DESC] [, expression [ASC|DESC]] ...
```

Sort by one column in ascending sequence

```
SELECT productName, listPrice, discountPercent
FROM products
WHERE listPrice < 500
ORDER BY productName
```

productName ▲	listPrice	discountPercent
Hofner Icon	499.99	25.00
Rodriguez Caballero 11	415.00	39.00
Washburn D10S	299.00	0.00
Yamaha FG700S	489.99	38.00

Sort by one column in descending sequence

```
SELECT productName, listPrice, discountPercent
FROM products
WHERE listPrice < 500
ORDER BY listPrice DESC
```

productName	listPrice ▼	discountPercent
Hofner Icon	499.99	25.00
Yamaha FG700S	489.99	38.00
Rodriguez Caballero 11	415.00	39.00
Washburn D10S	299.00	0.00

Sort by two columns

```
SELECT productName, listPrice, discountPercent
FROM products
WHERE categoryID = 1
ORDER BY discountPercent, listPrice DESC
```

productName	listPrice	discountPercent
Washburn D10S	299.00	0.00
Gibson Les Paul	1199.00	30.00
Fender Stratocaster	699.00	30.00
Yamaha FG700S	489.99	38.00
Rodriguez Caballero 11	415.00	39.00
Gibson SG	2517.00	52.00

Description

- The ORDER BY clause specifies how you want the rows in the result set sorted. You can sort by one or more columns, and you can sort each column in either ascending (ASC) or descending (DESC) sequence. ASC is the default.

- By default, in an ascending sort, special characters appear first in the sort sequence, followed by numbers, then by letters (which are *not* case-sensitive), and then by NULL values. In a descending sort, this sequence is reversed.

Figure 18-8   How to sort rows with an ORDER BY clause

How to select data from multiple tables

Now that you know how to select data from a single table, you're ready to learn how to select data from multiple tables. To do that, you code a join. A *join* lets you combine columns from two or more tables into a single result set. This topic shows how to use the most common type of join, an *inner join*.

MySQL also provides an *outer join* that you can use to retrieve all rows from the tables involved in the join, whether or not the join condition is TRUE. However, since outer joins aren't commonly used in web applications, they aren't presented in this book.

How to code an inner join

Figure 18-9 presents the *explicit syntax* for coding an inner join. To use this syntax, you code the names of the two tables in the FROM clause along with the optional INNER keyword, the required JOIN keyword, and an ON phrase that specifies the *join condition*. The join condition indicates how the two tables should be compared. In most cases, they're compared based on the relationship between the primary key of the first table and a foreign key of the second table.

The SELECT statement in this figure, for example, joins data from the customers and orders tables based on the customerID column in each table. Since this join condition uses the equals (=) operator, the value of the customerID column in a row in the customers table must match the customerID in a row in the orders table for that row to be included in the result set. In other words, only customers with one or more orders are included.

In this example, the customers table is joined with the orders table using a column that has the same name in both tables: customerID. Because of that, the columns must be qualified to indicate which table they come from. To do that, you can code a *qualified column name* by entering the table name and a period in front of the column name. Although this example uses qualified column names only in the join condition, you must qualify a column name anywhere it appears in the statement if the same name occurs in both tables. If you don't, MySQL returns an error indicating that the column name is ambiguous. Of course, you can also qualify column names that aren't ambiguous. However, we recommend you do that only if it clarifies your code.

MySQL also provides an *implicit syntax* that you can use to code inner joins. To do that, you can code a list of tables in the FROM clause and the join condition in the WHERE clause. However, there are several advantages to using the explicit syntax, so the implicit syntax is not presented in this book.

The explicit syntax for an inner join

```
SELECT select_list
FROM table_1
    [INNER] JOIN table_2
        ON join_condition_1
    [[INNER] JOIN table_3
        ON join_condition_2]...
```

A SELECT statement that joins the customers and orders tables

```
SELECT firstName, lastName, orderDate
FROM customers
    INNER JOIN orders
        ON customers.customerID = orders.customerID
ORDER BY orderDate
```

firstName	lastName	orderDate
Allan	Sherwood	2010-05-30 09:40:28
Barry	Zimmer	2010-06-01 11:23:20
Allan	Sherwood	2010-06-03 09:44:58

Description

- A *join* is used to combine columns from two or more tables into a result set based on the *join conditions* you specify. For an *inner join*, only those rows that satisfy the join condition are included in the result set.

- A join condition names a column in each of the two tables involved in the join and indicates how the two columns should be compared. In most cases, you use the equal operator to retrieve rows with matching columns.

- In most cases, you want to join two tables based on the relationship between the primary key in one table and a foreign key in the other table. However, you can also join tables based on relationships not defined in the database. These are called *ad hoc relationships*.

- If the two columns in a join condition have the same name, you have to qualify them with the table name so MySQL can distinguish between them. To code a *qualified column name*, type the table name, followed by a period, followed by the column name.

- The INNER keyword is optional.

- This syntax for coding an inner join can be referred to as the *explicit syntax*. It is also called the *SQL-92 syntax* because it was introduced by the SQL-92 standards.

- You can also code an inner join using the *implicit syntax*. To do that, you list the tables in the FROM clause and code the join condition in the WHERE clause.

Figure 18-9   How to code an inner join

When and how to use table aliases

When you name a table to be joined in the FROM clause, you can refer to the table by an *alias*. *Table aliases* are used to reduce typing and to make a query more understandable, particularly when table names are lengthy.

A table alias is similar to a column alias. However, for tables, it's common to use the AS keyword for columns, and it's not common to use the AS keyword for tables. After you assign a table alias, you must use the alias in place of the original table name throughout the query. This is illustrated in figure 18-10.

The first statement in this figure joins data from the customers and orders tables. This statement assigns both tables aliases that consist of a single letter. The customers table has an alias of c, and the products table has an alias of p.

The second statement joins data from four tables. This statement assigns three of the tables aliases that consist of a single letter, and it assigns the orderItems table an alias of oi. Since the orderID column is available from two tables (orders and orderItems), this statement uses a table alias of o to qualify this column in the SELECT, FROM, and ORDER BY clauses. This shows that you can qualify a column name in any part of a SELECT statement.

The syntax for an inner join that uses table aliases

```
SELECT select_list
FROM table_1 n1
    [INNER] JOIN table_2 [AS] n2
        ON n1.column_name operator n2.column_name
    [[INNER] JOIN table_3 [AS] n3
        ON n2.column_name operator n3.column_name]...
```

An inner join with aliases for all tables

```
SELECT firstName, lastName, orderDate
FROM customers c
    INNER JOIN orders o
        ON c.customerID = o.customerID
ORDER BY orderDate
```

firstName	lastName	orderDate
Allan	Sherwood	2010-05-30 09:40:28
Barry	Zimmer	2010-06-01 11:23:20
Allan	Sherwood	2010-06-03 09:44:58

An inner join with aliases for four tables

```
SELECT firstName, lastName, o.orderID, productName, itemPrice, quantity
FROM customers c
    INNER JOIN orders o
        ON c.customerID = o.customerID
    INNER JOIN orderItems oi
        ON o.orderID = oi.orderID
    INNER JOIN products p
        ON oi.productID = p.productID
ORDER BY o.orderID
```

firstName	lastName	orderID	productName	itemPrice	quantity
Allan	Sherwood	1	Gibson Les Paul	399.00	1
Barry	Zimmer	2	Yamaha FG700S	699.00	1
Allan	Sherwood	3	Rodriguez Caballero 11	549.99	1
Allan	Sherwood	3	Gibson SG	499.00	1

Description

- A *table alias* is an alternative table name assigned in the FROM clause.

- The AS keyword is optional.

- If you assign an alias to a table, you must use that alias to refer to the table throughout your query. You can't use the original table name.

- Use table aliases whenever they simplify or clarify the query. Avoid using them when they make a query more confusing or difficult to read.

Figure 18-10   When and how to use table aliases

How to code summary queries

When working with a database, you may sometimes want to get summary information about the values that are stored in a column. To do that, you can use an *aggregate function*. An aggregate function is a function that operates on a series of values and returns a single summary value. Since aggregate functions return summary values, a query that contains one or more aggregate functions is often referred to as a *summary query*.

How to code aggregate functions

Figure 18-11 presents the syntax of the most common aggregate functions. Most of these functions operate on an expression. However, the COUNT function can operate on the asterisk (*) wildcard character.

The first statement uses the COUNT(*) function to return a count of the number of rows in the result set. To limit the number of rows in the result set, you can include a WHERE clause like this:

```
SELECT COUNT(*) AS productCount
FROM products
WHERE listPrice > 500
```

The second statement shows how the aggregate functions work with NULL values. Here, the first column uses the COUNT(*) function. As a result, it counts all rows including rows that contain NULL values. However, the second column uses the COUNT(shipDate) function. As a result, it doesn't count a row if the shipDate column for the row contains a NULL value.

The third statement uses the MIN, MAX, and AVG functions to calculate the lowest, highest, and average list price for a product. If the listPrice column contains a NULL value, that column is not included in the calculation.

The fourth statement uses the SUM function to get the total of all orders. To do that, this function operates on an expression that includes three columns connected by arithmetic operators. This expression calculates the total for each row by multiplying the price and the quantity and subtracting the discount amount. Then, the SUM function gets the total for all rows in the result set.

This statement shows that a MySQL expression can be a *calculated value*. In this case, an arithmetic expression is used to derive a calculated value from the data in three columns in the base table. You can also use a string expression to combine two or more string values. And you can use MySQL's built-in functions within expressions.

In general, MySQL's operators and functions work similarly to PHP's operators and functions. As a result, you should be able to figure out how to use them by searching the online MySQL Reference Manual. Although you can always use PHP to code your arithmetic and string expressions after you retrieve the data from a database, it is often more efficient to let MySQL do the calculations so less data needs to be extracted from the database.

The syntax of the aggregate functions

Function syntax	Result
AVG(expression)	The average of the non-NULL values in the expression.
SUM(expression)	The total of the non-NULL values in the expression.
MIN(expression)	The lowest non-NULL value in the expression.
MAX(expression)	The highest non-NULL value in the expression.
COUNT(expression)	The number of non-NULL values in the expression.
COUNT(*)	The number of rows selected by the query.

Count all products

```
SELECT COUNT(*) AS productCount
FROM products
```

productCount
10

Count all orders and orders that have been shipped

```
SELECT COUNT(*) AS totalCount,
       COUNT(shipDate) AS shippedCount
FROM orders
```

totalCount	shippedCount
3	1

Find lowest, highest, and average prices

```
SELECT MIN(listPrice) AS lowestPrice,
       MAX(listPrice) AS highestPrice,
       AVG(listPrice) AS averagePrice
FROM products
```

lowestPrice	highestPrice	averagePrice
299.00	2517.00	841.895000

Get the total of the calculated values for all orders

```
SELECT SUM(itemPrice * quantity - discountAmount) AS ordersTotal
FROM orderItems
```

ordersTotal
1987.29

Description

- *Aggregate functions* perform calculations on the values in a set of selected rows. You specify the values to be used in the calculation by coding an expression as the argument.

- In many cases, the expression for an aggregate function is just the name of a column, but it can also be a *calculated value* that operates on the values in two or more columns.

- A SELECT statement that includes an aggregate function can be called a *summary query*.

- If you code an aggregate function in the SELECT clause, the SELECT clause can't include non-aggregate columns from the base table.

Figure 18-11 How to code aggregate functions

How to group queries by column

Now that you understand aggregate functions, you're ready to learn how to group data and use aggregate functions to summarize the data in each group. To do that, you need to learn about two new clauses of the SELECT statement: the GROUP BY clause and the HAVING clause.

Figure 18-12 presents the syntax of the SELECT statement with the GROUP BY and HAVING clauses. The GROUP BY clause determines how the selected rows are grouped, and the HAVING clause determines which groups are included in the final results. These clauses are coded after the WHERE clause but before the ORDER BY clause. That makes sense because the search condition in the WHERE clause is applied before the rows are grouped, and the sort sequence in the ORDER BY clause is applied after the rows are grouped.

In the GROUP BY clause, you list one or more columns or expressions separated by commas. Then, the rows that satisfy the search condition in the WHERE clause are grouped by those columns or expressions.

The first statement counts the products in each category and calculates the average list price for each category. To do that, it uses the COUNT and AVG aggregate functions for the second and third columns, and it uses the GROUP BY clause to group the aggregate functions on the first column. This displays one row for each category.

Although the first statement only uses data from one table, it's common to need to use data from multiple tables. To do that, you can join two or more tables. For example, the second statement joins data from the categories and products table and groups them by category name. This provides a result set that's similar to the first statement, but it allows you to use the category name instead of the category ID in the result set.

The second statement also includes a HAVING clause. The search condition in this clause only includes those categories with an average list price over $400. In this case, all of the categories that have products have an average list price over that amount so they are all included.

The third statement includes a search condition in the WHERE clause instead of the HAVING clause. This search condition limits the products within the groups to those that have a list price greater than $400. In other words, the search condition in the third statement is applied to every row. In the second statement, it was applied to each group of rows.

Beyond this, there are two more differences in the expressions that you can include in the WHERE and HAVING clauses. First, the HAVING clause can include aggregate functions as in the second statement, but the WHERE clause can't. That's because the search condition in a WHERE clause is applied before the rows are grouped. Second, the WHERE clause can refer to any column in the base tables, but the HAVING clause can only refer to columns included in the SELECT clause. That's because it filters the summarized result set that's defined by the SELECT, FROM, WHERE, and GROUP BY clauses. In other words, it doesn't filter the base tables.

The syntax of the GROUP BY and HAVING clauses

```
SELECT select_list
FROM table_source
[WHERE search_condition]
[GROUP BY group_by_list]
[HAVING search_condition]
[ORDER BY order_by_list]
```

Calculate the average list price by category

```
SELECT categoryID, COUNT(*) AS productCount,
       AVG(listPrice) AS averageListPrice
FROM products
GROUP BY categoryID
ORDER BY productCount
```

categoryID	productCount	averageListPrice
2	2	649.990000
3	2	749.990000
1	6	936.498333

Use columns from multiple tables

```
SELECT categoryName, COUNT(*) AS productCount,
       AVG(listPrice) AS averageListPrice
FROM products p JOIN categories c
   ON p.categoryID = c.categoryID
GROUP BY categoryName
HAVING averageListPrice > 400
```

categoryName	productCount	averageListPrice
Basses	2	649.990000
Drums	2	749.990000
Guitars	6	936.498333

Use a WHERE clause to filter rows before grouping them

```
SELECT categoryName, COUNT(*) AS productCount,
       AVG(listPrice) AS averageListPrice
FROM products p JOIN categories c
   ON p.categoryID = c.categoryID
WHERE listPrice > 400
GROUP BY categoryName
```

categoryName	productCount	averageListPrice
Basses	2	649.990000
Drums	2	749.990000
Guitars	5	1063.998000

Description

- The GROUP BY clause groups the rows of a result set based on one or more columns or expressions. It's typically used in SELECT statements that include aggregate functions.

- The HAVING clause specifies a search condition for a group or an aggregate. MySQL applies this condition after it groups the rows that satisfy the condition in the WHERE clause.

Figure 18-12   How to use the GROUP BY and HAVING clauses

How to code subqueries

A *subquery* is a SELECT statement that's coded within another SQL statement. The trick to using subqueries is knowing where and when to use them.

Where to use subqueries

Figure 18-13 shows that a subquery can be coded, or *introduced*, in the WHERE, HAVING, FROM, or SELECT clause of a SELECT statement. For example, the first statement in this figure uses a subquery in a WHERE clause. This statement retrieves all the products that have a list price that's greater than the average list price for all the invoices. To do that, the subquery calculates the average list price of all products. Then, the search condition tests each product to see if its list price is greater than the average list price.

The second statement also uses a subquery in the WHERE clause. Here, the subquery returns the category ID for the category named Basses. Then, the WHERE condition returns all products in that category.

When a subquery returns a result set that contains a single value as it does in both of the statements in this figure, you can use it anywhere you would normally use an expression.

However, a subquery can also return a result set that includes a single column with multiple values. In that case, you can use it anywhere you would normally use a list of values. For example, a list of values can be used in an IN clause. To see two examples of the IN clause, you can view figures 18-16 and 18-17.

In addition, a subquery can return a result set that includes multiple columns with multiple rows. In other words, a subquery can return a table of data. In that case, you can use it anywhere you would normally code a table. For example, you can code the subquery in a FROM clause.

Finally, you can code a subquery within another subquery. In that case, the subqueries are said to be nested. Because *nested subqueries* can be difficult to read, you should use them only when necessary.

Four ways to introduce a subquery in a SELECT statement

1. In a WHERE clause as a search condition
2. In a HAVING clause as a search condition
3. In the FROM clause as a table specification
4. In the SELECT clause as a column specification

Use a subquery in the WHERE clause

```
SELECT productName, listPrice
FROM products
WHERE listPrice > (SELECT AVG(listPrice) FROM products)
ORDER BY listPrice DESC
```

The value returned by the subquery

```
841.895
```

The result set

productName	listPrice ▾
Gibson SG	2517.00
Gibson Les Paul	1199.00

Use another subquery in the WHERE clause

```
SELECT productName, listPrice
FROM products
WHERE categoryID = (SELECT categoryID FROM categories
                    WHERE categoryName = 'Basses')
```

The result set

productName	listPrice
Fender Precision	799.99
Hofner Icon	499.99

Description

*   A *subquery* is a SELECT statement that's coded within another SQL statement.
*   A subquery can return a single value, a column that contains multiple values, or multiple columns that contain multiple values.
*   A subquery that returns a single value can be coded, or *introduced*, anywhere an expression is allowed. A subquery that returns a single column can be introduced in place of a list of values, such as the values for an IN clause. And a subquery that returns one or more columns can be introduced in place of a table in the FROM clause.

Figure 18-13   Where to use subqueries

How to code correlated subqueries

The subqueries presented in the previous figure are executed only once for the entire query. However, you can also code subqueries that are executed once for each row that's processed by the outer query. This type of query is called a *correlated subquery*, and it's similar to using a loop to do repetitive processing in a procedural programming language.

Figure 18-14 shows how to code a correlated subquery. The first statement retrieves rows from the categories table and it includes a count of the number of products for each category. To do that, the search condition in the WHERE clause of the subquery refers to the categoryID value of the current category. That way, only the products for the current category are included in the count.

Each time a row in the outer query is processed, the value in the categoryID column for that row is substituted for the column reference in the subquery. If the categoryID value is 1, for example, this subquery is executed:

```
SELECT COUNT(*) FROM products
WHERE products.categoryID = 1
```

The second SQL statement in this figure shows how to use the EXISTS operator with a correlated subquery. This operator tests whether or not the subquery returns a result set. In other words, it tests whether the result set exists. In this example, the statement retrieves all the rows in the customers table that don't have corresponding rows in the orders table. To do that, this statement uses the NOT keyword with the EXISTS operator. Because the subquery doesn't actually return a result set, it doesn't matter what columns are included in the SELECT clause. As a result, it's common to just code an asterisk.

As you study these examples, note how the column names in the WHERE clause of the inner query are qualified to indicate whether they refer to a column in the inner query or the outer query. In these examples, the inner and outer queries use different tables. As a result, you don't need to use a table alias. However, if the same table is used in both the inner and outer queries, you must assign aliases to the tables. Then, those alias names are used to qualify the column names.

Because correlated subqueries can be difficult to code, you may want to test a subquery separately before using it within another SELECT statement. To do that, you can substitute a constant value for the variable that refers to a column in the outer query. Then, once you're sure that the subquery works on its own, you can replace the constant value with a reference to the outer query so you can use it within a SELECT statement.

Use a correlated subquery in the SELECT clause

```
SELECT categoryID, categoryName,
    (SELECT COUNT(*) FROM products
       WHERE products.categoryID = categories.categoryID) AS productCount
FROM categories
```

categoryID	categoryName	productCount
1	Guitars	6
2	Basses	2
3	Drums	2

The syntax of a subquery that uses the EXISTS operator

```
WHERE [NOT] EXISTS (subquery)
```

Get all customers that don't have any orders

```
SELECT c.customerID, firstName, lastName
FROM customers c
WHERE NOT EXISTS
    (SELECT * FROM orders o
     WHERE c.customerID = o.customerID)
```

customerID	firstName	lastName
3	Christine	Brown

Description

- A *correlated subquery* is a subquery that is executed once for each row processed by the outer query.

- A correlated subquery refers to a value that's provided by a column in the outer query. Because that value varies depending on the row that's being processed, each execution of the subquery returns a different result.

- To refer to a value in the outer query, a correlated subquery uses a qualified column name that includes the table name from the outer query. If the subquery uses the same table as the outer query, you must assign a table alias to one of the tables to remove ambiguity.

- You can use the EXISTS operator to test that one or more rows are returned by the subquery. You can also use the NOT operator with the EXISTS operator to test that no rows are returned by the subquery.

Figure 18-14   How to code correlated subqueries

How to insert, update, and delete rows

Now that you know how to code subqueries, you're ready to learn the details of coding the INSERT, UPDATE, and DELETE statements. You can use these three statements to add new rows to a table, to modify existing rows in a table, or to delete rows from a table.

How to insert rows

To add new rows to a table, you use the INSERT statement as shown in figure 18-15. To start, this figure shows a CREATE TABLE statement for a products table. This table has seven columns, and two of these columns have default values.

Then, the second statement in this figure uses an INSERT statement to add a single row to the products table. This statement uses the INSERT INTO clause to specify the name of the table. Then, it uses the VALUES clause to specify the values for each column.

There are four points to note about this VALUES clause. First, it includes a value for every column in the table. Second, it lists the values in the same sequence that the columns appear in the table so MySQL knows which value to assign to which column. Third, it uses the DEFAULT keyword for two columns to use the default value for that column. As a result, the first column uses the integer value that's automatically generated for the productID column, and the sixth column uses the default value of 0.00 for the discountPercent column. Fourth, it uses MySQL's built-in NOW function to insert the current date and time into the dateAdded column.

The third statement includes a column list in the INSERT clause. Note that this list doesn't include the productID or discountPercent columns since they provide default values. Similarly, you can omit any columns that allow NULL values. Note also that you don't need to code the columns in the same sequence as the columns in the products table when you include a list of columns. Instead, you can code the columns in any sequence you like as long as you make sure that you use the same sequence for the values in the VALUES clause.

The fourth statement adds multiple rows to the categories table. To do that, it separates each list of values with a comma.

When you specify the values for the columns to be inserted, you must be sure that those values are compatible with the data types of the columns. In this figure, note how the values for the products table have data types that are compatible with the column definitions of the products table.

The syntax of the INSERT statement

```
INSERT INTO table_name [(column_list)]
VALUES (expression_1 [, expression_2]...) [,
        (expression_1 [, expression_2]...)]...
```

The table definition

```
CREATE TABLE products (
  productID          INT            NOT NULL    AUTO_INCREMENT,
  categoryID         INT            NOT NULL,
  productCode        VARCHAR(10)    NOT NULL,
  productName        VARCHAR(255)   NOT NULL,
  description        TEXT           NOT NULL,
  listPrice          DECIMAL(10,2)  NOT NULL,
  discountPercent    DECIMAL(10,2)  NOT NULL    DEFAULT 0.00,
  dateAdded          DATETIME       NOT NULL
)
```

Add a single row without using a column list

```
INSERT INTO products
VALUES (DEFAULT, 1, 'tele', 'Fender Telecaster', 'NA',
        '949.99', DEFAULT, NOW())
```

Add a single row using a column list

```
INSERT INTO products
    (categoryID, productCode, productName, description,
     listPrice, dateAdded)
VALUES
    (1, 'tele', 'Fender Telecaster', 'NA',
     '949.99', NOW())
```

Add multiple rows

```
INSERT INTO categories (categoryID, categoryName) VALUES
(4, 'Keyboards'),
(5, 'Brass'),
(6, 'Woodwind')
```

Description

- You use the INSERT statement to add a new row to a table.

- In the INSERT clause, you specify the name of the table that you want to add a row to, along with an optional column list.

- If you don't include a column list, you must specify the column values in the same order as they appear in the table, and you must code a value for each column in the table.

- If you include a column list, you must specify the column values in the same order as they appear in the column list. You can omit columns with default values and columns that accept NULL values.

- To insert a default value, you can use the DEFAULT keyword.

- To insert a NULL value into a column, you can use the NULL keyword.

Figure 18-15   How to insert rows

How to update rows

To modify the data in one or more existing rows in a table, you use the UPDATE statement. Although most UPDATE statements perform simple updates, you can also code more complex UPDATE statements that include subqueries.

Figure 18-16 presents the syntax of the UPDATE statement. The UPDATE clause names the table to be updated, the SET clause names the columns to be updated and the values to be assigned to those columns, and the WHERE clause specifies the condition a row must meet to be updated. Although the WHERE clause is optional, you almost always include it. If you don't, all of the rows in the table are updated, which usually isn't what you want.

The first statement in this figure modifies the values of the discountPercent column in the products table. Because the WHERE clause in this statement identifies a single product, this statement only updates the discount percent for that single product.

The second statement in this figure modifies the values of two columns in the products table: discountPercent and description. Like the first statement, this statement only modifies a single row.

The third statement modifies the discountPercent column in the products table. This time, however, the WHERE clause selects all of the products with a categoryID of 2. As a result, this statement updates all products in this category.

The fourth statement works like the third statement, but it doesn't include a WHERE clause. As a result, this statement updates all products.

The fifth UPDATE statement uses a subquery in the WHERE clause. This subquery returns a list of the customerID values for all customers with a last name of Sherwood. Then, the IN operator is used to update all the orders with customerID values in that list.

Before you execute an UPDATE statement, you can check to make sure that it selects the correct rows by executing a SELECT statement with the same search condition. Then, if the SELECT statement returns the correct rows, you can change it to an UPDATE statement.

In this figure, the SET clauses assign literal values to the columns. However, you can also code an expression that returns a value in a SET class. In addition, you can use the NULL keyword to assign a NULL value to a column that allows NULL values, and you can use the DEFAULT keyword to assign the default value to a column that's defined with one.

The syntax of the UPDATE statement

```
UPDATE table_name
SET column_name_1 = expression_1 [, column_name_2 = expression_2]...
[WHERE search_condition]
```

Update one column of one row

```
UPDATE products
SET discountPercent = '10.00'
WHERE productName = 'Fender Telecaster'
```

Update multiple columns of one row

```
UPDATE products
SET discountPercent = '25.00',
    description = 'This guitar has great tone and smooth playability.'
WHERE productName = 'Fender Telecaster'
```

Update one column of multiple rows

```
UPDATE products
SET discountPercent = '15.00'
WHERE categoryID = 2
```

Update one column of all rows in the table

```
UPDATE products
SET discountPercent = '15.00'
```

Use a subquery to update multiple rows

```
UPDATE orders
SET shipAmount = 0
WHERE customerID IN
    (SELECT customerID
     FROM customers
     WHERE lastName = 'Sherwood')
```

Description

- You use the UPDATE statement to modify one or more rows in the table named in the UPDATE clause.

- You name the columns to be modified and the value to be assigned to each column in the SET clause. You can specify the value for a column as a literal or an expression.

- You can specify the conditions that must be met for a row to be updated in the WHERE clause.

Warning

- If you omit the WHERE clause, all rows in the table are updated.

Figure 18-16   How to update rows

How to delete rows

To delete one or more rows from a table, you use the DELETE statement. Just as you can with the UPDATE statement, you can use subqueries in a DELETE statement to help identify the rows to be deleted.

Figure 18-17 presents the syntax of the DELETE statement. Here, the DELETE clause specifies the name of the table that contains the rows to be deleted. When you code this clause, you can omit the FROM keyword since it is optional.

To identify the rows to be deleted, you code a search condition in the WHERE clause. Although this clause is optional, you almost always include it. If you don't, all of the rows in the table are deleted. This is a common coding mistake, and it can be disastrous if you're working with live data.

If you want to make sure that you've selected the correct rows before you issue the DELETE statement, you can issue a SELECT statement with the same search condition. Then, if the correct rows are retrieved, you can use the same search for the DELETE statement.

The first statement in this figure deletes a single row from the products table. To do that, it uses the WHERE clause to specify a value of 6 for the productID column. Since the WHERE clause only specifies one row, the DELETE statement only deletes one row.

The second statement deletes multiple rows from the products table. To do that, it uses the WHERE clause to specify a value of 3 for the categoryID column. Since the WHERE clause specifies multiple rows, the DELETE statement deletes multiple rows.

The third statement deletes multiple rows from the categories table. To do that, this statement uses the greater than operator (>) to delete all categories that have a category ID that's greater than 3. If, for example, you insert the three categories shown in figure 18-15, this DELETE statement deletes those rows.

The fourth statement uses a subquery in its WHERE clause to delete all rows from the orderItems table for the customer that has an ID of 1. Here, the subquery returns a list of values from the orderID column of the orders table for the customer with the ID of 1. Then, the DELETE statement uses that list of values in the WHERE clause. To do that, it uses the IN clause to introduce the subquery. As a result, the DELETE statement deletes all rows that have an orderID value that's in the list of orderID values that are returned by the subquery.

By default, MySQL doesn't enforce referential integrity. As a result, MySQL usually allows you to delete any rows you want, even if that violates referential integrity. However, if you configure MySQL to enforce reference integrity, MySQL might not allow you to delete some rows. For example, if you attempt to delete a row from the customers table that has child rows in the orders and orderItem tables, MySQL might not allow you to delete that customer. In that case, you must delete the order items and orders before you can delete the customer.

The syntax of the DELETE statement

```
DELETE [FROM] table_name
[WHERE search_condition]
```

Delete one row

```
DELETE FROM products
WHERE productID = 6
```

Delete multiple rows

```
DELETE FROM products
WHERE categoryID = 3
```

Another way to delete multiple rows

```
DELETE FROM categories
WHERE categoryID > 3
```

Use a subquery to delete all order items for a customer

```
DELETE FROM orderItems
WHERE orderID IN
    (SELECT orderID FROM orders
    WHERE customerID = 1)
```

Description

- You can use the DELETE statement to delete one or more rows from the table you name in the DELETE clause.
- You specify the conditions that must be met for a row to be deleted in the WHERE clause.
- You can use a subquery within the WHERE clause.

Warning

- If you omit the WHERE clause from a DELETE statement, all the rows in the table are delcted.

Figure 18-17   How to delete rows

Perspective

In this chapter, you learned how to use the SELECT, INSERT, UPDATE, and DELETE statements to work with the data in a database. These are the statements that you will use in your PHP applications. At this point, you have the essential skills you need to write SQL statements at a professional level.

However, there's a lot more to learn about working with data in MySQL. For example, MySQL provides arithmetic operators and functions that you can use to perform calculations on two or more columns in the base table. MySQL provides string operators and functions that you can use to code string expressions. And MySQL provides functions that you can use to work with dates.

Often, you can use PHP instead of MySQL to do this type of processing. As a result, you might not need these operators and functions for some web applications. However, if you want to have MySQL do more of the processing so PHP does less, you can start by learning more about these operators and functions. In some cases, this will also improve the performance of your database applications.

Terms

base table	explicit syntax
column alias	implicit syntax
logical operators	join condition
compound condition	ad hoc relationships
NULL value	qualified column name
wildcards	table alias
string pattern	aggregate function
mask	summary query
nested sort	calculated value
join	subquery
inner join	nested subqueries
outer join	correlated subquery
SQL-92 syntax	

Summary

- By default, a column in the result set is given the same name as the column in the base table. If that's not what you want, you can specify a *column alias* for the column.

- You can use the AND and OR *logical operators* to create *compound conditions* that consist of two or more conditions.

- You can use the LIKE operator to retrieve rows that match a *string pattern*, called a *mask*. Within the mask, you can use special characters, called *wildcard* characters, that determine which values in the column satisfy the condition.

- A *join* is used to combine columns from two or more tables into a result set based on the *join conditions* you specify. For an *inner join*, only those rows that satisfy the join condition are included in the result set.

- If the two columns in a join condition have the same name, you have to qualify them with the table name so MySQL can distinguish between them. To code a *qualified column name*, type the table name, followed by a period, followed by the column name.

- For a join, coding the join condition in a JOIN clause is known as the *explicit syntax*. It is also called the *SQL-92 syntax* because it was introduced by the SQL-92 standards. Coding the join condition in the WHERE clause is known as the *implicit syntax*.

- A *table alias* is an alternative table name assigned in the FROM clause.

- An *aggregate function* performs a calculation on the values in a set of selected rows. A SELECT statement that includes an aggregate function can be called a *summary query*.

- A *subquery* is a SELECT statement that's coded within another SQL statement. A subquery can be *introduced* anywhere in a SQL statement as long as it returns a value, a list of values, or a table of values that are appropriate for the place in the statement.

- A *correlated subquery* is a subquery that is executed once for each row processed by the outer query.

Exercise 18-1   Work with the data in a database

In this exercise, you can run some of the examples in this chapter. Then, you can write some of your own SQL statements to work with the data in a database.

Run some of the examples from this chapter

1. Start phpMyAdmin.

2. Use your text editor to open the script named my_guitar_shop2.sql that's stored in the book_apps/_db_create directory. Note that this script ends with INSERT statements that load data into the database.

3. Use phpMyAdmin to run this script as shown in figure 3-10 of chapter 3.

4. Use your text editor to open the script named fig18-01.sql that's in the book_apps/ch18_db_scripts directory. Then, use phpMyAdmin to run the first SELECT statement in this script. To do that, you can select that statement in your text editor and copy it into phpMyAdmin. (Don't forget to use phpMyAdmin to select the correct database.) Then, run the next three statements to limit the number of columns and rows.

5. Open the script named fig18-10.sql in your text editor, and use phpMyAdmin to run the first SELECT statement in this script. Note how this statement selects data from two tables. Then, run the second SELECT statement. Note how this statement selects data from four tables.

6.   Open and run any of the other examples in this chapter that you're interested in reviewing.

Write your own SELECT statements

7.   Use phpMyAdmin to write and test a SELECT statement that selects the productName, description, and listPrice columns for all rows in the products table.

Add code to this statement so it sorts the result set by list price. Then, run this statement again to make sure it works correctly. This is a good way to build and test a statement, one clause at a time.

Add code to this statement so it only selects rows that have the word "electric" in the description column, and run this statement again to make sure it works correctly. Then, save this statement in a file named select_products.sql in the ex_starts/ch18_ex1 directory.

8.   Write a SELECT statement that joins data from the customers and addresses tables. This statement should select these columns: firstName, lastName, line1, line2, city, state, zipCode. It should only select the billing addresses for customers who have a last name of "sherwood". Then, save this statement in a file named select_billing_addresses.sql in the ex_starts/ch18_ex1 directory.

9.   Write a SELECT statement that returns a count of the number of products in the category that has a name of "Guitars". To do this, use a subquery to get the category ID. Then, save this statement in a file named count_products_by_category.sql in the ex_starts/ch18_ex1 directory.

Write your own INSERT, UPDATE, and DELETE statements

10.   Write an INSERT statement that adds a customer named John Smith to the customers table. Use an email address of "johnsmith@example.com" and a password of "sesame". Then, save this statement in a file named insert_customer.sql in the ex_starts/ch18_ex1 directory.

11.   Write an UPDATE statement that changes the password for John Smith to "5e5ame!". Then, save this statement in a file named update_customer.sql in the ex_starts/ch18_ex1 directory.

12.   Write a DELETE statement that deletes the customer named John Smith. Then, save this statement in a file named delete_customer.sql in the ex_starts/ch18_ex1 directory.

13.   To restore the database to the way it was initially, run the creation script again as you did in step 3.

19

Professional PHP for working with MySQL

In chapter 4, you learned how to use PDO (PHP Data Objects) to work with a MySQL database. Now, this chapter shows the rest of the skills you need to use PDO at a professional level. It also shows you how to use the mysqli extension instead of PDO in case you need or want to do that.

Three ways to use PHP to work with MySQL 612
PDO (PHP Data Objects) 612
PHP's mysqli extension 612
PHP's MySQL extension 612

How to work with PDO 614
How to work with prepared statements 614
How to set the error mode for PDO 618
A model in PDO 620

How to work with mysqli 626
How to connect to a database 626
How to select data 628
How to insert, update, and delete data 630
How to work with prepared statements 632
The object-oriented style compared to the procedural style 636
A model in mysqli 638

Perspective 642

Three ways to use PHP to work with MySQL

An *Application Programming Interface* (*API*) provides a way for an application to work with other applications. MySQL, for example, provides an API that specifies how languages like PHP can work with MySQL.

To use the MySQL API, PHP provides three *extensions*, as summarized in figure 19-1. Here, the PDO MySQL driver extension is used by *PHP Data Objects* (*PDO*), but PDO itself isn't an extension. Instead, it is a *database abstraction layer* that can use different extensions to communicate with different databases.

PDO (PHP Data Objects)

PDO is relatively new to PHP, and it has several advantages over the older ways of working with a database. The main advantage of PDO is that it defines a consistent object-oriented interface that supports most popular databases. As a result, PDO allows you to write code that is portable across different database servers such as Oracle, DB2, Microsoft SQL Server, PostgreSQL, and others.

One disadvantage of PDO is that it doesn't take advantage of all of the advanced features found in MySQL 4.1.3 and later, such as multiple statements. For most web applications, that isn't an issue. However, if you need to take advantage of these features, you can use the mysqli extension.

PHP's mysqli extension

The mysqli extension (the *i* is for *improved*) is included with PHP 5 and later. This extension provides an *object-oriented interface* and a *procedural interface*. One advantage of mysqli is that it takes advantage of all new features found in MySQL 4.1.3 and later. As a result, if you need to use these features, you can use mysqli instead of PDO.

One disadvantage of mysqli is that it is designed to work with the MySQL database and can't be used with other database servers. As a result, if you want to write code that can be used with other database servers, you should use PDO instead of mysqli.

PHP's MySQL extension

The MySQL extension is the oldest PHP interface for working with MySQL and is no longer under active development. As a result, you'll only want to use this extension if you're using an old version of PHP or maintaining legacy code. If you need to use it, it is similar to the procedural version of the mysqli extension that's described later in this chapter.

PDO (PHP Data Objects)

Pros

- Is included with PHP 5.1 and later and available for 5.0.
- Provides an object-oriented interface.
- Provides a consistent interface that's portable between other database servers such as Oracle, DB2, Microsoft SQL Server, and PostgreSQL.
- Takes advantage of most new features found in MySQL 4.1.3 and later.

Cons

- Doesn't work with versions of PHP 4.x, 3.x, or earlier.
- Doesn't take advantage of some advanced features found in MySQL 4.1.3 and later, such as multiple statements.

mysqli (MySQL improved extension)

Pros

- Is included with PHP 5 and later
- Provides both an object-oriented interface and a procedural interface.
- Takes advantage of all new features found in MySQL 4.1.3 and later.

Cons

- Can't be used with other database servers.

MySql (MySQL extension)

Pros

- Is included with PHP 3.x, 4.x, and 5.x.

Cons

- Doesn't take advantage of the advanced features found in MySQL 4.1.3 and later.
- Is not under active development.

Description

- An *Application Programming Interface* (*API*) provides a way for your application to communicate with other applications. MySQL provides an API for PHP.
- PHP provides three *extensions* for working with the MySQL API: the mysql extension, the mysqli extension, and the PDO MySQL driver extension.
- *PHP Data Objects* (*PDO*) is a *database abstraction layer* specifically for PHP applications. It uses the PDO MySQL driver extension to communicate with MySQL, and it can use other drivers to communicate with other databases.

Figure 19-1   Three ways to work with a MySQL database

How to work with PDO

In chapter 4, you learned how to use PDO to connect to a database and execute SQL statements. You also learned that we recommend PDO for new development. Now, this topic shows two new PDO skills that are used in professional database applications.

How to work with prepared statements

In chapter 4, you learned how to execute *dynamic SQL statements*. That's a simple way to get started with database programming.

For production applications, though, you should use *prepared statements* because they improve both database performance and security. Prepared statements improve performance when a statement is executed multiple times, because they allow the database server to reuse some of the work that it does when it prepares a statement. Prepared statements also improve security because they can prevent most types of SQL injection attacks. For more information about SQL injection attacks, you can search the Internet.

Figure 19-2 shows how to work with prepared statements. Here, the first example shows how to execute a prepared SELECT statement that doesn't have any parameters. To do that, you call the prepare method of the PDO object to prepare the query and return a PDOStatement object. Then, you can call the execute, fetchAll, and closeCursor methods of the PDOStatement object to execute the statement, return a result set, and free the connection to the server. In this example, all rows in the result set are stored in the variable named $products. As a result, you can use a foreach loop to access each row in the result set.

Although the fetchAll method works well for small result sets, you usually don't use it for large result sets since it causes PHP to use more memory than the fetch method. That's why the second example shows how to use the fetch method. Here, the first call to the fetch method returns the first row in the result set or a NULL value if the result set doesn't contain any rows. Then, you can use a while loop to process each row. In this example, the while loop just displays the value that's stored in the name column, but you can display every column or do more complex processing whenever that's necessary. After you're done processing the row, you can call the fetch method to return the next row. When you reach the end of the result set, the fetch method returns a NULL value, and the code exits the loop.

Some methods of the PDO class

Method	Description
prepare(*$sql_statement*)	Prepares the specified SQL statement for execution and returns a PDOStatement object. The specified statement can contain zero or more named (:name) or question mark (?) parameters.
lastInsertId()	After an INSERT statement has been executed, this method gets the ID that was automatically generated by MySQL for the row.

Some methods of the PDOStatement class

Method	Description
bindValue(*$param*, *$value*)	Binds the specified value to the specified parameter in the prepared statement. Returns TRUE for success and FALSE for failure.
execute()	Executes the prepared statement. Returns TRUE for success and FALSE for failure.
fetchAll()	Returns an array for all of the rows in the result set.
fetch()	Returns an array for the next row in the result set.
rowCount()	Returns the number of rows affected by the last statement.
closeCursor()	Closes the cursor and frees the connection to the server so other SQL statements may be issued.

How to use the fetchAll method to return a result set

```
$query = 'SELECT * FROM products';
$statement = $db->prepare($query);
$statement->execute();
$products = $statement->fetchAll();
$statement->closeCursor();
foreach ($products as $product) {
    echo $product['productName'] . '<br />';
}
```

How to use the fetch method to loop through a result set

```
$query = 'SELECT * FROM products';
$statement = $db->prepare($query);
$statement->execute();
$product = $statement->fetch();        // get the first row
while ($product != null) {
    echo $product['productName'] . '<br />';
    $product = $statement->fetch();     // get the next row
}
$statement->closeCursor();
```

Figure 19-2   How to work with prepared statements (part 1 of 2)

Of course, most prepared statements include one or more parameters. That's why the first example in part 2 of this figure shows how to use *named parameters*. A named parameter begins with a colon (:) followed by the name of the parameter. In this example, the first named parameter is :category_id and the second named parameter is :price. After you code the named parameters in a query, you use the bindValue method of the PDOStatement object to bind the values to the parameters. In this example, the first bindValue statement binds the value in the $category_id variable to the parameter named :category_id, and the second bindValue statement binds the value in the $price variable to the parameter named :price.

The second example in this part works the same as the first example, but it uses *question mark parameters* (also known as *unnamed parameters*) instead of named parameters. A question mark parameter uses a question mark (?) to indicate the location of the parameter in the SQL statement. In this example, the SQL statement includes two question marks. Then, you use the bindValue method to bind values to these parameters by using integer values for the parameters. In this example, the first bindValue statement binds the $category_id variable to the first question mark parameter in the SQL statement, and the second bindValue statement binds the $price variable to the second question mark parameter.

One advantage of using named parameters is that they continue to work even if you add more parameters to the SQL statement later on. Another advantage is that they make your prepared statements easier to read since it's easy to see how the values correspond to the named parameters. On the other hand, question mark parameters do require less code so you may want to use them if you're confident that the SQL statement won't be changed later on.

The third example prepares and executes an INSERT statement to insert a row into the database. This is similar to using a prepared SELECT statement with three differences. First, when you execute an INSERT statement, PDO returns a TRUE or FALSE value that indicates whether the statement executed successfully. Second, you can use the rowCount method of the PDOStatement object to get the number of rows that were affected by the statement. Third, after you execute an INSERT statement, you can use the lastInsertId method of the PDO object to get the ID that MySQL generated for that INSERT statement. Except for the use of the lastInsertId method, prepared UPDATE and DELETE statements work the same.

How to use named parameters

```
$category_id = 1;
$price = 400;

$query = 'SELECT * FROM products
          WHERE categoryID = :category_id
          AND listPrice > :price';
$statement = $db->prepare($query);
$statement->bindValue(':category_id', $category_id);
$statement->bindValue(':price', $price);
$statement->execute();
$products = $statement->fetchAll();
$statement->closeCursor();
```

How to use question mark parameters

```
$query = 'SELECT * FROM products
          WHERE categoryID = ?
          AND listPrice > ?';
$statement = $db->prepare($query);
$statement->bindValue(1, $category_id);
$statement->bindValue(2, $price);
$statement->execute();
$products = $statement->fetchAll();
$statement->closeCursor();
```

How to modify data

```
// Sample data
$category_id = 2;
$code = 'hofner';
$name = 'Hofner Icon';
$price = '499.99';

// Prepare and execute the statement
$query = 'INSERT INTO products
             (categoryID, productCode, productName, listPrice)
          VALUES
             (:category_id, :code, :name, :price)';
$statement = $db->prepare($query);
$statement->bindValue(':category_id', $category_id);
$statement->bindValue(':code', $code);
$statement->bindValue(':name', $name);
$statement->bindValue(':price', $price);
$success = $statement->execute();
$row_count = $statement->rowCount();
$statement->closeCursor();

// Get the last product ID that was automatically generated
$product_id = $db->lastInsertId();

// Display a message to the user
if ($success) {
    echo "<p>$row_count row(s) was inserted with this ID: $product_id</p>";
} else {
    echo "<p>No rows were inserted.</p>";
}
```

Figure 19-2   How to work with prepared statements (part 2 of 2)

How to set the error mode for PDO

Figure 19-3 shows how to set the error mode for PDO. By default, PDO uses the "exception" mode when it connects to the database. As a result, if there's an error when connecting to the database, PDO emits a standard PHP warning message, and it throws an exception that you can catch and handle.

After that, however, PDO uses the "silent" error mode by default when executing SQL statements. As a result, if there's an error executing a SQL statement, PDO doesn't throw an exception and it doesn't issue a standard PHP warning. Instead, it sets the error in the database object (for dynamic SQL statements) or in the statement object (for prepared SQL statements). Then, to view the error, you can use the errorCode and errorInfo methods on the database or statement object. However, this requires that you check for errors after each database call.

Since "silent" mode doesn't emit a PHP warning, it's more difficult to debug than the other two modes. As a result, you'll typically want to use one of the other two modes when you're testing and debugging. That way, PDO emits a traditional PHP warning that PHP displays on your web page if you encounter an error. This makes it easy for you to view the error message and debug the problem. However, you usually don't want to display these error messages to the users of your production applications.

For new web applications, it makes sense to use the "exception" error mode. This error mode allows you to use a try/catch statement to catch any exceptions that are thrown by PDO. Since this approach doesn't require you to check for errors after each database call, it provides a flexible way to handle errors. In addition, if you catch all the exceptions that might be thrown and handle them appropriately, this works well for production applications.

The first example in this figure shows how to use the PDO class to set the error mode. Here, the code creates an array of options. This array contains a single element that sets the error mode attribute of the PDO object to the "exception" mode. Then, this code passes that array as the optional fourth parameter to the constructor of the PDO class. Although this example only sets a single option, you can include multiple options in the options array if that's necessary.

The second example shows another way to set the error mode. This technique allows you to set the error mode after you create the PDO object. To do that, you use the setAttribute method of the PDO object to set the error mode attribute to the correct error mode.

The third example shows how to use a try/catch statement to catch the PDOException objects that might be thrown when you attempt to execute a SQL statement. Here, the SELECT statement incorrectly refers to the "product" table instead of the "products" table. As a result, when the code attempts to execute the prepared SELECT statement, it throws a PDOException. Then, execution jumps into the catch block. Within the catch block, the code uses the getMessage method of the exception to get the error message. Then, it displays the message and exits the script.

The three error modes for PDO

Name	Description
ERRMODE_SILENT	This is the default error mode. PDO sets the error in the database or statement object, but it doesn't emit a PHP warning message or throw an exception. To access the error, you can use the errorCode() and errorInfo() methods on the database or statement object. However, this requires you to check the error code after each database call.
ERRMODE_WARNING	PDO sets the error and doesn't throw an exception as in "silent" mode, but does emit a PHP warning message. This setting is useful during testing and debugging.
ERRMODE_EXCEPTION	PDO sets the error as in "silent" mode and throws a PDOException object that reflects the error code and error message. This setting is also useful during testing and debugging, and it makes it easier for you to structure your error-handling code.

How to use the constructor of the PDO class to set the error mode

```
$dsn = 'mysql:host=localhost;dbname=my_guitar_shop1';
$username = 'mgs_user';
$password = 'pa55word';
$options = array(PDO::ATTR_ERRMODE => PDO::ERRMODE_EXCEPTION);

try {
    $db = new PDO($dsn, $username, $password, $options);
} catch (PDOException $e) {
    $error_message = $e->getMessage();
    echo "<p>Error connecting to database: $error_message </p>";
    exit();
}
```

How to use the setAttribute method to set the error mode

```
$db->setAttribute(PDO::ATTR_ERRMODE, PDO::ERRMODE_EXCEPTION);
```

How to use a try/catch statement to catch PDOException objects

```
try {
    $query = 'SELECT * FROM product';
    $statement = $db->prepare($query);
    $statement->execute();
    $products = $statement->fetchAll();
    $statement->closeCursor();
} catch (PDOException $e) {
    $error_message = $e->getMessage();
    echo "<p>Database error: $error_message </p>";
    exit();
}
```

Description

- When you use PDO to execute SQL statements, you can choose between one of three error modes. Of these error modes, we recommend the "exception" error mode.

Figure 19-3   How to set the error mode for PDO

A model in PDO

Figure 19-4 shows the code for a model that works with the database named my_guitar_shop2. This model uses prepared statements as described in figure 19-2, and it uses the "exception" error mode as described in figure 19-3. In the next chapter, you'll see how you can use this model with the Product Manager application. For now, though, you can focus on the functions that it provides for retrieving, adding, updating, and deleting the data in the categories and products tables.

This figure begins by showing the code for the database.php file. Although this code isn't technically part of the model, I have included it here because it creates the database connection variable ($db) that's used by the functions in the model. This code uses the database named my_guitar_shop2 and sets the error mode to the "exception" mode. As a result, if PDO encounters an error when executing SQL statements, it throws an exception.

The database.php file also defines a function named display_db_error that's used by the other functions in the model to display a database error to the user. To start, this function uses the global keyword to get access to the $app_path variable. This variable is needed by the header for the db_error.php file, and you'll learn more about how this works in the next chapter. Then, this function displays the db_error.php file and exits the script.

The category_db.php file contains the get_categories function that returns a two-dimensional array of categories from the database. In addition, it contains the get_category method that returns a one-dimensional array for the specified category. Both of these methods use prepared statements. They use the fetchAll and fetch methods of the statement object to return arrays. And they use try/catch statements to catch and handle any errors that occur. If an error occurs, they call the display_db_error function of the database.php file to display the error and exit the script.

The benefit of returning an array instead of the PDOStatement object is that it separates the database layer (the model) from the presentation layer (the view). Another approach would be to return the PDOStatement object. Although this approach mixes the database layer (the model) with the presentation layer (the view), it can run more efficiently for result sets that are large. In this case, though, the categories table is small enough that there's little downside to returning a two-dimensional array.

The model/database.php file

```php
<?php
$dsn = 'mysql:host=localhost;dbname=my_guitar_shop2';
$username = 'mgs_user';
$password = 'pa55word';
$options = array(PDO::ATTR_ERRMODE => PDO::ERRMODE_EXCEPTION);

try {
    $db = new PDO($dsn, $username, $password, $options);
} catch (PDOException $e) {
    $error_message = $e->getMessage();
    include 'errors/db_error_connect.php';
    exit;
}

function display_db_error($error_message) {
    global $app_path;
    include 'errors/db_error.php';
    exit;
}
?>
```

The model/category_db.php file

```php
<?php
function get_categories() {
    global $db;
    $query = 'SELECT * FROM categories
            ORDER BY categoryID';
    try {
        $statement = $db->prepare($query);
        $statement->execute();
        $result = $statement->fetchAll();
        $statement->closeCursor();
        return $result;
    } catch (PDOException $e) {
        display_db_error($e->getMessage());
    }
}

function get_category($category_id) {
    global $db;
    $query = 'SELECT * FROM categories
            WHERE categoryID = :category_id';
    try {
        $statement = $db->prepare($query);
        $statement->bindValue(':category_id', $category_id);
        $statement->execute();
        $result = $statement->fetch();
        $statement->closeCursor();
        return $result;
    } catch (PDOException $e) {
        display_db_error($e->getMessage());
    }
}
?>
```

Figure 19-4   A model in PDO (part 1 of 4)

The product_db.php file contains the functions for retrieving, adding, updating, and deleting the products in the database. For the most part, these statements work like the functions in the category_db.php file.

The first two functions retrieve product data. Here, the get_products_by_category function returns a two-dimensional array of products for the specified category ID. Then, the get_product function returns a one-dimensional array for the product with the specified product ID.

The next three functions allow the user to add, update, and delete a product. To start, the add_product function accepts six parameters. Then, it binds these parameters to the named parameters in the INSERT statement, and it executes the statement. Last, it returns the product ID that MySQL automatically generates when it inserts the row in the database.

The update_product function accepts seven parameters, it binds these parameters to the named parameters in the UPDATE statement, and it executes the statement. Then, it returns the number of rows that were affected by the UPDATE statement. Since each product has a unique product ID, this function returns a value of 1 if an existing product ID is specified. Otherwise, it returns a value of 0. As a result, the code that calls this function can check this value and take an appropriate action.

The delete_product function accepts the product ID as a parameter, it binds the value for this parameter to the named parameter in the DELETE statement, and it executes the statement. Like the update_product function, this function returns a value of 1 if one row was deleted and a value of 0 if no rows were deleted.

The model/product_db.php file

```php
<?php
function get_products_by_category($category_id) {
    global $db;
    $query = 'SELECT * FROM products
                WHERE categoryID = :category_id
                ORDER BY productID';
    try {
        $statement = $db->prepare($query);
        $statement->bindValue(':category_id', $category_id);
        $statement->execute();
        $result = $statement->fetchAll();
        $statement->closeCursor();
        return $result;
    } catch (PDOException $e) {
        $error_message = $e->getMessage();
        display_db_error($error_message);
    }
}

function get_product($product_id) {
    global $db;
    $query = 'SELECT *
                FROM products
                WHERE productID = :product_id';
    try {
        $statement = $db->prepare($query);
        $statement->bindValue(':product_id', $product_id);
        $statement->execute();
        $result = $statement->fetch();
        $statement->closeCursor();
        return $result;
    } catch (PDOException $e) {
        $error_message = $e->getMessage();
        display_db_error($error_message);
    }
}
```

Figure 19-4   A model in PDO (part 2 of 4)

The model/product_db.php file (continued)

```php
function add_product($category_id, $code, $name, $description,
        $price, $discount_percent) {
    global $db;
    $query = 'INSERT INTO products
                (categoryID, productCode, productName, description,
                 listPrice, discountPercent, dateAdded)
              VALUES
                (:category_id, :code, :name, :description, :price,
                 :discount_percent, NOW())';
    try {
        $statement = $db->prepare($query);
        $statement->bindValue(':category_id', $category_id);
        $statement->bindValue(':code', $code);
        $statement->bindValue(':name', $name);
        $statement->bindValue(':description', $description);
        $statement->bindValue(':price', $price);
        $statement->bindValue(':discount_percent', $discount_percent);
        $statement->execute();
        $statement->closeCursor();

        // Get the last product ID that was automatically generated
        $product_id = $db->lastInsertId();
        return $product_id;
    } catch (PDOException $e) {
        $error_message = $e->getMessage();
        display_db_error($error_message);
    }
}

function update_product($product_id, $code, $name, $description,
                        $price, $discount_percent, $category_id) {
    global $db;
    $query = 'UPDATE Products
                SET productName = :name,
                    productCode = :code,
                    description = :description,
                    listPrice = :price,
                    discountPercent = :discount_percent,
                    categoryID = :category_id
                WHERE productID = :product_id';
    try {
        $statement = $db->prepare($query);
        $statement->bindValue(':name', $name);
        $statement->bindValue(':code', $code);
        $statement->bindValue(':description', $description);
        $statement->bindValue(':price', $price);
        $statement->bindValue(':discount_percent', $discount_percent);
        $statement->bindValue(':category_id', $category_id);
        $statement->bindValue(':product_id', $product_id);
        $row_count = $statement->execute();
        $statement->closeCursor();
        return $row_count;
```

Figure 19-4   A model in PDO (part 3 of 4)

The model/product_db.php file (continued)

```php
        } catch (PDOException $e) {
            $error_message = $e->getMessage();
            display_db_error($error_message);
        }
    }

    function delete_product($product_id) {
        global $db;
        $query = 'DELETE FROM products WHERE productID = :product_id';
        try {
            $statement = $db->prepare($query);
            $statement->bindValue(':product_id', $product_id);
            $row_count = $statement->execute();
            $statement->closeCursor();
            return $row_count;
        } catch (PDOException $e) {
            $error_message = $e->getMessage();
            display_db_error($error_message);
        }
    }
?>
```

Figure 19-4   A model in PDO (part 4 of 4)

How to work with mysqli

Although we recommend PDO for new development, many programmers prefer mysqli and have used it for years for existing web applications. As a result, if you need to maintain legacy code that uses mysqli, you can use the skills presented in this topic to do that. Of course, if you are using PDO and don't need mysqli, you can skip or skim this topic.

When you use mysqli, you can choose between a *procedural style* that uses functions and an *object-oriented style* that uses objects, methods, and properties. In this topic, the first figure shows how to use either style to connect to a database, and the next three figures show how to use the object-oriented style. Then, the last figure shows how the object-oriented style compares with the procedural style. Once you learn one style, it's pretty easy to switch to the other style whenever that's necessary.

How to connect to a database

Figure 19-5 shows how to use mysqli to connect to a database. The first example uses the object-oriented style to create a mysqli object that represents a connection to the database. The second example uses the procedural style to return a variable that represents a connection to the database.

For both styles, you need to specify four parameters: host, username, password, and database name. Most of the time, the MySQL database runs on the same server as PHP. As a result, you can usually use the localhost keyword to specify the host computer.

In the first two examples, the statement that gets a connection to the database begins with the *error suppression operator* (@). As a result, PHP doesn't display a warning if it encounters an error. Although this is probably what you want for a production application, you might want to display warnings when you're testing and debugging the application. To do that, you can remove the error suppression operator from the start of this line.

After you attempt to connect to a database, you typically want to check to make sure the you were able to connect successfully. That way, if your code wasn't able to connect successfully, you can display an appropriate error message and exit the script.

With the object-oriented style, you can use the connect_errno and connect_error properties of the mysqli object to get the error number and message if they exist. With the procedural style, you can use the mysqli_connect_errno and mysqli_connect_error functions to get the error number and message if they exist. Either way, you can test the error number and method, display an appropriate message, and take an appropriate action. In this figure, the examples display the error message to the user and exit the script, which is an appropriate action for many types of applications.

How to connect to a MySQL database (object-oriented)

```
$host = 'localhost';
$username = 'mgs_user';
$password = 'pa55word';
$db_name = 'my_guitar_shop1';

@ $db = new mysqli($host, $username, $password, $db_name);
```

How to connect to a MySQL database (procedural)

```
$host = 'localhost';
$username = 'mgs_user';
$password = 'pa55word';
$db_name = 'my_guitar_shop1';

@ $db = mysqli_connect($host, $username, $password, $db_name);
```

Two properties of the mysqli object for checking connection errors

Property	Description
connect_errno	Returns the error number if an error occurred. Returns a NULL value if no error occurred.
connect_error	Returns the error message if an error occurred. Returns a NULL value if no error occurred.

How to check for a connection error (object-oriented)

```
$connection_error = $db->connect_error;
if ($connection_error != null) {
    echo "<p>Error connecting to database: $connection_error</p>";
    exit();
}
```

How to check for a connection error (procedural)

```
$connection_error = mysqli_connect_error();
if ($connection_error != null) {
    echo "<p>Error connecting to database: $connection_error</p>";
    exit();
}
```

Description

- The mysqli extension includes a *procedural style* that uses functions to work with the database, and it includes an *object-oriented style* that uses objects, methods, and properties to work with the database.

- To suppress errors, you can begin the line of code that connects to the database with the *error suppression operator* (@).

Figure 19-5   How to connect to a database

How to select data

Figure 19-6 shows how to use mysqli to execute a SELECT statement. To start, you can use the query method of the mysqli object to return a result set. This result set is actually a mysqli_resultset object.

If the result set contains a FALSE value, an error occurred. In that case, you can handle the error. In this figure, for example, the code uses the error property of the mysqli object to get an error message, it displays the error message, and it exits the script.

If the result set doesn't contain a FALSE value, you can use the num_rows property of the result set object to get the number of rows in the result set. Then, you can loop through each row in the result set. Within that loop, you can use the fetch_accoc method to get the current row.

When you're done using the result set, you can free the resources used by the result set by calling the free method of the result set object. Then, if you're done using the database connection, you can free the resources used by that object by calling the close method of the mysqli object.

A method of the mysqli class for returning a result set

Method	Description
query(*$select_statement*)	Executes the specified SQL statement and returns a mysqli object for the result set. If no result set is returned, this method returns a FALSE value.

A property and a method of the mysqli_resultset class

Property/Method	Description
num_rows	The number of rows in the result set.
fetch_assoc()	Returns the result set as an associative array.

How to execute a SELECT statement

```
// Execute the statement
$category_id = 2;
$query = "SELECT * FROM products
          WHERE categoryID = $category_id";
$result = $db->query($query);

// Check the result set
if ($result == false) {
    $error_message = $db->error;
    echo "<p>An error occurred: $error_message</p>";
    exit();
}

// Get the number of rows in the result set
$row_count = $result->num_rows;
```

How to display the results

```
<?php for ($i = 0; $i < $row_count; $i++) :
        $product = $result->fetch_assoc();
?>
<tr>
    <td><?php echo $product['productID']; ?></td>
    <td><?php echo $product['categoryID']; ?></td>
    <td><?php echo $product['productCode']; ?></td>
    <td><?php echo $product['productName']; ?></td>
    <td><?php echo $product['listPrice']; ?></td>
</tr>
<?php endfor; ?>
```

How to free resources used by the result set and database connection

```
$result->free();    // close the result set
$db->close();       // close the db connection
```

Figure 19-6   How to select data

How to insert, update, and delete data

Figure 19-7 shows how to use mysqli to execute an INSERT statement. However, the same techniques can be used to execute UPDATE and DELETE statements.

The code in this figure begins by using the query method of the mysqli object to execute the INSERT statement. Then, it checks the value that was returned by the query method to check whether it executed successfully.

If the query executes successfully, this code calls the affected_rows property of the mysqli object to get the number of affected rows. Then, this code displays the number of affected rows to the user. In this case, the number should be 1, but it could be more than that if you executed an INSERT, UPDATE, or DELETE statement that affected multiple rows. Similarly, it could be 0 if you executed a statement that didn't affect any rows.

If the query fails, this code calls the error property of the mysqli object to get an error message that describes why the query failed. Then, this code displays that error message to the user. Although this code doesn't use the errno property, the errno property works similarly to the error property. However, it returns an integer for the error number instead of a string for the error message.

When you execute an INSERT statement, you sometimes need to get the row ID that's automatically generated by MySQL when the row is inserted. To do that, you can call the insert_id property of the mysqli object after you execute the INSERT statement. In this example, the code gets the ID that MySQL generated for the productID column of the products table.

Properties of the mysqli class for checking the result

Property	Description
`affected_rows`	Returns the number of affected rows. If no rows were affected, this property returns zero.
`insert_id`	Returns the auto generated ID used in the last query. If no ID was generated, this property returns zero.
`error`	Returns the error message if an error occurred. Otherwise, it returns an empty string.
`errno`	Returns the error number if an error occurred. Otherwise, it returns zero.

How to execute an INSERT statement

```
// Sample data
$category_id = 2;
$code = 'hofner';
$name = 'Hofner Icon';
$price = 499.99;

// Execute the statement
$query = "INSERT INTO products
            (categoryID, productCode, productName, listPrice)
          VALUES
            ($category_id, '$code', '$name', $price)";
$success = $db->query($query);

// Check the result
if ($success) {
    $count = $db->affected_rows;
    echo "<p>$count product(s) were added.</p>";
} else {
    $error_message = $db->error;
    echo "<p>An error occurred: $error_message</p>";
}

// Check the product ID that was automatically generated
$product_id = $db->insert_id;
echo "<p>Generated product ID: $product_id</p>";
```

Figure 19-7   How to insert, update, and delete data

How to work with prepared statements

Like PDO, mysqli provides support for prepared statements. Since prepared statements improve the performance and security of your application, you should use them whenever possible.

Figure 19-8 shows how to use mysqli to work with prepared statements. To start, you can use one or more question mark (?) parameters to specify the parameters for the query. In this figure, the first example specifies one parameter in a SELECT statement. Then, you can use the prepare method of the mysqli object to prepare the statement. If it executes successfully, this method returns a mysqli_stmt object.

Once you have the mysqli_stmt object, you can use the bind_param method of the mysqli_stmt object to bind a value to the parameter. Within this method, the first parameter is a format string that includes one character for each parameter with s for string, i for integer, d for double, and b for BLOB. In this example, the format string uses a value of "i" to indicate that the SELECT statement contains one integer parameter.

After you have bound the values to the parameters, you can bind the columns in the result set to the variables that provide access to their values. To do that, you can use the bind_result method of the mysqli_stmt object. In this example, the bind_result method binds the productCode, productName, and listPrice columns to the $code, $name, and $listPrice variables.

Once you have completed binding the variables, you can use the fetch method of the mysqli_stmt object to copy the values from the current row into the bound variables. To do that, you typically use a while loop as shown in the second example. Then, when you're done working with the prepared statement, you can call the close() method of the mysqli_stmt object to free the resources that are used by the statement as shown in the third example.

A method of the mysqli class

Method	Description
`prepare($sql_statement)`	Prepares the specified SQL statement for execution and returns a mysqli_stmt object. The specified SQL statement can contain zero or more question mark (?) parameters. If an error occurs, this method returns a FALSE value.

Four methods of the mysqli_stmt class

Method	Description
`bind_param($fs, $v1[, $v2]...)`	Binds the specified values to the parameters in the prepared statement. The first parameter is a format string that specifies the data types for all parameters (s for string, i for integer, d for double, b for BLOB).
`bind_result($v1[, $v2]...)`	Binds the columns in the result set to the specified variables.
`execute()`	Executes the prepared statement. Returns TRUE for success and FALSE for failure.
`fetch()`	Gets the values for the result set columns and stores them in the bound variables.
`close()`	Closes the prepared statement.

How to execute a prepared statement that returns a result set

```php
$category_id = 2;
$query = "SELECT productCode, productName, listPrice FROM products
          WHERE categoryID = ?";
$statement = $db->prepare($query);
$statement->bind_param("i", $category_id);
$statement->bind_result($code, $name, $listPrice);
$statement->execute();
```

How to display the result set

```php
<?php while($statement->fetch()) : ?>
<tr>
    <td><?php echo $code; ?></td>
    <td><?php echo $name; ?></td>
    <td><?php echo $listPrice; ?></td>
</tr>
<?php endwhile; ?>
```

How to close the statement

```php
$statement->close()
```

Figure 19-8   How to work with prepared statements (part 1 of 2)

The next example shows how to create and execute a prepared INSERT statement. In general, this works like creating and executing a prepared SELECT statement. However, when you execute this statement, it doesn't create a result set. Instead, it updates the data. Then, you can use the properties of the mysqli object to get the number of affected rows, error messages, and so on just as you do with dynamic SQL statements. Although this figure doesn't show how to work with prepared UPDATE and DELETE statements, the principles are the same as working with a prepared INSERT statement.

Since this example uses four question mark parameters, it clearly shows how the first argument of the bind_param function works. In this example, the format string uses a value of "issd" to indicate that the SQL statement contains four parameters: an integer, a string, another string, and a double.

How to execute a prepared statement that modifies data

```
$category_id = 2;
$code = 'hofner';
$name = 'Hofner Icon';
$price = 499.99;
$query = "INSERT INTO products
            (categoryID, productCode, productName, listPrice)
         VALUES
            (?, ?, ?, ?)";
$statement = $db->prepare($query);
$statement->bind_param("issd", $category_id, $code, $name, $price);
$success = $statement->execute();
if ($success) {
    $count = $db->affected_rows;
    echo "<p>$count product(s) were added.</p>";
} else {
    $error_message = $db->error;
    echo "<p>An error occurred: $error_message</p>";
}
$statement->close();
```

Figure 19-8   How to work with prepared statements (part 2 of 2)

The object-oriented style compared to the procedural style

Once you know how to use the object-oriented style, it's easy to convert it to the procedural style if that becomes necessary. To help you understand how the object-oriented style compares to the procedural style, figure 19-9 presents ten common database calls in the object-oriented and procedural styles.

To start, you should realize that mysqli provides a procedural call for every object-oriented call. These procedural calls always begin with "mysqli_" and include the parentheses at the end of the function. In addition, these calls usually pass the database connection, the result set, or the prepared statement to the function as its first argument.

On the other hand, the object-oriented calls don't include parentheses when they call a property, but they do include parentheses when they call a method. In addition, with object-oriented calls, you don't need to start the call with "mysqli_", and you don't need to pass the database, result set, or statement object as an argument. As a result, the object-oriented calls are shorter than the corresponding procedural calls. This makes the object-oriented calls easier to read and maintain.

Object-oriented statements compared to procedural statements

```
$result = $db->query($query);                         // oo
$result = mysqli_query($db, $query);                  // procedural

$error_message = $db->error;                          // oo
$error_message = mysqli_error($db);                   // procedural

$row = $result->fetch_assoc();                        // oo
$row = mysqli_fetch_assoc($result);                   // procedural

$row_count = $result->num_rows;                       // oo
$row_count = mysqli_num_rows($result);                // procedural

$count = $db->affected_rows;                          // oo
$count = mysqli_affected_rows($db);                   // procedural

$result->free();                                      // oo
mysqli_free_result($result);                          // procedural

$statement = $db->prepare($query);                    // oo
$statement = mysqli_prepare($db, $query);             // procedural

$statement->bind_param("i", $category_id);            // oo
mysqli_bind_param($statement, "i", $category_id);     // procedural

$success = $statement->execute();                     // oo
$success = mysqli_execute($statement);                // procedural

$db->close();                                         // oo
mysqli_close($db);                                    // procedural
```

Description

- For every object-oriented call to the mysqli extension, there is a corresponding procedural call.

- The object-oriented calls don't include parentheses when they call a property, but they do include parentheses when they call a method.

- The procedural calls always begin with "mysqli_" and include the parentheses at the end of the function.

- The procedural calls usually pass the database connection, the result set, or the prepared statement to the function as its first argument.

- The object-oriented calls require less code than the corresponding procedural calls.

Figure 19-9   The object-oriented style compared to the procedural style

A model in mysqli

Figure 19-10 shows the model in figure 19-4 after it has been converted from PDO to mysqli. As a result, if you understand the PDO version of the model, you shouldn't have much trouble understanding the mysqli version of the model. However, there are several significant differences.

The first significant difference is that the functions that retrieve data don't use prepared statements. That's because mysqli's prepared statements don't provide methods for returning arrays. Because this makes it difficult to separate the model from the view, I decided to not use prepared statements for these functions.

This allows the functions that retrieve data to use the fetch_assoc method of the result set to get an associative array for each row. Then, if necessary, the code can add that row to an array to create a two-dimensional array. For example, the get_categories method loops through the rows in the result set, gets an associative array for each row, and adds that array to the categories array. Then, it returns the categories array.

Another approach would be to use prepared statements and return the mysqli_stmt object. The advantage of this approach is that it allows you to use prepared statements, which improves the security and efficiency of your code. In addition, since you don't store the entire result set in an array, the code runs more efficiently and uses less memory when you're working with large result sets. Of course, the disadvantage is that it mixes the model and the view, which makes your code more difficult to maintain.

Note that the functions that modify data use prepared statements. As a result, these functions prepare the statement, bind the parameters to the statement, and execute the statement.

The second significant difference between PDO and mysqli is how these functions handle database errors. Here, the mysqli functions detect errors by checking the return values after making calls to the database. As a result, the functions that work with prepared statements check for errors twice, once after the statement is prepared and again after the statement is executed. Then, if an error has occurred, these functions handle the error appropriately by getting the error message from the mysqli object and passing that message to the display_db_error function.

The model/database.php file

```php
<?php
$host = 'localhost';
$username = 'mgs_user';
$password = 'pa55word';
$database = 'my_guitar_shop2';

$db = new mysqli($host, $username, $password, $database);

$error_message = $db->connect_error;
if ($error_message != null) {
    include 'errors/db_error_connect.php';
    exit;
}

function display_db_error($error_message) {
    global $app_path;
    include 'errors/db_error.php';
    exit;
}
?>
```

The model/category_db.php file

```php
<?php
function get_categories() {
    global $db;
    $query = 'SELECT * FROM categories ORDER BY categoryID';
    $result = $db->query($query);
    if ($result == false) {
        display_db_error($db->error);
        exit;
    }
    $categories = array();
    for ($i = 0; $i < $result->num_rows; $i++) {
        $category = $result->fetch_assoc();
        $categories[] = $category;
    }
    $result->free();
    return $categories;
}

function get_category($category_id) {
    global $db;
    $query = "SELECT * FROM categories
                WHERE categoryID = $category_id";
    $result = $db->query($query);
    if ($result == false) {
        display_db_error($db->error);
        exit;
    }
    $category = $result->fetch_assoc();
    $result->free();
    return $category;
}
?>
```

Figure 19-10   A model in mysqli (part 1 of 3)

The model/product_db.php file

```php
<?php
function get_products_by_category($category_id) {
    global $db;
    $query = "SELECT * FROM products WHERE categoryID = $category_id";
    $result = $db->query($query);
    if ($result == false) {
        display_db_error($db->error);
    }
    $products = array();
    for ($i = 0; $i < $result->num_rows; $i++) {
        $product = $result->fetch_assoc();
        $products[] = $product;
    }
    $result->free();
    return $products;
}

function get_product($product_id) {
    global $db;
    $query = "SELECT * FROM products WHERE productID = '$product_id'";
    $result = $db->query($query);
    if ($result == false) {
        display_db_error($db->error);
    }
    $product = $result->fetch_assoc();
    return $product;
}

function add_product($category_id, $code, $name, $description,
        $price, $discount_percent) {
    global $db;
    $query = 'INSERT INTO products
            (categoryID, productCode, productName, description,
             listPrice, discountPercent, dateAdded)
          VALUES
            (?, ?, ?, ?,
             ?, ?, NOW())';
    $statement = $db->prepare($query);
    if ($statement == false) {
        display_db_error($db->error);
    }
    $statement->bind_param("isssdd", $category_id, $code, $name, $description,
                            $price, $discount_percent);
    $success = $statement->execute();
    if ($success) {
        $product_id = $db->insert_id;
        $statement->close();
        return $product_id;
    } else {
        display_db_error($db->error);
    }
}
```

Figure 19-10   A model in mysqli (part 2 of 3)

The model/product_db.php file (continued)

```php
function update_product($product_id, $code, $name, $description,
                        $price, $discount_percent, $category_id) {
    global $db;
    $query = 'UPDATE Products
        SET categoryID = ?,
            productCode = ?,
            productName = ?,
            description = ?,
            listPrice = ?,
            discountPercent = ?
        WHERE productID = ?';
    $statement = $db->prepare($query);
    if ($statement == false) {
        display_db_error($db->error);
    }
    $statement->bind_param("isssddi", $category_id, $code, $name,
            $description, $price, $discount_percent, $product_id);
    $success = $statement->execute();
    if ($success) {
        $count = $db->affected_rows;
        $statement->close();
        return $count;
    } else {
        display_db_error($db->error);
    }
}

function delete_product($product_id) {
    global $db;
    $query = "DELETE FROM products
                WHERE productID = ?";
    $statement = $db->prepare($query);
    if ($statement == false) {
        display_db_error($db->error);
    }
    $statement->bind_param("i", $product_id);
    $success = $statement->execute();
    if ($success) {
        $count = $db->affected_rows;
        $statement->close();
        return $count;
    } else {
        display_db_error($db->error);
    }
}
?>
```

Figure 19-10   A model in mysqli (part 3 of 3)

Perspective

Now that you've finished with this chapter, you have the skills that you need for using PHP to work with a MySQL database at a professional level. In the next chapter, you'll learn more about how you can apply those skills.

Terms

Application Programming Interface
    (API)
PHP extension for the MySQL API
PHP Data Objects (PDO)
database abstraction layer
dynamic SQL statement
prepared SQL statement

named parameter
question mark parameter
unnamed parameter
object-oriented style
procedural style
error suppression operator

Summary

- MySQL provides an *Application Programming Interface* (*API*) that specifies how any application can work with MySQL.

- PHP provides three *extensions* for working with the MySQL API: the mysql extension, the mysqli extension, and the PDO MySQL driver extension.

- *PHP Data Objects* (*PDO*) is a *database abstraction layer* specifically for database applications. PDO uses the PDO MySQL driver extension to communicate with MySQL, but it can use other drivers to communicate with other databases.

- When you use PDO to execute SQL statements, you can choose between three error modes.

- When compared to *dynamic SQL statements*, using *prepared statements* provides improved performance and security.

- A *named parameter* begins with a colon (:) followed by the name of the parameter. An *unnamed parameter* (also known as a *question mark parameter*) uses a question mark (?) to indicate the location of the parameter in the SQL statement.

- The mysqli extension includes a *procedural style* that uses functions to work with the database, and it includes an *object-oriented style* that uses objects, methods, and properties to work with the database.

Exercise 19-1   Use PHP to work with a database

This exercise lets you use some of the skills that were presented in this chapter. In particular, it lets you use the functions from the products_db.php file that's presented in this chapter.

Review and test the code

1. Run the application in the ex_starts/ch19_ex1 directory. This should display the names of the products in the Basses category, a delete message, and an insert message.

2. Open the database.php file, the product_db.php file, and the index.php file. Then, review the code. Note that this code uses PDO.

3. If you want to use mysqli instead of PDO, replace the database.php and product_db.php files with the database.php and product_db.php files that are in the book_apps/ch20_guitar_shop_mysqli/model directory.

Modify the code

4. Modify the index.php file so it displays the products that are in the Guitars category.

5. Modify the index.php file so it uses a function from the model to add a product. When you do that, use the sample data that's already in the index.php file. Make sure this code displays an appropriate message that indicates whether the product was inserted. Note that the products table requires a unique product code for each product. As a result, you can't insert the same product code twice.

6. Add a function to the model named get_product_by_name. This function should have a parameter for the product name and it should return a product array for the product with the specified name. This provides a way to get the product ID and other product data that corresponds to the product name.

7. Modify the index.php file so it uses a function from the model to delete the product named "Fender Telecaster". To do that, you can use the function that you created in the previous step to get the product ID. Make sure this code displays an appropriate message that indicates whether the product was deleted.

8. Test the code to make sure it works correctly. If it does, it should display the products, delete a product, add a product, and display appropriate messages.

20

A database-driven web site

The last chapter showed how to use PHP to code the model for a database-driven web application. Now, this chapter shows how to use that model to build a database-driven web site for a store, and it presents enhanced versions of the two primary applications within that web site: the Product Catalog and Product Manager applications. But first, this chapter shows you how to work with database columns that store large amounts of text.

How to work with large text columns 646
A simple content management system 646
How to add HTML tags to text 648

The include files for the Guitar Shop web site 650
The Home page 650
The directory structure 650
The utility files 652
The view files 652

The Product Catalog application 658
The user interface 658
The controller 658
The view 658

The Product Manager application 662
The user interface 662
The controller 664
The view 666

Perspective 670

How to work with large text columns

When you develop a database-driven application, you often need to store large amounts of text in the columns of the database. For example, the description column for each product may consist of several paragraphs and may include bulleted lists and other types of formatting. This topic presents a simple but effective approach for working with columns like that.

A simple content management system

When you store large amounts of text in a column, you need to format it before you can display it on a web page. If, for example, the text contains multiple paragraphs, you need to add <p> tags to the paragraphs before you display them on a web page. Similarly, if the text contains an unordered list, you need to add <ul> and <li> tags to the items in the list. In addition, you may need to add other types of HTML formatting to the text such as tags for headings, links, boldfacing, italics, and so on.

One solution to this problem is to store the HTML tags that format the text in the database along with the text. From the programmer's point of view, this is an easy solution. All the programmer has to do is to *not* use the htmlentities or htmlspecialchars function to convert special characters to their equivalent HTML entities. That way, the HTML tags are stored in the database. However, when you use this approach, the person who enters the text must know HTML and must be able to code the HTML tags without making errors. Since that's a lot to ask, this usually isn't the way you want your web site to work.

To get around this problem, you can create a *content management system* for your web site. A content management system is a series of web pages that make it easy for users with little knowledge of HTML to manage the content of the web site. Figure 20-1 shows how a simple content management system works. This content management system allows the user to enter a large amount of text for the description column of a products table.

When the user enters text, he or she can use two returns to start a new paragraph, an asterisk to mark items in an unordered list, and standard HTML tags for bold and italics. This stores the end of line characters in the database, and it stores the HTML tags in the database.

When the application gets this text from the database, it uses PHP to apply the rest of the HTML tags. In particular, it adds the appropriate <p> tags when it finds two return characters, and it adds the appropriate <ul> and <li> tags when it finds a line that begins with an asterisk.

In this example, the content management system is a hybrid system that requires that the user have some knowledge of HTML tags. In particular, it requires that the users know how to use HTML tags to identify text that should be displayed in bold or italics. However, this system automatically handles the tags for paragraphs and unordered lists.

The text that's entered by the user

```
The Fender Stratocaster is <i>the</i> electric guitar design that changed
the world. This guitar features a thicker bridge block for increased sus-
tain and a more stable point of contact with the strings.

Features:

* Thicker bridge block
* 3-ply parchment pick guard
* Tinted neck
```

The HTML that's generated by the content management system

```
<p>The Fender Stratocaster is <i>the</i> electric guitar design that
changed the world. This guitar features a thicker bridge block for in-
creased sustain and a more stable point of contact with the strings.</p>

<p>Features:</p>

<ul>
    <li>Thicker bridge block</li>
    <li>3-ply parchment pick guard</li>
    <li>Tinted neck</li>
</ul>
```

The rules for this content management system

- Use two returns to start a new paragraph.
- Use an asterisk to mark items in a bulleted list.
- Use one return between items in a bulleted list.
- Use standard HMTL tags for bold and italics.

Description

- A *content management system* for a web site is a series of web pages that make it easy for users with little knowledge of HTML to manage the content of the web site.
- To allow the user to use HTML tags, you must not use the htmlentities or htmlspecialchars function to convert special characters to their equivalent HTML entities.
- *Bulletin Board Code* (*BBCode*) is a markup language that's used by many bulletin board or message board systems to format text. BBCode is similar to HTML, but it has a simplified syntax that uses square brackets ([ ]) instead of angled brackets (< >).

Figure 20-1   A simple content management system

Another approach to content management is to have the users use *Bulletin Board Code* (*BBCode*) to format the text. BBCode is a markup language that's used by many bulletin board and message board systems. It's similar to HTML, but it has a simplified syntax that uses square brackets ([ ]) instead of angled brackets (< >).

BBCode is more secure than HTML since it doesn't allow users to enter HTML tags. As a result, it's appropriate for web applications that are open to anybody, such as bulletin boards. However, more users are already familiar with HTML than BBCode. As a result, allowing HTML is appropriate for web applications where the users are administrative users who can be trusted not to enter HTML tags that contain malicious code. To get more information about BBCode, you can search the Internet.

How to add HTML tags to text

Figure 20-2 shows the PHP for the tag.php file that's stored in the util directory. This file defines a function named add_tags that adds <p>, <ul>, and <li> tags to a large amount of text as described in the previous figure.

The add_tags function begins by searching the text and converting the new line characters for Windows and Mac systems to the new line characters for a Unix system. This is necessary because Windows systems use return and new line characters ("\r\n") to mark a new line, and Mac systems use a single return character ("\r") to mark a new line. In contrast, a Unix system just uses a single new line character ("\n") to mark a new line. After this code executes, you can be sure that the text contains a single new line character ("\n") for each new line, no matter what operating system you are using.

After setting up the new line characters, this code uses the explode function to split the text into an array of paragraphs and stores this array in a variable named $paragraphs. Here, each paragraph is delimited by two new line characters ("\n\n"). Then, this code clears the $text variable and uses a loop to process each paragraph.

Within the loop, the first statement trims any white space from the left side of the paragraph. Then, the code gets the first character in the paragraph. If this character is an asterisk (*), this code adds the appropriate <ul> and <li> tags to the paragraph. Otherwise, this code adds the appropriate <p> tags to the paragraph. Either way, the paragraph is appended to the end of the $text variable.

After the loop, this function returns the $text variable. At this point, the $text variable contains the HTML tags that mark paragraphs and unordered lists. It also contains any HTML tags that were stored in this database.

As you review this code, note that it could easily be expanded to account for other HTML tags. For example, if you wanted to insert links, you could automatically check for any text that begins with "http://" and "www." and add the appropriate <a> tag. Or, if you wanted to provide for ordered lists, you could check if the first line in the paragraph starts with a number and add the appropriate <ol> and <li> tags.

The util/tags.php file

```php
<?php
function add_tags($text) {

    // Convert return characters to the Unix new lines
    $text = str_replace("\r\n", "\n", $text);    // convert Windows
    $text = str_replace("\r", "\n", $text);      // convert Mac

    // Get an array of paragraphs
    $paragraphs = explode("\n\n", $text);

    // Add tags to each paragraph
    $text = '';
    foreach($paragraphs as $p) {
        $p = ltrim($p);

        $first_char = substr($p, 0, 1);
        if ($first_char == '*') {
            // Add <ul> and <li> tags
            $p = '<ul>' . $p . '</li></ul>';
            $p = str_replace("*", '<li>', $p);
            $p = str_replace("\n", '</li>', $p);
        } else {
            // Add <p> tags
            $p = '<p>' . $p . '</p>';
        }
        $text .= $p;
    }

    return $text;
}
?>
```

Code that uses the add_tags function

```php
$description = add_tags($description);
```

Description

- To add HTML tags to the text in a column of a database, you can parse the code by using PHP's string functions that were presented in chapter 9 and add the tags wherever necessary.

Figure 20-2   How to add HTML tags to text

The include files for the Guitar Shop web site

The rest of this chapter presents an enhanced version of the Guitar Shop applications that were presented in chapter 5. To start, it presents the *include files* for the web site. These are the files that are used throughout the web site, and these files are used by both the Product Catalog and Product Manager applications that are part of the Guitar Shop web site. To include these files wherever they're needed, you can use the include and require functions.

To give you a better idea of how the include files work, part 1 of figure 20-3 shows the Home page and the directory structure for the Guitar Shop web site. Then, the next three parts show some of the include files.

The Home page

The Home page in this figure is displayed when a user accesses the web site. This page displays some featured products, and it lets the user browse to a product by clicking on the category links in the sidebar. Note that the code for this sidebar is stored in an include file.

Note also that the Home and Admin links in the sidebar wouldn't be included in a production application. However, in the development and testing stages of an application, links like these makes it easier for developers and testers to jump between the Product Catalog and Product Manager applications.

Remember too that the focus of these applications is to develop and test the PHP code for the applications. Later, when all of the code is working right, you or a web designer can enhance the HTML and CSS so the graphics and navigation are appropriate for the end users. For instance, the header would probably include a logo, a tag line, and a navigation bar that included the link to the Home page.

The directory structure

This figure also presents the directory structure of this application. Here, the model and view directories contain the files for the model and the view that are used in multiple parts of the web site. The directories named admin, cart, and catalog contain the PHP files for the applications within the web site. The images directory contains all of the images that are used by the web site. The errors directory contains the PHP files for handling errors. And the util directory contains the general-purpose files that can be used throughout the web site.

Within the root directory for the application, the index.php file is run when the users access the web site in their browsers. This file includes all of the util and model files that are used by the Home page. Then, it does some processing before it includes the home_view.php file to display the Home page.

The Home page for the Guitar Shop web site

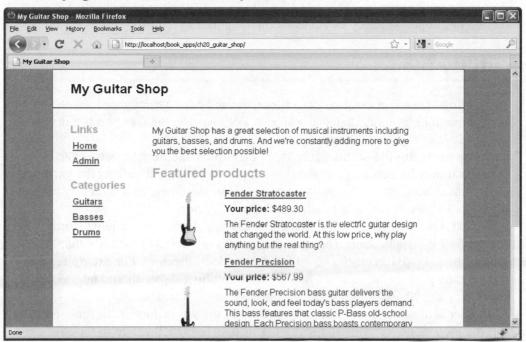

The directory structure for the web site starting from htdocs/book_apps

Files in the application's root directory

```
index.php
home_view.php
main.css
```

Description

- *Include files* contain code that is used throughout a web site. Then, those files can be included whenever they're needed.

- For the Guitar Shop web site, the include files are stored in the util, model, view, and errors subdirectories. These files are usually used by the files that drive the applications of the web site, like the files in the admin, cart, and catalog directories.

Figure 20-3   Include files for the Guitar Shop web site (part 1 of 4)

Note that the main CSS file is stored in the root directory. However, on a large system that requires multiple CSS files, these files would probably be stored in a separate directory named something like styles.

The utility files

Utility files are general-purpose files that can be used throughout a web site and sometimes by more than one web site. For instance, the tags.php file in figure 20-2 is a typical utility file.

The main.php file in this figure is another utility file. It defines two variables that may be needed throughout the application. First, it defines the variable named $doc_root. This variable points to the document root directory of the Apache server, which is usually the htdocs directory.

Next, this file defines the variable named $app_path. This variable stores the path of the application. The code that creates this variable assumes that the application is two directories down from the htdocs directory. For example, the application path for the Guitar Shop web site for this chapter should be book_apps/ch20_guitar_shop/.

After setting these variables, this code uses the set_include_path function to set the *include path* for the application. This path tells PHP where to look for the files specified in include and require functions. In this case, the path is set to the document root directory plus the application path. Then, because PHP always checks the include path, you can code include and require functions relative to the include path like this:

```
include 'errors/db_error.php';
```

This is helpful when you need to include a file from different depths in the directory structure of an application. For example, this code includes the db_error.php file in the errors directory no matter what directory it's called from.

The view files

The rest of the include files in this figure are stored in the view directory and define various components of a web page. To start, the header.php file contains the HTML tags that begin every page in the web site. This file works like it did in chapter 5 except that it uses the $app_path variable to get the path to the CSS file for the web site. Since this code doesn't require you to hard code the application path in the header file, it's more flexible and easier to maintain. Although it isn't shown in this chapter, the footer.php file is another one of the view files.

The util/main.php file

```php
<?php
// Get the document root
$doc_root = $_SERVER['DOCUMENT_ROOT'];

// Get the application path
$uri = $_SERVER['REQUEST_URI'];
$dirs = explode('/', $uri);
$app_path = '/' . $dirs[1] . '/' . $dirs[2] . '/';

// Set the include path
set_include_path($doc_root . $app_path);
?>
```

The view/header.php file

```html
<!DOCTYPE html PUBLIC "-//W3C//DTD XHTML 1.0 Transitional//EN"
    "http://www.w3.org/TR/xhtml1/DTD/xhtml1-transitional.dtd">
<html xmlns="http://www.w3.org/1999/xhtml">

    <!-- the head section -->
    <head>
        <title>My Guitar Shop</title>
        <link rel="stylesheet" type="text/css"
            href="<?php echo $app_path ?>main.css" />
    </head>

    <!-- the body section -->
    <body>
    <div id="page">
        <div id="header">
            <h1>My Guitar Shop</h1>
        </div>
        <div id="main">
```

Description

- General-purpose files like the tags.php file in figure 20-2 are often called *utility files* because they can be used by many applications.

- View files like the header.php and sidebar.php files in this figure are included by more than one of the other view files.

Figure 20-3   Include files for the Guitar Shop web site (part 2 of 4)

The sidebar.php file contains the HTML for displaying the <div> tag for the sidebar that contains the links for the Product Catalog application. To start, this code defines a <ul> tag that starts with a heading for links. Within this tag, the first <li> tag defines a link to the Home page, which is the page that's displayed by default when a browser requests the application path. Then, the second <li> tag defines a link to the default page for the admin directory of the web site.

Next, this code uses a loop to display one <li> tag for each category. Within each <li> tag, this code includes an <a> tag that displays the name of the category and passes two parameters to the default file in the catalog directory. Here, the first parameter has a name of "action" and a value of "list_products". The second parameter has a name of "category_id" and a value of the ID for the category. As a result, clicking on this link lists the products for the specified category.

The sidebar_admin.php file works like the sidebar.php file. However, it displays the sidebar for the Product Manager application. Here again, the Home link goes to the default page for the application, and the second link goes to the default page in the admin directory of the web site. Then, the category links call the controller in the admin/product directory.

The view/sidebar.php file

```php
<div id="sidebar">
    <ul>
        <!-- These links are for testing only.
            Remove them from a production application. -->
        <h2>Links</h2>
        <li>
            <a href="<?php echo $app_path; ?>">Home</a>
        </li>
        <li>
            <a href="<?php echo $app_path; ?>admin">Admin</a>
        </li>
        <h2>Categories</h2>
        <!-- display links for all categories -->
        <?php foreach ($categories as $category) : ?>
        <li>
            <a href="<?php echo $app_path .
                'catalog?action=list_products' .
                '&amp;category_id=' . $category['categoryID']; ?>">
                <?php echo $category['categoryName']; ?>
            </a>
        </li>
        <?php endforeach; ?>
        <li> </li>
    </ul>
</div>
```

The view/sidebar_admin.php file

```php
<div id="sidebar">
    <ul>
        <h2>Links</h2>
        <li>
            <a href="<?php echo $app_path; ?>">Home</a>
        </li>
        <li>
            <a href="<?php echo $app_path; ?>admin">Admin</a>
        </li>

        <h2>Categories</h2>
            <!-- display links for all categories -->
        <?php foreach ($categories as $category) : ?>
        <li>
            <a href="<?php echo $app_path .
                'admin/product?action=list_products' .
                '&amp;category_id=' . $category['categoryID']; ?>">
                <?php echo $category['categoryName']; ?>
            </a>
        </li>
        <?php endforeach; ?>
        <li> </li>

    </ul>
</div>
```

Figure 20-3   Include files for the Guitar Shop web site (part 3 of 4)

The product.php file contains the HTML tags that display a product and its image. This file begins with PHP code that sets up the variables that store the data for the product. To start, this code gets the elements that are stored in the product array and stores them in variables. Then, it calls the add_tags function that's in the util/tags.php file to add the appropriate HTML tags to the description. After that, this code calculates and formats the discount.

The last three statements of this file use the product code to create a path to the appropriate PNG image for the product. In addition, these statements set up some text that can be used for the alt attribute of the <img> tag. Here, the code that creates the filename for the image uses an underscore followed by an *m* to indicate that the image is *medium* size. This is necessary because this web site also provides for small images that are indicated by an underscore followed by an *s*.

The HTML tags for the product.php file begin with an <h1> tag that displays the name of the product. Then, this code uses two <div> tags to create two columns. In the left column, this code uses an <img> tag within a <p> tag to display the image for the product. In the right column, this code uses <p> tags to display the data for the product. Note, however, that it isn't necessary to include any tags for the description since the content management system automatically adds the appropriate tags to the description. Just before the tags for the description, a <form> tag is used to define a form that contains an Add to Cart button that lets the user add the product to the Shopping Cart application that's stored in the cart directory.

The view/product.php file

```php
<?php
    // Parse data
    $category_id = $product['categoryID'];
    $product_code = $product['productCode'];
    $product_name = $product['productName'];
    $description = $product['description'];
    $list_price = $product['listPrice'];
    $discount_percent = $product['discountPercent'];

    // Add HMTL tags to the description
    $description = add_tags($description);

    // Calculate discounts
    $discount_amount = round($list_price * ($discount_percent / 100), 2);
    $unit_price = $list_price - $discount_amount;

    // Format discounts
    $discount_percent = number_format($discount_percent, 0);
    $discount_amount = number_format($discount_amount, 2);
    $unit_price = number_format($unit_price, 2);

    // Get image URL and alternate text
    $image_filename = $product_code . '_m.png';
    $image_path = $app_path . 'images/' . $image_filename;
    $image_alt = 'Image filename: ' . $image_filename;
?>

<h1><?php echo $product_name; ?></h1>
<div id="left_column">
    <p><img src="<?php echo $image_path; ?>"
            alt="<?php echo $image_alt; ?>" /></p>
</div>

<div id="right_column">
    <p><b>List Price:</b>
        <?php echo '$' . $list_price; ?></p>
    <p><b>Discount:</b>
        <?php echo $discount_percent . '%'; ?></p>
    <p><b>Your Price:</b>
        <?php echo '$' . $unit_price; ?>
        (You save
        <?php echo '$' . $discount_amount; ?>)</p>
    <form action="<?php echo $app_path . 'cart' ?>" method="post">
        <input type="hidden" name="action" value="add" />
        <input type="hidden" name="product_id"
               value="<?php echo $product_id; ?>" />
        <b>Quantity:</b>
        <input type="text" name="quantity" value="1" size="2" />
        <input type="submit" value="Add to Cart" />
    </form>
    <h2>Description</h2>
    <?php echo $description; ?>
</div>
```

Figure 20-3   Include files for the Guitar Shop web site (part 4 of 4)

The Product Catalog application

Figure 20-4 presents an enhanced version of the Product Manager application that was presented in chapter 5. This version of the application uses the description column that's provided by the database named my_guitar_shop2, which has a large text column for product description. The application works equally well with either of the models (PDO or mysqli) that were described in chapter 19.

The user interface

Part 1 shows the user interface. On the Product List page, the user can click on the category links to display a list of products for each category. Then, the user can click on the link for a product to display the Product View page. There, the user can view an image of the product, read more about the product, or use the Add to Cart button to add the product to his or her cart.

The controller

Part 2 shows the code for the controller of the application. This code is stored in the index.php file of the catalog directory. To start, the first five statements load the code that's stored in the util and model directories. Then, an if statement gets the action parameter from the GET or POST request. Next, a switch statement executes the appropriate action.

For the list_products action, this code starts by getting the category ID from the GET request or by setting this ID to a default value of 1. Then, this code uses the functions from the model to get the necessary category and product data, and it displays the Product List page.

For the view_product action, this code gets the category and product data that corresponds to the selected product. Then, it displays the Product View page.

The view

Part 3 shows the code for the view that's stored in the catalog directory. Since most of the code for the view is stored in the view directory, the code in the catalog directory is short. For example, the product_list.php file includes the code for the header, sidebar, and footer. As a result, the only new code it provides is the code that displays the name of the current category and the list of links for each product. Similarly, the product_view.php file includes the header, sidebar, and footer files, plus the product.php file that displays the product data.

The Product List page

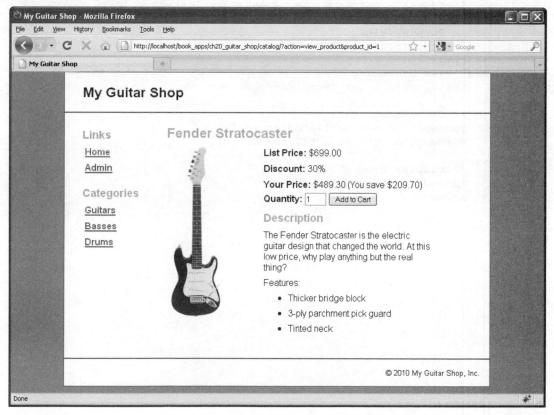

The Product View page

Figure 20-4   The Product Catalog application (part 1 of 3)

The catalog/index.php file

```php
<?php
require_once('../util/main.php');
require_once('../util/tags.php');
require_once('../model/database.php');
require_once('../model/product_db.php');
require_once('../model/category_db.php');

if (isset($_POST['action'])) {
    $action = $_POST['action'];
} else if (isset($_GET['action'])) {
    $action = $_GET['action'];
} else {
    $action = 'list_products';
}

switch ($action) {
    case 'list_products':
        // get current category
        $category_id = $_GET['category_id'];
        if (empty($category_id)) {
            $category_id = 1;
        }

        // get categories and products
        $current_category = get_category($category_id);
        $categories = get_categories();
        $products = get_products_by_category($category_id);

        // Display view
        include('product_list.php');
        break;
    case 'view_product':
        $categories = get_categories();

        // Get product data
        $product_id = $_GET['product_id'];
        $product = get_product($product_id);

        // Display product
        include('product_view.php');
        break;
}
?>
```

Figure 20-4   The Product Catalog application (part 2 of 3)

The catalog/product_list.php file

```php
<?php include '../view/header.php'; ?>
<?php include '../view/sidebar.php'; ?>
<div id="content">
    <h1><?php echo $current_category['categoryName']; ?></h1>
    <?php if (count($products) == 0) : ?>
        <p>There are no products in this category.</p>
    <?php else: ?>
        <?php foreach ($products as $product) : ?>
        <p>
            <a href="?action=view_product&amp;product_id=<?php
                    echo $product['productID']; ?>">
                <?php echo $product['productName']; ?>
            </a>
        </p>
        <?php endforeach; ?>
    <?php endif; ?>
</div>
<?php include '../view/footer.php'; ?>
```

The catalog/product_view.php file

```php
<?php include '../view/header.php'; ?>
<?php include '../view/sidebar.php'; ?>
<div id="content">
    <!-- display product -->
    <?php include '../view/product.php'; ?>
</div>
<?php include '../view/footer.php'; ?>
```

Figure 20-4   The Product Catalog application (part 3 of 3)

The Product Manager application

Figure 20-5 presents an enhanced version of the Product Manager application that was presented in chapter 5. This version provides for more product data, including the long description column. In addition, it allows the user to edit existing products (instead of only being able to add or delete them).

The user interface

Part 1 shows the user interface. On the Product View page, the user can review the image and data for a product. Note that this displays the same content with the same formatting as the Product View page in the Product Catalog application. However, it also displays an Edit Product button that allows the user to edit the product, and a Delete Product button that allows the user to delete the product.

On the Product Add/Edit page, the user can add a new product or edit the data for an existing product. This figure shows the Product Edit page that's displayed when the user clicks on the Edit Product button. This page is similar to the Product Add page that's displayed when the user clicks on the Add Product link. However, the Product Add page displays different text in the heading and it doesn't display any data in the controls. Either way, the user can use this form to work with the product data, and the user can click the Submit button to save the data.

The Product View page

The Product Add/Edit page

Figure 20-5   The Product Manager application (part 1 of 5)

The controller

Parts 2 and 3 show the code for the controller of the application. This code is stored in the index.php file of the admin/product directory. If you compare this code to the controller for the Product Catalog application, you'll see that much of the code is similar. For example, both controllers start by loading the PHP files needed by the application and by getting the action to be performed. In addition, the code for the list_products and view_product action is similar for both controllers. However, this controller contains four new actions: delete_product, show_add_edit_form, add_product, and update_product.

The delete_product action deletes the specified product and displays the Product List page for the current category. To do that, this code gets the product ID and the category ID from the POST request. Here, the product ID identifies the product to be deleted, and the category ID identifies the current category.

The show_add_edit_form action shows the Product Add/Edit page. To do that, this code gets the product ID from the GET or POST request. Then, it uses the functions from the model to get the product and category data. Here, the product ID identifies the product to be edited. But if this ID isn't set, this code returns an empty array, which is appropriate for adding a product.

The admin/product/index.php file

```php
<?php
require_once('../../util/main.php');
require_once('../../util/tags.php');
require_once('../../model/database.php');
require_once('../../model/product_db.php');
require_once('../../model/category_db.php');

if (isset($_POST['action'])) {
    $action = $_POST['action'];
} else if (isset($_GET['action'])) {
    $action = $_GET['action'];
} else {
    $action = 'list_products';
}

$action = strtolower($action);
switch ($action) {
    case 'list_products':
        // get categories and products
        $category_id = $_GET['category_id'];
        if (empty($category_id)) {
            $category_id = 1;
        }
        $current_category = get_category($category_id);
        $categories = get_categories();
        $products = get_products_by_category($category_id);

        // display product list
        include('product_list.php');
        break;
    case 'view_product':
        $categories = get_categories();
        $product_id = $_GET['product_id'];
        $product = get_product($product_id);
        include('product_view.php');
        break;
    case 'delete_product':
        $category_id = $_POST['category_id'];
        $product_id = $_POST['product_id'];
        delete_product($product_id);

        // Display the Product List page for the current category
        header("Location: .?category_id=$category_id");
        break;
    case 'show_add_edit_form':
        if (isset($_GET['product_id'])) {
            $product_id = $_GET['product_id'];
        } else {
            $product_id = $_POST['product_id'];
        }
        $product = get_product($product_id);
        $categories = get_categories();
        include('product_add_edit.php');
        break;
```

Figure 20-5   The Product Manager application (part 2 of 5)

The add_product action adds a new product to the database. To start, it gets the data for the product from the POST request. Then, it performs some simple validation on that data. If the data is valid, this code adds the data to the database and displays the Product View Page for that product. Otherwise, it uses the error.php page in the errors directory to display an error message to the user.

The update_product action updates an existing product in the database. This code works much like the code for the add_product action except that it uses the update_product function to update the current product.

The view

Parts 4 and 5 show the code for the view that's stored in the admin/product directory. Here, the product_view.php file displays the Product View page. This page uses the product.php file from the view directory to display the product. As a result, the product has the same content and formatting as the product displayed in the Product Catalog application. However, this page adds an <h1> tag above the product that indicates it is part of the Product Manager application, and it displays the Edit Product and Delete Product buttons below the product.

The product_add_edit.php file displays the Product Add/Edit page. This page begins with some PHP code that checks whether the product ID has been set by the controller. If the product ID is set, the user must be editing an existing product. As a result, this code sets the $heading_text variable to 'Edit Product'. But if the product ID isn't set, the user must be adding a new product. As a result, this code sets the $heading_text variable to 'Add Product'. Then, this page uses that variable to display an <h1> tag with a title that's appropriate for the current action.

After displaying the <h1> tag, this code defines a form that provides the controls that allow the user to work with the data for the product. To start, this code uses an if statement to set up the appropriate hidden fields for the form. If the user is editing the product, this form uses a hidden field to set the action to update_product and to set the product_id parameter to the product ID for the current product. But if the user is adding a product, this form just sets the action to add_product.

After displaying the hidden tags, this code displays a drop-down list of options for the category. If the user is editing an existing product, this drop-down list must select the correct category for the current product. To do that, this page adds some code within the loop that outputs the <option> tags for the categories. This code also outputs the selected attribute for the <option> tag if the category ID for the option matches the category ID for the product.

After displaying the drop-down list, the rest of the code displays the controls needed to work with the other fields. Note that these fields get data from the product array and display that data in the control. As a result, if the user is editing an existing product, this page displays the existing data on the form. But if the user is adding a new product, this doesn't display any data on the form.

The admin/product/index.php file (continued)

```php
    case 'add_product':
        $category_id = $_POST['category_id'];
        $code = $_POST['code'];
        $name = $_POST['name'];
        $description = $_POST['description'];
        $price = $_POST['price'];
        $discount_percent = $_POST['discount_percent'];

        // Validate inputs
        if (empty($code) || empty($name) || empty($description) ||
            empty($price) ) {
          $error = 'Invalid product data.
                    Check all fields and try again.';
          include('../../errors/error.php');
        } else {
            $categories = get_categories();
            $product_id = add_product($category_id, $code, $name,
                    $description, $price, $discount_percent);
            $product = get_product($product_id);
            include('product_view.php');
        }
        break;
    case 'update_product':
        $product_id = $_POST['product_id'];
        $code = $_POST['code'];
        $name = $_POST['name'];
        $description = $_POST['description'];
        $price = $_POST['price'];
        $discount_percent = $_POST['discount_percent'];
        $category_id = $_POST['category_id'];

        // Validate inputs
        if (empty($code) || empty($name) || empty($description) ||
            empty($price) ) {
          $error = 'Invalid product data.
                    Check all fields and try again.';
          include('../../errors/error.php');
        } else {
            $categories = get_categories();
            update_product($product_id, $code, $name, $description,
                            $price, $discount_percent, $category_id);
            $product = get_product($product_id);
            include('product_view.php');
        }
        break;
    }
    ?>
```

Figure 20-5   The Product Manager application (part 3 of 5)

The admin/product/product_view.php file

```php
<?php include '../../view/header.php'; ?>
<?php include '../../view/sidebar_admin.php'; ?>
<div id="content">
    <h1>Product Manager - View Product</h1>

    <!-- display product -->
    <?php include '../../view/product.php'; ?>

    <!-- display buttons -->
    <div id="buttons">
        <form action="" method="post" id="edit_button_form">
            <input type="hidden" name="action" value="show_add_edit_form">
            <input type="hidden" name="product_id"
                value="<?php echo $product['productID']; ?>" />
            <input type="hidden" name="category_id"
                value="<?php echo $product['categoryID']; ?>" />
            <input type="submit" value="Edit Product" >
        </form>
        <form action="" method="post" >
            <input type="hidden" name="action" value="delete_product">
            <input type="hidden" name="product_id"
                value="<?php echo $product['productID']; ?>" />
            <input type="hidden" name="category_id"
                value="<?php echo $product['categoryID']; ?>" />
            <input type="submit" value="Delete Product">
        </form>
    </div>
</div>
<?php include '../../view/footer.php'; ?>
```

The admin/product/product_add_edit.php file

```php
<?php include '../../view/header.php'; ?>
<?php include '../../view/sidebar_admin.php'; ?>
<div id="content">
    <?php
    if (isset($product_id)) {
        $heading_text = 'Edit Product';
    } else {
        $heading_text = 'Add Product';
    }
    ?>
    <h1 class="top">Product Manager - <?php echo $heading_text; ?></h1>
    <form action="index.php" method="post" id="add_edit_product_form">
        <?php if (isset($product_id)) : ?>
            <input type="hidden" name="action" value="update_product" />
            <input type="hidden" name="product_id"
                value="<?php echo $product_id; ?>" />
        <?php else: ?>
            <input type="hidden" name="action" value="add_product" />
        <?php endif; ?>
            <input type="hidden" name="category_id"
                value="<?php echo $product['categoryID']; ?>" />
```

Figure 20-5   The Product Manager application (part 4 of 5)

The admin/product/product_add_edit.php file (continued)

```php
            <label>Category:</label>
            <select name="category_id">
            <?php foreach ($categories as $category) :
                if ($category['categoryID'] == $product['categoryID']) {
                    $selected = 'selected';
                } else {
                    $selected = '';
                }
            ?>
                <option value="<?php echo $category['categoryID']; ?>"<?php
                        echo $selected ?>>
                    <?php echo $category['categoryName']; ?>
                </option>
            <?php endforeach; ?>
            </select>
            <br />

            <label>Code:</label>
            <input type="input" name="code"
                    value="<?php echo $product['productCode']; ?>" />
            <br />

            <label>Name:</label>
            <input type="input" name="name"
                    value="<?php echo $product['productName']; ?>" />
            <br />

            <label>List Price:</label>
            <input type="input" name="price"
                    value="<?php echo $product['listPrice']; ?>" />
            <br />

            <label>Discount Percent:</label>
            <input type="input" name="discount_percent"
                    value="<?php echo $product['discountPercent']; ?>" />
            <br />

            <label>Description:</label>
            <textarea name="description" rows="10">
                <?php echo $product['description']; ?></textarea>
            <br />

            <label> </label>
            <input type="submit" value="Submit" />
        </form>
        <h2>How to format the Description entry</h2>
        <ul>
            <li>Use two returns to start a new paragraph.</li>
            <li>Use an asterisk to mark items in a bulleted list.</li>
            <li>Use one return between items in a bulleted list.</li>
            <li>Use standard HMTL tags for bold and italics.</li>
        </ul>
    </div>
    <?php include '../../view/footer.php'; ?>
```

Figure 20-5   The Product Manager application (part 5 of 5)

Perspective

If you understand the web site presented in this chapter, you are well on your way to developing your own database-driven web sites. Also, if you would like to review a mysqli version of this web site, it is included with the downloads for this book. The only difference in the two web sites is the code for the database functions.

Of course, there's still more to learn about developing web sites. In section 4, for example, you will learn how to restrict access to an application like the Product Manager application so only the administrative users of the company can access that application.

Terms

content management system
Bulletin Board Code (BBCode)
include file

include path
utility file

Summary

- For a web site, a *content management system* is a series of web pages that make it easy for users with limited knowledge of HTML to manage the content of the site.

- *Bulletin Board Code* (*BBCode*) is a markup language that is used by many bulletin board systems. It is easier to use than HTML, but it needs to be converted to HTML before it can be displayed by a browser.

- An *include file* is a file that can be included whenever it's needed within an application. The *include path* is the path that tells PHP where to look for files that are specified in include and require functions.

- A *utility file* is a general-purpose file that can be used throughout a web site.

Exercise 20-1 Enhance the Guitar Shop application

This exercise has you enhance the Guitar Shop web site. That will give you a chance to use some of the skills that your learned in chapter 19.

Test the Guitar Shop web site

1. Run the web site in the ex_starts/ch20_ex1 directory. This is the Guitar Shop web site that you reviewed in this chapter.

2. Use the Product Catalog application to view the existing products.

3. Use the Product Manager application to add a new product to the database and to delete the product you just added.

4. Use your editor to open the database.php file and the products.php file in the model directory. Then, review the code. Note how the PDO exceptions are handled.

5. Modify the first SELECT statement in the products.php file so it refers to the "product" table instead of the "products" table. Then, test the error handling by running the application. It should display the error message to the user.

6. Fix the SELECT statement, so the application works correctly again.

Add a Category Manager section

Now, you'll add a page to the Product Manager application that lets you add or delete categories. This is similar to what exercise 4-1 and exercise 5-1 asked you to do. So if you did those exercises, you may be able to reuse some of your code in this exercise.

7. Open the admin/product/product_list.php file for this application. Then, add a "List Categories" link to the bottom of the Product List page.

8. Create a Category List page in the admin/product directory named category_list that displays the category data in a table as shown above. Here, the first column displays the names of all categories, and the second column displays a Delete button that allows the user to delete the category. If you give this table an id of "category_table", the main.css file for the exercise should format it as shown above.

9. After the table, add a form that lets the user add a category. Use a text box for the name of the category and a submit button to add the category to the database. If you give this form an id of "add_category_form", the main.css file for this exercise should format it as shown above.

10. Open the category_db.php file in the model directory, and add two functions that add and delete categories. These functions should use prepared statements with named parameters.

11. Open the index.php file in the admin/product directory, and add three new actions to it. The first action should display the Category List page. The second action should add a category to the database. And the third action should delete a category from the database.

12. Test the application by adding two or more categories. Note that the sidebar includes the categories that you added.

13. Test the application by deleting one or more of the categories that you added. However, don't delete any of the existing categories because that will lead to products without categories, which destroys the referential integrity of the database If necessary, though, you can restore the database by running the create_db.sql script again as described in the appendix.

14. If the formatting of your page isn't exactly like the one above, don't worry about that. The focus here is on web programming, not HTML and CSS.

Use application code to protect referential integrity

15. Open the category_db.php file in the model directory, and add a function to it that counts the number of products for the specified category. This function should use prepared statements with named parameters.

16. Open the index.php file in the admin/product directory, and modify the "delete_category" action so it doesn't delete a category if the category contains one or more products. In that case, this action should display an error message that says, "This category can't be deleted because it contains products."

17. Test the changes to make sure they work correctly.

Section 4

Master the advanced skills for building web sites

In sections 1 through 3, you learned the professional skills you need to use PHP and MySQL to build database-driven web sites. Now, this section presents some advanced PHP skills that are commonly needed for real-world web sites.

In chapter 21, you'll learn how to create secure web sites by using secure connections, authentication, and encryption. In chapter 22, you'll learn how to send email from your web site and how to access other web sites whenever that's necessary. In chapter 23, you'll learn how to read and write files, how to upload files, and how to work with images.

Then, in chapter 24, you'll be introduced to the Guitar Shop web site that's available as part of the download for this book. This eCommerce web site shows how all of the skills in this book come together, and the download provides all of its code so you can review it and use it in your own applications.

21

How to create secure web sites

If your application requires users to enter sensitive data such as credit card numbers and passwords, you should use a secure connection when you send data between the client and the server. Otherwise, a hacker might be able to intercept and view this data.

In addition, many web applications only allow authorized users. For example, many web sites have an administrative section that can only be accessed by a user who logs in to the site with an authorized username and password.

Finally, if you store sensitive data such as credit card numbers or passwords, you should encrypt that information before you store it in the database. That way, even if hackers are able to access the database, they won't be able to easily read that data. In this chapter, you'll learn how to use a secure connection, how to restrict access to parts of your application, and how to encrypt data.

How to use a secure connection **676**
An introduction to secure connections 676
How SSL authentication works 678
How to get a digital secure certificate 680
How to request a secure connection 682
How to redirect to a secure connection 684
How to use authentication **686**
Three types of authentication 686
How to store and validate a password 688
How to use form-based authentication 690
How to use basic authentication 696
How to work with encrypted data **700**
How to encrypt and decrypt data 700
A class for storing encrypted data 702
Perspective **704**

How to use a secure connection

To prevent others from reading data that is transmitted over the Internet, you can use a *secure connection*. Due to the time it takes to encrypt and decrypt the data that's sent across a secure connection, secure connections are noticeably slower than regular HTTP connections. As a result, you usually use secure connections only when your application passes sensitive data between the client and the server.

An introduction to secure connections

Figure 21-1 shows a web page that transfers data between the server and the client over a secure connection. To determine if you're transmitting data over a secure connection, you can read the URL. If it starts with https rather than http, then you are using a secure connection. In addition, a small lock icon appears in the lower right of the browser when you're using a secure connection.

With a regular HTTP connection, all data is sent as unencrypted plain text. As a result, if a hacker intercepts this data, it is easy to read. With a secure connection, though, all data is encrypted before it's transferred between the client and server. Although hackers can still intercept this data, they won't be able to read it unless they can break the encryption code.

The *Secure Sockets Layer* (*SSL*) protocol is an older Internet protocol that lets you transfer data between the server and the client over a secure connection. In contrast, *Transport Layer Security* (*TLS*) is a newer protocol that's used for working with secure connections. As a user, it's hard to tell whether you're using an SSL connection or a TLS connection. Although TLS is only supported by newer browsers, any server that implements TLS also implements SSL. That way, the newer browsers can use TLS, and the older browsers can still use SSL.

When you're working with secure connections, you'll find that SSL is often used to describe the connection instead of TLS. That's because SSL is the older, more established protocol for working with secure connections. In this chapter, the term SSL is used even though the connection could also be a TLS connection.

A request made with a secure connection

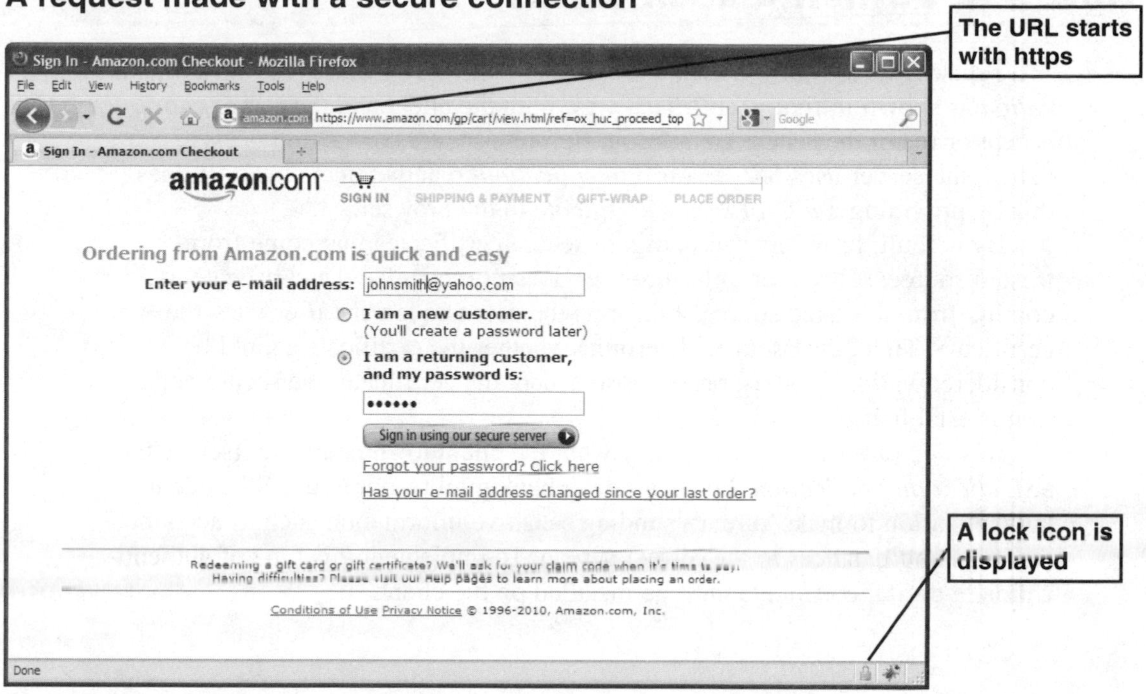

The URL starts with https

A lock icon is displayed

Description

- *Transport Layer Security* (*TLS*) and *Secure Sockets Layer* (*SSL*) are the two protocols used by the Internet that allow clients and servers to communicate over a *secure connection*.

- TLS is the successor to SSL. Although there are slight differences between SSL and TLS, the protocol remains substantially the same. As a result, they are sometimes referred to as the TLS/SSL protocol or these terms are used interchangeably.

- With SSL, the browser encrypts all data that's sent to the server and decrypts all data that's received from the server. Conversely, the server encrypts all data that's sent to the browser and decrypts all data that's received from the browser.

- SSL is able to determine if data has been tampered with during transit. It is also able to verify that a server or a client is who it claims to be.

- The URL for a secure connection starts with HTTPS instead of HTTP.

- A web browser that is using a secure connection displays a lock in the lower right corner.

Figure 21-1 An introduction to secure connections

How SSL authentication works

To use SSL to transmit data, the client and the server must provide *authentication* as shown in figure 21-2. That way, both the client and the server can accept or reject the secure connection. Before a secure connection is established, the server uses *SSL server authentication* to authenticate itself. It does this by providing a *digital secure certificate* to the browser.

By default, browsers accept digital secure certificates that come from trusted sources. However, if the browser doesn't recognize the certificate as coming from a trusted source, it informs the user and lets the user view the certificate. Then, the user can determine whether the certificate should be considered valid. If the user chooses to accept the certificate, the secure connection is established.

In some rare cases, a server may want the client to authenticate itself with *SSL client authentication*. For example, a bank might want to use SSL client authentication to make sure it's sending sensitive information such as account numbers and balances to the correct person. To implement this type of authentication, a digital certificate must be installed on the client.

A digital secure certificate

Certificate Viewer:"www.amazon.com"

General | Details

This certificate has been verified for the following uses:

SSL Server Certificate

Issued To
Common Name (CN)   www.amazon.com
Organization (O)   Amazon.com Inc.
Organizational Unit (OU) <Not Part Of Certificate>
Serial Number   1A:C7:DB:93:E5:18:0A:C5:96:B8:A2:F9:2D:A7:20:6E

Issued By
Common Name (CN)   VeriSign Class 3 Secure Server CA - G2
Organization (O)   VeriSign, Inc.
Organizational Unit (OU) VeriSign Trust Network

Validity
Issued On   7/29/2009
Expires On   7/30/2010

Fingerprints
SHA1 Fingerprint   A8:FD:FE:05:9A:72:68:08:9A:77:C3:FE:54:61:C8:CE:94:7B:3D:49
MD5 Fingerprint   72:E9:E1:D3:32:61:3C:B6:06:9C:A4:9C:24:1D:0A:FE

Close

Types of digital secure certificates

Certificate	Description
Server certificate	Issued to trusted servers so client computers can connect to them using secure connections.
Client certificate	Issued to trusted clients so server computers can confirm their identity.

How authentication works

* *Authentication* is the process of determining whether a server or client is who and what it claims to be.

* When a browser makes an initial attempt to communicate with a server over a secure connection, the server authenticates itself by providing a *digital secure certificate*.

* If the digital secure certificate is registered with the browser, the browsers won't display the certificate by default. However, the user still has the option to view the certificate.

* In some rare cases, the server may request that a client authenticate itself by presenting its own digital secure certificate.

Figure 21-2   How SSL authentication works

How to get a digital secure certificate

If you want to establish a secure connection with your clients, you must get a digital secure certificate from a trusted source such as those listed in figure 21-3. These *certification authorities (CAs)* verify that the person or company requesting the certificate is a valid person or company by checking with a *registration authority (RA)*. To obtain a digital secure certificate, you'll need to provide an RA with information about yourself or your company. Once the RA approves the request, the CA can issue the digital secure certificate.

A digital secure certificate from a trusted source isn't free, and the cost of the certificate will depend on a variety of factors such as the level of security. As a result, when you purchase a digital certificate, you want one that fits the needs of your web site. In particular, you'll need to decide what *SSL strength* you want the connection to support. SSL strength refers to the level of encryption that the secure connection uses when it transmits data.

In the early days of web programming, many web servers used certificates with 40-bit or 56-bit SSL strength. At this strength, it's possible for a determined hacker to break the encryption code. However, most browsers support these strengths, these strengths are appropriate for some sites, and these certificates are reasonably priced.

Today, most web servers use 128-bit or higher SSL strength. Although these certificates are more expensive than 40-bit certificates, it's extremely hard for a hacker to break the encryption code. Since most modern web browsers support 128-bit and 256-bit encryption, they are able to use this SSL strength. Meanwhile, older browsers that don't support this strength can use whatever lesser strength they support.

Once you purchase a secure certificate, you typically send it to your web host who installs it for your site. Once the certificate is installed, you can use SSL to transmit data over a secure connection.

Common certificate authorities that issue digital secure certificates

```
www.verisign.com
www.thawte.com
www.geotrust.com
www.instantssl.com
www.entrust.com
```

SSL strengths

Strength	Pros and Cons
40-bit	Most browsers support it, but it's relatively easy to break the encryption code.
56-bit	It's thousands of times stronger than 40-bit strength and most browsers support it, but it's still possible to break the encryption code.
128-bit	It's over a trillion times a trillion times stronger than 40-bit strength, which makes it extremely difficult to break the encryption code, but it's more expensive and not all browsers support it.
256-bit	It's virtually impossible to break the encryption code, but it's more expensive and not all browsers support it.

Description

- To use SSL in your web applications, you must first purchase a digital secure certificate from a trusted *certification authority* (*CA*). Once you obtain the certificate, you send it to the people who host your web site so they can install it on the server.

- A CA is a company that issues and manages security credentials. To verify information provided by the requestor of the secure certificate, a CA must check with a *registration authority* (*RA*). Once the RA verifies the requestor's information, the CA can issue a digital secure certificate.

- Since SSL is built into all major browsers and web servers, installing a digital secure certificate enables SSL.

- *SSL strength* refers to the length of the generated key that is created during the encryption process. The longer the key, the more difficult to break the encryption code.

- The SSL strength that's used depends on the strength provided by the certificate, the strength supported by the web server, and the strength supported by the browser. If a web server or browser isn't able to support the strength provided by the certificate, a lesser strength is used.

- It's considered a best practice to use 128-bit or better SSL strength if you process payments or collect personal information such as social security number, address, date of birth, and so on.

Figure 21-3   How to get a digital secure certificate

How to request a secure connection

If you install XAMPP as described in appendix A, the Apache server provides a secure connection for the local server with a digital certificate that can be used for testing. To test the secure connection on your local system, you can use the first URL shown in figure 21-4. Note that this URL begins with https.

If the secure connection works, your browser might display a message or two. To start, you might get a message that indicates that you're about to view pages over a secure connection. This is normal, and you can continue. Then, if you're using a temporary testing certificate, you might get a warning that indicates that the certificate doesn't come from a trusted source. At this point, you can read the warning and click the appropriate button or link to continue. If you can view the page, your secure connection is working properly. Otherwise, you'll need to troubleshoot your connection.

Once a commercial or local server has been configured to work with SSL, you can request a secure connection by coding an absolute URL that begins with https. Then, you can return to a regular connection by coding an absolute URL that begins with http. In this figure, all of the URLs request a directory, but a URL can also be used to request any type of file including PHP files, HTML files, XML files, and so on.

When a secure connection is requested, the server authenticates itself by sending its secure certificate to the browser. Then, if the certificate doesn't come from a certification authority that's registered with the browser, the browser usually displays a warning message. Even if the certificate does come from a certification authority that's registered with the browser, you may get a message that indicates that you are about to view pages over a secure connection. However, this depends on the security settings for the browser.

URLs for working with secure connections on a local system

Test if secure connections are configured correctly
```
https://localhost/
```

Request a secure connection
```
https://localhost/book_apps/ch21_ssl/
```

Return to a regular connection
```
http://localhost/book_apps/ch21_ssl/
```

URLs for working with secure connections over the Internet

Request a secure connection
```
https://www.murach.com/
```

Return to a regular connection
```
http://www.murach.com/
```

Description

- To request a secure connection, use an absolute URL that starts with https.
- Once you establish a secure connection, you can use relative URLs to continue using the secure connection.
- To return to a regular HTTP connection after using a secure connection, use an absolute URL that starts with http.

Figure 21-4   How to request a secure connection

How to redirect to a secure connection

If you want to make sure that a page is always viewed over a secure connection, you can include code at the top of the page that redirects the page to a secure connection as shown in figure 21-5. That way, if the user requests the page over a regular connection, the web server redirects the request to the same page but over a secure connection.

To perform a redirect, you can begin by using the $_SERVER array to check if the current request is using a secure connection. Then, you can use the $_SERVER array to get the host and the URI for the current request, and you can use them to create an absolute URL that uses a secure connection. Next, you can use the header function to redirect the current page to that URL. Finally, you can use the exit function to exit the current script.

Since the data that's stored in the $_SERVER array is set by the web server, there's no guarantee that every web server will set this data the same. Although the code in this figure works for most versions of the Apache web server, it doesn't work on all versions and it may not work on web servers like IIS. If it doesn't work, of course, you need to modify it so it works correctly with your web server.

The $_SERVER array

Index	Description
HTTPS	Returns a non-empty value if the current request is using HTTPS.
HTTP_HOST	Returns the host for the current request.
REQUEST_URI	Returns the URI (Uniform Resource Identifier) for the current request.

A utility file (util/secure_conn.php) that redirects a page to a secure connection

```php
<?php
    // make sure the page uses a secure connection
    if (!isset($_SERVER['HTTPS'])) {
        $url = 'https://' . $_SERVER['HTTP_HOST'] . $_SERVER['REQUEST_URI'];
        header("Location: " . $url);
        exit();
    }
?>
```

Description

- The $_SERVER array contains information about headers and paths. This data is set by your web server, and the code above works for most versions of Apache.

- Unfortunately, all web servers don't set the values in the $_SERVER array the same way. So, if this code doesn't work for your web server, you need to adjust it so it does.

Figure 21-5   How to redirect to a secure connection

How to use authentication

For some web applications, you need to restrict access to some or all of the pages so that only authorized users can access those pages. To do that, you begin by determining whether a client is who and what it claims to be. This process is known as *authentication*, and it's typically done by asking the client to enter a username and password.

Three types of authentication

Figure 21-6 presents three common types of authentication. *Form-based authentication* uses a web form to request a username and password from the user. This type of authentication gives the developer the most control over the authentication process and allows the developer to control the look and feel of the web page. As a result, it's the most common type of authentication for production web sites. However, it also requires the developer to do the most work since the developer must develop the login form and write the code that controls the authentication process.

Basic authentication causes the browser to display a dialog box that requests a username and password. Then, when the user enters a username and password, it sends this data to the server so the server can attempt to authorize the user. Since you don't have to code a form for this type of authentication, it is easy to implement. However, you can't control the appearance of the dialog box that's displayed. As a result, this type of authentication usually isn't used for production applications.

Since form-based authentication and basic authentication both send the username and password as plain text, a hacker can possibly intercept an unencrypted username and password and gain access to a restricted web resource. As a result, you usually use a secure connection with these types of authentication. That way, the username and password are encrypted before they are sent to the server.

Like basic authentication, *digest authentication* also causes the browser to display a dialog box that requests a username and password. However, when the user enters a username and password, digest authentication encrypts the username and password before it sends them to the server. Although this seems to be more secure, it isn't as secure as using basic authentication with a secure connection, and you don't have a much control over the encryption that's used. As a result, digest authentication isn't used as often as the other types of authentication.

Form-based authentication

- Allows the developer to code a login form that gets the username and password.
- Allows the developer to only request the username and password once per session.
- By default, it doesn't encrypt the username and password before sending them to the server.

Basic authentication

- Causes the browser to display a dialog box that gets the username and password.
- Requires the browser to send the username and password for every protected page.
- By default, it doesn't encrypt the username and password before sending them to the server.

Digest authentication

- Causes the browser to display a dialog box that gets the user name and password.
- Encrypts the username and password before sending them to the server.

Description

- Since *basic authentication* and *form-based authentication* don't automatically encrypt the username and password before sending them to the server, these types of authentication are typically used over a secure connection.
- Since *digest authentication* isn't as secure as using a secure connection, it isn't used as often as basic authentication or form-based authentication over a secure connection.

Figure 21-6   Three types of authentication

How to store and validate a password

For most types of authentication, you store the usernames and passwords in a database. Also, it's considered a best practice to encrypt the passwords before you store them in the database. That way, if a hacker gains access to the data in the database, he won't be able to easily read the passwords for your users.

Figure 21-7 begins by showing a script that creates a table named administrators that stores the email addresses and passwords for administrative users. Here, the administrator's email address is used instead of a username. This works because both an email address and a username uniquely identify the user. In this script, the passwords have already been encrypted.

To encrypt a password, you can use the sha1 function to convert the password to a 40-character hexadecimal string. The sha1 function uses the *Secure Hash Algorithm 1* (*SHA-1*). This function is a *hash function* that accepts a variable-size string and returns a fixed-size string known as the *hash value*. The original string is often called the *message*, and the hash value is sometimes called the *message digest* or *digest*.

There are three types of SHA: SHA-0, SHA-1, and SHA-2. Of these, SHA-1 is the most widely used. In addition, SHA-3 is being developed and is due to be completed in 2012.

After you create a table to store usernames and passwords, you can write database code that works with that table. For example, the admin_db.php file in this figure contains two functions that work with a table like that: the add_admin function and the is_valid_admin function.

The add_admin function adds an email address and password to the database. To do that, it accepts the email address and password as parameters. Then, the second statement concatenates the email address with the password and uses the sha1 function to encrypt this data. Here, the email address has been included to make the password longer and more complex, which makes it more difficult to crack. However, in many cases, it's acceptable to just encrypt the password. After encrypting the password, this function uses standard database code to add the username and password to the administrators table.

The is_valid_admin function checks whether the email address/password combination is valid for an administrative user. To do that, it accepts the email address and password as parameters. Then, the second statement concatenates the email address with the password and uses the sha1 function to encrypt this data. As a result, this encrypted password should match the encrypted password that's stored in the database. After that, this function uses standard database code to check whether the specified email address/password combination exists in the database. If so, this function returns a TRUE value. Otherwise, it returns a FALSE value.

When you use this technique to store passwords, there's no need to decrypt the password. Instead, you compare the passwords in their encrypted form. That's good because the sha1 function doesn't provide for decryption. As a result, if a user forgets his or her password, you can't decrypt it and send it to the user. Instead, you need to create a new password for the user.

A function that encrypts a string

Name	Description
sha1(*$string*[, *$bin*])	Uses the Secure Hash Algorithm 1 (SHA-1) to calculate the hash value for the specified string. By default, this function returns a 40-character hexadecimal value. If the second parameter is set to TRUE, the function returns raw binary data with a length of 20.

A script that creates a table for storing usernames and passwords

```
CREATE TABLE administrators (
    adminID             INT             NOT NULL   AUTO_INCREMENT,
    emailAddress        VARCHAR(255)    NOT NULL,
    password            VARCHAR(60)     NOT NULL,
    firstName           VARCHAR(60),
    lastName            VARCHAR(60),
    PRIMARY KEY (adminID)
);

INSERT INTO administrators (adminID, emailAddress, password) VALUES
(1, 'joelmurach@yahoo.com', '446b9db5b3f1d38bo64e3a4bde284196f77000df'),
(2, 'ray@harris.net', 'ba7294056da6cfb82cabe5f85a31eed548979611'),
(3, 'mike@murach.com', '3f2975c819cefc686282456aeae3a137bf896ee8');
```

The admin_db.php file

```php
<?php
function add_admin($email, $password) {
    global $db;
    $password = sha1($email . $password);
    $query = 'INSERT INTO administrators (emailAddress, password)
              VALUES (:email, :password)';
    $statement = $db->prepare($query);
    $statement->bindValue(':email', $email);
    $statement->bindValue(':password', $password);
    $statement->execute();
    $statement->closeCursor();
}

function is_valid_admin_login($email, $password) {
    global $db;
    $password = sha1($email . $password);
    $query = 'SELECT adminID FROM administrators
              WHERE emailAddress = :email AND password = :password';
    $statement = $db->prepare($query);
    $statement->bindValue(':email', $email);
    $statement->bindValue(':password', $password);
    $statement->execute();
    $valid = ($statement->rowCount() == 1);
    $statement->closeCursor();
    return $valid;
}
?>
```

Figure 21-7   How to store and validate a password

How to use form-based authentication

Form-based authentication lets you code a form within an HTML or PHP file that gets the username and password. When you use form-based authentication, requesting a restricted resource causes your browser to display a web page like the one in figure 21-8. This page begins by displaying a form that has a text box for a username, a text box for a password, and a Login button. When the user clicks the Login button, the username and password are sent to the server. Beneath this form is a message to the user that may change depending on the user's action.

This figure also shows a page that's protected by the login form. This page is a menu that provides links to administrative applications. It also provides a link that allows the user to log out. That way, if an administrative user is using a public computer, he can log out when he's done. This prevents unauthorized users from being able to access those administrative applications.

As you review these pages, note that they both use a secure connection. That way, the email address and password are encrypted before they're sent from the browser to the server. Similarly, any sensitive administrative data is encrypted before it's sent from the browser to the server.

A login form

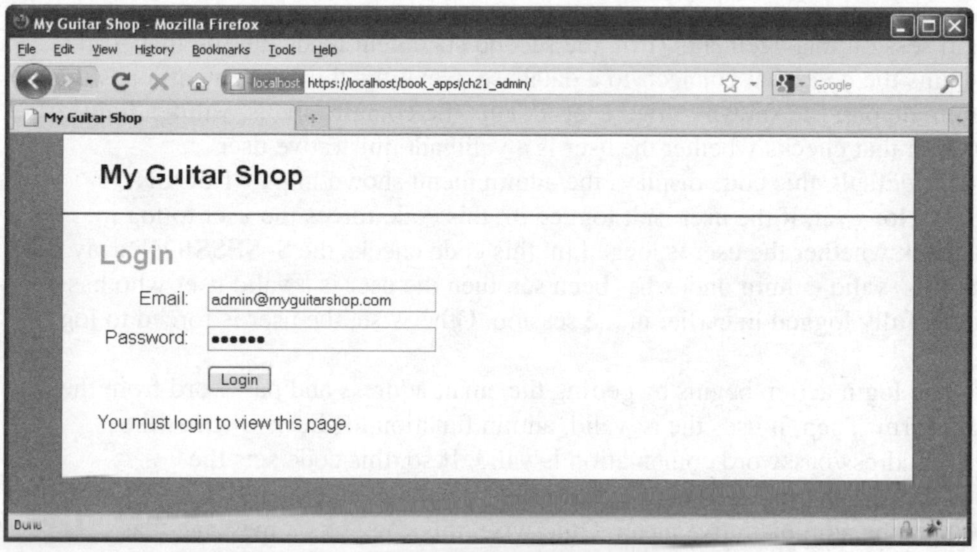

A protected page

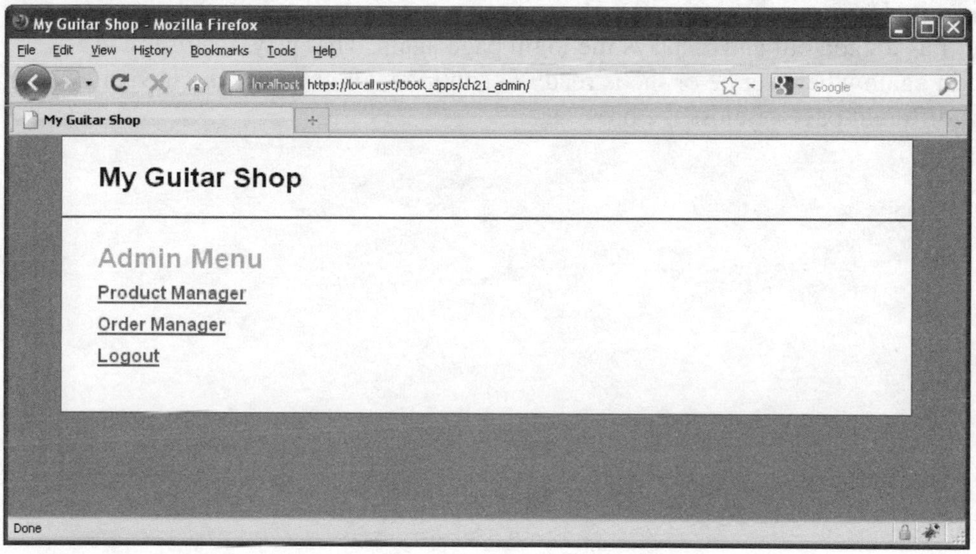

Figure 21-8   How to use form-based authentication (part 1 of 3)

Part 2 of figure 21-8 shows the code for the controller for the pages that are shown in part 1. To start, the first statement calls the session_start function to begin session management. Then, the second statement loads the file that contains the code that connects to a database. Next, the third statement loads the admin_db.php file shown in figure 21-7. This file contains the is_valid_admin function that checks whether the user is a valid administrative user.

By default, this code displays the admin menu shown in part 1 of this figure. However, if the user isn't logged in, this code forces the user to log in. To check whether the user is logged in, this code checks the $_SESSION array. If the 'is_valid_admin' index has been set, then the user is a valid user who has successfully logged in earlier in the session. Otherwise, the user is forced to log in.

The login action begins by getting the email address and password from the login form. Then, it uses the is_valid_admin function to check whether the email address/password combination is valid. If so, this code sets the 'is_valid_admin' index of the $_SESSION array to a value of TRUE and displays the administrative menu. Otherwise, this code sets a message that indicates that the user must log in and displays the login page again.

The logout action begins by clearing all data from the $_SESSION array. Then, it cleans up the session ID. Next, it sets a message that indicates that the user has logged out and displays the login page again. That way, the user can log in again whenever he or she is ready to continue. Or, the user can navigate to a different page or close the browser.

The controller for the protected pages

```php
<?php
// Start session management and include necessary functions
session_start();
require_once('model/database.php');
require_once('model/admin_db.php');

// Get the action to perform
if (isset($_POST['action'])) {
    $action = $_POST['action'];
} else if (isset($_GET['action'])) {
    $action = $_GET['action'];
} else {
    $action = 'show_admin_menu';
}

// If the user isn't logged in, force the user to login
if (!isset($_SESSION['is_valid_admin'])) {
    $action = 'login';
}

// Perform the specified action
switch($action) {
    case 'login':
        $email = $_POST['email'];
        $password = $_POST['password'];
        if (is_valid_admin_login($email, $password)) {
            $_SESSION['is_valid_admin'] = true;
            include('view/admin_menu.php');
        } else {
            $login_message = 'You must login to view this page.';
            include('view/login.php');
        }
        break;
    case 'show_admin_menu':
        include('view/admin_menu.php');
        break;
    case 'show_product_manager':
        include('view/product_manager.php');
        break;
    case 'show_order_manager':
        include('view/order_manager.php');
        break;
    case 'logout':
        $_SESSION = array();   // Clear all session data from memory
        session_destroy();     // Clean up the session ID
        $login_message = 'You have been logged out.';
        include('view/login.php');
        break;
}
?>
```

Figure 21-8   How to use form-based authentication (part 2 of 3)

Part 3 of figure 21-8 begins by showing the code that's stored in the valid_admin.php file that's in the util directory. This file checks whether the user has logged in during the current session. To do that, it checks the value at the 'is_valid_admin' index of the $_SESSION array. If the user has logged in, this code doesn't do anything. However, if the user hasn't logged in this code redirects the user to the controller.

This figure continues by showing the code that's included at the top of the login page. This loads the code that's stored in the secure_conn.php file described in figure 21-5, which forces the login page to use a secure connection. As a result, even if you use a regular HTTP connection to request the login page, this page uses a secure connection.

The last example in this figure shows the code that's included at the top of the other protected pages. This loads the code that forces a secure connection. In addition, it loads the code shown in this figure that forces a valid admin user. As a result, if the user attempts to skip the login form by requesting any of the protected pages directly, this code redirects the user to the controller, which forces the user to log in. Similarly, if the user attempts to use a regular connection instead of a secure connection, this code redirects the user to the secure connection.

A utility file that forces a valid admin user (util/valid_admin.php)

```php
<?php
    // make sure the user is logged in as a valid administrator
    if (!isset($_SESSION['is_valid_admin'])) {
        header("Location: ." );
    }
?>
```

Code that's included at the top of the login page

```php
<?php
    require_once('util/secure_conn.php');  // require a secure connection
?>
```

Code that's included at the top of the other protected pages

```php
<?php
    require_once('util/secure_conn.php');  // require a secure connection
    require_once('util/valid_admin.php');  // require a valid admin user
?>
```

Description

- You can use a utility file like the valid_admin.php file to redirect to the controller if the user isn't logged in as a valid administrator.

- The code at the top of the login page should force the page to use a secure connection.

- The code at the top of each protected page should force a secure connection. To do that, it can include a utility file that forces the connection like the file in figure 21-5.

- The code at the top of each protected page should also force a valid admin user. To do that, it can include a utility file like the valid_admin.php file in this figure.

Figure 21-8   How to use form-based authentication (part 3 of 3)

How to use basic authentication

Figure 21-9 shows how to use basic authentication to provide access to a restricted resource. In particular, it shows how to use basic authentication to provide access to the same administrative applications that were described in the previous figure.

If you request a restricted web resource that uses basic authentication, your browser displays an authentication dialog box. This figure, for example, shows the authentication dialog box Firefox displays. However, if you're using a different web browser, the dialog box may vary. This dialog box requests a username and password. Then, when you enter a username and password, the browser sends them to the server. As a result, the server can check the username and password to see whether they are valid.

This figure also shows a protected page. This page works much like the corresponding page in the previous figure. However, it doesn't provide a logout link. As a result, the user must close the web browser to log out of this application.

The last page is displayed by the browser when basic authentication determines that the user has not been authenticated. Most of the time, the browser displays this page because the user has clicked the Cancel button in the authentication dialog box, but the browser may also display this page for other reasons. At this page, the user can click on the Refresh button to request the original page again. This causes the browser to display the login dialog box again and gives the user another chance to log in.

As you review these pages, note that they all use a secure connection. In particular, note that the dialog box includes a message that indicates the server is using a secure connection, even though the original browser request was for a regular connection. This shows that the username and password are encrypted before they're sent from the browser to the server.

A login dialog box

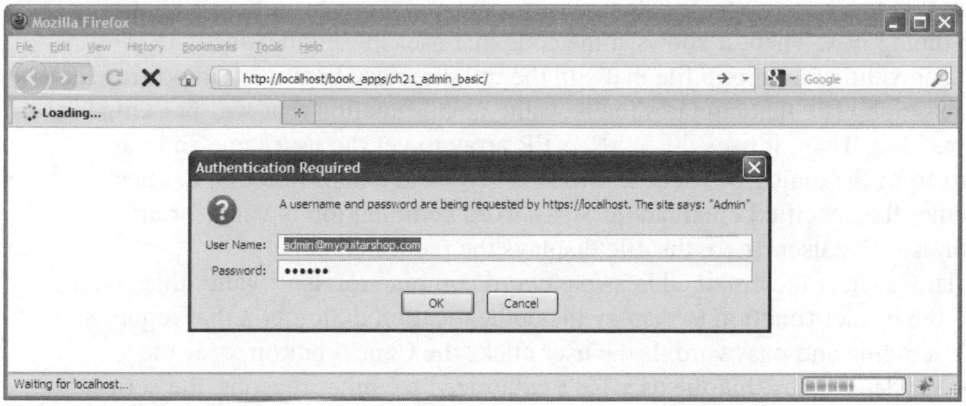

A protected page

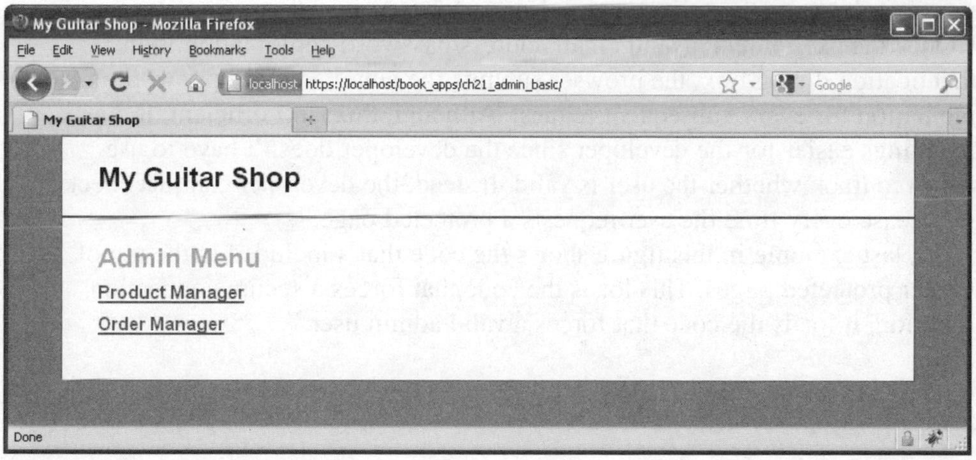

The unauthorized page

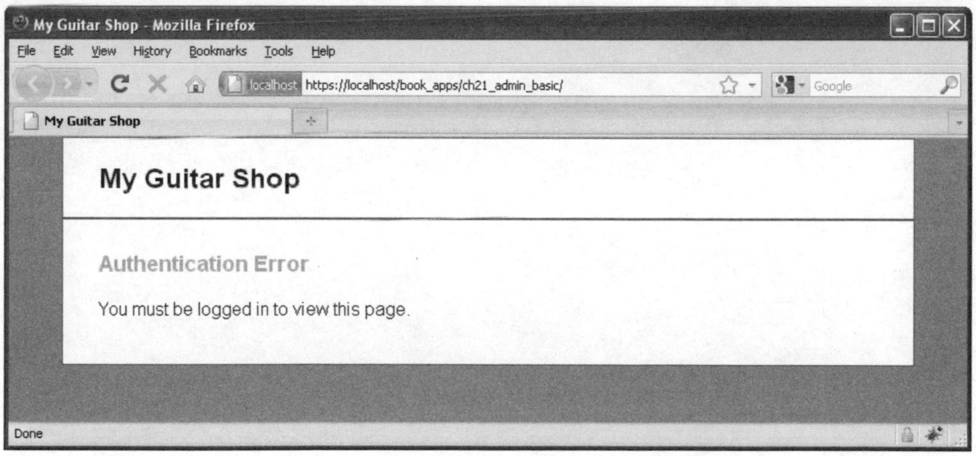

Figure 21-9   How to use basic authentication (part 1 of 2)

Part 2 of figure 21-9 begins by showing the two indexes of the $_SERVER array that you can use to get the username and password from the authentication dialog box. Then, it shows some code that uses these indexes.

The valid_admin.php file that's in the util directory begins by importing the database.php file that contains the is_valid_email function that was presented in figure 21-7. Then, it uses the $_SERVER array to get the username and password from the dialog box. Next, it uses the is_valid_email function to check whether the specified email address/password combination is valid for an administrative user. If so, this file displays the requested page.

However, if the email address/password combination isn't valid, this code uses the header function to display the authentication dialog box that requests the username and password. If the user clicks the Cancel button, or if the browser determines that the user isn't authorized for other reasons, the script continues and uses the header function to set an HTTP header that indicates that the user is unauthorized. Then, it includes a page that displays the unauthorized message and it exits the script.

Once the user enters a valid email address/password combination in the authentication dialog box, the browser submits the email address/password combination for every subsequent request. Although this isn't efficient, it does make things easier for the developer since the developer doesn't have to use sessions to track whether the user is valid. Instead, the developer can just check the database every time the user requests a protected page.

The last example in this figure shows the code that's included at the top of the other protected pages. This loads the code that forces a secure connection. In addition, it loads the code that forces a valid admin user.

The $_SERVER array

Index	Description
PHP_AUTH_USER	Returns the username from the authentication dialog box or a NULL value if the dialog box hasn't been displayed.
PHP_AUTH_PW	Returns the password from the authentication dialog box or a NULL value if the dialog box hasn't been displayed.

Code that forces a valid admin user (util/valid_admin.php)

```php
<?php
require_once('model/database.php');
require_once('model/admin_db.php');

$email = $_SERVER['PHP_AUTH_USER'];
$password = $_SERVER['PHP_AUTH_PW'];
if (!is_valid_admin_login($email, $password)) {
    header('WWW-Authenticate: Basic realm="Admin"');
    header('HTTP/1.0 401 Unauthorized');
    include('unauthorized.php');
    exit();
}
?>
```

Code that's included at the top of each protected page

```php
<?php
    require_once('util/secure_conn.php');   // require a secure connection
    require_once('util/valid_admin.php');   // require a valid admin user
?>
```

Description

- The 401 (Unauthorized) response header doesn't display the requested page and causes most modern browsers to display a dialog box that prompts the user for a username and password.

- The WWW-Authenticate header must also be included in a 401 (Unauthorized) response. This header can specify the type of authentication (usually Basic) and a name for the authentication realm.

- The code at the top of all protected pages should force a secure connection. To do that, it can include a secure_conn.php file like the one shown in figure 21-5.

- The code at the top of all protected pages should also force a valid admin user. To do that, it can include a valid_admin.php file like the one shown in this figure.

Figure 21-9   How to use basic authentication (part 2 of 2)

How to work with encrypted data

In figure 21-7, you learned how to use the sha1 function to encrypt passwords. However, the sha1 function doesn't allow you to decrypt the encrypted password. As a result, it isn't appropriate for encrypting certain types of data such as credit card numbers. For that type of data, you need to encrypt the data before you store it in the database, and you need to decrypt the data after you retrieve the data from the database.

To do that, you can use the functions in the mcrypt library that's included with PHP. This library provides functions that support a wide variety of encryption and decryption algorithms. These algorithms are known as *ciphers*.

This topic shows how to use *Advanced Encryption Standard* (*AES*), an encryption standard adopted by the U.S. government in 2002. This standard uses the *Rijndael cipher* that was developed by was developed by two Belgian cryptographers. The Rijndael ciphers are *block ciphers* that operate on blocks that have a fixed length.

To control how the cipher operates on a block, you can choose a *mode of operation* such as *cipher-block chaining* (*CBC*). CBC was invented by IBM in 1976. In addition, you can use an *initialization vector* (IV) to allow the cipher to produce a unique stream independent from other streams produced by the same encryption key.

How to encrypt and decrypt data

Figure 21-10 shows the functions, constants, and code for using the Rijndeal cipher in CBC mode to encrypt and decrypt data. To start, this code sets up the variables that are needed to encrypt and decrypt a credit card number. For example, the $cipher variable is set to value of the constant for the Rijndael cipher with a 128-bit key size, and the $mode variable is set to the value of the constant for the CBC mode. Then, the $key variable is set to the raw binary data that's returned by the sha1 function after it encrypts the specified string for the key. Finally, the $ivs variable is set to the correct size for the initialization vector, and the $iv variable is set to the initialization vector that's returned by the mcrypt_create_iv function.

After you set up the variables, you can use the mcrypt_encrypt function to encrypt the data. Since this function returns a string of binary data, it's often helpful to use the base64_encode function to convert the binary data to base64. This increases the size of the data by 33%, but it helps the data survive going through the transport layers.

Conversely, you can use the mcrypt_decrypt function to decrypt the data. However, since this function accepts a string of binary data, you need to use the base64_decode function to convert any base64 data to binary data before you pass it to the mcrypt_decrypt function.

Some functions from the mcrypt library

Name	Description
`mcrypt_get_iv_size($cipher, $mode)`	Gets the size of the initialization vector (iv).
`mcrypt_create_iv($ivs)`	Creates the initialization vector for the specified size.
`mcrypt_encrypt($cipher, $key, $data, $mode, $iv)`	Encrypts the specified data using the specified cipher, key, mode, and initialization vector.
`mcrypt_decrypt($cipher, $key, $data, $mode, $iv)`	Decrypts the specified data using the specified cipher, key, mode, and initialization vector.

Some constants from the mycrpt library

Name	Description
`MCRYPT_RIJNDAEL_128`	The Rijndeal cipher with a 128-bit key size.
`MCRYPT_RIJNDAEL_192`	The Rijndeal cipher with a 192-bit key size.
`MCRYPT_RIJNDAEL_256`	The Rijndeal cipher with a 256-bit key size.
`MCRYPT_MODE_CBC`	The CBC (Cipher-Block Chaining) mode of operation.

Two functions for converting between binary and base64

Name	Description
`base64_encode($data)`	Accepts a string of binary data and returns a string of base64 data.
`base64_decode($data)`	Accepts a string of base64 data and returns a string of binary data.

Code that encrypts and decrypts data

```php
$credit_card_no = '4111111111111111';

// Set up the variables
$cipher = MCRYPT_RIJNDAEL_128;
$mode = MCRYPT_MODE_CBC;
$key = sha1('secrectKey', true);    // use the sha1 function to generate a key
$ivs = mcrypt_get_iv_size($cipher, $mode);
$iv = mcrypt_create_iv($ivs);

// Encrypt the data
$data = mcrypt_encrypt($cipher, $key, $credit_card_no, $mode, $iv);
$data = base64_encode($data);
echo 'Encrypted data: ' . $data . '<br />';

// Decrypt the data
$data = base64_decode($data);
$credit_card_no = mcrypt_decrypt($cipher, $key, $data, $mode, $iv);
echo 'Decrypted data: ' . $credit_card_no . '<br />';
```

Figure 21-10   How to encrypt and decrypt data

A class for storing encrypted data

If you intend to encrypt and decrypt data in multiple places in an application, it's helpful to use a class like the one shown in figure 21-11. That way, you can store the details about the encryption and decryption process in a single location.

The Crypt class begins with a constructor that initializes all of the properties necessary to use the 128-bit version of the Rijndael cipher in CBC mode to encrypt and decrypt data. Then, the encrypt method accepts an unencrypted string of data and returns an encrypted string of base64 data. Conversely, the decrypt method accepts a string of base64 data and returns an unencrypted string.

Once you code the Crypt class, you can use it in multiple places in your application to encrypt or decrypt data with two simple statements. To start, you code the statement that creates the Crypt object from the Crypt class. Then, you call the encrypt or decrypt method to encrypt or decrypt the data.

As you review this code, note that the encrypted data is only safe as long as the hacker isn't able to access your source code. If the hacker is able to access your source code and the data in the database, he has access to the encryption key that's needed to decrypt the encrypted data. As a result, it's important to make sure that hackers won't be able to access both the data in your database and your source code.

One way to do that is to make sure that the source code and the database aren't stored in the same location. Another way to do that is to encode your PHP files so that they are difficult to decode even if a hacker can access them. To do that, you can search the Internet for various software products that are designed to encode PHP scripts.

The Crypt class (crypt.php)

```php
<?php
class Crypt {
    private $key;
    private $ivs;
    private $iv;
    private $cipher;
    private $mode;

    public function __construct() {
        $this->cipher = MCRYPT_RIJNDAEL_128;
        $this->mode = MCRYPT_MODE_CBC;
        $this->key = sha1('secrectKey', true);
        $this->ivs = mcrypt_get_iv_size($this->cipher, $this->mode);
        $this->iv = mcrypt_create_iv($this->ivs);
    }

    public function encrypt($data) {
        $data = mcrypt_encrypt($this->cipher, $this->key, $data,
                               $this->mode, $this->iv);
        $data = base64_encode($data);
        return $data;
    }

    public function decrypt($data) {
        $data = base64_decode($data);
        $data = mcrypt_decrypt($this->cipher, $this->key, $data,
                               $this->mode, $this->iv);
        return $data;
    }
}
?>
```

Code that uses the Crypt class to encrypt and decrypt data

```php
require 'crypt.php';

$credit_card_no = '4111111111111111';

// Create the Crypt object
$crypt = new Crypt();

// Use the Crypt object to encrypt the data
$data = $crypt->encrypt($credit_card_no);
echo 'Encrypted data: ' . $data . '<br />';

// Use the Crypt object to decrypt the data
$credit_card_no = $crypt->decrypt($data);
echo 'Decrypted data: ' . $credit_card_no . '<br />';
```

Figure 21-11   A class for encrypting and decrypting data

Perspective

Now that you're done with this chapter, you should be able to modify your applications so they use a secure connection whenever that's needed. In addition, you should be able to restrict access to certain portions of your web site by requiring the user to supply a username and a password. Finally, you should be able to encrypt data before you store it in a database, and you should be able to decrypt it when you get that data out of the database.

For many web sites, this is all you need to know about securing web pages. But if you need additional security, there's a lot more to it. For example, there are other libraries that you can use to provide authentication. In addition, the mcrypt library provides for dozens of ciphers...and each one has its advantages and disadvantages. In short, if the techniques in this chapter aren't adequate for your application, you can search the Internet for more information or get a book that's dedicated to security considerations.

Terms

secure connection	hash function
Secure Sockets Layer (SSL)	hash value
Transport Layer Security (TLS)	message
SSL server authentication	message digest
SSL client authentication	digest
digital secure certificate	cipher
certification authority (CA)	Advanced Encryption Standard
registration authority (RA)	(AES)
SSL strength	Rijndael cipher
authentication	block cipher
form-based authentication	mode of operation
basic authentication	cipher-block chaining (CBC)
digest authentication	initialization vector (IV)
Secure Hash Algorithm 1 (SHA-1)	

Summary

- *Transport Layer Security* (*TLS*) and *Secure Sockets Layer* (*SSL*) are the two protocols used by the Internet that allow clients and servers to communicate over a *secure connection*.

- *Authentication* is the process of determining whether a server or client is who and what it claims to be. When a browser makes an attempt to communicate with a server over a secure connection, the server authenticates itself by providing a *digital secure certificate*.

- To use SSL in your web applications, you must first purchase a digital secure certificate from a trusted *certificate authority* (*CA*). To verify information provided by the requestor, the CA must check with a *registration authority* (*RA*). When you get the certificate, you send it to the people who host your web site so they can install it on the server.

- *SSL strength* refers to the length of the generated key that is created during the encryption process. The longer the key, the more difficult to break the encryption code.

- Since *basic authentication* and *form-based authentication* don't automatically encrypt the username and password before sending them to the server, these types of authentication are typically used over a secure connection.

- Since *digest authentication* isn't as secure as using a secure connection, it isn't used as often as basic authentication or form-based authentication over a secure connection.

- The *Secure Hash Algorithm 1* (*SHA-1*) accepts a variable-length string and returns a fixed-length string known as the *hash value*. The original string is often called the *message*, and the hash value is sometimes called the *message digest*.

- Encryption and decryption algorithms are known as *ciphers*. The *Advanced Encryption Standard* (*AES*) is an encryption standard that uses the *Rijndael cipher*. The Rijndael ciphers are *block ciphers* that operate on blocks that have a fixed length.

- To control how a cipher operates on a block, you can choose a *mode of operation* such as *cipher-block chaining* (*CBC*). In addition, you can use an *initialization vector* (IV) to allow the cipher to produce a unique stream independent from other streams produced by the same encryption key.

Exercise 21-1   Use secure connections

This exercise gives you a chance to experiment with secure connections.

Test the application

1. Use Firefox to test a secure connection on your local system by entering

   `https://localhost/`

   into your browser's address bar. This should display a web page that includes a lock icon in the lower right corner as shown in figure 21-1.

2. Click on the lock icon to display security information about the page. Then, view the certificate for the secure connection.

3. Run the application in the ex_starts/ch21_ex1 directory. Then, click on the "View sensitive information" link. Note that this displays a page that uses a secure connection.

4. Change the URL so it attempts to use a link that isn't secure. To do that, change "https" to "http". Note that this page uses a secure connection despite the request for a regular connection.

5. Click on the "Return to a regular connection" link. Note that this displays a page that doesn't use a secure connection.

Review the code

6. Open the index.php file in your editor. Note how it uses a relative URL to display the secure.php file.

7. Open the secure.php and secure_conn.php files. Note how the code at the top of the secure.php file forces a secure connection by requiring the secure_conn.php file. Note also that the "Return to a regular connection" link uses an absolute URL to specify a regular HTTP connection.

Exercise 21-2   Use authentication

This exercise gives you a chance to use form-based authentication to restrict access to some pages in a web site.

Test the application

1. Run the application in the ex_starts/ch21_ex2 directory.

2. Test the application by entering an invalid email/password combination, and note that the Login page is displayed again.

3. Test the application by entering a valid email/password combination such as "admin@myguitarshop.com" and "sesame". This should give you access to the restricted pages. After you view some of these pages, use the Logout link to log out. Note that this returns you to the Login page.

Review the code

4. Open the model/admin_db.php file. Note that it uses the sha1 function to encrypt the email/password combination for both of its functions.

5. Open the view/admin_menu.php, view/product_manager.php, and view/order_manager.php files. Note that these files require a secure connection and a valid administrator.

6. Open the util/valid_admin.php file. Note that it redirects to the controller if the user isn't a valid admin user.

7. Open the index.php file. Note that it displays the Login page if the user isn't a valid admin user. Otherwise, it performs the appropriate action.

22

How to send email and access other web sites

When you create a web application, you often need to send email to your users. For example, when a user makes a purchase from an eCommerce site, the application usually sends an email that confirms the order.

Some web applications also need to get data from other web sites. To facilitate that, many major web sites such as Google, Yahoo, and YouTube provide a way for other web applications to get data from their web servers.

In this chapter, you'll first learn how to send email and get data from other web servers. Then, the application at the end of the chapter will show you how to combine the two skills in a useful application.

How to send email **708**
How email works 708
How to install the PEAR Mail package 710
How to set up a test email account 712
How to use PEAR Mail to send an email 714
A helper function for sending an email 718
How to use the helper function to send an email 722

How to get data from other servers **724**
How to enable the cURL library 724
How to use cURL to connect to another web server 726
How to use an API provided by another server 728

The YouTube Search application **730**
The user interface 730
The controller 732
Search view 736
Email view 738

Perspective **740**

How to send email

This topic shows you how to send email using the PEAR Mail package. But first, this topic introduces you to some basic email concepts, shows you how to install the PEAR Mail package, and shows you how to set up a test environment.

How email works

You're probably familiar with *email client* software such as Microsoft Outlook, Mozilla Thunderbird, or Eudora that allows you to send and retrieve email messages. This type of software communicates with the *email server* software that actually sends and retrieves your email. Most likely, your email server software is provided by your Internet Service Provider (ISP) or through your company's information technology department.

The diagram in figure 22-1 shows how the process of sending and receiving email works. The protocol that's used to send email is *Simple Message Transfer Protocol* (*SMTP*). When you send an email, it's first sent from your email client to your email server using SMTP. Then, your email server uses SMTP to send the email to the recipient's email server. Finally, the recipient's email client uses either the *Post Office Protocol* (*POP*) or *Internet Message Access Protocol* (*IMAP*) to retrieve the email from the recipient's email server.

Web applications can also be used to build email clients. You're probably familiar with web-based email clients such as Gmail, Yahoo Mail, and Hotmail. Web mail applications communicate with the email server by using the web server as an email client. PHP has several features that allow it to communicate with email servers. In this topic, you'll learn how to use the PEAR Mail package to send an email message from the server.

How email is sent

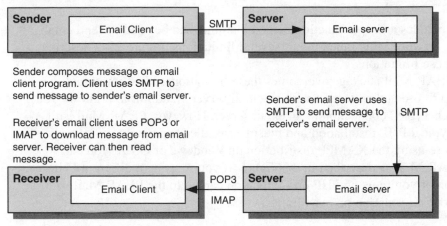

Protocols used in sending email

Protocol	Description
SMTP	Used to send messages to an email server. It is used by an email client to send the original message and by an email server to forward a message from one server to another.
POP3	Used to download messages from an email server. The message may be left on the server or deleted.
IMAP	Used to manage messages on an email server. It provides the ability to organize messages into folders on the server. Messages are typically left on the server until the user explicitly deletes them.

Description

- An *email client* allows a user to send and receive email messages. It can be a desktop application running on the user's computer. It can also be an application running on a smart phone or a web-based application. In web-based email, the web server acts as the email client.

- An *email server* sends and receives email on behalf of the user. When a user sends an email, it stores the message until it can be forwarded to all of the recipients' servers. When a user receives an email, it stores the message until the user logs in to download and read email.

Figure 22-1   How email works

How to install the PEAR Mail package

PHP includes a simple function named mail that can be used to send email messages. However, this function has several limitations. Figure 22-2 describes some of these limitations.

The PEAR Mail package overcomes these limitations. Most important, it allows you to use authentication with an email server. In addition, it allows you to use an encrypted connection to an email server. However, PEAR Mail isn't part of a typical PHP installation and must be installed separately.

If you're using the XAMPP distribution on Windows or OS X, you can install PEAR Mail as described in this figure. If you're using a different PHP distribution or you're using PHP on Linux, you can go to the PEAR Mail web site for more information on installing it.

The PEAR Mail web site

`http://pear.php.net/package/Mail/`

Limitations of the built-in PHP mail function

- You must modify the php.ini file to change email servers.

- You cannot use an encrypted connection to the email server.

- You cannot provide a username and password when connecting to the email server.

How to install the PEAR Mail package in Windows

1. Click the Start menu, select the Programs→Accessories group, and click on Command Prompt to open a command prompt window.

2. In the Command Prompt window, type these commands:

```
cd \xampp\php
pear install --alldeps Mail
exit
```

How to install the PEAR Mail package in Mac OS X

1. In Finder, open the Applications folder, open the Utilities folder, and double click the Terminal icon to open a Terminal window.

2. In the Terminal window, type these commands:

```
cd /Applications/XAMPP/xamppfiles/bin
sudo ./pear install --alldeps Mail
exit
```

Description

- PHP provides a built-in function named mail that allows you to send email messages with PHP. However, this function has several limitations.

- The PEAR Mail package overcomes the limitations of the built-in mail function. However, you must install it before you can use it.

Figure 22-2   How to install the PEAR Mail package

How to set up a test email account

As with any email client software, PHP needs to be able to access an SMTP server before it can send email. In a production environment, the company hosting your web server usually provides an SMTP server that you can use. If so, you can check their documentation for information on how to connect to this server.

In a development environment, though, you may not have access to a SMTP server. Then, you may need to find a remote SMTP server that you can use. For instance, an Internet Service Provider (ISP) often provides an email account that includes an SMTP server, and you can sometimes use that server for testing. Otherwise, you can set up a free email account on Gmail and use its SMTP server with PEAR Mail for testing as shown in figure 22-3

No matter how you get access to an SMTP server, you need to know several pieces of information before you can connect to it. These pieces of information are listed in this figure along with values that you can use to connect to Gmail's SMTP server.

To start, you need to know the host name of your SMTP server. Typically, the host name is a subdomain name such as smtp.gmail.com. However, the host name may also be an IP address such as 192.168.1.10.

Next, you need to know if your SMTP server uses SSL encryption and what port number you need to use. If the server uses SSL, the port number is usually 465. Otherwise, the port number is usually 25. An SMTP server can use any port number, however, so you need to specify the correct port number for your SMTP server.

Finally, you need to know if your SMTP server uses authentication. If it does, you need the username and password for your account on the server. The SMTP username may or may not include the "@" portion of the account's email address.

When you use a test email account, don't abuse your SMTP server by sending too many emails or by sending unsolicited email. Doing so can result in your account being closed and legal action being taken against you. Make sure to read the terms of service with any hosting company you use. That way, you can stay within their guidelines of acceptable use.

How to create a Gmail account for email testing

1. If you don't already have a Gmail account, create one. To do that, you can go to www.gmail.com, click on the "Create an Account" link, and follow the instructions.

2. Login to your Gmail account and go to your Inbox.

3. Click the "Settings" link at the top of the page.

4. On the Settings page, click the "Forwarding and POP/IMAP" link.

5. In the POP download section, select the "Enable POP for all mail" option.

6. Click the "Save Changes" button.

Configuration information for a Gmail SMTP server

Setting	Value	Note
Host name	smtp.gmail.com	
Encryption	SSL	
Port number	465	
Authentication	Yes	
Username	*username*@gmail.com	For example: johndoe@gmail.com
Password	*yourGmailPassword*	For example: pa55word

Description

- Before you can use PHP to send email, you need to connect to an SMTP server. If you have an Internet Service Provider (ISP) or a web hosting company, it will often provide access to an SMTP server. In addition, web-based email services such as Gmail typically provide access to an SMTP server.

- During development, you may not have access to an SMTP server. In this case, you can set up a free Gmail account as described above and use the Gmail SMTP server to test your application.

- During testing, make sure that you don't abuse the SMTP server by sending unsolicited emails. Otherwise, access to the server may be terminated, and you may be reported to your ISP as a possible spammer.

Figure 22-3   How to set up a test email account

How to use PEAR Mail to send an email

Now that you've installed PEAR Mail and set up your test environment, you're ready to use PEAR Mail to send email as described in figure 22-4.

To start, you need to load the PEAR Mail package so your application has access to it. To do that, you can use a require_once statement to load the Mail.php file. This file doesn't need to be copied into your application's folder. That's because all PEAR packages are stored in a separate folder that's part of the include path that's searched when you use any include or require statements. As a result, once you install PEAR Mail, you should avoid naming conflicts by not using the Mail.php filename for any of your PHP files.

After you load the PEAR Mail package, you need to define the parameters for your SMTP server. To do that, you can store these parameters in an array. In this figure, for instance, there are three examples of parameter arrays for an SMTP server.

The first example shows how to connect to an SMTP server that doesn't use encryption or authentication. In this example, you only need to set the host element of the array. However, if your server uses a port number other than 25, you need to set the port element of the array to that port number.

The second example shows how to connect to an SMTP server that uses authentication but doesn't use encryption. In this example, you also need to set the auth element to TRUE, the username element to your SMTP account username, and the password element to your SMTP account password.

The third example shows how to connect to an SMTP server that uses both encryption and authentication. In this example, the host name is prefixed with a string of "ssl://" and the port number is set to 465. Although 465 is a common port number for an encrypted SMTP connection, an SMTP server can use other nonstandard port numbers.

Once you create the array that stores the SMTP parameters, you can pass this array to the static factory method of the Mail class. This method creates and returns a mailer object that you can use to send an email. Typically, you store this object in a variable for later use.

Step 1: Load the PEAR Mail package

```
require_once 'Mail.php';
```

Step 2: Set the parameters for the mailer object

Example 1: A simple SMTP server

```
$options = array();
$options['host'] = 'mail.example.com';
```

Example 2: An SMTP server with authentication

```
$options = array();
$options['host'] = 'mail.example.com';
$options['auth'] = true;
$options['username'] = 'sample.user@example.com';
$options['password'] = 'Sup3r*S3cr3+';
```

Example 3: An SMTP server with authentication and SSL encryption

```
$options = array();
$options['host'] = 'ssl://mail.example.com';
$options['port'] = 465;
$options['auth'] = true;
$options['username'] = 'mail.account@example.com';
$options['password'] = 'Sup3r*S3cr3+';
```

Step 3: Create the mailer object

```
$mailer = Mail::factory('smtp', $options);
```

Description

- Before you can use the PEAR Mail package, you must load it. To do that, you can code a require_once statement that loads the file named Mail.php.

- The static factory method of the Mail class returns a mailer object that you can use to send an email. If it isn't able to create a mailer object, it returns a PEAR_Error object.

- To avoid naming conflicts, don't use the name Mail.php for any of your PHP files.

Figure 22-4   How to use the PEAR Mail package to send an email (part 1 of 2)

Once you create a mailer object, you can use it to send an email. But first, you need to create an array to hold the SMTP headers for the email. For example, you need to set the From, To, Cc, Bcc, and Subject headers. The case of these headers isn't important, but this figure shows the most common usage. For example, you can use CC instead of Cc if you want. When you add email addresses to headers, you shouldn't add an email address more than once.

After you create the headers, you need to create a comma-delimited list of all the email addresses to send the email to. This list combines the addresses in the To, Cc, and Bcc headers. When you create this list, you should make sure that each email address only appears once.

After you create the recipient list, you can create the text for the body of the message. To do that, you can use all the standard skills for coding a string. If you use a double-quoted string, you can use the new line (\n) character to specify a new line in the body of the message.

To send the email, you call the send method of the mailer object and pass it the recipient list, the header array, and the body of the message. This sends the message. If successful, this method returns TRUE. Otherwise, it returns a PEAR error object.

After you call the send method, you can check whether the result of that method is a PEAR_Error object by using the static isError method. If it is an error object, you can call the getMessage method of the PEAR_Error object to get an error message, and you can use that message in your application. When you're testing an application, this message often provides information that can help you debug and troubleshoot problems.

If you don't set the Content-type header, it is set to "text/plain" by default. This indicates that the email is in plain text. As a result, you can't use HTML tags to format the body of the email. However, if you want to use HTML tags to format the email, you can set the Content-type header to "text/html". Then, you can use HTML tags as shown in this figure. Here, the email uses a <p> tag to identify a paragraph and an <a> tag to specify a link. Of course, once you set the Content-type header correctly, you can use any of the HTML tags in your email.

In this figure, the email addresses are specified without a corresponding name. However, you can specify a name that corresponds with the email address by using this format:

```
Full Name <username@example.com>
```

That way, most email clients display the full name in the email inbox instead of the email address, which is usually what you want.

Step 4: Send the message

```
// 1. Set the SMTP headers
$headers = array();
$headers['From'] = 'sample.user@example.com';
$headers['To'] = 'john.doe@example.com, jane.doe@example.com';
$headers['Cc'] = 'fsmith@example.org';
$headers['Bcc'] = 'jsmith@example.net';
$headers['Subject'] = 'How to use PEAR Mail';

// 2. Set the recipient list
$recipients  = 'john.doe@example.com, jane.doe@example.com, ';
$recipients .= 'fsmith@example.org, jsmith@example.net';

// 3. Set the text for the body of the message
$body  = "The Murach PHP and MySQL book has a chapter on\n";
$body .= "how to use the PEAR Mail package to send email.";

// 4. Send the message
$result = $mailer->send($recipients, $headers, $body);

// 5. Check the result and display an error if one exists
if (PEAR::isError($result)) {
    $error = 'Error sending email: ' . $result->getMessage();
    echo htmlspecialchars($error);
}
```

How to use HTML formatting in the body of the message

```
// 1. Set the Content-type header
$headers['Content-type']  = 'text/html';

// 2. Use HTML tags to format the body of the message
$body = '<p>The Murach PHP and MySQL book has a chapter on how to use
        the <a href="http://pear.php.net/Mail/">PEAR Mail package</a>
        to send email.</p>';
```

Description

- The send method of the mailer object sends an email. It accepts three arguments:
  (1) a comma-delimited list of recipients, (2) an array of headers, and (3) the text
  for the body of the message. If this method encounters an error, it returns a
  PEAR_Error object.

- The static isError method of the PEAR class checks whether the specified object is
  a PEAR_Error object. If it is, you can use the getMessage method of that object to
  get the error message.

- By default, the text for the body of the message must be plain text with no attachments. However, if you set the Content-type header to a value of "text/html", you
  can use HTML tags to format the text.

- To create email messages with in-line images and attachments, you can use the
  PEAR Mail_Mime package. For more information about that package, you can
  visit this URL:

  http://pear.php.net/package/Mail_Mime/

Figure 22-4   How to use the PEAR Mail package to send an email (part 2 of 2)

A helper function for sending an email

Figure 22-5 presents the code for a helper function named send_email that you can use to make it easier to create and send an email message. This function validates the email addresses that are passed to it, connects to the SMTP server, and sends the email.

This code in this file starts by loading two files. The first file (Mail.php) is the PEAR Mail package. The second file (RFC822.php) is another PHP file. It provides a method named parseAddressList that validates a list of email addresses where each email address may be in this format:

```
Full Name <username@example.com>
```

This method is used by the valid_email function that's in part 2 of this figure.

The send_email function accepts five parameters. Here, the first four parameters are required: the From address, the To address, the subject line, and the body of the email. However, the fifth parameter is optional. This parameter specifies whether the body of the email is formatted with HTML tags. By default, this parameter is set to FALSE so the body of the message isn't formatted with HTML tags.

This function begins by checking whether the From and To addresses are valid. To do that, it uses the valid_email function that's in part 2. If an email address isn't valid, this code throws an Exception object that contains an appropriate error message.

After validating the email addresses, this function sets the parameters for an SMTP server. When you use this code, you need to modify the $smtp array elements to match the values for your own SMTP server. If you don't change the values, the code won't work.

Once the parameters are set, the Mail::factory method is used to create a mailer object. Then, it uses the PEAR::isError method to check whether this method returned a PEAR_Error object. If it did, this code throws an exception that indicates that the code couldn't create the mailer object.

After creating the mailer object, this code creates an array named $recipients. This array stores the addresses for all recipients of the email. For this function, this array only contains a single recipient, the To address. If necessary, though, you could create an enhanced version of this function that allows for multiple To, Cc, or Bcc addresses.

After creating the recipients list, this code sets the HTTP headers. Here, the code checks the $is_body_html parameter to determine whether to set the Content-type header. If this parameter is set to TRUE, this code sets the Content-type header to a value of "text/html". This indicates that the body is formatted with HTML tags. Otherwise, this code leaves the Content-type header at its default value of "text/plain".

After setting the headers, this code sends the email by calling the send method of the mailer object. To do that, this code passes the recipients array, the header array, and the message body to the send method, and it stores the return

The message.php file   **Page 1**

```php
<?php
require_once 'Mail.php';
require_once 'Mail/RFC822.php';

function send_email($to, $from, $subject, $body, $is_body_html = false) {
    if (! valid_email($to)) {
        throw new Exception('This To address is invalid: ' .
                            htmlspecialchars($to));
    }
    if (! valid_email($from)) {
        throw new Exception('This From address is invalid: ' .
                            htmlspecialchars($from));
    }

    $smtp = array();
    // **** You must change the following to match your
    // **** SMTP server and account information.
    $smtp['host'] = 'ssl://smtp.gmail.com';
    $smtp['port'] = 465;
    $smtp['auth'] = true;
    $smtp['username'] = 'example@gmail.com';
    $smtp['password'] = 'supersecret';

    $mailer = Mail::factory('smtp', $smtp);
    if (PEAR::isError($mailer)) {
        throw new Exception('Could not create mailer.');
    }

    // Add the email address to an array of all recipients
    $recipients = array();
    $recipients[] = $to;

    // Set the headers
    $headers = array();
    $headers['From'] = $from;
    $headers['To']   = $to;
    $headers['Subject'] = $subject;
    if ($is_body_html) {
        $headers['Content-type']  = 'text/html';
    }

    // Send the email
    $result = $mailer->send($recipients, $headers, $body);

    // Check the result and throw an error if one exists
    if (PEAR::isError($result)) {
        throw new Exception('Error sending email: ' .
                            htmlspecialchars($result->getMessage()) );
    }
}
```

Figure 22-5   A helper function for sending an email (part 1 of 2)

value in the variable named $result. Then, if the $result variable is an error, this code throws an exception. If not, it doesn't do anything since no error indicates that the email has been sent successfully.

The valid_email function in part 2 of this works similarly to the valid_email method presented in chapter 15. However, the valid_email function in this chapter uses the parseAddressList method provided by the PEAR Mail package to parse email addresses that are in this form:

```
Full Name <username@example.com>
```

This method accepts an address or a list of addresses and returns an array of email objects with one object for each address.

If the parseAddressList method returns a PEAR_Error object, the valid_email function returns FALSE. Or, if the parseAddressList method returns multiple email objects, the valid_email function returns FALSE. Otherwise, the email address parts are copied from the first email address object and stored in the $mailbox and $host variables.

Unfortunately, the parseAddressList method doesn't catch all invalid email addresses. For example, this method treats

```
last..first@example.com
```

as a valid email address. That's why the rest of the valid_email function performs address validation as described in chapter 15. In other words, this code is primarily using the parseAddressList method to split apart addresses that are in the form of "Full Name <username@example.com>".

For an explanation of how this code works, you can refer back to chapter 15. Another alternative, though, is to accept the fact that the code does work and use it in your own applications whenever you need to validate email addresses.

The message.php file   **Page 2**

```php
function valid_email($email) {
    $emailObjects = Mail_RFC822::parseAddressList($email);
    if (PEAR::isError($emailObjects)) return false;

    // Get the mailbox and host parts of the first email object
    $mailbox = $emailObjects[0]->mailbox;
    $host = $emailObjects[0]->host;

    // Make sure the mailbox and host parts aren't too long
    if (strlen($mailbox) > 64) return false;
    if (strlen($host) > 255) return false;

    // Validate the mailbox
    $atom = '[[:alnum:]_!#$%&\'*+\/=?^`{|}~-]+';
    $dotatom = '(\.' . $atom . ')*';
    $address = '(^' . $atom . $dotatom . '$)';
    $char = '([^\\\\"])';
    $esc  = '(\\\\[\\\\"])';
    $text = '(' . $char . '|' . $esc . ')+';
    $quoted = '(^"' . $text . '"$)';
    $localPart = '/' . $address . '|' . $quoted . '/';
    $localMatch = preg_match($localPart, $mailbox);
    if ($localMatch === false || $localMatch != 1) return false;

    // Validate the host
    $hostname = '([[:alnum:]]([-[:alnum:]]{0,62}[[:alnum:]])?)';
    $hostnames = '(' . $hostname . '(\.' . $hostname . ')*)';
    $top = '\.[[:alnum:]]{2,6}';
    $domainPart = '/^' . $hostnames . $top . '$/';
    $domainMatch = preg_match($domainPart, $host);
    if ($domainMatch === false || $domainMatch != 1) return false;

    return true;
}
?>
```

Figure 22-5   A helper function for sending an email (part 2 of 2)

How to use the helper function to send an email

Figure 22-6 shows how to use the helper function named send_email to send an email. This function makes it easy to send an email to a single recipient, which is what you typically need to do when coding web applications.

To use the send_email function, you begin by importing the message.php file that's in the previous figure. Then, you code the five arguments that specify the From address, the To address, the subject line, the body of the message, and whether the body of the message contains HTML formatting. Finally, you use the send_email function within a try/catch statement to catch any exceptions that are thrown if the function isn't successful.

When you use a helper function like this, it shields the rest of the application from the details of the code that sends an email. In other words, as long as you don't change the name or the parameters of the function, you can change the internal details of how this function sends an email without disrupting the rest of the application. For example, you could switch to a different SMTP server. To do that, you just modify the message.php file that's described in the previous figure.

How to use the send_email function

```
require_once 'message.php';

$from = 'John Doe <john.doe@example.com>';
$to = 'Jane Doe <jane.doe@example.com>';

$subject = 'How to use PEAR Mail';

$body = '<p>The Murach PHP and MySQL book has a chapter on how to use
         the <a href="http://pear.php.net/Mail/">PEAR Mail package</a>
         to send email.</p>';

$is_body_html = true;

try {
    send_email($to, $from, $subject, $body, $is_body_html);
} catch (Exception $e) {
    $error = $e->getMessage();
    echo $error;
}
```

Description

- To make it easier to send an email, you can use the send_email function in the message.php file that's presented in figure 22-5.

- Since the send_email function throws exceptions if it encounters invalid email addresses or other problems sending the email, you can use a try/catch statement to handle these exceptions.

Figure 22-6   How to use the helper function to send an email

How to get data from other servers

Just as the PEAR Mail package lets you turn your web server into an email client, the *cURL library* lets you turn your web server into a web browser. This allows you to retrieve information from another web server and format it for display in your own web application.

How to enable the cURL library

The cURL library is part of the XAMPP distribution, but it isn't enabled by default for Windows or Mac OS X. That's why figure 22-7 shows you how to enable cURL for these operating systems. If you're using Linux, cURL is probably already enabled. But otherwise, you can search the Internet for instructions on how to install cURL for your Linux distribution.

The default location of the PHP initialization file in Windows

```
c:\xampp\php\php.ini
```

How to configure PHP to use the cURL library in Windows

1. Open the php.ini file in a text editor.
2. Find the line that contains the text "php_curl.dll".
3. Remove the semicolon from the beginning of the line. It should read as follows:

```
extension=php_curl.dll
```

4. Restart the Apache web server as described in the appendix.

The default location of the PHP initialization file in Mac OS X

```
/Applications/XAMPP/xamppfiles/etc/php.ini
```

How to configure PHP to use the cURL library in Mac OS X

1. Open the php.ini file in a text editor.
2. Find the line that contains the text "curl.so".
3. If necessary, remove the semicolon from the beginning of the line. It should read as follows:

```
extension=curl.so
```

4. Restart the Apache web server as described in the appendix.

Description

- The *cURL library* lets you connect to other servers on the web. It supports protocols such as HTTP, FTP, IMAP, POP3, and SMTP.
- By default, cURL is installed with XAMPP, but it's not enabled.

Figure 22-7   How to enable the cURL library in XAMPP

How to use cURL to connect to another web server

Once you have enabled cURL, you can use the four functions described in figure 22-8 to connect to a web server. To start, you need to call the curl_init function to initialize the cURL session. This function takes a URL as its parameter and returns a reference to the cURL session. In the example in this figure, the curl_init function initializes a cURL session for this URL:

`http://www.example.com`

After you initialize a cURL session, you can use the curl_setopt function to set the options for the session. Most of the time, you only need to set the CURLOPT_RETURNTRANSFER option. If this option is set to FALSE, as it is by default, it sends the data that's returned from the web server directly to the web page as if it were sent using the echo statement. If this option is set to TRUE, you can modify the data that's returned from the web page before you send it to the web browser. That's why this option is commonly set to TRUE as shown in the example in this figure.

The curl_exec function executes the download from the URL stored in the cURL session. When the cURL return transfer option is set to TRUE, this function returns the contents of the URL as a string. In the example in this figure, the HTML source code for the specified URL is stored in a variable named $page.

When you finish a cURL session, you need to call the curl_close function to close the cURL session. This frees all resources associated with the cURL session.

After closing the cURL session, the data in the $page variable is still available for processing. In the example in this figure, the code just uses the htmlspecialchars and nl2br functions to format this string to make it easier to read. However, you could perform other types of processing on this data. Then, this code uses an echo statement to send this string to the browser. If this echo statement is coded within a web page, this causes the source code for the home page of www.example.com to be displayed in the browser.

When you call the curl_exec function, you should know that it is a "blocking call." That means that your PHP script stops executing until the function returns the content of the URL. As a result, if the server for the specified URL runs slowly, your PHP script will also run slowly.

Common cURL functions

Function	Description
curl_init(*$url*)	Initializes a cURL session for the specified URL and returns a reference to that session.
curl_setopt(*$curl, OPTION, $value*)	Sets the options for the specified cURL session. If the CURLOPT_RETURNTRANSFER option is set to a value of TRUE, the session returns data. Otherwise, the session echoes data to the page.
curl_exec(*$curl*)	Executes the cURL session and downloads data.
curl_close(*$curl*)	Closes the cURL session.

How to use the cURL functions

```
// Initialize the cURL session
$curl = curl_init('http://www.example.com');

// Set the cURL options so the session returns data
curl_setopt($curl, CURLOPT_RETURNTRANSFER, true);

// Transfer the data and store it
$page = curl_exec($curl);

// Close the session
curl_close($curl);

// Process the data
$page = nl2br(htmlspecialchars($page));
echo $page;
```

Description

- The functions in the cURL library let you connect to another web server and get data from that server.

Figure 22-8   How to use cURL to connect to another server

How to use an API provided by another server

Now that you know how to use cURL to connect to a web server, you're ready to learn how to use cURL to work with an API (*Application Programming Interface*) that's provided by another web server. An API provides a way to work with the data on another server, and many major web sites provide APIs. For example, figure 22-9 shows how to use the API for the YouTube web site.

The YouTube API lets you send a request to the YouTube server using HTTP. Then, the YouTube server returns the result as an HTTP response. By default, the result is returned as XML, but you can use the YouTube API to change this default so YouTube returns the data as *JavaScript Object Notation* (*JSON*). This makes it easier for PHP to process the data that's returned.

When you use the YouTube API, you can append one or more parameters to the base URL for the API. In this figure, for example, the URL appends the alt parameter with a value of json to specify a JSON data format. It also appends the q (query) parameter with a value of "space shuttle". Note that this URL uses a plus sign (+) for the space between the words.

The code example in this figure shows how to search YouTube and access the data that's returned by the YouTube API. To start, the code creates the query string that performs the search. Then, it uses the urlencode function to encode the query. This function converts text into the proper format to be included in a URL. For example, spaces are converted to plus signs (+) and other special characters are converted to a percent sign followed by the character's Latin-1 value in hexadecimal. In this example, "space shuttle" becomes "space+shuttle".

Once this code builds the full URL, it uses cURL to get the data in JSON format. To do that, the first statement initializes a cURL session for this URL. The second statement sets an option for the session so it returns data. The third statement executes the search and stores the JSON data that's returned in a variable named $json_data. And the fourth statement closes the cURL session and frees all associated resources.

Next, this code gets an associative array of videos from the JSON data. To do that, the first statement uses the json_decode function to parse the JSON data into a series of nested associative arrays. Here, the second parameter of TRUE causes the json_decode function to create nested associative arrays instead of nested objects. Then, the second statement copies the array of videos from the nested arrays to the $videos variable. To do that, this statement accesses the entry element of the feed element.

Finally, this code processes the common data for each video. In particular, it gets a URL to a thumbnail for the video, a URL to watch the video, and a text description of the video.

How to do all this is covered in the documentation for the API. However, the complete API is much too complex to examine in detail here. To learn more about the YouTube API, though, you can read its documentation. You can also learn how to use the APIs for other web sites by searching the Internet for their documentation.

The URL for the documentation of the YouTube API

```
http://code.google.com/apis/youtube/2.0/reference.html
```

The base URL for the YouTube Video Search API

```
http://gdata.youtube.com/feeds/api/videos
```

Four parameters that you can add to the base URL

Option	Description
alt	Specifies an alternate data format. The default is "atom" which returns XML data, but you can use "json" to return data in the JavaScript Object Notation (JSON) format.
q	Specifies the search string.
orderby	Specifies how to sort the results of the search. The default is "relevance", but you can specify other values such as "published", "viewCount", and "rating".
safeSearch	Filters videos by removing restricted content. The default value is "moderate", but you can specify other values such as "none" and "strict".

A URL for a YouTube query

```
http://gdata.youtube.com/feeds/api/videos?alt=json&q=space+shuttle
```

How to use cURL to query YouTube

```php
// Set up the URL for the query
$query = 'space shuttle';
$query = urlencode($query);
$base_url = 'http://gdata.youtube.com/feeds/api/videos';
$params = 'alt=json&q=' . $query;
$url = $base_url . '?' . $params;

// Use cURL to get data in JSON format
$curl = curl_init($url);
curl_setopt($curl, CURLOPT_RETURNTRANSFER, true);
$json_data = curl_exec($curl);
curl_close($curl);

// Get an array of videos from the JSON data
$data = json_decode($json_data, true);
$videos = $data['feed']['entry'];

// Access the data for each video
foreach ($videos as $video) {
    $image_url = $video['media$group']['media$thumbnail'][0]['url'];
    $video_url = $video['link'][0]['href'];
    $text      = $video['title']['$t'];

    // Code to output these values
}
```

Description

- Many web sites provide an *Application Programming Interface* (*API*) that lets other sites use their data, and *JavaScript Object Notation* (*JSON*) is often used for this data transfer.

- PHP's json_decode function can be used to parse JSON data into nested arrays.

Figure 22-9   How to use an API provided by another server

The YouTube Search application

To illustrate the skills you've just learned in the context of a complete application, this chapter ends by presenting an application that lets the user search for a video on YouTube. Then, the user can view the video or send an email that includes a link to the video.

The user interface

Figure 22-10 shows the two main views of the YouTube Search application. The Search view starts with a search form. If the user enters a search string and clicks on the Search button, this form sends the search string to YouTube for processing. Then, if YouTube returns one or more videos that match the search, the Search view displays those results in a table below the form

Each row in this table includes a thumbnail image of the video, a button, and a text description of the video. If the user clicks the image or text, the application navigates to YouTube's site to view that video. If the user clicks the button, the application displays the Email view.

The Email view presents a form that lets the user send an email that includes the video's link to someone. In this view, the video's description and link are embedded, and the user can't change these values. In contrast, the subject and message have default values that the user can change. As a result, the only data that a user must enter are the email addresses for the From and To fields.

When the user clicks on the Send button, the application attempts to send the email. If it's successful, it displays the Search view for the current query. Otherwise, the application displays the Email view again with an error message at the top of the page.

Search view

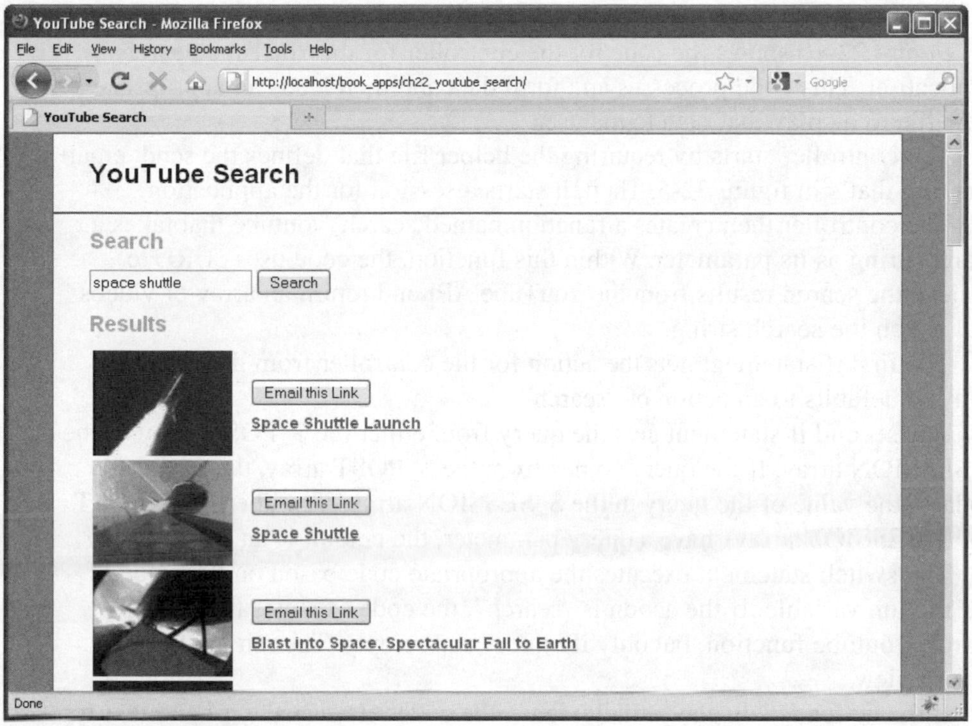

Email view

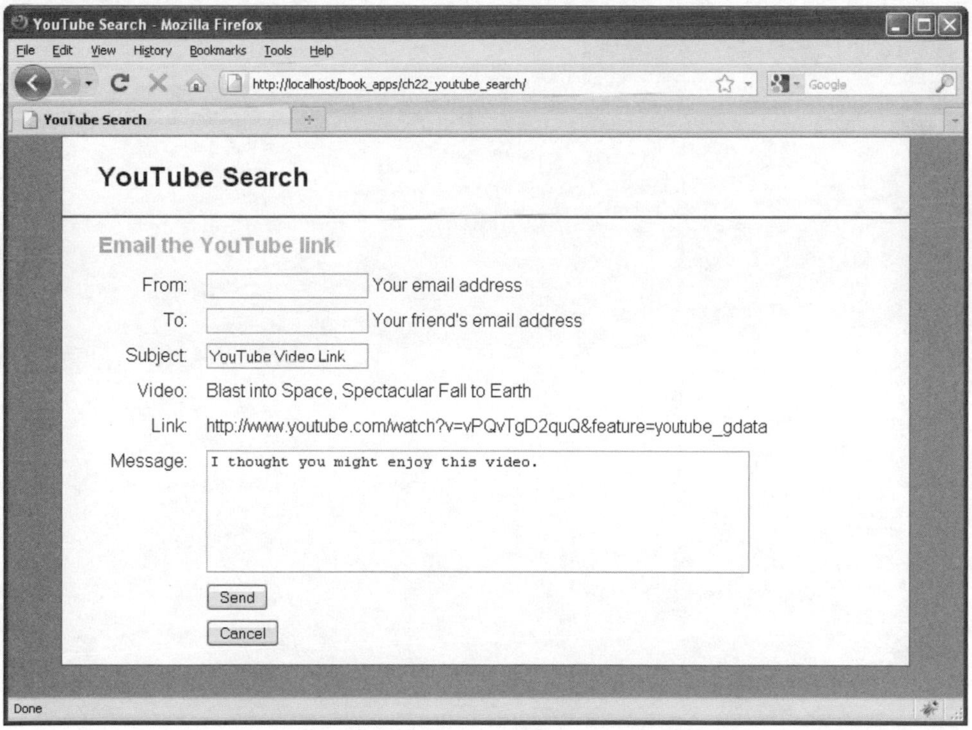

Figure 22-10   The YouTube Search application (part 1 of 5)

The controller

Figure 22-10 shows the code for the controller for the YouTube Search application. This code processes any form data and then loads an appropriate view file to display that data to the user.

The controller starts by requiring the helper file that defines the send_email function that's in figure 22-5. Then, it starts a session for the application.

The controller then creates a function named search_youtube that takes a search string as its parameter. Within this function, the code uses cURL to retrieve the search results from the YouTube API and return an array of videos that match the search string.

The first if statement gets the action for the controller from the $_POST array or defaults to an action of "search".

The second if statement gets the query from either the $_POST array or the $_SESSION array. If the query comes from the $_POST array, this code updates the value of the query in the $_SESSION array. If neither the $_POST nor $_SESSION arrays have a query parameter, the default is an empty string.

The switch statement executes the appropriate code based on the value of the $action variable. If the action is "search", the code executes the search_youtube function, but only if $query isn't empty. Then, it loads the Search view.

If the action is "display_email_view", the code retrieves the url and text for the video from the $_POST array. Then, it includes the Email view to display the form for emailing a YouTube link.

The controller (index.php)

```php
<?php
require_once 'message.php';
session_start();

function search_youtube($query) {
    // Set up the URL for the query
    $query = urlencode($query);
    $base_url = 'http://gdata.youtube.com/feeds/api/videos';
    $params = 'alt=json&q=' . $query;
    $url = $base_url . '?' . $params;

    // Use cURL to get data in JSON format
    $curl = curl_init($url);
    curl_setopt($curl, CURLOPT_RETURNTRANSFER, true);
    $json_data = curl_exec($curl);
    curl_close($curl);

    // Get an array of videos from the JSON data and return it
    $data = json_decode($json_data, true);
    $videos = $data['feed']['entry'];
    return $videos;
}

if (isset($_POST['action'])) {
    $action = $_POST['action'];
} else {
    $action = 'search';
}

if (isset($_POST['query'])) {
    $query = $_POST['query'];
    $_SESSION['query'] = $query;
} else if (isset($_SESSION['query'])) {
    $query = $_SESSION['query'];
} else {
    $query = '';
}

switch ($action) {
    case 'search':
        if (!empty($query)) {
            $videos = search_youtube($query);
        }
        include 'search_view.php';
        break;
    case 'display_email_view':
        $url = $_POST['url'];
        $text = $_POST['text'];
        include 'email_view.php';
        break;
```

Figure 22-10   The YouTube Search application (part 2 of 5)

If the action is "send_mail", the code retrieves the data that was posted by the Email view and copies that data into local variables. Then, this code creates the body of the email by combining the text description of the video, the URL for the video, and the message the user entered in the form. Note that these three elements are separated by two new line characters (\n\n).

Within the try/catch statement, the code attempts to send the email. To do that, this code uses the send_email function. Then, this code gets the results of the YouTube search and displays the Search view. However, if the send_email function throws an exception, the catch clause gets the error message from the Exception object and redisplays the Email view.

Finally, if the action isn't any of the previous actions, the switch statement displays the Search view without executing a YouTube search.

The controller (continued)

```
    case 'send_mail':
        // Get the data from the Mail View page
        $from = $_POST['from'];
        $to = $_POST['to'];
        $subject = $_POST['subject'];

        $text = $_POST['text'];
        $url = $_POST['url'];
        $message = $_POST['message'];

        // Create the body
        $body = $text . "\n\n" . $url . "\n\n" . $message;

        try {
            // Send the email
            send_email($to, $from, $subject, $body);

            // Display the Search view for the current query
            $videos = search_youtube($query);
            include 'search_view.php';
        } catch (Exception $e) {
            $error = $e->getMessage();
            include 'email_view.php';
        }
        break;
    default:
        include 'search_view.php';
        break;
}

?>
```

Figure 22-10   The YouTube Search application (part 3 of 5)

Search view

Figure 22-10 shows the code for the Search view of the YouTube Search application. The main <div> element is divided into two parts. The first part is a form that gets the query string from the user. The second part displays the results of the search as a table.

The search form displays a text box that lets the user enter a query string. If the user has previously performed a search, the text box displays the current query string. This form doesn't include a hidden field for the action since the controller uses a default action of "search". When the user clicks the submit button, the default file in the current directory (index.php) is executed so the search is done if the the text box contains a query string.

This view only displays the results table if the $videos array includes one or more videos. If it does, this view uses a foreach loop to display one table row for each video. Within each row, the thumbnail images and text descriptions are wrapped in <a> tags that link to the corresponding video on the YouTube site. Each Email button is stored within a form that submits the video's URL and text description to the controller. This form also submits a hidden field for the action that has a value of "display_email_view". As a result, when the user clicks on this button the controller displays the Email view.

Search view (search_view.php)

```php
<!DOCTYPE html PUBLIC "-//W3C//DTD XHTML 1.0 Transitional//EN"
    "http://www.w3.org/TR/xhtml1/DTD/xhtml1-transitional.dtd">
<html xmlns="http://www.w3.org/1999/xhtml">
    <head>
        <title>YouTube Search</title>
        <link rel="stylesheet" type="text/css" href="main.css">
    </head>
    <body>
        <div id="page">
            <div id="header"><h1>YouTube Search</h1></div>
            <div id="main">

<h2>Search</h2>
<form action="." method="post">
    <input type="text" name="query" value="<?php echo $query; ?>">
    <input type="submit" value="Search">
</form>
<?php if (count($videos) != 0) : ?>
    <h2>Results</h2>
    <table>
    <?php foreach ($videos as $video) :
        $imgsrc = $video['media$group']['media$thumbnail'][0]['url'];
        $url = $video['link'][0]['href'];
        $text = $video['title']['$t'];
    ?>
        <tr>
            <td>
                <a href="<?php echo $url; ?>">
                    <img src="<?php echo $imgsrc; ?>">
                </a>
            </td>
            <td>
                <form action="." method="post">
                    <input type="hidden" name="action"
                        value="display_email_view">
                    <input type="hidden" name="url"
                        value="<?php echo $url; ?>">
                    <input type="hidden" name="text"
                        value="<?php echo $text; ?>">
                    <input type="submit" value="Email this Link">
                </form>
                <a href="<?php echo $url; ?>">
                    <?php echo $text; ?>
                </a>
            </td>
        </tr>
    <?php endforeach; ?>
    </table>
<?php endif; ?>

            </div><!-- end main -->
        </div><!-- end page -->
    </body>
</html>
```

Figure 22-10   The YouTube Search application (part 4 of 5)

Email view

Figure 22-10 shows the code for the Email view of the YouTube Search application. This view displays a form that collects the data necessary to email a link to the video.

To start, this view checks if an error message has been set. If so, it displays the error message. This error message is set if the send_email helper method (figure 22-5) throws an exception. If, for example, the user submits an invalid email address in the form, the send_email function throws an exception that's caught by the controller. Then, this page displays that error message.

The first form is mostly HTML with only a little PHP. At the beginning of this form, a hidden field stores an action of "send_mail". Then, two more hidden fields store the URL and text description for the video. Since these values are also displayed as plain text within the form, the user can't edit these values.

After this form, this view has a second form that displays a Cancel button. If the user clicks on this button, the application executes the code in the controller without passing any action to it. This causes the controller to use the default action of "search" to display the search results for the current query string.

Email view (mail_view.php)

```
<!DOCTYPE html PUBLIC "-//W3C//DTD XHTML 1.0 Transitional//EN"
    "http://www.w3.org/TR/xhtml1/DTD/xhtml1-transitional.dtd">
<html xmlns="http://www.w3.org/1999/xhtml">
    <head>
        <title>YouTube Search</title>
        <link rel="stylesheet" type="text/css" href="main.css">
    </head>
    <body>
        <div id="page">
            <div id="header"><h1>YouTube Search</h1></div>
            <div id="main">

<h2>Email the YouTube link</h2>

<?php if (isset($error)) : ?>
    <p>Error Sending E-mail: <?php echo $error; ?></p>
<?php endif; ?>

<form action="." method="post" id="email_form">
    <input type="hidden" name="action" value="send_mail">
    <input type="hidden" name="url" value="<?php echo $url; ?>">
    <input type="hidden" name="text" value="<?php echo $text; ?>">

    <label>From:</label>
    <input type="text" name="from"> Your email address<br />

    <label>To:</label>
    <input type="text" name="to"> Your friend's email address<br />

    <label>Subject:</label>
    <input type="text" name="subject" value="YouTube Video Link"><br />

    <label>Video:</label>
    <?php echo $text; ?><br />

    <label>Link:</label>
    <?php echo $url; ?><br />

    <label>Message:</label>
    <textarea name="message">I thought you might enjoy this video.</textarea>
    <br />

    <label> </label>
    <input type="submit" value="Send">
</form>

<form action="." method="post" id="cancel_form">
    <label> </label>
    <input type="submit" value="Cancel">
</form>

            </div><!-- end main -->
        </div><!-- end page -->
    </body>
</html>
```

Figure 22-10   The YouTube Search application (part 5 of 5)

Perspective

In this chapter, you learned how to send both plain text emails and emails that are formatted with HTML from your PHP applications. This provides another level of interaction with your user. However, there is more to learn about sending email. For example, you may want to send email that has in-line images or attachments. To do that, you can use the PEAR Mail_Mime package. To learn more about that package, you can visit this URL:

`http://pear.php.net/package/Mail_Mime/`

In this chapter, you also learned how to use cURL to work with the API that's provided by the YouTube web site. However, you can use these skills to work with any web site that provides an API. As a result, if there's a web site that you want to access, you can search the Internet to see if that web site provides an API. If it does, you can read the documentation for that web site's API to learn how to use it.

Terms

email client
email server
Simple Mail Transfer Protocol (SMTP)
Post Office Protocol (POP)
Internet Message Access Protocol (IMAP)
cURL library
JavaScript Object Notation (JSON)
Application Programming Interface (API)

Summary

- An *email client* lets a user send and receive email messages. An *email server* sends and receives email on behalf of the user.

- An email server uses *Simple Message Transfer Protocol* (*SMTP*) to send emails. An email client uses either the *Post Office Protocol* (*POP*) or *Internet Message Access Protocol* (*IMAP*) to retrieve the email.

- The *cURL* library lets you connect to other servers on the web. It supports protocols such as HTTP, FTP, IMAP, POP3, and SMTP. Many major web sites provide *Application Programming Interfaces* (*APIs*) that let your web site use cURL to access their data.

- *JavaScript Object Notation* (*JSON*) is a data format based on JavaScript that allows two servers to exchange data.

Exercise 22-1 Send an email from a web page

In this exercise, you'll just set up your system so it can run the YouTube Search application that's presented in this chapter.

1. Install the PEAR Mail package as described in figure 22-2. Then, start the application in the YouTube Search application that's in the ex_starts/ch22_ex1 directory. If you've installed the Mail package correctly, you should be able to use the search feature of the opening page.

2. If you don't already have access to an SMTP server, set up a Gmail test account as described in figure 22-3. Then, try to send an email to yourself from the YouTube Search application.

3. Open the message.php file that's stored in the ex_starts/ch22_ex1 directory and review this code. Then, modify this code so it will work on your system. To do that, you need to enter an appropriate username and password.

4. Test the email portion of the YouTube Search application by trying to send an email to yourself. If this works, you should receive the email message. Otherwise, this application should display an error at the top of the web page. Then, you can use this error message to troubleshoot the problem.

23

How to work with files, uploads, and images

For some web applications, you need to work with files, uploads, and images. For instance, some applications let administrative users upload files that contain data or images that are used by the application. Some applications also process the uploaded images so they are sized correctly and have the proper transparency settings. In this chapter, then, you'll learn how to work with files, upload files, and process images.

How to work with files **744**
How to get a directory listing 744
How to read and write an entire file 746
How to read and write part of a file 748
How to read and write CSV data 750
How to copy, rename, and delete a file 752

How to upload a file **754**
HTML for uploading a file 754
PHP for working with an uploaded file 754

How to work with images **756**
How to get information about an image 756
How to read and write images 758
How to resize an image 760
How to work with transparency 762

The Image Upload application **764**
The user interface 764
The utility files 766
The controller 772
The view 774

Perspective **776**

How to work with files

The data that's used by most web sites is stored in a database. In some cases, though, some of the data might be stored in files. Then, you can use PHP to read data from the files and write data to the files.

How to get a directory listing

Figure 23-1 presents five PHP functions that you can use for working with directories. The three in the first table can be used to check whether a string is a valid path. The is_file function returns TRUE if the path points to a file, the is_dir function returns TRUE if the path points to a directory, and the file_exists function returns TRUE if the path points to either a file or a directory.

To get the current working directory, you can use the getcwd function. This returns the directory that contains the current PHP file. After you get the current directory, you can add code that moves up or down one or more directories and you can also add a filename to the path.

When building a path, the directory separator character varies depending on the operating system you're using. However, PHP provides the correct character in the constant named DIRECTORY_SEPARATOR. If you use this constant instead of hard coding a backslash (\) or front slash (/), your script will work correctly regardless of the operating system.

To get a listing of the files and directories in a directory, you can use the scandir function. This function returns an array containing all the files and directories in the path that is passed to the function. This array contains just the file and directory names, not the complete path to each item. It also contains the automatic directories "." and ".." that refer to the current directory and the directory above the current directory. If the path that's passed to this function isn't a valid directory, this function returns a value of FALSE instead of returning an array.

The first example in this figure shows how to use the scandir function to display the directories and files of a directory. To do that, the second statement uses the scandir function to get an array that contains the directories and files for the current working directory. Then, this code loops through this array and displays each item in an unordered list.

The second example shows how to filter out directories to display just the files of a directory. Here, the second line of code stores all files and directories in the array named $items. Then, it creates an empty array named $files. Next, it uses a loop to check whether each item in the array is a file. If so, it adds the item to the $files array. Once this code fills the $files array with filenames, it uses a second loop to display each file as an item in an unordered list.

Three functions to determine if a file or directory exists

Function	Description
`is_file($path)`	Returns TRUE if $path exists and is a file.
`is_dir($path)`	Returns TRUE if $path exists and is a directory.
`file_exists($path)`	Returns TRUE if $path exists and is either a file or a directory.

A function to get the current directory

Function	Description
`getcwd()`	Returns a string that specifies the current working directory.

A constant that contains the correct path separator

Constant	Description
`DIRECTORY_SEPARATOR`	A backslash on Windows servers or a forward slash on Mac OS and Linux servers.

A function to get a directory listing

Function	Description
`scandir($path)`	Returns an array containing a list of the files and directory in $path if $path is a valid directory name. Otherwise, it returns FALSE.

Display a directory listing

```php
$path = getcwd();
$items = scandir($path);
echo "<p>Contents of $path</p>";
echo '<ul>';
foreach ($items as $item) {
    echo '<li>' . $item . '</li>';
}
echo '</ul>';
```

Display the files from a directory listing

```php
$path = getcwd();
$items = scandir($path);
$files = array();
foreach ($items as $item) {
    $item_path = $path . DIRECTORY_SEPARATOR . $item;
    if (is_file($item_path)) {
        $files[] = $item;
    }
}
echo "<p>Files in $path</p>";
echo '<ul>';
foreach ($files as $file) {
    echo '<li>' . $file . '</li>';
}
echo '</ul>';
```

Figure 23-1   How to get a directory listing

How to read and write an entire file

Figure 23-2 presents three functions for reading an entire file with one statement. The file function reads each line of the file into a separate element in an array. The file_get_contents function reads the entire file into a single text string. And the readfile function reads a file and immediately echos it to the web page.

This figure also presents one function for writing an entire file. This file_put_contents function writes a text string to a file. If necessary, though, you can write an array of lines to a file by first using the implode function to convert the array to a string and then using the file_put_contents function.

The first example shows how to read text from a file. This code uses the file_get_contents function to read the file named message.txt and store its contents in the variable named $text. Since this code doesn't specify a directory for the file, this example looks for the file in the current directory. Then, this code uses the htmlspecialchars function to convert any special HTML characters to their corresponding character entities. Finally, this code uses an echo statement to send the text to the browser within a <div> tag.

The second example writes text to a file. First, this code stores the text in a variable named $text. Then, it uses the file_put_contents function to write the text to a file named message.txt.

The third example shows how to read the contents of a file into an array. First, this code uses the file function to read the file named username.txt. This stores each line of this file in an element of the $names array. Then, it uses a loop to display each element of the $names array inside of a <div> tag.

The fourth example shows how to write the contents of an array to a file. Here, the first statement creates the $names array and stores three elements in that array. Then, the second statement uses the implode function to concatenate the lines in the array in a single string with a new line character (\n) at the end of each line. Finally, this code uses the file_put_contents function to write the $names string to the file named message.txt. Note that the new line character (\n) must be in double quotes. If it's inside single quotes, this code will separate the lines with a backslash and an n, which isn't what you want.

Three functions to read an entire file

Function	Description
`file($name)`	Returns an array with each element containing one line from the file.
`file_get_contents($name)`	Returns the contents of the file as a string.
`readfile($name)`	Reads a file and echoes it to the web page.

A function to write an entire file

Function	Description
`file_put_contents($name, $data)`	Writes the specified data string to the specified filename.

How to read and write text

Read text from a file

```
$text = file_get_contents('message.txt');
$text = htmlspecialchars($text);
echo '<div>' . $text . '</div>';
```

Write text to a file

```
$text = "This is line 1.\nThis is line 2.\n";
file_put_contents('message.txt', $text);
```

How to read and write arrays

Read a file into an array

```
$names = file('usernames.txt');
foreach ($names as $name) {
    echo '<div>' . $name . '</div>';
}
```

Write an array to a file

```
$names = array('joelmurach', 'rayharris', 'mikemurach');
$names = implode("\n", $names);
file_put_contents('usernames.txt', $names);
```

Description

- PHP provides functions that let you read an entire file into a string variable and write a string variable to a file.
- PHP also provides functions that let you read the lines of a file into an array and write the elements of an array to the lines of a file.

Figure 23-2   How to read and write an entire file

How to read and write part of a file

For small files, you can use the functions in the previous figure to read or write the entire file. For large files, though, you may need to read and write portions of a file at a time since this can use large amounts of internal memory. In that case, you can use the functions in figure 23-3 to read or write portions of a file within a loop until the entire file is processed.

When opening a file, you must specify how you want the file opened. That's why this figure starts by describing the four modes you can use with the fopen function that opens a file. The two most common modes are the 'rb' and 'wb' modes.

If you use 'wb' mode to open a file and the file already exists, the fopen function deletes the existing contents of the file even if you don't write anything to the file. As a result, if you want to create a new file, but you don't want to accidentally erase an existing file, you should use the 'xb' mode.

To open and close a file, you can use these three functions: fopen, feof, and fclose. The fopen function opens a file and returns a file pointer that's used by the other file functions to access the file. The feof function returns TRUE when the end of a file is reached. And the fclose function closes a file.

Once you have opened a file, you can read and write data using these three functions: fread, fgets, and fwrite. The fread function reads from a file until it reads in the specified number of bytes or it reaches the end of the file. The fgets function reads from a file until it reaches either the end of a line or the end of the file. And the fwrite function writes the specified data to the file. This function doesn't automatically include new line characters. As a result, if you want to start a new line, you must add code that writes new line characters to the file.

The first example in this figure uses the fopen function with the 'rb' mode to open a file for reading. Then, it uses a while loop to read the file until it reaches the end of the file. Within this loop, the first statement uses the fgets function to get one line from the file. However, if the fgets function returns a FALSE value, which means that no line was read, the continue statement jumps to the top of the loop. Then, if the feof function returns a TRUE value, the loop ends.

Otherwise, this code trims any spaces from the name. Then, if the name is an empty string or begins with a pound sign, the continue statement jumps to the top of the loop. Otherwise, this code surrounds the name with a <div> tag and appends it to the $names variable. After the loop, this code closes the file and displays the list of names.

The second example starts by using the scandir function to retrieve a directory listing for the current working directory, and it stores this listing in an array named $items. Then, this code uses the fopen function with the "wb" mode to open the file named listing.txt for writing. Next, this code loops through the $items array and tests each item in the array. If an item is a directory, it is written to the file along with a new line character. After the loop, this code closes the file.

Modes used when opening a file with the fopen function

Mode	Description
'rb'	Opens the file for reading. If the file doesn't exist, fopen returns FALSE.
'wb'	Opens the file for writing. If the file exists, the existing data is deleted. If the file doesn't exist, it is created.
'ab'	Opens the file for writing. If the file exists, the new data is appended. If the file doesn't exist, it is created.
'xb'	Creates a new file for writing. If the file exists, fopen returns FALSE.

Functions that open and close a file

Function	Description
fopen(*$path, $mode*)	Opens the specified file with the specified mode and returns a file handle.
feof(*$file*)	Returns TRUE when the end of the specified file is reached.
fclose(*$file*)	Closes the specified file.

Functions that read from and write to a file

Function	Description
fread(*$file, $length*)	Reads up to the specified number of bytes from the specified file.
fgets(*$file*)	Reads a line from the specified file.
fwrite(*$file, $data*)	Writes the specified string data to the specified file.

Read from a file

```
$file = fopen('usernames.txt', 'rb');
$names = '';
while (!feof($file)) {
    $name = fgets($file);
    if ($name === false) continue;
    $name = trim($name);
    if (strlen($name) == 0 || substr($name, 0, 1) == '#') continue;
    $names .= "<div>" . $name . "</div>\n";
}
fclose($file);
echo $names;
```

Write to a file

```
$path = getcwd();
$items = scandir($path);
$file = fopen('listing.txt', 'wb');
foreach ($items as $item) {
    $item_path = $path . DIRECTORY_SEPARATOR . $item;
    if (is_dir($item_path)) {
        fwrite($file, $item . "\n");
    }
}
fclose($file);
```

Figure 23-3   How to read and write part of a file

How to read and write CSV data

When you work with text files, you may use a type of text file called a *comma-separated value (CSV) file*. This type of file is often exported from a spreadsheet or database table, and it can be imported into a spreadsheet or database table.

In a CSV file, each line represents one record, and each record contains values (or fields) that are separated by commas. If a field within a record contains a comma, double quote, or line break, the field must be surrounded by double quotes. In addition, any double quotes inside the field must be escaped by another set of double quotes.

Figure 23-4 describes two PHP functions that you can use to read from and write to CSV files. The fgetcsv function reads one line of comma-separated values and returns an array that contains the fields in the line. The fputcsv function writes each element in an array to a file as a line of comma-separated values.

In this figure, the examples work with a simple CSV file that consists of two lines of product data. Each line contains the product ID, description, and price of one product.

The first example writes product data to a CSV file. Here, the first statement creates an array named $products that stores two nested arrays that contain the data for two products. Then, the code opens a file named products.csv for reading and stores the file handle in the variable named $file. Next, the code uses a loop to write each element in the products array to the products.csv file. Within the loop, the putcsv function writes the data for each product to a line in the CSV file. After the loop, the code closes the file.

The second example reads product data from a CSV file and builds a nested array of product data named $products. First, the code opens the file named products.csv for reading and creates an empty array named $products. Then, the code loops through the file until it reaches the end of the file. Within the loop, the first statement reads one line of the CSV file and returns an array named $product. Then, the second statement checks whether there was an error reading the file. If so, the code executes a continue statement to skip the rest of the loop and try the next line. Otherwise, the code adds the $product array to the $products array. Finally, this code uses an echo statement to send the data for the product to the browser.

Functions that read and write CSV files

Function	Description
`fgetcsv($file)`	Reads in a line of comma-separated values and returns them in an array.
`fputcsv($file, $array)`	Writes the specified array to the specified file as a line of comma-separated values.

A simple CSV file

```
MMS-1234,Trumpet,199.95
MMS-8521,Flute,149.95
```

Write tabular data to a CSV file

```php
$products = array(array('MMS-1234', 'Trumpet', 199.95),
                  array('MMS-8521', 'Flute', 149.95));
$file = fopen('products.csv', 'wb');
foreach ($products as $product) {
    fputcsv($file, $product);
}
fclose($file);
```

Read tabular data from a CSV file

```php
$file = fopen('products.csv', 'rb');
$products = array();
while (!feof($file)) {
    $product = fgetcsv($file);
    if ($product === false) continue;
    $products[] = $product;
    echo "<div>$product[0] | $product[1] | $product[2]</div>";
}
```

Description

- In a *comma-separated value (CSV) file*, each line represents one record, and each record contains values (or fields) that are separated by commas.

- If a value in a CSV file contains commas, double quotes, or line breaks, the value must be enclosed within double quotes.

- CSV files are often exported from spreadsheets or database tables, and they can be imported to create spreadsheets or database tables.

Figure 23-4   How to read and write CSV data

How to copy, rename, and delete a file

When you work with files, you often need to copy, rename, or delete a file. To do that, you can use the three functions described in figure 23-5.

The first example in this figure shows how to use the copy function to make a copy of a file. Here, the first two statements create variables that store the old filename (the source) and the new filename (the destination). Then, this code checks whether the old file exists. If so, it uses the copy function to copy the old file to the new filename, and it stores the result in a variable named $success. If successful, this code sends a message to the browser.

Although you don't have to check whether the old file exists, it's usually a good practice. If you don't check and the file doesn't exist, PHP generates a warning message. In addition, you may want to check to make sure the new file doesn't exist. Otherwise, if this file exists, it will be overwritten by the old file.

The second example shows how to use the rename function to rename a file, and the third example show how to use the unlink function to delete a file. These examples work similarly to the first example, except that they use the rename and unlink functions instead of the copy function. As a result, the old file is renamed or deleted instead of copied.

Functions to copy, rename, and delete files

Function	Description
`copy($oldname, $newname)`	Copies the old filename to the new filename. If successful, returns TRUE.
`rename($oldname, $newname)`	Renames the old filename to the new filename. If successful, returns TRUE.
`unlink($name)`	Deletes the specified file. If successful, returns TRUE.

Copy a file

```
$name1 = 'message.txt';
$name2 = 'message_2.txt';
if (file_exists($name1)) {
    $success = copy($name1, $name2);
    if ($success) {
        echo '<div>File was copied </div>';
    }
}
```

Rename a file

```
$name2 = 'message_2.txt';
$name3 = 'message_copy.txt';
if (file_exists($name2)) {
    $success = rename($name2, $name3);
    if ($success) {
        echo '<div>File was renamed.</div>';
    }
}
```

Delete a file

```
$name3 = 'message_copy.txt';
if (file_exists($name3)) {
    $success = unlink($name3);
    if ($success) {
        echo '<div>File was deleted.</div>';
    }
}
```

Description

- PHP provides three functions that make it easy to copy, rename, or delete a file.

Figure 23-5   How to copy, rename, and delete a file

How to upload a file

Now that you know how to work with files, you're ready to learn how to let your users upload any type of file to a web server: text files, XML files, image files, sound files, video files, and so on. In a new XAMPP installation, the maximum upload file size is 128 MB, but most web hosting companies set this value much lower.

HTML for uploading a file

To upload a file, you code an HTML form like the one at the top of figure 23-6. Here, the method attribute must be set to "post" and the enctype attribute must be set to "multipart/form-data". Within the form, you must code an <input> tag that has its type attribute set to a value of "file". This is the tag that causes the text box and the Browse button to be displayed. The automatic behavior of this tag is to upload the file that's identified by the path in the text box.

You must also set the name attribute for this input tag. This is the name that you use in your PHP code to refer to the uploaded file. Here, the name has been set to "file1". If you want to let the users upload more than one file in a single form, you just code more <input> tags, but with different name attributes.

PHP for working with an uploaded file

When the user clicks on the submit button for the form, the file is uploaded, and the server saves it to a temporary file. Then, you can use PHP to get the temporary file and move it to a permanent location. To do that, you use the autoglobal $_FILES array to get information about each uploaded file. This array contains one nested array for each uploaded file that contains elements that provide the information shown in the table in this figure. Then, you can use the move_uploaded_file function to move each temporary file to a permanent location on the web server.

In the example, the first PHP statement uses the $_FILES array to get the temporary name ('tmp_name') of the uploaded file that corresponds to the <input> tag with 'file1' as its name attribute. The second statement creates a path to the 'images' subdirectory of the current directory. The third statement modifies that path so it includes the original filename ('name') of the uploaded file. The fourth statement uses the move_uploaded_file function to move the temporary file to the path on the server. And the fifth statement checks whether the file was moved successfully. If so, it stores a message that can be displayed to the user.

Although it isn't shown in this figure, you can also use the 'size', 'type', and 'error' indexes to get more information about the uploaded file. In particular, you can use the 'error' index to make sure the file was successfully uploaded.

An HTML form for uploading a file

```
<form action="upload.php" method="post" enctype="multipart/form-data">
    <input type="file" name="file1"><br />
    <input type="submit" value="Upload">
</form>
```

The browser display of the HTML

Elements of the nested arrays in the $_FILES array

Index	Description
`'name'`	The original name of the uploaded file.
`'size'`	The size of the uploaded file in bytes.
`'tmp_name'`	The temporary name of the uploaded file on the web server.
`'type'`	The MIME type of the uploaded file as sent by the user's browser.
`'error'`	The error code associated with the file. Common values are UPLOAD_ERR_OK (no error), UPLOAD_ERR_INI_SIZE (file was too large), and UPLOAD_ERR_PARTIAL (upload was not completed).

A function to save an uploaded file

Function	Description
`move_uploaded_file($tmp, $new)`	Moves an uploaded file from its temporary location to a permanent location. If successful, returns TRUE.

PHP for working with an uploaded file

```
$tmp_name = $_FILES['file1']['tmp_name'];
$path = getcwd() . DIRECTORY_SEPARATOR . 'images';
$name = $path . DIRECTORY_SEPARATOR . $_FILES['file1']['name'];
$success = move_uploaded_file($tmp_name, $name);
if ($success) {
    $upload_message = $name . ' has been uploaded.';
}
```

Description

- The <form> tag must have its method attribute set to "post" and its enctype attribute set to "multipart/form-data". Then, one <input> tag must have its type attribute set to a value of "file". This tag is displayed as a text box followed by a Browse button.

- The $_FILES array contains information about each uploaded file. The index for a file in the $_FILES array corresponds to the name attribute of the <input> tag for the file.

- The temporary file for the uploaded file is deleted when the script ends.

- In XAMPP, the maximum upload file size is 128 MB. However, web hosting companies typically set the value much lower.

Figure 23-6   How to upload a file

How to work with images

If you let your users upload images, you may want to process the images so they're appropriate for your application. For example, you often need a large, medium, and small size for each image that's used by an application. So, if a user uploads a large image, you may want to create medium and small sizes of that image. Also, if your application uses transparent images, you need to make sure that you don't lose the transparency of the images when you resize them.

PHP provides several image processing libraries that let you perform this type of processing. The one that you'll learn about in this chapter is the *GD library*. This library lets you to work with most image types including GIF, JPEG, and PNG. For this library to work properly, it must be installed with your version of PHP. But if you installed XAMPP as described in the appendix, this library should be ready for use.

How to get information about an image

Figure 23-7 shows how to use the getimagesize function. This function allows you to get the width and height of the image in pixels as well as other information such as the type of the image.

The example in this figure begins by setting the path to an image named gibson_sg.png. Then, it uses the getimagesize function to return an array that contains information about the image. Although this array contains seven elements that contain information about the image, this figure just shows the first three elements, which are the most commonly used. Index 0 returns the width of the image, index 1 returns the height of the image, and index 2 returns a constant that identifies the type of the image. For more information about the other indexes, you can look up the getimagesize function in the PHP documentation.

In this example, the image is a PNG image, so index 2 returns the IMAGETYPE_PNG constant. But if the image were a JPEG image, this index would return the IMAGETYPE_JPEG constant. Although this figure only shows the constants for the GIF, JPEG, and PNG types, the GD library also provides constants for many other types of images. For a complete list, look up the image_type_to_mime_type function in the online PHP documentation.

A function that gets information about an image

Name	Description
getimagesize(*$path*)	Returns an array that contains seven elements that provide information about the image. Index 0 gets the image width, index 1 gets the image height, and index 2 gets one of the IMAGETYPE_*XXX* constants that specifies the type of the image.

Common IMAGETYPE constants

```
IMAGETYPE_JPEG
IMAGETYPE_GIF
IMAGETYPE_PNG
```

Code that gets information about an image

```
// Set the path to the image
$image_path = getcwd() . DIRECTORY_SEPARATOR . 'gibson_sg.png';

// Get the image width, height, and type
$image_info = getimagesize($image_path);
$image_width = $image_info[0];
$image_height = $image_info[1];
$image_type = $image_info[2];

// Display the image type
switch($image_type) {
    case IMAGETYPE_JPEG:
        echo 'This is a JPEG image.<br />';
        break;
    case IMAGETYPE_GIF:
        echo 'This is a GIF image.<br />';
        break;
    case IMAGETYPE_PNG:
        echo 'This is a PNG image.<br />';
        break;
    default:
        echo 'File must be a JPEG, GIF, or PNG image.<br />';
        exit;
}
```

Description

- You can use the *GD library* to process existing images and to generate images from scratch.
- The GD library provides support for most image types including the GIF, JPEG, and PNG types.
- To be able to use the functions from the GD library, the GD library must be installed with your version of PHP. By default, the XAMPP installation includes the GD library.

Figure 23-7   How to get information about an image

How to read and write images

Figure 23-8 shows how to read and write images. To start, you can create an image from a file by using one of the imagecreatefrom*xxx* functions such as the imagecreatefromgif, imagecreatefromjpeg, and imagecreatefrompng functions. Then, if necessary, you can use the imagesx and imagesy function to get the width and height of the image, and you can do any processing on the image that you need to do.

When you're done processing an image, you can write the image to a file by using one of the imagexxx functions such as the imagegif, imagejpeg, and imagepng functions. Finally, since images take a substantial amount of memory, you can use the imagedestroy function to free the image from memory when you're done working with the image.

The example in this figure begins by getting the paths for two images. Then, this code gets a constant for the image type and uses a switch statement to set up the appropriate function names to read and write the image to and from a file. If the image isn't of the JPEG, GIF, or PNG type, this code displays an appropriate message.

After setting up the functions for the image type, this code creates the new image by reading it from the specified file. To do that, this code uses the function name that's stored as a string in the $image_from_file variable. In this case, the image is of the PNG type, so the code uses the imagecreatefrompng function. However, if the image were of the GIF or JPEG type, this code would use the appropriate function for that type.

After creating the image from a file, this code gets the height and width for the image. At this point, the code could do more processing on the image. For example, the code could resize the image as described in the next figure.

After this code processes the image, it uses the function that's stored in the $image_to_file variable to write the image to the second file path. Again, since this example uses a PNG image, this code uses the appropriate function for writing a PNG image: the imagepng function. Finally, this code uses the imagedestroy function to free any memory associated with the image.

Functions that work with images

Name	Description
imagecreatefrom*xxx*(*$path*)	Creates an image of the *xxx* type from the specified file path.
imagesx(*$image*)	Returns the width of the specified image.
imagesy(*$image*)	Returns the height of the specified image.
image*xxx*(*$image*, *$path*)	Writes the specified image of the *xxx* type to the specified file path.
imagedestroy(*$image*)	Frees any memory that's used for the specified image.

Code that reads and writes an image

```php
// Set the paths for the images
$image_path = getcwd() . DIRECTORY_SEPARATOR . 'gibson_sg.png';
$image_path_2 = getcwd() . DIRECTORY_SEPARATOR . 'gibson_sg_2.png';

// Get the image width, height, and type
$image_info = getimagesize($image_path);
$image_type = $image_info[2];

// Set up the function names for the image type
switch($image_type) {
    case IMAGETYPE_JPEG:
        $image_from_file = 'imagecreatefromjpeg';
        $image_to_file = 'imagejpeg';
        break;
    case IMAGETYPE_GIF:
        $image_from_file = 'imagecreatefromgif';
        $image_to_file = 'imagegif';
        break;
    case IMAGETYPE_PNG:
        $image_from_file = 'imagecreatefrompng';
        $image_to_file = 'imagepng';
        break;
    default:
        echo 'File must be a JPEG, GIF, or PNG image.';
        exit;
}

// Create a new image from the file
$image = $image_from_file($image_path);

// Check the image's width and height
$image_width = imagesx($image);
$image_height = imagesy($image);

// Write the image to a file
$image_to_file($image, $image_path_2);

// Free any memory associated with the image
imagedestroy($image);
```

Figure 23-8   How to read and write images

How to resize an image

Figure 23-9 shows how to resize an image. In particular, it shows how to resize a large image to a smaller size. This decreases the display size and file size of the image, which helps the image load faster, and it doesn't degrade the visual quality of the image. Although you can use similar techniques to create a larger image, this increases the file size and decreases the visual quality of the image. As a result, there's rarely a reason to increase the size of an image.

To resize an image, you can use the imagecreatetruecolor function to create a new truecolor image of a smaller size. A *truecolor image* uses *RGB values* that consist of 256 shades of red, green, and blue.

After you create a new image of a smaller size, you can use the imagecopyresampled function to copy the large image to the smaller image. This function resamples and resizes the image so it fits in the smaller image.

When you resize an image, you typically want to resize the height and width by the same ratio. Otherwise, the image gets stretched in a way that distorts the original image. To avoid this, you need to perform calculations like the ones in the example in this figure so you can get the correct height and width for the ratio.

This example begins by setting up two paths for the image. Then, it gets the height and width of the old image (the source image). Next, it calculates the ratio of the height and width of that image compared to a value of 100 pixels. For example, if the height of the image is 300, the height ratio is 3. And if the width of the image is 400, the width ration is 4.

After calculating the height and width ratios, this code checks whether either of the ratios is greater than 1. If so, it executes code that creates an image that's a maximum of 100 pixels by 100 pixels. To start, this code uses the max function to get the larger of the two ratios. Then, it uses that ratio to calculate the height and width of the new image (the destination image). Next, it creates the new image and copies the old image to the new image. To do that, this code uses a value of 0 for the x and y values of the old and new images to indicate that both images should start at the upper left corner. In addition, it specifies the correct values for the height and width of the old and new images.

After the image has been resized, this code writes the new image to a new file. Here, the filename (gibson_sg_100.png) indicates that the image is a maximum of 100 by 100 pixels. Then, this code frees any memory associated with the new and old images.

Functions that can resize an image

Name	Description
imagecreatetruecolor(*$w, $h*)	Returns an all black truecolor image of the specified size.
imagecopyresampled(*$di, $si,* *$dx, $dy, $sx, $sy,* *$dw, $dh, $sw, $sh*)	Copies a rectangular portion of the source image (s) to the destination image (d), resizing the image if necessary.

Code that resizes an image to a 100 by 100 pixel maximum

```
// Set some variables
$old_path = getcwd() . DIRECTORY_SEPARATOR . 'gibson_sg.png';
$new_path = getcwd() . DIRECTORY_SEPARATOR . 'gibson_sg_100.png';
$image_type = IMAGETYPE_PNG;

// Get the old image and its height and width
$old_image = imagecreatefrompng($old_path);
$old_width = imagesx($old_image);
$old_height = imagesy($old_image);

// Calculate height and width ratios for a 100x100 pixel maximum
$width_ratio = $old_width / 100;
$height_ratio = $old_height / 100;

// If image is larger than specified ratio, create the new image
if ($width_ratio > 1 || $height_ratio > 1) {

    // Calculate height and width for the new image
    $ratio = max($width_ratio, $height_ratio);
    $new_height = round($old_height / $ratio);
    $new_width = round($old_width / $ratio);

    // Create the new image
    $new_image = imagecreatetruecolor($new_width, $new_height);

    // Copy old image to new image to resize the file
    $new_x = 0;          // Start new image in upper left corner
    $new_y = 0;
    $old_x = 0;          // Copy old image from upper left corner
    $old_y = 0;
    imagecopyresampled($new_image, $old_image,
                    $new_x, $new_y, $old_x, $old_y,
                    $new_width, $new_height, $old_width, $old_height);

    // Write the new image to a file
    imagepng($new_image, $new_path);

    // Free any memory associated with the new image
    imagedestroy($new_image);
}

// Free any memory associated with the old image
imagedestroy($old_image);
```

Figure 23-9   How to resize an image

How to work with transparency

Transparency refers to the portions of an image that are transparent. If, for example, an image that contains a star is placed on a green background, the green background shows through the transparent parts of the image that surround the star. Although JPEG images don't allow parts of the image to be transparent, GIF and PNG images do provide for transparency.

A transparent image not only stores the RGB values for the colors, but also stores an *alpha channel* that provides additional information about the transparency. Then, the browser can combine the transparent parts of the image with the background to create the transparency effect. This process is known as *alpha blending*.

When you create a new truecolor image as described in the previous figure, the image has a black background by default. As a result, if you copy an image that uses transparency onto this black background, the background of the image is black and the transparency is lost. To avoid this, you can use the functions and techniques in figure 23-10 to control the transparency of the image.

In the example in this figure, the first if statement checks whether the image is a GIF image. If so, this code performs some processing that needs to be done for GIF images, but doesn't need to be done for PNG images. In particular, the first statement calls the imagecolorallocatealpha function to allocate the alpha color. In this case, the function sets the alpha color to black by specifying RGB values of 0, 0, and 0. In addition, it specifies an alpha value of 127 to indicate that the alpha color should be completely transparent. Then, the next statement uses the imagecolortransparent function to set the alpha color as the transparent color in the image.

The second if statement checks whether the image is a GIF image or a PNG image. If so, this code does the rest of the processing that's necessary for GIF images, and it does the only processing that's necessary for PNG images. Here, the first statement turns off alpha blending. This is necessary if you want the full alpha channel information to be saved. Then, the second statement attempts to save the full alpha channel information. If successful, this code creates an image that has parts that are completely transparent.

When you're done processing an image, you may want to view it to see how it looks. To do that, you can use Windows Explorer or Mac Finder to view the image. Or, you can open the image in a graphics editing program such as Photoshop. These programs typically use a background color or checkered pattern for the transparency portion of the image.

Functions that work with image transparency

Name	Description
imagecolorallocatealpha($i, $r, $g, $b, $a)	Returns an identifier for the transparent (alpha) color of the specified image. The RGB values specify the color. The alpha value specifies the amount of transparency. This value can range from 0 to 127 with 127 being completely transparent.
imagecolortransparent($i, $a)	Sets the transparent color in the specified image.
imagealphablending($i, $f)	To turn alpha blending mode off, set the second parameter to FALSE.
imagesavealpha($i, $f)	To attempt to save full alpha channel information, set the second parameter to TRUE. For this to work, alpha blending mode must be turned off.

Code that works with the transparency of an image

```
// code that calculates the width and height for the new image
// and sets the image type for the new image

$new_image = imagecreatetruecolor($new_width, $new_height);

// Set transparency according to image type
if ($image_type == IMAGETYPE_GIF) {
    $alpha = imagecolorallocatealpha($new_image, 0, 0, 0, 127);
    imagecolortransparent($new_image, $alpha);
}
if ($image_type == IMAGETYPE_PNG || $image_type == IMAGETYPE_GIF) {
    imagealphablending($new_image, false);
    imagesavealpha($new_image, true);
}

// code that writes the new image to a file
```

Description

- *Transparency* refers to portions of an image that are transparent. Although JPEG images don't provide for transparency, GIF and PNG images do provide for it.

- A transparent image stores RGB values for the colors, and it stores an *alpha channel* that provides additional information about the transparency.

- When a transparent image is displayed, the browser combines the transparent parts of the image with the background to create the transparency effect. This process is known as *alpha blending*.

Figure 23-10   How to work with transparency

The Image Upload application

To show you how the skills that you've just learned can be used in a application, figure 23-11 presents an Image Upload application. This application lets the user upload an image file from the client to the server. Then, if necessary, this application creates two smaller versions of the image. This application also lets the user view these images or delete them.

The user interface

The first page in the user interface starts with a form that lets the user upload a file. This form includes a Browse button that lets the user select the file. Then, after the user selects a file, this application displays the path to the file in the text box in the form. Last, this form includes an Upload button that lets the user upload the selected file.

After the form, this page displays a list of files that are already in the images directory. In this example, a user has already uploaded a file named gibson_sg.png, and the application has already generated two files from it. The first file is named "gibson_sg_100.png" and it has a maximum width of 100 pixels. The second file is named "gibson_sg_400.png" and it has a maximum width of 400 pixels.

In this list of images, the user can click on the delete icon to the left of the image to delete the image. Or, the user can click on the name of the image to view the image as shown by the second page of this application.

The user interface

An image displayed in the browser

Figure 23-11   The Upload Image application (part 1 of 6)

The utility files

Parts 2 through 4 of this figure show the code for the two utility files that are used by the controller of the Upload Image application.

The first file (file_util.php) contains the get_file_list function that returns an array of the filenames in the directory path that's passed to it. However, if the path that's passed to it isn't valid, this function returns an empty array. Since the code in this function is so similar to the code in figure 23-1, you shouldn't have any trouble understanding it.

The second file (image_util.php) contains a process_image function that is used to create 100- and 400-pixel versions of an image, if that's necessary, plus a helper function named resize_image that actually does the resizing.

The process_image function accepts two parameters: the directory for the image and the filename for the image. Then, the first four statements set up the variables that are needed throughout the function. The first statement adds a separator to the end of the directory parameter, so a directory named "images" becomes "images/". The second statement gets the index for the dot in the filename. The third statement stores the name of the file without its extension. And the fourth statement stores the extension of the file.

Then, the process_image function sets up the read path for the old image and the write paths for the new images. For the write paths, this code appends "_400" to the name of the file to indicate a maximum width of 400 pixels, and it appends "_100" to the name of the file to indicate a maximum width of 100 pixels.

Last, this code calls the resize_image function twice to create the two smaller versions of the image. This function is shown in parts 3 and 4 of this figure. Since its code is similar to the code in the last four figures, you shouldn't have much trouble understanding it. But here's a quick summary.

The file_util.php file

```php
function get_file_list($path) {
    $files = array();
    if (!is_dir($path)) return $files;

    $items = scandir($path);
    foreach ($items as $item) {
        $item_path = $path . DIRECTORY_SEPARATOR . $item;
        if (is_file($item_path)) {
            $files[] = $item;
        }
    }
    return $files;
}
```

The image_util.php file

```php
<?php
function process_image($dir, $filename) {
    // Set up the variables
    $dir = $dir . DIRECTORY_SEPARATOR;
    $i = strrpos($filename, '.');
    $image_name = substr($filename, 0, $i);
    $ext = substr($filename, $i);

    // Set up the read path
    $image_path = $dir . DIRECTORY_SEPARATOR . $filename;

    // Set up the write paths
    $image_path_400 = $dir . $image_name . '_400' . $ext;
    $image_path_100 = $dir . $image_name . '_100' . $ext;

    // Create an image that's a maximum of 400x300 pixels
    resize_image($image_path, $image_path_400, 400, 300);

    // Create a thumbnail image that's a maximum of 100x100 pixels
    resize_image($image_path, $image_path_100, 100, 100);
}
```

Figure 23-11   The Upload Image application (part 2 of 6)

In part 3, you can see that the resize_image function accepts four parameters: the path to the old image, the path to the new image, and the maximum width and height of the new image. Then, the first two statements get a constant that identifies the image type for the old image, and a switch statement sets up the appropriate functions for reading and writing an image of this type. For a PNG image, for example, it uses the imagecreatefrompng to read the image from a file, and it uses the imagepng function to write the image to a file.

After the switch statement, this function reads the old image into memory and gets its height and width. Then, it calculates the height and width ratios that correspond with the maximum height and width parameters.

The image_util.php file (continued)

```php
function resize_image($old_image_path, $new_image_path,
    $max_width, $max_height) {

    // Get image type
    $image_info = getimagesize($old_image_path);
    $image_type = $image_info[2];

    // Set up the function names
    switch($image_type) {
        case IMAGETYPE_JPEG:
            $image_from_file = 'imagecreatefromjpeg';
            $image_to_file = 'imagejpeg';
            break;
        case IMAGETYPE_GIF:
            $image_from_file = 'imagecreatefromgif';
            $image_to_file = 'imagegif';
            break;
        case IMAGETYPE_PNG:
            $image_from_file = 'imagecreatefrompng';
            $image_to_file = 'imagepng';
            break;
        default:
            echo 'File must be a JPEG, GIF, or PNG image.';
            exit;
    }

    // Get the old image and its height and width
    $old_image = $image_from_file($old_image_path);
    $old_width = imagesx($old_image);
    $old_height = imagesy($old_image);

    // Calculate height and width ratios
    $width_ratio = $old_width / $max_width;
    $height_ratio = $old_height / $max_height;
```

Figure 23-11   The Upload Image application (part 3 of 6)

In part 4, if either the height ratio or the width ratio is greater than 1, the old image is larger than maximum height or width. As a result, the code resizes the old image so it conforms to the maximum height or width that's specified. To do that, the code begins by getting the larger ratio of the two. Then, it uses that ratio to calculate the new height and width for the new image, and it creates a new truecolor image of that height and width.

After creating the new image, this code sets the transparency for GIF or PNG images. As a result, if the user uploads a GIF or PNG image that uses transparency, the images that are created also use transparency. Then, this code copies the old image to the new path, which creates and resizes a new image. Next, this code writes the new image to the specified file path. Finally, the last line within the if clause frees any memory used by the new image.

The else clause after the if clause is executed if the height ratio and the width ratio are both less than 1, which means the old image is smaller than the maximum height or width. Then, the code doesn't resize the old image. Instead, it writes a copy of the old image to the new path. Last, after the if statement ends, the imagedestory function is used to free any memory used by the old image.

The image_util.php file (continued)

```php
    // If image is larger than specified ratio, create the new image
    if ($width_ratio > 1 || $height_ratio > 1) {

        // Calculate height and width for the new image
        $ratio = max($width_ratio, $height_ratio);
        $new_height = round($old_height / $ratio);
        $new_width = round($old_width / $ratio);

        // Create the new image
        $new_image = imagecreatetruecolor($new_width, $new_height);

        // Set transparency according to image type
        if ($image_type == IMAGETYPE_GIF) {
            $alpha = imagecolorallocatealpha($new_image, 0, 0, 0, 127);
            imagecolortransparent($new_image, $alpha);
        }
        if ($image_type == IMAGETYPE_PNG || $image_type == IMAGETYPE_GIF) {
            imagealphablending($new_image, false);
            imagesavealpha($new_image, true);
        }

        // Copy old image to new image - this resizes the image
        $new_x = 0;
        $new_y = 0;
        $old_x = 0;
        $old_y = 0;
        imagecopyresampled($new_image, $old_image,
                           $new_x, $new_y, $old_x, $old_y,
                           $new_width, $new_height, $old_width, $old_height);

        // Write the new image to a new file
        $image_to_file($new_image, $new_image_path);

        // Free any memory associated with the new image
        imagedestroy($new_image);
    } else {
        // Write the old image to a new file
        $image_to_file($old_image, $new_image_path);
    }
    // Free any memory associated with the old image
    imagedestroy($old_image);
}

?>
```

Figure 23-11   The Upload Image application (part 4 of 6)

The controller

Part 5 shows the controller for the Upload Image application. To start, the controller imports the two utility files that you just reviewed. Next, it creates two variables that are used to work with the directory that's used to store the images. Then, it gets the current action.

This action has a default value of an empty string. As a result, the first time the controller runs, it skips over the switch statement, gets the list of uploaded files, and displays the view. However, if the action has been set to a value of "upload" or "delete", the controller executes the appropriate code.

For the "upload" action, the controller checks whether the file has been set in the autoglobal $_FILES array. If so, it gets the original name of the file. However, if this filename is an empty string, this code uses a break statement to exit the switch statement.

If the filename isn't an empty string, the controller gets the temporary name for the file. Then, it moves the temporary file to its new permanent location in the images directory. Finally, it calls the process-image function to create the smaller versions of the uploaded file.

For the "delete" action, the controller gets the name of the file that the user wants to delete. Then, it checks if that image exists. If so, it uses the unlink function to delete the image.

After the switch statement the code continues by getting the list of uploaded files and displaying the view. This displays the first page of the application so the user can upload another image.

The controller (index.php)

```php
<?php
require_once 'file_util.php';  // the get_file_list function
require_once 'image_util.php'; // the process_image function

$image_dir = 'images';
$image_dir_path = getcwd() . DIRECTORY_SEPARATOR . $image_dir;

$action = '';
if (isset($_POST['action'])) {
    $action = $_POST['action'];
} else if (isset($_GET['action'])) {
    $action = $_GET['action'];
}

switch ($action) {
    case 'upload':
        if (isset($_FILES['file1'])) {
            $filename = $_FILES['file1']['name'];
            if (empty($filename)) {
                break;
            }
            $source = $_FILES['file1']['tmp_name'];
            $target = $image_dir_path . DIRECTORY_SEPARATOR . $filename;
            move_uploaded_file($source, $target);

            // create '400' and '100' versions of the image
            process_image($image_dir_path, $filename);
        }
        break;
    case 'delete':
        $filename = $_GET['filename'];
        $target = $image_dir_path . DIRECTORY_SEPARATOR . $filename;
        if (file_exists($target)) {
            unlink($target);
        }
        break;
}

$files = get_file_list($image_dir_path);
include('uploadform.php');
?>
```

Figure 23-11   The Upload Image application (part 5 of 6)

The view

Part 6 shows the code for the view. Most of this code is HTML code that you shouldn't have any trouble understanding. However, take a close look at the code for the upload form. Here, the second <input> tag displays the text box and the Browse button for the image file. This tag gives the uploaded file a name of "file1". Then, the third input tag displays the submit button for the form, the Upload button.

The PHP code after this form uses an if statement to check if the images directory contains any files. If it doesn't, a message is displayed that indicates that no images have been uploaded.

Otherwise, a loop is used to process each of the files in the directory. For each file, this loop creates two URLs that are used in the links that follow. The first one is used to display the image in a browser window. That's the default behavior for a link that identifies an image file.

The second URL is used to delete the file. To do that, this URL calls the current page with an "action" parameter of "delete" and a filename parameter that contains the filename.

Next, the loop displays an unordered list where each item in the list corresponds to one of the files in the images directory. Within each of these list items are two links that use the URLs that were created earlier in the loop. The first link displays an image named delete.png that's in the current directory. Then, when the user clicks on this image, control is passed to the controller with the appropriate parameters for deleting the file. The second link displays the filename for the image. When the user clicks on this name, the image is displayed.

The view (uploadform.php)

```
<!DOCTYPE html PUBLIC "-//W3C//DTD XHTML 1.0 Transitional//EN"
    "http://www.w3.org/TR/xhtml1/DTD/xhtml1-transitional.dtd">
<html xmlns="http://www.w3.org/1999/xhtml">
    <head>
        <title>Upload Image</title>
        <link rel="stylesheet" type="text/css" href="main.css">
    </head>
    <body>
        <div id="page">
            <div id="header">
                <h1>Upload Image</h1>
            </div>
            <div id="main">
                <h2>Image to be uploaded</h2>
                <form id="upload_form"
                    action="." method="POST"
                    enctype="multipart/form-data">
                  <input type="hidden" name="action" value="upload">
                  <input type="file" name="file1"><br />
                  <input id="upload_button" type="submit" value="Upload">
                </form>
                <h2>Images in the directory</h2>
                <?php if (count($files) == 0) : ?>
                    <p>No images uploaded.</p>
                <?php else: ?>
                    <ul>
                    <?php foreach($files as $filename) :
                        $file_url = $image_dir . '/' .
                                    $filename;
                        $delete_url = '.?action=delete&filename=' .
                                        urlencode($filename);
                    ?>
                        <li>
                            <a href="<?php echo $delete_url;?>">
                                <img src="delete.png" alt="Delete"></a>
                            <a href="<?php echo $file_url; ?>">
                                <?php echo $filename; ?></a>
                        </li>
                    <?php endforeach; ?>
                    </ul>
                <?php endif; ?>
            </div><!-- end main -->
        </div><!-- end page -->
    </body>
</html>
```

Figure 23-11   The Upload Image application (part 6 of 6)

Perspective

In this chapter, you learned how to work with files, how to upload a file, and how to work with images. These are critical skills for many types of web applications. However, as always, there is more to learn about these topics.

If, for example, you need to upload large files such as video files, you may want to display a progress bar so the user can view the progress of the upload. To do that, you can use a combination of PHP, DOM scripting, and AJAX. For more information, you can search the Internet for "PHP upload progress".

Similarly, if you need to do other types of image processing or if you need to create images from scratch, PHP provides several libraries that allow you to do that. To learn more, you can search the function list in the PHP documentation for "image". There, you'll see the documentation for the various libraries that you can use.

Terms

comma-separated value (CSV)	RGB value
CSV file	alpha channel
GD library	alpha blending
truecolor image	

Summary

- PHP provides many functions for working with files, including *comma-separated value (CSV) files*. In CSV file, each line represents one record, and each record contains values (or fields) that are separated by commas.

- The *GD library* is a PHP library for processing images that includes functions for processing existing images in the JPEG, GIF, and PNG formats.

- A *truecolor image* uses *RGB values* that consist of 256 shades of red, green, and blue.

- *Transparency* refers to portions of an image that are transparent. A transparent image stores an *alpha channel* that provides information about the transparency. Then, the browser can combine the transparent parts of the image with the background to create the transparency effect. This process is known as *alpha blending*.

Exercise 23-1   Work with uploads and images

This exercise gives you a chance to enhance the Upload application presented in this chapter.

Test the application

1. Run the application in the ex_starts/ch23_ex1 directory.

2. Test the application by uploading one or more of the image files in the ex_starts/ch23_images directory. Note that this creates three files for every image that you upload (the original file plus a file that's a maximum of 100 pixels wide and one that's a maximum of 400 pixels wide).

3. Use the application to view the uploaded images.

4. View the files in the ex_starts/ch23_ex1/images directory. Note that the uploaded files have been copied to this directory and that the processed versions of the files have also been stored in this directory.

5. Use the application to delete one or more of the files that you have uploaded.

Modify the code

6. Open the uploadform.php and modify it so it allows you to upload three files at a time. When you're through, the form should look something like this:

7. Open the index.php file and modify it so it provides for uploading one, two, or three files at a time. To avoid code duplication, you can create a function that performs the upload for each file.

8. Open the image_util.php file and modify the process_image function so it creates three new images. The first two should be a maximum of 100 and 400 pixels wide, and the third one should be a maximum of 250 pixels wide.

24

An eCommerce web site

If you've mastered the skills in the first 23 chapters of this book, you have all of the skills that you need for developing professional web sites. Now, to give you some ideas for how you can apply your skills to the development of an eCommerce web site, this chapter presents another version of the Guitar Shop web site that you last saw in chapter 20. Besides the functions that you saw in that chapter, this version lets customers create accounts and place orders. It also lets administrative users view and process those orders.

Although this chapter doesn't present any of the code for this web site, the code is available in the download for this book. So, after you read this chapter, you can test the web site, review the code in any of its files, and modify that code so it better suits your purposes. That's a great way to learn.

An introduction to the web site **780**
The directory structure of the web site 780
Prototyping and stepwise refinement 782
The user interface for end users **784**
The Catalog application 784
The Cart application 786
The Checkout and Account applications 786
The My Account page 788
The user interface for administrators **792**
The Admin Login and Admin Menu pages 792
The Product Manager application 794
The Category Manager application 794
The Order Manager application 794
The Account Manager application 794
Perspective **798**

An introduction to the web site

Before you review the Guitar Shop web site, you should realize that it isn't a complete web site or a thoroughly tested web site. Instead, you should think of it as a prototype that you can use as a source of ideas. In the topics that follow you'll first learn why you should use prototyping. Then, you'll review the directory structure for this prototype of an eCommerce web site.

Prototyping and stepwise refinement

As I'm sure you realize by now, designing and programming a web site is a challenging process. To complicate that, a web site usually has to please several types of users and reviewers so you can't just develop the pages and be done with them. In particular, you have to coordinate the programming for a web site with the graphics design of the web site.

That's why *prototyping* is commonly used during the development of a web site. This just means that you develop a working model (*prototype*) of the web site or the critical portions of the web site as early in the development process as possible. Then, the users and reviewers can actually use the pages to see how they work. That usually will raise concerns that can be resolved early in the development process, when the cost of fixing the problems is relatively inexpensive.

Along with prototyping, *stepwise refinement* is commonly used during the development of a web site. This just means that you can't design and implement a web site in a single step. Instead, you need to work the web site through successive levels of refinement with review, evaluation, and adjustment after each step.

With that as background, you can think of the web site for this chapter as a prototype that provides most of the functionality of an eCommerce web site. At this stage, the reviewers can use the applications of the site, evaluate them, and make recommendations for improvements. In addition, the web designers and programmers can start to coordinate their views of how the web site should look and work.

For instance, the Home page in figure 24-1 is obviously just a prototype of a Home page. Before it's done, the web designers will most likely design a header that includes a logo, a tag line, a navigation bar, and so on. They are also likely to put the View Cart, Login/Register, and Home links in the header. And they will remove the Admin link because that shouldn't be part of the user interface for end users. In this prototype, it's included just to make it easy for the reviewers and developers to move between the end user and admin applications.

So remember to think of the web site in this chapter as a functional or programmer's prototype. As you review it, you will find that some of the coding is minimal, especially in data validation routines. You are likely to discover bugs since this application hasn't been user tested. And you should have many ideas for how this web site can be improved. No matter what, though, you should learn a lot by seeing how this prototype works.

The Home page for a prototype of the Guitar Shop web site

Description

- A *prototype* is a working model of a web site or portion of a web site. This model lets the intended users and members of the development team evaluate how the pages are going to work and make recommendations for improvements.

- *Stepwise refinement* refers to the process of making step-by-step improvements to the prototype with review and evaluation after each step.

- One benefit of *prototyping* and stepwise refinement is that you detect problems early in the development cycle when they cost less to fix. Another benefit is that the users are more likely to be satisfied by the final version of the web site because they've participated in the development process.

- The web site that's presented in this chapter can be thought of as a programmer's prototype. It shows how the web site is going to work in terms of function. Then, the programmers can work with the web designers to get the web site looking and working the way everyone wants it to.

Figure 24-1   Prototyping and stepwise refinement

The directory structure of the web site

Figure 24-2 presents the directory structure for this web site. Here, you can see that the files for each of the applications in the web site are stored in a separate directory. For instance, the files for the Catalog, Cart, Checkout, and Account applications are stored in the catalog, cart, checkout, and account directories. These are the applications for the end users of the web site.

In contrast, the four applications for the administrative users are stored in four subdirectories of the admin directory. Specifically, the applications for managing accounts, categories, products, and orders are stored in the account, category, product, and orders subdirectories.

Notice that each of these application directories contains a controller file named index.php. This is the default file that is run for each directory. That file in turn displays the view files that are stored in the directory. For instance, the catalog directory contains two view files named category_view.php and product_view.php that are controlled by the index.php file.

Similarly, the application root directory (ch24_guitar_shop) contains an index.php file that is executed when the application starts. This controller then displays the page for the home_view.php file.

The other directories for this web site contain files for special purposes. For instance, the errors directory contains PHP files for displaying error pages. The images directory contains the image files that are used by the web site. The model directory contains the files that provide the database functions that are the model in the MVC pattern.

Similarly, the util directory contains utility files like the tags.php file from chapter 20 that parses the description entry when the data for a product is entered or edited. This directory also contains the main.php file that sets some global variables, defines some global functions, and calls the start_session function to start a session. This file is included at the start of all of the controller files.

That leaves the view directory, which contains the view files that can be used by any of the applications. That includes header, footer, product, and sidebar files.

For a production application, more than one style sheet (CSS file) is likely to be used so the directory structure would also include a directory for those files, with a name like "styles". For this prototype, though, the application root directory contains the one CSS file that's used for all of the pages of the ite.

A directory structure like this in combination with the MVC pattern makes it easier to maintain and enhance a web site. Suppose, for example, that you decide to use two different headers, one for the end user applications and one for the admin applications. To do that, you just add a second header file to the view directory and modify the files that use it so they include the new header instead of the old one.

Or, suppose you want to change the way the cart application works. You'll find the controller and view files in the cart directory, and you can go from there. In short, the larger an application gets, the more you benefit by a logical directory structure and the use of the MVC pattern.

The directory structure of the Guitar Shop web site

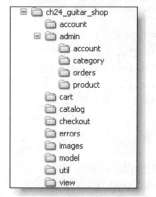

The files in the application root directory (ch24_guitar_shop)

```
home_view.php
index.php
main.css
```

The contents of the subdirectories

Directory	Description	Controller
account	PHP files that let users manage their accounts	index.php
cart	PHP files that show the user's shopping cart	index.php
catalog	PHP files that show category and product pages	index.php
checkout	PHP files that confirm orders and get payments	index.php
admin	PHP file for displaying the Admin Menu page	index.php
admin/account	PHP files for managing admin accounts	index.php
admin/category	PHP files for managing categories	index.php
admin/orders	PHP files for managing orders	index.php
admin/product	PHP files for managing products	index.php
errors	PHP files that display error pages	None
images	Image files	None
model	Database files that provide the database functions	None
util	Utility files for various purposes	None
view	Include files for views that can be used by any of the pages	None

Description

- The directory structure of a web site should group files in directories so it's easy to find the files for specific purposes.
- If a web site requires more than one CSS file, the CSS files are usually stored in a separate directory, often one named "styles".

Figure 24-2   The directory structure of the web site

The user interface for end users

With that as background, you're ready to take a quick look at the user interfaces for this prototype, starting with the interface for the end users. Since you've most likely bought something from more than one eCommerce web site, it should be easy to see how the interface for this prototype works.

The Catalog application

Part 1 of figure 24-3 shows the two pages of the Catalog application. The first one provides a way for the user to select a product. The second one displays the data for the product. This second page also provides an Add to Cart button that lets the user add the product to his or her cart.

If the user clicks this button, the Cart page in part 2 is displayed. Otherwise, the user can click on one of the links in the sidebar to view the cart, to log in or to register with the web site, to return to the Home page, or to display the products in other categories.

The user can also click on the Admin link to go to the Admin applications, but remember that button is for development only. It won't be available in the final version of the site.

The Category View page (catalog/category_view.php)

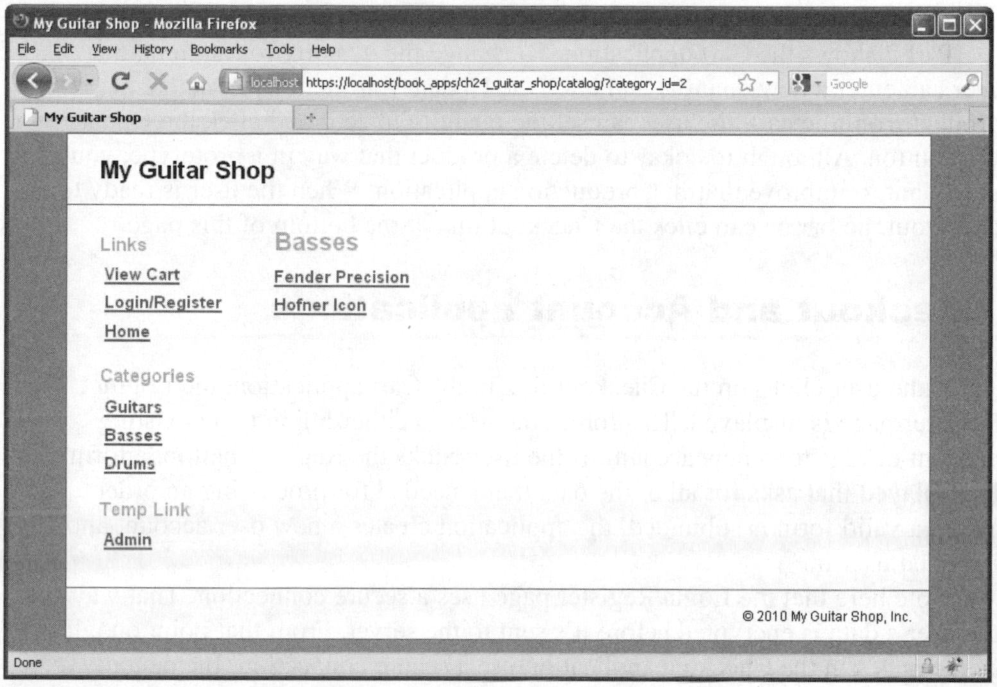

Product View page (catalog/product_view.php)

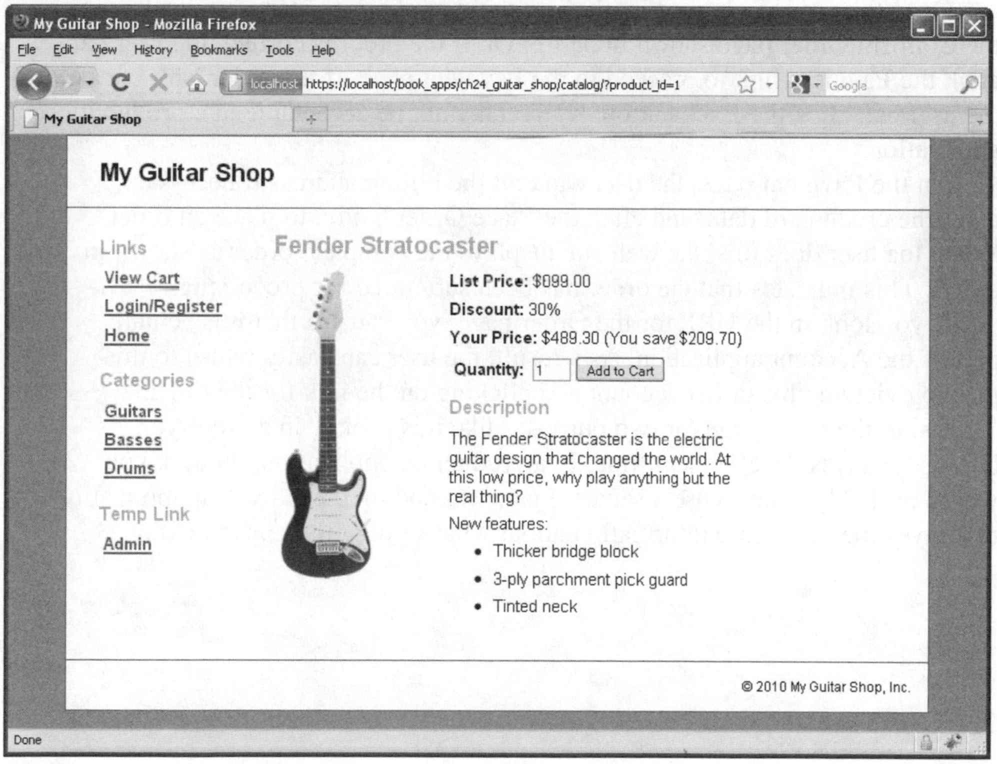

Figure 24-3   The user interface for end users (part 1 of 5)

The Cart application

Part 2 shows the Cart application. To change the quantity for an item, the user can enter a new quantity and click the Update Cart button. To delete a product from the cart, the user can set the quantity to zero and click the Update Cart button. Although it's okay to delete a product that way in a prototype, you may want to improve that in a production application. When the user is ready to check out, he or she can click the Checkout link at the bottom of this page.

The Checkout and Account applications

If the user clicks on the Checkout link in the Cart application, the Login/Register page is displayed. This forces the user to either log in to an existing account or register a new account. If the user clicks the Register button, a form is displayed that asks for all of the data that's needed for processing an order. When a valid form is submitted, the application creates a new user account and logs that user in.

Note here that the Login/Register page uses a secure connection. That way, the user's data is encrypted before it's sent to the server. From that point on, all of the pages in the Checkout application use a secure connection. Incidentally, the Login/Register page is actually a part of the Account application, which you'll learn more about in part 5 of this figure.

Once the user has logged in, the Checkout application starts by displaying the Confirm Order page shown in part 3. Or, if the order is correct, the user can click the Payment link to proceed to the Payment page. If the order isn't correct, the user can click the Back button, which may not be acceptable in a production application.

On the Payment page, the user can edit the billing address if necessary, enter the credit card data, and click the Place Order button to place an order. When the user does this, the web site displays the complete order as shown in part 4. This indicates that the order has been submitted for processing.

If you look in the URL for the Order page, you can see that it is actually part of the Account application. As a result, the user can easily return to this page by viewing his or her account and clicking on the link for the order.

Using the same page for two purposes like this is okay in a prototype because it saves development time. In a production application, though, you would probably want to use a separate page for ending the Checkout application that gives the user more information about what's going to happen next.

The Cart page (cart/cart_view.php)

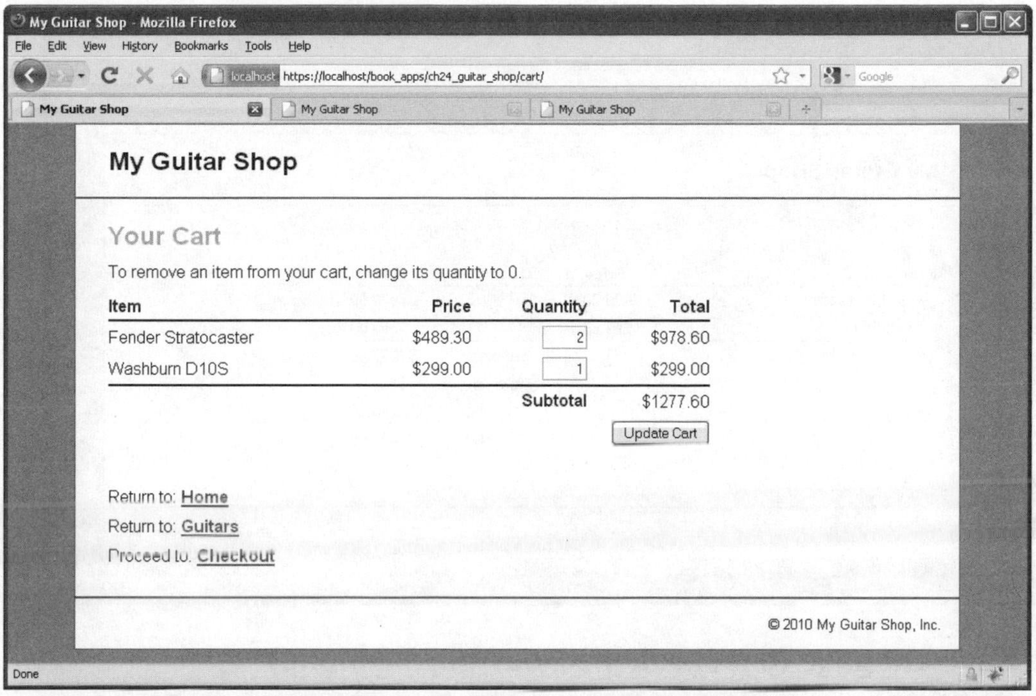

The Login/Register page (account/account_login_register.php)

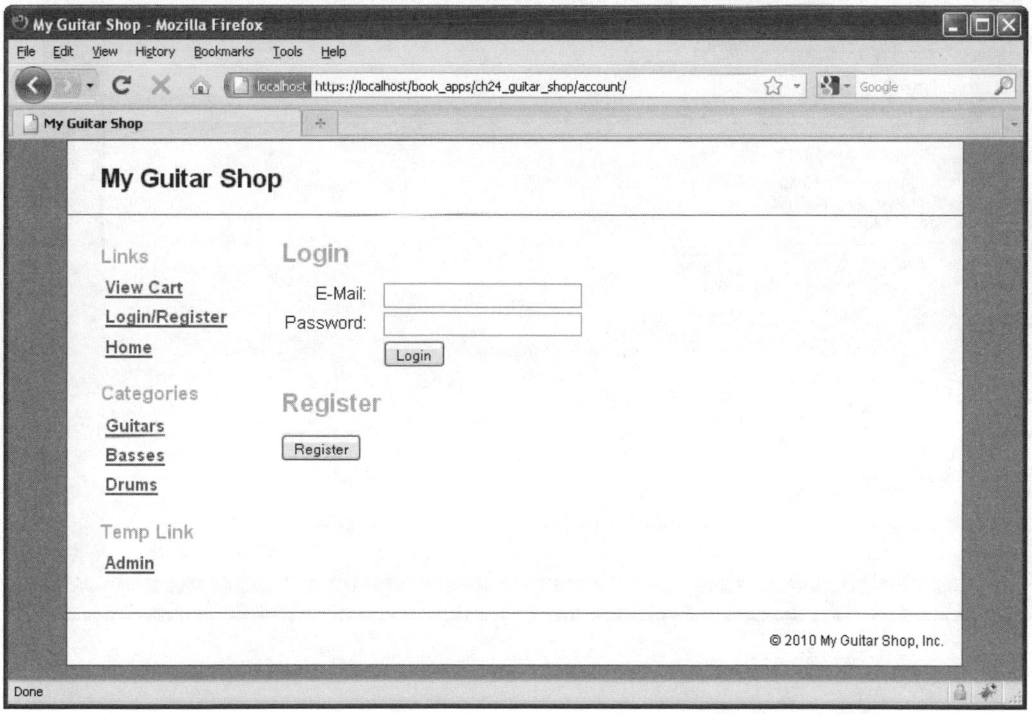

Figure 24-3   The user interface for end users (part 2 of 5)

The Confirm Order page (checkout/checkout_confirm.php)

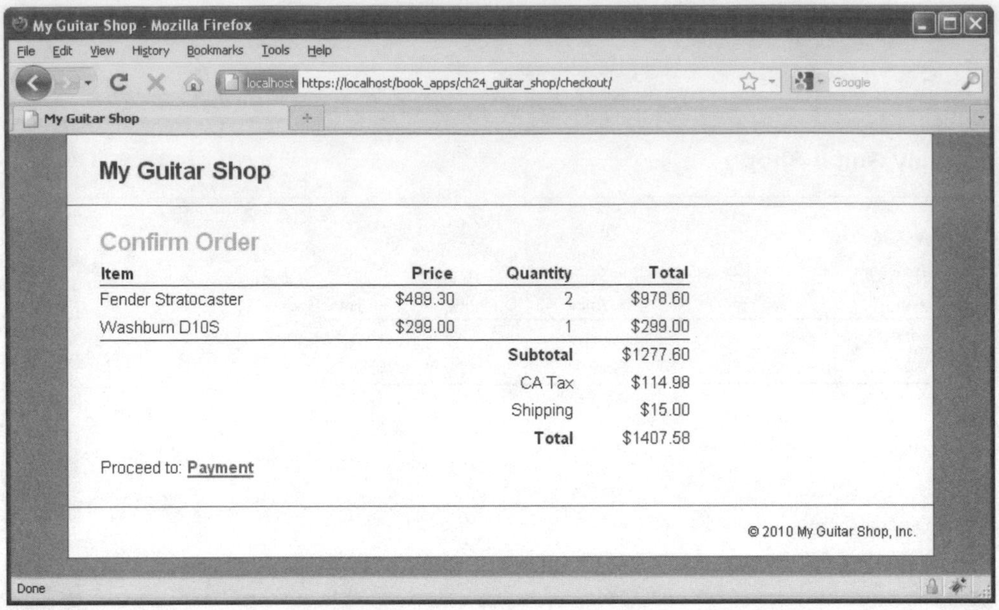

The Payment page (checkout/checkout_payment.php)

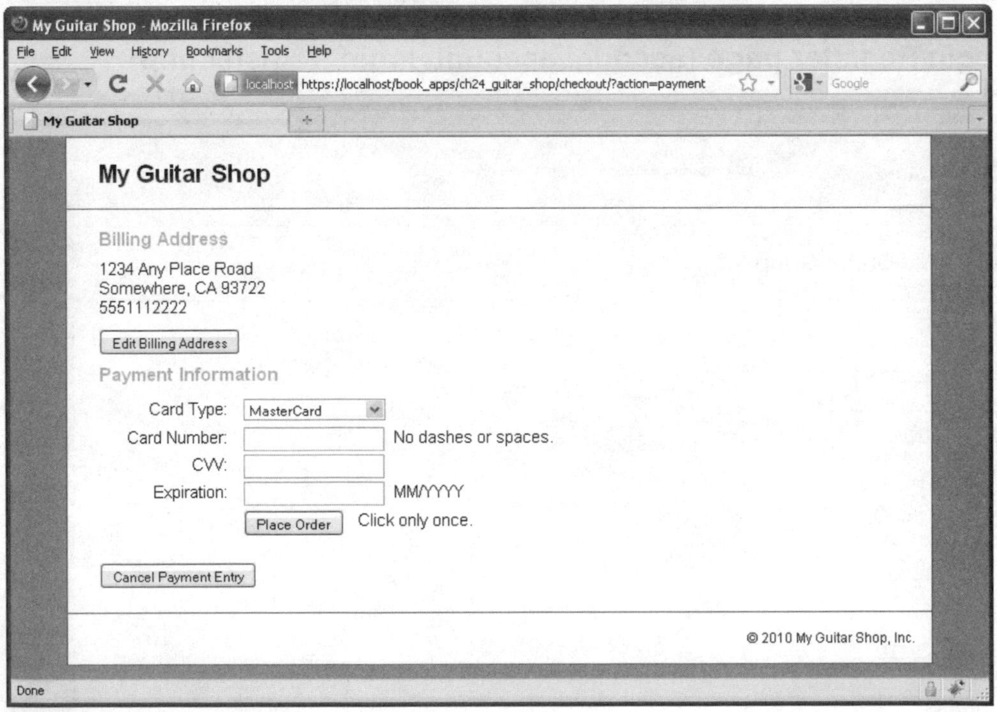

Figure 24-3 The user interface for end users (part 3 of 5)

The Order page (account/account_view_order.php)

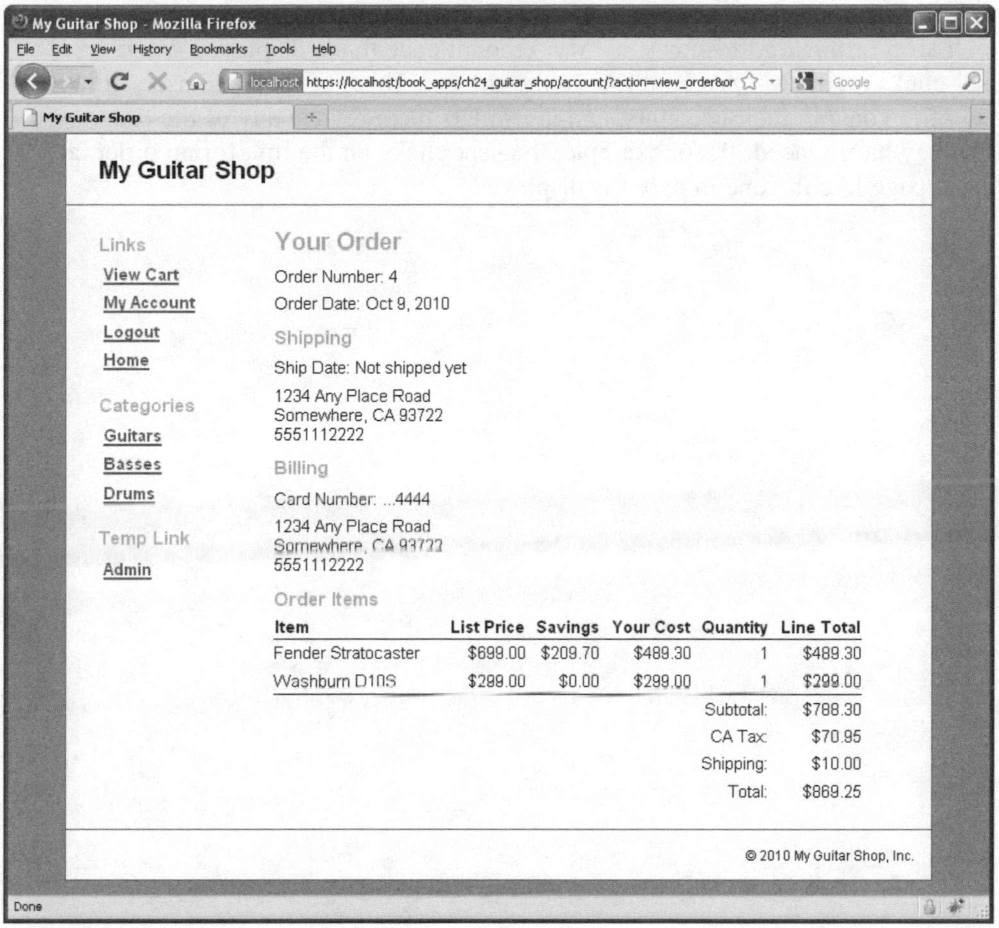

Description

- When the user clicks the Place Order button on the Payment page, the order is processed and this page is displayed.

- Note that this page is stored in the account directory. This page is also displayed if the user clicks on one of the order links in the My Account page, which is shown in the next figure.

- For a prototype like this, it's okay to use the same page for both applications. But for the final version of the web site, this should probably be a custom page that tells the user what has happened and what is going to happen next.

Figure 24-3   The user interface for end users (part 4 of 5)

The My Account page

Part 5 of this figure shows the My Account page that's displayed when the user clicks on the My Account link in the sidebar. This page lets the users edit any of the data in their accounts, and it also lets them review any of the orders that they have placed. If, for example, the user clicks on the link for an order, an Order page like the one in part 4 is displayed.

The My Account page (account/account_view.php)

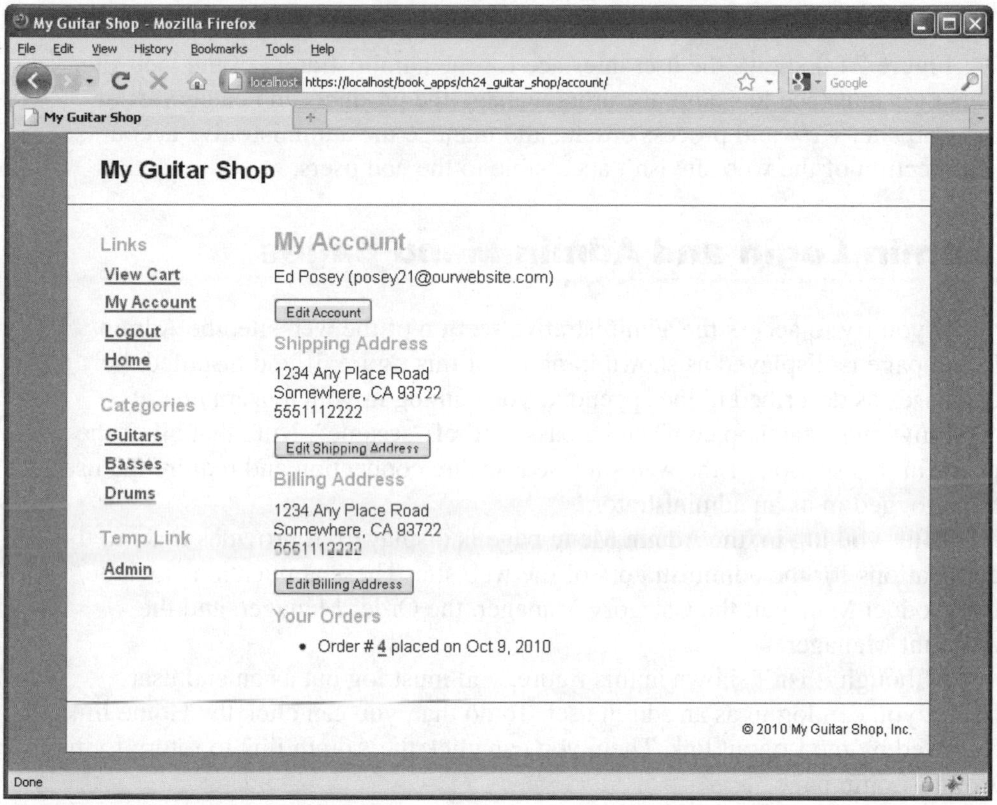

Description

- If the user clicks on the My Account link, this page is displayed. Then, the users can edit any of the account data, by clicking on the appropriate button. The user can also display any order by clicking on the order number link.

Figure 24-3   The user interface for end users (part 5 of 5)

The user interface for administrators

Figure 24-4 shows the user interface for the administrators of the web site. This user interface lets administrators manage the products and categories of the web site, view and process orders, and manage the administrative accounts. This section of the web site isn't accessible to the end users.

The Admin Login and Admin Menu pages

If you try to access the administrative section of the web site, the Admin Login page is displayed as shown in part 1 of this figure. If you installed the databases as described in the appendix, you can log in with a username of "admin@myguitarshop.com" and a password of "sesame". Note that all of the pages in this section of the web site use a secure connection and require the user to be logged in as an administrator.

After you log in, the Admin Menu page is displayed. It provides links to the applications for the administrators of the web site. These applications include the Product Manager, the Category Manager, the Order Manager, and the Account Manager.

Although it isn't shown in this figure, you must log out as an end user before you can log in as an admin user. To do that, you can click the Home link followed by the Logout link. Then, you can click the Admin link to return to the Admin Login page.

The Admin Login page (admin/account/account_login.php)

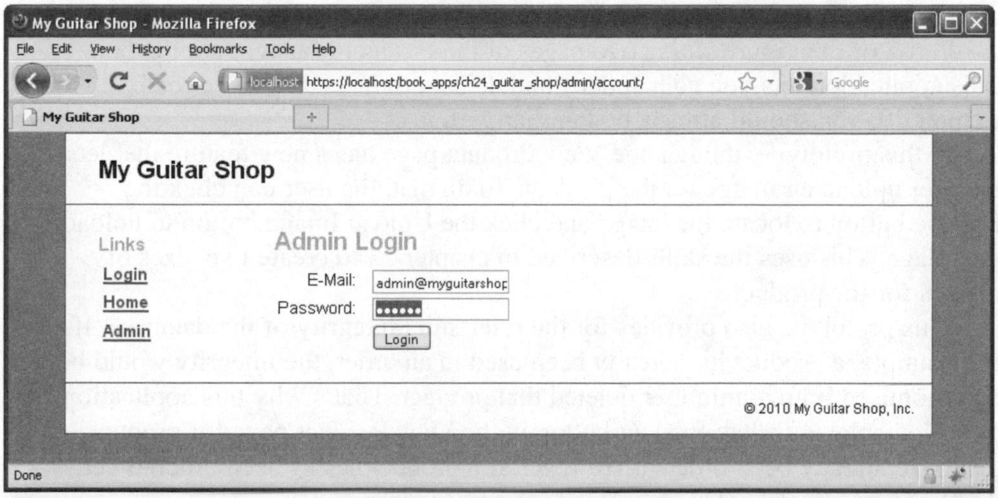

The Admin Menu page (admin/index.php)

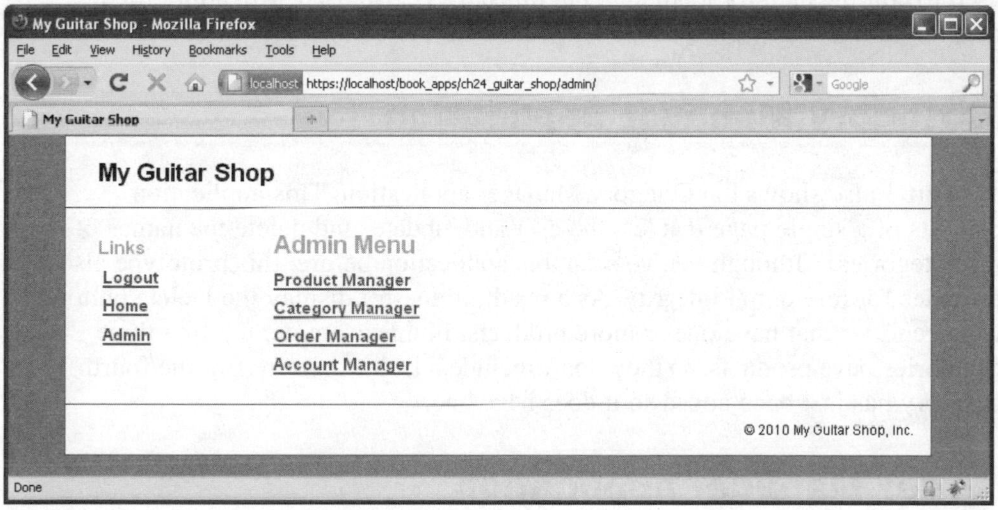

Figure 24-4   The user interface for administrators (part 1 of 4)

The Product Manager application

Part 2 of this figure shows two pages of the Product Manager application. This application lets you add, update, and delete products. If you've read chapter 20, you should already be familiar with it.

In this prototype, though, the View Product page has a new feature that lets the user upload an image for the product. To do that, the user can click the Browse button to locate the image and click the Upload Image button to upload the image. This uses the skills described in chapter 23 to create two sizes of images for the product.

This prototype also provides for the referential integrity of the database. If, for example, a product has already been used in an order, the integrity would be compromised if an admin user deleted that product. That's why this application doesn't display a Delete Product button in the View Product page for products that have already been ordered. However, if a product hasn't been ordered yet, the Product page does display a Delete Product button.

The third page of this application is in part 3 of this figure. Here, the page is used to edit the data for a product, but this page is also used with a modified heading to add a new product.

The Category Manager application

Part 3 also shows the Category Manager application. This application consists of a single page that lets the user add, update, and delete the names of the categories. Although you've seen this application before, this prototype also provides for referential integrity. As a result, it doesn't display the Delete button for categories that have one or more products. In this example, the first three categories have products, so they don't include a Delete button. But the fourth category has just been added so it does have one.

The Order Manager application

Part 4 shows the first page of the Order Manager application. This application lets the user view the outstanding orders as well as the orders that have been shipped. When an order is displayed, the user can either ship an order or delete it. If the user ships the order, the application processes the order. Then, it is moved to the list of shipped orders.

The Account Manager application

Part 4 also shows the first page of the Account Manager application. This lets an admin user create, edit, or delete the accounts for other administrators of the web site.

The List Products page (admin/product/product_list.php)

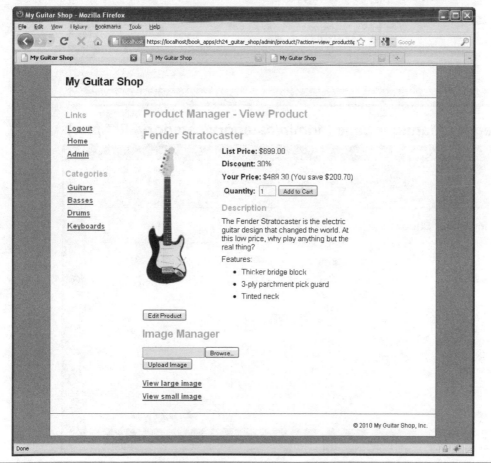

The View Product page (admin/products/product_view.php)

Figure 24-4   The user interface for administrators (part 2 of 4)

The Edit Product page (admin/product/product_add_edit.php)

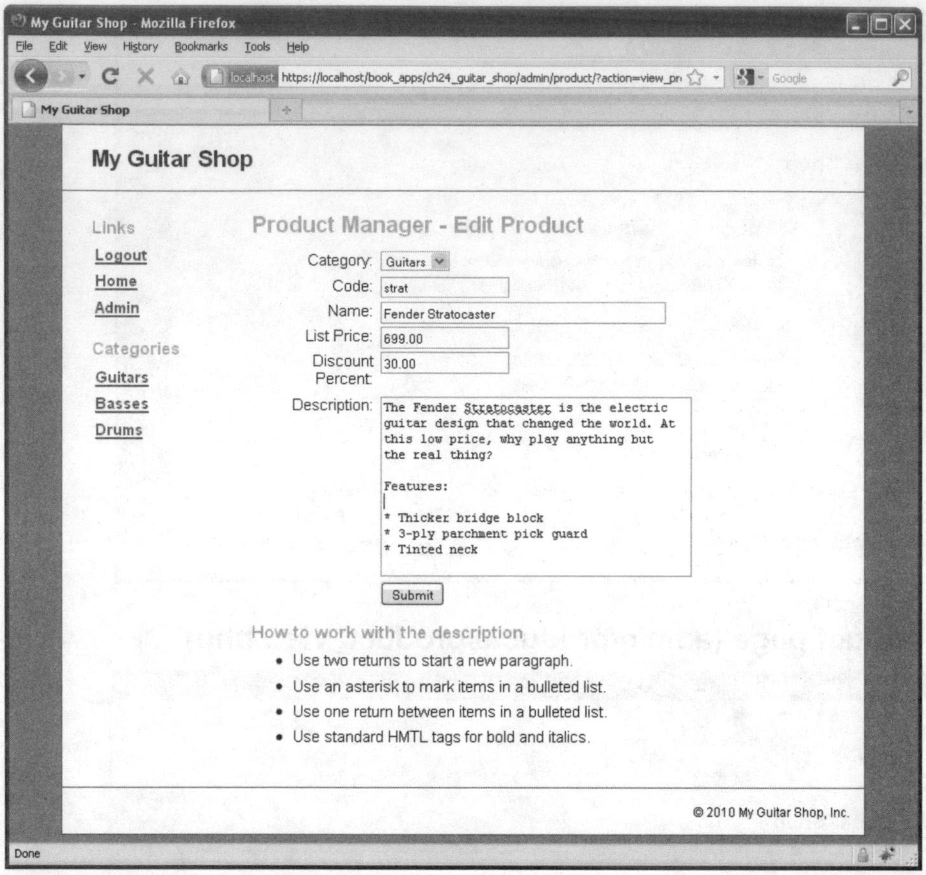

The Category Manager page (admin/category/category_list.php)

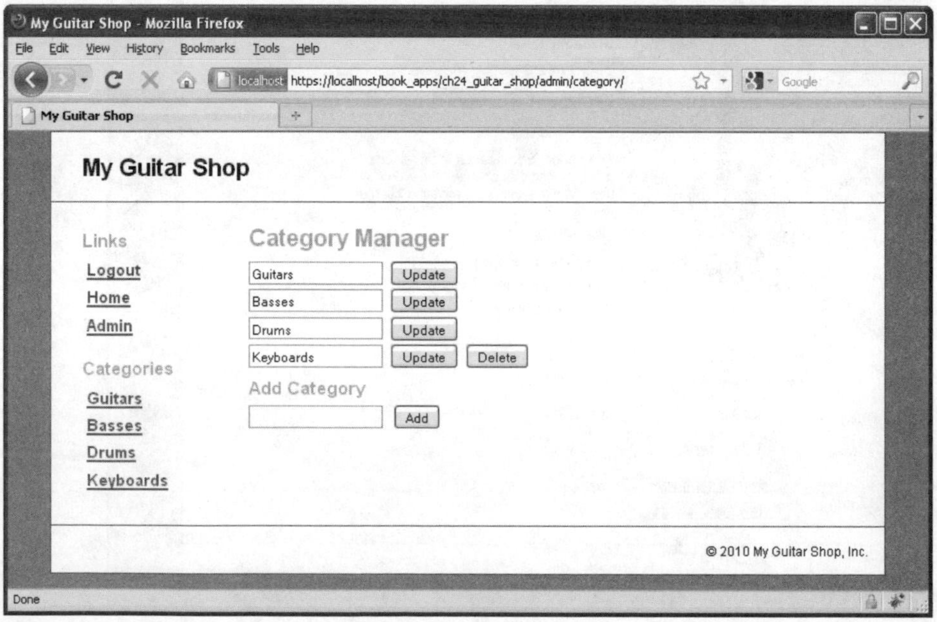

Figure 24-4   The user interface for administrators (part 3 of 4)

The Order Manager page (admin/orders/orders_view.php)

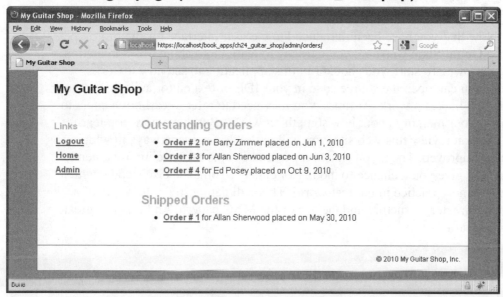

The Account Manager page (admin/account/account_view.php)

Figure 24-4   The user interface for administrators (part 4 of 4)

Perspective

Now that you have been introduced to the user interface for the prototype of the Guitar Shop web site, you're ready to learn more about this application on your own. To start, you should run this application to see how it works. Then, you can open the source code in your IDE or text editor and review the code that makes it work. At times, you may need to refer to earlier chapters to refresh your memory about how something works. But that's how you learn.

As you review this web site, you will probably see many ways in which it can be improved. Then, you should try to make some of those improvements. That will give you a chance to modify or enhance someone else's code, which is a common practice in the real-world. This will demonstrate the value of a logical directory structure and the use of the MVC pattern. And this is a great way to learn.

Terms

prototype   stepwise refinement
prototyping

Summary

- A *prototype* is a working model of a web site or portion of a web site. *Stepwise refinement* refers to the process of making step-by-step improvements to the prototype with review and evaluation after each step.

- The primary benefit of *prototyping* is that you detect problems early in the development cycle when they cost less to fix.

Exercise 24-1   Test and review the prototype

This exercise guides you through the process of testing the Guitar Shop prototype and reviewing its code. But if you prefer, you can do this on your own.

Test the end user section

1. Run the application in the book_applications/ch24_guitar_shop directory, which displays the Home page. Then, browse through the categories and view the products in each category.

2. Add several products to the cart. Then, delete one product by changing its quantity to 0, and change the quantity for another product to 2.

3. Click the Checkout link. If you haven't already created an account, you'll need to click the Register button to create an account and log in. Otherwise, you can enter your email address and password to log in. Note that the web site switches to a secure connection for this page.

4. After you register, confirm your order and enter your credit card information to complete the order. Because the data validation code for this is incomplete, you can enter a fake credit card and CVV number.

5. Click the My Account link and view the information for your account. Then, click the link for the order that you just placed to view that order.

6. Click the Logout link to log out. Note that the My Account link disappears.

Review the end user code

7. Open the util/main.php file and review its code. Note that it sets the $application_path variable and that it sets the include path to the application path, as shown in chapter 20. As a result, all included files can be specified relative to the application path. Note also that the last statement in this file calls the start_session function. As a result, any file that includes the main.php file can work with sessions.

8. Open the account/index.php file, and note the actions that this code provides for. Note also that the data validation uses the display_error function of the util/main.php file to display errors on a separate page.

9. Open the checkout/index.php file, and note the actions that this code provides for. Then, note that the "process" action uses the add_order and add_order_item functions of the model to add the order data to the database.

10. Open the model/order_db.php file and review its code. Note that the shipping_cost function uses a simple algorithm to calculate shipping costs of $5 per item with a maximum of $25 per order. Note also the that tax_amount function only calculates sales tax for orders from the state of California (CA). This simplification is typical for an early prototype.

Test the admin section

11. Click the Admin link to go to the admin section of the web site. Then, log in with an email address of "admin@myguitarshop.com" and a password of "sesame".

12. Click the Order Manager link to view the orders for the site. Note that the "Outstanding Orders" include any orders that you made earlier in this exercise. Then, view one of these orders.

13. Click the Ship Order button to ship the order. Note that this sets the ship date for the order and removes the two buttons. Then, click the Back button in your browser to view the list of orders again. Note that the order has been moved under the "Shipped Orders" heading.

14. Click the Admin link to return to the main Admin menu.

15. Click the Account Manager link to view the administrative accounts. Note that this displays the three administrative users that were created by the database script. Then, click the Admin link to return to the main Admin menu.

16. Click the Category Manager link. Then, add a new category named "Keyboards". Note that the new category includes a Delete button since it doesn't contain any products, but the other three categories don't include a Delete button since they do contain products. Next, return to the Admin menu.

17. Click the Product Manager link. Note that the Keyboards category is included in the list of categories. Use the Add Product link to add a new product to the Keyboards category. (You can make up your own test data.) After you add this product, note that it includes a Delete button since it hasn't been used by any orders yet. Navigate to the Gibson Les Paul guitar and note that it doesn't contain a Delete button since it has been used in an order.

18. Click the Logout link to log out of the administrative section.

Review the admin code

19. Open the admin/index.php file, and note that it uses the util/valid_admin.php file to only allow valid administrative users to view this page.

20. Open the util/valid_admin.php file and review its code. Note that it redirects to the admin/account directory if the user isn't logged in as a valid administrator.

21. Open the admin/account/index.php file and review its code. Note that this includes actions that display the Admin Login page and uses functions in the model/admin_db.php file to check whether the email/password combination is valid. Note also that this code includes actions that are used by the Admin Manager to create and maintain the admin accounts.

22. Open the admin/orders/index.php file, and note the actions that this code provides for. Note also that shipping an order uses a function from the model/order_db.php file to set the ship date for the order to the current date.

23. Open the admin/category/category_list.php file and note that it uses a column named productCount to determine whether to display the Delete button. Then, open the model/category_db.php file and note that the get_categories function uses a SELECT statement that includes a subquery that uses the aggregate COUNT function to create the column named productCount. This column contains a count of the number of products for each category.

Exercise 24-2   Review and enhance the prototype

1. Put yourself in the role of reviewer, and review either the end user or the admin user section of the web site. As you review, take notes on what improvements you would recommend.

2. Make the enhancements for one or more of the improvements that you've recommended. This is a great way to learn. If you don't want to modify the web site in the book_apps directory, you can find the same application in the ex_starts directory.

Appendix A

How to set up your PC for this book

This appendix shows how to install and configure the software that we recommend for developing PHP applications on a PC. This software includes the XAMPP package, the NetBeans IDE, Firefox as your default browser, and Notepad++ as your text editor. This appendix also shows how to install the book applications and the starting applications for the exercises in this book.

Please note that this appendix is designed for a PC that's running the Windows operating system. For directions on setting up a Mac, please see appendix B.

As you read this appendix, please remember that most web sites are continually updated. As a result, some of the procedures in this appendix may have changed since this book was published. Nevertheless, these procedures should still be good guides to installing the software. And if there are significant changes to these setup instructions, we will post updates on our web site (www.murach.com).

How to install Firefox and Notepad++ **802**
How to install the Firefox browser 802
How to install Notepad++ 802
How to install and configure XAMPP **804**
How to install XAMPP 804
How to configure phpMyAdmin 806
How to install and configure NetBeans **808**
How to install NetBeans 808
How to configure xDebug 808
How to install the book applications and databases **810**
How to install the source code for this book 810
How to create and restore the databases 812
How to fix a possible problem with the time zone **814**

How to install Firefox and Notepad++

As you do the exercises and work with the applications in this book, we recommend you that use Mozilla Firefox to test your applications. In addition, we recommend that you use Notepad++ as your text editor. Both of these components are free, and they don't take long to install.

How to install the Firefox browser

Figure A-1 shows how to download and install Firefox. As you respond to the dialog boxes for the installer, we recommend that you make Firefox your default browser.

How to install Notepad++

Figure A-1 also shows how to download and install Notepad++.

The Firefox web site

www.mozilla.com

How to install Firefox

1. Go to the web site address above.

2. Click on the Download Firefox - Free button.

3. Save the exe file to your hard drive.

4. Use Windows Explorer to find the exe file and double-click on it to run it. Then, follow the instructions.

The web site address for downloading Notepad++

http://notepad-plus.sourceforge.net

How to install Notepad++

1. Go to the web site address above.

2. Click on the Download link at the top of the page, click the "Binary files" link, and click the "Download Notepad++ executable files" link.

3. Click on the latest version of the Installer file (it should be named something like npp.5.6.4.Installer.exe) and save it on your hard drive.

4. Use Windows Explorer to find the exe file and double-click on it to run it. Then, follow the instructions.

Figure A-1   How to install Firefox and Notepad++

How to install and configure XAMPP

Before you can develop database-driven PHP applications, you need to install and configure a web server, a database server, and the PHP language. For this book, we recommend the Apache web server and the MySQL database server. Although you can install and configure these components individually, that can be tedious and error prone. As a result, we recommend using the XAMPP package to simplify the installation of Apache, MySQL, and PHP.

Be aware that the default installation of XAMPP is not secure. As a result, it should not be used as a production server until it is properly secured. As you progress through this book, you'll learn more about securing the XAMPP installation.

How to install XAMPP

Figure A-2 shows how to install XAMPP. Once you've completed the basic installation, you can test that installation by starting and stopping the Apache and MySQL servers as described in this figure. In addition, if you want the Apache and MySQL servers to start automatically when you start your computer, you can make them Windows services.

Once you've started the Apache server, you can test it by starting a web browser and navigating to this directory:

`http://localhost`

If this URL displays a web page, you have successfully installed and started the Apache server. By default, this page displays a page that provides some additional information about XAMPP.

The web site address for downloading XAMPP for Windows

www.apachefriends.org/en/xampp-windows.html

How to install XAMPP for Windows

1. Go to this URL:
   http://www.murach.com/books/phps/xampp.htm

2. Follow the directions there to download and install XAMPP

How to start and stop the Apache and MySQL servers

1. Start the XAMPP Control Panel by double-clicking the shortcut to the XAMPP Control Panel that's on your desktop.

2. Use the XAMPP Control Panel to start or stop a server by clicking on its Start or Stop button.

How to automatically start the Apache and MySQL servers

1. Start the XAMPP Control Panel by double-clicking the shortcut to the XAMPP Control Panel that's on your desktop.

2. If necessary, use the XAMPP Control Panel to stop the server.

3. Check the Srv checkbox for the server and click OK in the resulting dialog box to confirm your selection.

4. Start the server by restarting your computer or by clicking on the Start button for the server.

A URL you can use to test the Apache server

http://localhost

Description

- The XAMPP package includes the Apache web server, the MySQL database server, the PHP interpreter, and other software that's useful for developing PHP applications.

Figure A-2   How to install XAMPP

How to configure phpMyAdmin

XAMPP includes a web-based tool for working with MySQL named phpMyAdmin. By default, phpMyAdmin stores the username and password for MySQL's root user in its configuration file, which is a plain text file. Since this isn't secure, it's generally considered a good practice to modify these default settings.

We recommend changing the authentication type for phpMyAdmin from 'config' to 'cookie' as shown in figure A-3. When you use the 'cookie' authentication type, phpMyAdmin does not store any usernames or passwords in its configuration file. Instead, it prompts the user for a username and password when it starts, and it stores the username and password in a cookie in the user's browser. Once you've modified the configuration file for phpMyAdmin, you can use the second procedure in this figure to make sure the MySQL server is working correctly and to make sure that phpMyAdmin is configured correctly.

The default location of the config file for phpMyAdmin

```
C:\xampp\phpMyAdmin\config.inc.php
```

How to configure authentication for phpMyAdmin

1. Open the config.inc.php file in a text editor such as Notepad++.
2. Set the 'blowfish_secret' option to a random string up to 46 characters. This specifies the encryption key for the cookie.
3. Set the 'auth_type' option to a value of 'cookie'.
4. Set the 'user' and 'password' options to empty strings as shown below.
5. Save your changes.

The default settings

```
$cfg['blowfish_secret'] = 'xampp'; /* YOU SHOULD CHANGE THIS FOR A MORE
SECURE COOKIE AUTH! */

/* Authentication type and info */
$cfg['Servers'][$i]['auth_type']          = 'config';
$cfg['Servers'][$i]['user']               = 'root';
$cfg['Servers'][$i]['password']           = '';
```

The settings after phpMyAdmin has been configured for authentication

```
$cfg['blowfish_secret'] = 'dk20vc93ms28si29';

/* Authentication type and info */
$cfg['Servers'][$i]['auth_type']          = 'cookie';
$cfg['Servers'][$i]['user']               = '';
$cfg['Servers'][$i]['password']           = '';
```

How to use phpMyAdmin to test the MySQL server

1. Use the XAMPP Control Panel to start the Apache and MySQL servers as described in figure A-2.
2. Use the XAMPP Control Panel to start phpMyAdmin. To do that, click on the Admin button for MySQL. This should start phpMyAdmin and prompt you for a username and password. If it doesn't, click the "Log out" link to get to the log in page.
3. Log in as the root user by specifying a username of 'root' and the password for the root user. By default, the root user doesn't have a password, so you don't need to enter one. When you successfully log in as the root user, phpMyAdmin should display its Home page. At this point, both the MySQL server and phpMyAdmin are working correctly.

Description

- XAMPP includes a web-based tool for working with MySQL known as phpMyAdmin.
- For security reasons, we recommend changing the authentication type for phpMyAdmin from 'config' to 'cookie'. When you use the 'cookie' authentication type, phpMyAdmin prompts the user for a username and password when it starts.

Figure A-3   How to configure phpMyAdmin

How to install and configure NetBeans

We recommend that you use the NetBeans IDE for PHP with this book because it makes it easier for you to enter, edit, and run the various files that make up a web application. In addition, we recommend that you configure the xDebug debugger to work with NetBeans because it makes it easier to debug your PHP applications.

You should know, however, that NetBeans is a large application that may run slowly on an older, less powerful system. Nevertheless, we think it's worth installing because it illustrates the value of an IDE and the type of debugger that often comes with an IDE. Then, if you like using it, you can use it all the time. Otherwise, you can use it only when you want to use its debugger.

How to install NetBeans

Figure A-4 shows how to install the NetBeans IDE for PHP. Since this works like most installation programs, you shouldn't have any trouble with this procedure. If you encounter any problems, you can view the documentation that's available from the NetBeans web site and consult the troubleshooting tips.

How to configure xDebug

The xDebug debugger is included as a part of the XAMPP installation. However, it isn't enabled by default. As a result, you must enable this debugger before you can use it with NetBeans. To do that, you can use the procedure shown in this figure.

The NetBeans web site

www.netbeans.org

How to install NetBeans

1. Go to the NetBeans web site.

2. Download the NetBeans IDE that supports PHP. On a Windows system, the exe file should be named something like netbeans-6.9.1-ml-php-windows.exe.

3. Run the exe file and respond to the resulting dialog boxes.

The default location for the PHP initialization file

C:\xampp\php\php.ini

How to configure NetBeans to use the xDebug debugger

1. Open the php.ini file in a text editor such as Notepad++.

2. Search for the line of code that contains text of "php_xdebug.dll".

3. Remove the semicolon at the start of the line. After you do this, the line should look like this:

zend_extension = "C:\xampp\php\ext\php_xdebug.dll"

4. Search for the line of code that contains text of "xdebug.remote_enable=0".

5. Remove the semicolon at the start of the line, and change the 0 to a 1. After you do that, the line should look like this:

xdebug.remote_enable = 1

6. Save your changes.

7. Stop and restart Apache.

Description

- For this book, we recommend that you use NetBeans with xDebug as your primary development tool.

- For more information about installing NetBeans, you can refer to the documentation that's available from the NetBeans web site.

- The xDebug debugger is included as a part of the XAMPP installation. However, by default, this debugger is not enabled. As a result, if you want to use this debugger with NetBeans you must enable it.

Note

- NetBeans is a large application that may run slowly on an older, less powerful system.

Figure A-4   How to install NetBeans and configure xDebug

How to install the book applications and databases

To get the most from this book, you need to run the applications that it presents and do the exercises at the ends of the chapters. To do that, you need to download the book applications and exercise starts from our web site and you need to run a script that installs the databases that the applications use.

How to install the source code for this book

Figure A-5 shows how to download and install the source code for this book. This includes the source code for the applications that are presented in this book and the source code for the exercise starts and solutions.

When you finish this procedure, the book applications, exercise starts, and exercise solutions will be in the directories that are shown in this figure. Then, you'll be ready to do the exercises in this book.

The Murach web site

www.murach.com

The default installation directory for the source code

`c:\xampp\htdocs\`

The directories for the book applications, exercise starts, and solutions

```
c:\xampp\htdocs\book_apps
c:\xampp\htdocs\ex_starts
c:\xampp\htdocs\ex_solutions
```

How to download and install the source code

1. Go to www.murach.com, and go to the page for *Murach's PHP and MySQL*.

2. Click the link for "FREE download of the book applications." Then, click the "All book files" link for the self-extracting zip file. This will download a setup file named phps_allfiles.exe onto your hard drive.

3. Use the Windows Explorer to find the exe file on your hard drive. Then, double-click this file. This installs the source code into the directories shown above.

Description

- All of the source code for this book can be downloaded from www.murach.com.

Figure A-5   How to install the source code for this book

How to create and restore the databases

Before you can run the SQL statements presented in this book, you need to create the database tables and users on the database server. The easiest way to do that is to use phpMyAdmin to run the create_db.sql file described in figure A-6. When you run this script, it creates the databases and the user listed in this figure. This includes all of the tables for the databases.

As you work with the examples in this book, you may make changes to the database tables that you don't intend to make. In that case, you may want to restore the database to its original state so your results will match the results shown in this book. To do that, you can use phpMyAdmin to run the create_db.sql file a second time. This will drop both databases and create them again.

The create_db.sql file

`C:\xampp\htdocs\book_apps\_create_db\create_db.sql`

The databases that are created

Database	Description
my_guitar_shop1	A simple database that's used for the applications in sections 1 and 2.
my_guitar_shop2	An expanded version of the database that is used for the applications in sections 3 and 4.

A user that's created

User	Description
mgs_user	A user with privileges that allow only the use of SELECT, INSERT, UPDATE, and DELETE statements. This user is used for the database connections for most of the applications in the book.

How to create the databases and users for this book

1. Start phpMyAdmin as described in figure A-3.
2. Log in as the root user.
3. Click on the Import tab, click the Browse button, and select the create_db.sql file shown above. Then, click the Go button. If the script executes successfully, it creates both databases and the user shown above.

How to restore the databases and users for this book

- Run the create_db.sql script again. This drops both databases and creates them again.

Description

- If you have any problem following this procedure, chapter 3 provides a more detailed explanation of how to use phpMyAdmin to run scripts such as the create_db.sql script.

Figure A-6   How to create and restore the databases

How to fix a possible problem with the time zone

When you install XAMPP, it usually sets the time zone that's used by PHP correctly. However, in some rare cases, XAMPP doesn't set the time zone correctly. If that happens, you'll get an error when you try to use PHP to get the current date and time.

To check whether the time zone is set correctly on your system, you can use the first procedure shown in figure A-7 to run the specified application. If you don't see an error on the first page of this application, the time zone is set correctly. As a result, you don't need to take any further action.

However, if the first page of this application displays an error, you need to set the time zone as shown in the second procedure. To do that, you need to open the php.ini file in a text editor such as Notepad++ and set the time zone. For a list of supported time zones, you can view the PHP documentation that's available from the URL specified in this figure.

A URL for a local application that uses the date function

```
http://localhost/book_apps/ch05_guitar_shop/
```

How to check if your time zone is set correctly

1. Make sure the Apache and MySQL servers are started as described in figure A-2.
2. Start Firefox or another web browser.
3. Enter the URL for an application that uses the date function such as the application shown above. If the application displays a warning at the bottom of the first page, you need to set the time zone. Otherwise, you don't need to take any further action.

How to set the time zone

1. Open the php.ini file in a text editor such as Notepad++. On a Windows system, this file is stored here:

```
c:\xampp\php\php.ini
```

2. Search the file for 'timezone'.
3. Set the timezone correctly. For example, for Pacific Standard Time, you can set the time zone like this:

```
date.timezone = "America/Los_Angeles"
```

Where to find a list of supported time zones

```
http://us2.php.net/manual/en/timezones.php
```

Description

- If you get an error when you call the date function, you need to set the time zone in the php.ini file. Otherwise, the time zone is already set correctly.

Figure A-7   How to fix a possible problem with the time zone

Appendix B

How to set up your Mac for this book

This appendix shows how to install and configure the software that we recommend for developing PHP applications on a Mac. This software includes the XAMPP package, the NetBeans IDE, Firefox as your default browser, and TextWrangler as your text editor. This appendix also shows how to install the book applications and the starting applications for the exercises in this book.

Please note that this appendix is designed for a Mac that's running the OS X operating system. For directions on setting up a PC, please see appendix A.

As you read this appendix, please remember that most web sites are continually updated. As a result, some of the procedures in this appendix may have changed since this book was published. Nevertheless, these procedures should still be good guides to installing the software. And if there are significant changes to these setup instructions, we will post updates on our web site (www.murach.com).

How to install Firefox and TextWrangler 818
How to install the Firefox browser 818
How to install TextWrangler 818
How to install and configure XAMPP 820
How to install XAMPP 820
How to configure phpMyAdmin 822
How to install NetBeans and xDebug 824
How to install NetBeans 824
How to install xDebug 824
How to install the book applications and databases 826
How to install the source code for this book 826
How to create and restore the databases 828
How to fix a possible problem with the time zone 830

How to install Firefox and TextWrangler

As you do the exercises and work with the applications in this book, we recommend that you use Mozilla Firefox to test your applications. In addition, we recommend that you use TextWrangler as your text editor. Both of these applications are free, and they don't take long to install.

How to install the Firefox browser

Figure B-1 shows how to download and install Firefox. As you respond to the dialog boxes for the installer, we recommend that you make Firefox your default browser.

How to install TextWrangler

Figure B-1 also shows how to download and install TextWrangler.

The Firefox web site

www.mozilla.com

How to install Firefox

1. Go to the web site address above.

2. Click on the Download Firefox - Free button and save the disk image (dmg) file to your hard drive.

3. If the Firefox disk window doesn't appear, double-click the disk image file to open the disk window.

4. In the Firefox disk window, drag the Firefox icon on top of the Applications folder icon. Then, close the Firefox window.

5. Use Finder to browse to the Applications folder and double-click the Firefox icon to start Firefox.

The web site address for downloading TextWrangler

www.barebones.com/products/textwrangler

How to install TextWrangler

1. Go to the web site address above.

2. Click the Download Now button, click the Download link for the disk image (dmg) file that's right for your release of Mac OS, and save the disk image file to your hard drive.

3. If the TextWrangler disk window doesn't open, double-click the TextWrangler disk image file to open the TextWrangler disk window.

4. In the TextWrangler disk window, drag the TextWrangler icon on top of the Applications folder icon. Then, close the TextWrangler window.

5. Use Finder to browser to the Applications folder and double-click the TextWrangler icon to start TextWrangler.

Figure B-1   How to install Firefox and TextWrangler

How to install and configure XAMPP

Before you can develop database-driven PHP applications, you need to install and configure a web server, a database server, and the PHP language. For this book, we recommend the Apache web server and the MySQL database server. Although you can install and configure these components individually, that can be tedious and error prone. As a result, we recommend using the XAMPP package to simplify the installation of Apache, MySQL, and PHP.

Be aware that the default installation of XAMPP is not secure by default. As a result, it should not be used as a production server until it is properly secured. As you progress through this book, you'll learn more about securing the XAMPP installation.

How to install XAMPP

Figure B-2 shows how to install XAMPP. Once you've completed the basic installation, you can test that installation by starting and stopping the Apache and MySQL servers as described in this figure.

Once you've started the Apache server, you can test it by starting a web browser and navigating to this directory:

`http://localhost`

If this URL displays a web page, you have successfully installed and started the Apache server. By default, this page displays a page that provides some additional information about XAMPP.

The web site address for downloading XAMPP for Mac OS X

`www.apachefriends.org/en/xampp-macosx.html`

How to install XAMPP for Mac OS X

1. Go to the web site address above.
2. Scroll down to the "XAMPP for Mac OS X" section.
3. Click on the "XAMPP Mac OS X" link to start the download and save the file to your hard disk.
4. Use Finder to locate the disk image (dmg) file and double-click on it to open the installer window.
5. In the installer window, drag the XAMPP folder onto the Applications folder.

How to start and stop the Apache and MySQL servers

1. Use Finder to browse to your Applications folder and open the XAMPP folder.
2. Double-click the XAMPP Control program.
3. Use the XAMPP Control program to start or stop a server by clicking on its Start or Stop button.

A URL you can use to test the Apache server

`http://localhost`

Description

- The XAMPP package includes the Apache web server, the MySQL database server, the PHP interpreter, and other software that's useful for developing PHP applications.
- Once you start Apache and MySQL on Mac OS X, they may stop when you log out or restart your computer. In that case, you may need to restart Apache and MySQL before you do any PHP development.

Figure B-2   How to install XAMPP for Mac OS X

How to configure phpMyAdmin

XAMPP includes a web-based tool for working with MySQL named phpMyAdmin. By default, phpMyAdmin stores the username and password for MySQL's root user in its configuration file, which is a plain text file. Since this isn't secure, it's generally considered a good practice to modify these default settings.

We recommend changing the authentication type for phpMyAdmin from 'config' to 'cookie' as shown in figure B-3. When you use the 'cookie' authentication type, phpMyAdmin does not store any usernames or passwords in its configuration file. Instead, it prompts the user for a username and password when it starts, and it stores the username and password in a cookie in the user's browser. Once you've modified the configuration file for phpMyAdmin, you can use the second procedure in this figure to make sure the MySQL server is working correctly and to make sure that phpMyAdmin is configured correctly.

The default location of the config file for phpMyAdmin

`/Applications/XAMPP/xamppfiles/phpmyadmin/config.inc.php`

How to configure authentication for phpMyAdmin

1. Use TextWrangler to open the config.inc.php file shown above.

2. Set the 'blowfish_secret' option to a random string up to 46 characters. This specifies the encryption key for the cookie.

3. Set the 'auth_type' option to a value of 'cookie'.

4. Set the 'user' and 'password' options to empty strings as shown below.

5. Save your changes.

The default settings

```
$cfg'blowfish_secret'] = 'xampp'; /* YOU SHOULD CHANGE THIS FOR A MORE
SECURE COOKIE AUTH! */

/* Authentication type and info */
$cfg['Servers'][$i]['auth_type']           = 'config';
$cfg['Servers'][$i]['user']                = 'root';
$cfg['Servers'][$i]['password']            = '';
```

The settings after phpMyAdmin has been configured for authentication

```
$cfg['blowfish secret'] = 'dk20vc93ms28si29';

/* Authentication type and info */
$cfg['Servers'][$i]['auth_type']           = 'cookie';
$cfg['Servers'][$i]['user']                = '';
$cfg['Servers'][$i]['password']            = '';
```

How to use phpMyAdmin to test the MySQL server

1. Use the XAMPP Control Panel to start the Apache and MySQL servers as described in figure B-2.

2. Start Firefox and enter this URL:

   `http://localhost/phpmyadmin/`

   This should start phpMyAdmin and prompt you for a username and password. If it doesn't, click the "Log out" link to get to the log in page.

3. Log in as the root user by specifying a username of 'root' and the password for the root user. By default, the root user doesn't have a password, so you don't need to enter one. When you successfully log in as the root user, phpMyAdmin should display its Home page. At this point, both the MySQL server and phpMyAdmin are working correctly.

Permissions note

- If you don't have permission to save the config.inc.php file, give yourself the appropriate permissions. To do that, use Finder to select the config.inc.php file. Then, select the File menu, the Get Info item, and the Sharing and Permissions link. Next, click on the lock icon to allow changes, click on the plus sign (+), and add yourself as a user who has read and write privileges. If necessary, repeat this procedure for the phpmyadmin folder.

Figure B-3   How to configure phpMyAdmin

How to install NetBeans and xDebug

We recommend that you use the NetBeans IDE for PHP with this book because it makes it easier for you to enter, edit, and run the various files that make up a web application. In addition, we recommend that you configure the xDebug debugger to work with NetBeans because it makes it easier to debug your PHP applications.

How to install NetBeans

Figure B-4 shows how to install the NetBeans IDE for PHP. Since this works like most installation programs, you shouldn't have any trouble with this procedure. If you encounter any problems, you can view the documentation that's available from the NetBeans web site and consult the troubleshooting tips.

How to install xDebug

This figure also shows how to download and install the xDebug debugger. To make that easy for you, we have made the Mac OS X binary file for xDebug (xdebug.so) available from murach.com. Once you download this file, you can copy it into XAMPP's lib folder. Then, you can add the code shown in this figure to the php.ini file. At this point, the xDebug debugger should work as described in chapter 6.

The NetBeans web site

http://netbeans.org

How to install NetBeans

1. Go to the NetBeans web site.
2. Download the disk image (dmg) file for the NetBeans IDE that supports PHP. This file should be named something like netbeans-6.9.1-ml-php-macosx.dmg.
3. Double-click the disk image file and respond to the resulting dialog boxes.

A URL for downloading the xDebug binary file

www.murach.com/books/phps/xdebug.htm

The default location for the extensions folder

/Applications/XAMPP/xamppfiles/lib/

The default location for the PHP initialization file

/Applications/XAMPP/etc/php.ini

How to install xDebug and configure it for PHP

1. Go to the URL shown above.
2. Download the Mac OS X binary file for xDebug (xdebug.so).
3. Use Finder to find the xdebug.so file, and copy it to the extensions folder shown above.
4. Use TextWrangler to open the php.ini file shown above. Scroll down to the end of this file and and add these lines:

```
[xdebug]
zend_extension = /Applications/XAMPP/xamppfiles/lib/xdebug.so
xdebug.remote_enable=on
xdebug.remote_host=localhost
xdebug.remote_handler=dbgp
xdebug.remote_port=9000
```

5. Save your changes.
6. Stop and restart Apache.

Description

- For this book, we recommend that you use NetBeans with xDebug as your primary development tool.
- For more information about installing NetBeans, you can refer to the documentation that's available from the NetBeans web site.
- For more information about installing xDebug, you can search the Internet for "Mac OS X xDebug".

Figure B-4   How to install NetBeans and xDebug

How to install the book applications and databases

To get the most from this book, you need to run the applications that it presents and do the exercises at the ends of the chapters. To do that, you need to download the book applications and exercise starts from our web site and you need to run a script that installs the databases that the applications use.

How to install the source code for this book

Figure B-5 shows how to download and install the source code for this book. This includes the source code for the applications that are presented in this book and the source code for the exercise starts and solutions.

When you finish this procedure, the book applications, exercise starts, and exercise solutions will be in the directories that are shown in this figure. Then, you'll be ready to do the exercises in this book.

The Murach web site

`www.murach.com`

The default installation directory for the source code

`/Applications/XAMPP/htdocs`

The directories for the book applications, exercise starts, and solutions

```
/Applications/XAMPP/htdocs/book_apps
/Applications/XAMPP/htdocs/ex_starts
/Applications/XAMPP/htdocs/ex_solutions
```

How to download and install the source code

1. Go to www.murach.com, and go to the page for *Murach's PHP and MySQL*.
2. Click the link for "FREE download of the book applications." Then, click the "All book files" link for the regular zip file. This will download a zip file named phps_allfiles.zip onto your hard drive.
3. Use Finder to browse to this file and double-click on it to unzip it. This creates the book_apps, ex_starts, and ex_solutions folders.
4. Use Finder to move these three folders into the htdocs folder.

Description

*   All of the source code for this book can be downloaded from www.murach.com.

Figure B-5   How to install the source code for this book

How to create and restore the databases

Before you can run the SQL statements presented in this book, you need to create the database tables and users on the database server. The easiest way to do that is to use phpMyAdmin to run the create_db.sql file as described in figure B-6. When you use phpMyAdmin to run this file, it executes a script that creates the databases and the user described in this figure. This includes all of the tables for the databases.

As you work with the examples in this book, you may make changes to the database tables that you don't intend to make. In that case, you may want to restore the database to its original state so your results will match the results shown in this book. To do that, you can use phpMyAdmin to run the create_db.sql file a second time. This will drop both databases and create them again.

The create_db.sql file

```
/Applications/XAMPP/htdocs/book_apps/_create_db/create_db.sql
```

The databases that are created

Database	Description
my_guitar_shop1	A simple database that's used for the applications in sections 1 and 2.
my_guitar_shop2	An expanded version of the database that is used for the applications in sections 3 and 4.

A user that's created

User	Description
mgs_user	A user with privileges that allow only the use of SELECT, INSERT, UPDATE, and DELETE statements. This user is used for the database connections for most of the applications in the book.

How to create the databases and users for this book

1. Start phpMyAdmin as described in figure B-3.
2. Log in as the root user.
3. Click on the Import tab, click the Browse button, and select the create_db.sql file shown above. Then, click the Go button. If the script executes successfully, both databases were created.

How to restore the databases and users for this book

- Run the procedure for creating the tables and users again. This will drop all of the tables and users before creating them again.

Description

- If you have any problem following this procedure, chapter 3 provides a more detailed explanation of how to use phpMyAdmin to run scripts such as the create_db.sql script.

Figure B-6   How to create and restore the databases

How to fix a possible problem with the time zone

When you install XAMPP, it usually sets the time zone that's used by PHP correctly. However, in some cases, XAMPP doesn't set the time zone correctly. If that happens, you'll get an error when you try to use PHP to get the current date and time.

To check whether the time zone is set correctly on your system, you can use the first procedure in figure B-7 to run the specified application. If you don't see an error on the first page of this application, the time zone is set correctly. As a result, you don't need to take any further action.

However, if the first page of this application displays an error, you need to set the time zone as shown in the second procedure. To do that, you need to open the php.ini file in a text editor such as TextWrangler and set the time zone. For a list of supported time zones, you can view the PHP documentation that's available from the URL specified in this figure.

A URL for a local application that uses the date function

`http://localhost/book apps/ch05 guitar shop/`

How to check if your time zone is set correctly

1. Make sure the Apache and MySQL servers are started as described in figure B-2.

2. Start Firefox or another web browser.

3. Enter the URL for an application that uses the date function such as the application shown above. If the application displays a warning at the bottom of the first page, you need to set the time zone. Otherwise, you don't need to take any further action.

How to set the time zone

1. Use TextWrangler to open the php.ini file. On an OS X system, this file is stored here:

`/Applications/XAMPP/etc/php.ini`

2. Search the file for 'timezone'.

3. Set the timezone correctly. For example, for Pacific Standard Time, you can set the time zone like this:

`date.timezone = "America/Los_Angeles"`

Where to find a list of supported time zones

`http://us2.php.net/manual/en/timezones.php`

Description

- If you get an error when you call the date function, you need to set the time zone in the php.ini file. Otherwise, the time zone is already set correctly.

Figure B-7   How to fix a possible problem with the time zone

Index

$_COOKIE variable, 350-351
$_GET array, 54-55, 208-209
$_POST array, 56-57, 68-69, 208-209, 211, 213, 215, 217, 219
$_SERVER array, 684-685, 698-699
$_SESSION array, 358-359
$GLOBALS array, 384-385
401 (Unauthorized) response header, 699

A

abs function, 278-279
Absolute template (strtotime function), 296-297
Abstract class, 452-453
Abstract method, 452-453
Action query, 104-105
Ad hoc relationship (SQL), 590-591
add method (DateTime object), 304-305
add_tags function, 648-649
Address format (email address), 490
Advanced Encryption Standard (AES), 700-701
Aggregate function, 594-595
Alias
    column, 576-577
    table, 592-593
Alpha blending, 762-763
Alpha channel, 762-763
ALTER TABLE statement, 546-547
Anonymous function, 398-399
Apache web server, 10-11
    starting and stopping, 24-25
API (Application Programming Interface)
    MySQL, 612-613
    YouTube, 728-729
Append a string, 62-63
Application Programming Interface (see API)
Application root directory, 26-27
Application server, 10-11
Applications (see Book applications)
Argument (function), 64-65, 162, 380-381
    for creating object, 124-125
Arithmetic operator, 60-61
Array, 132-133, 311-344
    $_GET array, 54-55, 208-209
    adding elements, 314-315
    associative, 318-323
    built-in, 54-55

Array (continued)
    conversion, 270-271
    creating, 312-313
    deleting elements, 314-315
    for loops, 316-317
    jagged, 334-335
    multi-dimensional, 334
    rectangular, 334-335
    two-dimensional, 334-337
    variable substitution, 314-315
array function, 132-133
array_count_values function, 328-329
array_fill function, 324-325
array_key_exists function, 328-329
array_merge function, 324-325
array_pad function, 324-325
array_pop function, 326-327, 380-381
array_product function, 328-329
array_push function, 326-327
array_rand function, 332-333
array_reverse function, 332-333
array_search function, 328-329
array_shift function, 326-327
array_slice function, 324-325
array_splice function, 324-325
array_sum function, 328-329
array_unique function, 332-333
array_unshift function, 326-327
array_values function, 314-315
Array of arrays, 334-337
arsort function (array), 330-331
ASCII character set, 270-271
asort function (array), 330-331
ASP.NET, 10-11
Assertion (regular expression), 470-471
Assigning a value, 52-53
Assigning string values, 260-261
Assignment operator, 52-53, 192-193
Associative array, 318-323
    adding elements, 320-321
    creating, 318-319
    deleting elements, 320-321
    foreach loops, 322-323
    variable substitution, 320-321
Atom (email address), 490
Attribute (database), 504-505
Authentication, 678-679, 686-697
Auto-completion, 22-23
Autoglobal variable, 384
Auto-increment column, 98-99, 544-545, 602-603

B

Base class, 448-449
Base value, 274-275
Basic authentication, 686-687, 696-699
Binary operator, 242
bindValue method (PDOStatement class), 614-617
Block comment, 48-49
Book applications
   eCommerce, 779-798
   Future Value, 78-85
   Guitar Shop, 650-669
   Image Upload, 764-775
   installing (Mac), 826-827
   installing (Windows), 810-811
   Product Catalog, 178-185, 658-661
   Product Discount, 14-21, 66-69
   Product Manager, 146-155
   Product Manager (OOP), 432-441
   Product Manager (MVC), 166-177, 662-669
   Product Viewer, 138-141
   Registration (long), 482-495
   Registration (short), 482-495
   running, 28-29
   Shopping Cart (functions), 402-409
   Shopping Cart (sessions), 364-375
   Task List Manager, 338-341
   YouTube Search, 730-739
Book databases
   create and restore (Mac), 828-829
   create and restore (Windows), 812-813
Boolean data type, 50-51
Boolean literal, 52-53
Boyce-Codd normal form, 520-521
Bracket expression (regular expression), 466-467
break statement, 254-255
Breakpoint, 196-197
Browser, 4-5, 10-11
   cookies and security settings, 353
Bug, 30-31
Built-in array, 54-55
Built-in function, 64-65
Bulletin Board code (BBCode), 647-648

C

CA (Certification Authority), 680-681
Calculated value, 594-595
Callback, 396-397
Calling a function, 162-163, 380-381
Calling a method, 126-127

Camel casing, 52
Cascading Style Sheets (see CSS)
CASE (Computer-Aided Software Engineering), 510-511
Case-insensitive regular expression, 462-463
Casting (data type), 286-287
catch block, 130-131, 480-481
CBC (Cypher-Block Chaining), 700
ceil function, 278-279
Cell, 94-95
Certificate (digital secure), 678-679, 680-681
Certification authority (CA), 680-681
CHAR data type (MySQL), 98-99, 540-541
Character class (regular expression), 466-467
Character entity, 222-223
Check box, 212-213, 214-215
checkdate function, 294-295
Child class, 448-449
chr function, 270-271
Chrome, 10-11
Class, 124-125, 413-458
   for encrypting and decrypting, 702-703
Class constant, 428-429
Class method, 430-431
Class property, 430-431
class_exists function, 446-447
Client (MySQL), 4-5
   command-line, 108-109
   web-based, 108-109
Client certificate, 678-679
Clone an object, 444-445
closeCursor method (PDOStatement class), 614-617
Closure, 400-401
Column, 94-95
   alias, 576-577
   database design, 510-511
Column-level primary key, 544-545
Command-line client, 108-109
Comma-separated value (CSV) file, 750-751
Comment, 48-49
Composite index, 518-519
Composite key, 512-513
Compound assignment operator, 62-63
Compound condition (SQL), 582-583
Compound conditional expression, 70-71
Concatenate, 58-59
Concatenation operator, 58-59
Concrete class, 452-453
Conditional expression, 70-71, 232-237
Conditional include, 76-77
Conditional operator, 226-227, 242-243

Configuration (NetBeans), 38-39
Connection
    database, 124-125
    secure 676-685
Constant, 52-53
    class, 428-429
    PHP_INT_MAX, 274-275
Constraint, 514-515, 542-543, 544-545
Constructor, 414, 422-423
Content management system, 646-647
continue statement, 254-255
Control statements, 231-255
Controller (MVC), 160-161
Cookie, 348-353, 356-357
copy function, 752-753
Correlated subquery, 600-601
count function (array), 132-133, 316-317
CREATE DATABASE statement, 538-539
CREATE INDEX statement, 550-551
CREATE TABLE statement, 542-543
CREATE USER statement, 554-555
Creating, an array, 312-313
CSS, 18-19
CSV file, 562, 750-751
cURL library, 724-729
curl_close function, 726-727
curl_exec function, 726-727
curl_init function, 726-727
curl_setopt function, 726-727
Cypher (encryption algorithm), 700
Cypher-block chaining (CBC), 700

D

Data Definition Language (DDL), 100
Data element, 506-507
Data Manipulation Language (DML), 100
Data redundancy, 516-517
Data Source Name (DSN), 124-125
Data structure, 504
Data types
    MySQL, 98-99, 540-541
    PHP, 50-51
Data validation, 78, 82-83
    date, 294-295
    email address, 490-491
    object-oriented, 482-495
    with regular expressions, 476-477
    zip code, 476-477
Database
    column design, 510-511

Database (continued)
    creation, 537-570
    denormalization, 528-529
    design, 504-519
    diagram, 532-533
    extraction layer, 612-613
    index, 518-519
    installing, 112-113
    loading data, 562-563
    normalization, 516-517, 520-529
    performance, 100
    privileges, 552-553, 556-561
    relational, 94-99
    table design, 510-511
    table creation, 542-543
Database administrator (DBA), 504, 539, 547
Database server, 8-9
Database user, 554-555,
DATE data type (MySQL), 98-99, 540-541
Date formatting, 292-293
date function, 64-65, 292-293
Date interval, 302-303, 304-305
Date validation, 294-295, 476-477
DateInterval class, 302-303
Dates, 291-308
DateTime class, 300-301, 304-305, 306-307
DATETIME data type (MySQL), 98-99, 540-541
DBA, 504, 539, 547
DDL (Data Definition Language), 100
DDL statements (SQL), 537-570
Debugging, 30-31, 190-201
Decimal, 274-275
DECIMAL data type (MySQL), 98-99, 540-541
Decimal data type (PHP), 50-51
Declarative referential integrity (DRI), 514-515
Declaring a variable, 52-53
Decrypting data, 700-701
Default file, 28-29
Default value
    database column, 98-99, 542-543
    function, 386-387
    include path, 392-393
    INSERT statement, 602-603
DELETE statement, 104-105, 128-129, 606-607
Denormalization, 528-529
Dependencies, 520
Deploying a PHP application, 26-27
Derived class, 448-449
Deserialization, 358-359
Destructor, 422-423
die function, 76-77

diff method (DateTime object), 304-305
Digest, 688
Digest authentication, 686-687
Digital secure certificate, 678-679, 680-681
Directory functions, 744-745
Directory listing, 744-745
Directory navigation, 76-77, 164-165
Directory structure, 650-651, 782-783
Displaying data, 222-227
DML (Data Manipulation Language), 100
DML statements, 573-608
Document root directory, 26-27
Documentation (PHP), 86-87
Domain (email address), 490
Domain name, 28-29
Domain-key normal form, 520-521
Double data type, 50-51
Double value, 276-277
do-while loop, 250-251
do-while statement, 250-251
DRI (Declarative referential integrity), 514-515
DROP DATABASE statement, 538-539
DROP INDEX statement, 550-551
DROP TABLE statement, 548-549
DROP USER statement, 554-555
Drop-down list, 216-217
DSN (Data Source Name), 124-125
Dumping a database, 564-565
Dynamic SQL statement, 614
Dynamic web page, 8-9

E

echo statement, 194-195, 226-227
eCommerce web site, 779-798
Editing, 22-23, 36-37
Element (array), 132-133, 312-313
else clause, 72-73, 238-239
else if clause, 72-73, 240-241
Email, 708-723
Email address validation, 476-477, 490-491, 720-721
Email client, 708-709
Email helper function, 718-721, 722-723
Email server, 708-709
Embedding PHP, 46-47
empty function, 64-65, 264-265
Empty string, 58-59
Encapsulation, 414
Encrypted data, 700-703
Encrypted password, 688-689
end function (array), 316-317
Entity (database), 504-505

Entity-relationship (ER) modeling, 504-505
Equality operator, 232-233
    with objects, 444-445
ER (entity-relationship) modeling, 504-505
Error modes (PDO), 618-619
Error suppression operator, 626-627
Errors, 190-191, 192-193
Escape character (regular expression), 464-465
Escape sequence, 262-263
Exception, 130-131, 478-479
Exception class, 130-131, 478-479
Exception error mode, 618-619
Exception handling, 478-481
    PDO, 130-131
exec method (PDO object), 128-129
execute method (PDOStatement class), 614-617
exit function, 76-77
Explicit syntax (SQL join), 590-591
explode function, 270-271
Exponent, 50-51
Exponential notation, 276-277
Expression, 58
    conditional, 70-71, 232-237
    numeric, 60-61
    string, 58-59
Extend a class, 448-449
Extension (PHP), 612-613

F

fclose function, 748-749
feof function, 748-749
fetch method (PDOStatement class), 135-136, 614-617
fetchAll method (PDOStatement class), 614-617
fgetcsv function, 750-751
fgets function, 748-749
Field (database table), 94-95
FIFO, 326-327
file function, 746-747
File functions, 744-755
File handling, 744-753
File Transfer Protocol (FTP), 26-27
File uploading, 754-755
file_exists function, 744-745
file_get_contents function, 746-747
file_put_contents function, 746-747
Filename, 28-29
Final class, 454-455
Final method, 454-455
Firefox, 10-11
    cookies, 353
        ending a session, 356

Firefox (continued)
  install (Mac), 818-819
  install (Windows), 802-803
First normal form, 522-523
First-in, first-out, 326-327
Float value, 276-277
Floating-point number, 50
Floating-point value, 274, 276-277
floatval function, 286-287
floor function, 278-279
fopen function, 748-749
for loop, 74-75, 252-253
  with array, 316-317
for statement, 74-75, 252-253, 316-317
foreach loop, 132-133, 136-137
  for object properties, 442-443
  with associative array, 322-323
foreach statement, 132-133, 136-137, 322-323, 442-443
Foreign key, 96-97
  constraint, 514-515
  design, 512-513
Form, 208-221
Format code (sprintf function), 282-285
format method (DateInterval object), 302-303
format method (DateTime object), 300-301
Format string (sprintf function), 282-283
Formatting
  date, 64-65
  number, 64-65
  strings and numbers, 282-283
Form-based authentication, 686-687, 690-695
Forwarding a request, 76-77
fputcsv function, 750-751
fread function, 748-749
FROM clause, 100-101
FTP (File Transfer Protocol), 26-27
func_get_arg function, 388-389
func_get_ars function, 388-389
func_num_args function, 388-389
Function, 64-65, 379-410
  array, 132-133
  array conversion, 270-271
  array handling, 314-317, 324-333
  array sorting, 398-399
  binary and base64 conversion, 700-701
  calling, 162-163, 380-381
  count, 132-133
  creating, 162-163, 380-381
  cURL, 726-727
  date, 64-65, 292-293

Function (continued)
  die, 76-77
  directory, 744-745
  documentation, 86-87
  email helper, 718-721, 722-723
  empty, 64-65
  encrypting and decrypting, 700-701
  exit, 76-77
  file, 744-755
  for functions, 388-389
  formatting, 282-283
  header, 164-165
  htmlentities, 262-263, 646-647
  htmlspecialchars, 222-223, 646-647
  images, 756-763
  include, 76-77
  include path, 392-393
  include_once, 76-77
  infinity testing, 276-277
  inspecting objects, 446-447
  integer conversion, 270-271
  is_leapyear, 298-299
  is_numeric, 64-65
  isset, 64-65, 316-317, 358-359
  math, 278-279
  n12br, 224-225
  number_format, 64-65
  path, 744-745
  queues, 326-327
  random number, 280-281
  regular expressions, 462-463, 472-473, 474-475
  require, 76-77
  require_once, 76-77
  scope, 392
  session handling, 356-363
  set_cookie, 350-351
  sha1 (encryption), 688-689
  stacks, 326-327
  string and number conversion, 286-287
  string comparison, 272-273
  string conversion, 270-271
  string length, 264-265
  string modification, 268-269
  string replace, 266-267
  string search, 266-267
  substrings, 264-265
  timestamp, 294-295, 296-297
Future Value application, 78-85
fwrite function, 748-749

G

GD library (image handling), 756-757
GET method, 54-55
GET request, 54-55
GET vs. POST method, 56-57
get_class function, 446-447
get_include_path function, 392-393
getCode method (Exception object), 478-479
getcwd (directory) function, 744-745
getdate function, 294-295
getFile method (Exception object), 478-479
getimagesize function, 756-757
getLine method (Exception object), 478-479
getMessage method (Exception object), 130-131, 478-479
getrandmax function, 280-281
getTimestamp method (DateTime object), 300-301
getTrace method (Exception object), 478-479
getTraceAsString method (Exception object), 478-479
global keyword, 162-163
Global regular expression, 472-473
Global scope, 384-385
Gmail account for email testing, 712-713
GRANT statement, 554-555, 556-557
GROUP clause, 596-597
Guitar Shop applications, 650-669

H

Handling exceptions, 130-131, 478-481
Hard return, 220-221
Hash function, 688-689
Hash value, 688-689
HAVING clause, 596-597
header function, 164-165
heredoc, 260-261
Hexadecimal, 274-275
Hidden field, 208-209
Host name (email address), 490
HTML (Hypertext Markup Language), 6-7, 16-17
    character entity, 222-223
    check box, 212-213, 214-215
    drop-down list, 216-217
    form, 208, 221
    hidden field, 208-209
    in database columns, 646-649
    list box, 218-219
    password box, 208-209
    radio button, 210-211
    text area, 220-221
    text box, 208-209
    uploading file, 754-755

HTML/XHTML compatibility, 16
htmlentities function, 262-263, 646-647
htmlspecialchars function, 222-223, 646-647
HTTP (Hypertext transport protocol), 6-7
HTTP request, 6-7, 8-9
HTTP response, 6-7, 8-9
Hypertext Markup Language (see HTML)
Hypertext Transport Protocol (HTTP), 6-7

I

IDE (Integrated Development Environment), 34-35
Identity operator, 232-233
    with objects, 444-445
    with regular expression, 462-463
IE (see Internet Explorer)
if clause, 72-73
if statement, 72-73, 238-241
IIS (Internet Information Services), 10-11
Image functions, 756-763
Image handling, 756-763
Image Upload application, 764-775
Image utility file, 766-771
imagealphablending function, 762-763
imagecolorallocatealpha function, 762-763
imagecolortransparent function, 762-763
imagecopyresampled function, 760-761
imagecreatefromxxx function, 758-759
imagecreatetruecolor function, 760-761
imagedestroy function, 758-759
Images directory, 782-783
imagesavealpha function, 762-763
imagesx function, 758-759
imagesy function, 758-759
imagexxx function, 758-759
IMAP (Internet Message Access Protocol), 708-709
Implement an interface, 456-457
Implicit syntax (SQL join), 590-591
implode function, 270-271
Importing to NetBeans, 38-39
in_array function, 328-329
Include files, 650-651
include function, 76-77
Include path, 392-393, 652-653
include_once function, 76-77
Increment a counter, 62-63
Index
    array, 132-133, 312-313
    database, 94-95, 518-519, 550-551
    PDOStatement object, 135-136
    string, 264-265

Infinite loop, 248
Information hiding, 414
Inheritance, 448-457
Initialization vector (IV), 700
Inner join, 102-103, 590-591
InnoDB tables, 514
INSERT statement, 104-105, 128-129, 602-603
Instance, 426-427
    database entity, 504-505
Instantiation, 426-427
INT data type (MySQL), 98-99, 540-541
Integer, 50-51, 274-275
Integer data type, 50-51
Integrated Development Environment (IDE), 34-35
Interface, 456-457
Internal function, 64-65
Internet, 4-5
Internet exchange point (IXP), 4-5
Internet Explorer, 10-11
    cookies and security settings, 353
Internet Information Services (IIS), 10-11
Internet Service Provider (ISP), 4-5, 708
Interpolation, 58-59, 260-261
Intranet, 4-5
Introducing a subquery, 598-599
Introspection (objects), 446-447
intval function, 286-287
IS NULL operator (SQL), 584-585
is_a function (objects), 446-447
is_dir function, 744-745
is_file function, 744-745
is_finite function, 276-277
is_infinite function, 276-277
is_leap method (DateTime object), 306-307
is_leapyear function, 298-299
is_numeric function, 64-65
ISP (Internet Service Provider), 4-5, 708
isset function, 64-65
isset function (array), 316-317
isset function (session), 358-359
Iteration structures, 248-255
IV (Initialization Vector), 700
IXP (Internet exchange point), 4-5

J

Jagged array, 334-335
JavaScript Object Notation (JSON), 728-729
Join, 102-103, 590-591
JSON (JavaScript Object Notation), 728-729
JSP, 10-11

K

key function (array), 316-317
Keyword, 50, 192-193
    global, 162-163
krsort function (array), 330-331
ksort function (array), 330-331

L

LAN (Local area network), 4-5
Last-in, first-out, 326-327
lastInsertId method (PDO class), 614-617
Latin-1 character set, 540-541
lcfirst function, 268-269
Leap year test, 298-299, 306-307
Left outer join, 102-103
Length (string), 264-265
Library
    cURL, 724-729
    function, 390-395
    GD, 756-757
    mcrypt, 700-701
LIFO, 326-327
LIKE operator (SQL), 586-587
LIMIT clause, 578-579
Line break, 224-225
Linking table, 512-513
List box, 218-219
Literal, 52-53
Loading data into database, 562-563
Local (email address), 490
Local area network (LAN), 4-5
Local scope, 384-385
Logic error, 190-191
Logical operator, 70-71, 236-237
    SQL, 582-583
Look-ahead assertion (regular expression), 470-471
ltrim function, 268-269

M

Mac OS, 22-23, 817-831
Main project (NetBeans), 34-35
Many-to-many relationship, 96-97, 512-513
Mask (LIKE operator), 586-587
max function, 278-279
mcrypt library, 700-701
Message digest, 688
Metacharacter (regular expression), 464-465

Method, 126-127, 414-415, 424-425
  add (DateTime object), 304-305
  constructor, 414, 422-423
  destructor, 422-423
  diff (DateTime object), 304-305
  exec, 128-129
  fetch, 135-136
  format (DateInterval object), 302-303
  format (DateTime object), 300-301
  getMessage, 130-131
  getTimestamp (DateTime object), 300-301
  is_leap (DateTime object), 306-307
  modify (DateTime object), 300-301
  mysqli, 628-629, 632-633
  Exception class, 478-479
  PDO class, 614-617
  PDOStatement class, 614-617
  query, 126-127
  setDate (DateTime object), 300-301
  setTime (DateTime object), 300-301
  static, 430-431
  sub (DateTime object), 304-305
method_exists function, 446-447
min function, 278-279
mktime function, 294-295
Model (MVC), 160-161
  mysqli, 638-641
  PDO, 620-625
modify method (DateTime object), 300-301
Modulus operator, 60-61
Mozilla Firefox (see Firefox)
mt_getrandmax function, 280-281
mt_rand function, 280-281
Multiline regular expression, 472-473
Multiple inheritance, 456-457
Multiple-line comment, 48-49
Multivalued dependencies, 520-521
MVC pattern, 160-185
  switch statement in controller, 246-247
MyISAM tables, 514
MySQL, 12-13, 106-109
  connecting to, 124-125
  data types, 540-541
  extension, 612-613
  features, 106-107
  history, 12-13
  InnoDB tables, 514
  MyISAM tables, 514
  PHP coding, 611-642
  starting and stopping, 24-25
  versions, 12-13

MySQL Workbench, 530-533, 537
mysqli, 612-613, 626-641
  methods, 628-629, 632-633
  model, 638-641
  prepared statements, 632-635
  properties, 630-631

N

n12br function, 224-225
Named parameter (prepared statement), 616-617
Namespace, 394-395
Naming rules (variables), 52-53
Navigating directories, 76-77, 164-165
Negative look-ahead assertion (regular expression), 470-471
Nested if statements, 72-73
Nested subqueries, 598-599
NetBeans, 34-39
  configuration, 38-39
  debugging, 196-201
  error highlighting, 192-193
  importing, 38-39
  installing (Mac), 824-825
  installing (Windows), 808-809
  main project, 34-35
  project, 34-35
  run configuration, 38-39
  testing, 36-37
Netscape Navigator, 10
Network, 4-5
Network Interface Card (NIC), 4-5
NIC (Network Interface Card), 4-5
Non-primary key, 94-95
Normal form, 516-517, 520-521
Normalization, 516-517, 520-529
Normalized data structure, 516-517
Notepad++, 22-23
  install (Windows), 802-803
nowdoc, 260-261
Null value, 58-59
  database column, 98-99, 542-543, 602-603
Number, 274-281, 282-287
number_format function, 64-65
Numeric expression, 60-61
Numeric literal, 52-53

O

Object, 124-125, 413-458
  access operator, 422-423
  chaining, 426-427

Object (continued)
  creating, 124-125, 426-427
  deserialization, 358-359
  serialization, 358-359
Object-oriented interface (mysqli), 612-613
Object-oriented programming, 413-458
  Registration application, 482-495
Object-oriented style (mysqli), 626-627, 636-637
Octal, 274-275
One-to-many relationship, 96-97, 512-513
One-to-one relationship, 96-97, 512-513
Opera, 10-11
Operator
  arithmetic, 60-61
  assignment, 52-53
  binary, 242
  compound assignment, 62-63
  concatenation, 58-59
  conditional, 226-227, 242-243
  equality, 232-233, 444-445
  error suppression, 626-627
  identity, 232-233, 444-445
  IS NULL (SQL), 584-585
  LIKE (SQL), 586-587
  logical, 70-71, 236-237
  logical (SQL), 582-583
  modulus, 60-61
  object access, 422-423
  relational, 70-71, 234-235
  scope resolution, 428-429
  ternary, 242-243
  unary, 242
Oracle, 12-13
ord function, 270-271
ORDER BY clause, 100-101, 588-589
Order of precedence
  arithmetic expression, 60-61
  conditional expression, 236-237
  SQL, 582-583
Orphaned row, 514-515
Outer join, 102-103
Override a method, 448-449

P

Paamayim Nekudotayim, 428-429
Pad a string, 268-269
Parameter, 162-163, 380-381
  prepared statement, 616-617
Parameter list, 162-163, 380-381
  variable-length, 388-389

Parent class, 448-449
Passing arguments, 382-383
Password box, 208-209
Path, 28-29
Pattern (regular expression), 462-463
PDO (PHP Data Objects), 124-127, 612-625
  methods, 614-615
  model, 620-625
PDOException class, 130-131, 480-481, 618-619
PDOStatement class, 126-127, 135-136, 614-615
PEAR Mail package
  emailing, 714-717
  installation, 710-711,
Performance (database), 100
Perl, 10-11
Per-session cookie, 350-351, 356
Persistent cookie, 350-351
Phone number validation, 476-477
PHP, 10-11
  assigning a value, 52-53
  comment, 48-49
  connecting to database, 124-125
  control statements, 70-75
  data types, 50-51
  declaring a variable, 52-53
  documentation, 86-87
  errors, 193
  executing SQL queries, 124-129
  history, 12-13
  interpreter, 8-9
  keyword, 50
  statement, 48-49
  syntax, 48-49
  variable, 52-53
  versions, 12-13, 124-125
PHP Data Objects (see PDO)
PHP: Hypertext Processor, 12-13
phpMyAdmin, 108-109, 110-119
  changing password, 110-111
  configure (Mac), 822-823
  configure (Windows), 806-807
  creating users, 118-119
  dumping database, 564-565
  granting privileges, 118-119
  importing script, 112-113
  loading data, 562-563
  logging in, 110-111
  logging out, 110-111
  reviewing data, 114-115
  running SQL statements, 116-117
  starting, 110-111

pi function, 278-279
POP (Post Office Protocol), 708-709
Position (string), 264-265
POST method, 56-57, 66-67
POST request, 56-57
POST vs. GET method, 56-57
pow function, 278-279
Precision, 540-541
preg_match function (regular expression), 462-463
preg_match_all function (regular expression), 472-473
preg_replace function (regular expression), 474-475
preg_split function (regular expression), 474-475
prepare method (PDO class), 614-617
Prepared statement, 614-617
 mysqli, 632-635
Primary key, 94-97, 518-519, 544-545, 550-551
 design, 512-513
print statement, 226-227
Private method, 424-425
Private modifier, 450-451
Private property, 420-421
Privileges (database), 552-553, 556-561
Procedural interface (mysqli), 612-613
Procedural style (mysqli), 626-627, 636-637
Product Catalog application, 658-661
Product Discount application, 14-21, 66-69, 662-669
Product Manager application (OOP), 432-441
Project (NetBeans), 34-35
Property, 414-415, 420-421
 static, 430-431
Properties
 looping through, 442-443
 mysqli, 630-631
property_exists function, 446-447
Protected method, 424-425
Protected modifier, 450-451
Protected property, 420-421
Protocol, 28-29
 IMAP, 708-709
 POP, 708-709
 Secure Sockets Layer, 676-677
 SMTP, 708-709
 stateless, 354-355
 Transport Layer Security, 676-677
Prototyping, 780-781
Public method, 424-425
Public modifier, 450-451
Public property, 420-421
Python, 10-11

Q

Qualified column name (SQL), 590-591
Query, 100, 594-597
query method (PDO object), 126-127
Question mark parameter (prepared statement), 616-617
Queue, 326-327
Quotation marks, 192-193, 260-261
 single vs. double, 58-59
 SQL, 104
Quoted text format (email address), 490

R

RA (Registration Authority), 680-681
Radio button, 210-211
rand function, 280-281
Random number, 280-281
range function (array), 324-325
readfile function, 746-747
Read-only property, 418
Real number, 276-277
Record (database table), 94-95
Rectangular array, 334-335
Redirect a request, 164-165
 secure connection, 684-685
Reference (passing by), 382-383
Referential integrity, 106-107, 514-515, 548
Reflection (objects), 446-447
Registration application (long), 496-497
Registration application (short), 482-495
Registration authority (RA), 680-681
Regular expression, 462-463, 462-477
Relational database, 94-99
Relational operator, 70-71, 234-235
Relative template (strtotime function), 296-297
rename function, 752-753
RENAME USER statement, 554-555
Render, 8-9
require function, 76-77
require_once function, 76-77
Result set, 100-101, 132-137
Result table, 100-101, 132-137
return statement, 162-163, 380-381
Return, 220-221
REVOKE statement, 558-559
RFC822 email method, 718-721
RGB value, 760
Right outer join, 102-103
Root directory, 26-27
round function, 278-279

Round trip, 8-9
Router, 4-5
Row (database table), 94-95
rowCount method (PDOStatement class), 614-617
rsort function (array), 330-331
rtrim function, 268-269
Rule set (CSS), 18-19
Run configuration (NetBeans), 38-39
Runtime error, 190-191

S

Safari, 10-11
Scalar value, 386-387, 420-421
Scale, 540-541
Schema, 108
Scope resolution operator, 428-429
Scope, 384-385, 392
Script (SQL), 112-113
Scripting language, 10
Second normal form, 524-525
Secure connection, 676-685
Secure Hash Algorithm (SHA-1), 688-689
Secure Sockets Layer (SSL), 676-677
SELECT statement, 100-103, 126-127, 574-592
Selection structures, 238-247
send_email function, 718-723
Serialization (object), 358-359
Server, 4-5, 8-9, 10-11
Server certificate, 678-679
Server-side language, 10-11
Session hijacking, 362-363
Session, 354-363
Session tracking, 354-355
session_get_cookie_params function, 360-361
session_id function, 361-362
session_name function, 360-361, 362-363
session_regenerate function, 362-363
session_set_cookie_params function, 356-357
session_start function, 356-357
session_write_close function, 362-363
set_cookie function, 350-351
set_include_path function, 392-393
setDate method (DateTime object), 300-301
setTime method (DateTime object), 300-301
SHA-1 (Secure Hash Algorithm), 688-689
function (encryption), 688-689
copy, 444-445
application (functions), 402-409
application (sessions), 364-375
tement, 560-561

shuffle function (array), 332-333
Silent error mode, 618-619
Single-line comment, 48-49
SMTP (Simple Message Transfer Protocol), 708-709
    Gmail configuration, 712-713
SMTP specification (email address), 490
Soft return, 220-221
sort function (array), 330-331
Sort sequence (SQL), 588-589
Sorting (arrays), 330-331
Source code for a web page, 32-33
Special character, 222-223
sprintf function, 282-283
SQL (Structured Query Language), 100
SQL query, 100
SQL script, 112-113
    create Guitar Shop database, 566-569
    dump from database, 564-565
SQL statement
    ALTER TABLE, 546-547
    CREATE DATABASE, 538-539
    CREATE INDEX, 550-551
    CREATE TABLE, 542-543
    CREATE USER, 554-555
    DDL, 537-570
    DELETE, 104-105, 606-607
    DML, 573-608
    DROP DATABASE, 538-539
    DROP INDEX, 550-551
    DROP TABLE, 548-549
    DROP USER, 554-555
    GRANT, 554-555, 556-557
    INSERT, 104-105, 602-603
    RENAME USER, 554-555
    REVOKE, 558-559
    SELECT, 100-103, 574-592
    SHOW GRANTS, 560-561
    UPDATE, 104-105, 604-605
    USE, 538-539
SQL-92 syntax, 591
sqrt function, 278-279
SSL (Secure Sockets Layer), 676-677
SSL client authentication, 678-679
SSL server authentication, 678-679
SSL strength, 680-681
Stack, 326-237
Stack trace, 200-201, 478-479
Stateless protocol, 354-355
Statement (PHP), 48-49
    break, 254-255
    control, 231-255

Statement (continued)
    do-while, 250-251
    echo, 58-59, 194-195, 226-227
    for, 74-75, 252-253, 316-317
    foreach, 132-133, 136-137, 322-323, 442-443
    if, 72-73, 238-241
    print, 226-227
    return, 162-163, 380-381
    switch, 244-247
    throw, 478-479
    try/catch, 130-131, 480-481, 618-619
    while, 74-75, 248-249
Static method, 430-431
Static property, 430-431
Static web page, 6-7
Stepping through code, 198-199
Stepwise refinement, 780-781
str_ireplace function, 266-267
str_pad function, 268-269
str_repeat function, 268-269
str_replace function, 266-267
str_shuffle function, 268-269
strcasecmp function, 272-273
strcmp function, 272-273
String, 50-51, 260-273, 282-287
    comparison, 272-273
    conversion, 270-271, 286-276
    data type, 50-51
    expression, 58-59
    formatting, 282-283
    handling (regular expressions), 474-475
    index, 264-265
    length, 264-265
    literal, 52-53
    modification, 268-269
    padding, 268-269
    position, 264-265
    replace, 266-267
    search, 266-267
    trim, 268-269
String pattern (LIKE operator), 586-587
stripos function, 266-267
strlen function, 264-265
strnatcasecmp function, 272-273
strnatcmp function, 272-273
strpos function, 266-267
strrev function, 268-269
strripos function, 266-267
strrpos function, 266-267
strtolower function, 268-269
strtotime function, 296-297

strtoupper function, 268-269
Structured Query Language (SQL), 100
Styles directory, 782-783
sub method (DateTime object), 304-305
Subclass, 448-449
Subquery (SQL), 598-601
substr function, 264-265
Substring, 264-265, 266-267
Summary query, 594-597
Superclass, 448-449
Superglobal variable, 55
switch statement, 244-247
Syntax
    PHP, 48-49
    SQL join, 590-591
Syntax error, 30, 190-191, 192-193
Syntax highlighting, 22-23

T

Tab-delimited string, 270-271
Table (database), 94-95
    alias, 592-593
    database design, 510-511
    linking, 512-513
Table scan, 518
Table-level primary key, 544-545
Task List Manager application, 338-341
Template (strtotime function), 296-297
Ternary operator, 242-243
Testing a PHP application, 28-29, 30-31, 190-193
    with NetBeans, 36-37
Text area, 220-221
Text box, 208-209
Text column (database), 646-647
TEXT data type (MySQL), 540-541
Text editor, 22-23
TextWrangler, 22-23
    installing (Mac), 818-819
Third normal form, 526-527
Third-party cookie, 348
Throw an exception, 130-131, 478-479
throw statement, 478-479
TIME data type (MySQL), 98-99, 540-541
time function, 294-295
Time zone problem
    Mac, 830-831
    Windows, 814-815
Timestamp, 292-299, 300-301
    formatting, 292-293
    functions, 294-295

TINYINT data type (MySQL), 540-541
TLS (Transport Layer Security), 676-677
TLS/SSL protocol, 677
Tracing with echo statements, 194-195
Transaction processing, 106-107
Transitive dependencies, 520-521
Transparency, 762-763
Transport Layer Security (TLS), 676-677
Trim a string, 268-269
trim function, 268-269
Truecolor image, 760-761
try block, 130-131, 480-481
try/catch statement, 130-131, 480-481
    PDOException, 618-619
Type casting, 286-287
Type coercion, 232-233

U

ucfirst function, 268-269
ucwords function, 268-269
Unary operator, 242
Unicode character set, 540-541
Uniform Resource Locator (URL), 28-29
Unique constraint, 550-551
Unique key, 94-95
Unique value (database column), 542-543
Unix epoch, 292-293
unlink function, 752-753
Unnamed parameter (prepared statement), 616-617
Unnormalized data structure, 516-517
unset function (array), 314-315
unset function (session), 358-359
UPDATE statement, 104-105, 128-129, 604-605
Uploading files, 754-755
URL (Uniform Resource Locator), 28-29
URL encoding, 354-355
USE statement, 538-539
Users (database), 554-555
usort function (array), 398-399
Utilities directory, 782-783
Utility file, 652-653, 766-771

V

Validation
    date, 294-295
    email address, 490-491
    oriented, 482-495
    expressions, 476-477
    77

Value
    hash, 688-689
    of array, 312-313
    passing by, 382-383
    scalar, 386-387
VARCHAR data type (MySQL), 98-99, 540-541
Variable, 52-53
    autoglobal, 384
    naming rules, 52-53
Variable function, 396-397
Variable name, 192-193
Variable substitution, 260-261
    with arrays, 314-315, 320-321
View (MVC), 160-161
Viewing source code, 32-33

W

WAN (Wide area network) 4-5
Web application, 4-5
Web browser, 4-5, 10-11
Web server, 4-5, 8-9 10-11
Web-based client, 108-109
WHERE clause, 100-101, 580-587
while loop, 74-75, 248-249
while statement, 74-75, 248-249
Whole number, 274-275
Wide area network (WAN), 4-5
Wildcard character (SQL), 586-587
Windows (Microsoft), 22-23, 801-815
World Wide Web, 4

XYZ

XAMPP, 24-25, 106-107
    install (Mac), 820-821
    install (Windows), 804-807
XAMPP Control Panel, 24-25
xDebug, 196-201
    install (Mac), 824-825
    install (Windows), 808-809
XHTML, 16-17
Y2K38 problem, 292
Year 2038 problem, 292
YouTube Search application, 730-739
YouTube Video Search API, 728-729
Zend engine, 12-13
Zip code validation, 476-477

What software you need for this book

- The XAMPP distribution, which includes Apache 2.2, MySQL 5.1, PHP 5.3, and phpMyAdmin 3.2. You can download this software for free from the XAMPP web site.

- A good text editor. We recommend Notepad++ for Windows users and TextWrangler for Mac OS users, and both are free.

- A standards-compliant web browser. We recommend Mozilla Firefox, and it too is free.

- If you want to use an IDE for developing your PHP applications (this is optional), we recommend NetBeans and the xDebug debugger. Both are available for free.

- When new versions of this software become available, please check www.murach.com for updates that describe how to use this book with the new software.

- For complete instructions on how to install and configure this software, please see appendix A (for PC users) or appendix B (for Mac users).

The downloadable source code for this book

- Complete source code for the applications presented in this book, so you can view the code and run the applications as you read each chapter.

- Starting source code for the exercises that are presented at the end of each chapter, so you can get more practice in less time.

- Source code for the exercise solutions, so you can check your solutions.

- All source code is compatible with the NetBeans IDE, but this code can also be edited with a text editor or imported into other IDEs.

How to download the source code for this book

- Go to murach.com, and go to the page for *Murach's PHP and MySQL*.

- Click the link that lets you download the book applications. Then, click on the link that downloads a zip file for all book applications. This should download a file named phps_allfiles.zip to your computer.

- Unzip all files into XAMPP's htdocs directory. This will unzip all files into these three directories: book_apps, ex_starts, and ex_solutions.

- Use phpMyAdmin to run the create_db.sql script that's in the book_apps/_create_db directory.

  For more information, please see appendix A (for PC users) or appendix B (for Mac users).

www.murach.com